AF541211

EDUCATION

For UGC-NET/SLET

Objective Type Questions

Second Edition
Revised, Updated and Enlarged

Atlantic Research Division

Published by

ATLANTIC

PUBLISHERS & DISTRIBUTORS (P) LTD

7/22, Ansari Road, Darya Ganj, New Delhi-110002
Phones : +91-11-40775252, 40775214, 23273880, 23275880
Fax : +91-11-23285873
Web : www.atlanticbooks.com
E-mail : orders@atlanticbooks.com

First Edition: 2011

Printed & bound in India by Atlantic Print Services

General Information

About the NET

The National Educational Testing Bureau of University Grants Commission (UGC) conducts National Eligibility Test (NET) to determine eligibility for lectureship and for award of Junior Research Fellowship (JRF) for Indian nationals in order to ensure minimum standards for the entrants in the teaching profession and research. The Test is conducted in Humanities (including languages), Social Sciences, Forensic Science, Environmental Sciences, Computer Science and Applications and Electronic Science.

The Council of Scientific and Industrial Research (CSIR) conducts the UGC-CSIR NET for other Science subjects, namely, Life Sciences, Physical Sciences, Chemical Sciences, Mathematical Sciences and Earth Atmospheric Ocean & Planetary Sciences jointly with the UGC. The tests are conducted twice in a year generally in the months of June and December. For candidates who desire to pursue research, the Junior Research Fellowship (JRF) is available for five years subject to fulfillment of certain conditions. UGC has allocated a number of fellowships to the universities for the candidates who qualify the test for JRF. The JRFs are awarded to the meritorious candidates from among the candidates qualifying for eligibility for lectureship in the NET. JRFs are available only to the candidates who opt for it in their application forms.

The test for Junior Research Fellowship is being conducted since 1984. The Government of India, through its notification dated 22nd July, 1988 entrusted the task of conducting the eligibility test for lectureship to UGC. Consequently, UGC conducted the first National Eligibility Test, common to both eligibility for Lectureship and Junior Research Fellowship in two parts, that is, in December 1989 and in March, 1990.

NET Schedule

UGC conducts NET twice a year, i.e., in the months of June and December. The notifications announcing the June and December examinations are published in the months of March and September respectively in the weekly journal of nation-wide circulation, viz, Employment News.

NET Results Declaration Schedule

The result of June, UGC-NET is declared generally in the month of October. Similarly December, UGC-NET result is usually declared in the month of April. The UGC-NET results published in the Employment News are also available on UGC website.

UGC-NET in Objective Mode from June, 2012 Onwards

1. The UGC-NET will be conducted in objective mode from June 2012 onwards. The Test will consist of three papers. All the three papers will consist of only objective type questions and will be held on the day of Examination in two separate sessions as under:

Session	Paper	Number of Questions	Marks	Duration
First	I	60 out of which 50 questions are to be attempted	50 × 2 = 100	1¼ Hours (09.30 a.m. to 10.45 a.m.)
First	II	50 questions all of which are compulsory	50 × 2 = 100	1¼ Hours (10.45 a.m. to 12.00 Noon.)
Second	III	75 questions all of which are compulsory	75 × 2 = 150	2½ Hours (01.30 p.m. to 04.00 p.m.)

2. The candidates are required to obtain minimum marks separately in Paper-I, Paper-II and Paper-III as given below:

Category	Minimum marks (%) to be obtained		
	Paper-I	Paper-II	Paper-III
General	40 (40%)	40 (40%)	75 (50%)
OBC	35 (35%)	35 (35%)	67.5 (45%) rounded off to 68
PH/VH/SC/ST	35 (35%)	35 (35%)	60 (40%)

Only such candidates who obtain the minimum required marks in each Paper, separately, as mentioned above, will be considered for final preparation of result.

However, the final qualifying criteria for Junior Research Fellowship (JRF) and eligibility for Lectureship shall be decided by UGC before declaration of result.

3. The syllabus of Paper-I, Paper-II and Paper-III will remain the same.

4. The candidates will be allowed to carry the carbon printout of OMR Response Sheets with them on conclusion of the examination.

5. There will be no negative marking.

Preface

The book has been designed for students preparing for UGC-NET/SLET in the subject of Education. This second edition has been thoroughly revised, updated and sufficiently enlarged with the addition of questions in each chapter. Three sets each of Model Test Papers, Paper II and Paper III have been added. Previous Years Papers (December 2012) in Paper II and Paper III, with answers, have been included to give the students a feel of what type of questions are asked in the examination. The book is very comprehensive and covers almost all possible objective type questions for the exam. The questions set in UGC-NET/SLET examinations in the previous years have also been used for preparing this book.

In spite of our best efforts to cover all possible questions, the paper may contain some questions which are not covered in this book and can be answered only if the candidate has a thorough knowledge of the topics covered in the syllabus. For a thorough and elaborate knowledge of the subject, candidates are advised to read the following books published by Atlantic Publishers and Distributors (P) Ltd. (i) *Philosophy of Education* by S.S. Chandra and Rajendra Kumar Sharma; (ii) *Sociology of Education* by S.S. Chandra and R.K. Sharma; (iii) *Foundations of Education* by Srinibas Bhattacharya; (iv) *Fundamentals of Educational Psychology* by M. Dash and Neena Dash; (v) *Principles of Education* by S.S. Chandra and Rajendra Kumar Sharma; (vi) *Research in Education* by S.S. Chandra and R.K. Sharma; (vii) *Philosophical and Sociological Perspectives of Education* by R.P. Pathak; (viii) *Educational Thinkers* by V.R. Taneja and S. Taneja; (ix) *Essentials of Exceptionality and Special Education* by Neena Dash and M. Dash; (x) *Socio-philosophical Approach to Education* by V.R. Taneja; (xi) *Advanced Educational Psychology* by Ramnath Sharma and Rajendra Kumar Sharma; and (xii) *Advanced Educational Technology* by Ramnath Sharma and S.S. Chandra.

Atlantic Research Division

Contents

1

Philosophical Foundation of Education

1. According to Adams, education is the following aspect of philosophy
   (a) Dynamic (b) Idealistic
   (c) Practical (d) Theoritical
2. What is the origin of the word Education?
   (a) Word 'Educate'
   (b) 'E' and 'Catum'
   (c) Edu and 'Catum'
   (d) None of the these
3. As an educationist Gandhiji was
   (a) a pragmatist
   (b) a naturalist
   (c) an idealist
   (d) naturalist, an idealist and a pragmatist all together
4. "Philosophy is theory of Education." Whose statement is it?
   (a) Bertrand Russell (b) Adams
   (c) John Dewey (d) Fechte
5. Which of the following statements is correct?
   (a) Education is a science
   (b) To some extent it is art and to some extent it is science
   (c) It is neither an art nor science
   (d) Education is an art
6. Which of the following type represents M.K. Gandhi's contribution to education?
   (a) Education for international understanding
   (b) Education for man making
   (c) Basic education
   (d) Integral education.
7. Which of the following statements is of German Philosoper Fichte?
   (a) Philosophy is the principle of education
   (b) The main aim of philosophy is to acquire knowledge
   (c) Without philosophy the teaching art cannot reach perfection
   (d) Education is the dynamic aspect of philosophy
8. Which of the following type represents Aurobindo's contribution to education?
   (a) Basic education
   (b) Education for international understanding
   (c) Education for man making
   (d) Integral education.
9. The statement of Socrates—"The true philosophers are those who love true knowledge"—shows the following fact
   (a) Philosophy and education are closely related
   (b) Philosophy does not determine the objectives of education
   (c) Philosophy makes education impracticable
   (d) Philosophy and education are not closely related
10. Which one of the following sentences is correct about the nature of teaching?

(a) It is remedial
(b) It is diagnostic as well as remedial
(c) It is diagnostic
(d) All the above statements are correct

11. The person who has love for wisdom (truth) may be called as philosopher provided that
(a) his love is in the active form.
(b) his knowledge is correct.
(c) he has logical power.
(d) None of the above.

12. "All questions related to Education are really the questions of philosophy." Which educationist has this opinion?
(a) Gandhi (b) Ross
(c) Rousseau (d) Adams

13. What is the compulsory element of learning?
(a) Bright Mind
(b) Tendency to know
(c) Ability to read
(d) None of the these

14. The person who is curious to learn and is never satisfied may be termed as philosopher. It is the opinion of
(a) Descartes (b) John Locke
(c) Plato (d) Socrates

15. Which of the following aspects of education are based on philosophy?
(a) Teacher-pupil and teacher-guardian relation
(b) Extra-curricular activities and home-work
(c) Method of teaching and teaching-material
(d) Objectives and curriculum

16. What is the place of principal in an educational institute?
(a) Owner of the school
(b) Founder of the school
(c) Overall head of the school
(d) Manager of the school

17. The community influences the child's growth and development
(a) formally
(b) informally
(c) Both (a) and (b)
(d) None of the above

18. This ideology of philosophy is not the basis of education.
(a) Pregmatism (b) Idealism
(c) Naturalism (d) Terrorism

19. If a student failed in any class what should be done to him?
(a) He should be advised to leave studies
(b) He should be given a chance to improve and sent to the next class after he improves
(c) He should be kept in the same class
(d) All the above methods are right

20. Which institution has maximum control over education?
(a) Family (b) Economy
(c) Religion (d) State

21. According to Indian point of view, the form of "Idealism" is
(a) Pragmatism (b) Naturalism
(c) Spiritualism (d) Realism

22. Which of the following type represents Vivekananda's contribution to education?
(a) Education for international understanding
(b) Integral education
(c) Basic education
(d) Education for man making.

23. The following is not the fundamental principles of idealism.
(a) Unity in Diversity
(b) The individual is truth in the nature

(c) Spiritual Value
(d) Development of Personality

24. What are the three components of the educational process?
(a) Teaching, learning and practice
(b) Direction, instruction and skill
(c) Education, teacher and books
(d) Teacher, student and education

25. Which of the following statements is/are correct?
(a) Darshan in Sanskrit refers to metaphysical or intutional perception that leads to Moksha.
(b) Darshan is a logical exposition of the nature of reality.
(c) Only those are designated as philosophers who can guide others by influencing their ideas and actions.
(d) All of the above.

26. "The mind or soul is fundamental element of the whole universe and the meditation is mental"—Ross. What ideology of philosophy does this statement indicate?
(a) Marxism (b) Realism
(c) Existintialism (d) Idealism

27. What is teaching through deductive method?
(a) From macro to micro
(b) From easy to difficult
(c) From general to specific
(d) From specific to general

28. The purpose of all philosophical exercises is
(a) to provide base to all educational thoughts.
(b) to remove the doubts and wonders of the people.
(c) the enhancement of knowledge.
(d) All of the above.

29. According to idealism, the aim of education is
(a) full development the potentialities of the personality.
(b) to enable an individual for life-struggle.
(c) to make the present life happy and prosperous.
(d) to learn by one's own experience.

30. Mark out the reason that made Jawaharlal the great leader
(a) His leadership of the Congress
(b) His personal qualities
(c) His brahminical heritage
(d) His parentage

31. The word "Pragmatism" is derived from the Greek word "Pragatikos" which means
(a) Internal (b) Theoretical
(c) Natural (d) Practical

32. The future of education in India depends on
(a) Family (b) Society
(c) Government (d) Economy

33. "Education is regarded as reconstruction of experiences." John Dewey's this ideology is related to this Educational Philosophy.
(a) Naturalism (b) Pregmatism
(c) Realism (d) Idealism

34. In India, education is the responsibility of
(a) State Government
(b) Central Government
(c) Both Central and State Governments
(d) Neither Central or State Governments

35. According to Pragnatism, the principle of curriculum making is
(a) principle of child centred education.
(b) principle of comprehensive life.
(c) principle of activity.
(d) principle of self-realization.

36. What is the meaning of lesson plan?
(a) To prepare detailed answers of all the questions to be asked in the class

(b) To read the lesson before teaching it
(c) To prepare the list of questions to be asked
(d) To prepare all that the teacher wants to teach in a limited period

37. Etymologically, the word 'education' is derived from
(a) 'educare'
(b) 'e' and 'catum'
(c) 'edu' and 'catum'
(d) None of the above

38. The principle of "Discipline through natural consequences" is related to
(a) Idealism (b) Naturalism
(c) Realism (d) Marxism

39. On what depends the values of an educational experience in the eyes of the idealist?
(a) The extent to which it satisfies pupil desires
(b) Whether or not the pupil has been properly motivated
(c) The manner in which it affects future experience
(d) Whether or not it preserves accepted institutions

40. What is the place of principal in an educational institute?
(a) He is the owner of the school.
(b) He is the founder of the school.
(c) He manages the school.
(d) He is the overall head of the school.

41. The philosophy of idealism has the following basis.
(a) Practical (b) Soul
(c) Ideals (d) Idea

42. Which educational activity is most desirable to the pragmatist?
(a) That is beneficial effect upon the future experiences of the pupil
(b) Approximates the goals which educational scientists have set up
(c) That characterizes by spontaneous, active, continuously pleasurable and practical for the pupil
(d) Results from the indiscrimination of the pupil in democratic theory

43. The education acquired without any specific purpose, fixed period and place is called
(a) Formal Education
(b) Informal Education
(c) Individual Education
(d) Indirect Education

44. "The two aspects of education are fundamental—the meditation aspect and practical aspect." The two aspects of this statement are respectively the following.
(a) Philosophy and Teacher
(b) Ideas and Activity
(c) Theory and Practice
(d) Ideal and Purpose

45. The person who tried to synthesise mathematics with divine knowledge was
(a) Aristotle (b) Protagorus
(c) Socrates (d) Pythagoras

46. According to Idealism in the state of self-realization an individual has the following feeling.
(a) Natural development
(b) Skill development
(c) Attainment of happiness
(d) Truth welfare and beauty

47. Experimental method of education psychology is
(a) reliable but not regular.
(b) cannot be called reliable.
(c) very reliable, authentic and regular.
(d) None of the above.

48. In this educational philosophy instead of teacher's importance nature is regarded as teacher of a child.

(a) Existentialism (b) Naturalism
(c) Idealism (d) Marxism

49. What do you mean by curriculum?
(a) Sum total of the annual study
(b) Indicates the course to be taught by the teachers to the students throughout the year
(c) A child learns through curriculum
(d) Sum total of the activities of a school

50. The Ultimate Goal of education from a philosophic point of view in the east
(a) is a disciplined life to achieve unity among one's desires and aspirations.
(b) is not perfection of the individual but also becoming continuously beyond one self.
(c) is that a mind places high value in permanent opposition to continue to learn.
(d) is not solely becoming as the UNESCO commission says but expanding into the absolute.

51. In Pragnatism, the following teaching method is regarded as the best.
(a) Learning through experience
(b) Play-way method
(c) Inductive method
(d) Spontaneous self-activity

52. Man according to Charvaka Philosophy is
(a) the self
(b) the consciousness
(c) the physical body
(d) None of the above

53. Idealism believes in following type of discipline.
(a) Education through natural consequences
(b) Self-discipline
(c) Discipline based on happiness and suffering
(d) Social discipline

54. Who raised the slogan "Back to Nature"?
(a) Pragmatism (b) Naturalism
(c) Existentialism (d) Realism

55. Preparing the child for future life as an aim of education is preparing child for
(a) some suitable vocations.
(b) some particular course of study.
(c) a happy married life.
(d) facing all kinds of emergencies and situations of future life.

56. "Child-centred Education" is the contribution of the following educational philosophy.
(a) Pragmatism (b) Communism
(c) Naturalism (d) Idealism

57. Which statement is not correct about Naturalism?
(a) A reaction against sophistication, artificiality and paraphernalia in education.
(b) A reaction against the degenerated humanism of the Renaissance period.
(c) A reaction against a mere study of books and linguistic forms.
(d) A reaction against the degenerated humanism of the Renaissance period.

58. Dialogue method of discovering the truth was discovered by
(a) Heraclitus (b) Socrates
(c) Saint Augustine (d) Plato

59. Which educational philosophy includes science education in the curriculum?
(a) Existentialism (b) Idealism
(c) Pragmatism (d) Naturalism

60. Who said, "Reverse the usual practice and you will almost always do right"?

(a) Rousseau
(b) Plato
(c) Mahatma Gandhi
(d) Dewey

61. Harmonious development of the child means
(a) development of physical, mental, moral and spiritual potentialities of the child in a balanced manner.
(b) development of a sound mind in a sound body.
(c) development of the adjustment capacities of the child.
(d) development of all the qualities of the mind to the maximum possible extent.

62. "The centre of all knowledge should be a craft to which all the subjects be correlated and taught." Which scheme of education aspects this method of teaching?
(a) Gandhi's basic education scheme
(b) Education based on project method
(c) Child centred education scheme
(d) Learning be doing

63. "Human institutions are one mass of folly and contradiction." Whose statement is this?
(a) Dewey
(b) Ravindernath Tagore
(c) Bernard Shaw
(d) Rousseau

64. The nature of perception according to Charvaka can be said to be
(a) Authentic
(b) Inauthentic
(c) Both (a) and (b)
(d) Neither (a) nor (b)

65. What was the contribution of Mahatma Gandhi's Basic Education to the India education?
(a) The politicalization of education
(b) The complete self-supporting of the education
(c) The education for age group 7 to 14 years be free and compulsory
(d) The industrialization of education

66. According to which school of philosophy of education, exaltation of individual's personality is a function of education?
(a) Marxism
(b) Idealism and Marxism
(c) Pragmatism
(d) Idealism

67. The only valid Pramana according to Charvaka is
(a) Scriptures
(b) Inference
(c) Perception
(d) None of the above

68. "By education I mean all-round development of child's all the physical mental and spiritual powers." This statement relates to the following Indian educationist.
(a) Mahatma Gandhi (b) Dayanand
(c) Vivekanand (d) Arvindo

69. Which is not Naturalism's aim of education?
(a) To inculcate ethical and moral values in the pupils
(b) To help the pupils to learn to be in harmony with and well-adapted to their surroundings
(c) Education is the notion of man's evolution from lower forms of life
(d) To equip the individual or the nation for the struggle for existence so as to ensure survival

70. A curriculum is all the experiences a child has regardless of
(a) How they take place
(b) Where they take place
(c) When they take place
(d) Both (a) and (c)

71. The propagator of basic education was
    (a) Arvindo
    (b) Mahatma Gandhi
    (c) Dr. Zakir Hussain
    (d) Ravindranath Tagore

72. Which school held the view, "God makes all things good; man meddles with and they become evil"?
    (a) Naturalism (b) Pragmatism
    (c) Marxism (d) Existentialism

73. Adaptation to environment while facing its adversaries is
    (a) Teaching (b) Education
    (c) Moulding (d) All of the above

74. The basis of basic education is
    (a) Sarvodaya philosophy
    (b) Realism philosophy
    (c) Yoga philosophy
    (d) Vedic philosophy

75. Which school maintained self-expression with the accompanying cries of "no interference", "no restraints"?
    (a) Truest form of Naturalism
    (b) Most valid form of Naturalism
    (c) Extreme form of Naturalism
    (d) Most widely accepted form of Naturalism

76. Which of the following statements regarding education is correct?
    (a) Education is drawing out the innate capacities of man to enable him to adapt to the social environment.
    (b) Education is the other name of personality development.
    (c) Education is a continuous process starting from the first breath of life to the last.
    (d) All of the above.

77. Shri Arvind stressed on the development of this aspect of child.
    (a) Physical development
    (b) Bodily development
    (c) Spiritual and physical development
    (d) Spiritual development

78. Which is not the nature of philosophy?
    (a) It is the totality of man's creative ideas
    (b) It is a planned attempt on search for the truth
    (c) It is a collective ensemble of various viewpoints
    (d) It is a science of knowledge

79. In Indian philosophy the validity of scriptures has been challenged by
    (a) The Vedanta (b) Nyaya
    (c) The Charvaka (d) Samkhya

80. Gandhiji included in the basic education curriculum the teaching of following languages.
    (a) Mother tongue and Hindustani
    (b) Mother tongue and other one provincial language
    (c) Mother tongue and English
    (d) Mother tongue and Sanskrit

81. Which branch of philosophy deals with knowledge, its structure, method and validity?
    (a) Epistemology (b) Metaphysics
    (c) Logic (d) Aesthetics

82. Human consciousness, according to Charvaka Philosophy, is
    (a) body
    (b) combination of five elements
    (c) self
    (d) None of the above

83. "The man living a worldly life and serving the other men can transform his mind into super mind and himself into a Super Man." The statement relates to
    (a) Ravindranath Tagore
    (b) Vivekananda

(c) Mahatma Gandhi
(d) Arvindo

84. Which school maintained: "Natural impulses of the child are of great importance and are good in themselves"?
(a) Mechanical Naturalism
(b) Romantic Naturalism
(c) Biological Naturalism
(d) Naturalism of physical science

85. The important means for achievement of liberation according to Sankara is
(a) religious practices
(b) distinction of self and not-self
(c) concentration on Om
(d) All of the above

86. Maharshi Arvindo did not like to include the following subject in the curriculum of his education-scheme.
(a) Indian History and Culture
(b) Religion
(c) Science
(d) Psychology

87. Which branch of philosophy examines issues pertaining to the nature of "reality"?
(a) Axiology (b) Epistemology
(c) Ontology (d) Metaphysics

88. If education is a tripolar process, which is the third element after students and the teacher?
(a) Curriculum (b) School
(c) Parents (d) None of these

89. Where did Shri Arvindo do his meditation?
(a) Shantiniketan
(b) Vellor Math
(c) Pondicherry
(d) Sabarmati Ashram

90. On what is based the need for teaching philosophy of education?
(a) Different philosophies expressed different points of view on every aspect of education
(b) Different ways of teaching-learning
(c) All pupils are not alike
(d) Different systems of education found in different countries

91. Controlling and sublimation of instincts are done through the process of education. It is the opinion of
(a) Jerome Bruner (b) M.K. Gandhi
(c) McDougall (d) R.N. Tagore

92. "Education is the menifestation of all the perfection already present in man." This statement expresses the educational philosophy of this Indian thinker.
(a) Maharshi Arvindo
(b) Swami Vivekanand
(c) Ravindranath Tagore
(d) Mahatma Gandhi

93. What is the goal of education according to Idealism?
(a) Satisfaction of human wants
(b) Cultivation of dynamic, adaptable mind which will be resourceful and enterprising in all situations
(c) Realisation of moral values
(d) Perfect adaptation to the environment

94. Liberation as living in the country of God, according to Ramanuja is known as
(a) Sanidhya (b) Samipya
(c) Salokya (d) Sayujya

95. According to Swami Vivekanand, the aim of education is
(a) to be expert in Yoga.
(b) to develop oneself into Super Man.
(c) to attain the perfection already present.
(d) vocational efficiency.

96. The aim of education according to the Existentialists is

(a) a good understanding of the world outside.
(b) objective knowledge.
(c) humanitarian and humanist self-realization.
(d) adaptation to practical life.

97. Liberation as eternal contact with God, according to Ramanuja is known as
(a) Sayujya (b) Samipya
(c) Salokya (d) Sarupya

98. What institution did Swami Vivekanand establish in Vellor Math in memory of his teacher?
(a) Ram Krishna Mission
(b) Shantiniketan
(c) Sevashram
(d) Yoga Centre

99. The Realist's aim of education is
(a) happy and moral development.
(b) self-realization.
(c) total development of personality.
(d) spiritual and moral development.

100. Ramanuja's theory of causation is known as
(a) Asatkarayavada
(b) Brahman Parinamavada
(c) Prakrti Parinamavada
(d) Vivartavada

101. The Indian thinker who made correlated as the method of teaching was
(a) Ravindranath Tagore
(b) Mahatma Gandhi
(c) Swami Vivekananda
(d) Maharshi Arvindo

102. Naturalist's conception of man is
(a) it is spirit rather than animality that is most truly man.
(b) there exists in the nature of things a perfect pattern of each individual.
(c) nature would have them children before they are men.
(d) man's very essence of being is his spiritual nature.

103. In the 21st century, education is considered
(a) as a source of gaining material wealth.
(b) as a symbol of status.
(c) as a preparation for future life.
(d) All of the above.

104. What is the recommendation of Kothari Education Commission to replace rural craft as centre of Basic education?
(a) Socially productive work
(b) Work-experience
(c) Cottage Industry
(d) Modern Industry

105. Which philosophy of education considers psychology as an incomplete study of and an inadequate basis of educational theory?
(a) Idealism (b) Naturalism
(c) Realism (d) Pragmatism

106. Formal education differs from non-formal education in which of the following points?
(a) Curriculum is pre-determined in formal education.
(b) Formal education is controlled by definite time-table.
(c) Certificate is not issued after education is over.
(d) None of the above.

107. Arvindo believed that when man is physically, mentally and spiritually integrated, he develops this power in him.
(a) Mental Power (b) Physical Power
(c) Devine Power (d) Super Man

108. Which among the following does not fit into the scheme of educational goals of the Idealists?

(a) Skills (b) Self-expression
(c) Care of body (d) Moral values

109. Which is irrelevant to bringing the scheduled tribes at par with others?
(a) Developing the curricula and devise instructional materials in tribal languages.
(b) Opening centres of teaching Indian religions.
(c) Opening of anganwadis, non-formal and adult education centres on a priority basis in tribal areas.
(d) Opening of primary schools in the tribal areas.

110. Arvindo was a nationalist so he wanted to mould his educational system on the basis of
(a) Vedant philosophy
(b) Indian tradition
(c) Secular system
(d) Western system

111. Religious education is strongly advocated by
(a) Realist (b) Existentialists
(c) Pragmatists (d) Idealists

112. Values has been closely linked with interest by
(a) W.M. Urban (b) J.S. Mackenzie
(c) J.B. Perry (d) J.S. Mill

113. Arvindo wanted to form good habits in his students based on discipline by this method.
(a) Invitation method
(b) Inductive method
(c) Method of suggestion
(d) Brahmacharya

114. Which of the following is said about the idealists?
(a) They like "roses"
(b) They are content with "briars"
(c) They are satisfied neither with "briars" nor with "roses"
(d) They want "roses" and "briars" both

115. Value is concerned with liking, has been said by
(a) W.M. Urban (b) D.W. Prall
(c) J.S. Mill (d) J.S. Mackenzie

116. The aim of Arvindo's philosophy is "Realization of sublime truth" which is attained through
(a) Yoga Philosophy
(b) Integral View of Life
(c) Generous View of Life
(d) Vedanta Philosophy

117. Which school of philosophy of education advocated project method of teaching?
(a) Naturalism (b) Idealism
(c) Pragmatism (d) Realism

118. Which of the following is not an agency of informal education?
(a) Art galleries
(b) Church
(c) Social organization
(d) All of the above

119. "If the East tries to immitate West then it would be deceit."—By this statement what educational system did Ravindranath Tagore support?
(a) Buddh Educational System
(b) Vedanta Educational System
(c) Indian Educational System
(d) Western Educational System

120. Playway method of teaching has been emphasised in the scheme of the education of
(a) Realists (b) Existentialists
(c) Naturalists (d) Pragmatists

121. Education in India prepared by Central Board is general up to class
(a) VIIIth (b) Xth
(c) XIth (d) XIIth

122. The following institution is not working in Shantiniketan (Vishwa Bharti)—
(a) Music Bhawan (b) Russia Bhawan
(c) Shiksha Bhawan (d) China Bhawan

123. Which is the most widely accepted method of education, according to the pragmatists?
(a) Leaving the child free to learn
(b) Heuristic method
(c) Lecturing by the teacher
(d) Learning by doing

124. It is necessary in the interest of equality and social justice in India
(a) to provide technical education to all the students.
(b) to provide scholarships for education to all students.
(c) to provide employment to all educated persons.
(d) to provide incentives to all educationally backward sections of society, particularly in the rural areas.

125. What is Vinaya Bhawan in Ravindranath Tagore's Shanti Niketan?
(a) Graduation post graduation and research institution
(b) College Industry Training Institute
(c) Teachers Training College
(d) Primary and Secondary level institution

126. The pragmatists are against
(a) eternal spiritual values.
(b) breakdown of knowledge into separate subjects.
(c) the external examinations.
(d) the specialist teachers.

127. The social aims of education imply that
(a) the state has to give not to take anything from the individual.
(b) the state is superior to the individual transcending all his desires and aspirations.
(c) the state is above the individual citizen.
(d) the state is an idealized metaphysical entity.

128. One of the objectives of Shanti Niketan Institution is
(a) Study of village life and social service
(b) Nature-study
(c) Study of Western culture
(d) Following only Indian culture

129. Pragmatism has a greater sense of responsibility than Naturalism with regard to moral training because
(a) they do not want the teacher to abdicate from the scene.
(b) they consider education, basically, a social process.
(c) the free activity which pragmatic system of education entails does not mean licence; rather it means a guided activity.
(d) they emphasize teaching of values.

130. For strengthening democracy as a constitutional value through education it is necessary to ensure that
(a) people learn large-hearted tolerance, mutual give and take and appreciation of ways.
(b) all people have the freedom to live the life they think is the best for them.
(c) people are competitive for progress.
(d) None of the above.

131. Gandhiji and Ravindranath Tagore made the following language as medium of instruction.
(a) English Language
(b) Link Language
(c) Mother Tongue
(d) Provincial Language

132. Which of the following claims of the pragmatists is not acceptable?
   (a) Training in character through school's co-curricular activities is possible
   (b) The free activity of the pupil is likely to result in permanent attitudes of initiative and independence and moral discipline
   (c) Child's own experience is valuable for adequate development of child's personality
   (d) Training in citizenship is possible through school and community activities

133. Professionals are preferred to general people in every field today because
   (a) they can adopt research oriented techniques to solve a problem.
   (b) their theoretical knowledge is more sophisticated than mere technical people.
   (c) they can do their job better.
   (d) All of the above.

134. The basis of silent prayer by the students in Shantiniketan is
   (a) Idol-worship
   (b) Religious tolerance
   (c) Students own religion
   (d) Worship of Nirakar Brahma

135. Project method of teaching is an outstanding contribution of
   (a) Naturalism (b) Idealism
   (c) Realism (d) Pragmatism

136. Education is lame without philosophy because
   (a) education goes in the direction of goals of life and philosophy determines those goals.
   (b) philosophy can give birth to new sciences.
   (c) ideas and concepts are judged by philosophy.
   (d) All of the above.

137. Basic education enunciated by Gandhiji is also known as
   (a) Nehru Committee Report
   (b) Rural Education Scheme
   (c) Zakir Hussain Committee Report
   (d) Experimented and Tested Scheme by Vinoba Bhave

138. Which is the characteristic of the project method?
   (a) Carried in its natural setting
   (b) A voluntary undertaking
   (c) Problematic act
   (d) Used for all-round development of child's personality

139. In Indian philosophy, which of the following schools has not accepted the existence of soul?
   (a) The Buddhists (b) The Charvakas
   (c) Both (a) and (b) (d) Neither of them

140. Which Committee was constituted by Central Advisory Board of Education in 1939 to suggest changes in Basic Education?
   (a) B.G. Kher Education Committee
   (b) Dr. Zakir Hussain Education Committee
   (c) Sargent Education Committee
   (d) Vinoba Bhave Education Committee

141. Which among the following is not essentially desirable in the project method?
   (a) The task of the project should be full of message for the children
   (b) The task of the project should be interesting enough so that the pupil is genuinely eager to carry it out
   (c) The task of the project is as real as the task of the life outside the walls of the school

(d) The task of the project involves constructive effort or thought yielding objective results

142. According to Charvaka Philosophy, the relationship of consciousness and body is
(a) body is the product of consciousness.
(b) body has no consciousness.
(c) consciousness is the product of body.
(d) None of the above.

143. Which institution for the training of Basil Education teachers and inspectors was established by the Central Advisory Board of Education in 1956?
(a) DIET
(b) National Institute of Basic Education
(c) S.T.C. Schools
(d) NCERT

144. Which is a great disadvantage of the project method?
(a) Children are generally not interested in it
(b) Teachers, generally, do not like to teach through it
(c) It consumes much of the time of the child
(d) It leaves gaps in the knowledge of the child

145. The possibility of liberation while living has been accepted in Indian philosophy by
(a) Sankara (b) Jainas
(c) Ramanuja (d) All of the above

146. Learning by Project Method is technically known as
(a) Systematic learning
(b) Incidental learning
(c) Adequate learning
(d) Efficient learning

147. Liberation according to Sankara is the goal of
(a) Manushya (b) Atma
(c) Vijnana Atma (d) Parmatama

148. The subject not included in basic education was
(a) Computer literacy
(b) General Knowledge
(c) Drawing
(d) Social Studies

149. Education, according to the pragmatist, is
(a) wholly society-oriented.
(b) wholly interdisciplinary.
(c) wholly pupil-oriented.
(d) wholly purposive.

150. Education and philosophy are interrelated in which of the following points?
(a) Philosophy is a generalized study of all sciences.
(b) Most of the educational and moral values have been derived from philosophy.
(c) Both of them discuss the validity of laws and principles and their applications.
(d) All of the above.

151. The effect of naturalism philosophy on Ranvindranath Tagore is evident from the inclusion of it in his educational system.
(a) Mother-tongue
(b) Fine Arts
(c) Indian Culture
(d) Ban on physical punishment

152. Who among the following is not a follower of pragmatic philosophy?
(a) Kilpatrick (b) John Dewey
(c) Peshtalozzi (d) William James

153. Philosophy dominates over science in which of the following ways?

(a) Analysis dominates in science while synthesis dominates in philosophy.
(b) Philosophy is a generalized study while science is a specialized one.
(c) Science discusses what the nature of reality is and philosophy discusses both what it is and what it should be.
(d) All of the above.

154. The aim of educational system enunciated by Swami Vivekananda was this also
(a) to attain perfection.
(b) to make the student self-sufficient economically.
(c) to make the student aware of Western culture.
(d) to impose strict discipline on student.

155. What is not associated with pragmatism?
(a) Freedom-based education
(b) Education for self-realization
(c) Purposive education
(d) Experience-based education

156. Liberation as becoming a part of God, according to Ramanuja is known as
(a) Samipya (b) Sayujya
(c) Salokya (d) Sanidhya

157. Vivekanand supported this teaching method for spiritual knowledge.
(a) Supervision Method
(b) Lecture Method
(c) Yoga Method
(d) Discussion Method

158. Who emphasised realization of Truth, Beauty and Goodness as the aims of education?
(a) Realists (b) Naturalists
(c) Idealists (d) Pragmatists

159. The main centre of informal education is
(a) Radio and Television
(b) Family
(c) Society
(d) All of the above

160. "The teacher is a guide philosopher and friend of the child to mould him according to him." This statement is related to
(a) Vivekanand
(b) Swami Dayanand
(c) Arvindo
(d) Gandhi

161. Which statement about truth is not correct according to the philosophy of pragmatism?
(a) It is what emerges to be true in actual practice
(b) It is eternal
(c) It is made by man
(d) It is ever-changing

162. For a group to have high morals,
(a) the members must have self confidence and a sense of discipline.
(b) the members must be incapable for agreeing among themselves.
(c) the leader of the group should be man of status.
(d) All of the above.

163. This country does not have educational system according to Marxist ideology.
(a) Russia (b) America
(c) North Korea (d) China

164. In whose methodology of teaching "Experimentation" is the key-note of?
(a) Realism (b) Pragmatism
(c) Idealism (d) Existentialism

165. Which of the following societies had deep aesthetic sense in the ancient period?
(a) Indian (b) Arab
(c) Athens (d) Sparta

166. The following activities are specially encouraged in the curriculum of Russia according to Marxist ideology.
(a) Activities organised by 'Five Arts'
(b) Child-centred activities

(c) Activities based on labour
(d) Activities related to games and sports

167. The term "progressive education" related to
(a) Idealism (b) Existentialism
(c) Pragmatism (d) Realism

168. Mundane life is the cultivation of the world hereafter. It is the philosophy of
(a) Athens (b) Sankhya
(c) Islam (d) Christianity

169. The education based on Marxist philosophy develops the following.
(a) Probetariate internationalism
(b) Spiritualism
(c) Capitalism
(d) Socialism

170. Who said, "No fixed aims of education and no values in advance"?
(a) Marxists
(b) Realists
(c) Progressive educators
(d) Idealists

171. Which statement is not correct from the point of view of effect of heredity on the development of personality?
(a) The child of poor parents will be poor.
(b) The child has opposite qualities from the parents.
(c) The child of dullard parents will be a dullard.
(d) The child of parents of fair complexion will be fair.

172. The following institute directs teachers' training in Russia.
(a) National Advisory Council of Training
(b) DIET
(c) Academy of Pedogogical Services
(d) NCERT

173. Which school ot philosophy of education stresses the direct study of men and things through tours and travels?
(a) Marxism (b) Social realism
(c) Idealism (d) Existentialism

174. Curriculum activities are used in teaching in order to
(a) make teaching attractive.
(b) make teaching interesting, easy to understand and effective.
(c) assist the teacher.
(d) make teaching easy.

175. Which of the following institutions imports primary education according to Islam?
(a) Masjid (b) Maqtab
(c) Idara (d) Madarsas

176. Which school believes that all knowledge comes through the senses?
(a) Existentialism (b) Pragmatism
(c) Sense Realism (d) Idealism

177. The reliability of a test is determined on the principle of
(a) the correctness of the machine or the key used or the assessment of the test.
(b) the amount of chance efforts that have crept into an assessment.
(c) the consistency of marks obtained when a test is conducted.
(d) the objectivity of the items included in the test.

178. In the educational institutions based on Islam religion, the following ideology encourages terririst activities.
(a) Religious fanaticism
(b) Zehadi ideology
(c) Religious following
(d) Traditional ideology

179. Which school raised the slogan "Things as they are and as they are likely to be encountered in life rather than words"?

(a) Idealists (b) Existentialists
(c) Pragmatist (d) Realists

180. In the medieval period people rose up against the catholic church because
(a) church banned scientific experimentation.
(b) church denied them the freedom of thought and expression.
(c) Both (a) and (b).
(d) None of the above.

181. What is desirable to reform Islamic educational system?
(a) Quran teaching
(b) Traditional fanaticism
(c) Teaching of Modern subjects
(d) Development of humanity

182. As Huxley pleaded for the introduction of "a complete and thorough scientific culture" into schools, he is claimed to be
(a) a Pragmatist (b) a Naturalist
(c) an Idealist (d) a Realist

183. Who propounded the philosophy of inborn capacities of a child?
(a) John Dewey
(b) Kant
(c) John Locke
(d) None of the above

184. The government action to control terrorist activities in Islamic educational institutions should be
(a) to encourage them to adopt secularism.
(b) to appoint Hindu teachers in them.
(c) to ban them immediately.
(d) to ban religious teaching in them.

185. Realism in education was born out of
(a) a cleavage between the work of the schools and the life of the world outside that occurred during the 19th century.
(b) the enthusiasm of the Renaissance.
(c) the degeneration of humanism after Renaissance.
(d) the great religious movement of the 17th century.

186. Who was the supporter of Naturalism in Education?
(a) John Locke
(b) Rousseau
(c) Armstrong
(d) None of the above

187. What is desirable to be done to bring up the Islamic educational institutions in the mainstream?
(a) To derecognise them for adopting modern curriculum
(b) Muslim children should be educated in government schools
(c) To ban religious education in them
(d) To give them grants for introducing modern curriculum

188. Which of the following is not criticised by realism in education?
(a) Teaching which drifts away from life of the child
(b) Organizing schools in a way that is conducive to practical training in citizenship
(c) Teachers denying the value of school co-curricular activities
(d) Pupils cramming for knowledge from books for reproducing in examination

189. The first school for a child's education is
(a) Family (b) School
(c) Friends (d) Society

190. Gita's educational thought is influenced by this Indian philosophy.
(a) Buddha Philosophy
(b) Vedanta Philosophy
(c) Puranic Philosophy
(d) Western Philosophy

191. In the light of relevant past events, contemporary events and their understanding should find a place in the teaching of history. Who maintained this principle?
   (a) Marxists (b) Realists
   (c) Idealists (d) Naturalists

192. The book written by Plato on education is
   (a) *Education*
   (b) *Educational Philosophy*
   (c) *The Republic*
   (d) None of the above

193. Gita philosophy mainly propagated this ideology.
   (a) Secularism
   (b) Religious Tolerance
   (c) Bhakti Yoga
   (d) Nishkam Karmyoga

194. The most important thing to keep in mind for a teacher according to Realism in education is
   (a) the nature of the child.
   (b) the method of teaching.
   (c) organization of the content to be taught.
   (d) the value and significance of what is taught.

195. The process of carrying the related knowledge and experiences to the reach of students is called
   (a) teaching
   (b) method of teaching
   (c) curriculum
   (d) None of the above

196. According to Gita philosophy, the aim of education is to develop into this form.
   (a) Scholar of high calibre
   (b) Fully religious
   (c) "Stith Prangy"
   (d) Complete Scholar

197. Which school of philosophy very strongly advocates that education should be vocational in character?
   (a) Pragmatism (b) Realism
   (c) Existentialism (d) Naturalism

198. The child is not permitted even to think freely in the class. This is the example of
   (a) emancipatory discipline
   (b) impressionistic discipline
   (c) repressionistic discipline
   (d) None of the above

199. According to Gita or Vedant, the basis of teaching methods should be
   (a) selfless activity.
   (b) religious faith.
   (c) sensuous life .
   (d) natural tendencies and interests.

200. Which is not an aspect of mind according to the realists' theory of knowing?
   (a) Behaviour
   (b) Processing of awareness
   (c) Awareness
   (d) Consciousness

201. What type of questions should be asked in the examination for the evaluation of all the aspects of the total syllabus in a year?
   (a) Essay type questions
   (b) Objective questions
   (c) Descriptive questions
   (d) Critical questions.

202. According to Vedant or Gita, the subjects of the curriculum may be classified into these two categories.
   (a) Theoritical and practical
   (b) Worldly and spiritual knowledge
   (c) Knowledge and ignorance
   (d) Art and science

203. Who believe that "Objects have a reality independent of mental phenomena"?

(a) Existentialists (b) Idealists
(c) Realists (d) Naturalists

204. According to the idealists
(a) only they deserve education who are spiritualists.
(b) arrangement of education should be voluntary.
(c) education should be available to all and compulsory.
(d) education is meant for idealists only.

205. According to Gita, teacher should be like
(a) strict disciplinarian.
(b) "Stith Pragy".
(c) high level scholar.
(d) specialist of subject.

206. Marxist educational philosophy is closer to
(a) Pragmatism (b) Naturalism
(c) Idealism (d) Realism

207. What type of questions give knowledge of real ability of students of secondary and higher classes?
(a) Detailed essay type questions
(b) Critical questions
(c) Analytical questions
(d) Objective type questions.

208. According to Jainism for 'Hosueholder' instead of Brahmcharya this has been prescribed.
(a) Truth
(b) Ahinsa
(c) Self-control
(d) Non-collection of things

209. Which among the following statements is not a characteristic of Marxism?
(a) Its educational philosophy is essentially materialistic
(b) Its major objective is the development of child's personality
(c) It asserts that physical environment can definitely change the nature of the child
(d) It presupposes a reality independent of man's mind

210. Emancipatory discipline in the school system is approved if the society is
(a) Closed (b) Open and free
(c) Idealistic (d) Realistic

211. Which school of philosophy of education regrets dualism between cultural, and vocational curriculum?
(a) Idealism (b) Naturalism
(c) Marxism (d) Existentialism

212. Students are evaluated in the school in order to
(a) check the sense of responsibility among the persons concerned.
(b) promote the students to the next higher class.
(c) ascertain the maximum utilization of resources.
(d) All of the above.

213. In the three "Ratnas" of Jainism, 'right knowledge' means
(a) right knowledge Jainism and philosophy.
(b) to attain salvation by spiritual knowledge.
(c) faith in tirthankaras.
(d) spiritual knowledge through right knowledge.

214. According to which educational philosophy, socially useful labour must form the central pivot of the entire school?
(a) Naturalism (b) Existentialism
(c) Marxism (d) Idealism

215. The least hindrance in the way of the optimum development of a child's personality is

(a) free education for all and equal opportunity.
(b) mad scramble among various social groups for getting as much of the goods of education as possible.
(c) incompetent teachers.
(d) limited economic surplus that could be spent on education.

216. According to Jain educational system, the aim of education is not to have up this.
(a) Anger (b) Maya
(c) Ignorance (d) Pride of respect

217. Which of the following has been asserted about schools by Marxist educational philosophy?
(a) They should not be mere weapons in the hands of the ruling class
(b) They should function as deliberate instruments of state policy
(c) They should stand above politics
(d) They should disinterestedly serve society as a whole

218. Education should aim at provision of vocational training for students, at the
(a) Primary stage
(b) Secondary stage
(c) Tertiary stage
(d) University stage

219. Among the five categories of knowledge according to Jainism 'Motion' knowledge means
(a) Word knowledge
(b) Complete knowledge
(c) Sensation
(d) Direct knowledge

220. Which of the following characteristics is common to pragmatism, naturalism and existentialism?
(a) Emphasis on physical environment
(b) Emphasis on spiritual aims of education
(c) Emphasis on value education
(d) Emphasis on the individual

221. On whose leadership is founded the University at Pondicherry?
(a) Tagore (b) Gandhiji
(c) Sri Aurobindo (d) Vivekananda

222. In the Jain curriculum of education, arithmetic is included to study
(a) kaiwalya knowledge.
(b) study of matter or 'Pudgal'.
(c) study of 'Jiva or Soul'.
(d) spiritual knowledge.

223. Whose is the ultimate concern—"What is existence"?
(a) Existentialists and Idealists
(b) Idealists only
(c) Existentialists only
(d) Realists only

224. In evaluation, criterion of acceptability of behavioural change in learner is determined by
(a) educational technology
(b) philosophy
(c) the school
(d) None of the above

225. Aristotle, Thomas Accunos and Herbert were supporters of this philosophy.
(a) Idealism (b) Pregmatism
(c) Existentialism (d) Realism

226. Which of the following philosophies held that "Men in the world feel lonely and anxious, being unsure of their meaning and fearful of their annihilation"?
(a) Pragmatism (b) Marxism
(c) Idealism (d) Existentialism

227. Purpose of the creation of the universe and its relation to man and God is discussed in
(a) Ethics
(b) Epistemology

(c) Metaphysics
(d) None of the above

228. The aim of education according to realism is
(a) Spiritual Development
(b) Knowledge Development
(c) Physical Development
(d) Mental Development

229. According to existentialists, the essence of existence means
(a) continuous growth and development.
(b) tensions and contradictions which condition loneliness and anxiety.
(c) spiritual good and happiness.
(d) unity with the ultimate reality.

230. The nature of the differences in socio economic strata of the society such as the wealthy, middle class and the poor is that it
(a) affects negatively the morale of the teachers.
(b) affects adversely the quality of education.
(c) runs quite frequently, at cross purposes in the demands they make on education.
(d) vitiates the socio-emotional climate of the schools.

231. Realism regards the child as
(a) Realistic unit
(b) An ideal unit
(c) Centre of Education
(d) Source of Teacher

232. With which aspect of education does the educational sociology deals?
(a) Economic (b) Social
(c) Political (d) Psychological

233. The limitations of realism is
(a) more stress on student's development.
(b) emphasis on specialization of knowledge.
(c) incomplete ideas related to student.
(d) All of the above.

234. Who was twentieth century existentialist?
(a) Hegel
(b) Soren Kierkegaard
(c) D.J. O'Connor
(d) Jean Paul Sartre

235. The aims of Indian education should be
(a) to bring about social and national integration.
(b) to accelerate the process of modernization.
(c) to increase productivity.
(d) All of the above.

236. In the view of realism discipline enables the student to
(a) free himself from bondages.
(b) adjust himself in real world.
(c) acquire an ideal.
(d) None of these.

237. Which of the following is more generally acceptable by modern educationists?
(a) Education is bound to have several aims since its concerns are several such as the individual, the society, the family, the nation and so on
(b) There should be one single aim of education unchangeable over time and space
(c) There is one grand objective of education; and that is the development of the inner nature of the child
(d) Contribution to the welfare of the society should be the only aim of education

238. The group of pessimists in ethics is headed by
(a) Berkeley (b) Hegel
(c) Kant (d) None of the above

239. Education based on realism is centred around

(a) The Future (b) The Past
(c) The Present (d) All of these

240. What is development of human potentialities in education?
(a) Individual as well as social aim
(b) Specific aim
(c) Individual aim
(d) Social aim

241. "There is only one subject matter of education that is life in all its manifestation". Who said this?
(a) John Dewey (b) Percy Nunn
(c) Whitehead (d) None of the above

242. The "Universe and God" is central thought of this philosophy.
(a) Realism (b) Existentialism
(c) Pragmatism (d) Idealism

243. What is development of social sense and cooperation among the individuals through education?
(a) Constitutional aim
(b) National aim
(c) Social aim
(d) Individual aim

244. The Wardha Scheme in the 1930's was modern as it is
(a) topical
(b) revolutionary
(c) Both (a) and (b)
(d) None of the above

245. "Broudy" was the exponent of this school of philosophy.
(a) Naturalism (b) Pragnatism
(c) Neo-Realism (d) Idealism

246. Which among the following is not an acceptable criticism of social aims of education?
(a) They hinder the growth and development of art and literature
(b) Man, in them, becomes only a means to an end and interests of the individual
(c) They are anti-individual
(d) They are unpsychological as they do not take into account the capacities

247. The difference between the social groups, in the degree of cultural development; or the degree of antipathy manifested by individuals belonging to one group towards individuals belonging to the other is known as social
(a) Distance (b) Disorder
(c) Selection (d) Apathy

248. The exponent existentialism was
(a) Jean Paul Satre
(b) Fridrick Nietzce
(c) Soren Kirkgard
(d) All of the above

249. Which among the following is not emphasized by the individual aims of education?
(a) Development of values of tolerance and non-violence
(b) Individual freedom
(c) Self-expression
(d) Development of inner potentialities

250. While according to Samkhya Philosophy effect is the real modification of cause, according to Samkara it is
(a) real (b) indescribable
(c) unreal (d) None of these

251. The present thinker of existentialism is
(a) Kant (b) Hegel
(c) Rousseau (d) Karl Jespar

252. Which of the following statements does not go in favour of the individual aims of education?
(a) Every individual is unique; development of his potentialities is essential

(b) Society is supreme and all individuals are only parts of it
(c) The individual is an asset to the society; his development and growth are necessary
(d) The society is strong if the individual is strong

253. Formal education is different from non-formal in which of the following points?
(a) Formal education works out on the principle of weeding out failures.
(b) Formal education has fixed points of entry and exit.
(c) Both (a) and (b).
(d) None of the above.

254. Nietzce's assumption is
(a) Atheism
(b) Relativity
(c) To become powerful
(d) All of these

255. Which among the following is the most correct view about social and individual aims of education?
(a) Social aims should be preferred to individual aims
(b) Individual aims are implied in the social aims of education
(c) Individual and social aims are only two sides of the same coin
(d) Individual aims should be given preference to social aims

256. Who said this "Education is man making. It is that by which character is formed, strength of mind is increased, intellect is expanded and by which man can stand on his own feet"?
(a) Dayanand Saraswati
(b) Tagore
(c) Vivekananda
(d) None of the above

257. "God has died and we have killed him." This statement is of this philosopher.
(a) Kierkgaard (b) Hedemore
(c) Satre (d) Nietzce

258. Which statement is most acceptable to the academicians about "Bread and butter aim" of education?
(a) It is important for only a section of the society
(b) It is only partly acceptable
(c) It is the most important aim and should be given top priority by educationists
(d) It is equally important along with other aims of education

259. The relationship of the ultimate reality with the world in Indian philosophy has been explained by the theory of
(a) Error (b) Reality
(c) Falsehood (d) All of the above

260. The exponent of Existentialism was
(a) Satre (b) Niresh
(c) Hedemore (d) All of these

261. Which of the following does not pertain to intellectual development aim of education?
(a) Development of cognitive powers
(b) Cultivation of intelligence
(c) Training and "formation" of mind
(d) Spiritual development

262. Who was the founder of Shanti Niketan?
(a) Gandhi (b) Vivekananda
(c) Tagore (d) Sri Aurobindo

263. What philosophy desires the relations of teacher pupil simple straight and personal?
(a) Existentialism (b) Realism
(c) Idealism (d) Naturalism

264. The theory of causation advanced by Sankara has been proved by
(a) Logic (b) Experience
(c) Scriptures (d) All of the above

265. According to Marxists, the form of education is
(a) Individualist (b) Dictatorial
(c) Socialist (d) Humanist

266. The most effective method of character-formation is
(a) teaching by high character teachers.
(b) rewarding virtuous behaviours and presenting high character models in the schools.
(c) teaching virtues through religious books.
(d) organizing specialists lectures on importance of values in life.

267. Which of the following is not the function of education?
(a) Economic prosperity
(b) Leadership training
(c) Preservation, transmission and advancement of culture
(d) Development of personality.

268. Rousseau had used this method to familiarise "Emile" with nature
(a) Experimental method
(b) Supervision method
(c) Lecture method
(d) Project method

269. Harmonious development of the child aim of education means
(a) development of the adjustment capacities of the child.
(b) development of physical, mental, moral and spiritual potentialities of the child in a balanced manner.
(c) development of all the qualities of the mind to the maximum possible extent.
(d) development of a sound mind in a sound body.

270. Destiny of India is being shaped in the classrooms. It is the opinion of
(a) Hunter Commission
(b) Hurtog Committee
(c) Education Commission
(d) None of the above

271. The main exponent of logical empiricism was
(a) Aristotle (b) Compte
(c) Plato (d) Kant

272. The relation between the Jiva and Brahman according to Samkara can be explained as
(a) Reflection (b) Emanation
(c) Evolution (d) Identity

273. The following thinker was logical empiricist.
(a) Plato (b) Russall
(c) Moore (d) Both (b) and (c)

274. Examples of illusion in Indian philosophy have been utilized to explain the nature of
(a) Atman (b) Maya
(c) Brahman (d) All of the above

275. The study-method of logical empiricism is
(a) Logical Debate
(b) Logical Coordination
(c) Logical Analysis
(d) Logical Synthesis

276. The nature of world as illusion has been accepted in Indian philosophy by
(a) Advaita Vedanta (b) Mimamsa
(c) Vishishtadvaita (d) All of the above

277. The Muslims call the beginning of education of their children as
(a) Bismillah (b) Hohallah
(c) Mansha Allah (d) Insha Allah

278. Filtration theory of education was supported by
(a) Dewey (b) Kant
(c) Russell (d) Milton

279. The following gave financial grants to Madarsas in medieval periodic.
(a) Maulvi (b) Qazi
(c) The rich people (d) The Emperor

280. According to which philosophy of education, childhood is some thing desirable for its own sake and children should be children?
(a) Naturalism (b) Realism
(c) Idealism (d) Pragmatism

281. Which of the following is not the work of Russell?
(a) *Outline of Philosophy* (1928)
(b) *Education and the Social Order* (1932)
(c) *Democracy and Education* (1946)
(d) *Impact of Science on Society* (1952).

282. Who controls the "Maqtabs" these days?
(a) Muslim Board
(b) Madarsa Board
(c) Wakf Board
(d) Secondary Education Board

283. Who emphasized that education should be a social process?
(a) Dewey (b) Pestalozzi
(c) Rousseau (d) Vivekananda

284. Knowledge according to Mimamsa philosophy is
(a) Real (b) Unreal
(c) Neither (a) nor (b) (d) Both (a) and (b)

285. The teaching work is done in Maqtabs by
(a) Babarchi (b) Mufti
(c) Maulvi (d) Qazi

286. "Education is the process of natural development of the child into an enjoyable, rational, harmoniously balanced, useful and hence, natural life." Which school of philosophy of education believes that?
(a) Existentialism (b) Idealism
(c) Realism (d) Naturalism

287. The Ramamurti Report of 1990 laid down the goals or aims in education as
(a) sound knowledge base
(b) education must be techno-informative
(c) Both (a) and (b)
(d) None of the above

288. Evaluate the viewpoint—"The child knows better than any educator what he should learn, when and how he should learn it?"
(a) Correct, but not practical
(b) Hundred per cent correct
(c) Practical, but not correct
(d) Correct and practical both

289. In Vedic age, the ceremony of beginning of study was known as
(a) Upnayan (b) Anna Prashan
(c) Khshore Karm (d) None of these

290. It is industrial rather than other types of economy which most enhances the regard for education, because
(a) the industrialists belong to the upper class of the society.
(b) modern industry has become extremely technical, science based, knowledge-based and scientific and technical knowledge is gained only through education.
(c) each country has had tremendous development of industry.
(d) industrialization has led to the production of huge wealth.

291. The beginning of study according to Buddhism was admission to a Math and was called
(a) Upnanyan
(b) Pabajja
(c) Sangham Sharanam Gacchami
(d) Buddham Sharanam Gacchami

292. It is rational nature of man that places him above other living creatures in the world. It is called

(a) Sense realism
(b) Rational humanism
(c) Neorealism
(d) None of the above

293. The institutions of higher education in Islamic education were
(a) Wakf (b) Idara
(c) Madarasa (d) Maqtab

294. The aim of education advocated by Realistic humanism is
(a) Developing human values in man
(b) Cultivation of intellect for making man rational
(c) Both (a) and (b)
(d) None of the above

295. The teaching method of Maqtabs was
(a) to commit to memory the Ayats of Quran.
(b) to write on wooden slabs.
(c) to understand learn by role Quran.
(d) to study according to Islamic rites.

296. Illusion in Indian philosophy has been explained by the example of
(a) Snake in rope (b) The sky flower
(c) Silver in nacre (d) All of the above

297. The teaching method of Madaras was
(a) Experiment-Demonstration
(b) Lecture
(c) Dialogue
(d) Discussion

298. On whose philosophy is based the current primary education in India?
(a) Sri Aurobindo
(b) Vivekananda
(c) Tagore
(d) Mahatma Gandhi

299. The following subjects was also taught in the Madarsas.
(a) Philosophy (b) Arithmetic
(c) Handicraft (d) Science

300. To contribute to India's national integration education should
(a) be free and compulsory.
(b) be of high quality.
(c) make children familiar with the various aspects of national life.
(d) reach each and every child of the country.

301. In Medieval times who did the teaching work in the absence of the teacher?
(a) Temporary teacher
(b) Maulvi
(c) The Guardians of students
(d) Class-monitor

302. The indirect proofs for the existence of self, according to the Jain philosophers, are
(a) Efficient cause (b) Soul is mover
(c) Co-ordinator (d) All of these

303. The philosophy closer to Idealism is Scholastic Realism because it advocates that
(a) Truth is eternal and unchanging.
(b) God is central to its metaphysical theology and nature is His manifestation.
(c) Both (a) and (b).
(d) None of the above.

304. What were the centres of education in Vedic Age called?
(a) Chatshala (b) Vidyalaya
(c) Guru Kul (d) Guru Grah

305. The Jains have refused the Charvaka view of self on the basis of
(a) Against causation
(b) Illogical
(c) No evidence
(d) All of these

306. Neorealism states that
(a) knowledge should essentially benefit humans.

(b) true knowledge essentially comes through senses.
(c) Both (a) and (b).
(d) None of the above.

307. "सा विद्या या विमुक्तये"—This motto of the aim of education has been taken from this book.
(a) *Upnishad* (b) *Gita*
(c) *Yajur Veda* (d) *Rigveda*

308. Buddha's theory of self is known as
(a) Immutable self
(b) Eternal self
(c) Theory of no-soul
(d) None of these

309. According to the theory known as Avacchedavada, causation means
(a) Destruction
(b) Reflection
(c) Annihilation
(d) None of the above

310. In Vedic age, it was the part of elementary education.
(a) History (b) Kala
(c) Science (d) Grammar

311. Buddha's theory of self is similar to the theory propounded in the West by
(a) David Hume (b) Bertrand Russel
(c) William James (d) All of these

312. Indian education can promote national consciousness by
(a) breaking down regional and linguistic barriers.
(b) understanding and re-evaluating of India's cultural heritage.
(c) establishing more and more all India institutions which will admit students from different parts of the country.
(d) All of the above.

313. What celebration or ceremony was held in Vedic times at the end of education?
(a) Ann Prashan
(b) Sanavartam
(c) Convocation
(d) Upnanyan Sanskar

314. The existence of soul in Indian philosophy has not been accepted by the schools known as
(a) the Buddhists (b) the Charvakas
(c) Both (a) and (b) (d) None of these

315. Education is two-fold process and its two elements are
(a) aims and techniques.
(b) education centres and environment.
(c) teachers and textbooks.
(d) teachers and students.

316. The following name of a learned women is the proof of women education in Vedic times.
(a) Apala (b) Ghosa
(c) Gargi (d) All of these

317. Which of the following phrases conforms to Sense Realism?
(a) Inductive method of teaching
(b) Emphasis on nature study and natural sciences
(c) Observation and contact as the legitimate sources of knowledge
(d) All of the above.

318. In the ancient India educational context the following was well-known centre?
(a) Kashi (b) Dhar
(c) Taxila (d) Devband

319. Happiness and sorrow and other mental activities, according to Charvaka, are the attributes of
(a) Consciousness (b) Body
(c) Self (d) None of these

320. Which of the following philosophies supports education for the masses?

(a) Pragmatism (b) Existentialism
(c) Sense Realism (d) All of the above

321. In ancient times which peroid of student's life was meant for his education?
(a) Brahmacharya Ashram
(b) Adult age
(c) Young age
(d) Infacny

322. Charvaka philosophers have been classified into
(a) Susikshit (b) Dhurta
(c) Both (a) and (b) (d) None of these

323. Which one of the following statements is correct?
(a) Education is an art
(b) Education is a science
(c) It is neither an art nor science
(d) To some extent it is art and to some extent it is science.

324. In Vedic age, the closeness of teacher-pupil realizationship is evident by pupil's this relation to teacher.
(a) Successor (b) Adopted Son
(c) Mental Son (d) Son

325. The sage Vatsyayan belongs to the Charvaka school of
(a) Dhurta (b) Susikshit
(c) Both (a) and (b) (d) None of these

326. Which system of education was propounded by Mahatma Gandhi?
(a) Teaching by activities
(b) Teaching through listening, meditation, etc.
(c) Teaching through music
(d) All of the above.

327. The manual labour was an integral part of ancient educational system so that the students may understand its
(a) Compulsion (b) Attitude
(c) Dignity (d) Utility

328. Rebirth, according to Buddha, is connected with self as
(a) Fundamental (b) Relevant
(c) Irrelevant (d) None of these

329. Which one of the following education systems supports scientific progress?
(a) Naturalistic Education
(b) Idealistic Education
(c) Realistic Education
(d) None of the above

330. In Buddhist India in the east and west the Buddhistic centres of education were
(a) Nalanda and Vallabhi
(b) Taxila and Sarnath
(c) Amravati and Odantpuri
(d) All of these

331. Buddha's attitude towards self can be said to be
(a) Indifferent (b) Agnostic
(c) Dogmatic (d) Sceptic

332. Indian philosophy close to Realism is
(a) Jainism (b) Samkhya
(c) Advaita Vedanta (d) Both (a) and (b)

333. In Buddhistic educational centres after "Pabajja" the child had to obey this instruction.
(a) Not to take intoxicants
(b) To keep away from uncleanliness
(c) Not to tell a lie
(d) All of these

334. Man, according to Buddha, can be said to be
(a) Body (b) Sanghat
(c) Self (d) None of these

335. Anetantavada principle of Jainism implies
(a) liberal attitude towards the people and matter.
(b) flexible outlook in the pursuit of knowledge and truth.
(c) Both (a) and (b).
(d) None of the above.

336. This subject was included in the curriculum in Buddhist centres of higher education.
   (a) Science
   (b) Foreign Language
   (c) Logic
   (d) Medicine

337. The self, according to Samkhya theory, is
   (a) Intellect (b) Body
   (c) Mind (d) All of these

338. "Education is a process of man's adjustment to nature, to his fellows and the environment". This definition suits
   (a) a Pragmatist (b) a Realist
   (c) a Naturalist (d) an Idealist

339. In Buddhistic age, the medium of education was
   (a) Mother Tongue (b) Sanskrit
   (c) Prakrit (d) Pali

340. The self, according to Samkhya is different from
   (a) Mind (b) Intellect
   (c) Body (d) All of these

341. The viewpoint of progressive educators regarding the issue of liberal vs. vocational education is that
   (a) all subjects should have a vocational purpose.
   (b) vocational ends lead one to degrade learning.
   (c) vocational and liberal education should not be separated.
   (d) liberal arts subjects should precede vocational training.

342. The reason for the absence of military education in Buddhistic educational system was
   (a) emphasis on Ahinsa.
   (b) protest by the Brahman religion.
   (c) predominance of religious education.
   (d) the system was meant for common people.

343. The Samkhya theory of self, is based upon
   (a) *Puranas* (b) *Vedas*
   (c) *Bhagwad Gita* (d) None of these

344. Education in ancient India also meant
   (a) establishment of community.
   (b) the established customs of caste.
   (c) moral rectitude.
   (d) All of the above.

345. Who was the Chinese traveller who gave an account of Nalanda Buddhistic educational center?
   (a) Megasthenes (b) Fa-Hien
   (c) Xuanzang (d) Hiuen Tsang

346. The chief characteristics of the self, according to Samkhya philosophy, is
   (a) Rebirth
   (b) Eternity
   (c) Pure consciousness
   (d) None of these

347. Which of the following philosophies opposes bookish knowledge as the sole source of knowledge?
   (a) Pragmatism (b) Naturalism
   (c) Realism (d) All of the above

348. In the Nalanda Buddhistic education centre these students received education.
   (a) Buddhistic Sangh
   (b) All parts of the country
   (c) Local
   (d) Foreign

349. In evolution self aims at
   (a) Liberation (b) Enjoyment
   (c) Both (a) and (b) (d) None of these

350. Real knowledge comes from the social contact of man with material things. It is the belief of
   (a) Social Realism
   (b) Humanism
   (c) Socialism
   (d) None of the above

351. Who was that muslim ruler of India who sent his general to destroy Nalanda and Vikram Shila Buddhist centres of education?
(a) Qutbuddin Aibak (b) Babar
(c) Allauddin Khilji (d) Aurangzeb

352. The chief arguments to prove the existence of self-advance by Samkhya philosophies are
(a) Substratum of knowledge
(b) Structure of things
(c) The Gunas
(d) All of these

353. Ancient education enjoined on the pupils the tenets of dharma which implied the ideas of
(a) Duty (b) Sacred law
(c) Justice (d) All of the above

354. Who was that muslim ruler of India who established many Madarsas?
(a) Firoz Tuglaq (b) Sikander Lodi
(c) Balban (d) Altmash

355. The self is proved on the basis of the psychological tendencies of
(a) Salvation (b) Enjoyment
(c) Knowledge (d) All of these

356. The aim of Buddhist education was
(a) cultural development.
(b) religious development.
(c) scientific development.
(d) All of the above.

357. What changes did Akbar make due to his secular policy in Maqtab and Madarsa education?
(a) Introduced uniform syllabus for Hindus and Muslim
(b) Muslim children were asked to learn Hindu religion
(c) Introduced religious bigotry in education
(d) Made Islamic education compulsory for all

358. The plurality theory of self in Indian philosophy has been accepted by
(a) the Mimamsa (b) the Jainas
(c) the Samkhya (d) All of these

359. In ancient India when the caste system became rigid, a vocational aim was also added. Vocational training was
(a) for lower classes only.
(b) depended upon class of society.
(c) same for all castes.
(d) different for different castes.

360. What institutions were established by Firaoz Tughlaq and Akbar for vocational education?
(a) Art centres
(b) Crafts centres
(c) Work shops
(d) College industries

361. The unitary theory of self in Indian philosophy has been supported by
(a) the Samkhya (b) the Mimamsa
(c) Advaita Vedanta (d) the Jainas

362. Material and physical universe is an incomplete expression of reality. It is the idea of
(a) Idealism (b) Buddhism
(c) Islam (d) Both (a) and (b)

363. In ancient and medieval India education was
(a) Free
(b) Universal
(c) For rich people
(d) Compulsory for all

364. Samkhya theory of self has been criticised on the basis of
(a) Illogical.
(b) Confusion between Jiva and Atman.
(c) Proofs for practical self only.
(d) All of these.

365. Man is above all living and non-living creatures because of the rational mind given to him. It is the belief of
(a) Islam
(b) Idealism
(c) Both (a) and (b)
(d) None of the above

366. The Muslim education has this defect.
(a) Islamic education was compulsory
(b) It ignored women education
(c) Physical punishment was given
(d) All of these

367. The most important theory of self in Indian philosophy has been advanced by
(a) Jainas (b) Samkhya
(c) Advaita Vedanta (d) Buddhists

368. Buddhist education was primarily monastic in its
(a) Nature and Outlook
(b) Content and Outlook
(c) Nature and Content
(d) Nature, Content and Outlook

369. What Indian values have been provided in the Indian Constitution?
(a) Secularism values
(b) Democratic values
(c) Socialistic values
(d) All of these

370. Self, according to Samkara, is
(a) Eternal (b) Transcedent
(c) Brahman (d) All of these

371. Real life problems in science and technology will be solved in the
(a) college lab only
(b) school lab only
(c) college and school labs
(d) None of the above

372. The Article 45 of Indian constitution has made a provision for
(a) boys of 14 years to be given compulsory education.
(b) the period of introducing free and compulsory education be extended.
(c) compulsory education should be provided within 16 years.
(d) the free and compulsory education up to 14 years of age be provided within 10 years.

373. The most important characteristic of self, according to Samkara, is
(a) Axiological
(b) Metaphysical
(c) Epistemological
(d) All of these

374. The Kothari Commission's report was published in
(a) 1986 (b) 1996
(c) 1966 (d) 1976

375. What was that Indian educational scheme or plan which was introduced to make primary education free and compulsory?
(a) Sargent plan
(b) Montessory method
(c) Education through correspondence
(d) Basic education

376. The fundamental basis of Samkara's theory of self is
(a) Qualified monism
(b) Dualism
(c) Pluralism
(d) Non-dualism

377. Maya is indescribable, i.e. it is neither true nor false. This is the belief of
(a) Advaita Vedanta
(b) Realism
(c) Jainism
(d) All of the above

378. What is that article of constitution which provides primary education available to all sections of society?

(a) Article 38
(b) Article 45
(c) Articles 29 and 30
(d) None of these

379. Samkara's theory of self is based upon
(a) Logic (b) Metaphysics
(c) Epistemology (d) All of these

380. Education of Advaita Vedanta is different from western Idealism in which of the following points?
(a) Learning is restricted to the present world not to the world hereafter.
(b) Enabling the child to realize his real nature which is divine.
(c) Moksha can be obtained through knowledge.
(d) All of the above.

381. What are the backward classes called in the Articles 341 and 342 of Indian Constitution?
(a) Only Scheduled Tribe
(b) Only Scheduled Caste
(c) Both Scheduled Castes and Scheduled Tribes
(d) All of these

382. Causation in Indian philosophy has been explained by
(a) *Asatkaryavada*
(b) *Parinamavada*
(c) *Satkaryavada*
(d) All of these

383. Many Committees and Commissions on education were appointed and these gave a close look to
(a) education problem
(b) religious problem
(c) social problem
(d) All of the above

384. What is the provision for removal of untouchability in Article 17 of Indian Constitution?
(a) To introduce untouchability
(b) Untouchability is Sin
(c) Untouchability is legal crime
(d) All of these

385. The theory, that the effect is the real result of the cause, is known as
(a) *Parinamavada* (b) *Vivartavada*
(c) *Satkaryavada* (d) *Asatkaryavada*

386. National policy on education 1986 also emphasised on
(a) social understanding
(b) national understanding
(c) international understanding
(d) All of the above

387. The Article 15 of Indian Constitution make the provision of
(a) allowing the untouchables to touch the caste Hindus.
(b) allowing the untouchables to avail of all the public places.
(c) allowing the untouchables in the Hotels.
(d) allowing the untouchables to take water from the wells.

388. The theory, that the effect is only the apparent of the cause, is known as
(a) *Vivartavada* (b) *Parinamavada*
(c) *Asatkaryavada* (d) *Satkaryavada*

389. The language which is our window to the world is
(a) English (b) French
(c) German (d) Hindi

390. What is the provision for Scheduled Castes in Articles 16 and 35 of Indian Constitution?
(a) Reservation for the subordinate services
(b) Reservation for the Harijan services
(c) Reservation for the post of IV class servants
(d) Reservation for the public services

391. The theory that the effect is already implicit in the cause, is known as
(a) *Vivartavada* (b) *Satkaryavada*
(c) *Asatkaryavada* (d) *Parinamavada*

392. The ultimate aim of education according to Naturalist is
(a) bringing the child back to nature.
(b) adaptation to changing environment.
(c) development of the child in a free environment.
(d) All of the above.

393. What is the provision for Scheduled Caste/Tribe in Article 25 of Indian Constitution?
(a) Freedom of going to Hindu religious places
(b) Freedom of staying in hotels
(c) Freedom of participating in Hindu marriage celebrations
(d) Freedom of studying in schools

394. The theory, that the effect is not implicit but super-imposed upon cause, is known as
(a) *Parinamavada* (b) *Vivartavada*
(c) *Satkaryavada* (d) *Asatkaryavada*

395. The criterion of judging values and reality in Pragmatism is
(a) rational discourses
(b) utility and usefulness
(c) changing needs of the society
(d) None of the above

396. The Article 29 of Indian Constitution has provided it for Scheduled Caste/Tribe students.
(a) They can study in only government schools
(b) They can study in government as well as private schools
(c) They can establish their own schools
(d) They can study in private school

397. The theory of causation known as *Parinamavada* in Indian philosophy has been supported by
(a) Ramanuja
(b) Samkhya
(c) Both (a) and (b)
(d) None of these

398. Curriculum means
(a) towards a circle
(b) towards a society
(c) towards a goal
(d) All of the above

399. What interests of untouchables are protected by Indian Constitution in Article 46?
(a) Removal of untouchability
(b) Economic
(c) Educational
(d) Both (b) and (c)

400. The cause, according to Indian philosophy, can be classified as
(a) Efficient cause
(b) Material cause
(c) Immediate cause
(d) All of these

401. Education must further provide a climate for its
(a) catalyst values
(b) adventurous role
(c) natural values
(d) any kind of role

402. What provisions have been made for the welfare of untouchables in the states by Articles 164 and 338 of Indian Constitution?
(a) Reservation in Services
(b) Free education and boarding
(c) Advisory Councils and Separate Departments
(d) Separate educational institutions

403. The material and the efficient cause, according to Samkhya philosophy, are related as
(a) Different (b) Identical
(c) Contradictory (d) None of these

404. Development of self-confidence is a must to innovate and
(a) have good job
(b) solve social problems
(c) perform social functions
(d) face unfamiliar situations

405. The objective of educational provisions made in the Constitution for the Scheduled Castes/Tribes was
(a) to give equal opportunities of education to all.
(b) to give preference to the education of the untouchables.
(c) to remove their backwardness.
(d) None of these.

406. The *Mimamsa* theory of causation is known as
(a) Vivartavada
(b) Parinamavada
(c) Theory of energy
(d) None of these

407. The biggest reality according to Pragmatism is
(a) adaptive power of humans
(b) consequences of action
(c) progress and change
(d) None of the above

408. What facilities have been given to the backward classes for giving them opportunities of education?
(a) Hostel facilities (b) Scholarships
(c) Free education (d) All of these

409. The world, according to Samkara, is the result of
(a) Evolution
(b) Real causation
(c) Super-imposition
(d) None of these

410. Which of the following tenets does not belong to Pragmatism?
(a) If individual is developed, society will automatically develop.
(b) Idea devoid of action are meaningless.
(c) Experiment is needed for verification of truth.
(d) Only that knowledge is significant which has any relevance to man.

411. In 1977-78, Government of India started this scheme for the education of the handicapped children.
(a) Special schools
(b) The Integrated Education Scheme for the handicapped
(c) Blind schools
(d) Deaf and dumb schools

412. The theory known as *Satkaryavada* includes
(a) *Vivartavada* (b) *Parinamavada*
(c) Both of them (d) None of these

413. The students should study for national consciousness through
(a) Science
(b) Indian history
(c) the Constitution of India
(d) Both (a) and (c)

414. In the following articles of Indian Constitution, the backward classes have been indicated for giving educational facilities.
(a) Article 45 (b) Article 342
(c) Article 341 (d) Both (b) and (c)

415. The causal relation, according to Samkara, is
(a) Unreal change (b) Real change
(c) Both of them (d) None of these

416. The National Policy on Education focussed on

(a) creativity of individual
(b) competence of individual
(c) social well-being
(d) All of the above

417. In the Vedic times, the objective of alms-begging by the students was to enable the students
(a) to develop their sense of duty and obligation towards society.
(b) to give up their sense of ego and adopt sense of sacrifice.
(c) to remove their inferiority complex due to wealth.
(d) All of these.

418. The reflection of Brahman as according to Samkara, is due to
(a) *Vyavahara* (b) *Avidya*
(c) *Adhyasa* (d) All of these

419. While saying that education contributes to national cohesion furthering the goals of socialism, secularism and democracy enshrined in our constitution, the National Policy on Education assumes that
(a) democracy is the best form of government.
(b) secularism is the most cherished goal of democracy.
(c) education can be used as an instrument of social change.
(d) socialism is the best way of organizing Indian society.

420. The centres of Buddhistic education were
(a) Buddh-Viharas (b) Buddh-Math
(c) Buddh-Stupas (d) Buddh-Chaitya

421. According to Pranvadin Charvakas, the nature of self is
(a) Vital principle (b) Mind
(c) Body (d) Sense organs

422. Pragmatism considers education
(a) as the reconstruction of experiences to benefit the society as a whole.
(b) as a responsibility of the state to take it to the last man of the society.
(c) as an interactive process that takes place in a social matrix.
(d) All of the above.

423. These books give an account of Buddhistic primary education system.
(a) Textbooks (b) Philosophy
(c) Jatak (d) Tripitak

424. According to *Atma Manovadin*, *Charvakas* self is
(a) Mind (b) Vital principle
(c) Sense organs (d) Body

425. Pragmatism is also known by the name of
(a) Experimentalism
(b) Pragmatic Naturalism
(c) Instrumentalism
(d) All of the above

426. The Buddhistic educational celebration "Pabajja" was done at the age of
(a) 5 years (b) 6 years
(c) 8 years (d) 10 years

427. The *Charvakas* deny the existence of
(a) Merit and demerit
(b) Heaven and hell
(c) Self
(d) All of these

428. Power is the "capability to control others so that they will do what they are wanted to do". What among the following does not make people to obey?
(a) Man grows in the order of obligation and duty.
(b) For the pleasure of leader and authority.
(c) For reasons selfish and social.
(d) Disobedience would involve penalty.

429. After "Pabajja" celebration the student was admitted to
(a) Chaitya (b) Stupa
(c) Vihar (d) Math or Sangh

430. The *Charvaka* theory of self can be termed as
(a) Vitalist (b) Mentalist
(c) Materialist (d) All of these

431. Education as the sub-system of the larger Indian society can contribute to strengthening of democracy through
(a) cultivation of essential values
(b) a dedicated and competent leadership
(c) educated electorate
(d) All of the above

432. When did the "Upsampada" rite was celebrated after "Pabajja" rite at what age and after how many years?
(a) After 5 years at the age of 13 years
(b) After 10 years at the age of 18 years
(c) After 12 years at the age of 20 years
(d) After 15 years at the age of 23 years

433. The false knowledge, according to Samkara, is known as
(a) *Adhyasa* (b) *Maya*
(c) *Vidya* (d) *Avidya*

434. The ultimate aim of education according to Gandhiji was to help the individuals to be
(a) able to acquire as much as possible from the ocean of knowledge.
(b) peaceful and happy in life.
(c) able to grow into a divine human being by realizing Godliness.
(d) gainfully employed in life.

435. After "Upsampada" rite were the boys and girls called respectively?
(a) Bhikshu-Bhikshuni
(b) Brahmachari-Brahmcharini
(c) Shraman-Shramani
(d) All of these

436. The cause of the power of *Maya*, according to Samkara, is
(a) *Adhyasa* (b) *Vidya*
(c) *Aidya* (d) None of these

437. Which of the following is not the postulate of Humanism?
(a) Supernatural hand is also there to punish those who hinders in getting happiness.
(b) Achieving happiness on earth is the birth right of man.
(c) Man is the maker of his own destiny.
(d) Man is competent to solve all his problems by applying reason and scientific methods.

438. After "Pabajja" rite boy was called
(a) Sanyasi (b) Shraman
(c) Bhikshu (d) Brahmchari

439. The cause of bondage of the *Jiva* in the world, according to Samkara, is
(a) *Maya* (b) *Adhyasa*
(c) *Avidya* (d) *Vidya*

440. Harmonious blending of all the philosophies and their implication in the classroom according to need of the society is called
(a) Eclectic tendency in education
(b) Modern tendency in education
(c) Sociological tendency in education
(d) None of the above

441. The person who tested the students before their admission to the Buddhistic centre of education was called
(a) Vice-Chancellor (b) Chancellor
(c) Dwarpal (d) Registrar

442. The nature of *Avidya*, according to Samkara, can be described as
(a) Natural (b) Eternal
(c) Both (a) and (b) (d) None of these

443. Who gives the system of education in India?
(a) State (b) Society
(c) Family (d) Economy

444. The teaching-method used in Buddhistic education was

(a) Conference (b) Tourism
(c) Question-Answer (d) All of these

445. The aim of the study of *Vedanta* scriptures is
(a) Achievement of self
(b) Brahman realisation
(c) Liberation from *Avidya*
(d) All of these

446. The Wardha or Basic scheme of Education was set in
(a) 1986-90 (b) 1986-88
(c) 1964-66 (d) 1937-38

447. Ashoka sent his sister to Sri Lanka to propagated Buddhism. Her name was
(a) Gargi (b) Sanghmitra
(c) Gayatri (d) Loparnudra

448. Knowledge, according to Mimamsa philosophy, is
(a) Unreal (b) Real
(c) Both (a) and (b) (d) None of these

449. Our educational system has proved
(a) ineffective (b) inadequate
(c) very effective (d) Both (a) and (b)

450 According to Buddhistic educational system, women received education in
(a) Vihars
(b) Stupas
(c) Homes
(d) Separate Sanghas

451. Founder of Existentialism was
(a) Sartre (b) Augustine
(c) Kierkegaard (d) Heidegger

452. What cave-paintings represent the excellent art of painting of Buddhistic India?
(a) Ajanta (b) Kalinga
(c) Kanchi (d) Sanchi

453. Which of the following philosophies gives much more importance to man?
(a) Existentialism
(b) Humanism
(c) Both (a) and (b)
(d) None of the above

454. In Buddhistic education system what kind of life a 'Bhikshu' led after "Upsampada" rite?
(a) As a teacher
(b) Lifelong unmarried
(c) As a householder
(d) As an ascetic

455. Rigidity and inflexibility in thinking becomes apparent under the
(a) Social system
(b) Democratic system
(c) Totalitarian system
(d) Religious system

456. In India under the Muslim rule the women could not be educated due to
(a) Sati system (b) Child marriage
(c) Parda system (d) Both (b) and (c)

457. According to materialism, the only valid *Pramana* is
(a) Scriptures (b) Inference
(c) Perception (d) None of these

458. In ancient India religious and moral aims dominated the
(a) Brahmin system
(b) Vaishya system
(c) Kshatriya system
(d) None of the above

459. In the medieval India, the punishments given to students were
(a) Severe (b) Ordinary
(c) Generous (d) All of these

460. Perception coming through the contact of external senses with objects according to *Charvaka* is known as
(a) Internal (b) External
(c) Both (a) and (b) (d) None of these

461. 'Every man has in him something divine, something his own, a chance of perfection and strength in however small a sphere which God offers him to take or refuse', is described by
(a) Aurobindo (b) Tagore
(c) Kant (d) Plato

462. Swami Vivekananda's Guru was
(a) Swami Swaroopa Nand
(b) Arvindo
(c) Swami Dayanand
(d) Ram Krishna Paramhans

463. Courage, perseverance, respect for freedom and life, truthfulness, honesty of purpose etc. will lead to .... of an individual.
(a) practical efficiency
(b) social efficiency
(c) moral efficiency
(d) religious efficiency

464. In 1863, the person who attended the "Conference of Religious" held in the city Chicago of America was
(a) Swami Vivekananda
(b) Mahatma Gandhi
(c) Maharshi Arvindo
(d) Swami Dayananda

465. The *Charvakas* have challenged the validity of
(a) Scriptures (b) Inference
(c) Both (a) and (b) (d) None of these

466. Our education proved inadequate and ineffective because we have been
(a) Ignorant
(b) Unscientific
(c) Both (a) and (b)
(c) Uncertain to our aim

467. In 1887 Swami Vivekananda established this institution.
(a) Vedic Math
(b) Ram Krishna Math
(c) Sabarmati Ashram
(d) Sevashram

468. The validity of scriptures has been challenged by the *Charvakas* in the field of
(a) Imperceptible things
(b) Perceptible things
(c) Both (a) and (b)
(d) None of these

469. The philosophy antagonistic to Marxism is/are
(a) Naturalism
(b) Existentialism
(c) Both (a) and (b)
(d) None of the above

470. Swami Dayanand's educational ideas are available in this book.
(a) *Harijan Patrika*
(b) *Parmarth*
(c) *Vedanta Darshan*
(d) *Vedic Shiksha*

471. *Charvakas* have rejected the validity of scriptures on the basis of
(a) Criticism of inference
(b) Contradictions and tautologies
(c) Absence of physical proof
(d) All of these

472. Individual and self-evaluation in the school is advocated by
(a) Existentialism
(b) Realism
(c) Idealism
(d) None of the above

473. What formula has been adopted in school education for the development of languages?
(a) Secular Formula
(b) Minority Formula
(c) Three Language Formula
(d) All of these

474. *Charvaka* criticism of scriptures has been challenged by
(a) *Advaita Vedanta* (b) *Samkhya*
(c) *Nyaya* (d) All of these

475. The aims in education are framed by centralized authorities in the government in
(a) Spiritual system
(b) Democratic system
(c) Totalitarian system
(d) All of the above

476. It is an institution in Shantiniketan (Vishwa Bharti).
(a) Shilp Sadan (b) Shri Niketan
(c) China-Bhawan (d) All of these

477. The philosophers who have condemned *Charvaka*, challenge to Vedas include
(a) Samkara (b) Udayana
(c) Vainkathnath (d) All of these

478. In Navodaya Vidyalayas, admission to...were made under the scheme for children
(a) Class V (b) Class VI
(c) Class VII (d) Class VIII

479. 'Shri Niketan' established by Ravindranath Tagore was an institution of this education.
(a) Art
(b) Music
(c) Craft
(d) Rural higher education

480. The arguments presented in favour of the Vedas include
(a) character of the authors.
(b) purpose to the authors.
(c) authenticity of the authors.
(d) All of these.

481. Ramamurthi Report was published in the year
(a) 1960 (b) 1970
(c) 1980 (d) 1990

482. Shantiniketan has this characteristics
(a) Daily silent prayer and secular meditation
(b) Residential university
(c) Medium of instruction is mother-tongue
(d) All of these

483. The most important element in the Jain theory of *Pramanas* is
(a) Scriptures (b) Perception
(c) *Naya* (d) Inference

484. Which of the following is exclusively advocated by Humanism?
(a) Happiness of man is to be increased in whatever manner it is possible.
(b) Freedom to propagate and follow religion.
(c) Man is the centre and measure of all activities in the world.
(d) All of the above.

485. Mahatma Gandhi did his educational experiments at this place of South Africa.
(a) Seva Ashram
(b) Sevagram
(c) Tolstoy Farm
(d) Sabarmati Ashram

486. Knowledge according to Jain philosophers can be called
(a) *Naya* (b) *Pramana*
(c) Both (a) and (b) (d) None of these

487. Which of the following philosophies believe in eternal and absolute values
(a) Humanism
(b) Idealism
(c) Both (a) and (b)
(d) None of the above

488. Who was the ex-President of India who heared the Gandhiji's basic education committee?
(a) Dr. Zakir Hussain
(b) Dr. Rajendra Prasad

(c) Dr. Sanjiv Neelam Reddy
(d) Faqruddin Ali Ahmed

489. The theory of *Naya* is based upon
(a) *Ekantvada* (b) *Anekantvada*
(c) Both (a) and (b) (d) None of these

490. In interpreting the phrases 'needs of the pupil'
(a) the realist says that the needs of the pupil are his impulses or wishes of the moment.
(b) the experimentalist says the needs must involve intelligent consideration of probable outcomes.
(c) the pragmatist says that a need is that which adult feels is good for the pupil.
(d) all philosophic groups agree that education must be rooted in the pupil's own felt needs.

491. The education plan constituted in 1944 recognised basic education but did not accept its self-supporting aspects was
(a) Sargent Education Plan
(b) Mudaliar Education Plan
(c) Kothari Education Plan
(d) Hunter Education Plan

492. *Pramanas,* according to Jaina's include
(a) Indirect (b) Direct
(c) Both (a) and (b) (d) None of these

493. Equality of educational opportunity also exists for those who are
(a) Mentally Retarded
(b) Deaf
(c) Blind
(d) All of the above

494. In 1956, what education plan was accepted by the conference of State Education Ministers to be introduced at the national level?
(a) Multipurpose School Plan
(b) Work-experience Plan
(c) Buniyadi Education Plan
(d) Kothari Education Plan

495. The knowledge of the qualities of the *Paksha* through the *Hetu* is known as
(a) *Vyapti* (b) *Paramarsa*
(c) *Anuman* (d) None of these

496. Education changes the
(a) Values among people
(b) Objective
(c) Attitudes
(d) All of the above

497. "God is truth and Truth is God". This statement is of this thinker.
(a) Shri Arvindo
(b) Mahatma Gandhi
(c) Vivekanand
(d) Ravindranath Tagore

498. The invariable relation between the *Hetu* and the *Saddaya* in *Nyaya* Philosophy is known as
(a) *Anuman* (b) *Vyapti*
(c) *Paramarsa* (d) None of these

499. Downfall in history, according to Humanism, is due to
(a) Hunger and poverty
(b) Class struggle
(c) Decline in moral standard and values
(d) The downfall of educational standard

500. "Basic Education being implemented by State Governments is a deceit." It is the statement of
(a) Dr. Zakir Hussain (b) Mudaliar
(c) Dr. Kothari (d) Sargent

501. *Vyapti* can be properly defined as
(a) Sequence
(b) Invariable concomitant
(c) Causal relation
(d) None of these

502. Modern Humanism believes in

(a) Internationalism
(b) Human welfare at all costs
(c) Universal brotherhood
(d) All of the above

503. What characteristic of work-experience did Kothari Education Commission recongnise when he gave it a place in education instead of rural craft?
(a) Forward Looking
(b) Handicraft
(c) Cottage Industry
(d) All of these

504. The knowledge of the relation between a name and the thing named in *Nyaya* is known as
(a) Comparison (b) Testimony
(c) Perception (d) Inference

505. National policy on Education was declared in the year
(a) 1986 (b) 1990
(c) 1985 (d) 1885

506. "We should impart such education which may form character strengthen will power develop intellect and make a man self-supporting." It is a statement of this thinker.
(a) Mahatma Gandhi
(b) Swami Vivekananda
(c) Swami Dayanada
(d) Maharshi Arvindo

507. The knowledge gained through the testimony of the reliable statement of scripture is known as
(a) Testimony (b) Comparison
(c) Perception (d) Inference

508. A most important instrument of the development is
(a) Religion (b) Education
(c) Will power (d) None of the above

509. Swami Vivekananda prescribed this subject in the curriculum of his educational scheme for spiritual development.
(a) Ethics (b) Theology
(c) Philosophy (d) All of these

510. Words according to *Nyaya* can be classified as
(a) *Adrastartha* (b) *Drastartha*
(c) Both (a) and (b) (d) None of these

511. The number of Navodaya Vidyalays is
(a) 256 (b) 266
(c) 276 (d) 280

512. Vivekananda advocated this method of teaching in his educational curriculum for spiritual knowledge.
(a) Yoga (b) Thinking
(c) Meditation (d) All of these

513. The basis of the classification of scriptural words according to *Nyaya* can be
(a) Origin of words
(b) Meaning of words
(c) Both (a) and (b)
(d) Neither of these

514. Modern democracy is very much indebted to which of the following philosophies?
(a) Existentialism (b) Humanism
(c) Naturalism (d) All of the above

515. "गुरू ब्रह्म गुरू विष्णु गुरूर्देवों महेश्वरा:।
गुरू साक्षात परब्रह्म तस्मे गुरूवे नम:।।"
Guru's this dignity is according to this educational philosophy.
(a) Naturalism (b) Existentialism
(c) Idealism (d) Realism

516. The words which are given to the seers through the God himself are known as
(a) *Laukika* (b) *Vedic*
(c) Both of them (d) None of these

517. Humanism as a modern philosophy emerged in

(a) 15th century (b) 17th century
(c) 19th century (d) 20th century

518. The Limitation of Idealism is
(a) Child-centred education
(b) Use of project-method
(c) The aim of self-realization is impracticable
(d) Giving prominence to science

519. Words created by ordinary human beings are known as
(a) *Laukika* (b) *Vedic*
(c) Both (a) and (b) (d) None of these

520. Gandhiji's ashrams is/are situated at
(a) Porbandar and Sabarmati
(b) Sabarmati and Sevagram
(c) Sevagram and Porbandar
(d) Porbandar, Sabarmati and Sevagram

521. Naturalism is of following types.
(a) Physical Science Naturalism
(b) Biological Naturalism
(c) Mechanical Naturalism
(d) All of these

522. The nature of *Vedic* words can be described as
(a) False (b) True
(c) Both (a) and (b) (d) None of these

523. The outlook of many classes, people, towards lower classes changed due to
(a) Education
(b) Religious practices
(c) Industrialization
(d) All of the above

524. The exponent of biological naturalism was
(a) Palto (b) Marx
(c) Darwin (d) Rousseau

525. *Prama* literally means the experience which is
(a) Doubtful (b) Real
(c) Unreal (d) None of these

526. The provisions of better and expanded programmes for the education of minorities has been given priority by
(a) National Policy of Education 1986
(b) Ramamurti Report 1990
(c) Both (a) and (b)
(d) None of the above

527. The naturalists do not believe in God so they do not give this value any place in education.
(a) Moral Value
(b) Character-building
(c) Nature-Study
(d) Physical Education

528. Valid knowledge according to *Mimamsa* includes
(a) Non-perceptual (b) Perceptual
(c) Both (a) and (b) (d) None of these

529. Rousseau's aim of education was
(a) to develop good as well as bad sense of the child.
(b) to help the child in the acquisition of moral values by action.
(c) to develop the child according to his innate tendencies and capacity.
(d) All of the above.

530. The following educationist supported naturalism.
(a) Herbert Spencer
(b) Economics
(c) Roussean
(d) All of these

531. The perceptual knowledge, according to *Mimamsa,* can be classified as
(a) Nirvikalpa (b) Savikalpa
(c) Both (a) and (b) (d) None of these

532. Which of the following methods is not supported by Rousseau
(a) Project method
(b) Laboratory method

(c) Learning by doing
(d) Heuristic method

533. The immediate knowledge according to *Mimamsa* is known as
(a) Non-perceptual (b) Perceptual
(c) Both (a) and (b) (d) None of these

534. According to naturalists the aim of education is
(a) Mental Development
(b) Spiritual Development
(c) Natural Development
(d) Moral Development

535. The rapid expansion of educational facilities and educational opportunities has benefited
(a) poor classes the most
(b) middle classes the most
(c) upper classes the most
(d) equally to all classes

536. "Do not give the student any oral instruction or advice let him learn by his own experience." Rousseau's this statement indicated his faith in this educational philosophy.
(a) Naturalism (b) Pregnatism
(c) Idealism (d) Socialism

537. Knowledge of name, shape, quality, etc. is known as
(a) *Nirvikalpa* (b) *Savikalpa*
(c) Both (a) and (b) (d) None of these

538. The provision for large scale expansion of facilities for the education of the physically and mentally handicapped in both rural and urban areas has been made in
(a) National Policy on Education
(b) Ramamurti Report
(c) Both (a) and (b)
(d) None of the above

539. Knowledge arising out of similar cognition or perception is known as
(a) Perception (b) Testimony
(c) Comparison (d) Inference

540. Accordingto naturalism, this teaching-methods the best.
(a) Playway method
(b) Inductive method
(c) Project method
(d) Deduction method

541. In terms of the nature of the learning experience
(a) the pragmatist sees it as a recording of something on a blank mental table.
(b) the realist sees it as a mirroring, by the mind of a pre-existing something.
(c) the idealist sees it as a discovery of something dependent upon the learner.
(d) the supernaturalist sees it as a revamping of former experiences of the learner.

542. "Know yourself", what philosophy believes in this aim of education?
(a) Pragmatism (b) Vedanta
(c) Realism (d) Idealism

543. The *Pramana* of *Upmana* in Indian philosophy has been accepted by
(a) *Vedanta* (b) *Nyaya*
(c) *Mimamsa* (d) All of these

544. The philosopher(s) supporting Utopian tendencies is/are
(a) Pestalozzi (b) Kant
(c) Comenius (d) All of the above

545. The most important source of knowledge according to *Mimamsa* is
(a) Comparison (b) Testimony
(c) Perception (d) Inference

546. "Sankhya" philosophy believes in
(a) World (b) Human being
(c) Nature (d) Both (b) and (c)

547. Pestalozzi wanted to establish a/an
(a) modern society
(b) scientific society
(c) primitive society
(d) ethical society

548. "Vedanta" is related to
(a) Philosophy (b) "Vaishashik"
(c) Yoga (d) Mimasa

549. The *Vedic* statements, according to *Mimamsa*, can be classified as
(a) Vidhayaka (b) *Siddhartha*
(c) Both (a) and (b) (d) None of these

550. Scholarships for the talented and merit scholarships for bright students were established in the year
(a) 1950 (b) 1955
(c) 1957 (d) 1960

551. Sentences pertaining to objective existence are known as
(a) *Vidhayaka* (b) *Siddhartha*
(c) Both (a) and (b) (d) None of these

552. According to "Sankhya" philosophy, the meaning of salvation is
(a) Meditation (b) Knowledge
(c) Yoga (d) Religion

553. Any child, rich or poor has been able to compete for the scholarships which provide expenses for
(a) Lodging (b) Travel
(c) Tuition (d) All of the above

554. According to Shankarachary, the steps of self-expression are
(a) Study (b) Listening
(c) Meditation (d) All of these

555. Statements concerning the Mode of Performance of religious activity are known as
(a) *Siddhartha* (b) *Vidhayaka*
(c) Both (a) and (b) (d) None of these

556. Those who urge that religion should be taught in our public schools are assuming that
(a) non-communicational instruction can be given in religion.
(b) moral values cannot be taught apart from religion.
(c) the issue of separation of church and state is not involved.
(d) None of the above.

557. "Achieve heaven through charity for a whole month" is a statement which can be classified as
(a) *Atidesa* (b) *Upadesaka*
(c) Both (a) and (b) (d) None of these

558. This philosophy emphasises on scientific and practical thinking.
(a) Gita Philosophy
(b) Indian Philosophy
(c) Western Philosophy
(d) Jain Philosophy

559. Which of the following ideas has not been given by Pestalozzi?
(a) Fun games should be introduced in education.
(b) Growth of the child is more important than achievement.
(c) Mental development of the child through education.
(d) Even wrong conclusions if drawn by the child himself is acceptable.

560. Indian philosophy regards knowledge as
(a) Means (b) Best
(c) Deplorable (d) Third eye

561. The postulation of a fact by the impossibility of its opposite is known as
(a) Inference (b) *Arthapatti*
(c) Testimony (d) *Anupalabdhi*

562. Dewey differs from other philosophers of the 20th century in his concept of

(a) Experimentalism
(b) Activity centred education
(c) Mind
(d) All of the above

563. The immediate knowledge of the non-existence of an object is known as
(a) Testimony (b) Inference
(c) Anupalabdhi (d) Arthapatti

564. In this period of Indian History, the education was available to all.
(a) Modern Time (b) Ancient Time
(c) Medieval Time (d) All of these

565. The essentialists would get their aims of education from
(a) public interests
(b) our traditions
(c) the church
(d) the great books

566. According to Vedanta, "Knowledge" develops this quality in man.
(a) Pride (b) Humility
(c) Jealousy (d) Self-respect

567. *Prama,* according to *Vedanta,* is the knowledge which is
(a) Worldly
(b) Uncontradictory
(c) Other worldly
(d) Contradictory

568. The classical realists would stress as their aim in education
(a) adjustment to nature
(b) preparation for the vocational virtues
(c) realization of the self
(d) development of the intellectual virtues

569. *Pramanas,* according to *Vedanta*, can be classified as
(a) Scriptures (b) Perception
(c) Inference (d) All of these

570. In a good educational system, the best discipline is
(a) Self Discipline (b) Strict Discipline
(c) Free Discipline (d) None of these

571. In determining the aims of education the
(a) realist would accept only those aims which emerge from a study of the situation.
(b) supernaturalist would accept uncritically the aims listed by the church.
(c) idealist would use the interest and needs of pupils in the present.
(d) pragmatist would accept only those aims which resulted from a study of society.

572. The limitations of ancient education was
(a) Realism (b) Idealism
(c) Pragmatism (d) Spiritualism

573. The identity of the subject and object consciousness adopting the form of external object is known as
(a) Scriptures (b) Perception
(c) Inference (d) All of these

574. The test of truth and reality according to Dewey is
(a) usefulness through experimentation
(b) social significance
(c) individual benefits
(d) Both (a) and (b)

575. The relation of subject and object in perception, according to *Vedanta*, is
(a) Contradictory (b) Identical
(c) Different (d) None of these

576. The curriculum according to naturalists should be
(a) Informal (b) Natural
(c) Formal (d) Practical

577. Those desires and norms whose gratification hinders the economic efficiency of man is called
(a) Positive morality
(b) Instrumentalism

(c) Negative morality
(d) None of the above

578. The defect of the curriculum enunciated by Herbert spencer was
(a) physical education for self-defence.
(b) no place for language.
(c) to give prominence to science.
(d) fine arts for leisure.

579. The knowledge which results by the past impressions based upon the awareness of concomitance is known as
(a) Inference (b) Scriptures
(c) Perception (d) All of these

580. In the eyes of the idealist, the values of an educational experience depend upon
(a) the extent to which it satisfies pupil's desires.
(b) whether or not the pupil has been properly motivated.
(c) whether or not it preserves accepted institutions.
(d) the manner in which it affects future experience.

581. The most important *Pramana,* according to *Advaita Vedanta,* is
(a) Scriptures (b) Perception
(c) Inference (d) All of these

582. The main characteristic of naturalistic education is
(a) Child-centred Education
(b) Strict Discipline
(c) Dignity of Labour
(d) Practicability

583. The educative experience is desirable to the
(a) realist only if it is pleasurable and practical for the pupil.
(b) pragmatist only if, on the whole it is acceptable to the pupil.
(c) reconstructionist only if it helps the pupils earn failure.
(d) realist only if it is affective in attaining immediate goals.

584. This educational philosophy does not give any importance to the teacher.
(a) Pragmatism (b) Realism
(c) Naturalism (d) Idealism

585. While *Nyaya* admits as many as five stages in the process of inference, Samkara has admitted
(a) Seven (b) Two
(c) Three (d) None of these

586. As to the question of what kind of education should be given
(a) Hutchins would combine vocational training with general education.
(b) the realist sees different kinds of education secured incidentally through natural growth.
(c) the supernaturalist believes that moral education requires specific subject matter.
(d) the idealist sees both the method and training functions as necessary and related.

587. The best theory of *Pramanas* in Indian philosophy has been presented by
(a) *Advaita Vedanta* (b) *Nyaya*
(c) *Samkhya* (d) None of these

588. Rousseau was in favour of punishing the student by
(a) Guardian (b) Nature
(c) Teacher (d) All of these

589. The concept of neutral monoism was given by
(a) Kant (b) Sartre
(c) TP Nunn (d) Russell

590. "The teacher's place is behind the curtain". This statement of Ross indicates his faith in this philosophy of education.

(a) Existentialism (b) Idealism
(c) Pragmatism (d) Naturalism

591. The most, important source of knowledge, according to Indian philosophy is
(a) Inference (b) Perception
(c) Scriptures (d) All of these

592. Regarding method of teaching Russell advocates
(a) analysis as method of teaching.
(b) maximum use of senses for learning.
(c) scientific way of dealing the subject matter.
(d) All of the above.

593. The imposition of some external objects upon the self, according to Samkara, means
(a) *Akyativada*
(b) *Atmakhyativada*
(c) *Asatkhyativada*
(d) *Anyathakhyativada*

594. Herbert Spencer in naturalistic education seeks to find solution to the problem of discipline by this theory.
(a) Physical punishment
(b) Prevention Theory
(c) Hedomistic Theory
(d) All of these

595. The question of who shall be educated is inextricably tied to
(a) the kind of government
(b) the philosophy of education
(c) the aims of education
(d) All of the above

596. The limitation of naturalistic education is
(a) Artificiality
(b) Severe punishment
(c) Ignores natural consequences
(d) Ignores spiritualism

597. The theory of error known as *Atmakhyativada* in Indian philosophy has been presented by
(a) *Nyaya* (b) *Mimamsa*
(c) *Advaita Vedanta* (d) *Samkhya*

598. On the question of 'the kind of education to be imparted',
(a) the idealist sees both the method and training functions as unnecessary and unrelated.
(b) the realist sees different kinds of education as secured incidentally through natural growth.
(c) Hutchins would postpone vocational training until general education is finished.
(d) the supernaturalist believes that moral education requires no specific subject matter.

599. The theory of imposition of a mental concept upon the external world is known as
(a) *Asatkhyativada*
(b) *Mmyativada*
(c) *Akhathakhyativada*
(d) *Atmakhyativada*

600. The similarity between naturalistic and idealistic education is
(a) development of self-realization.
(b) child-centred education.
(c) prominent place of teacher.
(d) stress on "Learning by doing" principles.

601. Which of he following philosophers supports child-centred education?
(a) John Dewey and Plato
(b) Maria Montessori
(c) Froebel
(d) All of the above

602. "Man builds his values in his activity"— Ross. What philosophical beliefs does this statement show?
(a) Realism (b) Existentialism
(c) Idealism (d) Pragmatism

603. The imposition of an object upon another due to illusion is known as
(a) *Asatkhyativada*
(b) *Akhyativada*
(c) *Atmakhyativada*
(d) *Anyathakhyativada*

604. The ability to think, is the most important attribute which education should aim at developing in the school. This statement is attributed to
(a) Hegal (b) Kapila
(c) John Dewey (d) Plato

605. The imagination of quality in a thing which has been the subject of imposition of the object having that quality leads to the error known as
(a) *Anyathakhyativada*
(b) *Asatkhyativada*
(c) *Atmakhyativada*
(d) *Akhyativada*

606. The following is the form of pragnatism.
(a) Experimental Pragmatism
(b) Humanist Pragmatism
(c) Ideal Pragmatism
(d) Both (a) and (b)

607. The second amendment of 1976 of the Indian Constitution
(a) brought closer relationship between education and agriculture.
(b) declared the partial considerations as aims of education.
(c) insisted on the vocationalisation of education.
(d) stressed on the social aspect of knowledge to be imparted in schools.

608. One of the principles of pragmatism is
(a) truth is never static and final.
(b) the soul or God exists.
(c) man is the best creation of God.
(d) unity in diversity.

609. The imposition of some quality in a thing where it is not, is known as
(a) *Akhyati* (b) *Avidya*
(c) *Adhyasa* (d) None of these

610. The period known as renaissance in the history of civilization and produced great changes in education
(a) preceded the medieval period
(b) followed the medieval period
(c) was characterised by low standards of education
(d) None of the above

611. The proper cause of *adhyasa,* according to Samkara, is
(a) *Vyavahara* (b) *Avidya*
(c) *Maya* (d) All of these

612. It is not a principle of idealism.
(a) Idea is basis of physical world
(b) Nature depends on will
(c) Truth is not static in life
(d) God is the creator of world

613. In India the primary aim of education is
(a) to make the country educationally strong.
(b) to prepare individuals for employment.
(c) to provide whole some knowledge.
(d) to safeguard national interest.

614. The limitations of pragmatism is
(a) no uniformity in educational organisation.
(b) undue stress on utility principle.
(c) curriculum-making is difficult.
(d) All of these.

615. The world, according to Samkara, is
(a) Illusory (b) Real
(c) Unreal (d) None of these

616. Ministry of education for all the states and union territories of the country was set up during the

(a) 4th five year plan
(b) 3rd five year plan
(c) 5th five year plan
(d) 1st five year plan

617. In Indian philosophy, the theory of error has been mostly utilised in the field of
(a) Epistemology (b) Axiology
(c) Metaphysics (d) All of these

618. Pragmatism regards this methods as the best
(a) Lecture Method
(b) Discussion Method
(c) Project Method
(d) Story-telling method

619. What does the individual aim of education imply?
(a) It must contribute to the peace and happiness of the whole society.
(b) It should be by and large the concern of the private sector.
(c) Education must secure for everyone the conditions under which the individuality is most completely developed.
(d) More and more institutions should be added every year.

620. It is the contribution of pragnatism in the field of curriculum.
(a) It made it activity-based
(b) It made it idealistic
(c) It made it definite
(d) None of these

621. Naturalism emphasises it in the curriculum.
(a) Relation with Nature through science
(b) Truth useful and beauty
(c) Utility in life
(d) All of these

622. Students have to be concerned about the preservation of
(a) Animal life (b) Forests
(c) Bird life (d) All of the above

623. Samkara has utilised the *Adhyasa* to explain
(a) nature of world.
(b) nature of Brahman.
(c) nature of liberation.
(d) nature of self.

624. The proper nature of *Adhyasa* can be explained as
(a) Ignorance (b) Knowledge
(c) Both (a) and (b) (d) None of these

625. The care of its aged members is the responsibility of the family in
(a) U.S.A. (b) United Kingdom
(c) Canada (d) All of the above

626. Gita contains this principle of integration.
(a) Gyan Yoga and Bhakti Yoga
(b) Karma Yoga Gyan Yoga and Bhakti Yoga
(c) Karma Yoga and meditation
(d) Meditation and Bhakti Yoga

627. The right knowledge, according to Samkara, is known as
(a) *Adhyasa* (b) *Maya*
(c) *Vidya* (d) *Avidya*

628. Individual interests must be subordinate to those of state. This interpretation is best illustrated in the
(a) Ancient Indian system
(b) Roman system of education
(c) Spartan system of education
(d) None of the above

629. The knowledge known as *Pramana* is gained by
(a) Jiva (b) Sense organs
(c) Soul (d) None of these

630. सर्वभूतेषु यनै कम् भावभव्यमीक्ते।
अभिभक्तं विभक्तेषु तज्ज्ञानं विद्धि सात्विकम्।।

This complete (श्लोक) of Gita defines it.
(a) Bhakti (b) Gyan
(c) Karma (d) Nishkarma

631. Which of the following views about discipline would be acceptable to you if you are an idealist?
(a) Discipline should emphasise on factors external to the individual.
(b) Discipline is necessary only for idealists.
(c) Punishment is necessary to impose discipline.
(d) Discipline should grow with the child himself.

632. "ज्ञान कर्मसु कौशलम" in Gita means "to perform activity with skill". It has made this socially useful.
(a) Skillful activity
(b) Activity for other's welfare
(c) Nishkam Karma
(d) Activity with purpose

633. The knowledge which the *Jiva* attains without any help is known as
(a) *Paroksha* (b) *Pratyaksha*
(c) Both (a) and (b) (d) None of these

634. Irrespective of prevailing totalitarian or democratic governments, there is a great realization that exposure to vocational skills and knowledge are essential in the school to bring about
(a) Individual efficiency
(b) Group efficiency
(c) Social efficiency
(d) Economic efficiency

635. The knowledge of a thing by means of *Hetu,* according to Jain's is known as
(a) *Paroksha* (b) *Pratyaksha*
(c) Both (a) and (b) (d) None of these

636. Gita has divided the curriculum into two categories—"Apara" and "Para" knowledge. "Para" means
(a) Knowledge of God
(b) Physical world
(c) Spiritual
(d) All of these

637. Who among of the following is not the exponent of Humanistic Realism?
(a) Aristotle (b) Erasmus
(c) Rabelais (d) Milton

638. Gita desires this feeling of student towards his teacher.
(a) Humility (b) Self-control
(c) Dedication (d) All of these

639. Knowledge, according to *Nyaya,* can be properly described as
(a) *Aprama* (b) *Prama*
(c) Both (a) and (b) (d) None of these

640. Whitehead and Russell support
(a) Sense Realism
(b) Humanistic Realism
(c) Neorealism
(d) Social Realism

641. Uncontradicted knowledge arising out of the sense object contact is known as
(a) Testimony (b) Comparison
(c) Inference (d) Perception

642. Gita's contribution to the field of education is this.
(a) Yoga practice
(b) Spiritual development
(c) Socially useful work
(d) Selfless act

643. "Man is a spiritual being and the world of ideas and values is more important than the world of matter". This was said by
(a) Plato (b) Gandhiji
(c) Kapila Muni (b) All of the above

644. Jain Saint Tulsi's this moral movement is well known.
(a) Anu Vrat (b) Panch Mahavrat
(c) Right knowledge (d) Ahinsa

645. The most important source of knowledge according to *Nyaya* philosophy, is
(a) Comparison (b) Testimony
(c) Perception (d) Inference

646. Under all systems of government, the education systems have reacted to similar pressure in the
(a) 18th century (b) 19th century
(c) 20th century (d) 21th century

647. *Anuma* knowledge, according to *Nyaya*, is
(a) Inference (b) Perception
(c) Testimony (d) Comparison

648. In the Jain "Panch Mahavrat", this "Vrat" is main
(a) Truth (b) Asteya
(c) Ahinsa (d) All of these

649. According to Comenius "Ultimate end of man is eternal happiness" so, education should aim at
(a) helping him to enjoy life
(b) using the senses more and more
(c) making the child God fearing
(d) None of the above

650. It is one of the "Tri Ratnas" of Jainism.
(a) Right Education (b) Right Action
(c) Right Character (d) Right Speech

651. The proper means of *Anumana*, according to *Nyaya*, is
(a) *Sadhya* (b) *Paksha*
(c) *Perception* (d) *Hetu*

652. "The world is continuously evolving toward greater degree of perfection that is God". It is the opinion of
(a) Aristotle (b) Comenius
(c) Hegel (d) Russell

653. In Jainism, "Salvation" means
(a) freedom from both Jiva and Pudgal.
(b) the integration of Jiva and Pudgal.
(c) the freedom of 'Jiva' (soul) from matter (Pudgal).
(d) the meeting of Jiva and Pudgal.

654. This teaching-method is suitable to develop "Shruti-knowledge" in Jain educational system.
(a) Seminar (b) Study of books
(c) Interpretation (d) All of these

655. Liberation, as nearness to *Ishwara*, according to Ramanuja, is known as
(a) *Sanidhya* (b) *Sayujya*
(c) *Salokya* (d) *Samipya*

656. The chief aim of education shall be to help the growing soul to draw out that in itself which is best and make it perfect for a noble use, according to
(a) Religious aim (b) Moral aim
(c) Social aim (d) Spiritual aim

657. The important means for achievement or liberation, according to Samkara, is
(a) concentration on Om.
(b) religious practices.
(c) distinction of self and not-self
(d) All of these.

658. This teaching method is suitable for "Mati-Knowledge"
(a) Minute Study
(b) Supervised Study
(c) Discussion
(d) Methods of direct knowledge

659. Where is the pressure felt strong by the teacher?
(a) Form global government
(b) Large number of adults to educate
(c) Large number of children to educate
(d) Making religion strong

660. "Jainism accepts both soul and world as realities"—Dr. Oad. According to this view following types of subjects have been included in the curriculum.

(a) Spiritual Subjects
(b) Worldly Subjects
(c) Scientific Subjects
(d) Both (a) and (b)

661. The main theories concerning the intrinsic values are
(a) Objective theory
(b) Axiological subjectivists
(c) Both (a) and (b)
(d) None of these

662. There is a distinction between matter and form and their existence is independent of mind. This idea makes Aristotle
(a) a Humanist (b) a Realist
(c) a Pragmatist (d) an Existentialist

663. The extrinsic values mainly include
(a) Things (b) Property
(c) Wealth (d) All of these

664. The main source-book of Jain Philosophy is
(a) Pudgal
(b) Relativity
(c) "Syadbad"
(d) "Kalp Sutra" of Bhadra Bahu

665. According to Aristotle, education should aim at enabling man to attain his rational self and raise his level by increasing his divinity
(a) by living with the matter
(b) by realizing the rational self
(c) by forsaking the matter that restricts his upward movement
(d) Both (b) and (c)

666. According to Jain Philosophy, the education should make the following behavioural changes in the student.
(a) To have self-control by mind word and action
(b) To free from the four "Kashaya"
(c) To be interested in "Anu Vrat"
(d) All of these

667. Health can be classified as having the value of
(a) Instrumental (b) Extrinsic
(c) Intrinsic (d) None of these

668. The Wardha Scheme of education was an explosive plan in the year
(a) 1964 (b) 1956
(c) 1937 (d) 1930

669. Beauty can be classified as having the value of
(a) Extrinsic (b) Instrumental
(c) Ultimate (d) None of these

670. According to Jainism, the student who after completing his education becomes householder is called
(a) Brahmchari (b) Vidyarthi
(c) "Shrawak" (d) "Shraman"

671. Gandhiji believed in the absolute oneness of
(a) Country (b) Culture
(c) God (d) World

672. In Jain Educational System, this type of discipline is defined.
(a) Ordinary (b) Strict
(c) Free (d) Ideal

673. According to Jainism, a student has to give up the following "Kashayas".
(a) Pride, anger, maya and greed
(b) Knowledge, religion ethics and shame
(c) Sex anger, pride and love
(d) All of these

674. Tagore's aim of education was
(a) self-realization through nature study.
(b) self-realization through meditation.
(c) self-realization by establishing affinity between man, nature and God.
(d) self-realization through yoga.

675. Value can be properly defined as
(a) Object of effort
(b) Aim of life

(c) Something important
(d) All of these

676. Value is accompanied with
(a) Sacrifices (b) Beliefs
(c) Convictions (d) All of these

677. Tagore's belief that man is the centre and measure of all activities in the universe makes him a/an
(a) Existentialist (b) Idealist
(c) Naturalist (d) Humanist

678. "Syadbad" in Jainism means
(a) there should be different views to reach a conclusion.
(b) a conclusion can be reached by any view.
(c) different conclusion can be reached by different views.
(d) None of these.

679. Value has been closely linked with interest. This statement has been given by
(a) J.S. Mill (b) W.M. Urban
(c) J.S. Mackenzie (d) J.B. Perry

680. Gandhiji made a dramatic bid for temple entry rights for untouchables in the year
(a) 1940 (b) 1935
(c) 1930 (d) 1920

681. According to psychologists, value is primarily concerned with
(a) Sentiments (b) Drives
(c) Needs (d) All of these

682. The main elements of Jain Philosophy are
(a) Syadbad (b) Jiva
(c) Ajiva (d) All of these

683. After Gandhiji's assassination several Brahman homes were set on fire in
(a) Gujarat (b) Punjab
(c) West Bengal (d) Maharashtra

684. According to Jainism, this bondage of ignorance is removed by knowledge.
(a) Bondage of worldly pleasures
(b) Bondage of Maya and affection
(c) Bondage of Soul and 'Pudgal' (matter)
(d) Bondage of Maya and Soul

685. According to ethicists, values are concerned with
(a) Purposes (b) Morals
(c) Reasons (d) All of these

686. Gandhiji believes in the essential ______ of man and for that matter of all that life encompasses.
(a) unity (b) uncertainty
(c) certainty (d) None of these

687. Axiological judgement shows the characteristics of
(a) Obligatory
(b) Based upon judgement
(c) Inevitable
(d) All of these

688. One of the "Panch Mahavrat", "Aprigrah" means
(a) not to steal anything.
(b) not to tease others.
(c) not to speak lie.
(d) giving up worldly things.

689. The dimensions of reality, according to Tagore is three—man, nature and
(a) Rational thinking
(b) God
(c) Matter
(d) None of the above

690. What is that Jain "Panch Mahavrat" called which asks one to give up sex-attraction?
(a) Ahinsa (b) Brahmcharya
(c) Aprigrah (d) Asteya

691. The materialists define value as
(a) Spiritual (b) Material
(c) Mental (d) None of these

692. Which of the following beliefs makes Tagore an Idealist?
(a) Utilitarian aim of education
(b) Development of spirituality
(c) Bread butter aims of education
(d) None of the above

693. The spiritualists define value as
(a) Mental (b) Spiritual
(c) Material (d) None of these

694. Strict discipline and dedication towards teacher can develop it in the student.
(a) Brahamcharya (b) Humility
(c) Receptivity (d) Knowledge

695. Zeal and temperament to perform the stupendous task of educating children is the framework of
(a) Dr. De Youngs philosophy
(b) Tagore's philosophy
(c) Gandhiji's philosophy
(d) None of the above

696. The following are called "Tripitak" the Buddhism religious books.
(a) Adhimm Pitak (b) Vinaya Pitak
(c) Satra Pitak (d) All of these

697. Values have been classified as
(a) Extrinsic (b) Intrinsic
(c) Both (a) and (b) (d) None of these

698. Educational system in ancient Greece was based on
(a) Religion
(b) Cultural value
(c) Interesting study
(d) Development of physical strength

699. Goodwill, according to Immaniial Kant, is
(a) Instrumental value
(b) Extrinsic value
(c) Intrinsic value
(d) None of these

700. This emperor made a great contribution to the propagation of Buddhism.
(a) Ashoka
(b) Skandgupta
(c) Chandragupta Maurya
(d) Harsh

701. According to Tagore, knowledge should be communicated to children in
(a) an environment where free action is permitted.
(b) an environment of nature.
(c) a social and friendly environment.
(d) All of the above.

702. The ultimate good includes
(a) Intrinsic value
(b) Instrumental value
(c) Extrinsic value
(d) None of these

703. Gandhiji searched for truth as
(a) an humanist (b) a communist
(c) an egoist (d) an economist

704. The ultimate human values are of the nature of
(a) Spiritual (b) Physical
(c) Intellectual (d) None of these

705. Who organised Buddh Conference at Kundalvan?
(a) Harsha (b) Bimbsar
(c) Ashoka (d) Kanishk

706. Traditionally untouchables were not allowed to
(a) enter certain parks
(b) pass-through certain streets
(c) enter temples
(d) All of the above

707. In the fourth Buddh Conference, Buddhism was devided into these two seats.
(a) Hinyan and Mahayan
(b) Sakar and Nirakar

(c) Digambar and Shwetambar
(d) Grahast and Sanyasi

708. Values can be classified as
(a) Temporary (b) Permanent
(c) Both (a) and (b) (d) None of these

709. At the bottom of the social ladder is a group of castes officially known as the
(a) Backward castes (b) Upper castes
(c) Forward castes (d) Scheduled castes

710. The theory of liberation has been rejected in Indian philosophy by the school known as
(a) the Vedanta (b) the Buddhists
(c) the Jaina (d) the Charvaka

711. What was Siddharth's leaving his home called?
(a) Sanyas-Grahan
(b) Mahabhinish Kraman
(c) Mahaparinirwan
(d) Maha Dharm Chakra Pravartan

712. Parentheistic relationship between man and nature makes him, according to Tagore, a
(a) cosmic man
(b) happy man
(c) real man
(d) None of the above

713. The "Arya Satya" of Buddhism that influenced Buddhistic education was
(a) removal of sufferings—its way.
(b) origin of sufferings.
(c) removal of sufferings.
(d) All of these.

714. Liberation, according to Charvaka, can be said to be
(a) Foolish (b) Possible
(c) Impossible (d) None of these

715. Which of the following beliefs of Gandhiji makes him a liberal Idealist?
(a) Non-violence (absence of ill will against all living being), is the means of Satyagraha.
(b) Truth is God and vice versa, Satyagraha (insistence for truth) is the only way of self-realization.
(c) Both (a) and (b).
(d) None of the above.

716. Liberation, according to Jaina philosophy, is
(a) freedom from life and death.
(b) freedom from *Karma*.
(c) freedom of matter.
(d) All of these.

717. According to Buddhism one of the "Ashtang Marg" is
(a) Right determination
(b) Right food
(c) Right dress
(d) All of these

718. Gandhiji was a philosopher in the sense that he had certain
(a) Beliefs
(b) Life views
(c) Systematic approaches
(d) All of the above

719. In the "Ashtang Marg", the meaning of "Right Meditation" is
(a) to give up speaking lie.
(b) to implement Buddha's teachings.
(c) to achieve perfect happiness through concentration.
(d) to determine to try to achieve salvation.

720. Liberation, according to Jaina philosophy can be classified as
(a) *Dravya moksha* (b) *Bhava moksha*
(c) Both (a) and (b) (d) None of these

721. Which article of the constitution abolishes untouchability and forbades its practice in any form?

(a) Article 13 (b) Article 14
(c) Article 15 (d) Article 17

722. The state of *Jivan mukti* is included in
(a) *Bhava moksha* (b) *Dravya moksha*
(c) Both (a) and (b) (d) None of these

723. "To behave honestly in the earning of livelihood"—this "Ashtang-Marg" is known as
(a) Right livelihood (b) Right feeling
(c) Right action (d) Right view

724. "When learning is restricted to learning from direct experience and to learning from the teacher and excludes learning through self-study and general reading, it is bound to be limited and patchy". This has been remarked by
(a) Dewey (b) Dr. E.A. Pires
(c) Dr. H. Bhabha (d) Fichte

725. This was one of ten good conduct rules prescribed by Buddha for Bhikshus.
(a) To work hard
(b) Not to deceive others
(c) To do good to others
(d) To tell the truth

726. Liberation, according to Jaina, can be achieved by
(a) Self-control (b) Detachment
(c) Penance (d) All of these

727. Gandhiji believed in
(a) education for self-reliance
(b) education through crafts
(c) education through mother tongue
(d) All of the above

728. Liberation, according to Buddha, means
(a) Freedom (b) Detachment
(c) Extinction (d) None of these

729. The philosophical assumption of Buddhism is
(a) Faith in God (b) Faith in Soul
(c) Faith in Fate (d) Faith in Karm

730. By corelating schools with the local industry, Gandhiji supports
(a) Marxism (b) Pragmatism
(c) Existentialism (d) None of these

731. Buddha has shown this way or path for achieving salvation.
(a) Human Path (b) Medium Path
(c) Difficult Path (d) Easy Path

732. Liberation in Buddhist philosophy is known as
(a) *Mukti* (b) *Nirvana*
(c) *Moksha* (d) None of these

733. Mahatma Gandhi was
(a) Leader all his life
(b) Follower all his life
(c) Experimenter all his life
(d) Philosopher all his life

734. The most important means for achieving *Nirvana,* according to Buddha, is
(a) Detachment (b) Mortification
(c) Eight-fold path (d) Penance

735. The ancient Buddhistic education centres had this arrangement.
(a) Co-education (b) Games
(c) Supervision (d) Boarding

736. Gandhiji is more known in the domain of
(a) Social reform (b) Politics
(c) Education (d) None of these

737. In ancient Nalanda University, the duty of "Dwar-Pandit" was
(a) to test the student for admission.
(b) to work as Vice-chancellor.
(c) to work as watchman.
(d) to regulate the movement of students.

738. *Nirvana* in Buddhist texts has been described as
(a) Eternal health (b) Perfect freedom
(c) State of peace (d) All of these

739. In post-independent India the .... prominence is clearly visible

(a) Brahmin (b) Shudra
(c) Vaishya (d) Kshatriya

740. According to Chinese traveller Hiuen Tsang, the teaching-method in Buddhistic Education Centres was
(a) Micreo-teaching (b) Project
(c) Excursion (d) Discussion

741. *Nirvana* cannot be described as
(a) Nihilism (b) Eternalism
(c) Both (a) and (b) (d) None of these

742. Thales' lived in Miletus in Asia minor in
(a) 800 BC (b) 500 BC
(c) 700 BC (d) 600 BC

743. The famous preaching of *Nirvana* to king Milinda were given by
(a) Nagarjuna (b) Nagasena
(c) Gautam Buddha (d) None of these

744. The aim of Buddhistic education was to orient the student towards
(a) Successful householder
(b) Nirvan
(c) Salvation
(d) Sanyas

745. Buddha stressed
(a) Individual effort
(b) Responsibility
(c) Both (a) and (b)
(d) None of the above

746. According to Chinese travellers, the teacher-pupil relation in the Buddhistic education centres were
(a) as father and son.
(b) as scholar and ignorant.
(c) as master and servant.
(d) as Critic and subject of criticism.

747. The important forms of *Nirvana* include
(a) *Nirupadhi sesa* (b) *Sopadhi sesa*
(c) Both (a) and (b) (d) None of these

748. "Education as a force makes an individual self-reliant as well as selfless." This statement is related to
(a) Samveda (b) Upanishads
(c) Rigveda (d) Vedanta

749. The world as suffering has been postulated by
(a) Samkhya (b) Jainas
(c) Buddhism (d) All of these

750. The student in Buddhistic education centres had to follow the following course to attain freedom from sufferings.
(a) Ashtang Marg
(b) Four "Arya Satya"
(c) Panch Mahavrai
(d) Both (a) and (b)

751. Real education prepares a man for struggle for existence and social service. It is the opinion of
(a) Tagore
(b) Gandhiji
(c) Vivekananda
(d) None of the above

752. The cause of suffering, according to Samkhya, philosophy is
(a) Attachment (b) Fear
(c) Ignorance (d) None of these

753. The aim of teaching-method in Jain education is
(a) "Mati"
(b) "Kewaiya Gyan"
(c) "Shruti Gyan"
(d) "Avadhi"

754. Who among the following was a staunch supporter of practical and technical education?
(a) Vivekananda
(b) Gandhiji
(c) Both (a) and (b)
(d) None of the above

755. According to Jain Philosophy to attain knowledge the student has to adopt it.
(a) Self-control and humility
(b) Strict discipline

(c) Interest and attention
(d) All of these

756. Liberation, according to Samkhya, can be attained by
(a) Enjoyment (b) Knowledge
(c) Penance (d) None of these

757. A prophet of spiritual regeneration was
(a) R.N. Tagore (b) M.K. Gandhi
(c) Fichte (d) None of the above

758. In Jain Education System the punishment for violating the rules is
(a) Fasting
(b) Social Boycott
(c) Penance
(d) Physical Punishment

759. The self in Samkhya philosophy is known as
(a) *Atman* (b) *Jiva*
(c) *Purusa* (d) None of these

760. Raja Rammohan Roy advocated social changes which is/are
(a) removal of superstition and illiteracy
(b) widow remarriage
(c) abolition of *Sati*
(d) All of the above

761. The chief characteristics of *purusa* in Samkhya philosophy is
(a) Ever liberated (b) Non-attached
(c) Transcedent (d) All of these

762. In Buddhist education, it is desired that the teacher must orient the pupil towards
(a) Indifference to world
(b) Self-realization
(c) Salvation
(d) Nirwan

763. Gandhiji's opinion about the God is/are
(a) Truth (b) Life
(c) Light (d) All of the above

764. The reason for the decline of Buddhistic education centres in India was
(a) lack of government support.
(b) their destinction by Muslim rules.
(c) moral deterioration of Bhikshu and Bhikshuni.
(d) All of these

765. The liberation by living, according to Samkhya philosophy, can be termed as
(a) *Videhamukti* (b) *Jivanmukti*
(c) Both (a) and (b) (d) None of these

766. "Arise, awake and stop not till the goal is achieved" was the call given by
(a) Vivekananda (b) Gandhiji
(c) Tagore (d) None of these

767. Liberation after death, according to Samkhya philosophy, can be termed as
(a) *Videhamukti* (b) *Jivanmukti*
(c) Both (a) and (b) (d) None of these

768. Aurobindo's conscience has
(a) two levels (b) three levels
(c) four levels (d) five levels

769. The Mechanical Naturalism regards man as
(a) Self-supporting (b) Machine
(c) Living Creature (d) Judicious

770. The final state of liberation, according to Samkhya philosophy, is
(a) *Videhamukti* (b) *Jivanmukti*
(c) Both (a) and (b) (d) None of these

771. *My Experiment with Truth* is written by
(a) Jawaharlal Nehru
(b) Kabir
(c) Ramanand
(d) Mahatma Gandhi

772. Liberation and bondage, according to Samkhya philosophy, are of the nature of
(a) Like dream
(b) Ultimate reality
(c) Practical reality
(d) None of these

773. Naturalism of physical sciences regards all physical matter made up of
(a) Five elements (b) Nature
(c) Soul (d) Atom

774. Raja Rammohan Roy was a religious and social reformer who lived in
(a) eighteenth century
(b) twentieth century
(c) twenty-first century
(d) nineteenth century

775. "Naturalism is anti of Idealism so it regards mind under the effect of matter and the real entity as physical instead of spiritual." Who has defined naturalism like this?
(a) Thomas and Lang
(b) Rusk
(c) Hawking
(d) Bryce

776. The main objection against Samkhya concept of liberation is based upon
(a) no happiness in liberation.
(b) falacies of evolution.
(c) the *Purusa* as agent.
(d) All of these.

777. Who demonstrated the value of education in the vitalization of Indian society?
(a) Raja Rammohan Roy
(b) Swami Vivekananda
(c) Dayanand Saraswati
(d) Rabindranath Tagore

778. The best theory of liberation in Indian philosophy has been advanced by
(a) the *Samkhya*
(b) *Advaita Vedanta*
(c) the Jainas
(d) the Buddhists

779. "It accepts the existence of physical matter and it tries to solve all the problems according to the physical rules." What philosophy is this statement based?
(a) Existentialism (b) Realism
(c) Idealism (d) Naturalism

780. Vishva Bharti was established by Tagore in
(a) 1914 (b) 1913
(c) 1902 (d) 1901

781. Which book of Rousseau carried the Naturalistic philosophy to its climax?
(a) *Paradise Lost* (b) *Emile*
(c) *Republic* (d) *Das Capital*

782. According to *Advaita Vedanta,* the nature of liberation can be explained as
(a) Transcedental reality
(b) *Brahman*
(c) *Atman*
(d) All of these

783. Tagore was honoured with Knighthood by British government in
(a) 1902 (b) 1911
(c) 1915 (d) 1917

784. *Advaita Vedanta* theory of liberation is based upon
(a) *Brahmasutra* (b) *Bhagwadgita*
(c) the *Upanishads* (d) the *Vedas*

785. Besides Rousseau the other supporters of naturalism were
(a) Herbert Spencer (b) Bacon
(c) Comenius (d) All of these

786. The Republic which outlines a complete and remarkable plan of education is based on
(a) Humanism (b) Naturalism
(c) Idealism (d) Existentialism

787. "Perfection of human machine."—What educational philosophy has this aim of education?
(a) Naturalism (b) Idealism
(c) Pragmatism (d) Realism

788. The liberation in *Advaita Vedanta* is known as
(a) *Moksha* (b) *Nirvana*
(c) *Apavargh* (d) None of these

789. Rabindranath Tagore's idea of education is that
(a) Education for Man-Making
(b) Education for liberation
(c) Education for all
(d) Education for fullness

790. These aims are according to Naturalism Educational Philosophy
(a) To enable them to adjust to the environment
(b) To enable them face struggle for life
(c) To give happiness to the students
(d) All of these

791. The Indian Constitution was implemented in
(a) 1947 (b) 1948
(c) 1949 (d) 1950

792. "Education through spontaneous self-activity".—This teaching-method is according to this philosophy.
(a) Naturalism
(b) Pregmatism
(c) Existentialism
(d) Idealism

793. Man is a part of nature. It is believed by
(a) Radhakrishnan
(b) Tagore
(c) Aurobindo
(d) None of the above

794. The characteristics of naturalistic curriculum is
(a) child-centred.
(b) more place is given to activities and skills.
(c) provision of subjects related to necessities of life.
(d) All of these.

795. Tagore believed in
(a) values created by nature
(b) values created by man
(c) eternal and absolute values
(d) All of the above

796. According to Herbert Spencer the following principle can present solution to the problem of discipline
(a) Moral principle
(b) Individual freedom principle
(c) Learning by doing principle
(d) Pain-pleasure principle

797. The pioneer educational efforts of the Christian mission impressed by
(a) Rabindranath Tagore
(b) Raja Rammohan Roy
(c) Both (a) and (b)
(d) None of the above

798. "It ignores the spiritual aspects of child so it has no provision for moral education."—This statement is related to this philosophy.
(a) Naturalism (b) Realism
(c) Idealism (d) Pragmatism

799. An Untouchability Offence Act was passed in year
(a) 1955 (b) 1957
(c) 1964 (d) 1966

800. "According to it an individual adjusts himself to his environment by his abilities and capacities or he changes the environment according to his needs." What type of pragmatism does it happen?
(a) Experimental Pragmatism
(b) Theoritical Pragmatism
(c) Human Pragmatism
(d) None of these

801. "Material and spiritual knowledge is already present in man covered by a curtain of ignorance"—who said this?

(a) Gandhi (b) Tagore
(c) Plato (d) Vivekananda

802. The Mission which has some finest schools, hospitals, dispensaries and which spread rapidly is
(a) Arya Samaj
(b) Ramakrishna Mission
(c) Brahmo Samaj
(d) None of the above

803. Vivekananda included study of religion, philosophy, *Upnishadas* and *Puranas* to achieve
(a) propagation of Indian culture.
(b) complete development of child's personality.
(c) spiritual development of the child.
(d) development of intellect of the child.

804. In this type of pragmatism, "The truth should be determined on the basis of the fulfilment of man's needs and aspiration".
(a) Spiritual Pragmatism
(b) Experimental Pragmatism
(c) Human Pragmatism
(d) Physical Pragmatism

805. Which of the following is not the principle of education given by Tagore?
(a) Active communication between nature and man
(b) Internationalism
(c) Knowledge based on experimentation
(d) Freedom for self-expression and creativity.

806. "Experimental Pragmatism regards idea as the means of conditioning." This is the viewcil the following thinker.
(a) Dewey (b) Morley
(c) James Ward (d) Rusk

807. Which of the following was not suggested as a method of education by Vivekananda?
(a) Meditation
(b) Guided readings
(c) Lecture-cum-discussion
(d) Yoga

808. Which of the following is not the work of Gandhiji?
(a) *India of my Dream*
(b) *Character and Nation Building*
(c) *India Wins Freedom*
(d) *Towards New Education.*

809. Vivekananda's philosophy of life was derived from
(a) Sarakhya philosophy
(b) Plato's Idealism
(c) Buddhistic philosophy
(d) Vedanta philosophy

810. The principle of pragmatism is
(a) Humanistic outlook
(b) Rational will
(c) Knowledge is byproduct of action
(d) All of these

811. "If you want to find the value of any single fact or experience, you can never do so by dealing with the fact in isolation". Who said it?
(a) Fichte (b) Hegal
(c) Kant (d) None of these

812. This principle is related to pragmatism.
(a) Spiritual value
(b) Education according to nature
(c) Truth education is not final
(d) Man is the best creation of God

813. Which of the following types represents M.K. Gandhi's contribution to education?
(a) Education for international understanding
(b) Education for man making
(c) Integral education
(d) Basic education

814. Who advocated social service in all forms to be the real expression of religion?
(a) Kabir
(b) Swami Vivekananda

(c) Raja Rammohan Roy
(d) Swami Dayanand Saraswati

815. Which of the following types represents Vivekananda's contribution to education?
(a) Education for man making
(b) Integral education
(c) Education for international understanding
(d) Basic education

816. Following principle relates to naturalistic educational philosophy.
(a) Education should be pleasurable
(b) Truth is not static in life
(c) Soul and God exist
(d) Idea is basis of physical world

817. Idealism in education asserts that
(a) we cannot accept any knowledge as valid without antecedent sense impressions.
(b) we would come to know the world as it really exists through education.
(c) each learning mind would have to build up its own idea of the world.
(d) there should be no emphasis on the inner feelings of the individual but on copying the world.

818. "Development of the sense of unity in Diversity" is the objective of this educational philosophy.
(a) Experimentalism (b) Idealism
(c) Pragmatism (d) Realism

819. Which of the following types represents Aurobindo's contribution to education?
(a) Education for man making
(b) Education for international understanding
(c) Integral education
(d) Basic education

820. Ultimate aim of education according to Aristotle is
(a) search of matter and its details.
(b) the realization of complete happiness.
(c) Both (a) and (b).
(d) None of the above.

821. As an educationist, Gandhiji was
(a) a pragmatist.
(b) naturalist, an idealist and a pragmatist all together.
(c) an idealist.
(d) a naturalist.

822. What teaching-method is used in naturalistic philosophy of education?
(a) Lecture method
(b) Project method
(c) Inductive-Deductive method
(d) Learning by doing

823. Which of the following ideas does not belong to Aristotle?
(a) Virtues are to be judged by their consequences.
(b) Equality according to proportion, and for every man to enjoy his own.
(c) Virtues are of two kinds—intellectual virtues developed by teaching and moral virtues developed from habits.
(d) Happiness lies in the best activity which is nothing but contemplation.

824. It is the contribution of pragmatism to education.
(a) To develop self-discipline in students
(b) Respect for personality
(c) To make curriculum flexible and useful for life
(d) To make education child-centred

825. The system of child marriages and castes appalled
(a) Kabir
(b) Swami Dayanand Saraswati
(c) Raja Rammohan Roy
(d) Swami Vivekananda

826. What did Gandhiji's philosophy of education stress as aim of education?
(a) Individual aims
(b) A synthesis of individual and social aims
(c) Social aims
(d) Cultural aims

827. "Giving secondary place to scientific subjects in the curriculum obstructs the development of science and technology." This limitation relates to this educational philosophy.
(a) Naturalism
(b) Existentionalism
(c) Pragmatism
(d) Realism

828. Rationalism was a movement which called for
(a) the substitution of Aristotelian authority with that of the Church.
(b) faith in the power of unaided reason to discover truth.
(c) the substitution of reasoning for foolish utopias.
(d) the reconciliation of Church dogma with the new science.

829. The limitations of pragmatic educational philosophy is
(a) curriculum-construction is difficult.
(b) to regard nature as child's teacher.
(c) secondary place of scientific subjects in curriculum.
(d) to emphasis spiritual life.

830. Rabindranath Tagore was a naturalist because he said about children that
(a) they should be acquainted with the ideals and values of national culture.
(b) they should be educated for national integration.
(c) they should be given full freedom to live in natural environment and learn by doing.
(d) they should be made to develop into complete human being.

831. Who recommended that the years of secondary schooling be increased to the 10 + 2 pattern?
(a) The Kothari Commission
(b) Basic Scheme
(c) The Ramamurti Report
(d) All of the above

832. Tagore was an idealist because he emphasized
(a) vocational education.
(b) rigid control and discipline in schools.
(c) religious education in a formal manner.
(d) moral and spiritual development of the child.

833. "Do they duty reward is not they concern-is Karm-Yoga". This philosophy is available in
(a) Upnishad or Vedanta Philosophy
(b) Vivekananda Philosophy
(c) Shri Arvindo Philosophy
(d) Gita Philosophy

834. Practical measures needed for the introduction of the 10+2 plan were made by
(a) Government of Bengal
(b) Government of Bihar
(c) Government of India
(d) Government of Delhi

835. "Purposeful teaching-method or method suiting the child's natural tendencies". According to Gita, this means that
(a) child be motivated for free activity.
(b) child's interests be sublimated and made socially useful.

(c) child be developed freely.
(d) All of these.

836. In democracy, educational pattern is planned after the interests of the many because
(a) there are always too many illiterates in a democracy.
(b) democracy has tremendous faith in her men and their powers.
(c) democracy is the government of the many, by the many and for the many.
(d) the ultimate authority determining educational policy in democracy is imminent in man.

837. Mahatma Gandhi's Basic Education Scheme was characterised by
(a) strict supervision and control of activities.
(b) strict discipline and punishment for wrongs.
(c) opposition to strict control and punishment.
(d) education of children through sense training.

838. Aims of education are determined by human being for the good of the
(a) Society
(b) Individual
(c) Both (a) and (b)
(d) None of these

839. Gita Philosophy fulfils this objective.
(a) Individual and Social
(b) Individual
(c) Social
(d) None of these

840. Rabindranath Tagore lived in
(a) early nineteenth century
(b) late nineteenth century
(c) early twentieth century
(d) late twentieth century

841. The basis of Jain principle "Syadbad" is
(a) to view the world with one standpoint.
(b) indefiniteness of reality.
(c) Kewalya Gyan.
(d) to free Jiva from Pudgal.

842. India's constitutional value of "equality of all" is founded on several assumptions. Which of the following is not among these?
(a) All men are alike by nature
(b) All men are created equal
(c) Claim of human dignity
(d) All men have intrinsic worth

843. According to Aristotle, children should be given knowledge of difficult subjects through direct experiences. This is an approach
(a) from unknown to known
(b) from known to unknown
(c) from general to particular
(d) None of the above

844. In India's constitutional values, equality applied to education means
(a) to impart education to all upto the same level.
(b) to equalize the external or material circumstances of obtaining education.
(c) to have same kinds of institutions for all in the society.
(d) to impart same kind of education to all.

845. The seven-fold formula to express "Syadbad" has this element.
(a) Probably it is and it is not
(b) Probably it is
(c) Probably it is not
(d) All of these

846. Which of the following philosophers has influenced modern system of education very much?

(a) Dewey (b) Pestalozzi
(c) Aristotle (d) All of the above

847. Jainism is believed in 'Anekantbad' because it has faith in
(a) many 'Jivas' and physical elements existence.
(b) atomic Theory.
(c) strict Discipline.
(d) All of these.

848. Which of the following does not contribute to India's national integration?
(a) National curriculum
(b) National language
(c) Teaching history compulsorily in the school
(d) National system of education

849. The Negative Education suggested by Rousseau asserts that
(a) too much work and rules in schools should be modified.
(b) knowledge should not be based on books and symbols but on nature.
(c) there should be no compulsion for children to attend school.
(d) school education should enable children to desist doing negative things.

850. Which of the following is not a national objective to be achieved through education in India?
(a) Increasing children's creative ability
(b) Increasing productivity
(c) Accelerating process of modernization
(d) Achieving social and national integration

851. The "Right Character" in the "Tri-Ratnas" of Jainism means
(a) right knowledge of Jainism.
(b) faith in Jain "Trithankaras".
(c) to free soul from matter by good acts.
(d) All of these.

852. In Gandhi's opinion, God is the ultimate
(a) Objective (b) Authority
(c) Reality (d) Religion

853. "According to Jainism, when the soul indulges in four "Kashayas" it falls in the bondage of "Pudgal". What are these "Kashayas"?
(a) Sin, immorality, greed and sex
(b) Pride, envy, jealousy and greed
(c) Pride, anger, maya, and affection
(d) Untruth, violence, jealousy and envy

854. Development of which of the following is not an aim of democratic education?
(a) Democratic citizenship
(b) Scientific and technical education
(c) Vocational efficiency
(d) Educational leadership

855. "Education should aim at manmaking", this philosophy is given by
(a) Shankaracharya
(b) Guru Nanak
(c) Yajnavalakya
(d) Swami Vivekananda

856. The Vedas teach us that creation is
(a) without an end.
(b) has a definite beginning and also an end.
(c) without beginning.
(d) without beginning and without an end.

857. In Jain Philosophy, "Mati Gyan" means
(a) Recognition
(b) Direct Knowledge
(c) Recall
(d) All of these

858. "There is a real world of things behind and corresponding to the objects of our perception". This definition of Realism was given by
(a) Erasmus (b) Nunn
(c) Ross (d) Milton

859. In Jainism, "Shruti Gyan" is also of this type.
(a) Kewalya (b) Pudgal
(c) Kashaya (d) Upyog

860. Who said, "Without caring for all that is believed, reason it all out and having found that it will do good to you and all believe it, live upto it and help others to live upto it"?
(a) Buddha
(b) Vyas
(c) Swami Vivekananda
(d) Kapila

861. The role of teacher is minimum in
(a) Marxism (b) Pragmatism
(c) Naturalism (d) Realism

862. Which philosophy maintained "The soul is divine, only held in the bondage of matter"?
(a) Buddhism (b) Vedanta
(c) Sankhya (d) All of these

863. In Buddhistic Curriculum, it was one of the subjects included in it.
(a) Sanskrit (b) Science
(c) Arithmetic (d) Logic

864. 'Social aim of education' was stressed in
(a) Developing Countries
(b) Developed Countries
(c) North America
(d) All of the above

865. The word 'Philosophy' is made up of two Greek words "Philos" and "Sofia" which means
(a) Love and Knowedge
(b) Love and Hate
(c) Sufi and Spirituality
(d) God and Soul

866. What should be done so that the school is to be the guardian of democracy?
(a) Lessons on the importance of democracy should be included in the textbooks
(b) The teachers should have faith in democracy
(c) Democracy should, actually, be lived in the school
(d) Eminent leaders should be invited to school to talk about democracy to teachers and the students

867. Maria Montessori in her approach to childhood, bases her method of education on
(a) Idealism (b) Existentialism
(c) Humanism (d) Naturalism

868. As one of the Indian constitutional values, secularism means
(a) abolition of all personal religious laws.
(b) control of religious activities by the government.
(c) no respect for any religion.
(d) equal respect for all religions and no discrimination in any matter on the ground of religion.

869. The "Idealism" is made up of two Greek words "Idea" and "Ism" which means
(a) Ideal and Real
(b) Mind and Soul
(c) Idea and Ideology
(d) None of these

870. Philosophy is
(a) Love of thought
(b) Love of education
(c) Love of human resources
(d) Love of wisdom

871. "Idealism is the description of the feeling of regarding man as an integral part of mental world." This statement was made by
(a) Home (b) Brubacker
(c) Ross (d) Plats

872. *Emile* was written in
(a) 1812 (b) 1800
(c) 1782 (d) 1762

873. "Child is more important than all kinds of books". This viewpoint of Tagore represents his faith in the following aims of education
(a) social aims.
(b) cultural aims.
(c) individual aims.
(d) a synthesis of individual and social aims.

874. It is one of the fundamental principles of idealism.
(a) Utility Principle
(b) Truth is not static in life
(c) Unity in Diversity
(d) Real is Truth

875. Which of the following philosophers put Rousseau's educational ideas into practice?
(a) Montessori (b) Pestalozzi
(c) Froebel (d) All of the above

876. "The creator of world is God." It is a principle of this philosophy.
(a) Existentialism (b) Realism
(c) Idealism (d) Pragmatism

877. "Next to Nature the child should be brought into touch with the stream of social 'behaviour'." By saying this Tagore is trying to emphasize following aims of education
(a) social aims.
(b) intellectual development aim.
(c) individual aims.
(d) both individual and social aims.

878. Campaign against superstition and illiteracy was launched by
(a) Guru Nanak
(b) Ramanand
(c) Kabir
(d) Raja Rammohan Roy

879. Who said that the aim of education should be to develop in children feelings of international brotherhood and attitude of international understanding?
(a) Rousseau
(b) Dewey
(c) Mahatma Gandhi
(d) R.N. Tagore

880. The aim of education according to idealistic approach is
(a) conservation of culture and traditions.
(b) natural development.
(c) to give happiness.
(d) to help in the struggle for life.

881. 'Mudaliar Commission' on secondary education was set up in
(a) 1957-58 (b) 1955-56
(c) 1954-55 (d) 1952-53

882. This philosophy has made teacher-pupil relationship human by the idea of "Self-discipline".
(a) Pragmatism (b) Realism
(c) Idealism (d) Existentialism

883. Characteristics of Vivekananda's philosophy of education include
(a) Pragmatism
(b) Naturalism idealism and pragmatism all
(c) Naturalism
(d) Idealism

884. Who described nature as an aggregate of things outside our mind which is moving in space?
(a) Rousseau
(b) Leucippins
(c) Democritus
(d) Thomas Hobbes

885. According to Vivekananda's philosophy of education, the prime aim of education is
(a) fullness of perfection already present in the child.
(b) social development of the child.
(c) physical development of the child.
(d) mental development of the child.

886. One of the limitations of idealistic educational philosophy is
(a) to give importance to scientific subjects curriculum.
(b) to fulfil selfish desires through self-realization.
(c) it is impracticable to ignore physical needs.
(d) All of these

887. Which of the following is the work of Pestalozzi?
(a) *Leonard and Gertrude*
(b) *The Swans Song*
(c) *Evening Hours of a Hermit*
(d) All of the above.

888. The Western educationist who supported idealistic educational philosophy was
(a) Forebel (b) Rousseau
(c) Dewey (d) Marx

889. Which of the following books is similar to *Emile*?
(a) *The Swans Song*
(b) *Evening Hours of a Hermit*
(c) *Leonard and Gertrude*
(d) All of the above.

890. The influence of both philosophy and religion in the life of the human individual and society is
(a) Unfavourable (b) Favourable
(c) Both (a) and (b) (d) None of these

891. The Western propagators of idealism were
(a) Pestalozzi (b) Plato
(c) Cominius (d) All of these

892. Who said that it is for the good of the state that the individual should be allowed to develop along the line of his own greatest powers?
(a) Socrates
(b) Plato
(c) Aristotle
(d) None of the above

893. The Indian thinkers who were idealistc were
(a) Swami Vivekananda
(b) Swami Dayanand
(c) Both (a) and (b)
(d) None of these

894. Of the doctrine of immanence it can be said truthfully that it
(a) distrusts the senses and unaided reason.
(b) pictures the world as an unfriendly place.
(c) would locate the search for knowledge of the good in the world about us.
(d) supports Plato's theory of reality.

895. The important aspects of philosophical problems are
(a) Synthetic (b) Critical
(c) Both (a) and (b) (d) None of these

896. Idealism accepts existence of God so it emphasis the developments of
(a) Worldly attachments
(b) Materialism
(c) Spiritualism
(d) All of these

897. In the opinion of M.K. Gandhi 'non violence' is a
(a) Dynamic virtue (b) Negative virtue
(c) Positive virtue (d) Both (a) and (c)

898. Idealism gives paramount importance to teacher in the educational process while naturalism gives such importance to

(a) Teaching-method
(b) Subject-matter
(c) Above (a) and (b)
(d) Student

899. The philosophical attitude include
(a) Criticism (b) Wonder
(c) Doubt (d) All of these

900. *Anschauung* in English means
(a) Personal experience of the child
(b) Face to face knowledge of objects
(c) First hand experience of the child
(d) All of the above

901. The philosophical method includes
(a) Dialectical (b) Induction
(c) Deduction (d) All of these

902. Idealism regards lecture and discussion teaching-methods as most suitable while naturalism prefers
(a) Inductive-Deductive method
(b) Question-Answer
(c) Learning by doing
(d) All of these

903. Pestalozzi is distinguished from other Naturalists in his contribution of
(a) ability grouping
(b) stress on curriculum
(c) teacher training
(d) All of the above

904. Philosophising requires the processes of
(a) Criticism (b) Analysis
(c) Synthesis (d) All of these

905. Who has said 'Nothing good enters into the human world except in and through the free activities of individual men and women and educational practice must be shaped to accord with that truth'?
(a) Aristotle (b) Plato
(c) Socrates (d) Percy Nunn

906. The true nature of philosophy can be explained as
(a) Comprehensive science
(b) Synthetic science
(c) Critical method
(d) All of these

907. The contribution of 'Pragmatism' to education is
(a) Project method
(b) Learning by doing
(c) Deductive-Inductive method
(d) All of these

908. "Individuality is of no value and personality is a meaningless term apart from the social environment in which they are developed and made manifest". The statement is given by
(a) Aristotle (b) Ross
(c) Plato (d) Socrates

909. Mahavir Swami added this one more "Vrat" the three Vratas—Ahinsa, Truth and Asteya
(a) Brahmcharya (b) Aparigrah
(c) Sacrifice (d) Cleanliness

910. The important characteristics of philosophy are
(a) Philosophical attitude
(b) Philosophical conclusions
(c) Philosophical method
(d) All of these

911. In Gandhian philosophy, truth is the
(a) Means (b) End
(c) Beginning (d) Path

912. The nature of philosophy can be explained as
(a) Critical method
(b) Collection of science
(c) Universal science
(d) All of these

913. "The sufferings can be removed." This truth of the four "Arya-truths" is the principles of this philosophy.

(a) Vedanta Philosophy
(b) Buddha Philosophy
(c) Jain Philosophy
(d) Gita Philosophy

914. To have a true perspective of Gandhiji's philosophy of education we should at first consider his
(a) philosophy of religion
(b) philosophy of education
(c) philosophy of life
(d) philosophy of politics

915. Out of those three "H's which Gandhiji emphasised to develop one is
(a) Heart (b) Hand
(c) Head (d) All of these

916. The most important trait of philosophy is
(a) Analysis (b) Criticism
(c) Synthesis (d) None of these

917. According to Gandhian philosophy "Truth which is the end and which is all prevading can be realised only through"
(a) Truth (b) Light
(c) Power (d) Conscience

918. Philosophy is a comprehensive synthetic science, has been maintained by
(a) Herbert Spencer
(b) Roy Wood Seller
(c) Joseph A. Leighton
(d) All of these

919. "Naturalism is such an instrument whose characteristics is to boycott the whole spirituality." This definition was given up
(a) Rusk (b) Bryce
(c) Thomas and Lang (d) Hawking

920. God is truth because truth can't
(a) be accomplished (b) be achieved
(c) exist (d) be destroyed

921. One of the principles of naturalism is
(a) Human point of view
(b) Utility Principle
(c) Every thing is subject to change
(d) All of these

922. What is correct about the nature of philosophy in relation to science?
(a) Philosophy is a normative science
(b) Philosophy is science
(c) Philosophy is the mother of all sciences
(d) Philosophy is the science of science

923. Which of the following is not the work of Froebel?
(a) Essays on education
(b) Education of man
(c) Reminiscences
(d) Pedagogies of Kindergarten

924. Literally the term philosophy means
(a) Criticism
(b) A particular method
(c) Love of knowledge
(d) None of these

925. "Man is made up of matter." The principles related to
(a) Pragmatism (b) Naturalism
(c) Realism (d) Idealism

926. The idea that there is unity between man, nature and God was given by
(a) Plato (b) Aristotle
(c) Froebel (d) Both (b) and (c)

927. What educational philosophy does not regard teacher's importance?
(a) Naturalism (b) Realism
(c) Existentialism (d) Marxism

928. The meaning of the terms philosophy and *Darshan* are
(a) Dissimilar (b) Similar
(c) Both (a) and (b) (d) None of these

929. Ahimsa is the
(a) Beginning (b) End
(c) Path (d) Means

930. The philosopher is more concerned with
(a) dialectics (b) induction
(c) deduction (d) None of these

931. The naturalism curriculum emphasis the study of
(a) Spiritual Subject (b) Science
(c) Language (d) All of these

932. The idealistic philosophy of education supports
(a) Social ideas
(b) Moral ideas
(c) Physical strength
(d) All of the above

933. The curriculum propagated by Rousseu is
(a) Impracticable (b) Practicable
(c) Informal (d) Above (b) and (c)

934. The contemporary trend in philosophical method is
(a) Synthesis (b) Dialectics
(c) Analysis (d) None of these

935. Rabindranath Tagore's school in Shantiniketan upholds in many respects the chief principle of
(a) Pragmatism (b) Naturalism
(c) Idealism (d) Humanism

936. Philosophical activity is concerned with
(a) Synthesising (b) Criticising
(c) Thinking (d) All of these

937. The naturalistic educational approach prefer the following telling-method.
(a) Learning by doing
(b) Discussion
(c) Project
(d) None of these

938. Non-violence is preferred to violence by Gandhiji because
(a) it is needed to show love for living being which is actually love for God.
(b) it shakes the opponent's will and destroys his morales.
(c) it is needed for moral and spiritual victory.
(d) All of the above.

939. The following is the contribution of naturalism to education.
(a) Teacher-centred education
(b) Bookish knowledge
(c) Child-centered education
(d) Both (a) and (c)

940. Philosophical thinking is characterised by
(a) Philosophical conclusion
(b) Philosophical results
(c) Philosophical effect
(d) All of these

941. Gandhiji despised industrialization because
(a) he was obsessed with the inequalities of income and wealth.
(b) Indian condition was not suited to industrialization.
(c) he did not want to make India a rich country.
(d) All of the above.

942. The philosophical effect can be seen upon
(a) the group life
(b) the culture
(c) the Philosopher
(d) All of these

943. Idealism regards teacher responsible for discipline while naturalism regards
(a) no Teacher's interference in teaching-process.
(b) teacher has no place in teaching-process.
(c) Both (a) and (b).
(d) None of these.

944. Fichte was a/an
(a) American philosopher
(b) English philosopher
(c) Greek philosopher
(d) German philosopher

945. The limitations of naturalistic educational approaches is
(a) it regards discipline important.
(b) it regards natural tendencies of child important.
(c) Both (a) and (d).
(d) it emphasises Nature-study.

946. The chief differences among thinking beings are
(a) Philosophical (b) Physical
(c) Biological (d) None of these

947. The social efficiency of an individual is lead by
(a) Courage
(b) Honesty of purpose
(c) Truthfulness
(d) All of the above

948. A bad philosophy can be substituted by
(a) Science
(b) Religion
(c) Better philosophy
(d) None of these

949. John Dewey regards Pragmatism as 'Reconstruction' because education is regarded as
(a) Recreation of knowledge
(b) Reconstruction of life
(c) Both (a) and (b)
(d) Reconstruction of Experiences

950. The first to challenge the caste system was
(a) Buddha (b) B.G. Tilak
(c) M.K. Gandhi (d) Mahavir

951. "Pragmatism is fundamentally a humanistic philosophy which propagates that man determines his values while performing the activity." This definition was given by
(a) Sechiller (b) Rogen
(c) Jones Prett (d) Ross

952. The diversity of philosophical conclusions shows
(a) Strength (b) Weakness
(c) Both (a) and (b) (d) None of these

953. Gandhiji dreamed of a
(a) Saral Samaj
(b) Brahmo Samaj
(c) Sarvodaya Samaj
(d) None of the above

954. The philosophical thinking in a philosopher is
(a) Evolving (b) Kimited
(c) Permanent (d) None of these

955. What are the types of Pragmatism?
(a) Real Pragmatism
(b) Humanistic Pragmatism
(c) Experimental Pragmatism
(d) Both (a) and (b)

956. Who advocated a reunion between the spirituality of the East and materialism of the West?
(a) Vivekananda (b) Gandhiji
(c) Tagore (d) None of the above

957. "Truth is not static in life" and "Logical will" are the principles of this philosophy
(a) Realism (b) Existentialism
(c) Pragmatism (d) Ideolism

958. Philosophers are, "those who are lovers of the vision of truth". This was said by
(a) Aristotle (b) William James
(c) Socrates (d) Plato

959. Which of the following branches of philosophy studies the problem of value?
(a) Axiology
(b) Esthetics
(c) Epistemology
(d) None of the above

960. The most important difference between philosophy and science is
(a) Method (b) Scope
(c) Subject matter (d) None of these

961. The principle of Pragmatism—"Truth is not static and final"—means
(a) Truth is that which is useful for life
(b) Truth has no utility in life
(c) Both (a) and (b)
(d) None of these

962. Comte said that "Sociology is a fundamental science" because
(a) it has a method of exact application.
(b) it has a method of exact derivation.
(c) it has a method of exact investigation.
(d) None of the above.

963. Pragmatism supports the teaching methods based on the following principles.
(a) Learning by experience
(b) Children's interests
(c) Both (a) and (b)
(d) None of these

964. The goal of philosophy can be properly defined as
(a) Philosophising
(b) Achievement of success
(c) Solution of problem
(d) None of these

965. Sociologists collect data about
(a) Animals (b) Children
(c) Celestial bodies (d) Mankind

966. Which of the following is the contribution of Rousseau to education?
(a) Education for State control
(b) Education for Nationalism
(c) Education for Democracy
(d) Education for Freedom

967. "Project is a problematic act which reaches its completion in its natural setting." This statement is given by this educaitonist.
(a) Rosen (b) Pears C.S.
(c) Kilpatric (d) Ross

968. Out of four paths of liberation, i.e. Karma, Bhakti, contemplation and knowledge which is the best path of liberation?
(a) Karma alone
(b) Bhakti alone
(c) Karma and Bhakti
(d) Any of the four depending on the nature of man

969. The principle of pragmatic curriculum is
(a) Spiritual Development
(b) Utility
(c) Experience-centred
(d) Both (b) and (c)

970. Which of the following represents fascist ideal of education?
(a) Education for Democracy
(b) Education for Freedom
(c) Education for Nationalism
(d) Education for State control

971. Which of the following is the belief of Vivekananda?
(a) Strength is life and weakness is death, so, stand firm like a rock.
(b) Patriotism and universal brotherhood.
(c) Teacher is necessary to lead to the path of salvation.
(d) All of the above.

972. Which of the following represents 'communist ideal' of education?
(a) Education for Democracy
(b) Education for Nationalism
(c) Education for Freedom
(d) Education for State control

973. Comte used the word 'Sociology' in the year
(a) 1797 (b) 1837
(c) 1847 (d) 1857

974. The contribution of pragmatism to education is
(a) Project Method
(b) Discussion Method
(c) Play-Way Method
(d) All of these

975. Which of the following is ideal of education, according to idealism?
   (a) Social Adjustment
   (b) Self Realisation
   (c) Livelihood
   (d) Citizenship

976. Sociology is a study of
   (a) Environment and Society
   (b) Race and Society
   (c) Human nature and Society
   (d) Animal nature and Society

977. Which of the following is the naturalist ideal of education?
   (a) Inculcation of democratic values
   (b) Social adjustment
   (c) Livelihood
   (d) Self Realisation

978. The limitation of pragmatic educational philosophy is
   (a) over emphasis on child-centred education.
   (b) undue stress on utility principle.
   (c) over emphasis on spiritual development.
   (d) None of these.

979. Who declared "the whole aim of education could be summed up in the concept of morality"?
   (a) Herbert Spencer
   (b) Bertrand Russell
   (c) Mahatma Gandhi
   (d) Plato

980. According to Gita the aim of education is to enable an individual to feel
   (a) God (b) Happiness
   (c) Knowledge (d) All of these

981. Who among the following has propounded idealism in education?
   (a) Russell (b) Rousseau
   (c) John Dewey (d) Plato

982. Which of the following is an important cause of misery of Indian masses?
   (a) Lethargy (Inertia)
   (b) Narrow mindedness and casteism
   (c) Ignorance
   (d) All of the above

983. According to Gita, the teaching-method should suit this of the student.
   (a) Nature
   (b) Self-religion
   (c) Both (a) and (b)
   (d) None of these

984. "If education was identical to informations, the libraries would be the greatest saints of the world and encyclopaedias the greatest rishis". Who said this?
   (a) Aurobindo
   (b) Gandhiji
   (c) Tagore
   (d) Swami Vivekananda

985. The following provisions had to be followed by an individual to free himself from sufferings according to Buddhistic philosophy
   (a) Four Arya-Satya
   (b) Ashtang Marg
   (c) Both (a) and (b)
   (d) "Panch Mahavrat"

986. Who among the following propounded naturalism in education?
   (a) Bertrand Russell
   (b) Rousseau
   (c) Plato
   (d) John Dewey

987. According to *My Experiments with Truth*
   (a) There is little significance of Hinduism
   (b) Caste and classes have significance in Hinduism
   (c) Caste and classes are useless
   (d) Caste and classes are baseless

988. Who among the following propounded existentialism in education?

(a) Rousseau
(b) Bertrand Russell
(c) Sartre
(d) Plato

989. In Buddha philosophy the following teaching-method is prefered.
(a) Interpretation (b) Lecture
(c) Discussion (d) All of these

990. "The school is the function of constantly reorganising and reconstructing human experience", is said by
(a) R.N. Tagore (b) Patanjali
(c) M.K. Gandhi (d) John Dewey

991. Gita philosophy has classified the curriculum into the following types of subjects.
(a) Worldly Knowledge
(b) Spiritual Knowledge
(c) Above (a) and (b)
(d) None of these

992. Who among the following propounded socialism in education?
(a) Sartre (b) Stalin
(c) Russell (d) Dewey

993. Today which of the following has extensive educational organization of schools and colleges?
(a) Brahmo Samaj
(b) Arya Samaj
(c) Ramakrishna Mission
(d) None of the above

994. Who among the following made maximum impact on modern education?
(a) Stalin (b) Sartre
(c) Dewey (d) Russell

995. According to Jain Philosophy, the aim of education is to motivate the individual towards
(a) prientation towards "Ashtang Marg".
(b) freedom from sufferings.
(c) freedom of soul from matter (Pudgal).
(d) All of these.

996. Vivekananda recommends that education by which
(a) one can stand on one's own feet.
(b) character is formed.
(c) strength of mind is increased.
(d) All of the above.

997. According to Gita Philosophy, the aim of education is to orient an individual towards
(a) Better life.
(b) To give knowledge of four "Arya-Satya".
(c) To work selflessly.
(d) All of these.

998. Science can be properly defined as
(a) a subject matter
(b) a method
(c) a field of knowledge
(d) None of these

999. According to Vivekananda which of the following is most needed in the acquisition of knowledge?
(a) A real guru
(b) Concentration of mind
(c) Drill
(d) All of the above

1000. The distinctions between philosophy and science are
(a) distinction in problems
(b) distinction in method
(c) distinction in nature
(d) All of these

1001. Jain Philosophy regards following types of knowledge.
(a) Nirwan (b) Shruti
(c) Kewalya (d) Both (b) and (c)

1002. Gandhiji says Ahimsa and truth are so intertwined that it is practically impossible to

(a) corelate them
(b) separate them
(c) disintegrate them
(d) All of the above

1003. In which magazine did Mahatma Gandhi published his educational articles in 1937?
(a) *Young India* (b) *Kesari*
(c) *Harijan* (d) All of these

1004. The most important distinction between philosophy and science is
(a) distinction in method
(b) distinction in nature
(c) distinction in problem
(d) All of these

1005. The idea of natural goodness of man is supported by
(a) Froebel
(b) Prophet Mohammad
(c) Rousseau
(d) All of the above

1006. What educational scheme did Gandhiji present in the "Zakir Hussain Committee Report"?
(a) Indian Education Scheme
(b) Elementary Education Scheme
(c) Basic Education Scheme
(d) None of these

1007. Maria Montessori (1870-1952) was basically a
(a) Social worker (b) Lady doctor
(c) Teacher (d) None of these

1008. By what other name was Gandhiji's basic education known?
(a) Elementary Education Scheme
(b) Wardha Education Scheme
(c) Sabarmati Education Scheme
(d) All of these

1009. The term Sociology was used first time by
(a) Patanjali
(b) Rabindranath Tagore
(c) Auguste Comte
(d) Charles Darwin

1010. The fundamental principles of basic education were
(a) the medium of instruction be mother-tongue.
(b) all subjects be taught by correlating them a craft.
(c) education be self-supporting.
(d) All of these.

1011. Which of the following statements defuses Aristotle's theory of knowledge?
(a) Truth is non-existent until man creates it through re-organising his experience.
(b) The intellect has a sixth sense which automatically integrates analytical judgements.
(c) Knowledge of form and the knowledge of the good are different things.
(d) The good is the same for all who use right thinking.

1012. In pre-independent what was the educational plan to give free compulsory and universal education to children of age 7 to 14 years?
(a) Basic Education Scheme
(b) Elementary Education Scheme
(c) Zakir Hussain Scheme
(d) Sargent Plan

1013. Comte placed Sociology in the hierarchy of the
(a) Arts (b) Science
(c) Playways (d) Society

1014. Basic education curriculum included the following subjects
(a) English
(b) Mother tongue

(c) Hindustani (Undue and Nagori Script)
(d) Both (b) and (c)

1015. The fundamental concept behind Montessori method is
(a) students can be motivated for learning by games.
(b) that individuality of the child should not be crushed through collective teaching.
(c) Both (a) and (b).
(d) None of the above.

1016. By stressing sense training of the child, Montessori comes closer to
(a) Pragmatism (b) Naturalism
(c) Realism (d) Marxism

1017. In pre-independent India which education plan recongnised basic education?
(a) Sargent Education Plan
(b) Cripps Education Plan
(c) Mountbatten Education Plan
(d) None of these

1018. The aim of formation of Brahmo Samaj was removing the stigmas in
(a) Western ideas
(b) Hinduism
(c) Both (a) and (b)
(d) None of the above

1019. Arya Samaj was founded in the year
(a) 1875 (b) 1878
(c) 1888 (d) 1898

1020. In 1956 Government of India established the following institution to implement basic education.
(a) National Educational Administration Institute
(b) National Council of Educational Research and Training
(c) National Basic Foundation
(d) All of the above

1021. Swami Vivekananda was disciple of
(a) Ramakrishna Parmahansa
(b) Ramanand
(c) Guru Nanak
(d) Ramanuj

1022. Which of the following is not the work of Maria Montessori?
(a) *Education for a New World*
(b) *Reconstruction in Education*
(c) *The Discovery of the Child*
(d) *Emile.*

1023. "By education I mean drawing out the best in man and child mind body and soul." This statement is of
(a) Arvindo
(b) Mahatma Gandhi
(c) Swami Vivekananda
(d) Swami Dayananda

1024. In Montessori's system of education, the role of a teacher in the class is like a
(a) Directress
(b) Guide
(c) Helper
(d) Well prepared instructor

1025. The basis of Gandhiji's life-philosophy was
(a) Truth
(b) Non-violence
(c) Above (a) and (b)
(d) Both (b) and "Aparigrah"

1026. Swami Vivekananda lived in
(a) Nineteenth century
(b) Eighteenth century
(c) Seventeenth century
(d) Twentieth century

1027. The word Sociology was coined by an
(a) Indian Philosopher
(b) French Philosopher
(c) English Philosopher
(d) German Philosopher

1028. The aim of making craft the central subject in Basic education was
(a) to make the child a labourer.
(b) to make education self-supporting.
(c) Both (a) and (b).
(d) None of these.

1029. Montessori's method can be criticized on which of the following grounds?
(a) It is costly because method of teaching changes with the topic.
(b) It neglects play activities of children.
(c) It is centred around didactic apparatus.
(d) All of the above.

1030. Montessori and Froebel are not alike in which of the following points?
(a) Development of child on idealistic pattern of life
(b) Sense training for sharpening mind
(c) Play activities of the child
(d) Recognition of individuality of the child.

1031. Besides craft as central subject in basic education what other subject was made the central subject?
(a) Social
(b) Natural Environment
(c) Mother Tongue
(d) Both (a) and (c)

1032. According to Gandhian philosophy arbitrator of our fate is the
(a) Lawlessness (b) Religion
(c) Beliefs (d) Living law

1033. Swami Dayanand Saraswati saw the practical value of
(a) Western practices
(b) Modern scientific ideas
(c) Both (a) and (b)
(d) None of the above

1034. Who was the first tourge the granting of equality of status to women and the importance of women's education?
(a) Annie Besant (b) Sarojini Naidu
(c) Medha Patkar (d) Indira Gandhi

1035. The limitation of basic education which caused its failure was
(a) to make it self-supporting.
(b) to implement it in a defective manner.
(c) Both (a) and (b).
(d) to implement it in rural areas.

1036. For which of the following books Russell was awarded noble prize in 1950?
(a) *Education*
(b) *Marriage and Morals*
(c) *Principia mathematica*
(d) None of the above.

1037. Pitaks were compiled in written form in
(a) 140 BC (b) 120 BC
(c) 80 BC (d) 20 BC

1038. Rabindranath Tagore was awarded the Noble Prize for the contribution to
(a) the message of ancient Indian education.
(b) the cause of humanity through sevasadans.
(c) education in starting the Shantiniketan.
(d) literature for the English version of his *Gitanjali*.

1039. If we succeed in building the character of the individual, society will take care of itself. This idea was given by
(a) Plato
(b) Aristotle
(c) Ross
(d) Mahatma Gandhi

1040. "Basic Education which is being implemented by State Governments is a depeit." Whose statement is it?
(a) Pt. Jawaharlal Nehru
(b) Abul Kalam Azad
(c) Vinoba Bhave
(d) Dr. Zakir Hussain

1041. The stories and legends on the life of Lord Buddha have been compiled in
(a) Jatakas
(b) Tripitakas
(c) Both (a) and (b)
(d) None of the above

1042. Auguste Comte believed that sociology dealt with complex and intricate
(a) Biological phenomena
(b) Social phenomena
(c) Geographical phenomena
(d) None of the above

1043. The term Sociology is a modern adition to the
(a) Biological Sciences
(b) Social Sciences
(c) Geographical Sciences
(d) Natural Sciences

1044. Formation of Brahmo Samaj took place in the year
(a) 1809 (b) 1829
(c) 1858 (d) 1929

1045. What form of craft in basic education was recognised by Kothari Education Commission (1966)?
(a) Hobby
(b) Work-Experience
(c) Production Work
(d) Forward Looking

1046. Founder of Buddhism got Nirvana in
(a) 483 BC (b) 460 BC
(c) 563 BC (d) 663 BC

1047. Buddha got enlightenment under a Pipal tree in Bodh Gaya at the age of
(a) 40 (b) 38
(c) 35 (d) 29

1048. Education means "the development of character and usefulness in an individual" as regarded by
(a) Swami Vivekananda
(b) Yajnavalakya
(c) Shankaracharya
(d) None of the above

1049. Aristotle's theory of knowledge included the belief that
(a) true knowledge consists of universals.
(b) universals are established deductively.
(c) man is born with true knowledge in him.
(d) the syllogistic major premise is obtained through education.

1050. National Education Policy (1986) accepted craft in the educational curriculum as a subject in this form.
(a) Socially useful productive work
(b) Work-Experience
(c) Cottage Industry
(d) All of these

1051. The influence of Aristotle can be seen as the
(a) philosophy of catholic education.
(b) belief that the universe is constantly changing.
(c) theory that the good is many rather than one.
(d) educational programmes with vocational subjects.

1052. Which of the following does not belong to the four noble truths identified by Buddha?
(a) Salvation is necessary
(b) Life is suffering
(c) Suffering can be extinguished
(d) Desire is the cause of suffering.

1053. Buddhist philosophy is mainly aimed at
(a) coping with only physical problems of the world.
(b) ending the suffering of the people.
(c) making a caste free society.
(d) All of the above.

1054. The following Indian was well-known educational thinker.

(a) Pt. Jawaharla Nehru
(b) Ravindranath Tagore
(c) Bal Gangadhar Tilak
(d) All of these

1055. Which of the following reflects to the greatest extent the beliefs of Plato?
(a) The cosmopolitan high school
(b) The science laboratory
(c) The differentiate-curriculum
(d) The liberal arts college.

1056. The 1952-53 Secondary Education Commission in India recommended the following pattern of education:
(a) 11 + 2 + 3 scheme
(b) 10 + 3 + 2 scheme
(c) 10 + 2 + 3 scheme
(d) 12 + 3 scheme

1057. The roots of Hutchins philosophy of education can be found in
(a) Rousseau's insistence that nature must lead the way.
(b) Aquina's acceptance of the two-fold truth.
(c) Allen's emphasis upon vocational studies.
(d) Aristotle's belief in intellectualism for its own sake.

1058. Shri Arvindo established his Yoga-center at this place.
(a) Pondicheri (b) Calcutta
(c) Rishikesh (d) Goa

1059. The philosophy of Madhyam Marg (Middle path) has been supported by
(a) Buddhism
(b) Islamic religion
(c) Both (a) and (b)
(d) None of the above

1060. Non-violence as a belief is accepted mainly by
(a) Jainism (b) Christianity
(c) Buddhism (d) All of the above

1061. Aristotle's theories denied that
(a) the intellect can infer universal truths from particular subjects.
(b) nature endowed man with sense, perception and memory.
(c) the intellect intuits reliable judgements about cosmic design.
(d) the universe is orderly, reasonable and purposeful.

1062. "The excellent achievement of Indian spiritual knowledge can be attained only through strict discipline as it contains the complete education of soul and mind." The Indian educational thinker who said these words was
(a) Swami Dayananda
(b) Swami Vivekananda
(c) Mahatma Gandhi
(d) Shri Arvindo

1063. The dignity of labour was demonstrated in
(a) Ramakrishna Mission
(b) Shantiniketan
(c) Both (a) and (b)
(d) None of the above

1064. The *Gita* urges the
(a) Exercise of intelligence
(b) Exercise of action
(c) Exercise of faith
(d) All of the above

1065. Aims of education according to Buddhism is
(a) Pleasing God
(b) Extinction of sufferings
(c) Nirvana through eight fold paths
(d) None of the above

1066. Shri Arvindo regarded the use of the following for the development of human personality as the aim of education.
(a) Super mind (b) Superman
(c) Soul (d) All of these

1067. Which of the following was not approved by Buddha as method of instruction?
(a) Craft-centred instruction
(b) Oral instruction and discussion
(c) Educational tours
(d) Meditation.

1068. Who was one of the greatest reformers, who spoke strongly about the social equality and injustice of the caste system?
(a) Indira Gandhi
(b) Annie Besant
(c) Kiran Bedi
(d) Medha Patkar

1069. "Gandhiji made a nice synthesis of idealism, naturalism and pragmatism in his educational philosophy." On the basis of this statement in what form the idealism had its effect on Gandhiji's educational philosophy?
(a) Because Gandhiji wanted to make education child-centred
(b) Because Gandhiji regaded character building as the aim of education
(c) Because Gandhiji wanted to make education self-supporting
(d) All of these

1070. The school Shantiniketan was established by
(a) Raja Rammohan Roy
(b) Swami Vivekananda
(c) Swami Dayanand
(d) Rabindranath Tagore

1071. All are one and perform the task according to their aptitude in the
(a) Ramakrishna Mission
(b) Pondicherry Ashram
(c) Both (a) and (b)
(d) None of the above

1072. How did the effect of naturalistic philosophy reflect in Gandhiji's educational philosophy?
(a) He wanted to make education self-supporting
(b) He regarded self-realization as the aim of education
(c) He wanted make education child-centered
(d) Both (a) and (c)

1073. Which of the following is not the part of Vedas?
(a) Aranyakas (b) Mantras
(c) Samhitas (d) Brahmanas

1074. Which of the following statements about Vedangas is correct?
(a) They are in the form of prose.
(b) They are six in number.
(c) They give knowledge about 64 sciences.
(d) All of the above.

1075. There was no thought of caste or creed in
(a) Shantiniketan
(b) Ramakrishna Mission
(c) Both (a) and (b)
(d) None of the above

1076. Education at all levels is provided at
(a) Shantiniketan
(b) Ramakrishna Mission
(c) Both (a) and (b)
(d) None of the above

1077. Ashram at Pondicherry was established by
(a) Swami Dayanand
(b) Swami Vivekanand
(c) Rabindranath Tagore
(d) Aurobindo Ghosh

1078. The approach of Hinduism is
(a) Rational and realistic
(b) Pragmatic and empirical
(c) Both (a) and (b)
(d) None of the above

1079. Ultimate values proclaimed by Vedic religion is/are
(a) Dharma only
(b) Dharma and Artha
(c) Dharma, Artha and Karma
(d) Dharma, Artha, Karma and Moksha

1080. Gandhi's contribution to education was this in the form of basic education.
(a) As he wanted basic education to be child-centred.
(b) He synthesized idealism, pragmatism and naturalism.
(c) Basic education was motivated by idealism.
(d) As he wanted basic education to be self-supporting.

1081. Aurobindo Ghosh was
(a) The seer of Pondicherry
(b) Educator
(c) Philosopher
(d) All of the above

1082. The seer of Pondicherry is
(a) Aurobindo Ghosh
(b) Swami Dayanand
(c) Ramakrishna Paramahansa
(d) Ramanuja

1083. *Tamaso Ma Jyotirgamaya* means
(a) bringing from darkness to light
(b) bringing from disbelief to faith
(c) Both (a) and (b)
(d) None of the above

1084. The aim of Arvindo's inclusion of Indian History and culture in curriculum was
(a) to develop love for country in the child.
(b) to develop in the child a feeling of supermacy of his country in the world.
(c) to create historical sense in the child.
(d) None of these.

1085. The Brahmo Samaj established many
(a) Schools
(b) Colleges
(c) Both (a) and (b)
(d) None of the above

1086. "Natural surroundings and freedom are the important factors in the development of the child" is said by
(a) Charles Darwin (b) Thomas Hobbes
(c) R.N. Tagore (d) H. Spencer

1087. Shri Arvindo regarded it the best method of giving moral education.
(a) By presenting teachers ideal character
(b) By giving lecture on great persons
(c) By giving advice for moral qualities
(d) All of these

1088. The 1964-66 Indian Educational Commission has recommended that
(a) Class IX is the proper stage to start specialisation.
(b) the system of 'Streaming' in schools of general education at Class IX stage should be given up.
(c) specialisation of courses should commence at the Class X stage.
(d) None of the above.

1089. Theory of representative knowledge was accepted by
(a) Yoga (b) Samkhya
(c) Advaita Vedanta (d) All of the above

1090. The knowledge which is obtained by the interaction between a subject and an object is called
(a) Vrtti Jnana
(b) Antah Karan
(c) Saksi Jnana
(d) None of the above

1091. Shri Arvindo emphasised on the development of mind as he regarded it as

(a) the basis of man's developments.
(b) man's Sixth Sense.
(c) the source of man's meditation.
(d) All of these.

1092. The branch of philosophy which deals with spiritual problems is called
(a) Metaphysics (b) Metascience
(c) Maya (d) Metabiology

1093. Plato's philosophy of education gave
(a) greater importance to the individual than to the state.
(b) greater importance to the state than to the individual.
(c) greater importance to knowledge than virtue.
(d) greater importance to spiritual than moral values.

1094. Shri Arvindo wanted the purification of mind by
(a) 'Yoga'
(b) 'Samadhi'
(c) Discipline
(d) Meeting with great persons

1095. The number of educational objectives laid down by Herbert Spencer was
(a) Five (b) Seven
(c) Eight (d) Nine

1096. The Universe was classified by elements. How many Indian schools of philosophy recognized this?
(a) Four (b) Five
(c) Six (d) Seven

1097. According to Advaita Vedanta the levels of reality (satya) are
(a) Nine (b) Four
(c) Five (d) Three

1098. Shri Arvindo's aim of philosophy was
(a) Development of Superman
(b) Realization of Devine Power
(c) Knowledge of Sublime Truth
(d) All of these

1099. Aims of education, according to Vedantic philosophy is/are
(a) material gain
(b) liberation from the worldly life
(c) moral development of the child
(d) Both (b) and (c)

1100 The Darwinian concept of man is based on
(a) physical naturalism
(b) biological naturalism
(c) mechanical naturalism
(d) sociological naturalism

1101. What was according to Arvindo the means of realization of the sublime truth?
(a) Integral View of Life
(b) Deep Meditation
(c) Strict Discipline
(d) Practice of Yoga

1102. Who has described the education of a child close to nature?
(a) Charles Darwin
(b) J.J. Rousseau
(c) H. Spencer
(d) Thomas Hobbes

1103. "Education exists exclusively to develop man's intellect in a world of reality which men can know and understand". This statement was given by
(a) Aristotle
(b) Plato
(c) Auguste Comte
(d) None of the above

1104. What qualities of an Indian genius did Arvindo wanted to develop in this countrymen?
(a) Spirituality (b) Intellectuality
(c) Creativity (d) All of these

1105. In Advaita Vedanta, sarvana refers to
(a) true knowledge which is obtained only with the help of a guru.

(b) ultimate truth which is learnt only through the study of revealed text.
(c) Both (a) and (b).
(d) None of the above.

1106. In Jnana yoga methodology realising moksha needs everything except
(a) Nidhidhyasana (b) Manana
(c) Experimentation (d) Sarvana

1107. Who taught that "a person's worth is determined by right conduct and right knowledge"?
(a) Swami Vivekananda
(b) Mahavira
(c) Gautam Buddha
(d) Lord Krishna

1108. The childhood name of Vivekananda was
(a) Dharmendra (b) Surendranath
(c) Vijayanath (d) Narendranath

1109. Which of the following does not come under the three levels of reality in Advaita Vedanta?
(a) Pratihara satta
(b) Pratibhasica satta
(c) Parmarthica satta
(d) Vyaviharica satta

1110. Experts have observed that deliquency during later childhood
(a) does not make its appearance at all.
(b) could be easily controlled in this period than in adolescence.
(c) is more than in adolescence.
(d) is less than in adolescence.

1111. "The objective of attaining perfection" was according to this Indian thinker.
(a) Mahatma Gandhi
(b) Swami Vivekananda
(c) Ravindranath Tagore
(d) Shri Arvindo

1112. Education is regarded to be synonymous with 'self realisation' by
(a) Shankaracharya (b) Mahavira
(c) S. Vivekananda (d) Yajnavalakya

1113. Herbert Spencer in the early nineteenth century, used the word '*force*' to describe
(a) Reality (b) Quality
(c) Individuality (d) Serendipity

1114. Jainism is similar to Buddhism in which of the following aspects?
(a) Pessimism
(b) Non-violence as a philosophy
(c) Repudiation of Vedas
(d) All of the above.

1115. "Arise awake and stop not till the goal is achieved." Why did Vivekananda warn the youth in these words?
(a) To develop self-confidence and sacrifice in them
(b) To develop patriotism in them
(c) To ask them to free their country
(d) All of these

1116. The person who has successfully subdued his passions and obtained mastery over himself, according to Jainism is called
(a) Jiva (b) Mukta
(c) Jina (d) None of these

1117. Rousseau glorified
(a) Animals (b) Education
(c) Philosophy (d) Nature

1118. "The chief aim of education is the formation of character", has been said by
(a) Herbert Spencer
(b) Plato
(c) Mahatma Gandhi
(d) Bertrand Russell

1119. Vivekananda wanted to develop this aspect of the students by the subjects included in the curriculum.

(a) Moral aspect (b) Spiritual aspect
(c) Worldly aspect (d) Both (b) and (c)

1120. Herbert Spencer was a
(a) Physical naturalist
(b) Biological naturalist
(c) Mechanical naturalist
(d) None of the above

1121. Vardhaman is the real name of
(a) Bhaskara
(b) Buddha
(c) Mahavira
(d) None of the above

1122. Jain philosophy discards
(a) Meditation (b) Karma
(c) Yoga (d) None of these

1123. It was one of the objectives of education according to Swami Vivekananda.
(a) Seeking Unity in Diversity
(b) Economic Development
(c) Materialistic Development
(d) All of these

1124. "Nature is an aggregate of things moving from one place to another in that space which is beyond us" described by
(a) Thales (b) Leucippus
(c) Thomas Hobbes (d) Democritus

1125. According to Gandhian philosophy way of living is characterised by
(a) Poverty (b) Strict discipline
(c) Non-violence (d) All of the above

1126. Swami Vivekananda regarded teacher for this pupils as
(a) Guide (b) Philosopher
(c) Friend (d) All of these

1127. Education, liberal ideas and professional training in various vocation were provided in the Christian schools, colleges and hospitals which were opened all over the country in the
(a) nineteenth century
(b) early twentieth century
(c) twentieth century
(d) None of the above

1128. Which of the following philosophies are most tilted to individualism?
(a) Buddhism (b) Jainism
(c) Samkhya (d) None of these

1129. The conversion of Hindus to the Christian faith is due to
(a) Faith in missionaries
(b) Discipline of Christians
(c) Liberality
(d) None of the above

1130. Which institution was established by Vivekananda for public education?
(a) Vedant Society
(b) Brahm Samaj
(c) Arya Samaj
(d) Ram Krishna Samaj

1131. Gandhiji undertook a fast unto death on an issue involving the treatment of untouchable as an integral part of Hindu and Indian society in
(a) 1932 (b) 1935
(c) 1937 (d) 1940

1132. "To have an aim is to act" the statement is given by (for education)
(a) John Dewey (b) Aristotle
(c) Plato (d) Socrates

1133. Aim of education according to Jainism is/are
(a) attainment of triratna
(b) development of personality
(c) to enable the child to discriminate pap and punya
(d) All of the above

1134. Swami Vivekananda supported this educational system.

(a) Gurukul System
(b) Traditional System
(c) Western System
(d) None of these

1135. According to Jainism, knowledge is obtained through
(a) Meditation
(b) Senses
(c) Both (a) and (b)
(d) None of the above

1136. "Education should enable one to attain the highest good or God, through pursuit of inherent spiritual values of truth, beauty and goodness", was held by
(a) John Dewey (b) Aristotle
(c) Plato (d) M.K. Gandhi

1137. Vivekananda's following assumption is not practicable.
(a) Gurukul System
(b) Expectation from the student to be a Brahmchari
(c) Recognition of traditional teaching-methods
(d) All of these

1138. The Sri Prakasa Committee on Religious and Moral Instruction recommended that
(a) moral education should be permitted but religious instruction should not be allowed.
(b) moral and religious education could be imparted only at primary or elementary stages.
(c) religious and moral education should be imparted in all educational institutions.
(d) religious and moral education should not be imparted in educational institutions.

1139. The Buddha was the first to challenge the caste system in the
(a) 4th Century BC (b) 5th Century BC
(c) 6th Century BC (d) 7th Century BC

1140. What was the poem of Ravindranath Tagore for which he was awarded Nobel Prize?
(a) "Shrandhanjali" (b) "Kabuliwala"
(c) "Gitannjali" (d) None of these

1141. When three qualities of Prakriti come in contact with Purusha, universe was created. This is the belief of
(a) Buddha (b) Mimansa
(c) Samkhya (d) None of the above

1142. Dwadasa Nidan explains that
(a) there are 12 paths to remove sufferings.
(b) there are twelve causes of sufferings.
(c) Both (a) and (b).
(d) None of the above.

1143. Which of the following is most important for teacher?
(a) Students of the class
(b) Time available for teaching
(c) Classroom discipline
(d) Subject he is teaching

1144. The original name of the educational institution established by Ravindranath Tagore was
(a) Vishwa Bharti (b) Jadhav pur
(c) Shantiniketan (d) All of these

1145. The statement by the then Prime Minister Rajiv Gandhi that a new education policy would be framed so as to "Prepare Indians for the 21st Century" was in the year
(a) 1988 (b) 1987
(c) 1986 (d) 1985

1146. Who had observed that the art of education would never attain clearness in itself without philosophy?
(a) Fichte
(b) Gautam Buddha
(c) M.K. Gandhi
(d) John Dewey

1147. Vivekanand favoured religious education in schools which
(a) is purely secular
(b) is based on Upanishads
(c) includes essentials of all religions
(d) None of the above

1148. "The best education is that which brings in harmony between our lives and the whole universe." This statement is made by the Indian educationist.
(a) Mahatma Gandhi
(b) Ravindranath Tagore
(c) Vivekananda
(d) Dayananda

1149. To propagate revolutionary ideas among Indians, Aurobindo started
(a) Bande Mataram
(b) Inqilab
(c) Swadeshi
(d) None of the above

1150. The opinion that "our aim should be to produce men who possess both culture and expert knowledge" was given by
(a) Montaigue
(b) Froebel
(c) A.H. Whitehead
(d) All of the above

1151. How do we get knowledge and how can we be sure it is true and not error? This area of philosophy is called
(a) Aesthetics
(b) Metaphysics
(c) Epistemology
(d) None of the above

1152. Ravindranath Tagore emphasised this objectives of education also.
(a) Internationalism (b) Nationalism
(c) Physical labour (d) Both (b) and (c)

1153. All the levels of education are provided from the nursery to the university stage in
(a) Brahmo Samaj
(b) Arya Samaj
(c) Ashram at Pondicherry
(d) Shantiniketan

1154. Aurobindo Ashram is in
(a) Tamil Nadu (b) Kerala
(c) Pondicherry (d) West Bengal

1155. Karmyogi, a weekly paper was edited by
(a) Swami Dayanand
(b) Gandhiji
(c) Tagore
(d) Aurobindo

1156. In today's society school should give
(a) Ornamental base
(b) Vocational base
(c) Both (a) and (b)
(d) None of the above

1157. Ravindranath Tagore included these types of subjects in his educational scheme.
(a) Liberal subjects
(b) Technical Subjects
(c) Both (a) and (c)
(d) Foreign Language

1158. Which of the following attributes would correctly define learning?
(a) Belief, creativity, and endurance
(b) Understanding, imagination and workmanship
(c) Intuition, intelligence and memorisation
(d) Change of behaviour, practice and experience.

1159. The 1968 National Policy on Education adopted by the Indian Government laid stress on the following aspects of teachers education
(a) promotion and retirement facilities for teachers.
(b) in-service training and correspondence education for teachers.

(c) adequate emoluments and academic freedom for teachers.
(d) travel allowance and family pensions for teachers.

1160. The terrorist activity along with Islamic education being carried on in Kashmir cannot be sestified as
(a) Struggle for "Jihad"
(b) Struggle for acquiring it
(c) Both (a) and (b)
(d) Struggle for freedom

1161. Who among the following favoured development of senses as aim of education?
(a) Vivekananda (b) Gandhiji
(c) Tagore (d) Aurobindo

1162. Which of the following denotes empiricism?
(a) Psychological analysis of human experiences
(b) Physical verification of objects or ideas
(c) Both (a) and (b)
(d) None of the above.

1163. If we believe in the dualistic theory of the mind versus body nature of man, we have to arrive at the conclusion that
(a) education is purely a matter of mental training and development of the self.
(b) learning and education should cater to observable behaviour of man.
(c) education is mechanisation in process and theoretical in development.
(d) learning is purely a matter of material changes in the behaviour of man.

1164. Swami Vivekananda was famous for speaking on
(a) Gita (b) Vedas
(c) Vedanta (d) Upanishads

1165. Article 45 under the Directive Principles of State policy in the Indian Constitution, provides for
(a) free and compulsory primary education.
(b) giving financial assistance to less advanced states.
(c) rights of minorities to establish educational institutions.
(d) education for weaker sections of the country.

1166. Logical Positivism denies metaphysics because
(a) later is related to values
(b) later determines values
(c) later cannot be verified
(d) All of the above

1167. In Indian constitution Article 30(1) the following class of people have been given the right to have their educational institutions.
(a) Of All the religious
(b) Of all linguistic minorities
(c) Both (a) and (b)
(d) All the caste Hindus

1168. Vivekananda was a
(a) Poet (b) Philosopher
(c) Religious guru (d) All of the above

1169. The National Educational Policy of 1979, recommended about the public schools that
(a) they must be allowed the autonomy that was bestowed on them by the past system of education.
(b) their traditions have to preserve the interests of the best talents of the country.
(c) suitable ratio has to be maintained for admission of middle class and poor students also.
(d) they should be brought under laws and regulations of the government public education system.

1170. In Logical Positivism values are

(a) Absolute (b) Real
(c) Relative (d) Fixed

1171. Logical positivism is more close to
(a) Objective Idealism
(b) Mechanical Naturalism
(c) Scientific Humanism
(d) Neorealism

1172. The following elements are included in the common core curriculum as suggested by National Education Policy (1986).
(a) National identity
(b) Constitutional responsibilities
(c) History India's freedom struggle
(d) All of these

1173. Ramakrishna Mission was founded by
(a) Guru Nanak Dev
(b) Raja Rammohan Roy
(c) Swami Dayanand
(d) Swami Vivekananda

1174. Annie Besant inspired the opening of schools in many cities in
(a) early nineteenth century.
(b) end of nineteenth century.
(c) early twentieth century.
(d) end twentieth century.

1175. In ancient India religions and moral aims were dominated by
(a) Brahmanic system of education
(b) Kshatriya system of education
(c) Both (a) and (b)
(d) None of the above

1176. The concept of totalitarian education in the West was in favour of
(a) the education of the individual for development of his total personality.
(b) making the state responsible to evolve education as a means of satisfying individual's needs and interests.
(c) treating education as a binding factor of international understanding.
(d) making the education of the individual as an instrument for realising the ends of the state.

1177. All logical positivists are at consensus at
(a) analyzing the statements on logical principles.
(b) opposing metaphysics.
(c) Both (a) and (b).
(d) None of the above.

1178. If any word or phrase becomes meaningless in a concept, what will happen?
(a) The meaning of the concept will change.
(b) The concept will also become meaningless.
(c) Both (a) and (b).
(d) None of the above.

1179. National Education Policy (1986) includes the following classes of people for equal opportunities for education.
(a) Scheduled Castes/Tribes
(b) Women
(c) Both (a) and (b)
(d) Cast Hindus

1180. Regarding co-education at the secondary stage, the 1952-53 Education Commission has suggested that
(a) the situation in our country warrants establishment of more boys schools than co-educational school.
(b) several states could not afford to establish them.
(c) there should be objection to extend co-educational schooling.
(d) separate schools be established for boys and girls.

1181. Who formed Brahmo Samaj?
(a) Raja Rammohan Roy
(b) Ramanand
(c) Guru Nanak
(d) Kabir

1182. Tagore was well-known as a
(a) Philosopher (b) Musician
(c) Poet (d) Both (a) and (b)

1183. The topic method in education should be interpreted as
(a) a method suited better for arts subjects as compared to science subjects.
(b) a method of development of the syllabus in a subject.
(c) a concentric approach of teaching the classroom.
(d) a substitute for the project method of teaching.

1184. National Education Policy (1986) has made provision of the following schools for quality education for rural children.
(a) Sainik Schools
(b) Basic Education Schools
(c) Central Schools
(d) Navodaya Schools

1185. Method of teaching proposed by Logical Positivism is
(a) problem solving
(b) learning by doing
(c) discussion and argumentation
(d) All of the above

1186. Arya Samaj was founded by
(a) Swami Dayanand Saraswati
(b) Kabir
(c) Raja Rammohan Roy
(d) Swami Satyanand

1187. Intellectual aim in education was emphasised in
(a) Sparta (b) Athens
(c) Greece (d) All of the above

1188. "The change based on conflict between reason and tradition" idea was given by
(a) Auguste Comte
(b) Max Weber
(c) Vableins theory
(d) None of the above

1189. The new electronic technologies of the 20th century are the real forces which have shaped and are shaping modern culture, is said by
(a) Mahatma Gandhi
(b) Herbert Spencer
(c) Thomas Moore
(d) Marshall McLuhan

1190. Rigid system of state-education is justified on the basis that the state
(a) has better resources to manage education.
(b) is supreme to dictate what shall be taught and how it shall be taught.
(c) has absolute control over the lives and destinies of its individual members.
(d) has a right and it is bounden duty to mould the citizens to a pattern which makes for its own preservation and enhancement.

1191. In India customs in relation to education is/are
(a) Sleeping (b) Eating
(c) Daily bath (d) All of the above

1192. National Education Policy (1986) had provided for it in the higher secondary education.
(a) Indianization
(b) Westernization
(c) Industrialisation
(d) Vocationalisation

1193. The performers of the services have to be
(a) Recognized
(b) Criticized
(c) Rewarded
(d) None of the above

1194. The internal harmony required for a person's satisfactory life, comprises
(a) harmony of intelligence and emotions.
(b) harmony of intelligence and the environment.
(c) harmony of the environment and society.
(d) harmony of emotions and society.

1195. The classroom in India is based on
(a) Age grouping
(b) Mass grouping
(c) Subject grouping
(d) Economic criteria

1196. The National Institute of Basic Education at New Delhi was woundup in
(a) 1953 (b) 1962
(c) 1969 (d) 1974

1197. National Education Policy (1986) has adopted it for qualitative improvement of primary education.
(a) Operative Black Board
(b) Work-experience
(c) Basic Education
(d) Educational Guidance

1198. Hitler's Nazi theory and practices brought about years of war, bringing destruction and ruin in many countries of
(a) Asia (b) U.S.A.
(c) Africa (d) Europe

1199. Madam Montessori was
(a) a German psychiatrist
(b) an English educator
(c) a French philosopher
(d) an Italian physician

1200. In spite of the vast diversity of thoughts in an individual philosophers believed that
(a) he could be regarded as identifying with an unchanging unity.
(b) his perceptions of old are always stable.
(c) he is more or less an integrated individual.
(d) his emotional states could be regarded as stable.

1201. "Religion could not stand for a moment, if it did not support itself by intellectual presentation, however inadequate, of profound truths." This has been said by
(a) Rabindranath Tagore
(b) Immanuel Kant
(c) Sri Aurobindo
(d) F.H. Bradley

1202. Article 45 under the Directive Principles of State Policy in the Indian Constitution, provides for
(a) free and compulsory primary education.
(b) education for weaker sections of the country.
(c) rights of minorities to establish institutions.
(d) giving financial assistance to less advanced states.

1203. Practical, Parochial and utilitarian nature of education system was of
(a) the Spartans (b) the Athenians
(c) the Romans (d) the Indians

1204. What type of universities have been provided by National Education Policy (1986) for making higher education available to all concerned.
(a) Central Universities
(b) Open Universities
(c) Higher Study Universities
(d) National Universities

1205. According to whom, the whole life of the school becomes the curriculum which can touch the life of the students at all points and help in the evolution of a balanced personality.

(a) The Wardha Scheme
(b) Report of NPE
(c) The Kothari Commission
(d) The Ramamurti Report

1206. The introduction of career courses in schools and colleges aims at
(a) increasing G.K. in students.
(b) providing professional knowledge.
(c) developing the ability to make the intelligent choice of jobs.
(d) All of the above.

1207. Which of the following is indicated as a subject in the usual curriculum concept in the syllabi issued by various departments of instruction in India?
(a) Geography (b) History
(c) Mathematics (d) All of the above

1208. By the end of 1977-78 was adapted by
(a) All the states
(b) Union territories
(c) Both (a) and (b)
(d) None of the above

1209. The following principle has been recognised by the National Education Policy (1986) for the National Educational Organization.
(a) Man-power should be developed for national self-sufficiency
(b) Education should be available to all
(c) Constitutional values should be developed
(d) All of these

1210. "To have an aim is to act" is said by
(a) Auguste Comte
(b) John Dewey
(c) Max Weber
(d) None of the above

1211. Roman education looked to the welfare of the
(a) State (b) Society
(c) Both (a) and (b) (d) Individual

1212. Some knowledge of this basic subject is necessary for living a useful and successful life. The subject is/are
(a) Mathematics (b) Language
(c) Social science (d) All of the above

1213. The 10 + 2 pattern was introduced by the end of
(a) 1973 (b) 1974
(c) 1975 (d) 1977

1214. The emperor Ashoka's attitude to war, many centuries later was changed due the influence of
(a) Mahavir's teaching
(b) Buddha's teaching
(c) Both (a) and (b)
(d) None of the above

1215. The field of education is permeated by conflicts and misconception because
(a) problems encountered in teaching are not amenable to rigorous scientific investigation.
(b) of lack of good teaching methods and procedures.
(c) problems in education call for subjectivity of interpretation.
(d) teachers are not worthy of doing rigorous scientific investigation.

1216. This amendment of the Constitution has imposed a special duty upon the citizens of the country to protect and improve the natural environment. Therefore, education has now aimed at keeping the problems of environment in the courses of B.Ed and M.Ed classes and teachers are expected to inculcate in the students the spirit of fundamental duties including the duty under Article 51 A (g) of the Constitution to protect the environment. In the light of the above which one of the following is correct?
(a) Students at school should not be burdened with duties.

(b) Only colleges should concern with the duties.
(c) Only primary schools should be concerned about envirnment.
(d) None of the above.

1217. The Hartog Committee of 1929 had recommended that careers should be started at the end of the
(a) primary school stage
(b) matriculation
(c) high school stage
(d) graduation

1218. In India, First public examination is called
(a) Middle School certificate
(b) Secondary School certificate
(c) Sr. Secondary certificate
(d) Pre-university certificate

1219. Buddha changed the religion in
(a) China (b) India
(c) Japan (d) All of the above

1220. Who is to decide "the mode and type of education which an individual is to receive for its welfare"?
(a) Society (b) Citizen
(c) State (d) All of the above

1221. The Latin root term for the word 'curriculum' means
(a) collection of contents fixed for education.
(b) the subjects taught through school alone.
(c) the objects conducive to education of children.
(d) a path or course to be run.

1222. The isolated individual is a figment of the imagination, is said by
(a) Plato (b) Comte
(c) Socrates (d) Raymont

1223. Spartan system of education was in
(a) Ancient Greece
(b) Modern Greece
(c) Roman Empire
(d) None of the above

1224. Ancient education enjoined on the pupils the tenets of dharma which implied the ideas of
(a) Duty (b) Sacred law
(c) Justice (d) All of the above

1225. The national science policy resolution was adopted in the year
(a) 1957 (b) 1958
(c) 1960 (d) 1962

1226. The year 1986 is significant in the history of Indian education for the
(a) Reconstitution of the CABE
(b) Report of the Committee on Emotional Integration
(c) Reforms in the vocational and technical education
(d) Adoption of the New Education Policy

1227. Which of the following schools of philosophy regarded man as the centre and measure of all activities?
(a) Humanism (b) Realism
(c) Progressivism (d) Naturalism

1228. Educational aims are determined or laid down in most cases by persons, i.e.
(a) Other than the Class teachers
(b) Schools principals
(c) Class teachers
(d) None of the above

1229. During the days of education for the classes as opposed to education for the masses educational freedom meant
(a) subordination of the individual.
(b) emancipation of the individual.
(c) discrimination in favour of the individual.
(d) self-realization of the individual.

1230. Which of the following does not represent the concern of philosophers?
(a) Should one follow or fight group mores?
(b) Is man a part of or is he independent of nature?
(c) What is the goal of education?
(d) Should poetry be studied by the whole or part method?

1231. The utility of philosophy of religion can be seen in the forms of
(a) Anti-dogmatism
(b) Rational Approach
(c) Anti-superstitions
(d) All of the above

1232. Which of the following does not belong to the group?
(a) Naturalism (b) Dualism
(c) Traditionalism (d) Idealism

1233. National reconstruction in any country should
(a) familiarise the children with the nation's culture and philosophy.
(b) weed out the unsocial and unscientific practices at the top level.
(c) develop ambitions and looks of administrators.
(d) improve adjustability and adaptability of the people.

1234. The U.G.C. in our country was established under the act of Parliament on the recommendations of
(a) the University Education Commission.
(b) the National Board of University Education.
(c) the Central Board of Secondary Education.
(d) the Secondary Education Commission.

1235. Teachers should study educational philosophy because
(a) they may improve their work by clarifying their own philosophy.
(b) they do not have their own philosophy.
(c) they do not know it.
(d) philosophy is the backbone of all disciplines.

1236. Generally speaking, one would identify
(a) Breed with idealism
(b) Hutchins with experimentalism
(c) Brameld with reconstructionism
(d) Rousseau with supernaturalism

1237. The educational philosophy of Swami Dayananda suggests
(a) a formal approach to education at all stages.
(b) a non-formal approach to pre-primary education.
(c) a non-formal approach to co-education.
(d) a formal approach to pre-primary education.

1238. The 1979 Draft National Policy on Education recommended the language formula as follows for the non-Hindi speaking areas
(a) Hindi as a link language along with mother tongue and English.
(b) English as a link language along with mother tongue and a modern Indian language.
(c) regional language and English in addition to Hindi.
(d) a modern Indian language along with a regional language and English.

1239. The fifth five-year plan period started in the year
(a) 1974 (b) 1973
(c) 1972 (d) 1971

1240. Educational objectives such as knowledge, understanding and application come under the category of

(a) Cognitive Objectives
(b) Specific Objectives
(c) Functional Objectives
(d) General Objectives

1241. 'Education is the consciously controlled process whereby changes in behaviour are produced in the person and through the person within the group'. This statement is accorded to
(a) Linton (b) Brown
(c) R.N. Tagore (d) Moore

1242. The U.G.C. was established in our country in
(a) 1953 (b) 1954
(c) 1956 (d) 1962

1243. Concerning educational philosophy today, it can be said truthfully that
(a) complete exemplification of a philosophy is really found.
(b) the differences between the philosophies are clear cut.
(c) there are several different philosophies in practice.
(d) All of the above.

1244. Which of the following was not involved in the medieval controversy between the realists and nominalists?
(a) Claims that reason is subordinate to faith
(b) Differences respecting the nature of universal
(c) Challenges to the authority of church dogma
(d) Emphasis given to Aristotle's deductive logic.

1245. The secondary education commission in our country suggested reform of our examinations through
(a) giving importance to internal tests alone instead of conducting the annual public examinations.
(b) substituting the essay type examinations by the objective type tests.
(c) introduction of better grade system instead of the percentile marks system for declaring results.
(d) application of examinations and maintenance of cumulative records.

1246. Which of the following was not an origin of the Thomoistic supernaturalist philosophy of education?
(a) The writings of Thomas Aquinas
(b) Beliefs of the Deists, especially the doctrine of immanence
(c) The philosophy of Aristotle
(d) Early Christianity's exclusive concern with life after death.

1247. Plato's theory called for an educational program in which
(a) the validity of mental discipline was denied.
(b) his science was for workers, his dialectic for rulers.
(c) the unfit were to be eliminated and the fit located.
(d) education was life itself, not a preparation for life.

1248. Concerning the classification of philosophy of education it can truthfully be said that
(a) Bacon's revelation, reason, and experience covers all classifications.
(b) The generally accepted classification today involves four categories.
(c) The classification of essentialism and progressivism is generally accepted.
(d) None of the above is correct.

1249. The intimacy between philosophy and religion can be seen in the field of
(a) Aim of knowledge
(b) Goal of life

(c) Values
(d) All of the above

1250. Eclecticism is a belief or practice which
(a) denies the need for accepting any criteria.
(b) uses practical results as standards of value.
(c) borrows views from many different philosophies.
(d) considers that all philosophers are in error.

1251. Which of the following statement is incorrect?
(a) The rina theory emphasises, among other things, that one has to pay off, the rinas (debts) to rishis and to gurus, and it is best paid by studying the texts and by imparting education to one's children.
(b) The Western dictum has been, "Those who can, do; those who cannot, teach".
(c) Education has been given greater prominence in India than in Western or Islamic societies or in China.
(d) None of the above.

1252. Which of the following statements would be consistent with the theory that knowledge of the good is received through revelation?
(a) All learning should by subordinated to religious dogma.
(b) Education should consist of abstract subjects like dialectics.
(c) Formal reading instruction should be delayed until age 12.
(d) Education should exclude the study of foreign languages.

1253. The SUPW has been introduced in the school curriculum due to the recommendations of
(a) the Kothari Education Commission's report.
(b) the Easwar Bhai Patel Education Review Committee.
(c) the University Education Commission's report.
(d) the Secondary Education Commission's report.

1254. Which of the following is not a purpose of educational philosophy?
(a) To critically examine assumptions behind educational practice.
(b) To increase the teacher's love of and control over, the pupils.
(c) To professionalise the job of teaching.
(d) To clarify values and aims in teaching.

1255. The word 'transcendentalism' means
(a) doctrine of first principles derived from use of the senses.
(b) moving from deductive to inductive logic.
(c) going beyond man's experience for knowledge of truth.
(d) belief in the doctrine of immanence.

1256. That which educators criticise most severely in the practices of the so-called progressive schools might best be termed as
(a) Idealism (b) Scholasticism
(c) Laissez-faire (d) Realism

1257. Who said that members of the same species are not alike?
(a) Thomas Huxley (b) Charles Darwin
(c) Herbert Spencer (d) Haeckel

1258. Revelation differed among primitive people and among Hebrews, Catholics, and Protestants, in respect to
(a) the agent for transmitting true knowledge.
(b) the location of the source of true knowledge.

(c) the interpretation of the revealed knowledge.
(d) All of the above.

1259. Who challenged the superstitions and priestly ceremonies and changed the attitudes of people towards religion?
(a) Mahavira
(b) Buddha
(c) Mahatma Gandhi
(d) Both (a) and (c)

1260. To Plato, the main role of education was to
(a) develop the power of contemplation.
(b) strengthen the power of perception.
(c) cultivate the personality of each individual.
(d) train each person for a vocation.

1261. Originally, the family was the all-inclusive social institution, according to
(a) Ballard (b) Moore
(c) Dewey (d) Patanjali

1262. The educational philosophy which is rooted in revelation as a method of receiving knowledge of the good is called
(a) romantic naturalism
(b) naturalism
(c) classical realism
(d) supernaturalism

1263. According to the generally accepted classification of I.Q. the superiors are those whose I.Q. range is
(a) 110-119 (b) 120-129
(c) 130-139 (d) 140 and above

1264. Taking all the possible points of view about education into consideration, we are justified in concluding that the most perennial dimension of education is
(a) practical in nature
(b) philosophical in nature
(c) social in nature
(d) political in nature

1265. Which of the following is not a means of inducing the recall of knowledge according to Plato's theory?
(a) Conditioning of the mind
(b) A study of recollections by sense organs
(c) The method of contemplation
(d) The use of the Socratic method.

1266. The term 'instrumentalism' in educational philosophy means the same as
(a) Nationalism
(b) Progressivism
(c) Pragmatism
(d) Realistic naturalism

1267. In the ancient Indian educational tradition, education was regarded as
(a) tool for successful living
(b) tool for self-realisation
(c) means of social service
(d) None of the above

1268. In the opinion of the 1952-53 Secondary Education Commission in our country, the special function of the secondary school is
(a) to see that persons after secondary education address themselves to works of productivity.
(b) to equip students with adequate knowledge for further education.
(c) to prepare students to join vocational courses easily.
(d) to train students to assume leadership responsibility in their community or locality.

1269. Some thinkers recommend educational immunization to be practised in educational institutions. This should be correctly mean
(a) observing health programmes in schools for prevention of infectious disease.

(b) checking students from wrong practices and harmful habits.
(c) informing students about all 'isms' in the society to enable them to take their decisions freely.
(d) preventing spread of false information through teaching.

1270. Rousseau's naturalism was like the rationalism of the encyclopedist in respect to
(a) its glorification of the intellect.
(b) its emphasis upon the rights of the individual.
(c) its emphasis upon feeling.
(d) None of the above.

1271. Rousseau's philosophy of education contends that
(a) the education of children should start from the womb itself.
(b) modern civilisation is to be modified according to the needs of the environment.
(c) environmental facilities for play activities should be improved in schools.
(d) all evils of education are due to departure from nature.

1272. The history of education reveals that even as late as the 19th century, all the various divisions of knowledge were spoken of as branches of
(a) Logic (b) Philosophy
(c) Metaphysics (d) Epistemology

1273. The essentialists in education claim that
(a) it is essential to take the interests of individual students into consideration in dividing the aims and methods of education.
(b) we must teach what is common and essential for all instead of diverting our attention to individual differences.
(c) in conformity with Dewey, the practical needs of the society should be treated as essential in framing the curricula in education.
(d) education should essentially be adjusted to the requirements of the growing children.

1274. The Swaminathan study group's report of 1972 was concerned with
(a) the vocational aspects of primary education.
(b) in-service teachers.
(c) development of pre-school children's education.
(d) the technical education at the secondary level of education.

1275. From an instrumentalist's point of view, the values in education
(a) should prepare young people for adult life to post-school work and social relationships.
(b) are instrinsic to a subject or activity comprising education.
(c) have a standard hierarchy.
(d) have a superiority in objectives of education at any level.

1276. Aristotle disagreed with Plato in respect to the belief that
(a) slaves should be excluded from education.
(b) the state should control education.
(c) ideas are the reals.
(d) there are universals.

1277. Educational philosophy should be
(a) able to determine the why of education from a theoretical point of view.
(b) concerned with determining the aims of education only.
(c) a determining factor in the context of education.
(d) concerned with the relation between mind and matter.

1278. Religion and philosophy meet in
(a) Spirit (b) Matter
(c) Mind (d) Body

1279. The controversy between science and religion in the West started over which of the following theories?
(a) Pragmatism (b) Darwinism
(c) Naturalism (d) Essentialism

1280. Which of the following statements would be correct with regard to the policy of non-formal education?
(a) It is good only for lower and unskilled classes.
(b) It does not require any theoretical basis or intellectual preparation or trained teachers.
(c) It is not a substitute, but a supplement to formal education.
(d) It is education of an unplanned nature to be adopted only to selected situations.

1281. The 1972 International Commission on Education has entitled its report as
(a) Learning to Be
(b) Learning as a Living
(c) Education and National Development
(d) Learning: The Treasure Within

1282. The educational movement started by Acharya Vinoba Bhave and being pursued by some followers even now is
(a) Acharya Kul
(b) Gurukul
(c) Shikshak Kul
(d) None of the above

1283. According to Sri Aurobindo the training of our five senses
(a) is only secondary as compared to training of mind.
(b) has no importance in education.
(c) is hindrance for training and education of conscience.
(d) should be given great importance.

1284. Herbert, the originator of the formal steps of teaching, considered morality as
(a) a misfit in his teaching steps.
(b) a consideration to be borne in mind at higher stages of education only.
(c) the whole and the main task of education.
(d) a concept that cannot be grasped by children at younger ages.

1285. Who holds that economic purposes should be constructive or they may be used for exploitation
(a) Veblen
(b) Auguste Comte
(c) Max Weber
(d) None of the above

1286. Which of the following does not belong to the group?
(a) Pragmatism (b) Essentialism
(c) Instrumentalism (d) Progressivism

1287. The philosophy behind existentialism considers that
(a) the individuality is supreme and society is only a means for its development.
(b) the environment should be given greater importance as compared to natural and spiritual aspects of education.
(c) greater recognition should be given to nature and intelligence as compared to aspects of self.
(d) man should remain subordinated to the interests of the society.

1288. The Kothari Education Commission's report was entitled as
(a) Diversification of Education
(b) Education and Socialisation in Democracy
(c) Education and National Development
(d) Learning to Be

1289. The three language formula at the lower secondary stage of Classes VIII to X, recommended by the Indian Education Commission (1964-66) was
(a) Mother Tongue or Hindi + English + A Regional Language
(b) Mother Tongue + Regional Language + English
(c) Mother Tongue + Hindi + A Regional Language
(d) Mother Tongue or Regional Language + Hindi + English

1290. Which of the following interpretations would be correct according to the progressive philosophy of education?
(a) Encouragement of private enterprises in education.
(b) Emphasis on the importance of project based learning.
(c) Emphasis on incentives to make learning more attractive.
(d) Making learning a delightful activity.

1291. The gurukul system of education started during
(a) Ancient Period (b) Modern Period
(c) Medieval Period (d) British Rule

1292. Gandhi's real greatness in the field of education is to be found in the fact that
(a) he made his idealism and naturalism complementary to his pragmatism.
(b) his naturalism merged with his pragmatism.
(c) he made his idealism as complementary to his naturalism.
(d) he made both naturalism and pragmatism as complementary to his idealism.

1293. The Secondary Education Commission's suggestion about negligence of education in school, favoured
(a) combination of religious instruction with moral education relating to it.
(b) limiting free religious instruction to only those who wanted it, by creating the required facilities within the school timetable itself.
(c) religious instruction as an integral part of regular school work without appointing special teachers for the purpose.
(d) religious instruction only on voluntary basis outside school hours with the consent of parents and management.

1294. According to Swami Vivekananda, a teacher's success depends on
(a) his professional training and creativity.
(b) his renunciation of personal gain and service to others.
(c) his mastery of the subject and adeptness in controlling the students.
(d) his concentration on his work and duties with a spirit of obedience to God.

1295. The Pancha Kosha Theory of Education was elaborated by
(a) Sri Aurobindo
(b) Swami Vivekananda
(c) Patanjali
(d) Mahatma Gandhi

1296. Rousseau, who popularized the Naturalistic Philosophy of Education in the West, belonged to
(a) the 16th century
(b) the 17th century
(c) the 18th century
(d) the 19th century

1297. The Indian Education Commission (1964-66) has recommended compulsory social service for school children as follows:
(a) 30 days for the lower secondary and 20 days for the higher secondary stage

(b) 20 days for the lower secondary stage and 20 days for the higher secondary stage
(c) 10 days for the lower secondary stage and 20 days for the higher secondary stage
(d) 10 days for the primary stage and 30 days the secondary stage

1298. The idea of starting girls' University in our country occurred in the year 1970.
(a) Through the efforts of municipalities and local fund communities
(b) With the opening of the SNDT university at Bombay
(c) As an initiative of the UN
(d) None of the above

1299. A technical educational cess was recommended to be levied in our country for the first time by
(a) the Technical Education Commission.
(b) the Secondary Education Commission.
(c) the International Education Commission.
(d) the University Education Commission.

1300. The 1965-66 Indian Education Commission, recommended among other things
(a) complete separation between the general and vocational educational courses.
(b) general education as distinct from vocational education.
(c) general education containing elements of vocational and technical education.
(d) general education, a college preparatory course and vocational education leading to technical course.

1301. The famous seven cordial principles of education were formulated in the U.S.A. by
(a) the national federation of education.
(b) the new education fellowship.
(c) the progressive education association.
(d) American Association for Higher Education.

1302. Realism is really
(a) The basis of idealism
(b) Reverse of naturalism
(c) An epistemological philosophy
(d) Pragmatic epistemology

1303. The progressive education movement in U.S.A. was the direct outcome of
(a) Pragmatism in education
(b) Experimentalism of Education
(c) Socialism in education
(d) Naturalism in education

1304. For Tagore, the real education is that which
(a) makes one's life harmonious with all existence.
(b) inculcates regularity in habits and attitudes.
(c) has intellectual and emotional predominance.
(d) makes a realistic and pragmatic approach to life.

1305. The Higher Education Channel run by Consortium for Educational Communication on DTH platform is named
(a) Vyas (b) Valmiki
(c) Agastya (d) Pulatsya

1306. The criticism of the 1952-53 Secondary Commission, about the curriculum in the secondary school was that
(a) it envisaged education for the more liberal classes of the society instead of uplifting the rural areas of the country.
(b) it was more theoretical than practical as an unbearable burden for students at that age.

(c) it appeared to suit the interests and tests of the expert teachers amounting to neglect of the capacities and requirements of the taught.
(d) it was narrowly conceived mainly in terms of admission requirements of the colleges.

1307. Tagore was a
(a) Politician (b) Civil Servant
(c) Reformer (d) Poet

1308. Liberalism in education, when it was claimed by universities of the world since the 19th century, meant
(a) academic freedom for teachers in instruction.
(b) separation of education from religion.
(c) administrative freedom to universities to run their institutions.
(d) favouring liberal education as opposed to special education.

1309. The industrial revolution that started in the West to begin with had the following effect on education:
(a) Introduction of mass educational programmes
(b) Shifting the emphasis from the lower class culture to the middle class culture
(c) Introduction of vocationalisation of education
(d) Shifting the centre of gravity from the middle to the lower class culture.

1310. The doctrine of immanence
(a) distrusts the senses and unaided reason.
(b) pictures the world as an unfriendly place.
(c) supports Plato's theory of reality.
(d) searches for knowledge of the good in the world about us.

1311. A teacher who believes in the realistic philosophy of education would
(a) allow full freedom to students in learning, following a non-interference policy.
(b) support strict control and supervision to make children understand human race and culture.
(c) not allow control and pressure on students to learn what they want to learn.
(d) oppose supervision and interference of the teacher in the interests of students.

1312. Education cultivates faculties which are
(a) Intellectual (b) Moral
(c) Aesthetic (d) All of the above

1313. According to Emile Durkheim, the function of education is to
(a) reinforce social solidarity
(b) maintain social role
(c) maintain division of labour
(d) All of the above

1314. Who realised the urgent need for the reform of rigid, lifeless, meaningless curriculum?
(a) Subhas Chandra Bose
(b) Mahatma Gandhi
(c) Lal Bahadur Shastri
(d) Jawaharlal Nehru

1315. According to the recommendation of the Mudaliar Secondary Education Commission, the maximum number of pupils in a class at the secondary level
(a) should not exceed 30
(b) should not exceed 40
(c) should not exceed 50
(d) should not exceed 60

1316. The Basic Education Scheme was a
(a) Learning through productive work
(b) Work-oriented curriculum
(c) Both (a) and (b)
(d) Objective centred

1317. If you are an educational philosopher, which of the following would be your main consideration in establishing a school?
(a) The abilities of teachers
(b) The site for its building
(c) The accommodation to be provided
(d) The deed that it should fulfill.

1318. Mahatma Gandhi proposed the scheme of basic education in
(a) 1957 (b) 1950
(c) 1940 (d) 1937

1319. The secondary education commission of 1952-53 was also called the
(a) Basic Education Scheme
(b) National Policy on Education
(c) Mudaliar Commission
(d) Wardha Commission

1320. Schools became higher secondary and multipurpose schools due to implementation of
(a) the Mudaliar Commission Report.
(b) the Basic Education Scheme.
(c) the National Policy on Education.
(d) the Kothari Commission Report.

1321. Historically, vocational education in the West was introduced by the
(a) progressive educational scheme
(b) industrial Revolution
(c) renaissance
(d) middle class capitalistic system

1322. The basic Education scheme is also called the
(a) National scheme
(b) National Policy on Education
(c) Wardha scheme
(d) Kothari Commission report

1323. The 5 + 3 + 2 pattern was changed to 5 + 5 + 3 pattern by
(a) the Kothari Commission
(b) Wardha Pattern
(c) Mudaliar Commission
(d) combined effect of all

1324. The idea of Socially Useful Productive Work in the curriculum given by
(a) Lala Lajpat Rai
(b) Mahatma Gandhi
(c) Jawaharlal Nehru
(d) Rajendra Prasad

1325. The secondary education commission was set up in
(a) 1967-68 (b) 1962-63
(c) 1957-58 (d) 1952-53

1326. Article 45 under the Directive Principles of State policy in the Indian Constitution provides for
(a) education for weaker sections of the country.
(b) rights of minorities to establish educational institutions.
(c) free and compulsory primary education.
(d) giving financial assistance to less advanced states.

1327. The previous pattern of 5 + 3 + 2 was of
(a) 15 years (b) 14 years
(c) 12 years (d) 10 years

1328. In basic education curriculum the subject taught in isolation is
(a) Biology (b) Physics
(c) Social Sciences (d) Not any subject

1329. Indian philosophers like Manu opined that philosophy leads to
(a) practical perfection
(b) thinking in the abstract
(c) salvation
(d) a disciplined life

1330. Acts and movements for progress have been set afloat to achieve what we had hoped for after gaining independence. It is in the

(a) Creations of States
(b) Twenty year plans
(c) Five year plans
(d) Foreign Policy

1331. Under the Satellite Instructional Television Experiment, the Govt. of India developed,
(a) Data Bank
(b) Multi-media package
(c) Student training material
(d) Teacher training material

1332. Educational Philosophers feel that the conflict between capitalism and communism
(a) creates a healthy competitive spirit in education.
(b) leaves important educational issues without solving the conflict.
(c) gives a definite shape to common policies.
(d) creates gaps in many different stages of education.

1333. What is nowadays termed as non-formal education, is really
(a) a substitute for higher education.
(b) a substitute for formal education.
(c) not a substitute for formal education.
(d) non-technical education.

1334. The main recommendation of the Sadler Commission appointed in 1917 was that
(a) the intermediate colleges should be attached to Universities.
(b) the intermediate colleges were dividing line between the University and the Secondary Education.
(c) the intermediate course was for the better students completing their matriculation and qualifying for higher education.
(d) None of the above.

1335. The Industrial Revolution, whose effects shook the world took place in the
(a) 17th century (b) 18th century
(c) 19th century (d) 20th century

1336. Which of the following statements would be correct in comparing the educational methods of Froebel and Montessori?
(a) There is greater scope for social development in the Montessori method as compared to Froebel's method.
(b) There is scope for development of imagination in both methods.
(c) Froebel favours development of imagination while Montessori provides no scope for this.
(d) Both favour class-room instructional approach.

1337. The Renaissance in Europe which brought about tremendous social, cultural and intellectual changes was the result of many new and explosive?
(a) Actions (b) Culture
(c) Politics (d) Ideas

1338. The Secondary Education Commission, 1952-53, took the lead for introduction of technical education in the country, from
(a) the Hunter Commission report of 1882.
(b) the Hartog Committee report of 1929.
(c) the Abbot-Wood report of 1936-37.
(d) the Sargent report of 1944.

1339. The subjects included in the late medieval studies of the West under quadrivium were
(a) Philosophy, Logic, Arithmetic and Grammar.
(b) Logic, Astronomy, Arithmetic and Grammar.

(c) Logic, Grammar, Music and Arithmetic.
(d) Music, Arithmetic, Geometry and Astronomy.

1340. The main objective of education according to Acharya Vinoba Bhave is to
(a) make a clear distinction between learning and doing.
(b) make a student self-dependent within the shortest possible time.
(c) train students in intellectual self-reliance and make them endependent thinkers.
(d) None of the above.

1341. The group of philosophers who call themselves as reconstructionlists
(a) object to Utopian view of the education and blindly support the status quo approach.
(b) recommend progressive education as the only approach for the reconstruction of the society.
(c) think that the present is more important for reconstructing the society.
(d) object to progressive education as the only approach for the reconstruction of the society.

1342. Socrates was executed in Greece on the complain that
(a) he was conservative in the sense of the Athenian notions of knowledge.
(b) he was corrupting the youth by teaching them disrespect for gods.
(c) he was encouraging the youth to revolt against the government of the day.
(d) he was teaching men to be skeptical without refining their convictions.

1343. The 1968 National Policy on Education stressed
(a) the need of functional literacy at the elementary and secondary levels.
(b) the need for spread of literacy and Adult Education.
(c) the importance of continuing educational programmes for the needy.
(d) the need for expansion of correspondence courses of education.

1344. The philosophy behind the progressive education movement could be designated as
(a) developmental philosophy of education.
(b) realistic philosophy of education.
(c) individualistic philosophy of education.
(d) personalistic philosophy of education.

1345. The philosophy known as mechanical naturalism considers that
(a) there is no purpose of aim of education except making education a mechanical process.
(b) it is much better than naturalism because its suggests a materialistic philosophy.
(c) the purpose of education is only to understand the nature of man and his activities.
(d) education is governed by the purpose of understanding nature and its mechanism.

Question below is Multi-statement type. Choose the correct code as given below.

1346. Arrange the Pestalozzi's stages of intellectual development given below in sequence
1. Function of mind starts with impression
2. Sense impression makes form and qualities of things clear
3. Images of things are transformed into ideas

Codes:

(a) 3, 1, 2 (b) 3, 2, 1
(c) 1, 2, 3 (d) 2, 1, 3

Question Nos. 1347 and 1348 Matching Type Questions. Choose the correct code as given below.

1347. List I / List II

List I	List II
A. Republic	1. Descartes
B. Emile	2. Rousseau
C. Modern theory	3. John Dewey of dualism
D. Experimentalism	4. Plato

Codes:	A	B	C	D
(a)	1	3	4	2
(b)	4	1	2	3
(c)	4	2	1	3
(d)	1	2	3	4

1348. **(I) Role of the teacher**

A. Guide and helper
B. Instructor
C. Autocrat
D. Disciplined

(II) Philosophy

1. Marxism 2. Existentialism
3. Pragmatism 4. Idealism

Codes:	A	B	C	D
(a)	2	3	4	1
(b)	4	3	2	1
(c)	1	2	3	4
(d)	3	4	1	2

ANSWERS

1. (a)	2. (b)	3. (d)	4. (c)	5. (b)	6. (a)
7. (c)	8. (d)	9. (a)	10. (d)	11. (a)	12. (b)
13. (b)	14. (c)	15. (d)	16. (d)	17. (d)	18. (d)
19. (b)	20. (d)	21. (c)	22. (d)	23. (b)	24. (d)
25. (c)	26. (d)	27. (c)	28. (d)	29. (a)	30. (b)
31. (d)	32. (c)	33. (b)	34. (c)	35. (c)	36. (b)
37. (a)	38. (b)	39. (d)	40. (c)	41. (b)	42. (b)
43. (b)	44. (a)	45. (d)	46. (d)	47. (c)	48. (b)
49. (b)	50. (b)	51. (a)	52. (c)	53. (b)	54. (b)
55. (d)	56. (c)	57. (c)	58. (b)	59. (d)	60. (a)
61. (a)	62. (a)	63. (d)	64. (d)	65. (c)	66. (b)
67. (c)	68. (a)	69. (a)	70. (d)	71. (b)	72. (a)
73. (b)	74. (a)	75. (c)	76. (d)	77. (c)	78. (a)
79. (c)	80. (a)	81. (a)	82. (b)	83. (d)	84. (c)
85. (d)	86. (b)	87. (d)	88. (a)	89. (c)	90. (a)
91. (c)	92. (b)	93. (c)	94. (c)	95. (c)	96. (c)
97. (b)	98. (a)	99. (a)	100. (b)	101. (b)	102. (c)
103. (d)	104. (b)	105. (a)	106. (d)	107. (c)	108. (c)
109. (a)	110. (b)	111. (d)	112. (c)	113. (c)	114. (c)

115. (b)	116. (b)	117. (c)	118. (a)	119. (c)	120. (c)
121. (b)	122. (b)	123. (d)	124. (a)	125. (c)	126. (b)
127. (a)	128. (a)	129. (c)	130. (a)	131. (b)	132. (b)
133. (d)	134. (b)	135. (d)	136. (d)	137. (c)	138. (d)
139. (c)	140. (a)	141. (a)	142. (c)	143. (b)	144. (d)
145. (d)	146. (b)	147. (b)	148. (a)	149. (d)	150. (d)
151. (b)	152. (c)	153. (c)	154. (a)	155. (b)	156. (b)
157. (c)	158. (b)	159. (d)	160. (a)	161. (b)	162. (a)
163. (b)	164. (b)	165. (c)	166. (c)	167. (c)	168. (c)
169. (a)	170. (c)	171. (a)	172. (c)	173. (b)	174. (c)
175. (b)	176. (c)	177. (c)	178. (b)	179. (d)	180. (b)
181. (c)	182. (d)	183. (c)	184. (a)	185. (a)	186. (b)
187. (d)	188. (b)	189. (a)	190. (b)	191. (b)	192. (c)
193. (d)	194. (d)	195. (b)	196. (c)	197. (b)	198. (c)
199. (d)	200. (a)	201. (b)	202. (b)	203. (c)	204. (c)
205. (b)	206. (d)	207. (c)	208. (c)	209. (b)	210. (b)
211. (c)	212. (d)	213. (a)	214. (c)	215. (a)	216. (c)
217. (b)	218. (b)	219. (d)	220. (d)	221. (c)	222. (b)
223. (a)	224. (b)	225. (d)	226. (d)	227. (c)	228. (b)
229. (b)	230. (c)	231. (a)	232. (b)	233. (d)	234. (d)
235. (d)	236. (b)	237. (a)	238. (a)	239. (c)	240. (c)
241. (c)	242. (a)	243. (c)	244. (c)	245. (c)	246. (c)
247. (d)	248. (d)	249. (a)	250. (c)	251. (d)	252. (b)
253. (c)	254. (d)	255. (c)	256. (c)	257. (d)	258. (b)
259. (a)	260. (d)	261. (d)	262. (c)	263. (b)	264. (d)
265. (c)	266. (b)	267. (a)	268. (a)	269. (b)	270. (c)
271. (b)	272. (a)	273. (d)	274. (b)	275. (c)	276. (d)
277. (a)	278. (c)	279. (d)	280. (a)	281. (c)	282. (c)
283. (a)	284. (d)	285. (c)	286. (d)	287. (c)	288. (a)
289. (a)	290. (b)	291. (b)	292. (b)	293. (c)	294. (b)
295. (a)	296. (d)	297. (b)	298. (c)	299. (b)	300. (c)
301. (d)	302. (d)	303. (c)	304. (c)	305. (c)	306. (b)
307. (b)	308. (c)	309. (c)	310. (d)	311. (c)	312. (d)
313. (b)	314. (c)	315. (d)	316. (d)	317. (d)	318. (c)

319. (b)	320. (d)	321. (a)	322. (c)	323. (d)	324. (c)
325. (b)	326. (d)	327. (c)	328. (a)	329. (c)	330. (a)
331. (b)	332. (d)	333. (d)	334. (b)	335. (c)	336. (c)
337. (d)	338. (b)	339. (a)	340. (d)	341. (d)	342. (a)
343. (b)	344. (d)	345. (b)	346. (c)	347. (d)	348. (d)
349. (c)	350. (a)	351. (a)	352. (d)	353. (d)	354. (a)
355. (d)	356. (b)	357. (a)	358. (d)	359. (d)	360. (c)
361. (c)	362. (a)	363. (a)	364. (b)	365. (c)	366. (d)
367. (b)	368. (a)	369. (d)	370. (c)	371. (c)	372. (d)
373. (d)	374. (c)	375. (d)	376. (d)	377. (a)	378. (c)
379. (c)	380. (d)	381. (c)	382. (d)	383. (a)	384. (c)
385. (a)	386. (c)	387. (b)	388. (a)	389. (a)	390. (d)
391. (b)	392. (b)	393. (a)	394. (d)	395. (b)	396. (b)
397. (c)	398. (c)	399. (d)	400. (d)	401. (c)	402. (c)
403. (a)	404. (d)	405. (a)	406. (c)	407. (c)	408. (d)
409. (c)	410. (a)	411. (b)	412. (a)	413. (d)	414. (d)
415. (a)	416. (d)	417. (d)	418. (d)	419. (b)	420. (b)
421. (a)	422. (d)	423. (c)	424. (a)	425. (d)	426. (c)
427. (d)	428. (b)	429. (d)	430. (b)	431. (c)	432. (c)
433. (d)	434. (c)	435. (a)	436. (c)	437. (a)	438. (b)
439. (c)	440. (a)	441. (c)	442. (c)	443. (a)	444. (d)
445. (d)	446. (d)	447. (b)	448. (c)	449. (d)	450. (d)
451. (c)	452. (a)	453. (c)	454. (b)	455. (c)	456. (d)
457. (c)	458. (a)	459. (a)	460. (c)	461. (a)	462. (d)
463. (b)	464. (a)	465. (c)	466. (c)	467. (b)	468. (a)
469. (c)	470. (a)	471. (d)	472. (a)	473. (c)	474. (d)
475. (c)	476. (d)	477. (d)	478. (b)	479. (d)	480. (d)
481. (d)	482. (d)	483. (c)	484. (d)	485. (c)	486. (c)
487. (c)	488. (a)	489. (b)	490. (a)	491. (a)	492. (c)
493. (d)	494. (c)	495. (b)	496. (d)	497. (b)	498. (a)
499. (c)	500. (a)	501. (d)	502. (d)	503. (a)	504. (a)
505. (a)	506. (b)	507. (a)	508. (b)	509. (d)	510. (c)
511. (a)	512. (d)	513. (c)	514. (d)	515. (c)	516. (b)
517. (b)	518. (c)	519. (a)	520. (b)	521. (d)	522. (b)
523. (a)	524. (c)	525. (b)	526. (c)	527. (a)	528. (c)

529. (d)	530. (d)	531. (c)	532. (a)	533. (b)	534. (c)
535. (a)	536. (a)	537. (b)	538. (c)	539. (c)	540. (b)
541. (d)	542. (b)	543. (d)	544. (d)	545. (b)	546. (d)
547. (d)	548. (d)	549. (c)	550. (d)	551. (b)	552. (b)
553. (d)	554. (d)	555. (b)	556. (a)	557. (a)	558. (c)
559. (c)	560. (d)	561. (b)	562. (c)	563. (c)	564. (a)
565. (a)	566. (b)	567. (b)	568. (b)	569. (d)	570. (a)
571. (d)	572. (d)	573. (b)	574. (d)	575. (b)	576. (a)
577. (c)	578. (b)	579. (a)	580. (c)	581. (a)	582. (a)
583. (b)	584. (c)	585. (c)	586. (d)	587. (b)	588. (b)
589. (d)	590. (d)	591. (d)	592. (d)	593. (b)	594. (c)
595. (a)	596. (d)	597. (c)	598. (d)	599. (c)	600. (b)
601. (d)	602. (d)	603. (b)	604. (c)	605. (b)	606. (d)
607. (c)	608. (a)	609. (c)	610. (b)	611. (d)	612. (c)
613. (b)	614. (d)	615. (c)	616. (c)	617. (d)	618. (c)
619. (c)	620. (a)	621. (b)	622. (d)	623. (a)	624. (a)
625. (d)	626. (b)	627. (c)	628. (c)	629. (a)	630. (b)
631. (d)	632. (c)	633. (b)	634. (d)	635. (a)	636. (b)
637. (a)	638. (d)	639. (b)	640. (c)	641. (d)	642. (d)
643. (d)	644. (a)	645. (d)	646. (c)	647. (a)	648. (d)
649. (c)	650. (c)	651. (d)	652. (a)	653. (c)	654. (d)
655. (d)	656. (d)	657. (d)	658. (d)	659. (c)	660. (d)
661. (c)	662. (b)	663. (d)	664. (d)	665. (d)	666. (d)
667. (c)	668. (d)	669. (c)	670. (d)	671. (c)	672. (b)
673. (a)	674. (c)	675. (d)	676. (d)	677. (d)	678. (c)
679. (d)	680. (c)	681. (d)	682. (d)	683. (d)	684. (c)
685. (d)	686. (a)	687. (d)	688. (d)	689. (b)	690. (b)
691. (b)	692. (b)	693. (b)	694. (b)	695. (c)	696. (d)
697. (c)	698. (c)	699. (c)	700. (a)	701. (d)	702. (a)
703. (a)	704. (a)	705. (d)	706. (d)	707. (a)	708. (c)
709. (d)	710. (d)	711. (b)	712. (a)	713. (d)	714. (d)
715. (c)	716. (d)	717. (a)	718. (d)	719. (c)	720. (c)
721. (d)	722. (a)	723. (a)	724. (b)	725. (d)	726. (d)
727. (d)	728. (c)	729. (d)	730. (b)	731. (b)	732. (b)

733. (c)	734. (c)	735. (d)	736. (d)	737. (a)	738. (d)
739. (a)	740. (d)	741. (c)	742. (d)	743. (b)	744. (b)
745. (c)	746. (a)	747. (c)	748. (c)	749. (d)	750. (d)
751. (c)	752. (c)	753. (b)	754. (c)	755. (a)	756. (b)
757. (b)	758. (c)	759. (c)	760. (d)	761. (d)	762. (d)
763. (d)	764. (d)	765. (c)	766. (a)	767. (a)	768. (c)
769. (b)	770. (a)	771. (d)	772. (c)	773. (d)	774. (d)
775. (a)	776. (d)	777. (d)	778. (b)	779. (d)	780. (d)
781. (b)	782. (d)	783. (c)	784. (a)	785. (d)	786. (c)
787. (a)	788. (a)	789. (d)	790. (d)	791. (d)	792. (a)
793. (b)	794. (d)	795. (c)	796. (d)	797. (c)	798. (a)
799. (a)	800. (a)	801. (d)	802. (b)	803. (c)	804. (c)
805. (c)	806. (a)	807. (b)	808. (c)	809. (d)	810. (d)
811. (b)	812. (c)	813. (d)	814. (b)	815. (a)	816. (a)
817. (c)	818. (b)	819. (c)	820. (b)	821. (b)	822. (d)
823. (a)	824. (c)	825. (b)	826. (b)	827. (a)	828. (b)
829. (b)	830. (c)	831. (a)	832. (d)	833. (d)	834. (c)
835. (b)	836. (a)	837. (c)	838. (c)	839. (a)	840. (c)
841. (b)	842. (a)	843. (b)	844. (b)	845. (d)	846. (d)
847. (a)	848. (c)	849. (b)	850. (a)	851. (c)	852. (c)
853. (c)	854. (b)	855. (d)	856. (d)	857. (d)	858. (c)
859. (d)	860. (a)	861. (c)	862. (b)	863. (c)	864. (d)
865. (a)	866. (c)	867. (d)	868. (d)	869. (c)	870. (d)
871. (a)	872. (d)	873. (c)	874. (c)	875. (d)	876. (c)
877. (a)	878. (d)	879. (d)	880. (a)	881. (d)	882. (c)
883. (b)	884. (d)	885. (a)	886. (c)	887. (d)	888. (a)
889. (c)	890. (c)	891. (d)	892. (d)	893. (c)	894. (c)
895. (c)	896. (c)	897. (d)	898. (d)	899. (d)	900. (d)
901. (d)	902. (c)	903. (d)	904. (d)	905. (d)	906. (d)
907. (a)	908. (b)	909. (a)	910. (d)	911. (b)	912. (d)
913. (b)	914. (c)	915. (d)	916. (b)	917. (a)	918. (d)
919. (b)	920. (d)	921. (c)	922. (d)	923. (a)	924. (c)
925. (b)	926. (d)	927. (a)	928. (a)	929. (d)	930. (a)
931. (b)	932. (b)	933. (c)	934. (c)	935. (a)	936. (d)
937. (a)	938. (d)	939. (c)	940. (d)	941. (a)	942. (d)

943. (b)	944. (d)	945. (b)	946. (a)	947. (d)	948. (c)
949. (d)	950. (a)	951. (d)	952. (a)	953. (c)	954. (a)
955. (d)	956. (a)	957. (c)	958. (c)	959. (a)	960. (a)
961. (a)	962. (a)	963. (c)	964. (a)	965. (d)	966. (d)
967. (c)	968. (d)	969. (d)	970. (c)	971. (d)	972. (d)
973. (b)	974. (a)	975. (b)	976. (c)	977. (b)	978. (b)
979. (a)	980. (a)	981. (c)	982. (d)	983. (c)	984. (d)
985. (c)	986. (b)	987. (b)	988. (c)	989. (d)	990. (d)
991. (c)	992. (b)	993. (b)	994. (c)	995. (c)	996. (d)
997. (c)	998. (b)	999. (b)	1000. (d)	1001. (d)	1002. (d)
1003. (c)	1004. (d)	1005. (d)	1006. (a)	1007. (b)	1008. (b)
1009. (c)	1010. (d)	1011. (d)	1012. (a)	1013. (b)	1014. (d)
1015. (b)	1016. (c)	1017. (a)	1018. (c)	1019. (a)	1020. (c)
1021. (a)	1022. (d)	1023. (b)	1024. (a)	1025. (c)	1026. (a)
1027. (b)	1028. (b)	1029. (d)	1030. (c)	1031 (d)	1032. (d)
1033. (c)	1034. (a)	1035. (c)	1036. (b)	1037. (c)	1038. (d)
1039. (d)	1040. (d)	1041. (a)	1042. (b)	1043. (b)	1044. (b)
1045. (b)	1046. (a)	1047. (c)	1048. (b)	1049. (a)	1050. (a)
1051. (a)	1052. (a)	1053. (d)	1054. (b)	1055. (d)	1056. (d)
1057. (d)	1058. (a)	1059. (c)	1060. (d)	1061. (a)	1062. (d)
1063. (b)	1064. (d)	1065. (c)	1066. (a)	1067. (a)	1068. (a)
1069. (b)	1070. (d)	1071. (c)	1072. (c)	1073. (c)	1074. (d)
1075. (c)	1076. (c)	1077. (d)	1078. (c)	1079. (d)	1080. (b)
1081. (d)	1082. (a)	1083. (a)	1084. (a)	1085. (c)	1086. (a)
1087. (a)	1088. (b)	1089. (d)	1090. (a)	1091. (b)	1092. (a)
1093. (b)	1094. (a)	1095. (a)	1096. (a)	1097. (d)	1098. (c)
1099. (d)	1100. (b)	1101. (a)	1102. (b)	1103. (a)	1104. (d)
1105. (c)	1106. (d)	1107. (c)	1108. (d)	1109. (c)	1110. (c)
1111. (b)	1112. (a)	1113. (c)	1114. (c)	1115. (a)	1116. (c)
1117. (d)	1118. (d)	1119. (d)	1120. (b)	1121. (c)	1122. (b)
1123. (a)	1124. (c)	1125. (d)	1126. (d)	1127. (a)	1128. (b)
1129. (c)	1130. (d)	1131. (a)	1132. (a)	1133. (d)	1134. (a)
1135. (c)	1136. (c)	1137. (d)	1138. (c)	1139. (c)	1140. (c)
1141. (c)	1142. (b)	1143. (a)	1144. (c)	1145. (d)	1146. (a)

1147. (c)	1148. (b)	1149. (a)	1150. (c)	1151. (c)	1152. (d)
1153. (c)	1154. (c)	1155. (d)	1156. (b)	1157. (c)	1158. (a)
1159. (c)	1160. (d)	1161. (d)	1162. (c)	1163. (a)	1164. (a)
1165. (a)	1166. (c)	1167. (c)	1168. (d)	1169. (c)	1170. (c)
1171. (c)	1172. (d)	1173. (d)	1174. (b)	1175. (c)	1176. (d)
1177. (c)	1178. (d)	1179. (c)	1180. (b)	1181. (a)	1182. (c)
1183. (d)	1184. (d)	1185. (c)	1186. (a)	1187. (c)	1188. (a)
1189. (d)	1190. (d)	1191. (d)	1192. (d)	1193. (c)	1194. (a)
1195. (b)	1196. (c)	1197. (a)	1198. (d)	1199. (d)	1200. (c)
1201. (c)	1202. (a)	1203. (c)	1204. (b)	1205. (c)	1206. (c)
1207. (d)	1208. (c)	1209. (d)	1210. (b)	1211. (a)	1212. (d)
1213. (d)	1214. (c)	1215. (a)	1216. (d)	1217. (c)	1218. (b)
1219. (d)	1220. (c)	1221. (d)	1222. (d)	1223. (a)	1224. (d)
1225. (b)	1226. (d)	1227. (a)	1228. (d)	1229. (a)	1230. (d)
1231. (d)	1232. (a)	1233. (a)	1234. (a)	1235 (a)	1236. (c)
1237. (b)	1238. (b)	1239. (b)	1240. (d)	1241. (b)	1242. (c)
1243. (c)	1244. (a)	1245. (c)	1246. (c)	1247. (c)	1248. (d)
1249. (d)	1250. (c)	1251. (d)	1252. (a)	1253. (b)	1254. (b)
1255. (c)	1256. (c)	1257. (b)	1258. (b)	1259. (d)	1260. (a)
1261. (a)	1262. (d)	1263. (b)	1264. (c)	1265. (b)	1266. (c)
1267. (b)	1268. (d)	1269. (c)	1270. (d)	1271. (d)	1272. (b)
1273. (b)	1274. (c)	1275. (a)	1276. (c)	1277. (a)	1278. (a)
1279. (b)	1280. (c)	1281. (a)	1282. (a)	1283. (d)	1284. (d)
1285. (a)	1286. (b)	1287. (a)	1288. (c)	1289. (d)	1290. (b)
1291. (a)	1292. (d)	1293. (c)	1294. (b)	1295. (a)	1296. (c)
1297. (a)	1298. (b)	1299. (b)	1300. (c)	1301. (d)	1302. (c)
1303. (a)	1304. (a)	1305. (a)	1306. (d)	1307. (d)	1308. (a)
1309. (d)	1310. (d)	1311. (b)	1312. (d)	1313. (d)	1314. (b)
1315. (c)	1316. (c)	1317. (d)	1318. (d)	1319. (c)	1320. (a)
1321. (b)	1322. (c)	1323. (c)	1324. (b)	1325. (d)	1326. (c)
1327. (d)	1328. (d)	1329. (c)	1330. (c)	1331. (b)	1332. (b)
1333. (c)	1334. (c)	1335. (b)	1336. (c)	1337. (d)	1338. (c)
1339. (d)	1340. (c)	1341. (c)	1342. (a)	1343. (b)	1344. (d)
1345. (c)	1346. (c)	1347. (c)	1348. (d)		

2

Sociological Foundations of Education

1. The founder of sociology in Western world was
   (a) Megasthnese (b) Plato
   (c) Herodotus (d) Aristotle
2. Education is a
   (a) Psychological necessity
   (b) Biological necessity
   (c) Social necessity
   (d) All of the above
3. This grand Indian book has first and foremost description of society.
   (a) *Gita*
   (b) *Manusamriti*
   (c) *Parakshar Samriti*
   (d) *Economics* by Chanakya
4. Sociology aims at explaining man's
   (a) Group behaviour
   (b) Interpersonal relationship
   (c) Both (a) and (b)
   (d) None of the above
5. This French philosopher had conducted scientific study of society in 19th century.
   (a) Augest Comet (b) Gillen
   (c) Maclver (d) Gidding
6. The Central theme in Sociology is
   (a) Chemical interaction
   (b) Physical interaction
   (c) Biological interaction
   (d) Social interaction

   Who said that "Educational sociology is the study of those phases of sociology that are of significance for educative processes, specially the study of those that point to valuable programmes of learning and control of learning processes"?
   (a) Ottoway (b) T.P. Munn
   (c) Brown (d) Carter
8. "Sociology is the science which attempts the interpretative understanding of social action". Above said words are of which sociologist.
   (a) MacIver (b) Gillen
   (c) Max Weber (d) Giddings
9. Adjustment function of education mainly refers to
   (a) Adjustment to nature
   (b) Social adjustment
   (c) Biological adjustment
   (d) None of the above
10. The following are included in the scope of sociology.
    (a) Study of social internal activity
    (b) Scientific study of social relations
    (c) Study of basic social groups
    (d) All of the above
11. Sociology analyzes the concept of
    (a) Animal welfare
    (b) Civilization
    (c) Juvenile delinquency
    (d) All of the above
12. Specialisation and further distinctions in making a living within a given economy, within an industrial economy makes

(a) a demand for specialized courses and training programmes such as management training, etc.
(b) a greater demand for better education.
(c) a demand for better man-machine facilities.
(d) many kinds of pressures on the expansion of education.

13. Education and sociology are deep-rooted related because both are related with the following.
(a) Human behaviour (b) Human group
(c) Human religion (d) Human caste

14. Sociology also studies the possibility of directing changes in the ultimate interest of
(a) Human welfare (b) Family welfare
(c) Social welfare (d) All of the above

15. Sociology is the study of the individual only from
(a) Political angle
(b) Cultural angle
(c) Economic angle
(d) None of the above

16. Sociology depicts the structure of education and education
(a) it is the foundation of social development.
(b) is influenced by sociology.
(c) social development is the creator of education.
(d) None of the above.

17. The nature of the differences in socio-economic strata of the society such as the wealthy, middle class and the poor is that it
(a) affects adversely the quality of education.
(b) vitiates the socio-emotional climate of the schools.
(c) affects negatively the morale of the teachers.
(d) runs quite frequently at cross purposes in the demands they make on education.

18. The word "Sociology" was for the first time used by Comte in
(a) 1854 (b) 1890
(c) 1907 (d) 1937

19. Social life consists of
(a) Games
(b) Musics
(c) Participation in dramas
(d) All of the above

20. The aims of education should remain changing because society's
(a) changes are due to education.
(b) is changeable.
(c) structure is stable.
(d) social changes are difficult.

21. Sociology analyzes the 'process of interaction' as
(a) Conflict (b) Competition
(c) Co-operation (d) All of the above

22. The syllabus of education should remain changing because
(a) changes in society are due to it.
(b) syllabus follows social directives.
(c) the society binds education for it.
(d) the needs of society go on changing.

23. The least hindrance in the way of the optimum development of child's personality is
(a) free education for all and equal opportunity.
(b) limited economic surplus that could be spent on education.
(c) incompetent teachers.
(d) mad scramble among various social groups for getting as much of the goods of education as possible.

24. *Social development* includes the development of

(a) Social attitudes (b) Co-operativeness
(c) Friendliness (d) All of the above

25. Educational sociology deals with which aspect of education?
(a) Economic (b) Psychological
(c) Political (d) Social

26. The effect of education on sociology is shown by this.
(a) Education promotes sociology
(b) Education is effected by sociology
(c) Education is controlled by sociology
(d) All of the above

27. Education is a/an
(a) Modification of the whole society
(b) Interpretation of society
(c) Social sub system
(d) All of the above

28. The theory that study of sociology is human relationship is given by
(a) Merritt
(b) Eldridge
(c) Both (a) and (b)
(d) None of the above

29. The following American scholars are considered the founder of Educational Sociology.
(a) Gorge Pany (b) Brown
(c) John Dewy (d) Elvin Good

30. The least important challenge to Indian education today is presented by the
(a) high cost of education.
(b) low return on education.
(c) poverty of the masses.
(d) expanding population.

31. Sociology is the study of
(a) Cultural relationship
(b) Human relationship
(c) Psychological relationship
(d) All of the above

32. Culture is
(a) the totality of mutual understandings of the people of a group.
(b) the totality of the inter-relationships of the people of a group.
(c) the sum total of feelings of the people of a group.
(d) the characteristics and products of the learned behaviour of a group of people.

33. "Educational Sociology is the study of mutual relation between education and sociology". This definition of educational sociology is of
(a) Alwin Good (b) George Paney
(c) A.K.C. Ottaway (d) Brown

34. Educational sociology is the study of the interaction of the individual and his cultural environment, which includes other individuals, social groups, and patterns of behaviour. This definition was given by
(a) Francis James Brown
(b) Auguste Comte
(c) George Payne
(d) None of the above

35. Education Sociology is the study of following alterations.
(a) Changes in education by social changes
(b) Changes in society by education
(c) Control of state only, on education and society
(d) Both (a) and (b)

36. To which type of culture belong attitudes, religious beliefs, moral beliefs and etiquettes?
(a) Non-material culture
(b) Industrial culture
(c) Material culture
(d) Intellectual culture

37. Caste system weakened in the 20th century's
    (a) First fifty decades
    (b) Middle decades
    (c) Last fifty decades
    (d) None of the above
38. Social classes and their sub-cultures are most interesting and most important to a student of education because
    (a) teachers also come from different social classes.
    (b) schools may belong to different social classes.
    (c) social classes differ from one another in many ways which are important for education.
    (d) students belong to different social classes.
39. The necessity of study of educational sociology is because of
    (a) society's control over education becomes evident.
    (b) relation between education and sociology becomes strong.
    (c) it helps to achieve the aims of education.
    (d) it gets knowledge of social changes.
40. When one learns something and makes use of what he has learned, it is called
    (a) Co-operation (b) Conflict
    (c) Assimilation (d) Competition
41. The idea that people of high and low status were all equal in the eyes of God first comes with the
    (a) Portuguese (b) English
    (c) Huns (d) Muslims
42. The effect of society on education is in the following way
    (a) according to geographical state of society.
    (b) according to religious status of society.
    (c) according to political status of society.
    (d) All of the above.
43. High degree of inter-dependence between education and the rest of the society is very much emphasised, not because of
    (a) man's social nature.
    (b) social nature of education.
    (c) increasing number of students, requiring increasing financial support.
    (d) dramatic changes in the role of government in educational matters.
44. Human behaviour is determined by
    (a) Psychological factors
    (b) Social factors
    (c) Biological factors
    (d) All of the above
45. Sociology examines
    (a) Social change (b) Social control
    (c) Both (a) and (b) (d) All of the above
46. It is implied in the "Social nature" of education that it
    (a) educates the child for citizenship.
    (b) ensures desirable socialisation of the child.
    (c) enables the individual to find a job for himself.
    (d) ensures the development of child's potentialities.
47. The effect of education is visible in economical sound society
    (a) will be compulsory.
    (b) will be diversified.
    (c) will be expensive.
    (d) will be cost free.
48. In Ginsberg's view Sociology is
    (a) all that happens to animals
    (b) all that happens to society
    (c) all that happens to human beings
    (d) All of the above
49. Effect of culture of society on education is

(a) it will enhance cultural values.
(b) it will discard other cultural values.
(c) it will follow Western culture.
(d) will try for cultural amalgam.

50. Which of the following does not influence the process of education?
(a) Social class structures
(b) Political organization of the society
(c) The culture of the society and its social institutions
(d) The upper middle class of the society

51. Which of the following is not a biological factor affecting human behaviour?
(a) Neuro muscular reaction
(b) Nutrition
(c) Reproduction
(d) Growth and maturity

52. Incorporating learned behaviour into own personality and making them their 'style of life' is
(a) Competition (b) Conflict
(c) Assimilation (d) Co-operation

53. Which one of the following social institutions of India does not have a profound effect on education?
(a) The government
(b) The business class organisation
(c) The religion
(d) The family

54. What effect will be on democratic education those societies which have backward classes?
(a) Backward classes will be given all facilities for education.
(b) Backward classes will be debarred from education.
(c) Backward classes will be given separate education.
(d) All of the above.

55. The idea of equality was welcomed by the
(a) Brahmans
(b) Backward classes
(c) Kshatriyas
(d) Lower castes in Hindu society

56. Those countries which are geographically suitable for agriculture, their effect on education will be visible
(a) special emphasis will be given on agriculture based works.
(b) in education priority will be on agricultural profession.
(c) industrialization of education will be done.
(d) Both (a) and (b).

57. Which of the following statements is not true about the family?
(a) It is an essential agency for socializing and rearing the child
(b) It is the only socially recognized relationship for child bearing
(c) It is the only important agency that introduces the child to the culture of the society
(d) It is the only institution of society which caters to the development of child's personality

58. Which of the following living beings takes longest time for cultural assimilation?
(a) Animals (b) Humans
(c) Birds (d) None of the above

59. Sociology should reflect the
(a) Culture (b) Community
(c) Customs (d) All of the above

60. Which of the following functions of education is determined and guided by Educational Sociology?
(a) Cultural assimilation and enrichment of culture
(b) Development of new social pattern
(c) Adjustment with social environment
(d) All of the above

61. What type of education the family imparts to the child?
    (a) Informal (b) Regular
    (c) Formal (d) Deliberate
62. Education affects this aspect of society.
    (a) Political part (b) Economic part
    (c) Religious part (d) All of these
63. When a group of people learn something and change their behaviour and attitudes as a result then we can say that this group has
    (a) Assimilated learning
    (b) Conflicted learning
    (c) Co-operated learning
    (d) Competited learning
64. Who defines Sociology as the study of society that is of the web or tissue of human interactions and interrelations?
    (a) Duncan (b) Ginsberg
    (c) Merritt (d) Moore
65. Education will effect religious status of country that
    (a) it will canvas for all religions.
    (b) it will become secular.
    (c) it will become atheist (non-believer in God).
    (d) None of the above.
66. Education provided to the child by the schools is
    (a) Highly standardized
    (b) Formal
    (c) Traditional
    (d) Informal
67. Social interaction includes
    (a) interaction with society
    (b) interaction with family
    (c) interaction with culture
    (d) All of the above
68. Value conflicts in the minds of school children are often created by
    (a) conflicting value systems of the home and the school.
    (b) maladjusted teachers.
    (c) conflicting laws of the country.
    (d) unruly students.
69. Education will have the following effect on the politics of the country.
    (a) Citizens will stand in opposition
    (b) Citizens will support all political parties
    (c) Citizens will become aware of their rights and duties
    (d) Citizens will become leaders
70. Educational sociology contributes
    (a) to the development of curriculum.
    (b) to the establishment of school discipline.
    (c) to the formulation of educational aims.
    (d) All of the above.
71. Which of the following is not correct?
    (a) The aim of education is to help in all round growth of the child and development of his mind, spirit and body.
    (b) The effect of the polluted social environment is required to be washed away by the educational system.
    (c) An educator has a great role to play in moulding the personality of his pupils.
    (d) None of the above.
72. In the National Education Policy, 1986 the following are to be discarded.
    (a) Violence
    (b) Orthodoxism
    (c) Religious fanaticism
    (d) All of the above
73. Resolving children's conflicts caused by contradictory value systems of the home and the schools is
    (a) Easy
    (b) Impossible

(c) Very easy
(d) Difficult but not impossible

74. The school which is socialized by imparting social interaction is/are
(a) staff vs staff
(b) students vs staff
(c) students vs student of different age
(d) All of the above

75. Communities do not exert pressures on educational systems in the following way
(a) debates and discussions.
(b) through agitations.
(c) through legislation.
(d) through revolts.

76. The aim of core curriculum in National Educational Policy, 1986 is for the development of following values.
(a) Orthodoxism (b) Fatism
(c) Secularism (d) Fanaticism

77. From the sociological viewpoint the function of education is/are
(a) the creative and constructive role.
(b) assimilation of tradition.
(c) development of new social patterns.
(d) All of the above.

78. The fundamental principle of home or family is
(a) Joint successor (b) Married life
(c) Blood relation (d) All of these

79. Control of the government over education is unavoidable because
(a) the government is empowered to exercise control by the people themselves.
(b) education costs money; and money can be provided by the government only.
(c) the very term "govern" means control.
(d) the government is all powerful.

80. School, state, church, museum, library and art galleries are formal agencies of education because
(a) they have fixed time table and place for their activities.
(b) their supervision and evaluation procedures are fixed.
(c) they have been established with specific educational objectives to achieve.
(d) All of the above.

81. Which of the following is not correct about the role of government in schooling?
(a) It will diminish if schooling affects smaller domains of the public interest and welfare
(b) It will be affected by neither of the foregoing conditions
(c) It will swell if schooling affects larger domains of the public interest and welfare
(d) It will swell if the institutional arrangements in the society become more and more inter-dependent

82. For the best character of children in an ideal family
(a) essential good habits are formed.
(b) basic tendencies are shown.
(c) original.
(d) All of the above.

83. The caste system showed signs of lossening up under the impact of
(a) Rajendra Prasad
(b) Raja Rammohan Roy
(c) Gandhiji
(d) Jawaharlal Nehru

84. Robbins definition for sociology deals with
(a) Whole organism (b) Whole society
(c) Whole world (d) Whole man

85. The families that have religious environment, their children have the developments of
   (a) religious fanaticism.
   (b) secularism.
   (c) blindness of religion.
   (d) morality.

86. As a social institution, the essential function of the family is
   (a) increasing community's population.
   (b) imparting formal education at the initial stages of life.
   (c) rearing of children during their immaturity.
   (d) producing children.

87. Games and Sports are
   (a) Assimilative
   (b) Competitive
   (c) Co-operative
   (d) None of the above

88. In informal agencies of education
   (a) learners need not do efforts for learning.
   (b) no formal evaluation is done.
   (c) formalities of rules and regulations are reduced to the minimum.
   (d) All of the above.

89 Which of the following is not a correct statement about children's education in the family?
   (a) Parents inevitably modify the behaviour of their children in one direction or another
   (b) The parents willy-nilly produce
   (c) The rearing of children by the family is a form of education
   (d) Criminality is taught to children by their parents

90. Home or family cooperates the schools for this development of children
   (a) Economic (b) Character
   (c) Political (d) Religious

91. In view of all sociological principles, the curriculum should include the subject of
   (a) Health
   (b) Social studies
   (c) Physical educationHome or family cooperates
   (d) All of the above

92. The group or individual have competition in
   (a) Social (b) Political
   (c) Economic (d) All areas

93. If the ideals which are taught in school, do not match with home or family, then the effect on children is
   (a) their moral development stops.
   (b) no development of character.
   (c) they become immoral.
   (d) All of the above.

94. Caring for the cultivation of emotional health of children is as important for the schools as caring for the cultivation of their intellect, not because
   (a) rearing of children in most families is defective.
   (b) there cannot be any other social institution which can be entrusted with this job.
   (c) the family is not competent enough to do that.
   (d) the family, being ignorant of the principles of emotional health, can do nothing about it.

95. Informal agencies of education may be criticized on which of the following grounds?
   (a) Professional skills cannot be developed here.
   (b) It imparts vague and unsystematic knowledge.
   (c) It does not enforce discipline.
   (d) All of the above.

96. "Religion has an indispensable place in the good life and the good society." This is not supported by the argument that religion
   (a) alone can make people more spiritual, more devoted, more loving and more perfect.
   (b) can teach values to the community which are essential for good life and good society.
   (c) alone can prevent wars in the world and bring peace as a consequence.
   (d) can provide for common worship and religious orientation to the universe as a whole bringing unity and peace.
97. For the education of children, the cooperation of parents in the school should be
   (a) in the form of a home.
   (b) in the form of family.
   (c) in the form of a community centre.
   (d) None of the above.
98. During periods of prosperity and trade expansion in Indian history there appears to have been considerable
   (a) Caste mobility
   (b) Social mobility
   (c) Both (a) and (b)
   (d) None of the above
99. The following committee should be formed for the mutual cooperation of school and home or family
   (a) committee of teacher and guardian.
   (b) committee of teacher and principal.
   (c) committee of school and local village or city.
   (d) committee of principal and head of the home.
100. in some forms is essential because it
   (a) makes good life in a good society.
   (b) is the foundation stone on which rests the success of a democratic society.
   (c) develops essential values in children.
   (d) provides children with desirable knowledge.
101. Education should bring a change not only in the amount of knowledge gained but in the
   (a) ability to do
   (b) ability to think
   (c) ability to acquire habits
   (d) All of the above
102. Which is incorrect about the school as a social institution?
   (a) It stands for the satisfaction of the needs of the pupils who come for schooling
   (b) It stands for the professional ideals of the community rather than the ideals it practises and tolerates
   (c) It has to teach about the social order and its institutions in its instructional activities
   (d) As it stands for the good life in general, it is the critic of society and all its institutions
103. Help to make a school in the form of community centre is by
   (a) knowledge of school activities of their children to the parents.
   (b) mutual cooperation between parents and teachers.
   (c) knowledge of family status of children to the teachers.
   (d) All of the above.
104. How many types of social processes are involved in education?
   (a) Two (b) Three
   (c) Four (d) Five
105. Maximum effect of the environment of home on children's development is of
   (a) Economic (b) Religious
   (c) Culture (d) Education

106. Which of the following type of economy places higher value on education?
(a) Industrial economy
(b) Commercial economy
(c) Mixed economy
(d) Agricultural economy

107. Which of the following is not an active agency of education?
(a) Factory and workshop
(b) Family
(c) Religious and social organizations
(d) State.

108. Earlier educational values were lower and less widespread in an agrarian than in an industriai society. This was not because
(a) the agrarian society would get little time to take off to attend school.
(b) education served no purpose for them as they needed no knowledge.
(c) the agrarian society needed no employment for their members outside agriculture for which education is necessary.
(d) the agrarian society was always in need of hard physical labour and long hours of work instead of education.

109. Children get the initial vocational training in
(a) Homes (b) Village or city
(c) Schools (d) Local community

110. In many socialist countries, there is
(a) Co-operative housing
(b) Co-operative farming
(c) Both (a) and (b)
(d) Either (a) or (b)

111. First of all development of interest and attitude takes place among children in
(a) Village or city (b) Community
(c) Schools (d) Homes

112. Today agrarian society calls for considerably more schooling than formerly because
(a) agriculture has become a science which together with its mechanization calls for scientific knowledge.
(b) the farmers have become wiser now.
(c) agriculture is now considered by farmers more dignified a calling.
(d) the farmers have greater interaction with the people in the cities who motivate them to go to schools.

113. Education should train the
(a) Society first (b) Family first
(c) Individual first (d) Nation first

114. The common uniform dress abolishes all
(a) individual identity
(b) collective identity
(c) political identity
(d) None of the above

115. It is industrial rather than other types of economy which most enhances the regard for education, because
(a) modern industry has become extremely technical, science-based, knowledge-based; and scientific and technical knowledge is gained only through education.
(b) each country has had tremendous development of industry.
(c) the industrialists belong to the upper class of the society.
(d) industrialization has led to the production of a huge wealth.

116. The for the betterment of moral of a child is possible in
(a) Family (b) School
(c) Village or city (d) Community

117. The basic scheme of education emphasises the need of a predominantly
(a) Agrarian population
(b) Rural population

(c) Both (a) and (b)
(d) All social classes

118. "House—the centre of love and affection—is the first place of education and first school of child". These words are of which of the following educationalist.
(a) Pestolozzi (b) Montssory
(c) Gandhiji (d) Frobel

119. A social institution is defined as
(a) the totality of relationships, processes and facilities which people develop to meet a specific social interest or need.
(b) an institution established by the government.
(c) an institution established for achieving social purposes.
(d) an institution which serves the society.

120. Mass media, cinema and library are passive agencies of education because
(a) they provide informal education.
(b) they cannot come closer to the educant.
(c) learner cannot react to the feedback system of these agencies directly.
(d) All of the above.

121. Our social institutions are frequently in conflict with one another. Which is not the possible reason?
(a) Different individuals and groups with different needs are associated with them for quite different reasons
(b) People's points of view with regard to their functioning or value may vary greatly
(c) They are so complex that they are only partially understood by many people
(d) They are established by people for meeting their needs

122. "Mothers are the best teachers and the informal education given by the home is most effective natural". These words are of following educationalist.
(a) Frobel (b) Gandhiji
(c) Pastolozzi (d) Montessory

123. Social institution is/are—
(a) The school (b) The family
(c) The state (d) All of the above

124. A socially efficient individual conforms to
(a) Basic standards of conduct
(b) Right way of conduct
(c) Moral standards of conduct
(d) All of the above

125. To prevent the ill-effect of family disputes on the child, teacher should do the following.
(a) Pressurise guardians by their neighbours
(b) Those children should be rusticated from school
(c) Complain about those guardians to administration
(d) Give better advise to parents or guardian

126. The social institution that men create should be the best because
(a) best institutions are liked by all in the society.
(b) poor schools, poor churches, weak and indecisive government will have a negative effect on the society which brings them into being.
(c) poor institutions will make people still poorer.
(d) poor institutions are always ineffective and corrupt.

127. Which of the following is a non commercial agency of education as per Brown's classification?
(a) Non-Welfare Clubs
(b) NGOs
(c) Scouting
(d) Church

128. A level in society made up of people similar in certain respect is known as
(a) Social hierarchy (b) Social order
(c) Social system (d) Social class

129. The smallest agency of informal education is
(a) Community (b) Religion
(c) School (d) Family

130. The demands of society are given priority against the inclination of the
(a) State (b) Parents
(c) Individual (d) Community

131. The following option is justified for the improvement of condition of house to cooperate the children in their education.
(a) Suggestion for the elimination of family disputes
(b) Improvement in economic condition
(c) Expansion of adult education
(d) All of the above

132. Indian society can be divided into various levels of people. Which of the following is not one of those?
(a) Lower class (b) Middle class
(c) Hindus (d) Upper class

133. Social aims in education has been upheld in
(a) South Asia
(b) North America
(c) United Kingdom
(d) South Africa

134. If in a social set up people are working against others in order to obtain possession, they are said to have
(a) Competition
(b) Accommodation
(c) Conflict
(d) Cooperation

135. "When the members of a small or big group live collectively in such a way that they not only help each other in special works, but help in the basic needs of day-to-day life, then we call that group a community". This definition of community is by the following scholar.
(a) McIver and Page (b) Ginsberg
(c) Yeager, W.A. (d) Bogardus

136. Today enlighted thinking is needed, which can be promoted through
(a) Our schools
(b) Leadership of teachers
(c) Both (a) and (b)
(d) All of the above

137. Education of a child really begins
(a) once he attains the age of three
(b) once he learns to speak
(c) once he takes birth
(d) once he is admitted to post nursery schools

138. Community is a big social group in which people of group satisfy their
(a) Aspirations (b) Desires
(c) Common needs (d) All of these

139. The act of adopting oneself, and one's behaviour, to the conditions and requirement of the community in which one lives is called social
(a) Behaviour (b) Dynamic
(c) Adaptation (d) Adjustment

140. Several schools in different states are participating in the
(a) National Social Mission
(b) National Cultural Mission
(c) National Literacy Mission
(d) All of the above

141. Which of the following can serve as the suitable example of the primary group?
(a) Community (b) Family
(c) School (d) Church

142. Community satisfies the following aspects of a child's education.
(a) Moral development
(b) Physical development
(c) Mental development
(d) All of the above

143. If education is the result of social change it means that social change has created a demand for
(a) Conscience
(b) Economic prosperity
(c) Education
(d) Industrialisation

144. For the physical development of children the community makes below mentioned arrangement by opening
(a) Physical health clubs
(b) Schools
(c) Gardens
(d) Entertainment centres

145. Any collection of human beings who are brought into social relationship with one another, is called a/an
(a) Institution (b) Group
(c) Family (d) Office

146. Family is the original social institution from which all other institutions emerged, who said this?
(a) MacIver (b) F.J. Brown
(c) Ballard (d) None of the above

147. Participating in the removal of illiteracy is a
(a) Conscience change
(b) Cultural change
(c) Social change
(d) None of the above

148. "Group defined by a sex relationship, sufficiently precise and enduring to provide for the procreation and up-bringing of children." This definition given by MacIver refers to
(a) Family (b) Nursery Schools
(c) Community (d) Primary Group

149. If the change has great demand for education then the nature of education should be connected with the type of
(a) Social status
(b) Social change
(c) Both (a) and (b)
(d) None of the above

150. The following will be developed in a child by the religious integrity in a community.
(a) Secularism
(b) Disliking
(c) Faith in one's religion
(d) Religious fratanity

151. The difference between the social groups, in the degree of cultural development; or the degree of antipathy manifested by individuals belonging to one group towards individuals belonging to the other is known as social
(a) Selection (b) Distance
(c) Disorder (d) Apathy

152. Students at the secondary stage are acting as volunteer teachers to teach
(a) as part of their SUPW
(b) illiterate people in the slums
(c) Both (a) and (b)
(d) None of the above

153. Out of the following four branches of psychology, with which sociology has got maximum linkage?
(a) Social Psychology
(b) General Psychology
(c) Child Psychology
(d) Industrial Psychology

154. Due to following atmosphere in a community, there is development in character and moral of a child.

(a) Faith in social culture
(b) High religious environment
(c) Orthodox environment
(d) All of the above

155. Basis of relationship in the family is
(a) blood
(b) breast feeding
(c) sexual intercourse
(d) All of the above

156. The following feeling in a child is developed by the mutual understanding of people in a community.
(a) Adjustment in society
(b) Mutual sympathy and love
(c) Cooperation and goodwill
(d) All of the above

157. The maximum contribution to the process of socialization, in general comes from
(a) School (b) Community
(c) Teacher (d) Home

158. The ways of influencing society and bringing about social change is possible by
(a) parent-teachers meetings.
(b) other ways of meeting adults in the neighbourhood of the school.
(c) school open-house days.
(d) All of the above.

159. The following development occur in children by language, living and eating style, and customs in a community.
(a) Cultural development
(b) Historical development
(c) Physical development
(d) Mental development

160. The book *India's Changing Villages* is written by
(a) M.N. Srinivas
(b) Jayaprakash Narayan
(c) T.B. Bottomore
(d) S.C. Dube

161. What do children learn from the profession and industry existing in community?
(a) Agriculture work in fields
(b) Professional work
(c) To do business
(d) Work in a factory

162. Cooley's "face-to-face" group refers to
(a) A formal group
(b) An in group
(c) An out group
(d) A primary group

163. Which of the following informal systems is most effective for socialization?
(a) Church (b) Family
(c) Playground (d) Public library

164. Which among the following may be taught as the most important part of culture?
(a) Values (b) Customs
(c) Mores (d) Norms

165. The role that an individual plays in the development of social phenomenon is studied by
(a) Anthropology
(b) Social psychology
(c) Political sociology
(d) Sociology

166. How can a school protect children from the prevailing bad customs, corruption and vulgarism within the society?
(a) By taking help of influential persons of society
(b) By giving lecture to children
(c) By alerting the guardians
(d) All of the above

167. The primary aim of Shantiniketan is to teach
(a) International culture
(b) National culture
(c) Both (a) and (b)
(d) Neither

168. The word "Modernization" is derived from English word 'Modo' which means
   (a) prevail or prevalent in present society.
   (b) customs.
   (c) modern or modernization.
   (d) None of the above.

169. Which of the following is a norm?
   (a) I like to eat ice cream
   (b) Honesty is the best policy
   (c) Simple living and high thinking is a great virtue
   (d) Eat ice cream with a spoon

170. "Man takes his birth in a certain culture", the statements come in
   (a) Assimilation
   (b) Acculturation
   (c) Diffusion
   (d) None of the above

171. Social functions of the family are more important than economic or civic functions because
   (a) it teaches manners and traditions to children.
   (b) even sick and old people and widows are cared in the family.
   (c) Both (a) and (b).
   (d) None of the above.

172. Which of the following does not describe a norm?
   (a) It describes a value held by society
   (b) It is based on one or more of society's values
   (c) It is society's expectation for right and proper behaviour
   (d) It is behaviour that is most often followed

173. The definition of modernization is given by which Indian commission?
   (a) Mudaliar Education Commission (1953)
   (b) (1966)
   (c) Dr. Radhakrishan Commission (1948)
   (d) All of the above

174. The concept of 'life-long learning' is an outcome of
   (a) country's need for a large number of educated people.
   (b) the dynamics of the expansion of knowledge.
   (c) shortage of schools in the country.
   (d) people's desire to learn more.

175. It has its complete hold on education in a totalitarian state.
   (a) State
   (b) Public
   (c) Public and state both
   (d) All of the above

176. The concept of role involves
   (a) thinking, reflecting and deciding.
   (b) taking a role voluntarily.
   (c) performing rights and duties which derive from the function to be performed.
   (d) being appointed to a role.

177. The main function of education of the child is
   (a) Teaching of $3r^s$
   (b) Teaching of means of livelihood
   (c) Transmission of cultural heritage
   (d) Teaching of $3H^s$

178. A group in which one has a "we feeling" is called a
   (a) Secondary group
   (b) Inherited group
   (c) Primary group
   (d) Nationality group

179. In a liberal state, who has a hold on education?
   (a) Hold of public representatives
   (b) Hold of administrators
   (c) State but a person has freedom of expression
   (d) Hold of public

180. Common people in India got the opportunity of schooling during
(a) Medieval period (b) British period
(c) Buddhist period (d) Both (b) and (c)

181. In dictatorship, autocrat wants that all education should be according to his interest.
(a) Ruler (b) Subject
(c) Person (d) All of these

182. An individual who tends to withdraw from association with others is called
(a) Poorly socialised
(b) Very suggestible
(c) Hysterical
(d) Well socialised

183. Culture may be defined as the
(a) uncodified ideology of people.
(b) typical habit patterns of people.
(c) sum total of collective behaviour.
(d) pattern of arrangements, material and behavioural, adopted by a society.

184. A man is not educated unless he has
(a) Information (b) Wealth
(c) Culture (d) Knowledge

185. The notion of the "I: me: Generalised other" was developed by
(a) Thomas William
(b) Mead G.H.
(c) Morton Robert
(d) Cooley Charles

186. In monarchy, an administrator wants the education for the favour of
(a) King (b) Person
(c) Public (d) Society

187. Which is the least important aim of education in the context of Indian democracy?
(a) Development of democratic citizenship
(b) Development of leadership qualities
(c) Increasing the vocational efficiency of students
(d) Teaching 'democracy' in the class.

188. In an autocracy of feudalistic form, the education is divided in which two classes?
(a) Good families and common peoples
(b) Rich and poor
(c) Powerful and powerless
(d) All of the above

189. The notion of in group and out group was first used by
(a) MacIver (b) Mead
(c) Sumner (d) Freud

190. The future of a nation is decided in
(a) the military headquarters
(b) schools
(c) big factories
(d) All of the above

191. The rewards and ensure conformity called
(a) Deviations (b) Sanctions
(c) Ostracism (d) Laws

192. In a democratic administration, education works in favour of which class of public?
(a) Minority class
(b) Rich class
(c) Majority class
(d) All classes

193. The difference between the pace of progress of material and nonmaterial culture in which case material culture is much more developed is known as
(a) Social lag (b) Cultural lag
(c) Technological lag (d) All of the above

194. The following effect can be seen in educational institutions due to interference of political class.
(a) Ability of leadership
(b) Lack of discipline
(c) Political awakening
(d) Democratic feelings

195. The essence of secondary group experience is
   (a) casualness of contact
   (b) face-to-face contacts
   (c) intimate relationships
   (d) consciousness of kind

196. The Sarda Act of 1930,
   (a) restricted the age of marriageable boys and girls among Hindus.
   (b) permitted women to receive higher education.
   (c) permitted widow remarriage among Hindus.
   (d) prohibited divorce among Hindus.

197. Which of the following is not the primary function of schools?
   (a) Advancement of culture
   (b) To make the children self-reliant
   (c) All-round development of the child
   (d) Reorganization and reconstruction of human experiences.

198. Which of the following is normative integration in a group?
   (a) Directing individual efforts
   (b) Co-ordination of individual efforts
   (c) Socialisation
   (d) Choosing good leaders for projects

199. The following value is undeveloped in education in democracy.
   (a) Fraternity
   (b) Freedom
   (c) Equality
   (d) All of the above values

200. The book *Races and Cultures of India* is written by
   (a) T.B. Bottomore (b) K.M. Kapadia
   (c) D.N. Majumdar (d) P.N. Prabhu

201. In ancient India, formal instruction was provided by
   (a) Brahmins (b) Monks
   (c) Kshatriyas (d) Family elders

202. The aim of education in democracy is
   (a) development of national integrity.
   (b) economic development.
   (c) personality development.
   (d) religious development.

203. Which of the following is the best example of what Cooley referred to as a quasi-primary group?
   (a) Columbia University
   (b) A boy-scout-troupe
   (c) A mother and her child
   (d) A spontaneous play group

204. Physical education, military training and discipline are given great importance as aims in a
   (a) Social system
   (b) Totalitarian system
   (c) Democratic system
   (d) None of the above

205. A child develops a self-concept when he is able to see himself as an object. He develops a concept of himself as he
   (a) reflects on objects that are not present.
   (b) thinks about himself and his own behaviour.
   (c) thinks as others do.
   (d) responds to the behaviour of his parents.

206. The syllabus of democratic education is having characteristic.
   (a) Professional
   (b) Religious
   (c) Stable and strict
   (d) Breed and flialble

207. Which of the following is an important responsibility of schools toward home?
   (a) Enabling the child to appreciate the role of the family.
   (b) Equipping the child with social norms.
   (c) Supplementing the educative functions of the family.
   (d) All of the above.

208. The following educational methods are used in democratic education.
(a) Development methods
(b) Discussion method
(c) Speech method
(d) Question-answer method

209. Which of the following statements is not true about the members of a social group?
(a) They are involved in close interaction
(b) They have distinct relations with one another
(c) They are aware of shared memberships
(d) They are a casual collection of people

210. Which is most favourable for education?
(a) Caste system
(b) Social mobility
(c) Social stratification
(d) Social class.

211. The book *Marriage and Family in India* is written by
(a) P.N. Prabhu (b) K.M. Kapadia
(c) M.N. Srinivas (d) M.S. Gore

212. The process of acting in awareness of others and adjusting responses to the way others respond is called
(a) Social interaction
(b) Role awareness
(c) Social awareness
(d) Social organisation

213. This type of discipline is stressed in democratic education.
(a) Loose discipline
(b) Military discipline
(c) Strict discipline
(d) Self discipline

214. Character and nature of education in schools must be revised and reviewed very frequently because
(a) demographic composition of the society changes over a period of time.
(b) society is dynamic and changes very frequently.
(c) Both (a) and (b).
(d) None of the above.

215. In a democracy, the teacher is considered student's
(a) friend, philosopher and guide.
(b) disciplinarian.
(c) guardian.
(d) spiritual teacher.

216. Which of the following is an example of an aggregate?
(a) Tax-payers' meeting
(b) A Rotary Club gathering
(c) Air-line passengers
(d) Individuals at meetings

217. Muta among Muslims represents
(a) Temporary marriage
(b) Mehar
(c) Bride price
(d) Dowry

218. Which of the following is inevitably involved in the exercise of competent authority in any social group?
(a) Superior memory
(b) Superior skill
(c) The right to exact obedience
(d) Superior knowledge

219. In democracy, school should become
(a) religious and spiritual centre.
(b) community centre.
(c) politics training.
(d) sports centre.

220. Which is not a characteristic of modernization?
(a) Empathy (b) Participation
(c) Religious faith (d) Mobility

221. In a democratic country, schools should reflect
(a) Community related local aspirations
(b) National aspirations

(c) Both (a) and (b)
(d) None of the above

222. "All minority classes based on religion and language have right to set up and run educational institutions of their will." Which article of Indian Constitution provides for it.
(a) Article 75
(b) Article 45
(c) Article 32
(d) Article 30

223. Which of the following characteristics is essential in a primary group?
(a) It should have large membership
(b) Its membership usually must be limited to one sex
(c) Its members must be of the same age
(d) Its members must have a high rate of interaction with one another

224. The special Marriage Act was passed in the year
(a) 1954
(b) 1951
(c) 1940
(d) 1912

225. In the traditional Brahma type of marriage among Hindus.
(a) The father gives his daughter in marriage after receiving money from the bridegroom.
(b) The bride selects her partner in the assembly of noble men.
(c) The father gives his daughter to a person as Kanyadaan.
(d) The father gives his daughter in marriage after receiving a cow and a bull from the bridegroom.

226. Of the following, the definition of personality is most appropriate, according to the text would be
(a) the sum total of observed or observable characteristics of an individual.
(b) the personal qualities which tend to emphasize how different people really are.
(c) qualities of a person.
(d) popularity with one's peers.

227. Which type of education does Articles 28(1) and (2) of Constitution gives freedom to minorities for establishing non-government institutions?
(a) Religious education
(b) Primary education
(c) Minority education
(d) Rural education

228. Characteristic of joint family is
(a) Open-door
(b) Limited size
(c) Hierarchy
(d) A productive unit

229. A corrupt society like India's can best be reformed by
(a) judicial system
(b) legislative system
(c) schooling system
(d) All of them as a joint effort

230. Educational institutions who impart specific religious education and character building measures, are those in which emphasis is given on the education and treated by government as
(a) non-recognised and non-aided.
(b) recognised and aided.
(c) non-recognised.
(d) non-aided.

231. When we try to explain the behaviour of an individual, we find that his social environment is
(a) a necessary but not sufficient total explanation.
(b) a sufficient total explanation.
(c) both a necessary and sufficient total explanation.
(d) Neither a necessary nor sufficient explanation.

232. The most important function of education is
   (a) Industrial development
   (b) Political development
   (c) Economic development
   (d) Human resource development

233. Socialisation is a process of converting a biological organism into
   (a) Modern man
   (b) Social man
   (c) Human being
   (d) Super human being

234. Those private schools are recognised by the government that are run by religious institutions
   (a) no discrimination of religion.
   (b) religious education is not compulsory for all.
   (c) admission is given to students of all religion.
   (d) All of the above.

235. Choose the main difference between custom and fashion.
   (a) Fashion stands for individuality and distinction and custom stands for uniformity and identification.
   (b) Fashion is an agency of social change and custom is not.
   (c) Fashion is popular among the people; custom is not.
   (d) Fashion is changing and custom is not.

236. In some muslim Maktab and Madarsa's undesirable education is rendered which is against the democratic administration
   (a) their place.
   (b) their citizenship.
   (c) their political thoughts.
   (d) their language, script and culture.

237. The study of society is nothing but study of
   (a) Laws (b) Folkways
   (c) Mores (d) Conventions

238. Which of the following characteristics does not belong to a community?
   (a) People having common ideals of life.
   (b) Group of people serving each other.
   (c) People belonging to a particular religion.
   (d) A group of people living in a geographical place of land.

239. Which is the most important social factor that has adversely affected the examination reforms in India?
   (a) Unethical behaviours of students and teachers.
   (b) Unwieldy nature of the examination.
   (c) Ineffective university administration.
   (d) Inadequate classroom teaching.

240. The term "oral dependency" means
   (a) depending on eating.
   (b) a stage of child's dependency on mother.
   (c) unwritten promise.
   (d) depending on words.

241. In Indian Constitution the right of equality and educational opportunities is given due to which reason?
   (a) Political justice
   (b) Social justice
   (c) Economic justice
   (d) All of the above

242. Characteristic of secondary group is
   (a) Emphasis on interest and competition
   (b) Spontaneity of relations
   (c) Inclusive relationship
   (d) Personal relationship

243. Who said, "Western education leads to the modernization of perspectives in traditional, non-industrial societies"?
   (a) Alex Inkeles
   (b) Yogendra Singh

(c) Michael Armer and Robert Youtz
(d) Robert C. Williamson

244. In Article 29(1) of the Indian Constitution, Indian citizens are given permission for establishing educational institutions of their liking for whose protection?
(a) Their place
(b) Their citizenship
(c) Their political thoughts
(d) Their language, script and culture

245. A role conflict occurs when
(a) there is a mental conflict over the choice from a set of roles.
(b) the role being played is questioned.
(c) the ego occupies two conflicting roles.
(d) the roles of two persons different with each other.

246. The best teacher in a village school is he who
(a) prepares instructional programmes in the interest of the community.
(b) carries class room experiences to the community.
(c) carries community experiences to the classroom.
(d) All of the above.

247. George Simmel classified human aggregates units
(a) Institutions (b) Groups
(c) Communities (d) Societies

248. In Article 30(1) of Indian Constitution, all minority persons are given permission to open educational institutions of their liking on which basis?
(a) Their territory
(b) Their castism
(c) Their language and religion
(d) Their political belief

249. Biology is the result of the fusion of the principles and learnings in
(a) Zoology (b) Anatomy
(c) Botany (d) All of the above

250. Sociology of education is concerned with:
(a) teacher taught relationship.
(b) interaction within educational system.
(c) school as a social system.
(d) All of the above.

251. According to Article 30(2) of Indian Constitution, the state will not discriminate in giving aid to educational institution on the basis of
(a) religion and language.
(b) castism.
(c) political leanings.
(d) regional disparity.

252. The preferential feeling which individual have for their own group is called
(a) Fraternal (b) Primary
(c) Ethnocentrism (d) Egoism

253. Difference between the nature of activities of school and state lies in
(a) organizational structure, i.e. State is a political and school is a sovereign social organization.
(b) the enforcement of law (state) and rules (school).
(c) taking pain for the development of citizens.
(d) enforcement of law guided by the judiciary in case of the state.

254. A group of individuals having essentially the same social status in a given society is called a
(a) Struggle
(b) Secondary group
(c) Social group
(d) Social class

255. As per Article 29(2) of Indian Constitution for government-aided educational institution the following should not be discriminated between students.

(a) Their culture
(b) For their admission
(c) Their religion
(d) All of the above

256. Standard of living has maximum relationship with one of the following factors. Which is that?
(a) Population (b) Culture
(c) Environment (d) People

257. Dumb people are classed as a/an
(a) Associational group
(b) Statistical group
(c) Societal group
(d) Social group

258. For providing equal rights of education, what instructions are given as per Article 46 of Constitution.
(a) To protect the economic interests of scheduled tribes
(b) To spread education in women
(c) To protect the educational rights of backward classes
(d) Secure social justice for scheduled caste

259. Which one of the following is not strictly speaking, one of Freud's stages of psycho-sexual development?
(a) Oedipal (b) Phallic
(c) Oral (d) Genital

260. Adoption of the modern comfort and symbols of civilization with the help of wealth, cars, luxurious homes, fashion, etc. are examples of
(a) material changes
(b) non-material changes
(c) Both (a) and (b)
(d) None of the above

261. A situation where a student is expected by his parents to study his lessons and is expected by his room-mates to visit a movie house illustrates
(a) primary-secondary group conflict.
(b) role conflict.
(c) culture conflict.
(d) status conflict.

262. As per Article 28 of constitution which institutions cannot impart religious education?
(a) Aided by state
(b) Established on basis of religion
(c) Fully aided by the state
(d) Recognised by state

263. Which of the following is not included in Human Development Index—progress index of a nation?
(a) Per capita income
(b) Education
(c) Health
(d) Political stability

264. According to Article 15(3) of the Constitution for education of women, State Governments have the right for setting up
(a) rules or regulations.
(b) professional coaching.
(c) educational institution.
(d) student hostel.

265. Individual and society are considered as
(a) Supplementary
(b) Complementary
(c) Contradictory
(d) Interdependent

266. The relationship between Indian system of education and increasing social disorganization as reflected in the strikes, increasing lawlessness, disregard for public property, corruption in public life, etc. is most realistic because
(a) to some extent the weaknesses of the system of school education but largely, the political climate of the country should be held responsible for this.

(b) India's system of school education being irrelevant is solely responsible for this.
(c) education has nothing to do with such social disorganization.
(d) political life and the environment of the country are wholly responsible for this.

267. Human nature develops in man as a
(a) member of a society.
(b) member of an organisation.
(c) citizen of a state.
(d) member of a religion.

268. According to Article 350(A) of Constitution, the State Government has to arrange for primary education of the minority by this medium of
(a) regional language.
(b) mother tongue.
(c) national language.
(d) contact language.

269. Many religious ceremonies and customs, which have become obsolete and meaningless, are still carried on, because they are of
(a) cultural significance
(b) regional significance
(c) emotional significance
(d) All of the above

270. Universalisation of education is the concept adopted by
(a) democratic state
(b) religious state
(c) modern state
(d) totalitarian state

271. List of border issues on which union, state, can formulate laws are having mention in any of this article of the constitution
(a) 250 (b) 15
(c) 49 (d) 246

272. Man's behaviour in society is determined mainly by two forces, namely
(a) physical and social.
(b) formal and informal.
(c) psychological and philosophical.
(d) natural and unnatural.

273. Material culture change lies behind
(a) cultural change
(b) non-material change
(c) social change
(d) religious change

274. If the old customs and traditions have emotional significance they will
(a) alter a bit
(b) change with the time
(c) have no value
(d) not change

275. Identify a quasi-group among the following
(a) Mob (b) Crowd
(c) Status groups (c) Trade union

276. "Education consists of a methodical socialization of a young generation." This sociologist has given the above definition of socialization.
(a) Durkime
(b) Ross, J.S.
(c) Gillen and Gillen
(d) Orvilla and Wheeler

277. A culture area is a
(a) geographical area characterised by a high level of cultural development distinguishing cultural traits.
(b) segment of culture which cuts across particular societies, e.g. technology, generally.
(c) geographical area characterized by distinguishing cultural traits.
(d) geographical area with relatively homogeneous human activity.

278. "Children learn style of society by socialization processes and make it a part of their personality." This definition is given by the following sociologist.
(a) Ross J.S.
(b) Durkheim
(c) Havighurst and Newgarten
(d) Bogardus

279. An individual starts learning from
(a) Adolescence (b) Childhood
(c) Mother's womb (d) Adulthood

280. Which of the following agency regulates education?
(a) State (b) Library
(c) Church (d) School

281. When the social culture does not change at the same rate as the material culture then there is
(a) no adjustment
(b) good adjustment
(c) maladjustment
(d) None of the above

282. Suggestion is one of the basic principles of
(a) Class (b) Socialization
(c) Human behaviour (d) Caste

283. Based on definition of socialization below mentioned characteristics appear
(a) it arises from a person's harmonization with society.
(b) it comes from the collective influence of people on society.
(c) it is accomplished through the mutual interaction among people.
(d) it is created by the influence of a person on society.

284. Even with the education, the poor in villages, cannot easily give up their old ways of thinking due to
(a) high rate of non-material changes.
(b) high rate of material changes.
(c) low rate of material changes.
(d) low rate of non-material changes.

285. Elements helpful in socialization are a child's
(a) Imitation (b) Child rearing
(c) Cooperation (d) All of these

286. One of the basic principles of socialing individuals is
(a) Education (b) Imitation
(c) Religion (d) Caste

287. Rapid rate of change is usually seen in
(a) Material changes
(b) Non-material changes
(c) Both (a) and (b)
(d) None of the above

288 When the child is able to judge the response of a group as a whole, he is responding to a
(a) "significant other".
(b) "generalised other".
(c) "insignificant other".
(d) "particular other".

289. Punishment and reward are helpful in the following activities of a child.
(a) Socialization (b) Separation
(c) Social mobility (d) All of these

290. Secular education in India means
(a) an education indifferent to religion.
(b) an education emphasizing equality of religions.
(c) an education opposed to religion.
(d) None of the above.

291. Muslim law has restricted the number of wives a man can have at a time to
(a) One (b) Two
(c) Three (d) Four

292. The following factors are also helpful in socialization of a child.
(a) Identification (b) Suggestion
(c) Sympathy (d) All of these

293. Internalization means that the individual
(a) has adopted the norms and values of the group and uses them.
(b) conforms to group norms.
(c) has standards to judge his own behaviour.
(d) has identity, social location, aspiration and values.

294. Change in culture may be brought about by
(a) Ideas (b) Acculturation
(c) Diffusion (d) All of the above

295. The school environment is
(a) Aggressive (b) Compassive
(c) Progressive (d) Seducive

296. The process which aims to destroy the opponent is
(a) Competition
(b) Accommodation
(c) Co-operation
(d) Conflict

297. Prime element in the socialization of a child is
(a) Environment (b) Heredity
(c) Education (d) Both (a) and (b)

298. In the three stages of family life cycle—beginning family, expanding family and contracting family—role of education becomes dominant in which of the following stages?
(a) First stage
(b) Second stage
(c) Third stage
(d) All of the above

299. The following instincts received from heredity, are helpful in the socialization of a child.
(a) Aptitudes
(b) Emotions
(c) Both (a) and (b)
(d) None of the above

300. When a group of clans get merged together, then the resultant grouping is called
(a) Family (b) Gotra
(c) Lineage (d) Siblings

301. Which of the following is not an important consideration in the planning of the development of education in India?
(a) Equity (b) Relevance
(c) Religion (d) Quality

302. Smoking cigarettes, tea-drinking, wearing Western dress, etc. are results of
(a) ideas of culture
(b) religion of culture
(c) diffusion of culture
(d) acculturation

303. Adjustment problem is most seen between husband and wife in which stage of family cycle?
(a) Beginning family
(b) Expanding family
(c) Contracting family
(d) Both (a) and (b)

304. The preferences and aversions amongst the various members of a group is shown by
(a) sociological analysis.
(b) interactional analysis.
(c) sociogram.
(d) social psychology.

305. The process of socialization
(a) begins with adulthood.
(b) intensifies in the old age.
(c) is life long process/continues for the whole of life.
(d) lasts only till the student life.

306. Material changes often need certain adaptive
(a) Material changes
(b) Social changes

(c) Both (a) and (b)
(d) None of the above

307. The process of socialization begins from the birth and continues throughout life. Many simultaneous processes do come which form various aspects of socialization. This aspect is worth mentioning with respect to above saying.
(a) Skill-learning (b) A language
(c) A feeling of self (d) All of these

308. The technique of measurement of the patterns of social behaviour in a group is known as
(a) social distance scale.
(b) sociometry.
(c) sociogram.
(d) interactional analysis.

309. Ogburn suggests that social and cultural evolution or change needs
(a) Favourable environment
(b) Challenging environment
(c) Unfavourable environment
(d) None of the above

310. Sex education to adults is needed in order to
(a) reduce mis-conceptions about sex and its related problems.
(b) get them adjusted in their own families.
(c) Both (a) and (b).
(d) None of the above.

311. "Birds of the same feather flock together" refers to the idea of a socialising process known as
(a) Identification (b) Sympathy
(c) Suggestion (d) Imitation

312. The meaning of sublimation of instincts with the point of view of socialization is
(a) channelisation of socially accepted instincts.
(b) prohibition on the display of antisocial basic instincts.
(c) Both (a) and (b).
(d) None of the above.

313. Social mobility according to Bogardus is
(a) change on the same status level.
(b) not movement but change of movement.
(c) movement as also change of movement.
(d) movement but not change of movement.

314. Common Schools should be opened which
(a) provide Free Education
(b) are Tax-supported
(c) provide Education for all
(d) All of the above

315. In socialization, formation of character is an important
(a) Aspect (b) Principle
(c) Element (d) All of these

316. The price paid to the Muslim bride is called
(a) Mehar (b) Compensation
(c) Dowry (d) Bride price

317. Cultural lag is the term used by Ogburn to describe how
(a) Moral changes occur
(b) Culture changes occur
(c) Social changes occur
(d) One phase of culture may change more rapidly than another phase

318. In early Hindu society, widow remarriage was
(a) Prohibited (b) Promoted
(c) Protected (d) Permitted

319. School is not only an agency of socialization, but also this of society's cultural progress.
(a) Favourer (b) Criticizer
(c) Reformer (d) Preserver

320. A society is identified by its
(a) culture
(b) economic progress
(c) military power
(d) All of the above

321. A teacher can be helpful by being this of the child's socialization process.
(a) Obstructor (b) Agent
(c) Aspect (d) Element

322. The laws of Muslim marriage are based on
(a) Indian contract act
(b) Constitution of India
(c) Quran
(d) Muslim law

323. The term 'Cultural lag' has been used by
(a) Comte (b) Ogburn
(c) Weber (d) Merritt

324. The difference in the material surroundings of the school and home is very great, and contrast between the ideas taught in school and those prevalent in his home surroundings cause a great conflict in students mind, in this case the lag is
(a) Large (b) Too large
(c) Small (d) Too small

325. Mehar given by husband to the wife immediately after marriage is known as
(a) Muwajjal Mehar
(b) Settled Dower
(c) Dower after dissolution of marriage
(d) Meharul Misl

326. For the purpose of socialization, a teacher can influence students through the following technique.
(a) Through examples from personal experiences encourage them to emulate
(b) Stimulate them to take part in intellectual activities
(c) Giving feedback and suggestions regarding acceptable behaviour
(d) All of the above

327. Whose definition of social class rested entirely on "relationship to the means of production"?
(a) Weber (b) Comte
(c) Marx (d) Warner

328. In the absence of law which of the following help in maintaining social order in simple societies?
(a) Mores (b) Folkways
(c) Customary rules (d) All of the above

329. For the socialization of a child, education should
(a) develop teacher guardian relationship.
(b) try to promote transmission of culture.
(c) to make them aware of scientific and technological progress.
(d) Both (a) and (b).

330. Dissolution of Muslim Marriage Act was passed in the year
(a) 1947 (b) 1953
(c) 1939 (d) 1912

331. School works as a social sub system for
(a) advancement of culture
(b) transmission of culture
(c) preservation of culture
(d) All of the above

332. The basic features of a community according to MacIver are
(a) Co-operation side by side with conflict
(b) Geographic territory and uniformity of conduct
(c) Like-men and difference
(d) Geographic territory and sense of solidarity

333. Identify the forms of marriage widely prevalent in tribal society.
(a) Asura marriage
(b) Probationary marriage
(c) Service marriage
(d) Gandharva marriage

334. By encouraging healthy competition a teacher can promote the following in children.
(a) Socialization
(b) Secularism
(c) National unification
(d) None of the above

335. Which of the following is not correct about schools?
(a) They are social agencies of cultural transmission.
(b) They are necessarily affected by the social and economic situations and changes in our civilization.
(c) They are powerful instruments of social change.
(d) They are potential agents of conflicts and disintegration.

336. Socio-cultural change is complete when change occurs in this field.
(a) Non-material culture
(b) Material culture
(c) World culture
(d) Both (a) and (b)

337. Some of the modern changes which have taken place in the Hindu Marriage are
(a) widow remarriage permitted.
(b) marriage is held as compulsory.
(c) two living wives permissible to a husband.
(d) no provision for divorce.

338. Biological function of family is
(a) perpetuation of race
(b) transmission of human experience
(c) nurturance of children
(d) division of labour

339. "Society is nothing but a process of interaction among people." Who said this?
(a) Reuter (b) Payne
(c) Lapier (d) Cuber

340. When changes take place in material culture but not in non-material culture, the following undesirable situation is created.
(a) Material change (b) Desired change
(c) Cultural lag (d) Cultural decline

341. Of the following, which is a primary group?
(a) Family (b) School
(c) Factory (d) Political party

342. Community means a group of individuals who are
(a) having the same caste
(b) living in the same territory
(c) informally organized
(d) living in two or more villages

343. Cultural lag is that time period which is between the acceptance of an innovation and the organization and integration of that innovation into social culture.
Who has defined cultural lag in the above given terms?
(a) Orburn
(b) Miller and Woock
(c) Rusk
(d) Drever

344. In the traditional Arsha type of marriage among Hindus
(a) the father gives his daughter in marriage after receiving money from the bridegroom.
(b) the father gives his daughter to a person as kanyadana.
(c) the bride selects her partner in the assembly of noble men.
(d) the father gives his daughter in marriage after receiving a cow and a bull from the bridegroom.

345. Conflicts in the society occur when
(a) undue domination of a section prevails.
(b) interest of the people do not match.

(c) justice is not maintained.
(d) All of the above.

346. Example of a community is a/an
(a) Prison (b) Caste
(c) Orphanage (d) Village

347. "Expansion of technological culture and lag in value culture is called social and cultural lag." In context to this statement the following example is of cultural lag.
(a) The married propagate family planning and themselves keep small families
(b) The present-day youth is educated and opposes malpractices
(c) Though rural Indian society watches TV, its values are traditional
(d) All of the above

348. Social stratification means
(a) differentiation which carries social prestige.
(b) groups of different sex, age and intelligence.
(c) traits that are socio-economic in nature.
(d) All of the above.

349. An example of a secondary group is
(a) Association of workers
(b) Playgroup
(c) Family
(d) Neighbourhood

350. The main cause of cultural lag is
(a) cultural inertia.
(b) narrow loyalties.
(c) fear of new things.
(d) All of the above.

351. A territorial community refers to an area that has a geographical location and which is a source for all the social and cultural needs of its members. Which of the following is not true of a territorial community?
(a) Its members have a sense of belonging in it
(b) It may encompass several groups
(c) It is a formal organisation
(d) Its members can live a satisfying life within it

352. Remarkable change/changes brought about in Indian society is/are
(a) rise of a new capitalist class.
(b) employment guarantee to poor.
(c) evolution of a strong middle class.
(d) All of the above.

353. Which of the following groups is under the greatest pressure of social change through education?
(a) Middle class people living in the cities.
(b) Scheduled castes and scheduled tribes.
(c) Rural masses.
(d) Labour class of the industry.

354. Standard of living has maximum relationship with one of the following factors. Which is that?
(a) Environment (b) Culture
(c) People (d) Population

355. Why do vested interests become the cause of cultural lag?
(a) Because of these selfish motives the rate of change increases
(b) Because these are helpful in selfish changes
(c) Because social changes hamper their interests
(d) All of the above

356. Aiming at national unity and social progress, social change in India is threatened by
(a) Caste
(b) Poor political leadership
(c) Joint family system
(d) Student unrest in schools and colleges

357. What is not true about a community project?
 (a) It aims at the involvement of the village community with the village uplift.
 (b) It is an attempt to bring about a social and economic transformation of village life "through the efforts of the people themselves".
 (c) It is more official and less local, it is more formal than basic.
 (d) It aims at effecting the required changes in the social and economic fields.

358. Due to cultural lag, 'the fear of new things' means
 (a) modernisation is incapable of removing old beliefs.
 (b) conventionalists are scared of breaking traditions due to modernisation.
 (c) by accepting modernisation changes will come to a halt.
 (d) All of the above.

359. Custom is an important
 (a) way of political behaviour.
 (b) social control.
 (c) way of thinking of Marxists.
 (d) social institution.

360. The most influential social engineer in the country is
 (a) the teacher
 (b) priest
 (c) the social worker
 (d) None of the above

361. Which is not the aim of education for citizenship?
 (a) To think clearly and effectively without and kind of prejudice.
 (b) To do everything for the good of the family as the family is the basic unit of the society.
 (c) To make decisions independently.
 (d) To understand the social, economic and political forces that shape the present and the future of the nation.

362. Main function of economic structure is
 (a) maintenance of a sense of purpose.
 (b) replacement of population.
 (c) production and distribution of goods and services.
 (d) socialisation of new population.

363. How can education help in the eradication of cultural lag?
 (a) Education brings about changes in material culture
 (b) Education guards old values
 (c) Education helps in adoption of new values
 (d) None of the above

364. Which of the following factors has contributed most to the falling standards of Indian education?
 (a) Government's apathy
 (b) Less competent teachers
 (c) Too much political interference with education
 (d) Non-availability of sufficient funds.

365. For the removal of cultural lag, Kothari Education Commission has desired the following.
 (a) Education based on science and technology
 (b) Education that develops traditional values
 (c) Both (a) and (b)
 (d) None of the above

366. Function of political structure is
 (a) maintenance of a sense of purpose.
 (b) system maintenance.
 (c) replacement of population.
 (d) socialization of new population.

367. Which of the following statements regarding the relationship of society and education is not correct?

(a) The best school reflects the worst society.
(b) Society determines the model and structure of education.
(c) Education changes the ideals of the society.
(d) Education can reduce regional disparities.

368. Main function of religious structure is
(a) production and distribution of goods and services.
(b) maintenance of a sense of purpose.
(c) replacement of population.
(d) socialization of new population.

369. For the removal of cultural lag only the following mentality can help.
(a) Modernisation (b) Indianisation
(c) Traditionalism (d) All of these

370. What cannot be helpful in the improvement of villages?
(a) Cultivating the spirit of self-help among the villagers.
(b) Politics in the panchayat, and giving speeches.
(c) Rural reconstruction schemes.
(d) Involvement of the panchayat in the village uplift.

371. "Social change may be defined as modification in the way of doing and thinking of people." Who has given the above definition of social change?
(a) Gillen and Gillen (b) Sir Johns
(c) Jenson (d) K. Devis

372. Function of educational structure is
(a) maintenance of a sense of purpose.
(b) system maintenance.
(c) replacement of population.
(d) socialisation of new population.

373. Educators must have some understanding of the social forces because
(a) the individual and the society are two sides of same coin.
(b) education is influenced by the social setting in which it takes place.
(c) social forces shape the future of the society.
(d) education is a psychological process.

374. The state is a National Institution, was maintained by
(a) Aristotle (b) T.H. Green
(c) Plato (d) Herbert Spencer

375. A field of study which includes history, philosophy, sociology of education and comparative education is known as
(a) Social Foundations of Education
(b) Social Sciences of Education
(c) Sociology of Education
(d) Educational Sociology

376. The best model of schooling is
(a) self reliant society by education
(b) reflection of openness by schools
(c) close interaction between education and society
(d) All of the above

377. This change brings about disparity in the old and the new generation. This is the result of which change?
(a) Social change
(b) Fundamental change
(c) Economical change
(d) Occupational change

378. One of the most important functions of the state is to
(a) maintain the spirit of nationalism.
(b) maintain law and order in a complex society.
(c) maintain the democratic process.
(d) provide means of recreation to the people.

379. Value is accompanied with

(a) Convictions (b) Sacrifices
(c) Beliefs (d) All of the above

380. Athenian education emphasised on
(a) Religional Value (b) Soldier Value
(c) Cultural Value (d) All of the above

381. Almost all societies, at some stage or the other, of their development have passed through
(a) educational conditions
(b) political conditions
(c) rural conditions
(d) economic conditions

382. "Cultural change is an important form of social change and there is no difference in it." What is the meaning of this Brown's statement?
(a) Cultural change is a part of social change
(b) Cultural change is a must after social change
(c) Social and cultural changes are chips of the same block
(d) All of the above

383. All of the following have a role in determining the direction of school, except
(a) Religion (b) State
(c) Society (d) None

384. Knowledge about changes in the methods of production and exchange is the knowledge of the effect of
(a) rapid growth of economy
(b) rapid democracy
(c) rapid urbanisation
(d) rapid industrialization

385. If cultural change does not take place after social change, which situation arises.
(a) Educational lag (b) Economic lag
(c) Social lag (d) Cultural lag

386. Social equality is supported by
(a) Domestic Institution
(b) Marxism
(c) Socialism
(d) Capitalism

387. Because of the increasing knowledge which an individual needs to acquire the important agency of education is
(a) School (b) Gurudwara
(c) Family (d) Church

388. Which of the following is not a characteristic of Indian society?
(a) People are open minded.
(b) Status is determined by birth.
(c) People are liberal to embrace any religion.
(d) Occupation and profession determine the status of a person.

389. Which of the following is a dynamic organisation of purposive individuals?
(a) Social behaviour
(b) Sociology
(c) Social relations
(d) Society

390. It is helpful in achieving changeable activity by evading cultural lag.
(a) Modern education
(b) Education of ancient values
(c) Traditional education
(d) All of the above

391. Who considered "education to be the process of discerning the truth about things as they really are"?
(a) Aristotle
(b) John Calvin
(c) St. Thomas Aquinas
(d) Martin Luther

392. Social change ascertained by Murdock is concluded by the following process.
(a) Selective elimination
(b) Social acceptance
(c) Innovations
(d) All of the above

393. The most important characteristic of a society is
(a) Mutual influence
(b) Inter-communication
(c) Individual approach
(d) Interpersonal relationship

394. What is the result of the existence of different socio-economic strata in the society with various class interests?
(a) Causing a lot of indiscipline in the classroom.
(b) Setting up mutually incompatible tensions in the educational programme.
(c) Generating a lack of responsibility in the teachers.
(d) Creating a lot of politics in the school.

395. The fundamental unit of human society is known as
(a) Individual (b) Family
(c) Social group (d) Tribal group

396. According to Murdock, what is meant by 'Integration', a process of social change.
(a) Co-existence of the old and the new habits
(b) Combination of the old and new habits
(c) New habit becoming a part of culture
(d) None of the above

397. The most effective method of character-formation is
(a) rewarding virtuous behaviours and presenting high character models in the schools.
(b) teaching virtues through religious books.
(c) organizing specialists' lectures on importance of values in life.
(d) teaching by high character teachers.

398. One hindrance factor in social change—cultural inactiveness—means
(a) slavery to old traditions and the possibility to leave them.
(b) cultural obstinacy.
(c) to strengthen the old values.
(d) to leave cultural fanatism.

399. Human society differs from animal society because of
(a) provision of nutriment.
(b) cultural heritage.
(c) reproduction of new organism.
(d) protection against injury.

400. Happiness and sorrow and other mental activities, according to Charvaka, are the attributes of
(a) Consciousness (b) Body
(c) Self (d) None of these

401. An example of formal norm is
(a) Law (b) Mores
(c) Custom (d) Tradition

402. An example of the Degree of Isolation as a factor of social change is
(a) the egoists separate themselves from the average people.
(b) the rich forming a coterie.
(c) the people from schedule tribes do not come in contact with other casts by separating themselves.
(d) None of the above.

403. Caste distinction in India is rooted in
(a) Religion
(b) Culture
(c) Both (a) and (b)
(d) None of the above

404. The Basic scheme of education was designed as an instrument of
(a) cultural change
(b) social change
(c) religious change
(d) economic change

405. Narrow allegiance are a hindrance to social change. An example of such narrow allegiance is
(a) dedication towards one's field.
(b) allegiance towards once's own religion.
(c) attachment to one's caste.
(d) All of the above.

406. Characteristic of society is
(a) definite geographical area.
(b) mutual awareness.
(c) interrelations.
(d) specific aims.

407. Application of principles of sociology to education is known as
(a) Educational Sociology
(b) Social Foundations of education
(c) Sociology of education
(d) Social Science of education

408. In public opinion, there is no higher court than that of the
(a) Mores (b) Laws
(c) Folkways (d) Customs

409. When a person reaches a higher or a lower range of a social group, then that is his social mobility. An example of P. Sorokin's statement can be
(a) a person marries into a cast higher than his own.
(b) a person becomes notorious due to some.
(c) a tribal due to his ability becomes a magistrate.
(d) All of the above

410. "The greatness of a nation is to be measured not only by its material power and wealth, but by the inter cultural relationship of its people". Who said this?
(a) Swami Vivekananda
(b) Dr. S. Radhakrishnan
(c) Sri Aurobindo Ghosh
(d) None of the above

411. Schools are social institutions because they
(a) suggest solutions to social problems.
(b) suggest ways and means of social progress.
(c) are established by the society.
(d) preserve and instill in future generations the knowledge, ideas, and customs of our culture.

412. c in social structure.
According to the above definition given by Young and Mark an example of social structure is
(a) a person gets demoted from a higher rank to a lower rank.
(b) a person gets promoted from a lower rank to a higher rank.
(c) a cast receives distinction for its good deeds.
(d) All of the above.

413. The members of the society share sentiments highly favourable to
(a) Mores (b) Nation
(c) Laws (d) Government

414. Family, school, club, gymnasium, sports and games, etc. constitute social groups known as
(a) Dynamic groups
(b) Temporary groups
(c) Permanent groups
(d) State groups

415. A society is a network of
(a) Social attitude
(b) Inter-personal relationships
(c) Religious-cultural attitudes
(d) Socio-political relationships

416. A form of social mobility is
(a) Diagonal (b) Downward
(c) Vertical (d) All of these

417. Greatest contribution of organizing co-curricular and community activities like camps, common meals, social services, etc. is towards
(a) students' acquisition of knowledge.
(b) international understanding.

(c) strengthening of school-community relationship.
(d) social development of the student.

418. An example of vertical downward social mobility is, when a person
(a) stays at the same level in his rank status.
(b) reaches a lower stage in his rank status.
(c) reaches a high rank.
(d) All of the above.

419. So thoroughly have norms become a part of human mode of existence that they are to a high degree
(a) Specialised (b) Internalised
(c) Regulated (d) Standardised

420. In a culturally pluralistic country which type of education is suitable?
(a) Education developing tolerance to other cultures.
(b) Education free from culture.
(c) Education emphasizing national culture.
(d) Both (a) and (b).

421. The analysis of human society must certainly be carried out on the level
(a) Psychological (b) Cultural
(c) Sociological (d) Biological

422. When a person gets transferred to another post equal to his previous rank status, what kind of mobility is that?
(a) Diagonal
(b) Horizontal
(c) Vertical
(d) None of the above

423. Which among the following is the most powerful constraint upon universalization of primary education in India?
(a) Politics in general
(b) Cost of universalization
(c) Regional politics
(d) Shortage of teachers.

424. According to Lipsetand Ziterberg, the following is also one of the fields of social mobility.
(a) Isolation
(b) Narrow loyalty
(c) Occupational ranking
(d) Historical

425. The study of Human society involves the study of
(a) Environment (b) Heredity
(c) Mind (d) Man

426. The least important linkage that needs to be brought about through education for future India is
(a) linkage between educational institutes and industry.
(b) linkage between industry and agriculture.
(c) linkage between the urban elite and the rural masses.
(d) linkage between science and spirituality.

427. Norms are society's expectations or rules specifying appropriate and inappropriate behaviour. Which of the following is not a norm?
(a) Eat soup with a soup spoon
(b) Keep to the left on the road
(c) Honesty is the best policy
(d) Stop at a red light

428. Power ranking is also this of social mobility.
(a) Factor (b) Cause
(c) Type (d) Class

429. Which of the following qualities a teacher should have for developing inter cultural understanding in children?
(a) He should be able to relate the subject with national culture.
(b) He should have knowledge about the origin of various cultures and sub cultures.

(c) He should be very progressive and open minded.
(d) All of the above.

430. One of the fields of social mobility is this also.
(a) Consumption Ranking
(b) Social Class
(c) Innovation
(d) Both (a) and (b)

431. Both nature and necessity compel man to live in
(a) Church (b) College
(c) Society (d) Forest

432. The salient feature of Indian economy is
(a) Mixed economy
(b) Taxation economy
(c) Industrial economy
(d) Rural economy

433. What is the nature of man, according to Aristotle?
(a) Cultural (b) Religious
(c) Social (d) Political

434. In the field of consumption ranking, why is social mobility evaluated on the basis of expense?
(a) Because more expenditure is related to higher living standard
(b) Because excess expenditure is considered waste
(c) Because excess expenditure is considered ostentation
(d) All of the above

435. "Material culture change lies behind social change" is said by
(a) Comte (b) Weber
(c) Ogburn (d) Bottomore

436 Distribution of cultural traits from one culture to another is
(a) Acculturation (b) Ideas
(c) Diffusion (d) All of the above

437. In the field of consumption ranking, social mobility is measured by expenditure because
(a) more expenditure is related to high standard of living.
(b) more expenditure is considered spendthrift.
(c) more expenditure is considered show-off.
(d) All of the above.

438. All human beings have to interact with the other human beings in order to
(a) Quarrel (b) Compete
(c) Survive (d) Gossip

439. Which of the following is not included in the material culture of a country?
(a) Houses
(b) Industrial growth
(c) Warfare technology
(d) Software technology

440. The understanding and analysis of any social organisation like restaurant becomes possible and relatively simple by knowing
(a) functional imperatives.
(b) many people in it.
(c) norms and status.
(d) order of the society.

441. Give an example of 'Social Mobility' in occupational ranking field.
(a) Change of a thief to a dacoit
(b) Change of a farmer into a big businessman
(c) Gentleman becoming a bad man
(d) All of the above

442. Private bodies often ignore their function of promoting social change consciously through their
(a) Educational programmes
(b) Sports activities
(c) Both (a) and (b)
(d) None of the above

443. According to Lipset and Zeterberg, the following is also a cause of social mobility.
   (a) Mutual change in level of grades
   (b) Filling up of vacant higher posts
   (c) Both (a) and (b)
   (d) All of the above

444. The idea of society's division as proletarian and bourgeoise is given by
   (a) Park and Burgess
   (b) Freud
   (c) Marx
   (d) GillinandGillin

445. The teachers of private bodies too, do not always realize their function of promoting
   (a) Cultural change
   (b) Functional change
   (c) Social change
   (d) All of the above

446. Philosophy of experimentalism gave the
   (a) core theory of curriculum
   (b) basic theory of curriculum
   (c) Both (a) and (b)
   (d) None of the above

447. Society preserves our
   (a) Philosophical ideas
   (b) Civilization
   (c) Interrelation
   (d) Culture and transmits it to succeeding generation

448. Due to social mobility—structural cause—give an example.
   (a) Children from middle class after getting education work on similar posts
   (b) Children from middle class after getting education work on lower posts
   (c) Children from lower class after getting education work at higher posts
   (d) All of the above

449. Which of the following comes under non-material culture?
   (a) Literary and scientific progress
   (b) Group behaviour pattern, i.e. dance, music, drama, etc.
   (c) Ideals of life and moral values
   (d) All of the above

450. Philosophy of experimentalism was given by
   (a) Fichte (b) John Calvin
   (b) Popper (d) John Dewey

451. What do you understand by motivation being a cause of social mobility?
   (a) When a person gets higher post due to motivation or ambition
   (b) When a person without any inspiration gets higher post
   (c) When a person gets motivation after getting higher post
   (d) None of the above

452. A school is a miniature
   (a) Society (b) Organisation
   (c) State (d) Family

453. Language Arts includes
   (a) Speed (b) Writing
   (c) Spelling memory (d) All of the above

454. A correlated curriculum assumes that
   (a) a fixed syllabus existed
   (b) two or more syllabus existed
   (c) two subjects exist in schools side by side
   (d) two or more subjects exist

455. The most potent instrument of social development is
   (a) Education (b) Culture
   (c) Law (d) Religion

456. Interchange of ranks due to social mobility—give one example.
   (a) When lower grade person gives a bribe to get high level grade.
   (b) When lower grade person achieves higher grade position by competition.

(c) When a lower grade person gets recommendation for gaining higher grade.
(d) All of the above.

457. Which of thc following is an important characteristic of culture?
(a) Culture can be preserved and transmitted.
(b) Culture is cumulative form of all non material aspects.
(c) Culture is the cumulative product that people have acquired in centuries.
(d) All of the above.

458. Factors affecting social mobility are
(a) economic success.
(b) opportunity structure.
(c) demographic structure.
(d) All of the above.

459. The educational institution is a
(a) Social institution
(b) Organisation
(c) Community
(d) Family

460. Fused or integrated means
(a) Blended together
(b) Correlated
(c) Separated
(d) None of the above

461. Which aim of education is most useful for the community?
(a) Socialization (b) Technological
(c) Cultural (d) Livelihood

462. Education is a cause of social mobility because
(a) highly educated people are more reputed than less educated people.
(b) highly educated people do not get any job.
(c) poor people have lesser education.
(d) None of the above.

463. How to make a living is fusion of
(a) Mathematics (b) Sciences
(c) Economics (d) All of the above

464. Which of the following is the characteristics of culture?
(a) Growth and change
(b) Continuity
(c) Unconscious adoption
(d) All of the above.

465. How does administration became a cause of social mobility?
(a) Monarchy is more supportive to it
(b) Democracy is more supportive to it
(c) Feudalism is more supportive to it
(d) All of the above

466. Land reforms have brought
(a) advantages to the landlords to exploit the tenants.
(b) drastic changes in urban areas.
(c) decrease in output.
(d) fragmentation of land.

467. The integrated or fused curriculum plan is also called the
(a) fixed fields curriculum
(b) narrow fields curriculum
(c) broad fields curriculum
(d) None of the above

468. Which Indian economy is based on village economy?
(a) National (b) International
(c) Agriculture (d) Household

469. Why does aspiration level inspire one for social mobility?
(a) Most people have high aspiration level for the improvement of their condition
(b) All have similar aspiration level
(c) Others aspiration level inspires a person
(d) People for improvement in their condition develop mutual aspiration level

470. The difference of rate of change is called
   (a) Material lag (b) Cultural lag
   (c) Regional lag (d) Moral lag

471. An intelligent and educated temple priest has an importance in the village community. To what do you attribute his role and status?
   (a) He is the judge of good and bad.
   (b) Being an educated man, he is friend, philosopher and guide.
   (c) Besides performing his priestly function, he is conductor of the community prayer.
   (d) All of the above.

472. Give an example of 'Occupational Improvement' being a cause of social mobility.
   (a) A shoe maker becomes a lawyer after passing LLB
   (b) When two people, one from high profession and another from lower profession inter-change their profession
   (c) A person deceitfully portrays himself to be of a high profession
   (d) All of the above

473. Usually, rural people's behaviour is
   (a) Cultured (b) Aggressive
   (c) Highly civilized (d) Very simple

474. When a person adopts any thing from a dominant culture, it is called
   (a) Acculturation
   (b) Cultural Lag
   (c) Universalization of culture
   (d) None of the above

475. The need for a national system of education in India is emphasized because
   (a) India is a developing country.
   (b) India is one nation and one people.
   (c) India needs a strong central government.
   (d) local, regional, linguistic and state loyalties tend to make the people forget India.

476. Rural society is
   (a) Literate
   (b) Densely populated
   (c) Small in size
   (d) Big in size

477. How can the 'Effect of Automation' become a cause of social mobility?
   (a) Due to the use of automatic machines people are removed from their services
   (b) When people due to automatic machines become jobless and then they take up higher professions
   (c) Both (a) and (b)
   (d) All of the above

478. Change is necessary to eliminate unsatisfactory conditions and situations which are produced by the conflict between ends that are beneficial or which tend to exploit. This idea given by
   (a) Veblen (b) Auguste Comte
   (c) Max Weber (d) None of the above

479. Economic success is a cause of social mobility because people
   (a) they are unsuccessful in their ambition to earn more.
   (b) due to their ambition to earn more, they are unable to improve their condition.
   (c) desire to earn more, makes them rich and of higher status.
   (d) All of the above.

480. What type of society is rural society?
   (a) Homogeneous society
   (b) Complex society
   (c) Primitive society
   (d) Heterogeneous society

481. In non-material changes the low-speed of change is due to

(a) Involvement of religion
(b) Involvement of society
(c) Involvement of materials
(d) Involvement of emotion

482. Main distinguishing factors between rural and urban societies in India are
(a) differences in the density of population.
(b) political differences.
(c) language differences.
(d) familial differences.

483. What is the meaning of 'Demographic Structure' being a reason for social mobility?
(a) Population distribution figures show the change in the rich and the poor people
(b) It shows that people coming from villages to cities are able to raise their standard by virtue of their work
(c) Population distribution figures show occupational change
(d) None of the above

484. The process by which an individual learns to behave in accordance with social norms and culture is called
(a) Socialization (b) Assimilation
(c) Acculturation (d) None of the above

485. The role of education in India seems to be much more important to bring about
(a) a change in the lifestyle of the people.
(b) a change in the attitudes of the people towards education.
(c) social and national integration.
(d) a change in the religious beliefs of the people.

486. Education encourages vertical social-mobility in that way that it ______ in the people.
(a) awakens high ambitions for improving own condition
(b) improves conditions by higher education
(c) creates disinterest for labour
(d) helps in maintaining status quo

487. The role of caste in village is
(a) Insignificant
(b) Based on colour
(c) Having less importance
(d) Very much significant

488. Each generation of human beings acquires culture in a similar way from the
(a) Country
(b) Latest generation
(c) Society in part
(d) Previous generation

489. The role of religion in rural society
(a) has nothing to do with the rural administration.
(b) is of greater importance even today.
(c) is responsible for family disorganisation.
(d) has its hold on the behaviour of the people.

490. Kothari Education Commission desired reconstruction of education for making what kind of society?
(a) To construct society based only on Indian values
(b) To make close society into a free society
(c) Protection of ancient beliefs and orthodox
(d) All of the above

491. Socialization is a/an
(a) social training for adoption of culture.
(b) behaviour training in social situations.
(c) adjustment training to social environment.
(d) All of the above.

492. Social responsibility, building of character, inculcation of discipline and a dignity of labour can be achieved through
   (a) Social service for all
   (b) National service for all
   (c) Both (a) and (b)
   (d) None of the above

493. From the social mobility point of view an important work of education is to develop among people this feeling.
   (a) Raise dissatisfaction for status quo
   (b) Allegiance for Indian values only
   (c) Create desire to bring about social change
   (d) Both (a) and (b)

494. Zamindari system of village administration was first introduced by
   (a) Guptas (b) British
   (c) Moghuls (d) Peshwas

495. "Education is the most powerful factor in making men modern". This was said by
   (a) M.S. Gore
   (b) Margaret L. Cormack
   (c) Robert C. Williamson
   (d) Alex Inkeles

496. Language, customs, caste and other barriers have created many obstacles to
   (a) National feelings of oneness
   (b) Social oneness
   (c) Both (a) and (b)
   (d) None of the above

497. Panchayatraj system is based on the principle of
   (a) administration through hereditary rulers.
   (b) democratic decentralisation of administration.
   (c) administration through government officials.
   (d) effective central administration for the improvement of villages.

498. With reference to social mobility, guardians put their wards in English medium schools so that later on their children
   (a) qualify in competitive exams and get higher posts.
   (b) having studied in English medium school gain expertise in the English language.
   (c) are considered respectable for having studied in English medium schools.
   (d) None of the above.

499. Process of socialization of a child will become slow if
   (a) child cannot communicate due to language barriers.
   (b) child is handicapped and he is hated by the society.
   (c) he is not allowed to go to neighbourhood due to social evils rampant there.
   (d) All of the above.

500. Social control is that process by which a group controls the behaviour of its members.

   This definition of social control is of
   (a) Ross (b) Smith
   (c) Bogards (d) Bandis

501. Characteristics of the urban industrial family are
   (a) isolation.
   (b) separation of place of work and home.
   (c) great degree of equality in roles.
   (d) All of these.

502. Indian education in future should fight as the first priority against
   (a) degeneration of educational standards.
   (b) inequality of opportunities in education.
   (c) dangers of communal and caste fragmentation.
   (d) ignorance.

503. It should be compulsory for students in all the levels of education, primary, secondary school and university to participate in
(a) National service
(b) Social services
(c) Both (a) and (b)
(d) Religious services

504. Modern urban industrial families are usually based upon
(a) Conjugal relationships
(b) Non-conjugal relationships
(c) Paternalistic relationships
(d) Maternalistic relationships

505. Which of the following is not the means of socialization?
(a) Association (b) Counseling
(c) Segregation (d) Imitation

506. The existence of private and public, government and other schools side by side strengthened
(a) barrier between upper & middle classes.
(b) barrier between rich and poor.
(c) Both (a) and (b).
(d) caste system.

507. Social control is necessary because
(a) diversities among people in society remain diverse.
(b) it brings about uniformity among the diversities in people of society.
(c) there is prohibition on diversities among people in society.
(d) All of the above

508. Which one of the following does not distinguish urban communities from rural ones?
(a) Population density
(b) Mobility
(c) Stratification
(d) Differentiation

509. Uniformity in appearance (through uniform dress) and a co-operative ideology are encouraged in
(a) Social system
(b) Democratic system
(c) Totalitarian system
(d) None of the above

510. "Women must always be honoured and respected by father, brother, husband and brother-in-law who desire their welfare" was a statement made by
(a) Vinoba Bhave
(b) Manu
(c) Tilak
(d) Mahatma Gandhi

511. If social control is not there in society, in that case
(a) a condition of disorder and anarchy will arise.
(b) democratic feelings will develop.
(c) unity among diversities will arise.
(d) society will be ruined by violence and strife.

512. On whose help are the educational institution depend maximum?
(a) State (b) Community
(c) Society (d) Family

513. How is the process of socialization similar to that of teaching?
(a) Both require interactions
(b) Both are an automatic processes
(c) Both start from the family
(d) Both (a) and (b).

514. The role of education in social control is
(a) stop a person from anti-social behaviour.
(b) teach a person to follow socially accepted traditions.
(c) None of the above.
(d) Both (a) and (b).

515. Hindu Marriage Act was passed in the year

(a) 1954 (b) 1961
(c) 1955 (d) 1956

516. After Buddha, the next challenge to caste system came with the
(a) English
(b) Hun invasion
(c) Portuguese
(d) Muslim invasion

517. The abolition of 'Sati' system was mainly due to the efforts of
(a) M.G. Ranade
(b) Dayananda Saraswati
(c) Mahatma Gandhi
(d) Raja Ram Mohan Roy

518. Education should not take social control to the limit that
(a) superstitions in society terminate.
(b) it becomes a hindrance to modern democratic society.
(c) expansion of western culture stops.
(d) All of the above.

519. Sociology is described as a study of '*plural behaviour*' by
(a) Darwin and Lamarck
(b) H. Spencer and Darwin
(c) Moore and Cole
(d) None of the above

520. Process of socialization increases when the child is brought to
(a) attend classes
(b) do experiment in the laboratory
(c) participate in co curricular activities
(d) All of the above

521. The meaning of socialization is that a person
(a) learns to live according to the principles of society.
(b) learns to live in social control.
(c) tries to change society.
(d) None of the above.

522. According to the Hindu Marriage Act 1955, the minimum age of marriage for boys is
(a) 18 years (b) 14 years
(c) 25 years (d) 21 years

523. Sociology analyses the concept of
(a) Civilization and Culture
(b) Civilization and Nature
(c) Civilization and Poverty
(d) Both (a) and (c)

524. According to the Hindu Marriage Act of 1955, a wife can seek divorce if her husband
(a) is regularly away from home.
(b) does not speak to her.
(c) beats her occasionally.
(d) is guilty of adultery.

525. The meaning of socialization is that it is a process by which a person becomes an active member of some social class and works according to it, also he associates himself with public relations, traditions and social conditions. Above noted defination is by whom of the following.
(a) Durkheim
(b) Guskin
(c) Orville and Wheeler
(d) Gillin and Gillin

526. Of the following, which is an informal agency?
(a) Arya Samaj (b) The family
(c) The temple (d) Gurudwara

527. In ancient times castes had elaborated restriction on
(a) Diet
(b) Social mixing
(c) Both (a) and (b)
(d) None of the above

528. Education is a systematic socialization of the young generation. This definition was given by

(a) Durkhim (b) Smith
(c) Bandis (d) Bogardus

529. In recent times, inter-caste marriages are increasing because of
(a) arrangement of marriages by elders.
(b) education and enlightenment.
(c) arrangement of marriages by friends.
(d) force used by the government.

530. Which of the following play a vital role in the process of socialization?
(a) Competition
(b) Group activities in the school
(c) Co-operation
(d) All of the above

531. According to the Hindu Marriage Act of 1955, which of the following is a legal ground for divorce?
(a) Absence of husband at regular intervals
(b) Misunderstanding between husband and wife
(c) Frequent quarrels with the in-laws
(d) Insanity for more than three years

532. Socialization is that process by which a person learns to play the role set for him and is ready for that role. This is the belief of which writer?
(a) Ross, J.S.
(b) Bogards
(c) Dr. S.S. Mathur
(d) Havingherst and Newgartan

533. Man is a member of some group or other by
(a) Any means (b) Birth
(c) Choice (d) All of the above

534. In the definition of socialization, the following fact emerges on the basis of its definitions.
(a) By this process, a person learns values to recognise the society.
(b) A person accepted by society becomes its able member.
(c) It is a process of mutual interaction.
(d) All of the above

535. The law forbidding dowry is ineffective because
(a) it lowers the status of women.
(b) it has not been enacted by the government.
(c) it cannot be easily enforced.
(d) it is not sufficiently clear.

536. Harijans or untouchables are at the...... of social ladder
(a) Bottom (b) Top
(c) Middle (d) None of these

537. According to Muslim law, "khula" is the form of divorce which is
(a) granted by the religious heads.
(b) obtained from a court of law.
(c) arranged by the friends.
(d) None of these.

538. A factor helpful in socialization is
(a) cooperation.
(b) nurturing of a child rearing.
(c) Both (a) and (b).
(d) None of the above.

539. By the process of socialization, we make the child
(a) aware of the social norms
(b) cultured
(c) acceptable to the society
(d) All of the above

540. 'Punishment and Reward' and 'Suggestion' are factors of which social activity?
(a) Westernization (b) Socialization
(c) Indianization (d) All of these

541. Hindu woman in a joint family has
(a) more freedom than men.
(b) complete freedom.

(c) greater freedom than Muslim women.
(d) lack of freedom.

542. The social ties in caste system give feelings of
(a) Security
(b) Belongingness
(c) Both (a) and (b)
(d) None of the above

543. Every caste is limited to
(a) Region (b) State
(c) Linguistic area (d) Village

544. In the process of socialization, how is identification factor occurs?
(a) By getting sympathy, a child accepts social behaviour
(b) A child imitates others behaviour
(c) A child cooperates with others
(d) None of the above

545. Sociology does not study the individual only from the political or economic angle but as a
(a) whole Society (b) whole Nation
(c) whole Man (d) whole World

546. "Punishment and reward" are helpful towards socialization process due to following reasons.
(a) They help him to be anti-social
(b) These do not tend him to do social works
(c) Due to their fear and encouragement the child do not do anti-social activity and he does social work
(d) All of the above

547. Which of the following Acts has legalised divorce on certain grounds?
(a) Abolition of Dowry Act of 1966
(b) S.I.T. Act of 1956
(c) Hindu Marriage Act of 1955
(d) Protection of Civil Liberties Act of 1976

548. Who wrote the book *Modernizing Effects of University Education*?
(a) A.R. Desai (b) Yogendra Singh
(c) S.L. Sharma (d) S.N. Eisenstadt

549. Which of the following will promote social change?
(a) Privatization (b) Liberalization
(c) Globalization (d) All of the above

550. Which of the following sections of IPC makes a person liable for two years imprisonment if he assaults or uses criminal force on a woman?
(a) IPC Section 375
(b) IPC Section 310
(c) IPC Section 354
(d) IPC Section 325

551. What can one understand by rearing a factor helpful in the process of socialization?
(a) It should be proper
(b) It should be strict
(c) It should be free
(d) None of the above

552. Which of the following simple socieities possess distinct political institutions?
(a) The Zulu
(b) The Banyankole
(c) The Bamangwato
(d) All of the above

553. Custom is an important
(a) way of thinking of Marxists
(b) way of political behaviour
(c) social control
(d) social institution

554. The following are the elements of socialization.
(a) Environment
(b) Heredity
(c) Sympathy
(d) Both (a) and (b)

555. Advisory committee on social and moral hygiene was set up in 1954 under the chairmanship of
(a) Smt. Rameshwari Nehru
(b) Dhanwanthi Rama Rao
(c) Rukminidevi Arundale
(d) Smt. Vijayalaxmi Pandit

556. LPG (Liberalization, Privatization and Globlization) policy in India was adopted since
(a) 1991 (b) 1996
(c) 2000 (d) 2002

557. Which is the pattern of modernization through education?
(a) Capitalist (b) Non-capitalist
(c) Both (a) and (b) (d) Neither

558. Suppression of Immoral Traffic in Women and Girls Act was passed by Indian Parliament in the year
(a) 1955 (b) 1956
(c) 1966 (d) 1945

559. What factors are there in environment which help in the socialization of a child?
(a) People from other societies
(b) Earned tradition and culture
(c) Friends
(d) Both (a) and (b)

560. What should govern the aim of education?
(a) Religion (b) Politics
(c) Culture (d) Caste

561. Example of a community is a/an
(a) Orphanage (b) Caste
(c) Prison (d) Village

562. What do you understand by various aspects of socialization?
(a) Processes of various societies
(b) Western effect
(c) Other processes taking place along with socialization
(d) Processes against it

563. Sexual intercourse by a person with the wife of another man amounts to offence of adultery liable for punishment according to
(a) IPC Section 497
(b) IPC Section 350
(c) IPC Section 499
(d) IPC Section 318

564. Social change refers to
(a) change in social structure
(b) change in social ideals
(c) cultural change
(d) All of the above

565. Political aim of education is
(a) Cosmopolitanism
(b) Secularism
(c) Democracy
(d) Constitutionalism

566. Of the following kinds of marriages, which one is the result of mutual love and affection of bride and bridegroom?
(a) Arsha marriage
(b) Gandharva marriage
(c) Brahma marriage
(d) Prajapatya marriage

567. In the socialisation process sublimation of instincts means
(a) praising of the appearance of basic instincts.
(b) to check out anti-social instincts.
(c) encouragement to the appearance of socially approved instincts.
(d) Both (b) and (c).

568. The essential attributes of a state are
(a) Government (b) Population
(c) Sovereignty (d) All of the above

569. Which of the following types of social stratification is seen in India?
(a) Occupational stratification
(b) Income based stratification

(c) Caste based stratification
(d) All of the above.

570. In formation of character how does the feeling of 'self and 'ego' help in socialisation?
(a) To talk proudly of good character and self-doings
(b) To accept good character by strict discipline
(c) To adopt good character on the basis of self-respect
(d) Development of good character and self-control in the norms of society

571. International women's year was celebrated during the year
(a) 1971 (b) 1975
(c) 1850 (d) 1950

572. Socialization process in human beings takes place
(a) during young age
(b) during childhood
(c) at different intervals
(d) for the whole life

573. The rapid progress in women's education took place
(a) during last 25 years.
(b) during British regime.
(c) during 15th century.
(d) after Muslim invasion.

574. Role of teacher in process of socialization should be any of one below.
(a) By giving examples of own behaviour to children.
(b) Feedback to children for proper behaviour.
(c) Both (a) and (b)
(d) None of these

575. Sociology of education is based on the faith in
(a) Anarchism (b) Democracy
(c) Dictatorship (d) Autocracy

576. The example of a community is
(a) a group (b) a town
(c) a classroom (d) a family

577. Role of teacher in the process of socialization should be as below.
(a) Installation of free discipline
(b) Agent
(c) Strict administrator
(d) All of the above

578. The progress for education of women in India was initiated by
(a) Robert Clive
(b) Lord Dalhousie
(c) Raja Ram Mohan Roy
(d) Iswar Chandra Vidya Sagar

579. Which of the following is the characteristic of social change?
(a) It is affected by material and non-material culture both.
(b) It is a slow but continuous process.
(c) It is an automatic and universal process.
(d) All of the above.

580. The difference between the pace of progress of material and non-material culture in case of a developed material culture is known as
(a) Social lag
(b) Cultural lag
(c) Technological lag
(d) Social and cultural lag

581. A teacher do socialization of students in the following ways.
(a) To put before students their own behaviour
(b) Feedback of students regarding moral character
(c) Both (a) and (b)
(d) None of the above

582. As the needs of society are dynamic the curriculum will be

(a) Dynamic
(b) Progressive
(c) Both (a) and (b)
(d) None of the above

583. Current concept of sociology is given by
(a) Moore and Cole
(b) Merritt and Eldridge
(c) Duncan
(d) All of the above

584. How can a teacher, for the sake of socialization influence children establishing close relations?
(a) By punishing them for their objectionable attitude
(b) By encouraging them to analyse their attitude
(c) By scolding them for their objectionable attitude
(d) All of the above

585. National Policy on Education (1986) makes a recommendation (8.1) that "The existing schism between the formal system of education and the country's rich and varied cultural tradition needs to be bridged." This assumes that
(a) there is insufficient progress of education in India.
(b) there is a social and cultural lag in Indian society.
(c) there is great need for social change in India.
(d) there is enough socio-cultural progress in India.

586. At present jobs are more easily available to Harijans in all
(a) Employment categories
(b) Professions
(c) Both (a) and (b)
(d) None of the above

587. Social education refers to
(a) education encompassing social change.
(b) education arousing national awareness.
(c) education accelerating social mobility.
(d) All of the above.

588. Among the scheduled castes of India, which is the main cause of social mobility?
(a) Education
(b) Television
(c) Migration
(d) Political awakening

589. How can a teacher contribute in the socialization of children by encouraging them to take part in intellectual activities?
(a) By criticising of ill-mannered students by good-mannered children
(b) By motivating the behaviour of children by these activities
(c) For socialization, giving speech
(d) All of the above

590. As society became more complex and culture developed various specialized expressions it became necessary to have a/an
(a) informal agency (b) formal agency
(c) efficient agency (d) new agency

591. Harijan students have a tendency to drop out before finishing their schooling due to
(a) poverty
(b) strict rules of schools
(c) lack of memorizing ability
(d) None of the above

592. For increasing the intensity of the process of socialization of children, the following means are used.
(a) Teacher-parent cooperation
(b) By social boycotting of undisciplined children
(c) Punishing undisciplined children
(d) All of the above

593. A social system invariably has a
(a) culture of its own.
(b) personality.

(c) social structure.
(d) All of these.

594. Which of the following is an important technological factor of social change?
(a) Opening domestic markets for international trade.
(b) Improvement in communication and transport.
(c) Mechanization of daily life.
(d) All of the above.

595. Sociology of education is
(a) an analysis of sociological process involved in the institutions of education.
(b) a branch of educational technology.
(c) a science which studies primitive societies.
(d) a study of the society.

596. By organising healthy competition socialization of children by organizing healthy competition can be done in any of the following.
(a) There will be a control on their objectionable attitude
(b) They will learn to act in a socially accepted manner
(c) Both (a) and (b)
(d) None of the above

597. Sociology focuses on total relationship of
(a) Animal and Man (b) Society
(c) Countries (d) Man

598. A teacher can adopt methods to realise the objectives of education with the help of
(a) suitable technology
(b) suitable material for instruction
(c) Both (a) and (b)
(d) None of the above

599. Democratic ways of thinking in world came during
(a) the last 400 years or so
(b) the last 300 years or so
(c) the last 200 years or so
(d) the last hundred years or so

600. The primary meaning of Equality of Educational Opportunities is
(a) backward classes of the society also attain educational equality.
(b) all social classes attain educational equality.
(c) preference be given to backward classes of the society also.
(d) Both (a) and (b).

601. Social structure, culture and personality combined together to form
(a) Tradition (b) The folkways
(c) A social system (d) An association

602. Which of the following functions of education is not related to social change?
(a) Education should accelerate the process of social change.
(b) Education should check undesirable social change.
(c) Education should change with social change.
(d) All of the above.

603. Which is not a threat to the desired social change in India pertaining to national unity and social progress?
(a) Social distance between different classes
(b) Educational system
(c) Religions
(d) Caste

604. According to "Kothari Education Commission" society of equality, exploitation of weak class should be minimum as per following measures.
(a) To provide separate education to this class
(b) To provide primary education to this class

(c) Some measures should be available for this class of education
(d) Establishment of equality for the opportunity of education of this class

605. Education should make each individual socially efficient, and this social efficiency must be achieved by the positive use of
(a) individual capacities
(b) individual powers
(c) Both (a) and (b)
(d) negative constraints

606. The basic scheme of education was framed with the objective of making people realize that education was not merely for
(a) Intellectual perfection
(b) Knowledge and culture
(c) the purpose of individual
(d) All of the above

607. The reason for providing equal opportunities in education is, that our society
(a) their is narrow classification due to closed society.
(b) is influenced by backward classes.
(c) is influenced by people similar castes.
(d) All of the above.

608. What is more crucial for bringing about a desired social change in India?
(a) Development of social resources
(b) Development of natural resources
(c) Development of physical resources
(d) Development of human resources

609. Process of defining different categories of people in the society is called
(a) socialization
(b) social stratification
(c) social mobility
(d) None of the above

610. A socially efficient individual is able to earn
(a) Prestige (b) Face value
(c) Livelihood (d) All of the above

611. Who said, "Western education leads to the modernisation of perspectives in traditional, non-industrial societies"?
(a) Alex Inkeles
(b) Michael Armer and Robert Youtz
(c) Yogendra Singh
(d) Robert C. Williamson

612. From the point of view of social justice the exploitation of backward class, what should they now be provided to them.
(a) Reservation in allotment of land
(b) Necessity of separate education
(c) Equal rights of education
(d) Priority in jobs

613. Democratic ways of thinking have resulted in
(a) schools for leaders
(b) schools for priests
(c) schools for royal classes
(d) schools for all

614. The social aim in education is directed towards the attainment of
(a) social sufficiency
(b) social efficiency
(c) Both (a) and (b)
(d) not related to social stigmas

615. "Some societies have closed working. Indian society is considered the same in which stress is given on these type of values which promote stratification based on caste, religion and class." What are the comments of Kothari Education Commission.
(a) Separate school for backward class
(b) All section of society should have equal rights of education
(c) The percentage of passed students of backward class should be less
(d) Backward class gets reservation in next class

616. Which of the following is not the characteristic of social stratification?

(a) Social and economic inequality
(b) Permanent grouping and ranking of the society
(c) Group behaviour according to the norms and ideals of the class
(d) Birth distinction.

617. The Basic scheme of education emphasises
(a) Social efficiency
(b) Ability to make a significant contribution
(c) Both (a) and (b)
(d) None of the above

618. In the traditional classification of Indian society, for the social mobility of the following people it is necessary to provide equality of educational opportunities.
(a) People from all backward classes
(b) To ladies
(c) People from scheduled tribes
(d) People from scheduled castes

619. Social institutions exist only for bettering the life of
(a) the individual
(b) the state
(c) the society
(d) None of the above

620. Which of the following does not specify Max Weber's concept of social stratification?
(a) Political power
(b) Social prestige
(c) Educational status
(d) Income and wealth

621. Only through equality of educational opportunity the following process can be accelerated.
(a) Social exploitation
(b) Social disintegration
(c) Social change
(d) None of the above

622. The subject not available to study in ancient schools was
(a) Philosophy (b) Geography
(c) Religion (d) Mathematics

623. Which of the following might be taken as contribution to sociological foundations of education for curriculum construction?
(a) Growth and mental development
(b) Life-centeredness
(c) Emotional development
(d) Child's interest.

624. Education affects the following type of social mobility.
(a) Upward (b) Downward
(c) Horizontal (d) All of the above

625. Which of the following arrangements would you think would be correct for running a guidance programme in a school?
(a) Entrusting the guidance programme to any one teacher in the school.
(b) Treating it as extra curricular activity.
(c) Making provision for it in the school time table itself.
(d) Running the programme as per instructions to be received from higher officers.

626. Equal opportunities of education should be available to anyone of the following classes.
(a) Only the privileged class
(b) Minority class
(c) Only the rich class
(d) None of the above

627. "Religious education" and "education about religions" are
(a) not, at all, different from each other.
(b) such a comparison between them is irrelevant.
(c) two different concepts entirely.
(d) little different from one each other.

628. Conflict is the fundamental form of
   (a) opposition-oriented relationship
   (b) dissociative interaction
   (c) Both (a) and (b)
   (d) None of the above

629. The form of government is said to be of the people, by the people and for the people is
   (a) Autocracy (b) Democracy
   (c) Oligarchy (d) Anarchism

630. Cultural diffusion means
   (a) an exogeneous source of change.
   (b) borrowing of the society's culture by another one.
   (c) historically important source of change.
   (d) All of these.

631. By education the following feeling arises among the neglected classes giving encouragement to upward social mobility.
   (a) Will for changing one's own norms
   (b) Dissatisfaction over status quo in present social set up
   (c) Strong desire for changes in current circumstances
   (d) All of the above

632. Independent thinking is replaced by thinking along the lines approved by the authorities in
   (a) democratic system
   (b) totalitarian system
   (c) spiritual system
   (d) All of the above

633. During British rule jolted
   (a) occupational stratification
   (b) caste based stratification
   (c) educational stratification
   (d) Both (a) and (b)

634. Kothari Education Commission—"If drastic changes are to be brought in society without violence, then there is only one solution that can be experimented and that is—education". In this context what changes are needed to be done in education system?
   (a) Reservation for only women in education
   (b) Separate education for backward classes
   (c) Equal opportunity to all classes, for education
   (d) All of the above

635. Modernization as a process of social change requires
   (a) decreased structural differentiation.
   (b) structural fusion.
   (c) increased structural differentiation.
   (d) None of these.

636. In sparta, due to its internal and external insecurity, education aimed at the development of
   (a) Courage (b) Obedience
   (c) Physical strength (d) All of the above

637. Value can be properly defined as
   (a) Aim of life
   (b) Object of effort
   (c) Something important
   (d) All of the above

638. The realization of the aspirations of the people of India involves
   (a) change in the knowledge, skills, interests and values of the people as a whole through education.
   (b) economic growth.
   (c) agricultural innovations.
   (d) industrialization.

639. Necessity of equality of educational opportunities is due to following reasons.
   (a) By it diversification of finding of exceptional quality of the people of a country

(b) By it establishment of equal society is possible
(c) By it democratic system will be successful
(d) All of the above

640. Which social class led the freedom movement in India?
(a) Middle class (b) Proletariat class
(c) Feudal class (d) Upper class

641. The educational sociologist favours the use of
(a) tabulation of opinions of experts to build the curriculum.
(b) 'subject matter' and 'curriculum' as interchangeable terms.
(c) pressure groups to bring about changes in subject matter.
(d) studies of groups behaviour patterns to determine the goals of education.

642. In India, the following are the obstacles of social change.
(a) Class (b) Caste
(c) Both (a) and (b) (d) Poverty

643. One of the several features of Indian education promoting divisive tendencies and thwarting national integration is
(a) rivalry among teachers being encouraged by teachers' associations.
(b) caste loyalties being encouraged by private and public schools.
(c) indifference to education being encouraged by unemployment.
(d) rivalry among students being encouraged by students' unions.

644. Which of the following is not a contributory factor for modernization?
(a) Reorientation of education
(b) Social changes
(c) Conservatism
(d) Rapid industrialization

645. Which of the following characteristics is possessed by a modern society?
(a) Upholding justice
(b) Open mindedness
(c) Stiff competition for material progress
(d) All of the above.

646. Transformation of the educational system means
(a) improving the socio-emotional climate of the schools.
(b) revolutionising its curriculum.
(c) relating it to the life, needs and aspirations of the people and making it an instrument of needed social change.
(d) changing the theory and practice of education.

647. Because of the following malpractice, caste system oppose social change.
(a) Language dispute
(b) Poverty
(c) Religious discord
(d) Untouchability

648. Which of the following characteristics makes India a traditional country even today?
(a) Regional aspirations and self centred politics.
(b) Blind loyalty to caste and creed.
(c) Superstition in the name of religion.
(d) All of the above.

649. The sociology of education is most concerned with the public schooling systems of modern industrial societies, including the expansion of
(a) higher education
(b) adult education
(c) continuing education
(d) All of the above

650. The following is considered backward class due to its giving equal rights of education to backward classes.

(a) The class which was kept aloof from education previously
(b) Those who were helpless to gain education due to their business in earning their livelihood
(c) Those classes who weren't taking interest in education previously
(d) For whom there wasn't separate educational arrangement

651. Educators must have a good understanding of the social forces because
(a) educators are themselves social beings.
(b) education is influenced by the social forces.
(c) education is a social process.
(d) education is one of the activities carried on in the social setting amidst social forces.

652. Which of the following sections of society was once cansidered to be the wealthiest and most powerful?
(a) Vaishyas (b) Shudras
(c) Brahmanas (d) None of the above

653. All of the following are important agencies of modernization except
(a) Adult Education centres
(b) Religious institutions
(c) Primary schools
(d) Universities and colleges

654. Religion is an institution because
(a) it performs an important social function.
(b) it teaches religion to people.
(c) it performs functions which satisfy important specific needs of people.
(d) it imparts moral and spiritual education to people.

655. According to the Articles 341 and 342 of the Indian Constitution which castes come under backward castes,
(a) to whom the states consider backward in their area.
(b) scheduled castes.
(c) scheduled tribes.
(d) All of the above.

656. Which of the following characteristics of Indian society makes it a backward traditional society?
(a) Reservation given to SCs
(b) Caste based marriages
(c) Laws against conversion of religion
(d) All of the above.

657. Which of the following steps should be taken in order to make India a developed country?
(a) Development oriented politics
(b) Maximum exploitation of resources
(c) Education according to the need of the economy
(d) All of the above.

658. For education, which classes have been considered for reservation and special facilities by the state?
(a) Those laid down by neighbouring states
(b) According to the order of educational director
(c) Those published in the gazette
(d) Those laid down by the centre

659. Family is said to be a primary social institution because
(a) a high degree of importance is attached to it by all societies of people.
(b) there is high degree of face-to-face relationship within this.
(c) it is a basic social unit.
(d) all these above characteristics are found in it.

660. Culture refers to
(a) Habit (b) Attitudes
(c) Tradition (d) All of the above

661. Socio-economic status of a person can change due to
   (a) Education
   (b) Promotion in job
   (c) Change in income
   (d) All of the above

662. Which is the most important factor which seems to be acting to reduce class differences in India?
   (a) Government's legal and social welfare efforts on improving the lot of the weaker sections of the society
   (b) Rise in standard of living of the working class
   (c) Spread of information through mass-media such as the TV
   (d) Missionaries of social workers

663. Which article of the Constitution has laid down the provision for providing protection to the untouchables from educational injustice and exploitation
   (a) Article 2 (b) Article 26
   (c) Article 164 (d) Article 46

664. Education should enable a person to make his life
   (a) Better
   (b) Significant to all concerned
   (c) More meaningful
   (d) Satisfying

665. The attempt to obtain similar or identical aims by two or more persons, or social system or institutions is called
   (a) Competition (b) Co-operation
   (c) Assimilation (d) Conflict

666. Under which article of Constitution, admission to all in government or government-aided institutions is compulsory?
   (a) Article 16 (b) Article 29
   (c) Article 15 (d) Article 338

667. Indian government's legislation concerning educational opportunities for the weaker sections of the society is an evidence which brings into focus the
   (a) cultural nature of education.
   (b) economic nature of education.
   (c) social nature of education.
   (d) political nature of education.

668. Which of the following works as a powerful barrier against vertical mobility in India?
   (a) Occupation (b) Caste
   (c) Jobs (d) Class

669. Which of the following is not included in the implied conception of the school as a social agency?
   (a) The curriculum should be focussed on the child, not the adult.
   (b) The curriculum should be directed at predetermined social goals.
   (c) The curriculum should be organized in terms of social values.
   (d) None of the above.

670. The schools help the people to
   (a) protest against culture.
   (b) enjoy culture.
   (c) assimilate culture.
   (d) ignore culture.

671. In 'Co-operation' people
   (a) do not work at all
   (b) work together
   (c) work separately
   (d) work at night only

672. Which of the following is/are example of healthy competition and rivalry?
   (a) Debate (b) Dramatics
   (c) Inter-class games (d) All of the above

673. The areas in which the people of Schedule Caste and Schedule Tribes are scattered,

which schools the government has opened for their free education and free residence?

(a) Ashram school
(b) Hostel of backward class
(c) School of Schedule Caste
(d) School of Schedule Tribe

674. Which is not relevant for achieving vertical social mobility?

(a) Religion
(b) Education
(c) Family background
(d) Wealth

675. All of the following are examples of horizontal social mobility except,

(a) a farmer becoming a primary teacher.
(b) promotion of a peon to the post of clerk.
(c) a shopkeeper turning to supply trade.
(d) an SC student becoming IAS.

676. The most emotional charged of all social processes is

(a) Co-operation (b) Conflict
(c) Competition (d) None of the above

677. In Rajasthan, in far-flung villages primary education is given in these schools.

(a) Antyodya schools
(b) Indra Gandhi schools
(c) ashram schools
(d) Rajeev Golden Jubilee schools

678. In Co-operation, there is

(a) energy
(b) a sharing of thought
(c) synthesis of thought
(d) All of the above

679. Which of the following societies is conducive to vertical social mobility?

(a) Open society
(b) Pluralistic society
(c) Closed society
(d) None of the above

680. Due to shortage of teachers, the following are given appointments in Rajeev Golden Jubilee Schools.

(a) Trained teachers sitting ideal
(b) Only guardians
(c) Local middle passed education helper
(d) Primary educated people of same village

681. Modernisation implies mobility which may be of any kind except

(a) Scientific mobility
(b) Physical mobility
(c) Psychic mobility
(d) Social mobility

682. In 'Competition' individual or group work

(a) At nights (b) Together
(c) Separately (d) None of the above

683. To develop the personality of the child we should build up

(a) Security (b) Adequacy
(c) Self-confidence (d) All of the above

684. Which is not the characteristic of modernisation?

(a) Empathy (b) Mobility
(c) Religious faith (d) Participation

685. It is reasonable to appoint local less educated teachers in Rajeev Gandhi School because they

(a) know the local dialect.
(b) know local customs and traditions.
(c) can work on less salaries also.
(d) work under local Gram Panchayat.

686. Students get more work done in

(a) Assimilative work situation
(b) Competitive work situation
(c) Co-operative work situation
(d) Same work in all situations

687. For effective learning, the situation should be

(a) Motivated
(b) Rewarding

(c) Both (a) and (b)
(d) None of the above

688. Which scheme has been implemented in Rajasthan for promotion of primary education system?
(a) District Primary Educational Plan by centre
(b) Lok Jumbish Educational Plan
(c) Both (a) and (b)
(d) None of the above

689. Which article of the Indian Constitution proclaims that "untouchability is abolished"?
(a) Article 46 (b) Article 16
(c) Article 14 (d) Article 17

690. A closed society is one where
(a) people are orthodox and rigid
(b) inter caste marriages are prohibited due to difference in status
(c) Both (a) and (b)
(d) None of the above

691. The chief basis of the social pattern in India is
(a) Religion (b) Job
(c) Status (d) Caste

692. For equal opportunity of higher primary education of women, they are being given following facilities?
(a) Scholarship (b) Free hostel
(c) Free education (d) School dress

693. Social development will help in
(a) Social science
(b) Social adjustment
(c) Knowledge
(d) None of the above

694. The caste system has a varying pattern of
(a) Custom
(b) Tradition
(c) Both (a) and (b)
(d) None of the above

695. How regional imbalance become hindrance in providing equal educational opportunity?
(a) In some areas have more schools than their requirement
(b) In some areas have no school
(c) In some areas illiteracy prevails
(d) Some areas have low percentage of education as compared to others

696. Which of the following steps have been taken after independence to promote social mobility?
(a) Equality of educational opportunity
(b) Political and social equality
(c) Equality before law
(d) All of the above.

697. Mark out the reason that made Jawaharlal a great leader
(a) his leadership of the Congress.
(b) his parentage.
(c) his personal qualities.
(d) his brahmanical heritage.

698. For providing equal opportunities of primary education, at present the government is running a campaign?
(a) Mid-day meals
(b) Free of cost distribution of school dress
(c) Registration campaign
(d) Nutrition programme

699. Culture may refer to institutionalised ways of dealing with the various problems like
(a) Attitudes
(b) Bringing up of children
(c) Traditions
(d) Social learning

700. In ancient times castes were thought to convey .... in varying degrees
(a) fight (b) conflict
(c) population (d) pollution

701. For providing equal opportunity for education to women, Rajasthan Government has given the following facilities.
(a) Free books upto eighth class
(b) Hostel at district headquarters
(c) Free education at all education levels
(d) All of the above

702. In India, education is the responsibility of
(a) State Government
(b) Central Government
(c) Both (a) and (b)
(d) None of these

703. In the words of Martin and Stendlar 'Culture' means
(a) Arts (b) Beliefs
(c) Morals (d) All of the above

704. In which of the following ways education can promote social mobility?
(a) It can make the person liberal in his attitude and thinking.
(b) It can help to change occupation.
(c) It can enable us to get administrative power.
(d) All of the above.

705. Which institution has maximum control over education?
(a) Religion (b) Economy
(c) Family (d) State

706. For reducing educational imbalances what recommendations have been given by Kothari Education Commission
(a) district should be considered fundamental unit for educational development.
(b) to adopt equal educational development policy in all district at state level.
(c) Both (a) and (b).
(d) None of the above.

707. In extreme cases the caste council may outcaste
(a) educated people
(b) the whole society
(c) a member
(d) None of the above

708. The school as a formal agency of education imparts the minimum general
(a) Religion
(b) Philosophy
(c) Culture
(d) None of the above

709. A list of scheduled castes was first prepared in India in
(a) 1971 (b) 1950
(c) 1935 (d) 1928

710. What suggestions are given by development of Kothari Educational Commission, regarding education of disabled
(a) they should be given education in general schools.
(b) to make arrangement after their separate education in special schools.
(c) to make arrangement of their education as per general education system.
(d) Both (b) and (c).

711. The future of education in India depends on
(a) Family (b) Economy
(c) Government (d) Society

712. The family fulfils the parental role in
(a) Higher castes (b) Lower castes
(c) Few cultures (d) All cultures

713. Tradition and custom are reflected in the
(a) Family
(b) Society
(c) Both (a) and (b)
(d) None of the above

714. Who gives the system of education in India?
(a) Society (b) Economy
(c) Family (d) State

715. provided these facilities to State Government under "Integrated Educational Programme for the Handicapped"
(a) total expanses will be born by the World Bank under this scheme.
(b) total expenditure will be given by local people.
(c) every state will get fifty per cent expenses in six cities.
(d) every state will get full expanses for their education in six cities by the centre.

716. In ancient times the most polluting castes were the
(a) Untouchables (b) Brahmins
(c) Vaishyas (d) Kshatriyas

717. Knowledge and interpretation of the religious writings has been the sole privilege of
(a) Brahmins (b) Shudras
(c) Vaishyas (d) Kshatriyas

718. Under Integrated Educational Programme for the Handicapped, the following aid is given to the handicapped
(a) in each school ₹ 500 are given for each student as grant for the equipments.
(b) each handicapped is given ₹ 250 as grant for books and other stationary.
(c) each handicap is given ₹ 25 per month as conveyance allowance.
(d) All the above facilities.

719. What is the status of political interference in education?
(a) Society (b) Justified
(c) Both (a) and (b) (d) Economy

720. Literacy rate in scheduled castes is
(a) 65.3% (b) 48.2%
(c) 41.2% (d) 37.41%

721. Varna refers to the original fourfold division into
(a) Religion (b) Caste
(c) Group (d) None of the above

722. The Central Government has opened a national workshop at Dehradun for providing the following facilities to the blind.
(a) A workshop for making Braille press and other equipments.
(b) For providing training to teachers for blind schools.
(c) Both (a) and (b).
(d) None of the above.

723. The first to benefit by English education during the British was
(a) Brahmans (b) Vaishyas
(c) Both (a) and (b) (d) Kshatriyas

724. Warnock Committee which was organised under Handicapped Education 1978 proposed organisational change besides the changes in the following.
(a) Attitude of the general public towards the handicapped regarding education
(b) Attitude of the teachers regarding education
(c) Views of administrators regarding education
(d) Views of parents regarding education

725. Socialisation is a process by which the individual is adapted to his
(a) natural environment
(b) school environment
(c) social environment
(d) All of the above

726. The following feelings of the handicapped must be respected.
(a) We are handicapped we need your pity
(b) We are helpless, give us food and shelter

(c) We are helpless, give us alms
(d) Don't pity, accept us

727. The highest percentage of scheduled castes live in
(a) UP (b) Bihar
(c) MP (d) AP

728. Hereditary trade, crafts or skills are carried on according to the caste system in certain cases in
(a) Rural areas (b) Urban areas
(c) Industrial areas (d) All over India

729. UNO has declared in 1981 while celebrating "handicapped year" that
(a) disabled should be given alms with free hand.
(b) disabled should get equality with total opportunity.
(c) donations should be given for rehabilitation of disabled.
(d) All of the above.

730. Which of the following sanctions can be applied for an offence by an individual in simple societies?
(a) Moral sanctions
(b) Ritual sanctions
(c) Penal sanctions
(d) All of these

731. Industrialization and urbanization have tended to produce
(a) New classes
(b) Caste system
(c) New status
(d) None of the above

732. How much percentage of population belonging to scheduled castes live below poverty line?
(a) 37% (b) 48%
(c) 51% (d) 61%

733. In simple societies, deviations from an appropriate day-to-day behaviour are corrected by such social controls as
(a) Mild Ostracism (b) Gossip
(c) Ridicule (d) All of these

734. In Rajasthan, the oldest school for the deaf and dumb is at
(a) Udaipur (b) Bikaner
(c) Jaipur (d) Bhilwara

735. When there is a large scale of social system then bureaucratic discipline becomes necessary. This statement is given by
(a) Veblen (b) Kroeber
(c) Max weber (d) Spencer

736. Position of Brahmins has been challenged
(a) Always
(b) Every now and then
(c) Never so far
(d) Rarely

737. Equal opportunities for women in education, the constitution has given provision under this article.
(a) Articles 16(1) and (2)
(b) Article 15(3)
(c) Article 45
(d) All of the above

738. The school socializes the child by providing social control through
(a) Regulation (b) Rules
(c) Social values (d) All of the above

739. Representation of scheduled castes people in government jobs including IAS, IPS and IFS at present is
(a) 17% (b) 26%
(c) 20% (d) 12%

740. What suggestion was given by "Durgabai Deshmukh Mahila Shiksha Samiti (1958-59)" with respect to women education development?
(a) They should be given more and more opportunity for primary and secondary education

(b) The formation of women education committees at state and centre level
(c) Both (a) and (b)
(d) All of the above

741. The skills and knowledge acquired in the classroom are actually utilized by the individual in his adjustment to
(a) Social science
(b) Social behaviour
(c) Social situations
(d) Social culture

742. Education is process of
(a) Direct learning
(b) Indirect learning
(c) Both (a) and (b)
(d) None of the above

743. The following are the activities of the National Women's Educational Council 1950.
(a) Generate public opinion about women's education
(b) Showing priority in women's educational policy, programmes, targets and development
(c) Open institutes for women's education
(d) Both (a) and (b)

744. A state has a large population, but not sufficient territory. What among the following it cannot do?
(a) Let its people migrate to other countries
(b) Raise multi-storey buildings
(c) Destroy all the new-born
(d) Popularise check on the growing population

745. The largest concentration of scheduled tribes (94.5%) live in
(a) Nagaland
(b) Meghalaya
(c) Mizoram
(d) None of the above

746. The effectiveness of learning for social competency depends on the suitability of
(a) Objective (b) Procedures
(c) Motives (d) Both (a) and (b)

747. In which of the following works, the theory of Social Contract was first propounded?
(a) Leviathan
(b) Social Contract
(c) Mahabharata
(d) Two Treatises of Civil Government

748. The chief desire of the 'Srimati Hansa Mehta Women's Educational Organisation 1962' was
(a) separate syllabus for girl-education.
(b) accept co-education.
(c) abandoning of the sex discrimination policy and providing equal opportunity.
(d) Both (b) and (c).

749. Theoretically each caste has its own
(a) Status
(b) Marriage group
(c) Hereditary occupation
(d) All of the above

750. Administration of pure tribal areas is mentioned in Article
(a) 251 (b) 244(2)
(c) 51 (d) 222(a)

751. The main suggestion of 'Bhaktavatsalyan Samiti—1963' for women's education was
(a) there would be separate primary schools for girls.
(b) there should be co-education at primary level.
(c) centre should give grants to states backward in women's education.
(d) None of the above.

752. Who, among the following thinkers, is not associated with the theory of Social Contract?

(a) Locke (b) Kautilya
(c) Hobbes (d) Rousseau

753. The divorce is not so difficult or uncommon among the
(a) Rich people
(b) Lower castes
(c) Higher castes
(d) Poor people

754. Socialization requires
(a) Punishment (b) Teachers
(c) Rewards (d) All of the above

755. The state of nature is
(a) a state of equality for all men.
(b) the state when Devas were troubled by Asurs.
(c) such a state did not exist historically.
(d) supremacy of might on right.

756. What suggestions were given by 'Dhebar Ayog' for the removal of linguistic difficulties in education of scheduled tribes?
(a) The languages of area-special should be included in the curricular of class 1 and 2
(b) The teachers should be trained with languages of area-special and related to there livelihood
(c) Teacher should be appointed to the people of area-special
(d) Both (a) and (b)

757. The methods of teaching must seek to utilize the social forces operative in the social life in order to develop capacity for
(a) Social attitude
(b) Social problems
(c) Social adjustment
(d) Social behaviour

758. Education of tribal people has been especially stressed in
(a) NPE (revised) 1992
(b) The tenth plan
(c) NPE 1986
(d) None of the above

759. What kind of schools have been proposed for the education of the children of nomadic tribes?
(a) Mobile school
(b) Rajiv Golden Jubilee School
(c) Single teacher school
(d) All of the above

760. Due to Social Contract, man
(a) became part of the whole.
(b) state came into existence.
(c) lost his freedom.
(d) gained his freedom.

761. "Socialisation is a process by which the individual is adapted to his social environment" the statement given by
(a) Thorstein Veblen
(b) Maria Montesseri
(c) Herbert Spencer
(d) James Drever

762. Brahmins have seldom been
(a) Teachers (b) Priests
(c) Kings (d) All of the above

763. "We, the people...having solemnly resolved to constitute...into a Sovereign, Socialist, Secular, Democratic, Republic, and to secure to all its citizens: Justice, Social, Economic and Political: Liberty of thought, expression, faith, belief and worship; Equality of Status and Opportunity; and to promote among all, Fraternity assuring the dignity of the individual and unity and integrity of the nation." Who stated these words indicating the movement of man from the state of nature to political society?
(a) Rousseau
(b) Constitution of India
(c) Kautilya
(d) Manu

764. Caste membership is determined by
(a) Birth (b) Fight
(c) Conflict (d) Competition

765. The percentage of women population in India at present is
(a) 48.3% (b) 49%
(c) 47% (d) 46.6%

766. Which movement was started in 2001 for universal aided in primary education by Indian government?
(a) Education at the door
(b) Lok Jumbish
(c) All education movement
(d) Complete education movement

767. "Let every soul be subject unto the higher powers; for there is no power but of God: the powers, that be ordained. Whosoever resisteth the power, resisteth the ordinance of God, and they that resist shall receive to themselves damnation". Mark out the correct conclusion from this statement.
(a) Those who resist the Divine power shall be punished by God
(b) The Divine Origin theory pleads for status quo
(c) The temporal power, is dependent on the ecclesiastical power
(d) God, being supreme need alone be obeyed

768. Old concept of Sociology is given by
(a) Lamarck (b) Auguste Comte
(c) Herbert Spencer (d) Both (a) and (b)

769. 'Socialisation is a prossess as a result of which children take on themselves the various social roles' according to
(a) Radcliffe (b) Kroeber
(c) Cook (d) Linton

770. Christ said "Render unto Ceasar things that are Ceasar's and unto God the things that are God's Mark out the correct conclusion.
(a) One should be loyal to the King
(b) King is superior to God
(c) State is not of Divine origin
(d) Church and the state are two different institutions

771. The aim of "all education movement" is
(a) universal primary education.
(b) naming in all classes.
(c) primary education in city limit.
(d) All of the above.

772. Caste is an important factor in how people deal with
(a) Groups (b) Enemies
(c) Religion (d) Each other

773. National Mother Security Scheme was started in
(a) 1997 (b) 2003
(c) 2004 (d) 2009

774. With special reference to the rural children, this programme is effective in universalisation of education.
(a) Serva Shiksha Abhiyan
(b) Lok Jumbish
(c) District Primary Education Plan
(d) All of the above

775. Informal agencies is/are
(a) the play group (b) the community
(c) the family (d) All of the above

776. One of the important industries in a competitive economy is/are
(a) Movies (b) Games
(c) Advertising (d) Sports

777. The importance of the Patriarchal theory of the origin of state
(a) overlooks the other factors in the development of the state.
(b) is doubtful.
(c) emphasizes the concept of command and the obedience which is the basis of political obligation.

(d) provides the simplest explanation of the origin of state which really is the product of complex circumstances.

778. Effect of cost which hinders social change in India can be removed by
(a) organisation of personal education by communities.
(b) organisation of non-discriminatory communal education.
(c) organisation of separate education for communities.
(d) None of the above.

779. National Women Commission established in 1992 is a/an
(a) advisory body
(b) autonomous body
(c) constitutional body
(d) None of the above

780. The conservative function of education is/are
(a) Social heritage
(b) Cultural heritage
(c) Constructive role
(d) Both (a) and (b) only

781. For social change, hindrance of language in education can be removed by this way.
(a) By using the formula of triple language
(b) For the linguistic minorities, appointing teachers of their language
(c) By accepting regional language (mother tongue) at primary level
(d) All of the above

782. Indicate the manner in which the office of kingship may have first come into existence?
(a) People elected the king
(b) Manu, God's own representative was the first king
(c) Priest was the first king
(d) The ablest in the war was made the first king

783. The hold of caste system is strongest in
(a) Urban areas
(b) Towns
(c) Metropolitan cities
(d) Rural areas

784. In the new social pattern, education has to play
(a) Cultural role
(b) Constructive role
(c) Creative role
(d) Both (a) and (b)

785. Which among the following primarily contributed to the concept of command and obedience?
(a) The priest kings by the use of magic
(b) Family
(c) The tribal heads who had to face the problems of numbers
(d) The group that first got engaged in war

786. The following are the chief elements in the socialisation of a child
(a) Effect of other societies
(b) Social conventions
(c) Social
(d) Social interaction

787. Constitution of India was adopted on
(a) 15 Aug. 1947 (b) 26 Aug. 1948
(c) 26 Jan. 1950 (d) 26 Nov. 1949

788. The method of teaching must place primary emphasis on
(a) Social culture (b) Social sciences
(c) Social behaviour (d) Religion

789. Unofficial units of socialization are
(a) Family
(b) Community
(c) Both (a) and (b)
(d) None of the above

790. Historical analysis indicates that the early kings were

(a) warlords.
(b) the founding father of diplomacy.
(c) wise men.
(d) God-fearing religious priests.

791. The meaning of initiative and independence is
(a) ability to adjust with society.
(b) ability to communicate with society.
(c) ability to conflict for society.
(d) ability to cope with problems independently.

792. Which of the following sections of the society is getting lion's share in central government jobs
(a) Upper castes people
(b) Scheduled castes
(c) Scheduled tribes
(d) Minorities

793. Community is helpful in the socialization of a child because
(a) in its contact children accept similar traditions of a community.
(b) they accept the religion of a society.
(c) community imposes their values and thoughts on them.
(d) community can levy harsh control over them.

794. Formal schooling, at first was confined chiefly to those areas having highest culture accumulation. They were
(a) Philosophy and Religion
(b) Religion and Mathematics
(c) Mathematics and Philosophy
(d) Mathematics, Philosophy and Religion

795. One of the most needed requirements of socialization, learning and education is
(a) Co-operation (b) Conflict
(c) Discipline (d) Competition

796. In a family, socialisation of a child is possible due to which tendency of his?
(a) Defence (b) Sports
(c) Sympathy (d) Initiation

797. What brought the people and the king in an agreement for mutual benefit?
(a) The existence of internal and external danger
(b) Faith in the supernatural forces
(c) The ancestral worship
(d) All in some degree

798. In all social systems, a person has to discipline himself to respect others
(a) Wishes (b) Right
(c) Desires (d) All of the above

799. What is the percentage of population of schedule castes people in India?
(a) 20.20% (b) 12.70%
(c) 16.20% (d) 32.50%

800. Who said: "The state is neither the handiwork of God, nor the result of the superior force, nor the creation of revolution of convention, nor a mere expansion of family"?
(a) Gamer (b) Maclver
(c) Burgess (d) Frazer

801. How is community an agency of the socialization of a child?
(a) If a child accepts the manners and customs of his caste he is ostracised
(b) Community forces a child to learn its traditions
(c) By participating in the functions of his community a child learns its manners and customs
(d) All of the above

802. With the development of written language and the number system, schools were established in
(a) China (b) America
(c) Africa (d) Australia

803. Learning is basically a/an
(a) Social process
(b) Group process
(c) Co-operational process
(d) Individual process

804. Neighbourers and friends are helpful in the socialization of a child in this way
(a) By criticising for unwanted behaviour of child
(b) To revolt if the child is not effected by self
(c) By effecting the child by self behaviour
(d) By giving punishment for unwanted behaviour of child

805. Which among the following statements considers state as the supreme authority, and an end in itself?
(a) Individual is free to disown his State
(b) He must submit to the laws of the State
(c) An individual is merely one among the so many that constitute the State
(d) He can challenge the laws which are against his conscience

806. What is the percentage of backward children in normal class?
(a) 10% (b) 20%
(c) 5% (d) 15%

807. Agriculture is open to
(a) Kshatriya (b) Brahmins
(c) Shudras (d) All castes

808. Who among the following belonged to the utilitarian school of thinkers?
(a) John Stuart Mill
(b) R.M. Maclver
(c) H.J. Laski
(d) Herbert Spencer

809. Such schools fail in the socialisation of a child which
(a) stress teaching of a particular language.
(b) are run on the basis of a particular religion.
(c) are run on the basis of a particular community.
(d) All of the above.

810. Peons, domestic workers, sweepers, etc. belong to
(a) Lower classes
(b) Lower employed classes
(c) Lower middle classes
(d) None of the above

811. Preamble to the Indian Constitution declares India a
(a) Democratic republic
(b) Secular republic
(c) Socialist republic
(d) All of the above

812. In the socialisation of a child, the following aspect is highly effective.
(a) School building
(b) School equipments
(c) Games facility
(d) Appropriate environment

813. "Nature has placed man under the governance of two sovereign masters, pain and pleasure. It is for them alone to point out what we ought to do. We refer to them all our judgments and all the determination of our life". To whom do you refer these words?
(a) Kant (b) Adam Smith
(c) Stuart Mill (d) Bentham

814. Social change is a
(a) conscious process
(b) discontinuous process
(c) continuous process
(d) None of the above

815. The position of Brahmins has been based largely on their monopoly of correct
(a) Education
(b) Learning

(c) Religious practices
(d) All of the above

816. Which among the following ideas is not connected with Socialism?
(a) The defects of social organisations arise from private ownership and the desire of profit
(b) The means of production and distribution must be in the hands of the community
(c) There should be a stateless society
(d) Private property should be abolished

817. Schools eliminate the following ill tendency acquired by children from their family, caste, neighbours, etc. and socialize them.
(a) Malpractices
(b) Narrow mindedness
(c) Superstition
(d) All of the above

818. Caste continues to play a unique role in
(a) America (b) China
(c) India (d) England

819. Democracy in India is grounded on which of the following principles
(a) Justice
(b) Liberty and equality
(c) Fraternity
(d) All of the above

820. For the socialization of a child, two factors are important.
According to Raman Bihari Lal these two factors are
(a) maximum members of a society should be educated.
(b) from birth to adolescence this process goes on at a faster rate.
(c) parents of a child should be more educated.
(d) Both (a) and (b).

821. Anarchism is
(a) an extreme form of individualism.
(b) an extreme form of socialism.
(c) it holds the state to be the good c
earth.
(d) an extreme form of communism.

822. Only an economic revolution can chan
the plight of people belonging to
(a) Upper classes
(b) Lower classes
(c) Upper middle class
(d) None of the above

823. Brahmins are divided into separate su
castes differing greatly from one anoth
in their
(a) Custom (b) Occupation
(c) Colour (d) Nature

824. The largest amendment to Indi
Constitution was made in
(a) 1995 (b) 1992
(c) 1982 (d) 1976

825. Who among the following is not
Anarchist thinker?
(a) Bakunin (b) Kropotkin
(c) Hegel (d) Proudhon

826. For the success of democracy, c
curricular activities of a child should
conducted in this manner.
(a) Democratic (b) Unrestrained
(c) Socialistic (d) Harshly

827. Brahmins are divided into separa
subcastes differing greatly from o
another in their
(a) Food habits (b) Customs
(c) Social standing (d) All of the abo

828. Ordinary people paid for the services
the Brahmins in
(a) Clothes (b) Grain
(c) Milk (d) All of the abo

829. Socialisation of a child is done when t
behavioural pattern of society

(a) is accepted.
(b) by doing adjustment with them.
(c) Both (a) and (b).
(d) Bone of the above.

30. Which thinker has not accepted that the state as an ethical purpose?
(a) Gandhi (b) Marx
(c) Laski (d) Aristotle

31. Anti-Brahmin sentiment has erupted occasionally in
(a) Madras (b) Maharashtra
(c) Calcutta (d) Both (b) and (c)

32. At which of the following levels of education, privatization is most successful?
(a) Technical education level
(b) Primary level
(c) Secondary level
(d) Higher education level.

33. Whom do you attribute the words: The State originates and continues to exist "for the sake of the best life"?
(a) Mahabharata (b) Plato
(c) Aristotle (d) Gandhi

34. "By socialisation human-being learns different behaviour magnitudes but in culturalisation he accepts only one behaviour model." Clarify this statement by an example.
(a) A person greets his mother-father and teacher differently but obey them according to Indian culture
(b) A person becomes polite in front of teacher but criticises him in his absence
(c) Both (a) and (b)
(d) None of the above

35. Students who join strikes and opposition movements in schools and colleges generally belong to
(a) Upper middle classes
(b) Lower classes
(c) Lower upper classes
(d) Lower middle classes

836. When a new habit is accepted by other members for social change, it is called
(a) imitation
(b) social pressure
(c) emulation
(d) social acceptance

837. Who said that the state exists and should aim at "the greatest good of all"?
(a) Laski (b) Sophists
(c) Socrates (d) Gandhi

838. A man without a caste is alone and cannot join
(a) any religion
(b) any company
(c) any school
(d) any other group

839. For success of democracy in India which of the following things is required at present?
(a) Abolition of reservation in education and employment.
(b) Tolerance and coexistence.
(c) Fair and transparent education and employment policies.
(d) All of the above.

840. "The state should enable men to realise the best that is in themselves". To whom do you attribute these words?
(a) Gandhi (b) Laski
(c) Arthasashtra (d) Plato

841. Social change implies changes in the
(a) structural units of society
(b) functional units of society
(c) Both (a) and (b)
(d) narrow sense

842. Which of the following castes remains one of the most extraordinary features of Indian social history?

(a) Kshatriyas (b) Vaishyas
(c) Shudras (d) Brahmins

843. The following thought is inherent in 'Modernisation'.
(a) Secularism
(b) Use of science and technology
(c) Socialism
(d) All of the above

844. In answer to the question, "What is Property", who said property is theft?
(a) Proudhon (b) Marx
(c) Bakunin (d) Engels

845. Secularism in India means
(a) an irreligious society
(b) an irreligious state
(c) equal weightage to all religions
(d) state keeps equal distance from all religions

846. Mark out the correct statement about modern state.
(a) It is a welfare state
(b) It is based on principle of *laissez-faire*
(c) It is a police state
(d) It does not interfere with social life

847. "Indian society should remain ready to accept the importance of science and to use it in every area of life." This view is indicative of the following process.
(a) Socialization
(b) Indianisation
(c) Modernisation
(d) All of the above

848. Caste system is still the framework of society among the
(a) Poor only
(b) Religious groups
(c) Illiterate masses only
(d) Poor and the illiterate masses

849. In the environment of a school, the following should be naturally encouraged for the propagation of modernization.s
(a) Secularisation
(b) Scientific point of view
(c) Socialisation
(d) All of the above

850. Which one of the following is done by modern state?
(a) Regulating divorce law
(b) Insisting on certain age requirement for marriage
(c) Prescribing limits of kinship within which marriage is prohibited
(d) All of these

851. The family in India was the source of
(a) Physical education
(b) Basic education
(c) Moral education
(d) All of the above

852. With development, religion becomes
(a) Individual matter
(b) Social matter
(c) Family matter
(d) All of the above

853. Which among the following operates as a limit on the functions of the state?
(a) The customs of the community
(b) The fear of resistance
(c) The means at its disposal
(d) All of these

854. At present, by making computer education compulsory in schools and universities students are integrated towards this.
(a) Modernisation (b) Indianisation
(c) Traditional living (d) Secularism

855. The policy of universalisation of elementary education is a
(a) Capitalist concept
(b) Autocratic concept
(c) Socialist concept
(d) None of the above

856. With culturalization through education this should be co-ordinated.

(a) Modernization (b) Indianization
(c) Socialism (d) Secularism

857. Caste system is deep rooted in the
(a) Rural areas
(b) The villages
(c) Lower strata of society
(d) All of the above

858. Woman's status in the family also varies according to
(a) Economic status
(b) Caste
(c) Education
(d) Can't say anything

859. The "conservation and the development of human capacities as well as of economic resources" is an important function of state. This is done by
(a) encouragements of art.
(b) regulating the exploitation of natural resources.
(c) providing education.
(d) leaving exploitation of natural resources in the hands of private individual.

860. According to social point of view, the work of education can be divided into the following two parts.
(a) Social control
(b) Social change
(c) Social revolution
(d) Both (a) and (b)

861. Education is included in which of the following lists
(a) Concurrent list (b) Residual list
(c) State list (d) Union list

862. The strength of caste councils varies greatly from
(a) Religion to religion
(b) Area to area
(c) Caste to caste
(d) None of the above

863. The meaning of social control is education social structure and working method.
(a) Orthodox (b) Protects
(c) Changes (d) All of the above

864. According to MacIver, there are certain functions which the state should not undertake. Which is not such a function?
(a) Interference with social customs
(b) Enforcing morality
(c) Regulating trade and commerce
(d) Controlling public opinion

865. Some thinkers identify social changes with
(a) Family changes
(b) Cultural changes
(c) The law of marriages
(d) All of the above

866. Rapid changes in the Indian family system during the last five decades or so is due to
(a) Technological upheavals
(b) Social upheavals
(c) Economic upheavals
(d) All of the above

867. The sphere of state activity should be limited because the state is
(a) Not omnicompetent
(b) Omnipotent
(c) Omnipresent
(d) Omnicompetent

868. An example of the effect of education on social change is
(a) freedom from superstition through English education.
(b) development of scientific through modern education.
(c) Both (a) and (b).
(d) None of the above.

869. An example of a formal agency is
(a) the community (b) the family
(c) the play group (d) libraries

870. Privatization in education and economy got momentum since
(a) 2005 (b) 1999
(c) 1991 (d) 1985

871. An example of the effect of social change on education is
(a) change in educational curriculum in modern age.
(b) teaching of ancient ideals in middle age.
(c) in modern age effect of religion on education.
(d) All of the above.

872. Who said that state is "a special repressive force for the suppression of the proletariat by the bourgeois, of millions of toilers by handful of rich"?
(a) Marx (b) Engels
(c) V.A. Lenin (d) MacIver

873. Education should bring a change in
(a) Skills (b) Interests
(c) Attitudes (d) All of the above

874. '*Jati*' refers to the numerous subcastes of each
(a) Religion (b) Society
(c) Varna (d) Region

875. Which of the following justifies that force is an instrument of state?
(a) To impose the will of the ruling class
(b) Since the state originated in warfare
(c) To eliminate the clash of interest between diverse groups
(d) To keep structure of society in working order

876. The meaning of social stratification is to divide society in the following categories.
(a) Religious and non-religious
(b) Social and non-social
(c) Civil and uncivil
(d) High and low

877. If there is any controversy on any matter of education between centre and any state what will be the final settlement?
(a) Law made by the Parliament will prevail.
(b) Both centre and state will choose separate line of action.
(c) State legislation will be accepted as education was in the state list before 1976.
(d) Both the laws will be rejected and matter will be decided by Supreme Court.

878. Social stratification is of the following two kinds.
(a) Educated and uneducated
(b) Uncivilized and civilized
(c) Communal and class
(d) None of the above

879. Force is
(a) the end of state.
(b) the basis of state.
(c) the origin of state.
(d) the element of state.

880. The older members of the family considered it their duty to acquaint the younger members with the family's
(a) Moral code
(b) Basic behaviour
(c) Cultural code
(d) All of the above

881. Central government maintains the quality and standard of education in the educational institutions of national importance like central universities, IITs, IIMs, etc. through
(a) All India Council of Technical Education (AICTE)
(b) Central Council of Indian Medicine
(c) University Grants Commission (UGC)
(d) All of the above

882. The basis of social stratification is
(a) Sex (b) Education
(c) Community (d) All of the above

883. The family has a virtual monopoly of the child's time and has opportunity for serving his needs because of
(a) dissatisfaction between members
(b) affection between members
(c) Both can be possible
(d) None of the above

884. Society based on this is called a closed society.
(a) Civilization
(b) Culture
(c) Education
(d) Caste and religion

885. Mark out the theory of Socialism that Karl Marx developed
(a) Communism
(b) Anarchism
(c) Socialism
(d) Functional Democracy

886. In India society has been organized according to a definite structure for
(a) only recently
(b) last three centuries
(c) many centuries together
(d) can't say anything about it

887. In classic Hindu thought, the king's duty was to rule justly in accordance with the principles laid down in the Sanskrit scriptures as interpreted by
(a) Kshatriyas (b) Vaishyas
(c) Shudras (d) Brahmins

888. In which of the following the essentials of communism are found?
(a) *Das Capital*
(b) *Communist Manifesto*
(c) *The Critique of Political Economy*
(d) *Guild Socialism*

889. Education abolishes such a society.
(a) Scientific society
(b) Democratic society
(c) Closed society
(d) Developed society

890. Our lives appear so different from those of our
(a) Fathers
(b) Fore Fathers
(c) There is no difference at all
(d) Cannot say

891. Which of the following is not included in the entry 13 of the union list?
(a) International association for culture
(b) Educational and cultural relations with foreign countries
(c) Maintenance of IIMs
(d) Participation in International conferences.

892. A factor of social mobility is
(a) Conservatism (b) Religion
(c) Community (d) Education

893. Which idea has most influenced the recent political thought?
(a) The dictatorship of the proletariat
(b) The materialistic interpretation of history
(c) The theory of class war
(d) That the state will 'wither away'

894. The class of people who generally have a great desire for education is
(a) lower middle classes
(b) lower classes
(c) upper classes
(d) None of the above

895. The children who become delinquents and join gangs which are anti-social generally belong to
(a) lower unemployed classes
(b) lower middle class

(c) lower classes
(d) None of the above

896. What is the scope of modern state, according to Gandhiji?
(a) Welfare of the Gandhian majority
(b) The welfare of the maximum number
(c) Welfare of all
(d) Welfare of the depressed classes

897. Professional prestige is an example of social mobility.
(a) Going from low profession to high profession
(b) Mutual changes in low professions
(c) Mutual changes in high professions
(d) All of the above

898. Vocational and technical training of workers comes under
(a) Union list
(b) Concurrent list
(c) State list
(d) None of the above

899. The child of a hardworking clerk or teacher tries his best to work his way up to becoming a doctor or an engineer and in many cases this has actually happened in
(a) Middle classes
(b) Lower classes
(c) Lower middle classes
(d) Upper classes

900. Social mobility which is chiefly among the educated is not seen in such situation when among the educated.
(a) There is laziness.
(b) There is idleness and indolence.
(c) There spreads unemployment.
(d) There prevails incapability.

901. The relation between an individual and body politics is
(a) to participate in all its activities as man is a political animal.
(b) to avoid politics as it is said to be the last resort of the scoundrels.
(c) to participate in body politic, as it is all around us.
(d) to avoid it, as it involves violence.

902. Article 351 is about
(a) Promotion of Hindi
(b) Education of tribals
(c) English as official language
(d) Promotion of secularism

903. Status of central university is given to any educational institution under union list of
(a) Entry 63 (b) Entry 64
(c) Entry 65 (d) None of these

904. It is repugnant to the Gandhian State
(a) to submit to the bad laws.
(b) not to accept the supremacy of state.
(c) to follow the laws.
(d) not to follow the laws.

905. Variety in educational curriculum is helpful in social mobility because people
(a) get education contrary to their interest.
(b) get education according to their capabilities.
(c) get education according to their capabilities and interest.
(d) Both (a) and (b).

906. After almost 20 or 25 years of extreme hardship, the father may be able to build and own a small house of his own in
(a) Lower middle classes
(b) Lower class
(c) Upper middle classes
(d) Upper class

907. The changes seen around us have also been contributed by
(a) Population explosion
(b) Wars
(c) Economic growth
(d) All of the above

908. The meaning of upward mobility is
   (a) a process of arriving from lower level to upper level.
   (b) mutual mobility among upper social status.
   (c) internal mobility among lower social strata.
   (d) None of the above.

909. According to Gandhiji, one can be slave to the state
   (a) by not expressing his views.
   (b) once one disobeys the laws.
   (c) by submitting to the laws which are against one's conscience.
   (d) by not participating in the body politic.

910. No citizen shall be denied admission in any educational institution maintained by the state or receiving aid out of state fund on grounds of religion, race, caste, language or any of them. It has been stated in
   (a) Article 30 (b) Article 29 (i)
   (c) Article 29 (ii) (d) Article 31

911. Which is the most important constituent of state, according to Gandhi?
   (a) Law
   (b) The State
   (c) Individual
   (d) The body politic

912. The meaning of downward mobility is
   (a) mutual mobility among higher and lower status.
   (b) mobility among lower social strata.
   (c) the process of reaching from higher social strata to lower social strata.
   (d) All of the above.

913. There are a few chances for the child of the lower middle class to rise into the category of the upper middle class, after succeeding in his struggles to get
   (a) good education
   (b) professional training
   (c) Both (a) and (b)
   (d) None of the above

914. Entry 25 of concurrent list states about
   (a) the education of disabled.
   (b) vocational and technical training of labour.
   (c) the education of working class.
   (d) None of the above.

915. An example of horizontal mobility is
   (a) an educational officer of a developed large district comes to a smaller district but at the same post.
   (b) a sub-strict officer becoming a district officer.
   (c) Both (a) and (b).
   (d) a district officer of a small district comes to a larger district but at the same post.

916. The aim of political institutions is
   (a) to serve the individual best.
   (b) to expand the authority of the state.
   (c) to enforce authority.
   (d) to sustain law and order.

917. Education in the mother tongue at primary stage to children belonging to linguistic minorities has been mentioned in Article
   (a) 349 (b) 351
   (c) 250 (d) 350

918. The children of teachers strive particularly hard and often do very well at school and college, and later succeed in getting good jobs. They belong to
   (a) Middle classes
   (b) Lower classes
   (c) Lower middle classes
   (d) Upper classes

919. Which among the following is the Gandhian way to deal with evil?
   (a) A little wrong to eliminate, it is not anti-Satyagraha

(b) It should be disregarded
(c) Standing by truth, one should go by Satyagraha
(d) It should be avoided

920. Example of vertical mobility is
(a) a watchman becoming a peon but at the same salary.
(b) promotion of a teacher to the post of Education Officer.
(c) a parliamentarian becoming a minister.
(d) Both (a) and (b).

921. Primary education in the mother tongue has been safeguarded in Article
(a) 220 (b) 351
(c) 29 (d) 350

922. Family is an important agency for developing
(a) Moral attitude
(b) Social attitude
(c) Both (a) and (b)
(d) Professional attitude

923. Classification of horizontal and vertical social mobility has been done by the following.
(a) Harold L. Hodgkinson
(b) John Dewey
(c) Miller
(d) Wook

924. Mark out the Gandhian State among the following
(a) Co-operative decentralisation
(b) Theocracy
(c) Swaraj
(d) Democracy

925. In the caste system at the top of the caste ladder are the
(a) Brahmins (b) Shudras
(c) Kshatriya (d) Vaishya

926. Educational and economic interests of SCs and STs have been safeguarded under Article
(a) 45(a) (b) 52
(c) 46 (d) 351

927. What is the true basis of Gandhian State?
(a) Co-operation (b) Satya
(c) Force (d) Non-violence

928. What is the effect on social mobility in a closed society?
(a) A person goes through descending social mobility
(b) A person mobilises on the basis of his ability
(c) Upward mobility is not there because a person is considered highly educated from the very birth
(d) All of the above

929. Education in union territories is administered by the central government under Article
(a) 50 (b) 239
(c) 350 (d) 229

930. The attempt of two or more persons or groups to attain identical aims through elimination of competitor is called
(a) Competition
(b) Co-operation
(c) Conflict
(d) None of the above

931. In a open society why do people go through ascending social mobility?
(a) Because a person of lower level is mobile in a lower level
(b) Because a person is considered of a lower caste by birth
(c) Because in such societies it is not birth but ability the basis of mobility
(d) None of the above

932. Gandhiji did not define the end of his Ideal State, because
(a) he deliberately avoided to define it.
(b) he was a religious man, who had strayed in politics.

(c) as a believer in good means, he was confident of the good ends.
(d) he had not the philosopher's capacity to plan for the future.

933. Central government can implement any policy on education ignoring State's wishes because
(a) Education is in the concurrent list
(b) India has parliamentary democracy
(c) Education is in the union list
(d) None of the above

934. At times conflict does not involve well defined
(a) People (b) Cause
(c) Aims (d) Both (a) and (b)

935. Every one is his own ruler "He rules himself in such a manner that he is never a hindrance to his neighbour". To which of the following does it refer?
(a) The conditions under our existing constitution
(b) To the sense of good neighbourliness
(c) The state of affairs is an Ideal State
(d) The Swiss democracy

936. If a society is based on democracy, then on the basis of ability a person will be able to go throw what kind of mobility?
(a) Downward
(b) Upward
(c) Lateral
(d) All of the above

937. Economic changes have brought about
(a) Social Mobility
(b) Caste system
(c) Both (a) and (b)
(d) None of the above

938. Central government must consult the state before beginning any legislation on any subject included in the concurrent list. This recommendation of Sarkaria Commission was accepted by Inter State board in
(a) 1982 (b) 1991
(c) 1995 (d) 1996

939. In an autocracy, why is a person on the basis of his ability unable to go through upward social mobility?
(a) Because he is considered high from the very birth
(b) Because he is from the ruling class
(c) Both (a) and (b)
(d) Because ruling class is considered low

940. 'All the children of all the people' should be educated in school is a development which originated
(a) in ancient times
(b) around 500 AD
(c) around 1200 AD
(d) very recently

941. Which of the following cannot be attributed to the state?
(a) It is based on voluntary co-operation
(b) It exercises authority through laws and coercion
(c) It is organised
(d) It is a territorial organisation

942. The reason for less social mobility in agricultural societies is
(a) scarcity of the educated.
(b) people are not hard-working.
(c) people are industrious.
(d) All of the above.

943. Education, industrialization and technology have changed
(a) Social system (b) Caste system
(c) Family system (d) All of the above

944. In conflict there is
(a) elimination of group
(b) elimination of other species

(c) elimination of competitor
(d) elimination of goal

945. In those societies where professions from the point of view of prestige are considered high or low, there what is the direction of social mobility?
(a) Within higher professions
(b) Within low professions
(c) From lower to higher professions
(d) None of the above

946. Common language, religion, race, etc. are important for presence of spirit of nationality. Which among the following can be considered a nation?
(a) People of Switzerland speaking different languages
(b) People of U.S.A. belonging to various racial groups
(c) People of India belonging to different religions
(d) All of these

947. Democratic socialism enshrined in our Constitution means
(a) reduction of inequalities of income through monetary and fiscal measures.
(b) absence of class distinction.
(c) mixed economy.
(d) Both (a) and (b).

948. Which is the most important element of nationality?
(a) Corporate sentiment
(b) Common religion
(c) Common language
(d) Common race

949. The availability of high posts and professions affect mobility in a society in such a manner.
(a) Due to more availability, mobility will be more
(b) Due to less availability, mobility will be less
(c) Both (a) and (b)
(d) None of the above

950. Caste is a
(a) Social class
(b) Social order
(c) Both (a) and (b)
(d) None of the above

951. The carpenter, the mason, the tanner, the priest were hereditary occupations based on
(a) Place (b) Caste
(c) Society (d) Work

952. In what kind of society do people's ambitions help in upward mobility?
(a) Religious (b) Licentious
(c) Materialistic (d) Idealistic

953. Nationality is a corporate sentiment. Which of the following factors is least significant to form a nation-state?
(a) They should organise themselves on a particular territory
(b) That people should be politically organised
(c) They should be either independent or desire to be independent
(d) They should have one leader

954. Which of the following is not an important characteristic of Indian democracy?
(a) Linguistic or religious minorities can run their own educational institutions in order to protect their culture and language.
(b) Every citizen in India has the right to develop his personality according to his own choice.
(c) Equality of educational opportunities but special safeguard to weaker sections of the society.
(d) None of the above.

955. Which among the following is a nation?

(a) People of Africa
(b) United Nations
(c) People of India
(d) Commonwealth

956. Education affects upward mobility in this manner.
(a) More education leads to higher mobility
(b) Less education leads to higher mobility
(c) Less education leads to higher general mobility
(d) Both (a) and (b)

957. The families who travel for sight-seeing together belong to
(a) Middle class
(b) Upper class
(c) Upper middle class
(d) Lower class

958. Approximately ten to fifteen per cent of the Indian population may be found in
(a) Upper middle class category
(b) Lower middle class category
(c) Upper class category
(d) None of the above

959. To increase social mobility, in education system the following change is expected.
(a) Giving admission to children in schools without discrimination
(b) Give freedom to choose subjects from curriculum according to ability
(c) Both (a) and (b)
(d) None of the above

960. What differentiates state from nation?
(a) Consciousness of political unity
(b) Sovereignty
(c) Government
(d) Territory and people

961. What you love and what you want for yourself, you must desire the same for others also. This is the opinion of
(a) Prophet Mohammad
(b) Justice Venkatchaliah
(c) Both (a) and (b)
(d) None of the above

962. Who among the following writers has/have recognised that the nation is distinctly a historical phenomenon?
(a) Karl Marx (b) Ernest Renan
(c) Hans (d) All of these

963. For social mobility what encouragement should be given to students?
(a) Textbooks should be given to brilliant students
(b) Scholarships should be given to brilliant students
(c) Free of cost education should be given to brilliant students
(d) All of the above

964. Whole of society and its functions were based in Ancient India on
(a) Trade
(b) Profession
(c) Rigid caste system
(d) Rigid religion

965. Which of the following subjects was taught in ancient times?
(a) Mathematics (b) Biology
(c) Physics (d) Chemistry

966. Nation is a
(a) religious group of people.
(b) territorial community.
(c) racial community.
(d) tribal community.

967. The owners of the largest business interests and magnets belong to
(a) Backward class (b) Harijans
(c) Lower class (d) Upper class

968. The purpose of democracy in India is to end

(a) Political inequalities
(b) Social inequalities
(c) Economic inequalities
(d) Both (a) and (b)

969. What constitutes the political sovereign?
(a) The electorate
(b) The people of a country
(c) The majority party in the Parliament
(d) The elected representatives of the people

970. Social science basis of education is important because a students interaction with the following leads to the development.
(a) Socially useful values
(b) International values
(c) Traditional values
(d) Conservative values

971. Snobbery also features in their attitudes and relationships with people outside their classes in
(a) Schedule tribes
(b) Backward class
(c) Upper class
(d) None of the above

972. Hard work and persistence in education are emphasised in
(a) Lower class (b) Upper class
(c) Middle class (d) All of the above

973. Preservation of culture by society is required so that this is maintained.
(a) Conservatism (b) Continuity
(c) Traditionalism (d) All of the above

974. What constitutes the legal sovereign?
(a) The President-in-Parliament
(b) The Speaker of Lok Sabha
(c) The Prime Minister-in-Parliament
(d) The Chairman of the Rajya Sabha

975. Which of the following points has been recommend by Education Commission (1964-66) in order to strengthen national unity and integrity through education?
(a) The development of an appropriate language policy.
(b) Common school system for public education.
(c) Making social and national services obligatory for all students.
(d) All of the above.

976. In modern India social order is based on
(a) Trade (b) Wealth
(c) Profession (d) All of the above

977. The view of Sovereignty is
(a) Historical (b) Pluralistic
(c) Legalistic (d) Sociological

978. The meaning of cultural transformation by education is that the following should continue.
(a) Modernisation
(b) Transportation from generation to generation
(c) Existence till older generations
(d) None of the above

979. The school socializes the child by imparting socially desirable
(a) Skills (b) Knowledge
(c) Experience (d) All of the above

980. Which of the following is an important characteristic of new social order?
(a) Increased role of women in education and employment sectors.
(b) Pressure and vote bank politics.
(c) Privatization of education including higher education.
(d) All of the above.

981. The meaning of remission of culture by education is that in it this should happen.
(a) Renunciation of old values
(b) Timely changes should take place
(c) Incorporation of new values
(d) All of the above

982. Which of the following statements is correct?
(a) The pluralistic conception is correct
(b) All associations are sovereign
(c) The notion of sovereignty cannot be discarded
(d) State is more sovereign than others

983. The percentage of lower classes in India is about
(a) 70% (b) 60%
(c) 40% (d) 50%

984. The children of lower middle classes are frustrated and become rebellious and join factions in schools and colleges due to
(a) Stain of poverty (b) Uncertain future
(c) Unemployment (d) All of the above

985. What is the position of state in sociology?
(a) State is omnipotent
(b) It is the first of the associations
(c) State is supreme
(d) It is one among the many associations

986. The meaning of creation of culture by education is the values of older traditions.
(a) Change in form according to the times
(b) Be renounced for the sake of modernisation
(c) Be substituted by values of Western culture
(d) All of the above

987. Education was transferred from state list of subjects to concurrent list in
(a) 1980 (b) 1979
(c) 1976 (d) 1972

988. The fundamental national values (objectives) has been given in the
(a) Articles of our constitution
(b) Entries of the lists of subjects
(c) Preamble to our Constitution
(d) All of the above

989. Co-ordination between formal and informal agencies of education should be there because they work for the following.
(a) Similar objectives
(b) Various objectives
(c) Opposed objectives
(d) None of the above

990. Which is not a limitation on sovereignty?
(a) The international law
(b) Constitution of the country
(c) Public opinion
(d) Laws of nature

991. Lower classes live in
(a) Slums (b) Huts
(c) Both (a) and (b) (d) None of the above

992. In the present political and social scenario in India positive autonomy is
(a) needed to raise quality of education.
(b) essential for the survival of democracy.
(c) the approach through which terrorism can be sublimated.
(d) All of the above.

993. Which is a correct statement?
(a) All laws are good
(b) Rules of conduct pre-existed the state
(c) Law regulates the conduct of man
(d) Existence of law, necessitated the formation of the state

994. For the mental and intellectual development of a child community provides
(a) reading room.
(b) information centre.
(c) library.
(d) All of the above.

995. Discipline is must to maintain
(a) Social setup
(b) Individual study
(c) Rules and regulations
(d) All of the above

996. Some believe that jati arose out of the organization of society into hereditary guild and
(a) Occupational groups
(b) Teachers
(c) Shudras
(d) Professional groups

997. The basis of democracy is
(a) Freedom (b) Equality
(c) Both (a) and (b) (d) Socialism

998. Which among the following is not an attribute of law in a civilised society?
(a) It must be certain
(b) It is meant for all
(c) Both (a) and (b)
(d) None of these

999. Parents set goal before their children and try to steer them into a proper career through their studies. These are characteristics of
(a) Upper class
(b) Lower class
(c) Lower middle class
(d) Upper middle class

1000. Which among the following is lawful?
(a) To seek settlement by methods other than lawful
(b) To disregard the law which one thinks is inconvenient
(c) To participate in law making
(d) To be law abiding and follow it

1001. For democracy, in the basis of education this is also important.
(a) Individual superiority
(b) Individual diversity
(c) Individual freedom
(d) Religious loyalty

1002. Illegal, arbitrary and unreasonable action of the executive is checked by Supreme Court under
(a) advisory jurisdiction
(b) the saviour and interpreter of the Constitution
(c) power of judicial review
(d) None of the above

1003. In competition the emphasis is on the
(a) Assimilator (b) Competitor
(c) Goal (d) Co-operator

1004. In personal and social objectives of education, this is desired.
(a) Coordination (b) Rivalry
(c) Competition (d) All of the above

1005. Which among the following is not a source of law?
(a) Equity
(b) Scientific commentaries
(c) Legislations
(d) Manners as those are more important than laws

1006. The ancient education is available to
(a) Childrens of priest
(b) Children of noble families
(c) Both (a) and (b)
(d) All castes and people

1007. Functional literacy programme has been started for
(a) illiterate farmers
(b) tribal people
(c) factory workers
(d) All of the above

1008. The law of the constitution may be stretched to meet the growing needs by
(a) the Supreme Court interpreting the law to meet the purpose.
(b) the President, according to his pleasure.
(c) methods other than these.
(d) an amendment to the Constitution.

1009. For the educational objective, 'Preparation for Life', which curriculum has been considered an integral part by the Kothari Educational Commission?

(a) Industry
(b) Work experience
(c) Some occupation
(d) None of the above

1010. Attempting to borrow the idea of equality and to synthesize it with Hinduism, teachers and religious thinkers of medieval India who attacked the caste system vigorously was/were

(a) Kabir (b) Ramanand
(c) Guru Nanak (d) All of the above

1011. When the skills of a particular caste were in short supply in relation to their demand then chances were greater for

(a) Economic betterment
(b) Religional betterment
(c) Social betterment
(d) None of the above

1012. For the educational objective, Preparation for Life, Kothari Educational Commission has given this suggestion for Higher Secondary Education.

(a) Commercialization
(b) Industrialisation
(c) Employmentation
(d) All of the above

1013. Which among the following statements is correct?

(a) Laws may be vindictive
(b) Society depends today more on law than on customs
(c) Laws are the manifestations of the powerful
(d) Custom is at the vanishing point of existence as a social discipline

1014. Social equality cannot be an easy task due to

(a) Attitudes (b) Emotions
(c) Traditions (d) All of the above

1015. Autonomy in the field of education can be dangerous for total education system if

(a) it is not guided by certain necessary laws.
(b) it is absolute as is the case of educational institutions maintained by minorities.
(c) it lacks accountability on the part of the authority.
(d) All of the above.

1016. In absence of Sharda Act, The Hindu Widow Remarriage Act 1956, The Hindu Marriage Act 1955, etc., the society would have remained, back looking, wooden, and inflexible. The changes, those and other social reforms brought about are immense. In view of this, mark out, the incorrect statement from among the following.

(a) It hinders the progress
(b) Men by nature are unprogressive
(c) Law is the instrument of progress; despite the time, it takes to effect the changes
(d) Custom is conservative

1017. For the attainment of national educational objectives, Kothari Educational Commission has suggested to relate secondary education with the following.

(a) Ancient culture
(b) Productivity
(c) Modernization
(d) Both (b) and (c)

1018. Top ranking university officials and executives may be included in

(a) Higher class
(b) Upper class
(c) Both (a) and (b)
(d) None of the above

1019. School teachers, shopkeepers, nurses, clerks, etc. belong to
(a) Lower classes
(b) Upper middle classes
(c) Upper class
(d) Lower middle classes

1020. Social change is the name of amendments in the methods of working and thinking of people.
This definition has been given by
(a) Davis
(b) Sir Jones
(c) Gillen and Gillen
(d) Jenson

1021. Who has defined bureaucracy as "a system of administration characterised by expertness, impartiality and the absence of humanity"?
(a) Lundberg (b) Arnold Green
(c) MacIver (d) Max Weber

1022. Which of the following objectives has not been mentioned in the Preamble of our Constitution
(a) Right to employment
(b) Justice and equality
(c) Liberty
(d) Fraternity

1023. The children remain illiterate in
(a) unemployed lower class families
(b) employed lower class families
(c) Both (a) and (b)
(d) None of the above

1024. Bureaucracy is
(a) administrative machinery dependent on few people.
(b) official class.
(c) a system of administration composed of hierarchy of sections, divisions, bureaus, and departments.
(d) a power wielding organisation.

1025. Brahmins were the majority in the nationalistic movement until
(a) 1930 (b) 1925
(c) 1920 (d) 1915

1026. Indian democracy, socialism and secularism have been explained by
(a) the preamble to the Constitution.
(b) the fundamental rights only.
(c) fundamental rights and other articles of the Constitution.
(d) All of the above.

1027. Cultural change is a significant part of this only.
(a) Social change
(b) Political change
(c) Economic change
(d) Religious change

1028. Which among the following is a feature of bureaucratic appointment?
(a) On the basis of merit
(b) On the basis of kinship
(c) Through elections
(d) On the basis of caste

1029. Which type of educational system is prevailing in India?
(a) Democratic
(b) Autocratic with red tapism
(c) Socialistic
(d) None of the above

1030. The source of income in lower middle classes are
(a) Business
(b) Salary
(c) Other revenue
(d) None of the above

1031. Bureaucracy is a professional calling, not demanding
(a) devotion to rules.
(b) devotion to person.
(c) devotion to job.
(d) devotion to office.

1032. When the changes in abstract culture fall behind changes in physical culture, the following process takes place.
(a) Cultural lag
(b) Physical lag
(c) Cultural intensity
(d) All of the above

1033. Which of the following terms was added to the Preamble of our Constitution in 1976?
(a) Secular (b) Integrity
(c) Socialist (d) All of the above

1034. An anti-brahmin Justice party was formed in the year
(a) 1920 (b) 1925
(c) 1930 (d) 1935

1035. Cultural lag can be removed by the following.
(a) Revolution (b) Preaching
(c) Law (d) Education

1036. Bureaucracy is a major social trend of modern society. This means that
(a) its becoming a dominant aspect of society is a modern phenomenon.
(b) it is modern phenomenon.
(c) its vastness in a modern phenomenon.
(d) it did not exist in pre-modern days.

1037. Government subordinates servants, salesmen and others belong to
(a) Upper classes
(b) Lower classes
(c) Lower middle classes
(d) Upper middle classes

1038. Special provisions have been made for socially and educationally backward classes of the nation under Article
(a) 15 (b) 19
(c) 29 (d) 31

1039. Mark out correct statement about bureaucracy
(a) It is found in both public and private organisations
(b) It is found only in private organisations
(c) It has nothing to do with private or public organisations
(d) It is found only in public organisations

1040. According to Murdock, social change is concluded by the following process.
(a) Social acceptance
(b) Selective elimination
(c) Innovation
(d) All of the above

1041. The Upper classes represent the aristocracy of wealthy families of
(a) Former rulers
(b) Jagirdars
(c) Large landowners
(d) All of the above

1042. The advancement of society is based on differention in their functions of
(a) Society
(b) Organism
(c) Individual
(d) None of the above

1043. When for social change, instead of the old habit, a new habit or work process is accepted, then it is called
(a) Discovery (b) Reform
(c) Innovation (d) Experiment

1044. Where does bureaucracy exist?
(a) It exists only in theocracy
(b) It exists only in democracy
(c) It exists in all the three forms of government
(d) It exists only in autocracy

1045. Religious education is prohibited in government schools and colleges under Article

(a) 39 (2) (b) 15 (a)
(c) 29 (d) 28 (1)

1046. The Upper middle classes are represented by
(a) Top Government officials
(b) Bankers
(c) Businessmen
(d) All of the above

1047. Bureaucracy in modern times is indispensable because
(a) it serves the needs of politicians.
(b) it fulfils the needs of mass administration.
(c) it is powerful.
(d) it has long traditions.

1048. When a new habit or work process is accepted by other members for social change, it is called
(a) Imitation
(b) Emulation
(c) Social pressure
(d) Social acceptance

1049. Four to five per cent of people in India belong to
(a) Upper class (b) Harijans
(c) Backward class (d) Lower class

1050. Their Children go to the most expensive and exclusive schools and colleges, they engage tutors to teach academics, skills, physical and artistic activities. They belong to
(a) Lower classes (b) Schedule tribes
(c) Upper classes (d) All of the above

1051. When a new habit or work process fails in satisfying needs, then for social change this is done.
(a) Selective Elimination
(b) Adoption
(c) Postponement
(d) None of the above

1052. Which factor among the following does not denote the difference between ancient and modern bureaucracies?
(a) Dominant aspect of society
(b) Greater specialisation of functions
(c) Hierarchy of command
(d) Vastness of modern bureaucracy

1053. Religious and linguistic minorities shall have the right to establish and administer their own educational institutions under Article
(a) 40 (b) 41
(c) 30 (1) (d) 31 (2)

1054. The parents have sufficient wealth, power and influence to steer them into a career closely connected with their family's interest in children of
(a) Upper class
(b) Lower class
(c) Middle class
(d) None of the above

1055. Which is a positive aspect of bureaucratic administration?
(a) Mechanical adherence to rules
(b) Indifference towards feelings of individuals
(c) Red tapism
(d) Its being objective oriented

1056. The meaning of integration in the process of social change is
(a) Acceptance of innovation by most of the people in a society.
(b) Abandonment of the innovation by most of the people in a society.
(c) Acceptance of the innovation by most of the people in a society.
(d) Both (b) and (c).

1057. Autonomy given to universities by the UGC is in accordance with
(a) Democratic principles
(b) Idealistic principles

(c) Socialistic principles
(d) None of the above

1058. Guardian of Indian Constitution and protector of fundamental rights of citizens is
(a) Judiciary
(b) Supreme Court only
(c) Parliament
(d) None of the above

1059. According to Ottaway, the cause of social change is the following.
(a) Interaction between a person and society.
(b) Interaction between greatmen and society.
(c) Interaction between scientific and technical interventions and social values
(d) Both (b) and (c)

1060. Jews could not have a state of their own, because
(a) they had no territory of their own.
(b) they had no government.
(c) they were not organised.
(d) they lived in different parts of the world.

1061. Out of 343 universities in India how many of them are Central Universities
(a) 20 (b) 22
(c) 14 (d) 18

1062. In which of following central universities 50% reservation was given to minorities in 2005 but it was later disapproved by Supreme Court?
(a) DU Delhi (b) JMI Delhi
(c) AMU Aligarh (d) BHU Varanasi

1063. Before the British withdrew from country, which among the following India did not possess?
(a) Government (b) Sovereignty
(c) Population (d) Territory

1064. Factors hindering social change are
(a) Cultural Inertia
(b) Vested Interests
(c) Narrow Loyalties
(d) All of the above

1065. The large joint families of earlier days are
(a) extended now
(b) continuing as usual
(c) developed now
(d) disappearing

1066. Due to the "fear of new things", people maintain status quo in their life, therefore this is hindered.
(a) Social intention
(b) Social change
(c) Cultural preservation
(d) None of the above

1067. Which among the following is a State?
(a) Punjab (b) U.N.
(c) Y.M.C.A. (d) India

1068. Hot media is
(a) A lecture (b) A book
(c) A movie (d) All of the above

1069. A significant aspect of society is its
(a) Social composition
(b) Family composition
(c) Religions composition
(d) Individual composition

1070. India became a State in 1947, because
(a) the country was partitioned.
(b) the Congress gained power.
(c) we assumed our sovereignty.
(d) Britishers left the country.

1071. An example of degree of isolation becoming an obstruction in social change is
(a) higher castes stay away from Scheduled Castes consider themselves of higher status.

(b) Scheduled Castes stay separated from higher castes and thus remain backward.
(c) Both (a) and (b).
(d) growth in mutual interaction between backward and higher castes.

1072. Efforts are directed in school towards providing
(a) Moral instruction
(b) Character education
(c) Physical education
(d) Both (a) and (b)

1073. The schools also cater to vocational education for a variety of
(a) Occupations (b) Trades
(c) Professions (d) All of the above

1074. Schools are a part of
(a) Family (b) Society
(c) Nation (d) Village

1075. On the basis of his capability or incapability when a person gets higher or lower position, this process is called.
(a) Social mobility
(b) Change in social prestige
(c) Both (a) and (b)
(d) None of the above

1076. What among the following, you think, the State of India can do?
(a) Stop the functioning of the Red Cross Society in the State of Nepal
(b) Order the people of USA not to contribute donations to the Red Cross
(c) Exercise authority on the Indian origin citizens of the other countries
(d) Stop Arya Samaj from enlisting its member to other countries

1077. In the high school stage boys get free from the influence of their families with regard to their
(a) Opinion
(b) Attitudes
(c) Both (a) and (b)
(d) None of the above

1078. The education of girls in India should receive emphasis because
(a) it accelerates social transformation.
(b) it needs social justice and social transformation.
(c) it is based on social justice.
(d) None of these.

1079. According to the 1991 population census literature in Ajmer district was 35% and in Banner was 12%, this is an example of the following imbalance.
(a) Regional (b) Rural
(c) Urban (d) All of the above

1080. The state is to control and direct all affairs including education in order to shape its citizens into
(a) Every mould
(b) Social mould
(c) Religious mould
(d) Particular mould

1081. A measure for the removal of regional imbalance is
(a) special central aid to less literate areas.
(b) efforts to increase literacy in less literate areas.
(c) for the increase in literacy, make a unit from a district.
(d) All of the above.

1082. "Women are human beings and have as much right to full development as men have". This was stated by
(a) Ravindranath Tagore
(b) Smt. Hansa Mehta
(c) Mahatma Gandhi
(d) Dr. Radhakrishnan

1083. Which is not an implication of the social aims of education?

(a) The individual receives higher education only if it is to the benefit of the society.
(b) The individual has no inherent right to education.
(c) Education is most powerful means of ensuring social progress and prosperity.
(d) The individual is educated as it is he who makes the society.

1084. "There cannot be educated people without educated women". This was indicated by
(a) The University Education Commission (1948-49)
(b) The Resolution on the National Policy on Education (1968)
(c) New Policy on Education (1986)
(d) The United Nations Declaration on the Elimination of Discrimination against Women (1967)

1085. To provide equal opportunities to the handicapped, the following measures can be taken
(a) special efforts in general educational techniques.
(b) they should be given separate education in special schools.
(c) Both (a) and (b).
(d) None of the above.

1086. Knowledge of and constructive attitudes towards our cultural and social heritage is/are
(a) Values (b) Attitudes
(c) Norms (d) All of the above

1087. The first important step in teaching is
(a) planning before hand.
(b) knowing the background of students.
(c) organizing material to be taught.
(d) None of the above.

1088. The children from the following categories come under the handicapped
(a) Dilinguents
(b) The poor
(c) Mentally retarded
(d) Blind and deaf and dumb

1089. The National Policy on Education (1986) recommendation that "In order to neutralize the accumulated distortions of the past, education will be used as an agent of basic change in the status of woman", implies Indian democracy's faith in
(a) equalization of educational opportunities for all.
(b) treating each individual always as an end.
(c) individuals' capacities, aptitudes, interests and intrinsic worth as against the discrimination on the basis of sex.
(d) All of these.

1090. Social classes has/have
(a) Functional characteristics
(b) Status systems
(c) Structural characteristics
(d) All of the above

1091. The movement from one social class to another is known as
(a) Social mobility
(b) Migration
(c) National movement
(d) Immigration

1092. While saying that education contributes to national cohesion furthering the goals of socialism, secularism and democracy enshrined in our Constitution, the National Policy on Education (1968) assumes that
(a) socialism is the best way of organizing Indian society.
(b) democracy is the best form of government.

(c) secularism is the most cherished goal of democracy.
(d) education can be used as an instrument of social change.

1093. In the year 1977-78, Indian Government had started the following educational plan for the handicapped.
(a) Samanvit Shiksha Yojna
(b) Ashram Vidhyalaya Yojna
(c) Lok Jumbish
(d) Shiksha Karmi

1094. The most appropriate meaning of learning is
(a) personal adjustment
(b) acquisition of skills
(c) modification of behaviour
(d) inculcation of knowledge

1095. "Educational programmes" are those that give pupils wholesome participating roles in
(a) Society
(b) Citizenship
(c) Both (a) and (b)
(d) None of the above

1096. Under the Integrated Educational Programme for the Handicapped, the following facilities are being given to the handicapped.
(a) For each handicapped ` 25 per month as vehicle allowance
(b) For writing material a sum of ` 250
(c) For hostel facility ` 250 per month
(d) Both (a) and (b)

1097. Education is a system in the sense that
(a) it acts upon these pupils and turns them out as outputs in the finished form.
(b) it is a complex of elements in mutual interaction.
(c) it has all the above characteristics.
(d) it receives pupils as inputs.

1098. Primary responsibility for the teacher's adjustment lies with
(a) the teacher's parents
(b) the children
(c) the principal
(d) the teacher himself

1099. The family provides individuals with group interaction of
(a) many kinds (b) some kinds
(c) different kinds (d) All of the above

1100. Education as the sub-system of the larger Indian society, can contribute to strengthening of democracy through
(a) a dedicated and competent leadership.
(b) cultivation of essential values.
(c) educated electorate.
(d) All of these.

1101. In Britain, which educational committee for the handicapped said in 1978 that a change in the attitude of people towards the handicapped should arise?
(a) Dr. Jakir Hussian Committee
(b) Simon Committee
(c) Warnock Committee
(d) Kher Committee

1102. According to sociological thinking education is equivalent to the development of
(a) Character
(b) Personality
(c) Both (a) and (b)
(d) All of the above

1103. A new teacher to start with, will have to
(a) tell the students about his qualifications.
(b) cut jokes with the students.
(c) establish rapport with the students.
(d) enforce discipline in the class.

1104. In the preservation of culture a child's help is received most by

(a) Community (b) School
(c) Family (d) State

1105. Expansion of educational facilities in India after independence as a result of the "explosion of expectations" of the masses demanding education, equality, higher standard of living and better civic amenities is an example of
(a) importance in the political and national life of a country its system of education.
(b) the psychology of people influences the course of social progress.
(c) the social change affects the system of education of a country.
(d) the schools and colleges change the life and values of the people.

1106. Which aims of education are emphasized in this statement, "The interests of the state are enhanced by the development of virtue and wisdom in the individuals, and individuals find their best chance of self-development in the service of the state."
(a) Individual aims
(b) Social aims
(c) More social aims, less individual aims
(d) A synthesis between social and individual aims

1107. What role education should play in achieving the objective that every citizen contributes his best to defence of freedom?
(a) Helping in the development of bold and competent political leadership
(b) Helping the country to achieve self-sufficiency in food
(c) Helping in achieving economic growth and full employment
(d) Developing in the citizens a strong sentiment and identification with country's freedom through the process of education

1108. "'Mothers are the ideal teachers, and the informal education given by the home is most effective and natural." This is a statement made by
(a) Montissory (b) Froebel
(c) Pestalozzi (d) Ross

1109. Teacher's professionalism may be assessed in terms of all of the following commitments except
(a) commitment to the profession and students.
(b) commitment to the religion and castes.
(c) commitment to the parents and community.
(d) commitment to the colleagues and employer.

1110. The group in which most members are of equal age and of similar social status are called
(a) Reference group
(b) Social group
(c) Peer group
(d) All of the above

1111. From a psychological point of view adaptation and adjustment could be distinguished as
(a) adaptation is limited to younger ones whereas adjustment is applicable to grown up individuals.
(b) psychologists use the term adaptation for personal requirements and adjustment for non-personal.
(c) adaptation is appropriate as a term for non-human beings, whereas adjustment is possible for human beings.
(d) adaptation is restricted to the physical aspect of the environment while adjustment is meant of the social relations.

1112. In the physical education of children, a community is helpful through the following equipments.
(a) Movie theatres
(b) Gymnasiums
(c) Sport fields
(d) Both (b) and (c)

1113. Education contributes to the efforts made by a traditional society on its economic development by
(a) establishing agricultural universities in the country.
(b) bringing about "human change on a grand scale" leading to a pervasive social transformation consisting of change in values, habits and existing life of the people.
(c) strengthening its programmes of science and technology.
(d) teaching the subject of "Economic Growth and Development" in the universities.

1114. Which of the following interpersonal relationships in the school is/are necessary?
(a) Headmaster and staff
(b) Staff and students
(c) Among the staff
(d) All types are necessary.

1115. As long as a human being is a social animal living in society and developing through contacts there will be some subordination of individuality to
(a) Social needs (b) Politics
(c) Criminals (d) Religion

1116. Being a multi-religious country, India needs to
(a) provide instruction in religious dogmas in the school of the country.
(b) define the attitude of the state to religion, religious education and the concept of secularism.
(c) utilize different religions and faiths as instruments of propagation of values and morals.
(d) allow freedom to all schools to adopt their own policy in this matter.

1117. In the mental development of a child, community is helpful through
(a) business and industry.
(b) panchayats and municipalities.
(c) library and auditorium.
(d) religious function.

1118. A sentiment could be correctly defined as
(a) a link between the likes and dislikes of an individual.
(b) a strong desire for an action with an inner motive.
(c) a sum total of a person's feelings and emotions about some object.
(d) a week point in individual's emotional life.

1119. Status implies
(a) Social position
(b) Higher or lower relationship
(c) Ranking
(d) All of the above

1120. In India, inequality in educational opportunity is seen in the following fields.
(a) Uneven distribution of educational institutions
(b) Diversity at district level
(c) Both (a) and (b)
(d) Illiteracy at the national level

1121. Adoption of a secularist policy in the field of education means
(a) all religious sects should have some freedom to run their own schools.
(b) that all people, irrespective of their religious faith, will enjoy equality of rights in political, economic and social matters.

(c) that the government adopt a policy of no intervention in matters of any faith.
(d) that religious minorities should be given certain privileges in regard to certain matters.

1122. One learns and is taught through
(a) Social interaction
(b) Technology
(c) Communication
(d) None of the above

1123. On which of the following statements there is consensus among educators?
(a) Disciplinary cases should be totally neglected in the class.
(b) Disciplinary cases should never be sent to the principal's office.
(c) Disciplinary cases should be sent to the principal only when other means have failed.
(d) None of the above.

1124. The Indian education should ensure primarily with reference to religion
(a) sufficient financial support to religious schools.
(b) development of national religion in some form, like the national language.
(c) effective administration of religious schools.
(d) promotion of religious tolerance and an active reverence for all religions.

1125. From the following it is clear that education is an investment.
(a) Increase in national income
(b) Development in the field of knowledge and science
(c) Increase in the working skill of people
(d) All of the above

1126. The best educational programme is one which is tailored according to the
(a) need of the child
(b) interest of child
(c) ability of the child
(d) all these along with the need of the society

1127. Which of the following statements would be correct about the spread of educational values, from a practical point of view?
(a) Educational values are lower and less wide spread in an agrarian than in an industrial society.
(b) Educational values are higher and more widespread in an agrarian than in an industrial society.
(c) Educational values have no place in both agrarian and industrial societies.
(d) Educational values have equal place in both agrarian and industrial societies.

1128. In the version of National Educational Policy, 1986, this part exists.
(a) Education for equality
(b) Making educational systems successful
(c) Commercialisation of education
(d) Both (a) and (b)

1129. One possible way of arresting the growing of inequality of educational opportunities is to
(a) motivate the people to educate their children.
(b) have widest dispersal of educational institutions throughout the country.
(c) force the communities to open their own institution.
(d) make reservation of seats in all institutions for the talented students.

1130. The search for aims in the process of education has deeply concerned the
(a) politicians (b) educators
(c) sociologists (d) All of the above

1131. The refusal to admit the existence of illusion is known as

(a) Asatkhyativada
(b) Atmakhyativada
(c) Anyathakhyativada
(d) Akhyativada

1132. Besides abolishing fees progressively, it is desirable to provide free books, stationery and even school meals in Indian schools because
(a) it may reduce the level of inequality of educational opportunities due to poverty of the people.
(b) India is a socialistic democracy.
(c) no other country charges fees and many have introduced the system of free books and free school meals.
(d) many people in India want the government to do this.

1133. In the third part of National Education Policy, 1986, the following basic principle has been mentioned.
(a) There should be compulsory occupational training in education
(b) Education should improve the present and construct an attractive future
(c) There should be similarity in education in the whole country
(d) All of the above

1134. The school should maintain a log book to register the
(a) pupil's case studies.
(b) records of special events and circumstances.
(c) income and expenditure.
(d) inspection and supervision reports.

1135. For better education system in rural areas, under National Education Policy, 1986, it has been resolved to open the following schools at district level.
(a) Navodaya Schools
(b) Ashram Schools
(c) Central Schools
(d) Military Schools

1136. When an American takes his meals seated at a table and uses a knife, fork and spoon to eat, he follows the USA cultural
(a) Peculiarities (b) Universals
(c) Alternatives (d) Specialities

1137. To educate "according to nature" means
(a) education according to the natural laws of human development.
(b) to study natural laws and apply them to the educational process.
(c) to return to the natural as opposed to the artificial in life.
(d) None of the above.

1138. Conflict in value makes for social
(a) maladjustment
(b) good adjustment
(c) beneficial adjustment
(d) can't say anything

1139. Which of the following is not a characteristic of culture?
(a) It is transmitted from generation
(b) It is changeable
(c) It is biologically inherited
(d) It is abstract

1140. Teacher should himself
(a) Be taller
(b) Be an example before students
(c) Be talkative
(d) All of the above

1141. Which of these is not the social aim of education?
(a) Social efficiency
(b) Social service
(c) Citizenship
(d) The perfection of the individual.

1142. The aim of 'Operation Black Board' is to strengthen the following side of primary education.
(a) Teaching aids (b) Quality
(c) Quantity (d) All of the above

1143. Within every society it is universally accepted that people shall work for a living but whether to follow a career in this occupation or that occupation, is left up to the individual. This exemplifies cultural
(a) Specialities (b) Peculiarities
(c) Universals (d) Alternatives

1144. A teacher in the class is
(a) the president of the group
(b) a leader and guide of the group
(c) a director of the group
(d) All of the above

1145. The supporters of the social aim do not believe that an individual can live and develop in
(a) cultural value of society
(b) isolation from society
(c) Both (a) and (b)
(d) None of the above

1146. Implicit culture may be defined as
(a) the model cognitions, wants, interpersonal response traits and attitudes existing in a society.
(b) the sum total of collective behaviour.
(c) typical habit patterns of people.
(d) the uncodified ideology of a people.

1147. For higher education, the following provision has been laid in the National Education Policy, 1986.
(a) Provision of open schools
(b) Separation of degree from service
(c) Providing autonomy to selective colleges
(d) All of the above

1148. In school, effective interpersonal relationship is
(a) not good for healthy developments
(b) necessary
(c) not necessary
(d) None of the above

1149. An effective teacher adopts the norms of the
(a) autocratic society
(b) laissez faire society
(c) democratic society
(d) All of the above according to the situation

1150. For the education of children in sparsely populated tribal or mountainous, or desert areas, there is a provision of the following schools.
(a) Central Schools
(b) Military Schools
(c) Navodaya Schools
(d) Ashram Schools
(d) pattern of arrangements, material and behavioural, adopted by a society.

1151. If there is conflict in any social institution its
(a) function has to recognized
(b) structure has to recognized
(c) Both (a) and (b)
(d) None of the above

1152. Kibbutz in Israel and the communes in communistic countries are substitute for the
(a) cultural revolution
(b) traditional family
(c) social organisation
(d) modern family

1153. A culture area is a
(a) geographical area characterised by distinguishing cultural traits.
(b) segment of a particular society's culture, e.g., Hopi technology.
(c) geographical area characterised by a high level of cultural development.
(d) segment of culture which cuts across particular societies, e.g. technology, generally.

1154. For the education and care of very small children of the country, the following institutes have been set up.
(a) Anganbari
(b) Nursery schools
(c) Montessary schools
(d) All of the above

1155. The cultural revolution in China in the 1960s was directed towards the achievement of
(a) Prosperity (b) Progress
(c) Plenty (d) All of the above

1156. Culture is considered to have an optional from also beside the universal and special forms. Therefore, the cultural progress of a society is depicted by
(a) a combination of the universal and the special forms.
(b) the universal form only.
(c) the optional form only.
(d) the special form only.

1157. Through the process of socialisation, children learn social manners and customs and they make them a part of their personality.
The above statement is of the following educationalist.
(a) Ross, J.S.
(b) Durkheim
(c) Havigharst and Newgarten
(d) Bogardus

1158. The main function of education of child is
(a) teaching of 3Rs.
(b) transmission of cultural heritage.
(c) teaching of means of livelihood.
(d) teaching 3Hs.

1159. One of the basic reasons for the existence of classes is that people require
(a) some kinds of services
(b) many kinds of services
(c) different skills
(d) Both (a) and (c)

1160. The basic purpose of school administration is
(a) to organise and operate the school for instructional conveniences.
(b) to provide the required equipment for the school.
(c) to advise and stimulate teachers in their functioning.
(d) to improve instructional programme.

1161. Which of the following may be taught as the most important part of culture?
(a) Mores (b) Customs
(c) Values (d) Norms

1162. The following type of social control is mentionable.
(a) Customs
(b) Reward and punishment
(c) Social education
(d) Both (a) and (b)

1163. When there is conflict in the mind of an individual, he may have to change his
(a) Class system
(b) Whole value system
(c) Functional system
(d) Cultural system

1164. In order to develop rapport with your pupils you should
(a) guide them
(b) have communicative ability
(c) behave with them in a democratic way
(d) All of the above

1165. Social control is that process by which social order is set up and maintained.
This statement is of the following socialist.
(a) Bogardus (b) Bandis
(c) Ross (d) Smith

1166. In the 1960s, the cultural revolution took place in
(a) Iran (b) India
(c) China (d) Russia

1167. The most important factor for education is
(a) Psychological (b) Religional
(c) Cultural (d) Sociological

1168. An example of horizontal social mobility is
(a) when a person reaches a lower rank.
(b) when a person rises in his rank.
(c) when a person works on the post similar to his previous rank.
(d) None of the above.

1169. Use of telecast materials
(a) increases retention power
(b) reduces the burden of the teacher
(c) enhances concentration and learning
(d) All of the above

1170. The term 'Functional Literacy' regarding the education of adult means that
(a) it should provide him access to written communication without much difficulty.
(b) the literacy of the adult should enable him for thoughtful reading in his social and professional life.
(c) the adults should be able to function as members of the adult franchise scheme.
(d) None of the above.

1171. TV is superior to radio as teaching aid because it
(a) is generally liked by pupils.
(b) is costly.
(c) invites two senses—hearing and vision simultaneously—leading to more accurate form of learning.
(d) All of the above.

1172. Which of the following shall be considered a non-cultural activity?
(a) Singing among the friends
(b) Singing in musical concert
(c) Singing among the family members
(d) Singing while passing through a lane

1173. The following are the dimensions of social mobility.
(a) Consumption Ranking
(b) Occupational Ranking
(c) Social Class
(d) All of the above

1174. Educationally speaking, the concept of democracy is based on
(a) the faith in the dignity and worth of every single individual as a human being.
(b) confidence in the worthfulness of education.
(c) helping the needy in the interest of the expectations of the better placed sections.
(d) the hope of being able to promote the talented characteristics of human beings.

1175. Social classes have existed in
(a) some countries (b) all societies
(c) some societies (d) All of the above

1176. A cause of social mobility is
(a) Interchange of ranks
(b) Motivation
(c) Both (a) and (b)
(d) None of the above

1177. What is culture?
(a) Whims of the conservative in the group
(b) Repetition of the most repeated
(c) Initiating an individual in the group ways
(d) A limitation on freedom

1178. One will be an effective communicator if he
(a) is very clear about what he wants to communicate.
(b) is a humorous speaker.
(c) communicates in his mother tongue.
(d) has histrionic talents.

1179. Communication may be defined as the transmission of meaning through the use of
(a) Digits (b) Figures
(c) Symbols (d) All of the above

1180. The chief vehicle of culture is language. It enables one
(a) to acquire and to transmit ideas and experiences.
(b) to learn.
(c) to study.
(d) to read.

1181. The following is the factor of 'effects of Automation'.
(a) Social inertia (b) Social mobility
(c) Social control (d) All of the above

1182. A sentiment could be correctly defined as
(a) a link between the likes and dislikes of an individual.
(b) a sum total of a person's feeling and emotions about some object.
(c) a weak point in individual's emotional life.
(d) a strong desire for an action with an inner motive.

1183. Which of the following is not a part of culture?
(a) Religious tolerance
(b) Our spirituality
(c) Rail Roads
(d) Observance of *Sanskaras*

1184. Which of the following does not represent the educational sociologists' point of view?
(a) The method of teaching must alter one's behaviour outside the school rather than merely develop skills.
(b) The method of teaching must be effective in aiding the pupil in his adjustment to social situations.
(c) The method of teaching must stress critical evaluation in reading rather than mere comprehension.
(d) The method of teaching must place primary emphasis upon social behaviour inside, not outside, the classroom.

1185. Which of the following is not a part of civilisation?
(a) Atomic energy
(b) The commercial banks
(c) Poetry and music
(d) The electrical devices

1186. The following are the difficulties considering education an investment.
(a) It is an illusion to assume positive relations between education and economic development
(b) It is not a means in itself
(c) It is a long term investment
(d) All of the above

1187. It is said that conflicts between persons of nations arise when feelings of despondency get strong. It is because
(a) they desire to achieve more than their means.
(b) their self appears to have been hurt by their opponents.
(c) their insight into the resources of other is defective.
(d) they lack in estimation of their own selves.

1188. Which of the following is not a successful communicator?
(a) One who knows a lot but is somewhat reserved in his attitude.
(b) One who is able to adapt himself according to the language of the person to with when he wants to communicate.
(c) One who sometimes becomes informal before the receiver and develops rapport.
(d) One who presents material in a precise and clear way.

1189. A democratic society is one which
(a) believes in equal educational opportunity.
(b) follows the principles of equality, freedom, fraternity and justice.
(c) respects the enlightened individuals.
(d) All of the above.

1190. It is said that education requires a period of social infancy. The implication is that
(a) there should be special attention towards societies in a state of infancy to their education.
(b) the society should realise its limitations in being able to educate the young.
(c) every effort should be made to enhance the educational standards of the infants of the society.
(d) the young should be released from the need of self supporting efforts.

1191. Family helps in shaping the child's basic
(a) Character
(b) Personality
(c) Structure of culture
(d) All of the above

1192. For equal educational opportunity, Kothari Education Committee has stressed on the planning of the following schools.
(a) Neighbourhood (b) Novodaya
(c) Central (d) Rajiv Gandhi

1193. In the growth of our society, which of the following were first taught formally on a level above the elementary schools?
(a) Social work and teaching
(b) Vocational and industrial training
(c) Liberal arts and sciences
(d) Business and commercial subjects

1194. The only institution which is an essential agency for child rearing, socialization and for introducing the child to the culture of its society is
(a) School (b) College
(c) Family (d) All of the above

1195. Mark out the cultural trait.
(a) Joint family system
(b) Touching the feet of an elderly person
(c) Performing the death ceremonies of the deceased
(d) Vaishnavism

1196. For productivity and national unity, National Education Policy (1986) has desired to join education with
(a) Vocation
(b) Learn and earn
(c) Work experience
(d) All of the above

1197. One may change his class position through
(a) Leadership (b) Monopoly
(c) Marriage (d) Illegal means

1198. The family is an important...but active agency of education
(a) Formal (b) Social
(c) Informal (d) Regional

1199. In early twentieth century, the radical leadership brought politics to our people because
(a) they drew upon the cultural heritage.
(b) they were radical.s

(c) they belonged to different parts of the country.

(d) they were popular leaders.

1200. The school is also a basis for reconstruction of society through

(a) Research (b) Study

(c) Both (a) and (b) (d) Religion

1201. Child at the primary school is strongly

(a) Self oriented

(b) Peer oriented

(c) Family oriented

(d) None of the above

1202. In the field of secondary education as a form of pacesetter schools, National Education Policy has decided to set up the following schools.

(a) Navodaya (b) Military

(c) Cocational (d) Central

1203. Which of the following methods of communication is the most effective?

(a) Multi-media method

(b) Presenting written material alongwith film projector

(c) Presenting written material

(d) Cannot be determined.

1204. What is the minimum population for which it is compulsory to open one primary school in all tribal, mountainous and desert areas under the National Education Policy?

(a) 200 (b) 800

(c) 300 (d) 600

1205. In the era of religious nationalism, there developed deep understanding between the leadership and the people due to

(a) their drawing upon the heritage and culture brought them closer to people.

(b) the use of English language made the leaders popular.

(c) their successful attempt in explaining the Western political thought to the people, gained the popularity for them.

(d) their high educational attainment and distinguished family background made them popular.

1206. Education for specialisation could be achieved through

(a) promoting the course included in the social studies.

(b) teaching schools maintained by social societies.

(c) continuous contacts with society and its members.

(d) teaching of social sciences in schools.

1207. There will be better communication in a lecture if a teacher

(a) talks extempore drawing examples from other disciplines.

(b) talks extempore without drawing examples from other disciplines.

(c) prepares the notes well in advance and uses them as a guide.

(d) reads from prepared notes.

1208. Even though brought up in the Western style of life, some of our leaders such as Sri Aurobindo and Sri Nehru were successful in establishing an excellent rapport with the people because

(a) they acquired popularity due to their intellectual transformation and for drawing on their heritage and culture.

(b) people liked their Western dress and were impressed by their oratorial gestures.

(c) they gave to the people a picture of British progress and greatness.

(d) they made people conscious of their poor standard of living.

1209. A family is an example of

(a) Secondary group

(b) In-group

(c) Out-group
(d) Primary group

1210. The home retains its influence much more in
(a) Communist society
(b) Indian society
(c) Western society
(d) None of the above

1211. What is the real strength of Indian culture?
(a) Having been patronised by the Indian National Congress
(b) Being original in character
(c) Its capacity to adjust to the changing conditions
(d) Being the product of Western impact

1212. The professionally acceptable definition of a backward child would be
(a) one who falls backward in achievement due to absenteeism.
(b) one who fails to follow the class room instructions.
(c) one who is not able to do the work two years below his class.
(d) one who cannot do the work of one class below his class.

1213. The beliefs of Francis Bacon included
(a) a refusal to discuss theology.
(b) the rejection of the hypothesis.
(c) consideration of "negative instances".
(d) the claim that Aristotle committed an error.

1214. In which article of the constitution it is mentioned that "any kind of religious education cannot be given in such schools which are completely aided by the government".
(a) Article 21 (b) Article 20
(c) Article 19 (d) Article 18

1215. When two or more people interact
(a) it is called Social Interaction.
(b) they influence each other's behaviour.
(c) they stimulate each other's behaviour.
(d) All of the above.

1216. Man has superiority over lower animals because of his
(a) Speech
(b) Learning ability
(c) Both (a) and (b)
(d) None of the above

1217. Culture change is
(a) restricted to primitive societies.
(b) an illusion.
(c) a universal phenomena.
(d) restricted to developed societies.

1218. Dominance could be discriminated from leadership in the following aspects:
(a) Dominance implies fear whereas leadership implies acquaintance among the followers.
(b) Leadership can be in different forms but dominance is uniform in nature.
(c) Leadership is generated by the weakness of a group whereas dominance speaks of the strength of the group.
(d) Dominance denotes willing acceptance whereas leadership is a matter of appeal for compliance.

1219. Characteristics of all informal and formal communication are
(a) same (b) structured
(c) different (d) unstructured

1220. The main distinction between aims and outcomes of education is that
(a) aims are a matter of impulse while the outcomes are a matter of determination.
(b) aims are a matter of hindsight whereas outcomes are a matter of foresight.

(c) aims are guided by outcomes whereas the outcomes are guided by experiences.
(d) aims are a matter of foresight while the outcomes are a matter of hindsight.

1221. In the Constitution, education has been accepted in this list.
(a) Concurrent list (b) Central list
(c) State list (d) All of the above

1222. Reconstruction and adaptation are necessary for urban as well as rural pattern of living because of
(a) Technological advancement
(b) Industrialization
(c) Scientific development
(d) All of the above

1223. Schools cannot be understood without the understanding of
(a) The family (b) The nation
(c) The religion (d) The society

1224. Nationalism in education has the aim of
(a) making education internationalists.
(b) enforcing obedience in the individuals.
(c) supporting the democratic educational objectives.
(d) development of individuality.

1225. We usually welcome a liberal outlook from the members of any society. This comprises
(a) believing others even if we do not understand them.
(b) accepting statements from people whom we know.
(c) not hesitating to accept a correct fact.
(d) not posing problems and objections to what others say or believe.

1226. In the Constitution, what has been given priority over fundamental rights?
(a) Fundamental duties
(b) Justice
(c) Education
(d) Constitution

1227. A teacher will become an effective communicator if
(a) he helps students get meaning out of what he teaches.
(b) he asks questions in between teaching.
(c) he uses instructional aids.
(d) he helps students get correct answers to the questions on the topic.

1228. Communication will be effective
(a) if it reaches the receiver completely.
(b) if it is delivered in a calm situation.
(c) if it reaches the receiver as intended by the sender.
(d) if it is delivered slowly and clearly.

1229. Both in the east and in the west, attempts are made to develop character and moral qualities in the school through
(a) practical situations
(b) pupil government
(c) Both (a) and (b)
(d) religious book

1230. In which of the following respects, a group and crowd differ from each other?
(a) Organisation (b) Intimacy
(c) Size (d) Suggestibility

1231. In the 42nd Constitutional Amendment the following was added.
(a) Socialist
(b) Secular
(c) Fundamental Rights
(d) Both (a) and (b)

1232. There is a call from some thinkers that there is great necessity to socialise school education. This could be correctly interpreted as
(a) formation of a common neighbourhood of schools to raise their academic standards.

(b) greater stress on social services to be rendered by the schools.
(c) the implementation of greater coordination between the schools and the society.
(d) establishment of more community schools by private venture.

1233. The traditional school is usually associated with the
(a) recitation of lessons
(b) great books theory
(c) integration of subjects
(d) activities program

1234. In the Constitution, the elements of state's directive policy are related to this.
(a) Helping the aged sick people
(b) Helping the unemployed
(c) Social security
(d) All of the above

1235. The group which is first in influencing on individual and in shaping his attitudes and behaviour patterns is the
(a) village (b) country
(c) society (d) family

1236. The medieval university was dominated by
(a) scholasticism (b) social realism
(c) nominalism (d) verbal realism

1237. During the days of informal education children used to get
(a) professional education through non-professional people.
(b) some kinds of education first through the process of living.
(c) education only at an advanced age through schools.
(d) education without any specific purpose.

1238. First of all, a child comes in contact with
(a) political environment
(b) family environment
(c) street environment
(d) school environment

1239. The superiority of man over animals is due to
(a) thinking capability
(b) exchange of ideas
(c) system of expression
(d) All of the above

1240. The right to vote is not given to those citizens of 18 years of age who are
(a) abnormal.
(b) accused of a grave crime.
(c) Both (a) and (b).
(d) None of the above.

1241. Without a knowledge of aims the educator is like a sailor
(a) with rudderless vessels
(b) who knows his destination
(c) who doesn't know his destination
(d) None of the above

1242. The following is social justice.
(a) Freedom
(b) Rights
(c) Equality to all in a society
(d) All of the above

1243. Modern Indian education at the Elementary school level can best be described as being
(a) Pupil-centered
(b) Project-centered
(c) Subject-centered
(d) Curriculum-centered

1244. For the attainment of the ideals of the Indian Constitution, people have been given
(a) judicial system.
(b) fundamental duties.
(c) fundamental rights.
(d) None of the above.

1245. The secular moral education is characterized by
(a) school, class and social motivations.
(b) social, humanistic and divine aspects of behaviour.
(c) pragmatic and theological considerations.
(d) humanistic and technological norms of behaviour.

1246. Sciences are taught in schools with the goals of
(a) providing the latest technological and logical process.
(b) preparing children to be creative.
(c) equipping schools with better laboratories and workshops.
(d) compensating for the conservative views of arts.

1247. In the following article of the constitution equality to opportunity has been mentioned.
(a) Article 17 (b) Article 15
(c) Article 16 (d) Article 14

1248. Subjects that are called sciences are all
(a) Hypothetical in nature
(b) Theoretical in nature
(c) Empirical in nature
(d) None of the above

1249. In this article of the constitution there is provision for the opposition to untouchability.
(a) Article 19 (b) Article 18
(c) Article 17 (d) Article 16

1250. Today, most educationists are substituting the term basic education by the concept of
(a) Community Education
(b) Evaluation
(c) Work Experience
(d) Learning Experience

1251. In the preface to the Indian Constitution on what stress has been laid?
(a) Freedom (b) Justice
(c) Equality (d) All of the above

1252. The term "wastage" in education indicates
(a) expulsion of teachers in schools at the Primary stage.
(b) expenditure on buildings for schools without encouraging children.
(c) wasting lot of money on note books and paper by children.
(d) dropping of children from school before the completion of the school course.

1253. Which process of communication is the best for controlling noise in a classroom?
(a) Remaining calm and just looking at students
(b) Raising one's voice above students voice
(c) Continue teaching without caring for noisy class
(d) Saying 'don't talk'.

1254. A means of informal socialisation is
(a) community.
(b) means of communication.
(c) state.
(d) All of the above.

1255. Which of the following steps would you consider first as an effective communicator?
(a) Identify various media for communication
(b) Plan the evaluation procedure
(c) Select the channels of communication
(d) Specify the objectives of communication.

1256. The process of socialisation goes on
(a) Always (b) Constantly
(c) Throughout life (d) All of the above

1257. Social development among children requires that
- (a) parents should give full freedom to children in their activities.
- (b) the classes of children should be enlarged for wider movement.
- (c) children's relations with other children and adults should be encouraged.
- (d) children should be prepared to move among right members of the society.

1258. Absenteeism in the class can be minimized by
- (a) teaching the class effectively and regularly.
- (b) ignoring the fact of absenteeism.
- (c) telling students that it is bad to be absent in the class.
- (d) punishing the students.

1259. In the backward classes, people seeking equal educational opportunities are
- (a) Scheduled Tribes
- (b) Women
- (c) Scheduled Castes
- (d) All of the above

1260. Which one of the following is not an attribute of culture?
- (a) Learnt (b) Transmittable
- (c) Shared (d) Innate

1261. Equalisation of educational opportunities means
- (a) providing the same kind of schools for all.
- (b) providing education suited to the natural abilities for all.
- (c) providing equal type of education for all.
- (d) planning similar curriculum and methods for all.

1262. National Literacy Mission was set up in the following year.
- (a) 1985 (b) 1980
- (c) 1988 (d) 1992

1263. A dogma is different from a theory in respect of
- (a) Acceptability
- (b) Conviction
- (c) Experimental verification
- (d) Assumptions

1264. Discussion in the class will be more effective if the topic of discussion is
- (a) written on the Board without introducing it.
- (b) informed to the students well in advance.
- (c) stated before the start of the discussion.
- (d) None of the above.

1265. The general criticism against education now-a-days is that
- (a) there is increase in the number of students with sub-standards attainments.
- (b) there is increase in the number of schools but decrease in the number of teachers.
- (c) the percentages of pass in public examinations are falling.
- (d) the number of students taking to formal education is falling.

1266. The term that describes the social heritage of people
- (a) Social norm
- (b) Culture
- (c) Human involvement
- (d) Transmission

1267. This is not a cause of the problem of stagnation in education.
- (a) Ineffective educational techniques
- (b) Students irregularity
- (c) Faulty educational technique
- (d) Proper availability of educational equipments

1268. Which one of the following characteristics could be regarded as the outstanding aspect of a scientific culture?
(a) Actualisation (b) Generalisation
(c) Quantification (d) Qualification

1269. In India, education means
(a) learning and understanding the importance of customs.
(b) the assimilation of tradition in language.
(c) respectful behaviour towards elders and teachers.
(d) All of the above.

1270. In which of the following respects is a theory 'not' different from a belief?
(a) Acceptability
(b) Antecedent consequent relationships
(c) Demonstrability
(d) Verifiability

1271. It is usually claimed that any subject that is taught in school has a disciplinary value. This means that
(a) it requires special and disciplined methods of teaching.
(b) it requires strict discipline among students to learn it.
(c) it teaches certain habits and qualities to train the minds of students.
(d) every subject is the outcome of the disciplined thinking and experience of experts.

1272. A measure for removing the problem of
(a) till the primary level syllabus is over, students school be detained in school.
(b) school should be close to the house.
(c) universal registration.
(d) All of the above.

1273. It is often complained that there is brain drain in our country. It implies that
(a) education that is imparted is a string to the brains average students.
(b) educated and capable people are seeking jobs in other countries because of unemployment here.
(c) students brains are unnecessarily burdened with education.
(d) the brains of educated persons are being utilised in unnecessary pursuits.

1274. A good communicator needs to be good at
(a) the use of language
(b) listening
(c) speaking
(d) All of the above

1275. Adult education's main objective is to
(a) help adults achieve literacy along with personal development.
(b) teach adults to be able to understand what they read.
(c) socialise the adults to move about freely.
(d) enable the adults to read and write.

1276. Vocationalisation of education has the object of
(a) converting liberal education into vocational education.
(b) preparing students for a vocation along with knowledge.
(c) creating an vocational bias among educational people.
(d) giving more importance to vocation than general education.

1277. The abbreviation SUPW means
(a) Socially Useful Productive Work
(b) Social Upsurge for Progress and Work
(c) Solution of Utilitarian Problems of Work
(d) Scientific Utilisation for People and World

1278. Drop outs are more likely to be
(a) engaged in antisocial behaviour.
(b) vulnerable to the requirement of public assistance.

(c) unemployed.
(d) All of the above.

1279. Concerning the application of education to the problem of intergroup relations in America, it can be said truthfully that
(a) there is evidence that the education of the Negroes will increase rather than solve conflict.
(b) the melting pot programme of assimilation was found applicable to Negroes and Chinese.
(c) equality in education alone will provide the Negroes with equality of job opportunity.
(d) None of the above.

1280. The effect of secularism on education is the following.
(a) Religion should not be the basis of admission
(b) Celebration of festivals of all religious
(c) Abolition of specific religious education in schools
(d) All of the above

1281. Effective communication will make the receivers
(a) accept it
(b) enjoy it
(c) think about it
(d) pass it on to others

1282. The special courts meant for dealing with juvenile delinquents look upon delinquency as
(a) a mistake of parents rather than of children.
(b) a crime rather than misbehaviour.
(c) a misbehaviour rather than a crime.
(d) an act of negligence on the part of the children.

1283. Acculturation is the process of
(a) being influenced by the cultural imperatives of a nation.
(b) accepting the innovations required for the development of nation's culture.
(c) following the latest trends of a culture as opposed to the past traditions.
(d) developing qualities that effect the culture of nation.

1284. This is not a type of social mobility.
(a) Horizontal (b) Vertical
(c) Triangular (d) All of the above

1285. Which of the following statement is not correct?
(a) A good communicator has a good sense of humour.
(b) A good communicator cannot be a good teacher.
(c) A good communicator has command over language.
(d) A good communicator has wide reading.

1286. An effective communication does not require
(a) mastery of content
(b) appropriate gestures
(c) handsome personality
(d) change in speech pattern

1287. Which of the following is not true of adult education in India?
(a) Its origin lies outside the formal agency of the school.
(b) It has included worker's education.
(c) It is a recent development within the last fifty years.
(d) It needs to adopt formal school methods if it is to succeed.

1288. The facial expressions of students relate to which element of the communication process?
(a) Channel (b) Receiver
(c) Message (d) Sender

1289. In the eyes of the educational sociologists, schools can best contrast prejudice by
(a) developing and extending primary group values.
(b) imparting the knowledge.
(c) developing the intellect.
(d) asserting loyalty to the "in-group" and hostility to others.

1290. The term 'sub-culture' is used to indicate
(a) the traditions and ideas of tribal groups of societies.
(b) the belief and customs of traditional social groups.
(c) the culture of the lower strata of the society.
(d) the culture of different groups of societies.

1291. Which of the following is not a method or approach commonly used in intergroup education?
(a) Socio-drama and role-playing
(b) Emphasis placed upon the contributions or minorities
(c) Criticism of the customs of minorities
(d) None of the above.

1292. Naturalism in education means
(a) giving more importance to mind than to matter.
(b) supporting both mind and consciousness equally.
(c) introduction of physical sciences in education.
(d) making discrimination between mind and consciousness.

1293. Any deterrents are negative in character
(a) when they are administered owing to some misunderstanding.
(b) when they prevent children from doing wrong.
(c) when they are administered with a negative motive.
(d) when they prevent doing wrong but do not reform children.

1294. Industries near the towns cause
(a) Happiness
(b) Employment problems
(c) Pollution
(d) Security concerns

1295. The following is not a means of social control.
(a) Religion (b) Traditions
(c) Morality (d) Development

1296. It is absurd to say that
(a) transport vehicles cause pollution.
(b) pollution occurs due to land noise.
(c) education causes pollution.
(d) All of the above.

1297. Which of the following will not hamper effective communication in the class?
(a) A statement which allows the listener to draw his own conclusions
(b) An ambiguous statement
(c) A lengthy statement
(d) A precise statement.

1298. The most powerful barrier of communication in the classroom is
(a) lack of teaching aids.
(b) noise in the classroom.
(c) more outside disturbance in the classroom.
(d) confusion on the part of the teacher.

1299. It is said that there is an urgent need of articulation among schools and colleges. This problem of articulation is concerned with
(a) communication and closer relationship among teachers.
(b) provision of better administrative facilities.
(c) better facilities for in-service training of teachers.
(d) appointment of talented teachers.

1300. The idea that Basic Education is education through crafts is

(a) the complete truth even for urban areas.
(b) true so far as the rural areas are concerned.
(c) true to some extent only because the concept is deeper.
(d) Not true at all.

1301. The term prejudice in a person is coloured by
(a) partial observation and acquaintance of a situation without any motives.
(b) a hasty judgement about a situation without due examination of facts.
(c) pre-judgement of a situation with a view to settle a conflict in haste.
(d) judgement and assessment of a situation without any favoritism.

1302. Suppose you are teaching in a minority college where casteism and narrow mindedness victimize you, for better adjustment you should
(a) be submissive and save your job at all costs.
(b) uplift the humanistic values beyond those narrow walls and develop scientific temper in your students.
(c) rebel against such attitudes as it is against the norms of the Indian society.
(d) None of the above.

1303. The sociologist feels that, if men expect to put an end to prejudice and race conflict, they will have to give major attention to
(a) putting into effect the "melting pot theory".
(b) re-establishing ethnocentrism.
(c) remedying social abuses and reducing conflict.
(d) legislating human rights for minorities.

1304. Boarding schools are considered to be better than the day schools because
(a) they are helpful in freeing parents from their responsibilities.
(b) they help children in their social development.
(c) they are meant for homeless and parentless children.
(d) they save the trouble for children to walk to school from homes.

1305. The aim of social control is
(a) check on arbitration.
(b) social stability.
(c) mass uniformity.
(d) All of the above.

1306. Cultural pluralism is based on the concept that
(a) our culture is variegated and dynamic, with each group of immigrants contributing towards its enrichment.
(b) America is the "Melting Pot" for various foreign stocks.
(c) culture differs from individual to individual.
(d) culture vanishes due to intermingling of people.

1307. As an idealist, which of the following maxim would you think to correct the problem of discipline?
(a) The child should be allowed full freedom without any restraint.
(b) The child should be trained to practice restraint with only limited freedom.
(c) The child be subjected to fear and control to train him to desist from doing wrong.
(d) Discipline should be imposed from outsiders and teachers with full control.

1308. Which of the following statement is incorrect?

(a) The purpose of population education is to develop awareness and understanding of the relations between population growth and national development both in short and long run and to develop an understanding of the consequences of individual decisions in the important area of reproductive behaviour.
(b) The term population education is applied either to increase or to decrease the rate of growth of population as per the need of situation of a nation of the world.
(c) 'Population Education' was first used in Sweden in 1935, the population education commission of the country to generate public awareness about the increase of the rate of growth.
(d) None of the above.

1309. A student centred plan is most favourable in the matter of
(a) Continuity (b) Articulation
(c) Balance (d) All of the above

1310. Forms of social control are
(a) positive and negative control.
(b) conscious and subconscious control.
(c) direct and indirect.
(d) All of the above.

1311. The term "Co-curricular activities" is a popular one for all educational institutions. Which of the following would you regard as a co-curricular activity
(a) collection of funds for school building
(b) debating competitions
(c) football matches
(d) None of the above

1312. The interaction between teachers and students or between buyers and sellers is classified by the sociologists as a social interaction of
(a) The primary type
(b) The secondary type
(c) The responsive type
(d) The multiple type

1313. A sentiment could be correctly defined as
(a) a sum total of a person's feeling and emotions about some object.
(b) a strong desire for an action with an inner motive.
(c) a weak point in individual's emotional life.
(d) a link between the likes and dislikes of an individual.

1314. Learning is a
(a) Dynamic process
(b) Reflective process
(c) Both (a) and (b)
(d) Organic process

1315. The process of expansion of an individual's capacities qualitatively, should be termed as
(a) Development (b) Equilibration
(c) Growth (d) Maturation

1316. The term 'curriculum' is used in education to indicate
(a) the courses prescribed for an examination.
(b) the contents of a broad subject selected for a particular class or grade.
(c) the sum total of all experiences provided for students by an educational institution.
(d) the field covered by a particular course of study.

1317. Elements of the core concept is/are
(a) ideas to develop resource units.
(b) teacher-pupil planning daily.
(c) co-operative pre-planning by teachers.
(d) All of the above.

1318. Who criticized the subject-centred traditional curriculum?
 (a) Alfred North Whitehead
 (b) John Dewey
 (c) Sigmund Freud
 (d) Rabindranath Tagore

1319. Which of the following distinctions between instruction and education would meet your approval as a teacher?
 (a) Instruction is specific whereas education is comprehensive.
 (b) Education depends upon the students abilities while instruction requires teacher's abilities.
 (c) Instruction requires a content matter whereas education requireds a methodical approach.
 (d) Education is for grown ups, but instruction is for younger ones.

1320. The emphasis in core concept is on total growth of the pupil
 (a) Intellectually (b) Socially
 (c) Physically (d) All of the above

1321. The approach of core pattern is
 (a) Core centred
 (b) Objective centred
 (c) Problem centred
 (d) All of the above

1322. Educational Administration is concerned with
 (a) the goals of educational practices.
 (b) the 'why' of educational processes.
 (c) the 'how' of achieving educational objectives.
 (d) the 'what' of educational programme.

1323. A school complex means
 (a) a number of schools with in a single building.
 (b) number of schools situated in any community area.
 (c) the superiority or inferiority complexes of schools.
 (d) schools within easily accessible radius.

1324. Which group of communication aspects does not distort the communication process in the class?
 (a) Focussing - illustrating - exaggerating
 (b) Evaluating - focussing - illustrating
 (c) Reversing - evaluating - focussing
 (d) Evaluating - focussing - exaggerating.

1325. The difference between moral and ethical education is that
 (a) morals emphasize knowledge while ethics emphasize performance.
 (b) teaching ethics can hinder moral stagnation while teaching morals advances discrimination.
 (c) morals can prematurely hinder ethical development whereas ethics need support of religion.
 (d) morals emphasize performance whereas ethics emphasize knowledge.

1326. Social stratification and rigid class structures brought about the
 (a) Cultural system
 (b) National integration
 (c) Caste system
 (d) United system

1327. Social changes may be speeded up by
 (a) Industrialization (b) Economy
 (c) Education (d) All of the above

1328. Educational inspection is different from educational supervision in the sense that
 (a) inspection is static whereas supervision is dynamic in approach.
 (b) inspection is prutive whereas supervision is corrective.
 (c) inspection assumes correction whereas supervision assumes status quo.
 (d) None of the above.

1329. One is most likely to lead to the desired goal through
(a) Education (b) Service
(c) Marriage (d) Election

1330. The most important factors in bringing about social change which may be found in inventions are
(a) Diffusion
(b) Ideas
(c) Acculturation
(d) None of the above

1331. The belief and ideas common to all societies represent
(a) sub-culture of the societies
(b) universal forms of culture
(c) optional forms of culture
(d) special forms of culture

1332. For minimizing classroom absenteeism, the most effective method is
(a) to punish the absentees.
(b) to see that the class is taught well and regularly.
(c) to tell students that cutting classes is a bad behaviour.
(d) to allow students to attend or not to attend the class.

1333. Castes are
(a) Cultural groups
(b) Service groups
(c) Religional groups
(d) Status groups

1334. Cool media are those that affect the senses in
(a) Depth (b) Sensation
(c) Mind (d) Light

1335. The correspondence or vacation courses in education are a form of
(a) Extension Education
(b) Pre-service Education
(c) Continuation Education
(d) In-service Education

1336. Classes are
(a) Socially mobile
(b) Hereditary
(c) Inborn
(d) None of the above

1337. Schools are a part of
(a) Village (b) Nation
(c) Society (d) Family

1338. Caste position is a status position into which one is
(a) Forcibly sent
(b) Married
(c) Born
(d) None of the above

1339. Of all routes to social upgrading the best route is by
(a) Education (b) Hard labour
(c) Election (d) Marriage

1340. Craftsmen like potters, weavers and woodcavers are trained in
(a) Hereditary skills
(b) Traditional skills
(c) Both (a) and (b)
(d) None of the above

1341. Modern media is
(a) Celluloid (b) Electronic
(c) Print (d) Digital

1342. The media is altering the
(a) meaning of life
(b) human interdependence
(c) Both (a) and (b)
(d) None of the above

1343. The relationship between education and social changes functions in
(a) Five ways (b) Four ways
(c) Three ways (d) Two ways

1344. The main difference between work and play is
(a) Play is carried on just for itself
(b) Work has a definite goal

(c) Work is worship
(d) Play gives satisfaction

1345. A hot medium of communication is one that imparts much information and is sharp in
(a) Location (b) Performance
(c) Presentation (d) Definition

1346. It has been pointed out by most thinkers, that education has much to do with social change and this will lead to
(a) non-material changes
(b) material changes
(c) other changes
(d) regional changes

1347. Classes are not completely
(a) Self perpetuating
(b) Restricted to marriage
(c) Rigid
(d) None of the above

1348. Without education there can be
(a) Social changes
(b) Material changes
(c) Non-material changes
(d) No social changes

1349. Education comes prior to
(a) Religion
(b) Material change
(c) Social change
(d) None of the above

1350. The machinery which is moulded to create conditions for a successful achievement of the ends of education could be called
(a) Educational inspection and supervision
(b) Educational Organisation
(c) Educational co-ordination and direction
(d) Educational administration

1351. The term 'Social Intelligence' could be correctly defined as
(a) techniques and emotions aroused in us by a social situation.
(b) ability to react to social situations of daily life correctly.
(c) controls and restrains that could be correctly adopted in dealing with social situation.
(d) the pressures exerted by the society for the development of one's intelligence.

1352. The discipline obtaining in any institution depends upon the
(a) attitudes of headmaster and teachers towards children.
(b) circumstances of the surrounding environment.
(c) philosophy behind its programmes.
(d) sufficiency of its staff members.

1353. One of the most important question to be decided in the language controversy in our country is the problem of
(a) expenditure to be incurred for the spread of the language.
(b) the link language for institutions of higher learning.
(c) languages of the minorities and their development.
(d) the medium of instruction at different levels.

1354. Joint family system is breaking. The religion is loosing its grip on the people. The school serves to fill the gap. The school builds up social, economic and democratic ideals. It has to develop the moral and aesthetic sense of the pupils. The end product must possess a sense of true application of truth, goodness and beauty. The home and the school must actively co-operate with each other in

the best interest of true education. The above statement pertains to
(a) ideals of education
(b) objectives of education
(c) role of education
(d) None of the above

1355. Necessity is the mother of invention. This saying indicates the phenomenon of
(a) intellectual flux in the population of any country.
(b) scientific development of society.
(c) social changes occurring as a result of man's efforts and attributes.
(d) progress in the industrial areas of nation.

1356. Education officers often speak about the tone of an institution. This concept of 'tone' refers to
(a) the disciplinary measures adopted by an institution for avoiding classes.
(b) the organisational and supervising set up of the institution.
(c) the programmes and activities planned by the institution.
(d) the healthy atmosphere of the institution from the sentimental point of view.

1357. Schools help in the establishment of a better and happier society. The child not only acquires knowledge but also develops the required habits, skills, and attitudes. School programme is so planned that the children are trained in democratic methods, so essential in a democratic society. It is a direct responsibility of the school to prepare each individual child for post school adjustments. After completing his school education he has to adjust himself in the society. The success or failure of a school system is judged by its end product. Keeping in view the above statement, which one of the following is correct?
(a) The statement applies to secondary education.
(b) The above pertains to education at primary level only.
(c) The above pertains to one of the primary objectives of education.
(d) None of the above.

1358. Population education means
(a) education for family planning.
(b) knowledge of the problems imposed by population growth.
(c) the characteristics to be grasped about different population growth.
(d) sex education from scientific point of view.

1359. All are the examples of two way communication except
(a) public meeting
(b) streetplays
(c) procession and rallies
(d) padyatra

1360. Which of the following statement would be acceptable to you as being correct, about the concept of the word 'culture'?
(a) It has implications for abstract and idealistic achievements rather than materialistic attainments.
(b) It includes all the progress made in the past.
(c) It includes all the progress of ideas and attainment of a society or nation achieved in the past.
(d) It is more prospective than retrospective in describing the status of nation or society.

1361. If a curriculum maker follows the subjective theory of values in education, he will
(a) implement the study of a subject for its inherent values to fulfill the needs of a student.

(b) not insist on the inclusion of any subject in the curriculum if pupils or parents are not interested in it.
(c) care more for the content aspect than for the methodological.
(d) disregard the interests of children and parents for the inclusion of any subject in the curriculum.

1362. If the moral duty of law in a society is interpreted as obedience to the will of the sovereign Lord, Teachers' method takes the form of
(a) an indoctrination approach.
(b) a problem solving approach.
(c) an appeal to conscience approach.
(d) an experimental approach.

1363. The term "Didactics" refers to
(a) artistic and cultural-cum-esthetic trends in education.
(b) the theory and art of teaching.
(c) the ethical and cultural aspects of education.
(d) organization and supervision in teaching activities.

Following Question is multi-statement type. Choose the correct code given.

1364. Arrange the following activities of interaction in logical order
1. Analysis of the work done
2. Planning and preparation
3. Presentation of material
4. Modification and improvement

Codes:
(a) 1, 3, 4, 2 (b) 4, 1, 2, 3
(c) 1, 2, 3, 4 (d) 2, 3, 1, 4

ANSWERS

1. (b)	2. (d)	3. (c)	4. (c)	5. (a)	6. (d)
7. (d)	8. (c)	9. (b)	10. (d)	11. (b)	12. (a)
13. (a)	14. (a)	15. (d)	16. (a)	17. (d)	18. (a)
19. (d)	20. (b)	21. (d)	22. (d)	23. (a)	24. (d)
25. (d)	26. (a)	27. (c)	28. (c)	29. (a)	30. (c)
31. (b)	32. (d)	33. (c)	34. (a)	35. (d)	36. (a)
37. (a)	38. (c)	39. (c)	40. (c)	41. (d)	42. (d)
43. (a)	44. (d)	45. (c)	46. (b)	47. (d)	48. (c)
49. (a)	50. (d)	51. (a)	52. (c)	53. (b)	54. (a)
55. (d)	56. (d)	57. (d)	58. (b)	59. (d)	60. (c)
61. (a)	62. (d)	63. (a)	64. (b)	65. (b)	66. (b)
67. (d)	68. (a)	69. (c)	70. (d)	71. (d)	72. (d)
73. (d)	74. (d)	75. (d)	76. (c)	77. (d)	78. (d)
79. (b)	80. (d)	81. (b)	82. (a)	83. (c)	84. (d)
85. (d)	86. (c)	87. (b)	88. (d)	89. (d)	90. (b)
91. (d)	92. (d)	93. (d)	94. (b)	95. (d)	96. (c)
97. (c)	98. (c)	99. (a)	100. (c)	101. (d)	102. (b)

103. (d)	104. (c)	105. (c)	106. (a)	107. (d)	108. (b)
109. (a)	110. (c)	111. (d)	112. (a)	113. (c)	114. (a)
115. (a)	116. (a)	117. (c)	118. (a)	119. (a)	120. (c)
121. (d)	122. (a)	123. (d)	124. (c)	125. (d)	126. (b)
127. (a)	128. (d)	129. (c)	130. (c)	131. (d)	132. (c)
133. (c)	134. (c)	135. (a)	136. (c)	137. (c)	138. (c)
139. (c)	140. (a)	141. (b)	142. (d)	143. (c)	144. (a)
145. (b)	146. (c)	147. (b)	148. (a)	149. (c)	150. (a)
151. (d)	152. (d)	153. (a)	154. (b)	155. (d)	156. (d)
157. (d)	158. (d)	159. (a)	160. (b)	161. (b)	162. (a)
163. (b)	164. (c)	165. (d)	166. (d)	167. (c)	168. (a)
169. (c)	170. (b)	171. (c)	172. (d)	173. (b)	174. (b)
175. (a)	176. (c)	177. (c)	178. (c)	179. (c)	180. (d)
181. (a)	182. (b)	183. (c)	184. (c)	185. (c)	186. (a)
187. (d)	188. (d)	189. (c)	190. (b)	191. (b)	192. (d)
193. (b)	194. (b)	195. (a)	196. (a)	197. (a)	198. (c)
199. (d)	200. (c)	201. (a)	202. (a)	203. (c)	204. (b)
205. (b)	206. (d)	207. (d)	208. (a)	209. (d)	210. (d)
211. (b)	212. (a)	213. (d)	214. (b)	215. (a)	216. (c)
217. (a)	218. (c)	219. (b)	220. (a)	221. (c)	222. (d)
223. (d)	224. (a)	225. (c)	226. (b)	227. (a)	228. (c)
229. (d)	230. (a)	231. (c)	232. (d)	233. (b)	234. (d)
235. (a)	236. (b)	237. (b)	238. (c)	239. (a)	240. (b)
241. (d)	242. (a)	243. (c)	244. (d)	245. (c)	246. (d)
247. (b)	248. (c)	249. (d)	250. (d)	251. (a)	252. (c)
253. (d)	254. (d)	255. (d)	256. (b)	257. (c)	258. (c)
259. (a)	260. (a)	261. (b)	262. (c)	263. (d)	264. (a)
265. (d)	266. (a)	267. (a)	268. (b)	269. (c)	270. (c)
271. (d)	272. (b)	273. (c)	274. (d)	275. (a)	276. (a)
277. (d)	278. (c)	279. (c)	280. (a)	281. (c)	282. (b)
283. (c)	284. (d)	285. (d)	286. (b)	287. (a)	288. (c)
289. (a)	290. (b)	291. (d)	292. (d)	293. (c)	294. (d)
295. (c)	296. (d)	297. (d)	298. (b)	299. (c)	300. (c)
301. (c)	302. (c)	303. (d)	304. (b)	305. (c)	306. (c)

307. (d)	308. (b)	309. (a)	310. (c)	311. (a)	312. (c)
313. (a)	314. (d)	315. (a)	316. (a)	317. (d)	318. (d)
319. (d)	320. (a)	321. (b)	322. (c)	323. (b)	324. (b)
325. (a)	326. (d)	327. (c)	328. (d)	329. (d)	330. (c)
331. (d)	332. (a)	333. (b)	334. (a)	335. (d)	336. (d)
337. (a)	338. (a)	339. (a)	340. (c)	341. (a)	342. (c)
343. (a)	344. (b)	345. (d)	346. (d)	347. (c)	348. (c)
349. (a)	350. (d)	351. (c)	352. (d)	353. (a)	354. (b)
355. (b)	356. (a)	357. (c)	358. (b)	359. (b)	360. (a)
361. (c)	362. (b)	363. (c)	364. (c)	365. (a)	366. (c)
367. (a)	368. (b)	369. (a)	370. (b)	371. (c)	372. (d)
373. (b)	374. (c)	375. (a)	376. (c)	377. (a)	378. (b)
379. (d)	380. (c)	381. (c)	382. (d)	383. (d)	384. (d)
385. (d)	386. (c)	387. (a)	388. (c)	389. (d)	390. (a)
391. (d)	392. (d)	393. (d)	394. (b)	395. (b)	396. (c)
397. (a)	398. (a)	399. (b)	400. (b)	401. (b)	402. (c)
403. (a)	404. (b)	405. (d)	406. (c)	407. (c)	408. (a)
409. (d)	410. (b)	411. (d)	412. (d)	413. (a)	414. (c)
415. (b)	416. (c)	417. (d)	418. (b)	419. (b)	420. (d)
421. (c)	422. (b)	423. (b)	424. (c)	425. (d)	426. (b)
427. (b)	428. (b)	429. (d)	430. (d)	431. (c)	432. (a)
433. (c)	434. (a)	435. (c)	436. (c)	437. (d)	438. (c)
439. (d)	440. (a)	441. (b)	442. (c)	443. (c)	444. (c)
445. (a)	446. (a)	447. (c)	448. (d)	449. (d)	450. (d)
451. (a)	452. (a)	453. (d)	454. (d)	455. (a)	456. (b)
457. (d)	458. (d)	459. (c)	460. (a)	461. (a)	462. (a)
463. (d)	464. (d)	465. (b)	466. (b)	467. (c)	468. (a)
469. (a)	470. (b)	471. (c)	472. (a)	473. (d)	474. (a)
475. (d)	476. (c)	477. (b)	478. (a)	479. (c)	480. (a)
481. (d)	482. (a)	483. (b)	484. (a)	485. (c)	486. (a)
487. (d)	488. (d)	489. (b)	490. (b)	491. (d)	492. (c)
493. (d)	494. (b)	495. (d)	496. (c)	497. (b)	498. (a)
499. (d)	500. (c)	501. (d)	502. (c)	503. (c)	504. (c)
505. (c)	506. (c)	507. (b)	508. (c)	509. (c)	510. (d)

511. (a)	512. (a)	513. (d)	514. (d)	515. (c)	516. (d)
517. (d)	518. (b)	519. (c)	520. (c)	521. (a)	522. (b)
523. (d)	524. (d)	525. (d)	526. (b)	527. (c)	528. (a)
529. (b)	530. (d)	531. (d)	532. (c)	533. (d)	534. (d)
535. (c)	536. (a)	537. (a)	538. (c)	539. (d)	540. (b)
541. (d)	542. (c)	543. (c)	544. (a)	545. (c)	546. (c)
547. (c)	548. (c)	549. (d)	550. (c)	551. (a)	552. (d)
553. (c)	554. (d)	555. (c)	556. (a)	557. (c)	558. (b)
559. (d)	560. (c)	561. (d)	562. (c)	563. (b)	564. (d)
565. (c)	566. (b)	567. (b)	568. (d)	569. (d)	570. (b)
571. (b)	572. (d)	573. (a)	574. (a)	575. (b)	576. (b)
577. (b)	578. (d)	579. (d)	580. (b)	581. (c)	582. (c)
583. (d)	584. (b)	585. (a)	586. (c)	587. (d)	588. (a)
589. (b)	590. (c)	591. (a)	592. (a)	593. (d)	594. (d)
595. (a)	596. (c)	597. (d)	598. (b)	599. (d)	600. (d)
601. (c)	602. (a)	603. (d)	604. (d)	605. (c)	606. (d)
607. (a)	608. (a)	609. (b)	610. (d)	611. (b)	612. (c)
613. (d)	614. (b)	615. (b)	616. (d)	617. (c)	618. (a)
619. (c)	620. (c)	621. (c)	622. (b)	623. (c)	624. (a)
625. (c)	626. (b)	627. (d)	628. (c)	629. (b)	630. (d)
631. (d)	632. (b)	633. (d)	634. (c)	635. (d)	636. (d)
637. (a)	638. (a)	639. (d)	640. (a)	641. (c)	642. (c)
643. (a)	644. (d)	645. (d)	646. (a)	647. (d)	648. (d)
649. (d)	650. (a)	651. (b)	652. (c)	653. (b)	654. (d)
655. (d)	656. (d)	657. (d)	658. (c)	659. (b)	660. (d)
661. (d)	662. (b)	663. (d)	664. (b)	665. (a)	666. (b)
667. (d)	668. (b)	669. (a)	670. (c)	671. (b)	672. (d)
673. (a)	674. (a)	675. (b)	676. (b)	677. (d)	678. (d)
679. (a)	680. (c)	681. (b)	682. (c)	683. (d)	684. (a)
685. (a)	686. (c)	687. (c)	688. (c)	689. (d)	690. (c)
691. (d)	692. (c)	693. (b)	694. (c)	695. (d)	696. (d)
697. (c)	698. (c)	699. (b)	700. (d)	701. (d)	702. (c)
703. (d)	704. (d)	705. (d)	706. (c)	707. (c)	708. (c)
709. (c)	710. (d)	711. (c)	712. (d)	713. (c)	714. (d)

715. (c)	716. (a)	717. (a)	718. (d)	719. (c)	720. (d)
721. (b)	722. (c)	723. (c)	724. (a)	725. (c)	726. (d)
727. (a)	728. (a)	729. (b)	730. (d)	731. (a)	732. (a)
733. (d)	734. (c)	735. (c)	736. (a)	737. (d)	738. (d)
739. (c)	740. (c)	741. (c)	742. (a)	743. (d)	744. (c)
745. (c)	746. (d)	747. (a)	748. (d)	749. (d)	750. (b)
751. (a)	752. (b)	753. (b)	754. (d)	755. (c)	756. (d)
757. (c)	758. (a)	759. (a)	760. (b)	761. (d)	762. (c)
763. (b)	764. (a)	765. (a)	766. (c)	767. (b)	768. (d)
769. (c)	770. (d)	771. (a)	772. (d)	773. (b)	774. (d)
775. (d)	776. (c)	777. (d)	778. (b)	779. (c)	780. (d)
781. (d)	782. (d)	783. (d)	784. (d)	785. (b)	786. (d)
787. (d)	788. (c)	789. (c)	790. (a)	791. (d)	792. (b)
793. (a)	794. (d)	795. (c)	796. (d)	797. (d)	798. (d)
799. (c)	800. (a)	801. (c)	802. (a)	803. (d)	804. (c)
805. (b)	806. (a)	807. (d)	808. (a)	809. (d)	810. (b)
811. (d)	812. (d)	813. (d)	814. (c)	815. (c)	816. (c)
817. (d)	818. (c)	819. (d)	820. (d)	821. (a)	822. (b)
823. (a)	824. (d)	825. (c)	826. (a)	827. (d)	828. (d)
829. (c)	830. (b)	831. (d)	832. (b)	833. (c)	834. (a)
835. (d)	836. (d)	837. (d)	838. (d)	839. (d)	840. (b)
841. (c)	842. (d)	843. (d)	844. (a)	845. (d)	846. (a)
847. (c)	848. (d)	849. (d)	850. (d)	851. (c)	852. (a)
853. (d)	854. (a)	855. (c)	856. (a)	857. (d)	858. (b)
859. (d)	860. (d)	861. (a)	862. (c)	863. (b)	864. (c)
865. (b)	866. (d)	867. (a)	868. (c)	869. (d)	870. (c)
871. (a)	872. (c)	873. (d)	874. (c)	875. (d)	876. (d)
877. (a)	878. (c)	879. (b)	880. (d)	881. (d)	882. (d)
883. (b)	884. (d)	885. (a)	886. (c)	887. (d)	888. (b)
889. (c)	890. (b)	891. (c)	892. (d)	893. (c)	894. (a)
895. (a)	896. (c)	897. (a)	898. (b)	899. (a)	900. (c)
901. (c)	902. (a)	903. (a)	904. (a)	905. (d)	906. (a)
907. (d)	908. (a)	909. (c)	910. (b)	911. (c)	912. (c)
913. (c)	914. (b)	915. (d)	916. (a)	917. (d)	918. (c)

919. (c)	920. (d)	921. (d)	922. (c)	923. (a)	924. (c)
925. (a)	926. (c)	927. (a)	928. (c)	929. (b)	930. (c)
931. (c)	932. (c)	933. (a)	934. (d)	935. (c)	936. (b)
937. (a)	938. (b)	939. (d)	940. (d)	941. (a)	942. (a)
943. (b)	944. (c)	945. (c)	946. (d)	947. (a)	948. (b)
949. (c)	950. (c)	951. (b)	952. (c)	953. (d)	954. (d)
955. (c)	956. (b)	957. (c)	958. (a)	959. (c)	960. (b)
961. (c)	962. (d)	963. (d)	964. (c)	965. (a)	966. (b)
967. (d)	968. (d)	969. (a)	970. (a)	971. (c)	972. (c)
973. (a)	974. (a)	975. (d)	976. (d)	977. (c)	978. (b)
979. (d)	980. (d)	981. (b)	982. (c)	983. (d)	984. (d)
985. (d)	986. (a)	987. (c)	988. (c)	989. (a)	990. (a)
991. (c)	992. (d)	993. (b)	994. (d)	995. (d)	996. (a)
997. (c)	998. (b)	999. (d)	1000. (d)	1001. (c)	1002. (c)
1003. (c)	1004. (a)	1005. (d)	1006. (c)	1007. (a)	1008. (d)
1009. (b)	1010. (d)	1011. (a)	1012. (a)	1013. (b)	1014. (d)
1015. (d)	1016. (c)	1017. (d)	1018. (d)	1019. (d)	1020. (d)
1021. (d)	1022. (a)	1023. (a)	1024. (c)	1025. (c)	1026. (c)
1027. (a)	1028. (a)	1029. (b)	1030. (b)	1031 (c)	1032. (a)
1033. (d)	1034. (a)	1035. (d)	1036. (a)	1037. (c)	1038. (a)
1039. (a)	1040. (d)	1041. (d)	1042. (c)	1043. (c)	1044. (c)
1045. (d)	1046. (d)	1047. (b)	1048. (d)	1049. (a)	1050. (c)
1051. (a)	1052. (c)	1053. (c)	1054. (a)	1055. (d)	1056. (a)
1057. (a)	1058. (b)	1059. (c)	1060. (a)	1061. (d)	1062. (c)
1063. (b)	1064. (d)	1065. (d)	1066. (b)	1067. (d)	1068. (d)
1069. (a)	1070. (c)	1071. (c)	1072. (d)	1073. (d)	1074. (b)
1075. (a)	1076. (d)	1077. (c)	1078. (b)	1079. (a)	1080. (d)
1081. (d)	1082. (a)	1083. (a)	1084. (c)	1085. (c)	1086. (d)
1087. (b)	1088. (d)	1089. (a)	1090. (d)	1091. (a)	1092. (c)
1093. (a)	1094. (c)	1095. (c)	1096. (d)	1097. (c)	1098. (d)
1099. (a)	1100. (c)	1101. (c)	1102. (c)	1103. (c)	1104. (c)
1105. (c)	1106. (d)	1107. (d)	1108. (b)	1109. (b)	1110. (c)
1111. (d)	1112. (d)	1113. (b)	1114. (d)	1115. (a)	1116. (b)
1117. (c)	1118. (c)	1119. (d)	1120. (c)	1121. (b)	1122. (c)

1123. (c)	1124. (d)	1125. (d)	1126. (d)	1127. (a)	1128. (d)
1129. (c)	1130. (d)	1131. (a)	1132. (a)	1133. (b)	1134. (b)
1135. (a)	1136. (b)	1137. (a)	1138. (a)	1139. (c)	1140. (b)
1141. (d)	1142. (b)	1143. (d)	1144. (b)	1145. (b)	1146. (d)
1147. (d)	1148. (b)	1149. (c)	1150. (d)	1151. (c)	1152. (b)
1153. (b)	1154. (a)	1155. (d)	1156. (d)	1157. (c)	1158. (b)
1159. (d)	1160. (a)	1161. (b)	1162. (d)	1163. (b)	1164. (d)
1165. (b)	1166. (c)	1167. (d)	1168. (c)	1169. (c)	1170. (b)
1171. (c)	1172. (d)	1173. (d)	1174. (a)	1175. (b)	1176. (c)
1177. (c)	1178. (a)	1179. (c)	1180. (a)	1181. (b)	1182. (b)
1183. (c)	1184. (d)	1185. (c)	1186. (d)	1187. (a)	1188. (a)
1189. (d)	1190. (a)	1191. (d)	1192. (a)	1193. (c)	1194. (c)
1195. (b)	1196. (c)	1197. (c)	1198. (c)	1199. (a)	1200. (c)
1201. (c)	1202. (a)	1203. (a)	1204. (a)	1205. (a)	1206. (c)
1207. (c)	1208. (a)	1209. (d)	1210. (b)	1211. (c)	1212. (c)
1213. (b)	1214. (c)	1215. (d)	1216. (c)	1217. (c)	1218. (a)
1219. (c)	1220. (d)	1221. (a)	1222. (d)	1223. (d)	1224. (b)
1225. (c)	1226. (a)	1227. (a)	1228. (c)	1229. (c)	1230. (a)
1231. (d)	1232. (c)	1233. (a)	1234. (d)	1235 (d)	1236. (c)
1237. (b)	1238. (b)	1239. (d)	1240. (c)	1241. (c)	1242. (c)
1243. (a)	1244. (c)	1245. (a)	1246. (b)	1247. (c)	1248. (c)
1249. (c)	1250. (c)	1251. (a)	1252. (d)	1253. (a)	1254. (d)
1255. (d)	1256. (d)	1257. (b)	1258. (d)	1259. (d)	1260. (d)
1261. (a)	1262. (c)	1263. (c)	1264. (b)	1265. (a)	1266. (b)
1267. (d)	1268. (c)	1269. (d)	1270. (a)	1271. (c)	1272. (d)
1273. (b)	1274. (d)	1275. (a)	1276. (b)	1277. (a)	1278. (d)
1279. (b)	1280. (d)	1281. (b)	1282. (c)	1283. (a)	1284. (c)
1285. (b)	1286. (c)	1287. (d)	1288. (c)	1289. (a)	1290. (d)
1291. (c)	1292. (c)	1293. (d)	1294. (c)	1295. (d)	1296. (c)
1297. (d)	1298. (d)	1299. (a)	1300. (c)	1301. (b)	1302. (b)
1303. (d)	1304. (b)	1305. (d)	1306. (a)	1307. (b)	1308. (d)
1309. (b)	1310. (d)	1311. (b)	1312. (b)	1313. (a)	1314. (c)
1315. (a)	1316. (c)	1317. (d)	1318. (a)	1319. (a)	1320. (d)
1321. (c)	1322. (c)	1323. (d)	1324. (a)	1325. (d)	1326. (c)

1327. (c)	1328. (a)	1329. (a)	1330. (b)	1331. (c)	1332. (b)
1333. (d)	1334. (a)	1335. (d)	1336. (a)	1337. (c)	1338. (c)
1339. (a)	1340. (c)	1341. (d)	1342. (c)	1343. (c)	1344. (a)
1345. (d)	1346. (c)	1347. (a)	1348. (d)	1349. (c)	1350. (d)
1351. (b)	1352. (c)	1353. (b)	1354. (c)	1355. (b)	1356. (d)
1357. (c)	1358. (b)	1359. (b)	1360. (d)	1361. (a)	1362. (a)
1363. (b)	1364. (d)				

3

Psychological Foundations of Education

1. The word 'Psychology' is formed by combination of Psyche' and 'Logos' which means
   (a) science of soul.
   (b) science of brain.
   (c) science of consciousness.
   (d) All of the above.
2. Who suggested that mental processes and events are unimportant or even totally non-existent?
   (a) Wundt (b) Hull
   (c) Jung (d) Waston
3. Psychology as a science of mind was rejected by philosophers because
   (a) mind could not be interpreted in behavioural terms.
   (b) mind could not be defined in definite terms.
   (c) Both (a) and (b).
   (d) None of the above.
4. General Psychology and Educational Psychology are dissimilar. In that educational psychology
   (a) is concerned with the various aspects of learning.
   (b) deals only with the applications and not with the theory.
   (c) selects and emphasises certain data from the general field.
   (d) is concerned with the child and not with the adult.
5. The scholar who told that psychology is 'Science of soul' was
   (a) William Wudnt (b) Plato
   (c) Aristotle (d) Both (b) and (c)
6. All are the characteristics of scientific knowledge except
   (a) future course of action can be predicted by it.
   (b) it cannot be repudiated in future.
   (c) it can be verified objectively.
   (d) it depends on observation and experiment.
7. William James considered psychology as the science of
   (a) Brain (b) Behaviour
   (c) Consciousness (d) Soul
8. Education psychology is oriented towards
   (a) the formulation of hypothesis and theories related to educational practice.
   (b) the study of the peculiarities of individual children.
   (c) the development on the part of the child of realistic goals and effective plans for their attainment.
   (d) the application of the principles and techniques of psychology to the solution of the problems of the classroom.
9. Behaviour is a collective name for all
   (a) Observation (b) Activities
   (c) Manifestation (d) All of the above

10. The main method of psychological study, as for all science is
    (a) Perception (b) Lab method
    (c) Record (d) Observation
11. The primary aim of educational psychology is
    (a) to provide the academic background essential for effective teaching.
    (b) to contribute to an understanding of sound educational practices.
    (c) to provide a theoretical framework for educational research.
    (d) to provide the teacher with a greater appreciation of his role in the education of the child.
12. Psychology is the science of brain, was considered by
    (a) Aristotle (b) Woodworth
    (c) James Selly (d) Pomponazzi
13. The first psychologist who systematically studied behaviour was
    (a) Ivon Pavlov
    (b) Wilhelm Wundt
    (c) J.B. Watson
    (d) None of the above
14. Mc. Dougal said that psychology is the science of
    (a) Behaviour (b) Conscience
    (c) Soul (d) Brain
15. Which of the following is not a function of educational psychology?
    (a) To define the goals for which education is to strive
    (b) To discover techniques by means of which educational goals can be attained effectively
    (c) To promote a greater understanding of the learner
    (d) To promote a greater understanding of the learning process
16. Psychology is a social science because
    (a) it studies human behaviour in social context.
    (b) it helps in moulding behaviour of the child according to the need.
    (c) its laws and principles are applicable to human life situations.
    (d) All of the above.
17. Educational psychology should provide prospective teachers with
    (a) research procedures by means of which to evaluate correct teaching procedures.
    (b) insight in to the various aspects modern education.
    (c) validate procedures to use in their teachings.
    (d) principles, insights and attitudes as points of departure for effective teaching.
18. "First of all psychology abandoned its soul, then its mind and finally its consciousness. But there is study of behaviour still in it." These words are of
    (a) William Wundt (b) Woodworth
    (c) Plato (d) Aristotle
19. In Brain white matter is composed of
    (a) Nerve fibres
    (b) Nerve cells
    (c) Ependymal cells
    (d) None of the above
20. "Educational psychology describe the learning and experience of a person from his birth to old age." This definition was given by
    (a) James Draver (b) Kolensik
    (c) Crow and Crow (d) Skinner, C.E.
21. By what types of theories of human nature, sexual behaviour and the conditions under which a person may be held legally responsible for his actions are influenced?

(a) Psychological (b) Sociological
(c) Physiological (d) Biological

22. Many of our observations, subjective and objective, turn out to be inaccurate and need to be tested, confirmed and amplified by
(a) Experiment (b) Society
(c) Environment (d) All of the above

23. Logos means knowledge and psyche means
(a) Consciousness (b) Behaviour
(c) Soul (d) Mind

24. Psychology is the science of behaviour and it has deep-rooted relation with education because education tries for changes in child's
(a) Soul (b) Behaviour
(c) Consciousness (d) Mind

25. After pin-prick, jumping is due to the
(a) Stimulus (b) Pain
(c) Emotion (d) Response

26. Educational psychology, is a branch of psychology in area of education in
(a) Theoretical (b) Applied
(c) Practical (d) Intimate

27. What level of consciousness the process of awareness indicates?
(a) Preconscious (b) Unconscious
(c) Conscious (d) Sub-conscious

28. How many ways are there for looking at the same object?
(a) One (b) Three
(c) Two (d) Four

29. The function and structure of nervous system includes
(a) P.N.S. and A.N.S.
(b) C.N.S. and P.N.
(c) A.N.S. only
(d) P.N.S. only

30. The study methods of education-psychology are
(a) Philosophical (b) Experimental
(c) Observatory (d) Both (b) and (c)

31. Mental activity which is controlled by the wishes of the individual is known as
(a) reality thinking
(b) introverted thinking
(c) autistic thinking
(d) extraverted thinking

32. The following is the method of educational psychology.
(a) Archeological (b) Numismatics
(c) Case history (d) All of the above

33. Which behaviour studies psychology as a science?
(a) Creative animal
(b) Social
(c) Overt
(d) Human and animal

34. Which of the following is not a subjective method of studying behaviour
(a) introspection (b) observation
(c) dream analysis (d) interview

35. What is the subject matter of psychology?
(a) Behaviour
(b) Development
(c) Perception of form
(d) Socialization

36. Sociometry and interview are study-method of following.
(a) Education-psychology
(b) Sociology
(c) History
(d) Education-philosophy

37. Participant method of observation is suitable for studying the behaviour of
(a) criminals
(b) small children

(c) Both (a) and (b)
(d) None of the above

38. Growth and development are indicators of
(a) Changes (b) Stability
(c) Maturity (d) All of the above

39. Greeks studied psychology as a branch of
(a) Biology (b) Religion
(c) Theology (d) Philosophy

40. Two children born in the same month of same year are bound to have the same
(a) chronological age
(b) performance age
(c) mental age
(d) intelligence quotient

41. Psychology began to be studied as a science in Germany in the year
(a) 1879 (b) 1839
(c) 1890 (d) 1820

42. Growth is of
(a) Physical parts (b) Intelligence
(c) Interests (d) Attitudes

43. The number of cranial nerves in man is
(a) 22 (b) 18
(c) 16 (d) 12

44. The cause of the aggression may be social rather than
(a) Psychological
(b) Biological
(c) Physiological
(d) Both (b) and (c)

45. The process of growth and development starts from pregnancy, which continues after birth with contact of
(a) Education (b) Environment
(c) Rearing (d) All of the above

46. Who established the first Psychological Laboratory?
(a) Wundt (b) Watson
(c) Galton (d) Kurt Lewin

47. Observation method is used in
(a) lab situation
(b) classroom situation
(c) sports situation
(d) All of the above

48. The study of occupational information should be
(a) introduced in connection with a programme of self-appraisal.
(b) postponed until the pupil is ready to choose a vocation.
(c) made a regular 10th and 12th grade subject.
(d) handled only by the school's occupation counsellor.

49. The following elements are in the concept of growth.
(a) Parts of body
(b) Rhythmic regular
(c) Continuous process
(d) All of the above

50. Which of the following techniques is used in educational survey? (to study the problems of education)
(a) Interview (b) Tests
(c) Questionnaire (d) All of the above

51. Growth in comparison to development is
(a) Diversified
(b) Narrow
(c) Equal
(d) None of the above

52. Experience has shown that the most feasible plan for utilizing occupational orientation programme broadcast by radio is
(a) the assignment of pupils to listen to and report on the programme.
(b) the recording of the programme for inter-communication playback.
(c) the bringing of pupils to listen to a direct hook-up in assembly.
(d) the direct hook-up of the programme with all classroom radios.

53. Teachers who are enthusiastic in the classroom teaching,
   (a) often lack proficiency in the subjects which stays hidden under their enthusiasm.
   (b) involve their students in the teaching learning process.
   (c) simply dramatize to hold the students' attention.
   (d) All of the above.
54. In making occupational field-trips, the pupils should
   (a) be prepared to ask questions from their guide.
   (b) discuss their visits upon returning to school.
   (c) be accompanied by the teacher at all times.
   (d) All of these.
55. The following elements are in the concept of development.
   (a) Towards maturity
   (b) Relatively qualitative
   (c) Relatively quantitative
   (d) Both (a) and (b)
56. The idea arose in psychology that thinking was actually a kind of
   (a) talking yourself under your breath
   (b) inner speech
   (c) linguistic speech
   (d) Both (a) and (b)
57. "Adolescent is the period of revolutionary changes, hard labour and stormy part of life"—Bigge and Hunt. This statement means that in adolescence
   (a) changes are very difficult.
   (b) a child becomes revolutionary.
   (c) changes are very fast.
   (d) All of the above.
58. In helping students to make educational plans, it is unwise for them to
   (a) take typing with college preparatory subjects.
   (b) mix general with vocational subjects.
   (c) plan their programmes more than a year ahead.
   (d) select all their subjects from one field.
59. The substance theory of personality was given by
   (a) G.W. Allport (b) Sigmund Freud
   (c) Kurt Lewin (d) F.H. Allport
60. A pupil should definitely be encouraged to go to college if
   (a) he has financial backing to see him through.
   (b) he has met high-schopl graduation requirements.
   (c) he has better than the average intelligence.
   (d) All the above are true and he wishes to go.
61. The reason to effect physical development is
   (a) Environment (b) Heredity
   (c) Sex difference (d) All of the above
62. In this system some task is given to the students regarding months, science or language. Students complete this task with the help of Teaching Machine. Question and all the problems are filled in the Teaching Machine. Student asks question to this machine and solves the problem like quiz machine. Which method is this?
   (a) Programmed Instruction
   (b) Remedial Teaching
   (c) Diagnostic Teaching
   (d) Micro Teaching
63. Studying the classroom problems is an example of
   (a) clinical survey
   (b) field study

(c) field experiment
(d) None of the above

64. This type of love and sympathy of parents towards a child has adverse effect on him.
(a) Lack of love and sympathy
(b) Too much of love and sympathy
(c) Both (a) and (b)
(d) None of the above

65. The problem child is generally one who has
(a) a poor heredity.
(b) an unsolved problem.
(c) a younger brother or sister.
(d) a poor home environment.

66. Educational psychology helps the teacher in which of the following ways
(a) he can modify his teaching in accordance with individual differences.
(b) he studies the personality of learners and then plans his way of action.
(c) he can motivate the learners for learning.
(d) All of the above.

67. By emotional maturity is meant a
(a) lack of patience or sympathy towards problems involving other people.
(b) low degree of sensitivity coupled with a high level of intellectual growth.
(c) lack of control or inhibition of the emotions appropriate to one's age-group.
(d) extreme patience or sympathy towards problems involving other people.

68. Mentality shows activeness and intellectual development of a child.
(a) Interest (b) Consciousness
(c) Physique (d) Intelligence

69. Purely motor nerve is
(a) Abducens (b) Ophthalamic
(c) Palatines (d) Optic

70. Evidence of mental development of a child is shown by development of
(a) Attitude (b) Language
(c) Personality (d) Intelligence

71. To educate according to nature means
(a) to educate according to the law of nature of human development.
(b) to study natural laws and apply them to the educational process.
(c) to return to the nature as opposed to the artificial in life.
(d) All of these.

72. Human activity may be studied in how many ways?
(a) Four (b) Three
(c) Two (d) One

73. The first philosopher who integrated psychology with education at least theoretically was
(a) Aristotle
(b) Pestalozzi
(c) John Locke
(d) None of the above

74. Which of the following is most likely to be characteristic of the ineffective teacher?
(a) Refusal to help children until they have helped themselves
(b) Emphasis upon standard
(c) Differential treatment of the students of his class
(d) Emphasis upon the control of the immediate situation

75. The mental development of a child after birth is on basis of
(a) Society (b) School
(c) Heredity (d) Environment

76. *Principles of Psychology* of William James was published in
(a) 1888 (b) 1890
(c) 1903 (d) 1906

77. In which stage a child develops his reasoning and thinking power?
(a) Adolescence (b) Babyhood
(c) Childhood (d) Both (a) and (b)

78. Which method of research probably contributes most to the advancement of educational psychology as a science?
(a) The survey method
(b) The experimental method
(c) The clinical method
(d) The historical method

79. Personality was beautifully remarked as "The same fire which melts the butter hardens the egg" by
(a) Allport (b) Hull
(c) Watson (d) Lindzey

80. Psychology is the science of
(a) Behaviour
(b) Attitude
(c) Human being
(d) Animal's behaviour

81. According to Freud in which age of child auto-eroticism is of
(a) Babyhood
(b) Childhood
(c) Adolescence
(d) None of the above

82. Human activity is commonly studied in terms of
(a) Goodness (b) Greatness
(c) Both (a) and (b) (d) Badness

83. The following quality is developed in a child in adolescence.
(a) Memory and imagination
(b) Generalization of facts
(c) Abstraction
(d) All of the above

84. Education requires general set of methods, focusing mainly on
(a) scientific method.
(b) systematic observation method.
(c) sociological method.
(d) direct-experimentation.

85. Which of the following is a specialized branch of educational psychology?
(a) Educational technology
(b) Special education
(c) Measurement and evaluation
(d) None of the above.

86. Who was the father of experimental psychology?
(a) Wundt (b) Hull
(c) Watson (d) Freud

87. Day-dreaming tendency in a child occurs at this age.
(a) Adult age (b) Childhood
(c) Babyhood (d) Adolescence

88. Psychological principles and theories can be applied in the field of
(a) business and trade
(b) medical treatment
(c) management
(d) All of the above

89. Maturity and IQ of a child are due to development of
(a) Moral (b) Physical
(c) Mental (d) Emotional

90. "Introspection Method" was used mainly in
(a) Behaviourism
(b) Gestalt psychology
(c) Functionalism
(d) Structuralism

91. Psychology is science of
(a) mental processes
(b) mental states
(c) mental functions
(d) All of the above

92. "Any manifestation of life can be called activity" is said by
(a) Patanjali (b) Socrates
(c) Woodworth (d) R.N. Tagore

93. Who rejected introspection as a legitimate method of study?
(a) Wundt (b) Bernstein
(c) Watson (d) Freud

94. IQ is indicative of child's which development?
(a) Emotional (b) Mental
(c) Physical (d) Personality

95. Personality, according to Allport, is the organisation of
(a) Physical systems
(b) Psychophysical systems
(c) Social systems
(d) Psychological systems

96. Below mentioned are the main reasons for the social development of a child.
(a) Effect of family
(b) Effect of community
(c) Effect of class
(d) All of the above

97. What is the value of process of socialisation?
(a) Biological perception
(b) Pognitive value
(c) Genetic development
(d) Perception of the situation

98. Which of the following statements about growth and development is not correct?
(a) Growth is determined by intrinsic and genetic factors of the organism.
(b) Growth generally refers to quantitative changes while development refers to qualitative changes.
(c) Growth is a function of the environment.
(d) Growth is not possible without development and vice versa.

99. The limit of growth is fixed by
(a) nutrition and exercise
(b) internal factors of the organism
(c) Both (a) and (b)
(d) None of the above

100. Behavioural changes which occur on the basis of physiological developments rather than learning and which appear in virtually all members of species are the result of
(a) Maturation (b) Fermentation
(c) Socialisation (d) Rationalisation

101. Due to following difference among the boys-girls they attract each other.
(a) sex difference.
(b) mental difference.
(c) physical difference.
(d) All of the above.

102. Which of the following is not a positive factor in the teacher's Mental-health?
(a) Personal and professional competence
(b) A strong need to love and to be loved by children
(c) A programme in which routine is routinized
(d) A schedule allowing for hobbies, friends and relaxation.

103. For the development of social principle in child, a teacher should develop this practice in him.
(a) Socialization (b) Indianization
(c) Discipline (d) Exercise

104. To trace the course of mental growth in an individual or the race is the problem of
(a) Genetic psychology
(b) Analytical psychology
(c) Physiological psychology
(d) Synthetic psychology

105. Subjective observation or self-observation is called
(a) Experiment
(b) Practical behaviour

(c) Introspection
(d) Super observation

106. There is an evidence of a hereditary component in development of the mental illness known as
(a) Schizophrenia
(b) Paralysis
(c) Paranoia
(d) Psychoneurotic disorders

107. Emotions in a child help in the following ways.
(a) Adjustment (b) Westernization
(c) Socialization (d) Indianization

108. When a question is answered wrongly the teacher should
(a) correct the answer with the help of the students.
(b) leave that question and proceed to the next question.
(c) punish the student for giving wrong answer.
(d) correct the fault in the answer and tell the students.

109. Emotions are the following stage of a person.
(a) Excited and scarred feelings
(b) Painful feelings
(c) Provocation of thought
(d) Good feeling

110. At what age the child takes his first step in walking?
(a) 4 to 5 years (b) 5 to 6 years
(c) 10 to 12 years (d) None of these

111. Development is
(a) Learning
(b) Synthesis of abilities
(c) Maturation
(d) All of the above

112. Development takes place when
(a) environmental forces interact with the hereditary forces in an organism.
(b) environmental forces work on the organism.
(c) Both (a) and (b).
(d) None of the above.

113. Maturation changes occur in a fairly predictable sequence and continue until
(a) Old stage (b) Adolescence
(c) Adulthood (d) None of these

114. The following are main emotions.
(a) Love (b) Anger
(c) Fear (d) All of the above

115. Which of the following statements about development is correct?
(a) Development may be positive and negative both.
(b) Development proceeds from general to specific.
(c) Process of development can be improved by exercise and nutrition.
(d) All of the above.

116. For a perfect emotional growth in a child, the following emotions should be eliminated.
(a) Ill-effects (b) Rise
(c) Excessive (d) All of the above

117. In the changes of body proportions, the ratio of head to height is 1:4 at birth, by the time of maturity it becomes
(a) 1:6 (b) 2:8
(c) 1:8 (d) 1:2

118. Logic is a normative science of
(a) Action (b) Thought
(c) Behaviour (d) None of the above

119. The word psychology has originated from
(a) the words 'Psycho' and 'Logus'.
(b) the words 'Logus' and 'Social'.
(c) the words 'Psycho' and 'Logis'.
(d) None of the above.

120. The concept of "a personality nucleus" was given by

(a) Stendler (b) Skinner
(c) Allport (d) Shirley

121. Good effect of emotions is
(a) source of tensions.
(b) source of entertainment.
(c) source of motivation.
(d) Both (a) and (b).

122. Which of the following is psychologically more sound?
(a) Success is always motivating and, hence, beneficial.
(b) Repeated failure, is undoubtedly, demotivating.
(c) A child should never have the experience of failure.
(d) Failure is always frustrating and, hence, harmful.

123. For emotional development of a child, the role of school should be
(a) coordination with environment.
(b) control over emotions.
(c) Both (a) and (b).
(d) None of the above.

124. A child is born with some
(a) Ego (b) Innate drives
(c) Qualities (d) All of these

125. The son of a goldsmith becomes an expert goldsmith. It is an example of a
(a) transfer of instinct
(b) biological heredity
(c) social heredity
(d) None of the above

126. The child becomes socialized
(a) After ego (b) Slowly
(c) Fast (d) Gradually

127. For the social development of a child, child should experience the following activities.
(a) Artistic activities (b) Individual
(c) Group-working (d) All of the above

128. The number of chromosomes in most cells of the human body is
(a) 46 (b) 42
(c) 36 (d) 26

129. DNA test helps us to know
(a) nature of personality and its composition.
(b) the genetic traits of a person.
(c) Both (a) and (b).
(d) None of the above.

130. The following has main role in the formation of character of a child.
(a) Control over anti-social feelings
(b) Increase in entertainment
(c) Formation of good habits
(d) Both (a) and (c)

131. What is the determinant of the scope of socialization of a child?
(a) Development of physique
(b) Environment
(c) Language development
(d) Excitement

132. The law of experience may be taken to mean
(a) Generalization (b) Repetitions
(c) Reward (d) Discriminations

133. Intelligence is the ability
(a) to learn
(b) to adjust oneself to new situations
(c) to think in terms of ideas
(d) to do all the three above

134. An individual adopts the way of living mores and religion of his society through
(a) Learning (b) Socialization
(c) Motivation (d) Not emotion

135. For the character-building of children in school, the option is
(a) character of principal.
(b) ideal of a teacher.
(c) good behaviour of guardian.
(d) None of the above.

136. The definition of psychology as the science of human behaviour set forth is more
 (a) Recent (b) Broad
 (c) Both (a) and (b) (d) Popular

137. Science deals with
 (a) particular type of subject
 (b) particular type of society
 (c) particular type of individual
 (d) None of the above

138. In which condition the development of concept occurs?
 (a) Adolescence (b) Childhood
 (c) Babyhood (d) All of the above

139. The main processes of socialization are
 (a) 3 (b) 8
 (c) 6 (d) 4

140. Many of our activities are responses to physical environment such as
 (a) breathing
 (b) closing our eyes to avoid dust
 (c) eating food
 (d) All of the above.

141. The socialization of an individual also depends on the manner in which he perceives
 (a) Attitude
 (b) Variables
 (c) Objective qualities
 (d) Situation

142. The following mental development occurs in adolescence.
 (a) Ability of abstraction
 (b) Development of playing instinct
 (c) Ability of taking decision
 (d) Both (a) and (b)

143. Which of the following illustrates conceptual development?
 (a) Concept changes with age
 (b) Perception is the beginning of concept formation
 (c) Concept changes with changes in experiences
 (d) All of the above.

144. The reason of individual differences.
 (a) Difference in mental power of a person
 (b) Difference in physical power of persons
 (c) Difference in education of a person
 (d) Both (a) and (b)

145. Indivual differences are found in
 (a) cognitive situations.
 (b) environmental situations.
 (c) emotional situations.
 (d) perceptual situations.

146. One thing that is common in language and physical development is
 (a) dependence on experience
 (b) dependence on training
 (c) spurts of development at different ages
 (d) None of the above

147. The socialisation of an individual takes place according to
 (a) cognitive learning.
 (b) perceptual learning.
 (c) dynamic learning in the perception of a situation.
 (d) dynamic learning in the emotion of stimulus.

148. Difference of person to person is called.
 (a) Internal or intro difference
 (b) External or inter difference
 (c) Both (a) and (b)
 (d) None of the above

149. Which of the following characteristics is not associated with emotional development?
 (a) Emotions are unrelated to physical development.
 (b) Emotion is accompanied by physiological changes.

(c) Emotions start immediately after birth.
(d) Intense form of emotions are seen during early childhood period.

150. Skinner has told two characteristics of individual differences.
(a) Commonality
(b) Similarity
(c) Variability
(d) Both (a) and (c)

151. How far does the mutual relationship of parents influence child's personality?
(a) Largely (b) Commonly
(c) Gradually (d) Speedily

152. Teach the child rather than the subject is the essential principle of
(a) Government
(b) School programme
(c) Old education
(d) New education

153. What is the result of emotional immaturity in the child?
(a) Frustration (b) Anger
(c) Struggle (d) Pain

154. "Today the meaning of individual differences is worth noticing aspect of collective behaviour." This definition is of the following.
(a) James Draver
(b) Tyler
(c) Skinner
(d) None of the above

155. The result of learning is
(a) modification and development.
(b) storing new knowledge in the mind.
(c) acquiring more information.
(d) utility to use old experiences.

156. The first to study the individual differences was
(a) Galton (b) Skinner
(c) McIver (d) Woodworth

157. What is the impact of other members of the family besides the parents, on the socialisation of the child?
(a) Intimate (b) Good
(c) External (d) None of these

158. The child acquires about three fourth of the brain weight by the age of
(a) 2 years (b) 6 years
(c) 8 years (d) 9 years

159. Social development of an infant depends on
(a) love and affection shown to the child.
(b) the extent to which he is able to attract the attention of others.
(c) his chance of interaction with others.
(d) All of the above.

160. How will the socialisation of the child be affected if he may follows the evil path?
(a) Intimately (b) Adversely
(c) Directly (d) Indirectly

161. The following is the area of individual differences.
(a) Character (b) Emotional
(c) Mental (d) All of the above

162. In which of the following stages the child looks self centred?
(a) Infancy (b) Early childhood
(c) Adolescence (d) Adulthood

163. Axiology comprises
(a) Ethics, Sociology and Philosophy
(b) Logic, Grammar and Rhetorics
(c) Logic, Ethics and Aesthetics
(d) Logic, Grammar and Mathematics

164. Interest, attitude, achievement and sex. To which different areas do they belong?
(a) Individual diversification
(b) Character diversification
(c) Internal diversification of a person
(d) Social diversification

165. How do brothers and sisters affect the socialisation of the child?
(a) Greatly (b) Commonly
(d) Continuously (d) Indirectly

166. The reply to that question or the behaviour aroused by that from or sneer will be the
(a) Stimulus (b) Action
(c) Reaction (d) Response

167. What does the youngest child receive all from the parents?
(a) Affection (b) Attention
(c) Drives (d) All requirement

168. The reason of individual differences are
(a) Maturity
(b) Environment
(c) Heredity
(d) All of the above

169. Chemistry deals with
(a) Matter (b) Material things
(c) Both (a) and (b) (d) Energy

170. Psychology is the science which underlines the art of
(a) Reading (b) Teaching
(c) Study (d) All of the above

171. Educational implications of individual differences are
(a) diversification in educational methods.
(b) flexibility in syllabus.
(c) Both (a) and (b).
(d) None of the above.

172. What shall be the child's position in the society. On the basis of social and economic conditions?
(a) Bad (b) Pre-supposed
(c) Reprehensible (d) Considerable

173. In the period of infancy, emotions are
(a) need based
(b) intense, frequent and unstable
(c) like an open book (overt)
(d) All of the above

174. Which of the following parts of the body shows rapid growth in infancy?
(a) fingers (b) hands
(c) head (d) legs

175. In what manner the child's socialisation proceeds in a school?
(a) A good manner (b) A bad manner
(c) Considerable (d) None of these

176. Why individual teaching is necessary?
(a) Due to environment
(b) Due to individual differences
(c) Due to heredity
(d) All of the above

177. The child should have a height of 43 inches and weight of 43 pounds by the age of
(a) Four years (b) Five years
(c) Six years (d) Eight years

178. Why bright or retarded child should be taught separately?
(a) Due to their individual differences
(b) Due to their individual similarities
(c) Both (a) and (b)
(d) None of the above

179. When does an individual make serious effort to pattern his behaviour according to social acceptance?
(a) 14 to 21 years (b) 13 to 20 years
(c) 15 to 23 years (d) 10 to 21 years

180. The influence which the environment exercises on the organism and reuses it to activity is called the
(a) Response (b) Stimulus
(c) Both (a) and (b) (d) Emotion

181. 'Micro teaching', one of the recent trends in education, insists on
(a) teaching of minutest points of a subject.
(b) teaching students by dividing them into smaller groups.

(c) mastering of various skills of teaching with special attention.
(d) finding out the subtle doubts in the minds of students.

182. Considering punishment as an insult, how do adolescents react to it?
(a) Abhore it very much
(b) Consider it command
(c) Fear it very much
(d) None of these

183. Due to individual differences of children the following should be different.
(a) Test (b) Home work
(c) Teaching (d) Both (b) and (c)

184. Lesson plan means
(a) to prepare all that the teacher wants to teach in a limited period.
(b) to read the lesson before teaching it.
(c) to prepare the list of questions to be asked.
(d) to prepare detailed answers of all the questions to be asked in the class.

185. This should be done by the teacher to the children for adjustment of individual differences.
(a) Diversification
(b) Socialization
(c) Teaching
(d) Instruction and advice

186. In order to escape punishments, the adolescent is cautious
(a) In socialisation
(b) In his behaviour
(c) In demand
(d) Of rebuke

187. Objective observation is especially useful in studying the mental life and behaviour of
(a) Animals (b) Children
(c) Savages (d) All of the above

188. Child's socialisation is influenced by
(a) Biological norm
(b) Brain pattern
(c) Ethnic status
(d) Communication

189. The teacher should adopt the following syllabus for intelligence children.
(a) Enriched (b) Simply
(c) Difficult (d) All of the above

190. Clear conception of size, weight, colour, time etc., is seen at the age of
(a) Seven (b) Six
(c) Five (d) Four

191. Due to individual differences a teacher can help retarded children.
(a) Group teaching
(b) Simple teaching
(c) Micro teaching
(d) Diagnostic and remedial teaching

192. School comes in socialisation of a child
(a) at oral stage.
(b) after society.
(c) through grouping.
(d) after family.

193. Applied aspects of social psychology include the development and perfection of techniques for measuring
(a) Opinion (b) Socialisation
(c) Attitude (d) Both (a) and (b)

194. Seriously handicapped children should be taught in this way.
(a) Specially separate
(b) In general classes
(c) In hospitals
(d) All of the above

195. Social development by the end of early childhood is marked by
(a) the temperament of co-operation and friendliness.
(b) the feeling of autonomy.

(c) the end of solitary plays.
(d) All of the above.

196. For the effective education of children due to individual differences, they should be taught in following groups.
(a) General intelligence
(b) Sharp intelligence
(c) Mentally retarded
(d) All of the above

197. The ability to think abstractly and to learn readily from experience is
(a) Learning (b) Thinking
(c) Memory (d) Intelligence

198. In the process of teaching a lesson, Thorndike's law of readiness finds applications in
(a) Recapitulation (b) Home work
(c) Introduction (d) Presentation

199. Who believed that performance on any cognitive task depended on a primary general factor(s) and on one or more specific factors(s) relating to that particular task?
(a) Cattell (b) Spearman
(c) Guilford (d) Thurstone

200. In the view of individual differences education should be centralized in
(a) syllabus centralized.
(b) guardian centralized.
(c) teacher centralized.
(d) child centralized.

201. Who is the best motivator at school?
(a) The Headmaster
(b) The Class Fellows
(c) The Class Teacher
(d) The Subject Teacher

202. "Adjustment between relative and new circumstances is called intelligence". This definition of intelligence in view of biological approach is given by
(a) Freeman (b) Calvin
(c) Burt (d) William Stern

203. Intelligence is a composite of seven distinct primary mental abilities was suggested by
(a) Binet (b) Thurstone
(c) Gardner (d) Sternberg

204. The state during which the individual is able to think in abstract and general terms and is intensely idealistic is
(a) adolescence (b) late childhood
(c) early childhood (d) adulthood

205. The law of inheritance was discovered by Gregor Mendel in
(a) 1811 (b) 1844
(c) 1866 (d) 1888

206. The first version of Binest and Simon's test was published in
(a) 1914 (b) 1814
(c) 1905 (d) 1904

207. "Intelligence is the power of attention". This definition is of
(a) Woodrow (b) Burt
(c) Mc Dougal (d) Stout

208. The traits of Kallikak family of USA were studied by
(a) Francis Galton
(b) Gregor Mendel
(c) Henry Goddard
(d) None of the above

209. The efficiency adjustment between relative and new circumstances is called intelligence". This definition of intelligence is by
(a) Burt (b) Weshler
(c) Cruz (d) Wels

210. The word Stanford in the Stanford-Binet test stands for
(a) a Psychiatrist (b) a Psychologist
(c) a Country (d) a University

211. Which of the following statements regarding personality traits is correct?
(a) Bad environment can surpass good inheritance but good environment is not a substitute for poor heredity.
(b) Traits of personality cannot be developed in isolation without taking the help of environment.
(c) Subjective traits of the individual are determined by genetic factors.
(d) All of the above.

212. The Stanford-Binet test a revision of Binet's original test was made by
(a) David Wechsler (b) Theodore Simon
(c) Alfred Binet (d) Lewis Terman

213. "Intelligence is the ability to learn". This definition is given by
(a) Terman (b) Balkigham
(c) Woodrow (d) Dearborn

214. A number of experiments have indicated that movements of the vocal apparatus may indeed accompany thought, but other experiments have made it clear that such movements are
(a) very necessary for thinking.
(b) not necessary for thinking.
(c) Both (a) and (b).
(d) sometimes necessary and not necessary at other times.

215. "Intelligence is the ability of abstract thinking". This statement is of
(a) Alfred Binet (b) Burt
(c) Spearman (d) Terman

216. The Wechsler Adult Intelligence scale consists of
(a) only non-verbal items.
(b) only verbal items.
(c) Both verbal and non-verbal items.
(d) Neither verbal nor non-verbal items.

217. Research has shown that the most frequent symptom of nervous instability among teachers is
(a) Digestive upsets
(b) Explosive behaviour
(c) Worry
(d) Absenteeism

218. The extent to which a test actually measures what it claims to measure is its
(a) Norms
(b) Reliability
(c) Split-half reliability
(d) Validity

219. On the basis of definitions, the following factors are shown of intelligence.
(a) This is an ability of abstract thinking
(b) This is an inborn power
(c) This is the ability of learning
(d) All of the above

220. What are the appreciation lessons?
(a) Science and Agriculture
(b) Language and Grammar
(c) Music and Poetry lessons
(d) History and Geography.

221. Ability of reasoning, thinking and decision is an element of following.
(a) Attitude (b) Intelligence
(c) Interest (d) Personality

222. The Stanford-Binet and the Wechsler scales are
(a) both group tests.
(b) both individual tests.
(c) Wechsler scale is group test.
(d) Stanford-Binet is group test.

223. For older psychologists who defined psychology as the science of consciousness alone the only method of enquiry is
(a) Introspection
(b) Reading and recording
(c) Observation
(d) By action

224. The intelligence test that includes items designed to be unaffected by specific cultural knowledge or experience is

(a) cultural bias test.
(b) cultural test.
(c) cultural-specific test.
(d) culture-fair test.

225. The following effects intelligence.
(a) Health
(b) Environment
(c) Heredity
(d) Both (b) and (c)

226. Which of the following characteristics denote infancy period?
(a) Head grows at relatively slower rate as compared to other parts of the body.
(b) Physical growth is curvilinear.
(c) Physical growth is rapid.
(d) All of the above.

227. Binet has founded the following theory of intelligence.
(a) Multi-factor theory
(b) Two-factor theory
(c) Uni-factor theory
(d) None of the above

228. The Raven Progressive Matrices consists of
(a) Fifty matrices (b) Eighty matrices
(c) Sixty matrices (d) Thirty matrices

229. Which gland controls the pitutary gland and hence the normal and proportionate growth of the body?
(a) urinary gland
(b) sex gland
(c) thyroid gland
(d) None of the above

230. The full form of the K-ABC Intelligence test for children is
(a) Kaufman-Assessment battery for children
(b) Kentman-Advancement battery for children
(c) Kaufman-Advancement box for children
(d) Kentman-Assessment box for children

231. The following has founded the multi-factor theory of intelligence.
(a) Thuston (b) Spearman
(c) Binet (d) Thorndike

232. Which of the following is not the characteristic of infancy period?
(a) Steady mental development
(b) From bilateral to unilateral trend in motor organs
(c) From general to specific trend in motor organs
(d) Emotional/social development is not associated with motor development.

233. Thuston has founded the following theory of intelligence.
(a) Group-factor theory
(b) Two-factor theory
(c) Uni-factor theory
(d) All of the above

234. Boys score _______ in intelligence tests as compared to girls.
(a) similar (b) lower
(c) higher (d) cannot be said

235. Parental indifferences to the child's behaviour is called
(a) withdrawal (b) overprotection
(c) aggression (d) identification

236. What is the most important contribution of psychology?
(a) Use of co-curricular activities
(b) Proper arrangement of discipline
(c) Student centred education
(d) Change in the time table.

237. An intelligence test that predicts how well you will do in college is an
(a) Aptitude test
(b) Achievement test

(c) Adjustment test
(d) Anxiety test

238. Spearman has proved the following factors in the unity of intelligence.
(a) Internal factor
(b) Specific factor
(c) General factor
(d) Both (b) and (c)

239. Fictional world of the child starts at the age of
(a) 3-4 (b) 4-5
(c) 5-6 (d) 6-8

240. This is the characteristic of the general factor of intelligence proved by Spearman.
(a) Its excess amount tells its success
(b) This is inborn
(c) Both (a) and (b)
(d) None of the above

241. Examinations given at the end of a course to see how much you have learned are
(a) Achievement tests
(b) Adjustment tests
(c) Anxiety tests
(d) Aptitude tests

242. Girls are more dominating than boys in social situations in which of the following periods?
(a) Early childhood period
(b) Pre-adolescent period
(c) Both (a) and (b)
(d) None of the above

243. Both Aptitude test and Achievement test are
(a) Anxiety tests (b) Attitude tests
(c) Adjustment tests (d) Ability tests

244. Specific factor of intelligence is important in these activities of a person
(a) Music (b) Handicraft
(c) Art (d) All of the above

245. In the period of early childhood, child is
(a) guided by his innate tendencies and instincts.
(b) helpless to hide his emotions.
(c) seen shifting his emotions very rapidly and frequently.
(d) All of the above.

246. According to Spearman, transfer of subjects is possible by this factor of intelligence.
(a) Specific factor (b) Group factor
(c) General factor (d) All of the above

247. The French psychologist Alfred Binet published the first intelligence test in 1905 in collaboration with
(a) Sir Francis Galton
(b) Theodore Simon
(c) David Wechsler
(d) None of these

248. Specialisation in any field of study involves
(a) reward (b) generalisation
(c) discrimination (d) punishment

249. 'Population Education' explains to us
(a) the problems being faced by different groups of people.
(b) the problem and their solution concerning the population growth.
(c) the type of education suited to different sections of population.
(d) the process of educating people on a large scale.

250. The need of group tests started with
(a) India Pakistan War
(b) World War I
(c) India China War
(d) World War II

251. According to the uni-factor theory of intelligence of Binet, intelligence activates a person to do one work at a time.

(a) Perform only one function
(b) To perform many functions
(c) To perform special functions
(d) All of the above

252. A nursery teacher should organize
(a) those games which help the child to manipulate the environment.
(b) group games in the school.
(c) those games which involve motor organs of the body.
(d) All of the above.

253. Thorndike has proved the following factors or ability in intelligence.
(a) General factor
(b) Common factor
(c) Primary factor
(d) Both (b) and (c)

254. Down syndrome, a genetic defect occurs when the cells in the body have an extra copy (trisomy) of chromosome
(a) number 20 (b) number 23
(c) number 22 (d) number 21

255. Later childhood is called latency period because
(a) it is a period of inactivity.
(b) creative potentials are dormant.
(c) sex remains dormant.
(d) All of the above.

256. Intelligence is expressed as a quotient and the formula used to arrive at I.Q. is
(a) $\frac{MA}{CA} \times 100$ (b) 100 – MA
(c) M.A. × C.A. (d) M.A. + CA

257. Human intelligence is affected by
(a) only environment.
(b) only heredity.
(c) Both heredity and environment.
(d) Neither heredity nor environment.

258. On the basis of factorial analysis, Thurston gave result that structure of intelligence is due to the primary factor of
(a) Coordination (b) Group
(c) Union (d) All of the above

259. The school exists for the pupil, not the pupil for the
(a) School (b) Society
(c) Family (d) All of the above

260. According to Thurston following primary factors make group in the structure of intelligence.
(a) Special ability (b) Verbal activity
(c) Numerical ability (d) All of the above

261. The first intelligence test was developed by
(a) Albert Sidney Beckham
(b) Lewis Terman
(c) Alfred Binet
(d) David Wechsler

262. Psychology tells us about understanding of
(a) Human culture
(b) National problems
(c) National leaders
(d) Human nature

263. Who invented the correlation coefficient and developed the ideas behind finger-printing and eugenics?
(a) Alfred Binet
(b) Charles Darwin
(c) Wechsler
(d) Sir Francis Galton

264. Thompson proved which theory of intelligence?
(a) Group-factor theory
(b) Uni-factor theory
(c) Multi-factor theory
(d) Sample theory

265. Physical development of later childhood is marked by

(a) Permanent teeth
(b) Excessive motor activity
(c) Ossification of bones
(d) All of the above

266. "Every work is a sample of fixed qualifications." This theory of intelligence is given by
(a) Spearman (b) Thorndike
(c) Thompson (d) Thurston

267. The Binet scale for intelligence which was published in 1905 was revised in the years
(a) 1908 and again in 1911
(b) 1906 and again in 1910
(c) 1909 and again in 1912
(d) 1907 and again in 1913

268. Girls surpass boys physically in
(a) early childhood (b) adolescence
(c) later childhood (d) infancy

269. A bright child's MA is above his CA; a dull child has a MA below his CA. This statement is
(a) False (b) Partly right
(c) True (d) Can't be said

270. The Hierarchical Theory of intelligence was founded by
(a) Guilford (b) Cattell
(c) Burt and Bunon (d) Thompson

271. The period of later childhood is marked by
(a) hero worship
(b) intellectual maturity
(c) high muscular energy
(d) All of the above

272. Guilford proved which theory of intelligence
(a) three dimensional
(b) multi factor
(c) hierarchical
(d) group factor

273. The formula for calculating IQ is
(a) $\frac{CA}{MA} \div 100$ (b) $\frac{MA}{CA} \times 100$
(c) $\frac{CA}{MA} \div 200$ (d) $\frac{MA}{CA} \times 200$

274. Psychology is a study of man in his several activities and states. It analyses his
(a) thoughts and feeling.
(b) fears and hopes.
(c) ideas and memories.
(d) All of the above.

275. According to the Guilford's (1967) model of Intelligence, the number of identifiable abilities are
(a) 100 (b) 130
(c) 120 (d) 110

276. According to Guilford, this class is included in mental qualification of intelligence.
(a) Products (b) Operation
(c) Contents (d) All of the above

277. Evaluation in education as an examination reform recommends
(a) careful scrutiny of the causes of errors in the student's answers.
(b) careful analysis of the student's responses to determine the common errors.
(c) objective type of questions in examinations instead of the essay type questions.
(d) clear-cut determination of objectives of teaching and testing their achievement.

278. This theory of intelligence was founded by Piaget.
(a) Hierarchical theory
(b) Fluid and crystallised theory

(c) Mental growth theory
(d) None of the above

279. "Intelligence is the aggregate or global capacity of the individual to act purposefully, to think rationally, and to deal effectively with his environment." The above definition was given by
(a) Anastasi (b) Wechsler
(c) Terman (d) Ebbinghaus

280. The soul is beyond
(a) Knowledge (b) Experience
(c) Action (d) Both (b) and (c)

281. Intelligence is the ability of
(a) adjusting in new situations.
(b) availing of past experiences.
(c) abstract thinking.
(d) All of these.

282. Spearman proved this principle of intelligence aiongwith two-factor theory.
(a) Three-factor (b) Uni-factor
(c) Group-factor (d) All of the above

283. Which of the following is not a characteristic of intellectual development of later childhood?
(a) Careful for future
(b) End of imaginary fears
(c) High interest in science fiction
(d) Increased logical power.

284. Children are very much hateful or indifferent to opposite sex at the age of
(a) 10-11 (b) 11-12
(c) 13-14 (d) 15-16

285. Who first formed the method of measurement of intelligence in 1905.
(a) Weschler (b) Spearman
(c) Binet and Simon (d) Wunt

286. To understand the intelligence, scientific approaches started around
(a) hundred years back.
(b) two hundred years back.
(c) recently.
(d) quarter of a century back.

287. Period of later childhood is marked by
(a) anger against injustice.
(b) slow and steady physical growth.
(c) stability in emotions.
(d) All of the above.

288. For testing purposes, the highest level at which all items of Binet's test are passed by a given child is that child's
(a) Ground age (b) Ceiling age
(c) Basal age (d) Mental age

289. The number of question in the scale of intelligence test of "Binet and Simon" of 1905 were
(a) 30 (b) 50
(c) 75 (d) 100

290. Which statement is correct regarding the use of audio-visual material?
(a) Audio-visual material should be used only when the students like it.
(b) Audio-visual material should be used as help in teaching of the subject.
(c) Audio-visual material should be used in beginning of the lessons.
(d) None of the above.

291. In the intelligent-test-scale of Binet and Simon which powers of a person are stressed most?
(a) Decision (b) Reasoning
(c) Appreciation (d) All of the above

292. The age level at which the child cannot pass any of the items of particular subtest is called
(a) Ceiling age (b) Mental age
(c) Specific age (d) Basal age

293. The importance of motivation and reciprocity was brought out in the learning theories by
(a) Wolfgang Kohler (b) Jean Piaget
(c) B.F. Skinner (d) Jerome Bruner

294. Psychology is the science of
(a) Emotion (b) Action
(c) Consciousness (d) Reaction

295. Intelligence is the property of recombining our behaviour pattern so as to act better in a novel situation. This definition is given by
(a) Binet (b) Hull
(c) William Stern (d) Wells

296. Decorated in 1908, by Binet-Simon intelligence-test-scale, was used to decide the following.
(a) Intelligence age
(b) Mental age
(c) Chronological age
(d) All of the above

297. At the end of later childhood period, the child
(a) becomes independent of his family.
(b) wants to become hero.
(c) feels himself superior to girls.
(d) All of the above.

298. The best place of social development for a 12 years old child is
(a) Family (b) School
(c) Neighbourhood (d) Playground

299. The following changes were made in the third edition of Binet-Simon intelligence-test-scale in 1911.
(a) Its extension was up to adult level
(b) Number of questions was increased
(c) Both (a) and (b)
(d) None of the above

300. As the infant grows, his mental ability
(a) Fluctuates (b) Stagnates
(c) Increases (d) Decreases

301. The extra Y chromosome apparently causes the adrenal glands to secrete an abnormally large amount of the male hormone (Testosterone) so that such individuals reach sexual maturity early and may have a higher than normal sex drive. In a sense they are
(a) Super female (b) Super male
(c) Dull male (d) Both (a) and (b)

302. Psychology as a science concerns itself with facts of
(a) Religion (b) Behaviour
(c) Cultural (d) All of the above

303. The most widely used test for adults was developed by
(a) Guilford (b) Wechsler
(c) Stanford (d) Terman

304. What is the speciality of Binet-Simon intelligence-test-scale?
(a) Its question are according to age group
(b) To find the mental age
(c) In its scale question increases from easy to hard
(d) All of the above

305. Group activities and group loyalties are at its peak at the age of
(a) 18-20 (b) 13-15
(c) 10-12 (d) 8-10

306. A teacher should not let a 12 year old child any time free because
(a) child is frustrated.
(b) child is always interested to get involved in physical or mental activities.
(c) spurts of creativity are seen at this age.
(d) All of the above.

307. In which intelligence-test scoring is according to age-norms?
(a) Stanford test
(b) Merill-Palmer test
(c) Binet-Simon test
(d) Terman

308. Which group test was designed during World War I for persons who could not read or who did not speak English?
(a) WAIS (b) Stanford-Binet
(c) Army Alpha (d) Army Beta

309. Which of the following is the most correct statement about the relation between marital status and the personal social adjustment of teachers?
(a) Marital status favours married male teachers.
(b) Marital status bears no relation to adjustment.
(c) Empirical evidence favours the married teacher.
(d) Empirical evidence favours the single teacher.

310. Which group test was designed during World War I for persons who could read?
(a) Army Beta (b) WAIS
(c) Army Alpha (d) Stanford-Binet

311. According to the favourable circumstances of our country, the correction of Binet-Simon intelligence-test is known as
(a) Minisota (b) Stamford
(c) Bobertaga (d) Terman

312. Each science tries to formulate
(a) New facts
(b) General principles
(c) General findings
(d) Both (b) and (c)

313. Difficulties of introspection are stressed mostly by behaviourists who deny that there is
(a) any form of life
(b) any physical life
(c) any expressive life
(d) any mental life

314. Binet-Simon intelligence-test-scale has following errors.
(a) It takes time for individual test
(b) It gives emphasis on words inspite of object
(c) It was tested on the students of Paris alone
(d) All of the above

315. "Intelligence is the ability to adjust oneself to a new situation." This definition was given by
(a) William Stern (b) Merrill
(c) Terman (d) Wells

316. Electra complex is psychoanalytic theory that a
(a) son's attachment to his mother.
(b) boy develops inferiority complex in the presence of girls.
(c) daughter's attachment to her father.
(d) None of the above.

317. According to Freud, super ego is properly developed during
(a) anal stage (b) phallic stage
(c) latency stage (d) genital stage

318. The WAIS like the Stanford-Binet is a/an ______ test.
(a) individual (b) social
(c) school (d) general

319. Merill-Parmer intelligence-test-scale is used for children of this age-group.
(a) One and half to five and half years
(b) Fifteen and half to 18 years
(c) 10 to 14 years
(d) 5 to 8 years

320. Development is a process of observable social interaction. This is the opinion of
(a) Robert Sears (b) Erikson
(c) Skinner (d) None of these

321. Observing the behaviour of other individual is
(a) Objective observation
(b) Objective introspection

(c) Subjective observation
(d) Subjective introspection

322. Minnesota pre-school-scale is used for children of which age?
(a) 2 to 6 years
(b) 3 to 4 years
(c) 5 to 10 years
(d) 18 months to 5 years

323. The deviation IQ is a type of
(a) Average score (b) Raw score
(c) Standard score (d) Mean score

324. The environment in which behaviour takes place need not necessarily be
(a) Material
(b) Chemical
(c) Physical
(d) Any of the above

325. History tells us of the changing
(a) Habits of nations
(b) Thoughts of nations
(c) Both (a) and (b)
(d) Social culture

326. Wechsler set the mean of the scores equal to an IQ of
(a) 150 (b) 50
(c) 100 (d) 120

327. Wechsler scale of 1949 is suitable for age group.
(a) 3 years (b) 5 years
(c) 8 years (d) 10 years

328. The Science of Psychology is concerned with
(a) Social problems
(b) Human relations
(c) Human nature
(d) National relations

329. Psychology helps us to understand the behaviour of
(a) Individual (b) People
(c) Society (d) Both (a) and (b)

330. Wechsler adult scale was make in which year?
(a) 1905 (b) 1949
(c) 1940 (d) 1955

331. Wechsler set one standard deviation in score prints equal to how many IQ points
(a) 15 (b) 25
(c) 20 (d) 5

332. The secondary behaviour of the child according to Robert Sears starts with
(a) imitation
(b) modeling
(c) reinforcement
(d) None of the above

333. Girls generally do better on verbal problems and boys in spatial, numerical and mechanical tasks. This statement is
(a) False (b) True
(c) Partially false (d) Cannot say

334. Group intelligence-tests developed in 1917 in name of
(a) Army omega (b) Army alfa
(c) Army gama (d) Army bita

335. Piaget's Sensory Motor stage occurs in children of
(a) 4-6 years (b) 3-5 years
(c) 1-3 years (d) 0-2 years

336. Which of the following is not the view point of cognitive theories of development?
(a) Moral principles are universal.
(b) Moral principles are acquired automatically with age.
(c) Super ego is formed during the period of adolescence.
(d) Moral values are determined by culture.

337. Army bita intelligence-test was of what type of test?
(a) Non-verbal (b) Numeral
(c) Pictorial (d) Verbal

338. People are appropriately regarded as mentally retarded if they attain IQ's below
(a) 100 (b) 120
(c) 90 (d) 70

339. The project method is based on the
(a) principle of inspiration
(b) principle of selection
(c) principle of learning by doing
(d) principle of regulation

340. Ability includes
(a) Observations (b) Achievement
(c) Aptitude (d) Both (b) and (c)

341. The following Indians contributed in the development of intelligence test.
(a) Mehrotra (b) Kamath
(c) Sharma (d) Both (a) and (b)

342. According to Herbert Spencer, four components of teaching are Clearness, association, system and method but his followers amended it and increased the number of components to
(a) Five (b) Six
(c) Seven (d) Eight

343. Economics teach us about the ways in which people
(a) Earn (b) Work
(c) Sell (d) All of the above

344. Decision of mental age by IQ for a child, shows his ability in comparison to which age-group?
(a) Of higher age-group
(b) Of lower age-group
(c) Of other age-group
(d) Of equal age-group

345. As compared to a dull child, mental age for bright children would generally grow
(a) more rapidly.
(b) less rapidly.
(c) at the same rate.
(d) can't be said.

346. Organization of sensory experiences about a particular object is called
(a) Reasoning (b) Concept
(c) Percepts (d) None of the above

347. The concept building in a person depends on
(a) past experiences of the learner
(b) intelligence of the learner
(c) the age and maturity of the person
(d) All of the above

348. Assume that subject is given a long list of unrelated words to study and is asked to recall the words at a later time. The content of thistest is
(a) Symbolic (b) Semantic
(c) Behavioural (d) Figural

349. Which formula is used for calculation of IQ?
(a) Mental age ÷ chronological age × 100
(b) Mental age ÷ age of other child × 100
(c) Chronological age ÷ mental age × 100
(d) All of the above

350. Agreement on a concept is possible because
(a) concepts are subjective
(b) concepts are objective
(c) concepts are hierarchical
(d) Both (b) and (c)

351. Range of IQ of idiot children is
(a) 0-25 (b) 25-50
(c) 50-70 (d) 120-140

352. The study of the characteristics of one person has been called the
(a) nomothetic approach.
(b) monologus approach.
(c) general approach.
(d) idiographic approach.

353. The chief purpose of the study of psychology is to know more about
(a) Social gatherings
(b) Human activity

(c) Human nature
(d) Both (b) and (c)

354. The Army Alpha and Army Beta tests were devised during
(a) 1950-60 (b) 1990-2000
(c) World War I (d) World War II

355. 80-90 IQ range is of which type of children?
(a) Average (b) Superior
(c) Dull (d) Feeble-minded

356. Psychology is a
(a) Science of magic
(b) Science of society
(c) Science of facts
(d) Science of mind

357. IQ range of genius children should be
(a) 50-70 (b) 90-110
(c) 120-140 (d) more than 140

358. The Otis-Lennon school Ability Test, the Henmon-Nelson Tests and the Cognitive Abilities Test (CAT) are all
(a) Adjustment test (b) Personality test
(c) Individual test (d) Group test

359. Which of the following statements about concepts is correct?
(a) All concepts are universal
(b) Concepts are differentiated on the basis of their attributes
(c) Some concepts are more powerful than others
(d) None of the above

360. The original Guilford's structure of intellect model suggests
(a) 120 unidentifiable abilities.
(b) lumping together of items to form tests.
(c) seven primary abilities.
(d) the general intelligence factor 'g'.

361. Constancy of IQ means that IQ
(a) gets changes.
(b) not increases or decreases.
(c) decreases with age.
(d) increases with age.

362. Which is the highest level of concept formation?
(a) concrete level
(b) sensory level
(c) formal level
(d) None of the above

363. The perceptual response to a stimulus is essentially
(a) Subjective (b) Learned
(c) Intuitive (d) Objective

364. The type of intelligence test is
(a) Group (b) Personal
(c) Non-verbal (d) All of the above

365. By giving tests in two different but equivalent forms, one can ascertain the
(a) Utility (b) Norms
(c) Validity (d) Reliability

366. The tests where use of written words is involved are called
(a) Verbal tests (b) Language tests
(c) Word tests (d) Written tests

367. The characteristic of personal intelligence-test is
(a) calculation of group.
(b) observing the working of a person.
(c) class-view.
(d) All of the above.

368. The standard visual-gestural sign language learned by the deaf have many features in common with
(a) stimulus vocal languages.
(b) auditory vocal languages.
(c) local vocal languages.
(d) visual vocal languages.

369. The entire life of an individual is expressed by
(a) Action (b) Behaviour
(c) Work (d) Thought

370. Group tests of intelligence are generally of following types.

(a) Practical type
(b) Paper-pencil type
(c) Oral type
(d) All of the above

371. Terman of Stanford University brought out are vision of Binet's test in
(a) 1915 (b) 1916
(c) 1960 (d) 1816

372. An individual consists of
(a) Body only
(b) Mind only
(c) Attitudes
(d) Both body and mind

373. How many steps of problem solving has been given by Gates?
(a) Five (b) Six
(c) Seven (d) Ten

374. In an intelligence test a 10-year-old child was found to have mental age of 12 years. His IQ is
(a) 105 (b) 95
(c) 100 (d) 120

375. Which type of intelligence-test are useful for selection and classification of persons?
(a) Group test (b) Individual test
(c) Non-verbal test (d) Verbal test

376. An individual possesses
(a) bulk of personality traits
(b) one personality trait
(c) few personality traits
(d) no personality trait

377. By and large psychology is a
(a) Science of society
(b) Science of magic
(c) Science of nation
(d) Science of behaviour

378. The characteristic of verbal intelligence test is
(a) there administration can be in both forms—personal and groupwise.
(b) a person can give answer in oral or written form.
(c) Both (a) and (b).
(d) None of the above.

379. Which of the following statements is true?
(a) If a test measures what it is intended to measure then by definition it is reliable
(b) A test can be valid without being reliable
(c) If a test gives consistent scores when administered repeatedly then it is valid
(d) A test can be reliable without being valid

380. Freeman considers intelligence as an ability to
(a) manipulate abstract materials
(b) adjust in an adverse situation
(c) learn better and faster
(d) All of the above

381. Mirror Drawing Apparatus is related to
(a) Span of memory
(b) Conditioning
(c) Forgetting
(d) Trial and error

382. The limitations of verbal intelligence test is
(a) effected by social, cultural and economy and of students.
(b) business in view of money and time.
(c) for those who know the language of test.
(d) Both (a) and (c).

383. Single factor theory of intelligence was given by
(a) Freeman (b) Alfred Binet
(c) Thorndike (d) None of the above

384. Animal psychology is also called
(a) Genetic psychology
(b) Physiological psychology

(c) Comparative psychology
(d) None of the above

385. In non-verbal intelligence tests the following are used in place of words.
(a) Geometrical shapes
(b) Pictorial figures
(c) Pictures
(d) All of the above

386. On which animal Pavlov conducted his experiment?
(a) Dog (b) Bird
(c) Cat (d) Rat

387. In a gang there is well defined
(a) Symbol (b) Leadership
(c) Status (d) Can't say

388. As children learn to co-operate they develop
(a) team-spirit (b) social attitude
(c) confidence (d) All of the above

389. Who said "we are born capable of learning"?
(a) Noam Chomsky
(b) Jean-Jacques Rousseau
(c) Ivan P. Pavlov
(d) Jean Piaget

390. Non-verbal intelligence tests can be divided into following parts.
(a) Performance
(b) Paper-pencil
(c) Performance and thinking
(d) Both (a) and (b)

391. Many of the attitudes of the teenagers are a result of
(a) Group influence (b) Stimulation
(c) Both (a) and (b) (d) Society

392. The peer group is primarily an
(a) Active group
(b) Playing group
(c) Over active group
(d) Inactive group

393. The limitation of non-verbal intelligence test is that
(a) it is effected by behaviour elements.
(b) it is unable to predict.
(c) Both (a) and (b).
(d) None of the above.

394. Skinner's best known apparatus is the teaching machine, invented by
(a) James (b) Thorndike
(c) Sidney Pressey (d) Watson

395. If the population on which a study is based is such that all its units can be reached, it is termed as
(a) accessible population
(b) homogeneous population
(c) target population
(d) heterogeneous population

396. Operant conditioning is associated with
(a) Skinner (b) Kohler
(c) Piaget (d) Pavlov

397. In performance intelligence test
(a) behaviour work is given at a place of answer.
(b) knowledge of language is not necessary.
(c) knowledge of language is necessary.
(d) Both (a) and (b).

398. Which of the following is not the characteristics of 'S' factor according to Spearman?
(a) It varies from activity to activity in the same individual.
(b) Individuals differ only in 'S' factor of intelligence.
(c) Specialization in only one trade is possible.
(d) It is the acquired capacity of the individual.

399. In performance intelligence test, directions are given by mono-acting or signs, thus

they are used to know the mental level of following.

(a) Blind (b) Deaf and dumb
(c) Retarded (d) Both (a) and (b)

400. Food in classical conditioning is called
(a) Unconditioned stimulus
(b) Conditioned stimulus
(c) Unconditioned response
(d) Conditioned response

401. In multifactor theory, range is related to
(a) general intelligence of learners.
(b) number of tasks that a person can do in a limited period of time.
(c) difficulty level of items.
(d) None of the above.

402. Differences in age of first walking or talking between children living in the same sort of environment are primarily due to differences in
(a) rate of maturation
(b) imitative learning
(c) amount of opportunity
(d) levels of motivation

403. What is the 'Bell' in Pavlov's classical conditioning?
(a) US (b) CR
(c) UCR (d) UCS

404. The quality of performance intelligence-test is
(a) a student can perform according to his will.
(b) useful for disabled or people not knowing language.
(c) the language of student is used in it.
(d) All of the above.

405. The film enquiry committee was established in
(a) 1981 (b) 1971
(c) 1958 (d) 1951

406. SI model of intelligence was given by J.P. Guilford in
(a) 1966 (b) 1975
(c) 1911 (d) 1904

407. Utility of intelligence-test is following.
(a) To know individual differences
(b) Guidance
(c) For entrance and job selection
(d) All of these

408. Which operant technique weakens behaviour?
(a) Positive and negative reward
(b) Positive and negative incentive
(c) Positive and negative punishment
(d) None of these

409. Hierarchy theory of intelligence was given by
(a) Burt and Vernon
(b) Spearman
(c) Thorndike
(d) None of the above

410. "Sampling frame" means
(a) identification of target and accessible population.
(b) fixing the sample size and drawing a sample.
(c) defining sample unit and selecting units.
(d) preparing a complete list of the units of finite population for drawing a sample.

411. A _______ is a brief involuntary reaction to some stimulus, typically a specific part of the body.
(a) reflection (b) response
(c) reflex (d) None of these

412. The formula to know IQ was given by which psychologist?
(a) Mc Dougal (b) Kohler
(c) Freud (d) Terman

413. Youth movement should be based on the
(a) social ideologies
(b) ideologies of nation as a whole
(c) cultural ideologies
(d) All of the above

414. In the pre-Binet period, intelligence was considered as
(a) associative ability of the individual
(b) sensory activity of the individual
(c) verbal ability of the individual
(d) All of the above

415. If Ram is 8 years old and by Binet test his mental age is proved 12 years then his IQ will be
(a) 150 (b) 90
(c) 75 (d) 120

416. A pigeon is trained to peck at green light. Now it peck at all lighted spots. It is a case of
(a) generalization gradient.
(b) stimulus generalization.
(c) discrimination.
(d) response generalization.

417. An age scale of intelligence was first developed by
(a) Binet-Simon (b) Spearman
(c) Lewis Terman (d) Stanford-Binet

418. In teenager groups, the group organisation is based on
(a) Physical shape (b) Sex
(c) Education (d) Age

419. In social learning theory, an instance in which the correct response appears on the first trial is called
(a) one trial learning.
(b) no trial learning.
(c) no learning.
(d) simple trial learning.

420. Formula to get IQ is
(a) Chronological age ÷ mental age ÷ 100
(b) Mental age ÷ chronological age ÷ 100
(c) Chronological age ÷ mental age × 100
(d) Mental age ÷ chronological age × 100

421. Many students who form gangs come from
(a) low income families
(b) deprived sections
(c) Both (a) and (b)
(d) None of the above

422. "Learning is changing of behaviour by experience and training". This definition was given by
(a) Cronback (b) Woodworm
(c) Gates (d) Skinner

423. Operant conditioning is also called
(a) classical conditioning.
(b) instrumental conditioning.
(c) simple conditioning.
(d) avoidance conditioning.

424. Binet-Simon scale of intelligence measures
(a) mental growth of the individual over a period of time.
(b) the aptitude or level of an examinee, not his speed.
(c) general mental abilities, not specific ones.
(d) All of the above.

425. WAIS came into being in
(a) 1955 (b) 1954
(c) 1939 (d) 1930

426. The structure of the brain which is involved in balance and coordination, and plays a key role in the formation of simple form of classically conditioned responses is
(a) Hypothalamus (b) Limbic system
(c) Cerebellum (d) Thalamus

427. "Learning is changing by pre-formed and experience by behaviour". This definition was given by which psychologist?

(a) Guilford, J.P. (b) Calvin
(c) Pavlov (d) Peel, E.A.

428. Peer groups during adolescence are very significant especially in
(a) Indian culture (b) Eastern culture
(c) Western culture (d) All cultures

429. Play group gives the experience in miniature form of the world of people of different
(a) Attitudes (b) Backgrounds
(c) Values (d) All of the above

430. The following elements are in nature of learning.
(a) This is formation of habit due to binding
(b) Behaviour changes by experience
(c) This is a process of post positive behaviour
(d) All of the above

431. Name the process in which a conditioned stimulus gradually ceases to elicit a conditioned stimulus.
(a) Classical conditioning
(b) Extinction
(c) Escape Conditioning
(d) Discrimination

432. Play group of children are
(a) Unorganized
(b) Organized
(c) Partially organised
(d) None of the above

433. Wechsler developed an intelligence test for children in
(a) 1949 (b) 1939
(c) 1936 (d) 1935

434. When a behaviour occurs consistently in the presence of a discriminative stimulus, it is said to be under
(a) delayed process.
(b) stimulus control.
(c) classical conditioning process.
(d) extinction.

435. Learning is a process of this kind.
(a) Process at the time of experience
(b) Lifelong
(c) It is result oriented
(d) Both (b) and (c)

436. At the age of seven or eight years play groups are generally
(a) Informal
(b) Leadership oriented
(c) Formal
(d) None of the above

437. Effecting directions or factors of classified learning are
(a) Motivation (b) Environment
(c) Physiological (d) All of these

438. The acquisition of new forms of behaviour, information or concepts through exposure to others and the consequences they experience is called
(a) operant learning.
(b) slow learning.
(c) observational learning.
(d) conditioning learning.

439. Play groups of young children exercise a considerable influence on their
(a) Religion (b) Society
(c) Personality (d) Culture

440. Popularity and effectiveness of the cinema may be due to
(a) story writers (b) the directors
(c) cinema stars (d) All of the above

441. The term classical means
(a) well planned.
(b) in the established manner.
(c) without planning.
(d) planned manner.

442. Types of motivation are
(a) Extrinsic (b) Intrinsic
(c) Spiritual (d) Both (a) and (b)

443. Play groups are useful in learning the
(a) status of group
(b) vocabulary of group
(c) religion of group
(d) All of the above

444. Physical factor of learning are
(a) Attitude (b) Maturity
(c) Personality (d) Intelligence

445. In Pavlov's experiments as the experiment progressed, the sight of the bowl, the sight of the experimenter and eventually even the sound of experimenter's footsteps produced salivation, Pavlov called these learned reactions as
(a) psychic secretions.
(b) natural reactions.
(c) unnatural reactions.
(d) neutral reactions.

446. Catell's culture fair test of intelligence was developed in
(a) 1945 (b) 1955
(c) 1960 (d) 1961

447. Non-verbal test of intelligence is suitable for
(a) backward children
(b) deaf and dumb
(c) illiterates
(d) All of the above

448. The classical conditioning has been described as
(a) neutral.
(b) response behaviour.
(c) stimulus substitution.
(d) unlearned behaviour.

449. Environmental factor of learning is
(a) School
(b) Home and family
(c) Age
(d) Both (a) and (b)

450. The Cinema is a very popular and powerful agency and an effective instrument in modifying
(a) cultural value
(b) human behaviour
(c) habits
(d) All of the above

451. Following law of learning is formed by Thorndike.
(a) Law of experience
(b) Law of success
(c) Law of nearness
(d) Law of readiness

452. The translation of Russian word ouslovny means
(a) Unconditioned (b) Operant
(c) Conditioned (d) Classical

453. In the opinion of the 1952-53 Secondary Education Commission in our country, the special function of the secondary school is
(a) to train students to assume leadership responsibility in their community or locality.
(b) to equip students with adequate knowledge for further education.
(c) to see that persons after secondary education address themselves to works of productivity.
(d) to prepare students to join vocational courses easily.

454. Which operant techniques strengthen behaviour?
(a) Positive and negative punishment
(b) Reward and incentive
(c) Positive and negative reinforcement
(d) None of these

455. The meaning of "Law of Readiness" of learning by Thorndike is

(a) preparation of nervous process.
(b) preparation for attention.
(c) preparation for physical health.
(d) preparation for attitude.

456. Intelligence testing is useful for knowing
(a) mental retardation
(b) educational backwardness
(c) individual difference
(d) All of the above

457. Scores on intelligence tests cannot be fully relied on because
(a) cultural factors can influence the score.
(b) they generally do not reveal all the mental abilities of a person.
(c) fatigue level can influence the performance.
(d) All of the above.

458. What should teacher do for a student ready for learning?
(a) He should calm the readiness of student
(b) Student should be made more ready
(c) The experience that help in the increase of readiness should be preformed
(d) All of the above

459. Habit interference is also known as
(a) negative transfer.
(b) bilateral training.
(c) positive transfer.
(d) None of these.

460. Gangs may be generally classified into
(a) Two categories (b) Three categories
(c) Four categories (d) Six categories

461. The programmes of youth should provide opportunities of
(a) creative self-expression
(b) new experience
(c) responsibility
(d) All of the above

462. Positive transfer greatly depends upon the presence of identical elements between the original and subsequent
(a) Process (b) Perception
(c) Learning (d) Attention

463. Readiness of student during the process of learning is
(a) Incurable (b) Curable
(c) Excited (d) Satisfactory

464. Which of the following is the sign of good memory?
(a) Ability to relate abstract materials with life situations.
(b) Ability to retain learnt material for a longer period of time and reproduce it.
(c) Quick ability to learn anything.
(d) All of the above.

465. For effective learning, teacher should infuse readiness in student in this way.
(a) By postulating the study material .
(b) Education by help aids
(c) By asking questions of pre-knowledge
(d) All of the above

466. Bilateral transfer is also called
(a) negative transfer.
(b) cross education.
(c) training programme.
(d) positive transfer.

467. Traditional theory of forgetting believed that
(a) Forgetting is the result of decay
(b) Forgetting is the result of interference
(c) Learning is the result of practice
(d) None of the above

468. A play group becomes a gang when it begins to arouse disapprovals and opposition from
(a) Adults (b) Schools
(c) Society (d) Groups

469. When a desired response is reinforced everytime it occurs we call it ______ reinforcement.
(a) intermittent (b) continuous
(c) partial (d) None of these

470. According to Law of Use, the relation between circumstance and reaction will be strong when
(a) is established again and again.
(b) it is established occasionally.
(c) is established strongly.
(d) All of the above.

471. The cinema makes an appeal to
(a) Our religion (b) Our culture
(c) Our senses (d) Our habit

472. Youth movement should be
(a) Social movement
(b) Regional movement
(c) National movement
(d) None of the above

473. The meaning of Law of Disuse is that when relation between circumstance and response is
(a) used continuously some time.
(b) not used for long time.
(c) used for long time.
(d) None of the above.

474. Law of exercise was introduced by
(a) Hull (b) Atkinson
(c) Kohler (d) Thorndike

475. In our daily life, we want to recall the name of a friend but we fail at that time but when condition changes, we recall the name. This is
(a) Retrieval theory
(b) Trace change theory
(c) Pleasure theory
(d) None of the above

476. Insight learning is basically a learning by
(a) Conditions (b) Imitation
(c) Trial and error (d) Cognition

477. After making amendments in his Law of Effect, Thorndike had said that relation of stimulus and reaction was getting effected by it
(a) Recency (b) Frequency
(c) Decency (d) Both (a) and (b)

478. In which of the following conditions we will forget a thing readily?
(a) If we are in a condition of fear or tension.
(b) If we have not given enough time to consolidate the material and go for physical activities immediately after learning.
(c) If importance has not been given to the material.
(d) All of the above.

479. According to Thorndike, Law of Exercise to strengthen the relations of stimulus and reaction this exercise should be done in primary classes.
(a) Play-activity (b) Drill
(c) Reading (d) All of the above

480. Salivation to the bell in the classical conditioning is called
(a) UCR (b) UCS
(c) CS (d) CR

481. Individual is
(a) Social unit
(b) Psycho-physical organism
(c) Both (a) and (b)
(d) Psycho-active organism

482. It is necessary that commercial cinema have to change their
(a) Money
(b) Motives
(c) Method of playing to the gallery
(d) All of the above

483. Who was the first person to conduct experiment on classical conditioning?
(a) Thorndike (b) Kohler
(c) Pavlov (d) Hull

484. As per educational implication of leaning law of Thorndike, education should be
(a) made aimful.
(b) made satisfactory.
(c) made pleasant.
(d) All of the above.

485. Movies modify the behaviour pattern of
(a) Group (b) Society
(c) Nation (d) Individual

486. *Understanding Media* is written by
(a) Rupert Murdoch
(b) Marshall McLuhan
(c) Bill Gates
(d) Subhash Chandra

487. This is included in the secondary laws of learning by Thorndike.
(a) Law of Interest
(b) Law of Disuse
(c) Law of Multiple Response
(d) All of the above

488. Out of the following methods which one is not used in studying verbal learning?
(a) Free recall
(b) Paired associate learning
(c) Free association
(d) Serial learning

489. In order to improve retention and learning which of the following methods can be adopted?
(a) Complete rest after learning
(b) Making the material to be learnt meaningful
(c) Over learning
(d) All of the above.

490. Thorndike is remembered for his contribution to
(a) methods of learning.
(b) trial and error.
(c) conditioning.
(d) insight theory.

491. The meaning of "Law of Mental Set or Attitude" by Thorndike is that learning is run by a person's
(a) Interest (b) Attention
(c) Cultural activity (d) Habit

492. Why it is said that a teacher should relate learnt material with life situation?
(a) Because the gap between past and present is reduced to zero level.
(b) Because association improves learning and retention.
(c) Because materials of life situations work as material aids.
(d) All of the above.

493. When learnt material is reproduced without any manipulation it is called
(a) perfect memory
(b) whole memory
(c) rote memory
(d) All of the above

494. "Law of Partial Activity"' by Thorndike means that eduction should be done in this series
(a) from part to whole.
(b) from whole to part.
(c) whole part once at a time.
(d) None of the above.

495. Spontaneous recovery will grow weaker and weaker if no reinforcement is provided after
(a) CR (b) CS
(c) US (d) None of these

496. The chairman of film enquiry committee of 1951 was
(a) Smita Patil (b) S.K. Patil
(c) V. Shantaram (d) Satyajit Ray

497. In this materialistic world, materialistic values are
(a) Significant for youth
(b) Little significant

(c) Highly significant
(d) None of the above

498. Negative conditioning is also known as
(a) escape learning.
(b) forward conditioning.
(c) reconditioning.
(d) backward conditioning.

499. "Law of Multiple Response" of Thorndike is based on which law of learning?
(a) Partial activity (b) Mental set
(c) Trial and error (d) All of the above

500. Who among the following psychologists is of the view that a learner can be motivated by satisfying his needs?
(a) Abraham Maslow
(b) Henry Murray
(c) Both (a) and (b)
(d) None of the above

501. This educational law is based on Thorndike's "Law of Analogy".
(a) Multi-method response
(b) Partial working
(c) From known to unknown
(d) Try and forget

502. The concept of experimental neuroses which threw light on various aspects of abnormal behaviour has been studied in depth by
(a) Hull (b) Guthrie
(c) Pavlov (d) Watson

503. Permanent change in behaviour brought about by experience or training is called
(a) Assimilation (b) Learning
(c) Motivation (d) None of these

504. The programme of youth should be flexible enough to allow for
(a) individual growth
(b) initiative
(c) Both (a) and (b)
(d) None of the above

505. Operant conditioning is usually studied in the laboratory using
(a) Skinner box (b) Cage
(c) Maze (d) Sticks

506. In the process of learning when response is as before but circumstances change. Thorndike has considered this under which law?
(a) Law of Disuse
(b) Law of associate changes
(c) Law of Use
(d) Law of Effect

507. Girls and boys at teenage prefer to have
(a) Cultural group (b) Same group
(c) Social group (d) Separate group

508. Play group is homosexual at the age of
(a) 5-7 years (b) 7-8 years
(c) 10 to 15 years (d) can't say

509. The following are important in theory of learning.
(a) Classical conditioning
(b) Operant conditioning
(c) Association
(d) All of the above

510. Pavlov was the founder of the most important type of learning called
(a) insight learning.
(b) classical conditioning.
(c) programme learning.
(d) instrumental learning.

511. The book *Theory of Motivation* has been written by
(a) Maslow (b) Murray
(c) K.B. Madsen (d) None of these

512. Motivated behaviour of a person is
(a) agitated until the goal is achieved.
(b) well directed and well guided toward the goal.
(c) Both (a) and (b).
(d) None of the above.

513. The concept of programme learning was introduced by
(a) Watson (b) Thorndike
(c) Skinner (d) Hull

514. According to association of learning theory by Herbert which mass of mind becomes a part of relative thoughts?
(a) Apperceptive mass
(b) Attution mass
(c) Learning mass
(d) All of the above

515. Process of motivation is affected by all except
(a) Mental sets and values
(b) Physical factors
(c) Habits
(d) None of the above

516. The following theory is stressed by the learning process of associatism or connectism.
(a) Trial and error
(b) Stimulus response
(c) Both of the above
(d) None of the above

517. When the experimentally extinguished response reappear again after a period it is called
(a) extinction.
(b) experimental neuroses.
(c) forgetting.
(d) spontaneous recovery.

518. The gang in which young boys are forcibly involved by older member's in crimes by the use of threats and violence is called
(a) Drug gang
(b) The criminal gang
(c) Conflict gang
(d) None of the above

519. Children learn in play groups to
(a) Conflict (b) Compete
(c) Co-operate (d) All of the above

520. An organism tends to repeat those behaviours that bring about satisfaction and it tends to discard those that bring about dissatisfaction. This is related to
(a) Thorndike's law of effect.
(b) the law of proximity of Hull.
(c) the law of similarity of Skinner.
(d) None of these.

521. Classical conditioning is the process in which neutral stimulai gets the characteristic of the following stimulaization.
(a) Self stimulus
(b) Artificial stimulus
(c) Secondary stimulus
(d) All of the above

522. In age group of 7-9 years the group leadership is done by
(a) Boys
(b) Girls
(c) Both (a) and (b)
(d) None of the above

523. By using the classical conditioning on a dog, Pavlov used which two stimulus?
(a) Giving food
(b) Ringing bell and giving food
(c) Ringing bell
(d) None of the above

524. Operant conditioning is also known as
(a) operative conditioning.
(b) condition after thought.
(c) instrumental conditioning.
(d) classical condition.

525. Youth organisations can include among their activities, programmes on
(a) International understanding
(b) Human behaviour
(c) Interpersonal relationship
(d) All of the above

526. Pavlov was a

(a) Neurologist (b) Zoologist
(c) Physiologist (d) Psychologist

527. In the experiment of Pavlov what was the response of dog on the ringing of the bell alone without food?
(a) Eating food
(b) Taking out of tongue
(c) Leaking of saliva
(d) All of the above

528. Among other things it is often the business of the school to do what other agencies have left undone. This is referred to as the
(a) delegated function
(b) primary function
(c) unique function
(d) residual function

529. In education disuse of classical conditioning theory can be done as follows.
(a) Satisfaction of students needs
(b) Formation of good habbits
(c) Leaving bad habbits
(d) All of the above

530. Zero transfer is also known as
(a) neutral transfer.
(b) positive transfer.
(c) negative transfer.
(d) None of these.

531. Which of the following does not come under the category of social motives?
(a) Money hoarding
(b) Prestige and status
(c) Social approval
(d) Personal goal

532. The S-O-R concept was developed by
(a) Pavlov (b) Wood worth
(c) Gestalt (d) Tolman

533. Critic of classical conditioning theory do not consider it useful because
(a) it was experimented on animals (dogs).
(b) it does not define the process of complex educational learning.
(c) Both (a) and (b).
(d) None of the above.

534. Our action and behaviour is motivated by the desire for getting pleasure and avoiding pain. This is the opinion of
(a) Kant (b) John Locke
(c) Thomas Hobbes (d) Descartes

535. The founder of theory of Operant Conditioning of learning was
(a) Watson (b) Skinner, S.E.
(c) Pavlov (d) Thorndike

536. In Pavlov's experiment, the UCS was _______ and UCR _______.
(a) salivation; bell
(b) meat powder; bell
(c) meat powder; salivation
(d) bell; salivation

537. The Heuristic method of teaching any subject insists on
(a) self experimentation for observation and discovery.
(b) verification of facts through exploration and analysis.
(c) the survey of a situation for arriving at conclusion.
(d) quantification of problems and planning for their solutions.

538. Which psychologist performed a series of experiments with Chimpanzees?
(a) Wertheimer (b) Thorndike
(c) Koffka (d) Kohler

539. The response of theory of operant conditioning is related to the following instead of stimulus?
(a) Conditioning (b) Stimulus
(c) Reinforcement (d) All of the above

540. The cinema stars, the directors, etc. are effective because they are
(a) all known people
(b) have great social prestige
(c) have a lot of wealth
(d) All of the above

541. Fundamental instincts of humans are inherited rather than acquired. These instincts are the spring of human behaviour. The above opinion was held by
(a) McDougall
(b) Charles Darwin
(c) Both (a) and (b)
(d) None of the above

542. Skinner experimented operant conditioning on the following.
(a) Dogs (b) Pigeon
(c) Rats (d) Both (b) and (c)

543. Who coined the concept of higher order conditioning?
(a) Watson (b) Hull
(c) Pavlov (d) Thorndike

544. Instinct theory of behaviour was rejected by psychologists on which of the following grounds?
(a) Human behaviour is affected by the cultural factors also.
(b) Human being is a rational animal. He is not supposed to be directed by instincts only.
(c) Adult behaviour is guided by experience and learning also. It is not always guided by instinct.
(d) All of the above

545. According to which principle a more preferred activity can be used to reinforce a less preferred activity?
(a) Recency principle
(b) Pinprick principle
(c) Law of effect principle
(d) Premack principle

546. In the experiment of Skinner the rat correlate which two things in "Skinner-box"?
(a) Light and to strike beak at grain
(b) Bell and food
(c) The sound of knock and food
(d) None of the above

547. The members of gang may be engaged in
(a) Drinking (b) Smoking
(c) Loitering around (d) All of the above

548. Play groups provide training in
(a) Society (b) Organisation
(c) Serving (d) Leadership

549. In the experiment of Skinner which drive was moved for operant conditioning?
(a) Self protection
(b) To come out of box
(c) Hungary
(d) All of the above

550. In operant conditioning the experimental animal is placed in a
(a) Skinner room (b) Skinner box
(c) Pavlov's lab (d) None of these

551. Central motive state was explained by
(a) McDougall
(b) Murray
(c) Morgan
(d) None of the above

552. Abraham Maslow was basically a
(a) Realist (b) Pragmatist
(c) Humanist (d) All of the above

553. The rate of response in operant conditioning is usually portrayed by a ________.
(a) poly curve
(b) serial learning curve
(c) cumulative curve
(d) None of these

554. The main difference between classical and operant conditioning is

(a) in first response is before reinforcement and in second after reinforcement.
(b) in first response is by condition stimulus but in second is self willed.
(c) Both (a) and (b).
(d) None of the above.

555. If youth organisations have been properly organized and their programmes are well planned they can help in character building of the
(a) Society (b) Youth
(c) Nation (d) All of the above

556. The disuse of operant conditioning in education can be following.
(a) Learning of students can be compared
(b) By the knowledge of result learning become easy
(c) Changes can be brought in the behaviour of students
(d) Both (b) and (c)

557. Tolman called his theoretical views as
(a) Behaviourism
(b) Radical behaviourism
(c) S.R. Theory
(d) Purposive

558. Physical, social, aesthetic and cultural education can be imparted by the provision of corresponding
(a) activity of youth movement
(b) organization
(c) religion of society
(d) can't say anything

559. Cinema makes an appeal to our imagination and arouses variety of
(a) Action (b) Emotion
(c) Fear (d) Sensation

560. Who proposed that the optimum level of arousal depends on the level of task difficulty?
(a) Yerkes and Dodson
(b) Miller
(c) Dollard
(d) None of these

561. Skinner has used the theory of operant conditioning to train the children of following types.
(a) Neurotic (b) Lunatic
(c) Disabled (d) All of the above

562. Some play groups if supervised may become remedial and therapeutic for certain types of children
(a) Aggressive (b) Timid
(c) Both (a) and (b) (d) Can't say

563. A self actualized person is one who
(a) always seeks perfection
(b) is very good in inter personal relationship with others
(c) does not accept restrictions imposed by the society
(d) All of the above

564. Theory of insight is based on the following concept of psychology?
(a) Psychoanalyst (b) Behaviourism
(c) Gestaltism (d) All of the above

565. The expectancy theory is related to ______ concept
(a) memory (b) learning
(c) emotion (d) motivation

566. The theory of achievement motivation was developed by McClelland of Harvard University in
(a) 1965 (b) 1944
(c) 1949 (d) 1951

567. Achievement motive in a child can be developed by
(a) setting a realistic goal for the child.
(b) proper guidance and high expectation from the child.
(c) telling the stories of great men to the child.
(d) All of the above.

568. According to Maslow physiological, safety and social needs are
(a) efficiency needs.
(b) proficiency needs.
(c) basic needs.
(d) deficiency needs.

569. The founder of theory of insight of learning was
(a) Wertheimer (b) Kohler
(c) Koffka (d) All of the above

570. Suppose the teachers are busy in cracking filthy jokes and you are also there but you are unable to stop them you should
(a) instruct them to mind their language while passing leisure time.
(b) persuade them decently not to waste their time in filthy jokes.
(c) be critical and remind them of the nobility of their jobs.
(d) live in isolation or change the group.

571. Kohler used the theory of insight on which animals
(a) Pigeons (b) Chimpanzees
(c) Rats (d) Dogs

572. At the base of hierarchy of needs, Maslow describes ________.
(a) social needs
(b) physiological needs
(c) growth needs
(d) safe needs

573. The main purpose of the first degrees in our universities should be to
(a) prepare students for social service and bring them to the threshold of knowledge.
(b) bring students to frontiers of knowledge and from there should be research.
(c) bring to the frontiers of research with necessary equipment of knowledge.
(d) equip students with necessary competencies for different work experiences.

574. Which part of the brain is related to hunger?
(a) Amygdala (b) Cortex
(c) Hypothalamus (d) Thalamus

575. Kohler disclosed the meaning of insight that the problem may be solved in this way.
(a) After cross questions
(b) Immediately and instantly
(c) After many difficulty
(d) All of the above

576. The general criticism against education now-a-days is that
(a) there is increase in the number of schools but decrease in the number of teachers.
(b) the number of students taking to formal education is falling.
(c) the pass percentage in public examinations is falling.
(d) there is increase in the number of students with sub-standard attainments.

577. Gestalt psychology initially emerged with an analysis of the
(a) attitudes and aptitudes
(b) testing of intelligence
(c) process of perfection
(d) emotional behaviour

578. The following are characteristics of theory of insight of learning.
(a) The solution of a problem is by stimulus conditioning
(b) The solution of a problem is of sudden
(c) The solution of a problem is by trial and error
(d) All of the above

579. Who propounded the theory of instincts?
(a) Watson (b) Skinner
(c) McDougall (d) Allport

580. Which of the following is not a characteristic of learning?

(a) Learning is directly observed
(b) Learning is a relatively permanent change in behaviour
(c) Learning is a goal directed process
(d) Learning is a growth of the organism.

581. In the beginning of life, the baby is guided by
(a) instincts (b) learning
(c) maturation (d) None of the above

582. Which part of the hypothalamus is responsible for activation and sustains eating in animals?
(a) Ventromedial hypothalamus
(b) Lateral hypothalamus
(c) Both (a) and (b)
(d) None of these

583. Insight is based on following.
(a) Growth
(b) Interest
(c) Trial and error
(d) Knowledge and intelligence

584. Accumulation of knowledge or facts becomes learning when
(a) it is done by the learner himself.
(b) it is provided by the teacher.
(c) it is applied in real life situation.
(d) None of the above.

585. Play group in teenagers can have great
(a) Religious value (b) Cultural value
(c) Educative value (d) Economic value

586. Clark C. Hull founded the following theory of learning.
(a) Operant conditioning
(b) Field theory
(c) Reinforcement theory
(d) None of the above

587. What is the function of lateral hypothalamus?
(a) Obesity
(b) Stop eating
(c) Activates sustain eating
(d) Over eating

588. What is the modern method of acquiring knowledge?
(a) Expert opinion
(b) Authority
(c) Personal experience
(d) Scientific method

589. Hawthrone effect is related to
(a) Habit (b) Learning
(c) Emotion (d) Motivation

590. "The relation between excitement and reaction depends upon the drive and reward"—this theory of learning of Hull was founded by which name?
(a) Reinforcement
(b) Drive
(c) Conditioning
(d) Operant conditioning

591. Dancing, driving, writing, etc. are the examples of
(a) mechanical learning
(b) perceptual motor learning
(c) psychomotor learning
(d) Both (b) and (c)

592. Tallman founded the theory of learning by name of
(a) Sign gestoct theory
(b) Field theory
(c) Reinforcement theory
(d) None of the above

593. The famous test to measure achievement motivation is
(a) Work test (b) TAT
(c) CAT (d) None of these

594. In Gagne's hierarchy, learning has been divided into
(a) six parts (b) seven parts
(c) eight parts (d) None of these

595. A smooth working democratic society depends on
(a) an equal distribution of economic resources among the body of citizens.
(b) a highly selective school system.
(c) unfair economic competition.
(d) widespread common interests and common attitudes among its citizens.

596. Electrical stimulation of certain areas of the ______ produces aggressive behaviour
(a) thalamus (b) hypothalmus
(c) limbic system (d) medulla

597. The field theory of learning by Lewin is based on
(a) reward and punishment.
(b) level of aspiration.
(c) dynamics of memory.
(d) All of the above.

598. Gangs are often a cause of
(a) truancy
(b) dropping out from family
(c) dropping out from school
(d) All of the above

599. An important feature of reference groups is that an individual relates himself to them or
(a) to religion
(b) to culture
(c) has aspiration to relate to them
(d) to society

600. "Motivation is the best way of learning". This definition of motivation is given by
(a) Gatts (b) Guildford
(c) Skinner (d) Woodworth

601. According to Maslow, the deficiency need is related to
(a) Security (b) Habit
(c) Interest (d) Affiliation

602. Reflexes are of two types according to Pavlov. They are physiological and
(a) Mental (b) Psychic
(c) Neural (d) None of the above

603. In classical conditioning extinction will take place when
(a) CS > UCS
(b) Organism is poor in generalization
(c) CS is given without UCS for a long time
(d) None of the above

604. ______ can be defined as "all internal processes that influences the direction, persistence and vigour of goal directed behaviour"
(a) Drive (b) Need
(c) Reinforcement (d) Motivation

605. Motivation is the process to start a work to continue it and control it, whose views are these about motivation.
(a) Atkinson (b) Goode
(c) Bernard (d) Skinner

606. For the development of the self and also in the learning of culture, which of the following groups is important for young?
(a) Social group
(b) Religious group
(c) Peer group
(d) All of the above.

607. The main elements of motivation are
(a) this is a path for desired behaviourial changes.
(b) this is an internal power of a person to stimulate.
(c) this is goal oriented.
(d) All of the above.

608. Maslow refers to physiological needs as
(a) primary needs.
(b) deficiency needs.
(c) secondary needs.
(d) growth needs.

609. A basic ideal of a democratic society is

(a) might makes right.
(b) respect for the enlightened individual.
(c) powerful leadership.
(d) belief in the opinion of the leaders.

610. Backward conditioning will take place when
(a) reward is not given to the organism.
(b) UCS is presented prior to CS.
(c) CS is presented prior to UCS.
(d) None of the above.

611. Maslow refers to self-actualization needs as _____.
(a) deficiency needs
(b) growth needs
(c) survival needs
(d) basic needs

612. The following method can be used to motivate learning.
(a) Use of reward and punishment
(b) Good and contented feeling
(c) Both (a) and (b)
(d) None of the above

613. When connection is not established between a CS and CR, due to any factor, that is called
(a) Inhibition
(b) Spontaneous recovery
(c) Extinction
(d) None of the above

614. "A teacher should teach the students in a class according to their aspiration level". For this process of learning student should be given
(a) Help (b) Facilities
(c) Motivation (d) None of these

615. "Push theories" of motivation refers to _____ of motivation.
(a) drive theories
(b) incentive theories
(c) needs theories
(d) motive theories

616. The gang engaged in use and selling of drugs is called a
(a) conflict gang
(b) drug gang
(c) criminal gang
(d) None of the above

617. Which of the following is not a social motive?
(a) Need for affiliation
(b) Need for approval
(c) Need for safety
(d) Need for achievement

618. A student should be motivated by encouraging instead of criticising him because criticising makes him
(a) mutual hatred and jealous.
(b) mutual anger and jealous.
(c) will develop mutual cooperation.
(d) Both (a) and (b).

619. The attitude of the educational sociologist towards vocational education generally is that
(a) distinctions between general and vocational education have no real basis.
(b) 'private-for-profit' vocational schools should be free from regulation.
(c) federal aid for vocational education should be discontinued.
(d) the apprenticeship system for vocational training should be abolished.

620. To promote learning competition is not good because this is developed in student.
(a) Discourage (b) Insulted
(c) Frighten (d) All of the above

621. _____ is a positive social phenomena.
(a) Anxiety (b) Laughter
(c) Anger (d) All of these

622. The George-Deen Act provided mainly for federal aid to

(a) Agricultural colleges
(b) Industrial education
(c) Public service occupations
(d) Distributive occupational training

623. When a child responds to all women who wear black suit because of the black suit of her mother, it is the example of
(a) assimilation
(b) internal inhibition
(c) generalization
(d) All of the above

624. By the age of 2 years all emotions develop. This is described by
(a) Thompson (b) Bridges
(c) Thorndike (d) Watson

625. In learning student gets motivation if he is told about its result.
(a) Reinforcement by feedback
(b) To say wrong and praise
(c) Information of failure
(d) Information of success

626. Who among the following is not a behaviourist?
(a) Pavlov (b) Lewin
(c) Watson (d) Skinner

627. Learning according to Watson is
(a) the result of connection between S-R formed in the brain.
(b) the shifting of old responses to the new stimuli.
(c) Both (a) and (b).
(d) None of the above.

628. To make educational process new and interesting, a student learning should be
(a) Satisfied (b) Operant
(c) Motivated (d) Alert

629. James Lange theory is related to
(a) Learning (b) Emotion
(c) Personality (d) Motivation

630. Other agencies of education is/are
(a) Radio (b) Cinema
(c) Print media (d) All of the above

631. Which of the following is least questionable as an assumption made in intergroup education?
(a) Modification in verbalisation of attitudes.
(b) Intergroup experiences in a school situation change behaviour in other situations.
(c) Prejudice is a result of ignorance of the facts and truth will remove one's prejudices.
(d) Having had favourable contacts with minorities one is apt to have a more favourable attitude towards them.

632. Which of the following is not related to emotional behaviour?
(a) Hypothalamus
(b) Mid brain
(c) Reticular formation
(d) Thalamus

633. The following is helpful in promotion of learning.
(a) Goal getting (b) Trying for goal
(c) Setting of goal (d) All of the above

634. Statistics collected in our country as late as 1976-77 reveals that the enrolment of girls as compared to boys
(a) is lower for the age group of 11 to 14 years than at the ages of 14 to 17 years.
(b) shows downward trend from the higher to lower classes.
(c) very rapidly falls down from the lower to the higher classes.
(d) falls slowly and gradually.

635. The following are the source of motivation.
(a) Environmental (b) Extrinsic
(c) Intrinsic (d) Both (b) and (c)

636. When anger is expressed outwardly in the form of aggressive activity there is increase in the secretion of ______.
(a) gonads (b) pancreas
(c) adrenal gland (d) thyroid gland

637. Which of the following points differentiates the theories of Watson and Guthrie?
(a) law of frequency
(b) law of contiguity
(c) law of recency
(d) generalization

638. In operant conditioning reward works as motives but in Guthrie's theory motives are
(a) actions done by the learner
(b) stimuli given to the learner
(c) Both (a) and (b)
(d) None of the above

639. Emotion is expressed through
(a) Gesture
(b) Facial expression
(c) Language
(d) All of these

640. Intrinsic source of motivation are
(a) Motives (b) Needs
(c) Interests (d) Both (a) and (b)

641. We forget something not by disuse but by other learning. This is the theory of
(a) learning by insight
(b) contiguity
(c) perception
(d) trial and error

642. The following can be the extrinsic source of motivation.
(a) Reward (b) Praise
(c) Speak ill (d) All of the above

643. In the development of emotion ______ plays a major role.
(a) maturation (b) intelligence
(c) learning (d) insight

644. The formal discipline theory of education is the outcome of
(a) Faculty psychology
(b) Genetic psychology
(c) Functional psychology
(d) Structural psychology

645. Sympathetic activation causes
(a) decrease in sweating.
(b) decrease in the pulse rate.
(c) an increase in the heart rate.
(d) decrease in the heart rate.

646 The option to motivate students for learning, reward should be
(a) Symbolic
(b) Way and not a goal
(c) Both (a) and (b)
(d) None of the above

647. Which of the following is not a basic problem faced by vocational education since World War II?
(a) The length of time and amount of training needed for economic life.
(b) The extent to which the vocation school should train for specific skills.
(c) The lack of a constant pattern in types of vocational training.
(d) The extent and nature of federal aid for vocational education.

648. "Exchange or transfer of experience is by related working in a learning without any conform learning or practice of experience by rectifying, generalization or correcting." This defination of "Transfer of learning" is given by
(a) Crow and Crow (b) Kolsnik
(c) Sorenson (d) Goode, Cater V.

649. Motive is a
(a) Trait (b) Behaviour
(c) Desire (d) Impulse

650. Which of the following is not an essential requirement for trial and error learning?

(a) Selective movement of the organism
(b) Chance success
(c) Drive
(d) Barrier

651. According to the law of trial and error, learning occurs when
(a) bond between S-R is strengthened by the repeated use.
(b) drive is there in the learner to act.
(c) it is satisfying for the learner.
(d) All of the above.

652. The motive to keep contact with others is called
(a) Mastery
(b) Dependency
(c) Gregariousness
(d) Self assertiveness

653. The use of knowledge already gained in same circumstances or different fields of life is called this of learning.
(a) Generalization (b) Changeable
(c) Change of path (d) Transfer

654. A vestibule school was a
(a) correspondence school
(b) school for apprentices
(c) school run by a factory
(d) public trade school

655. Peer groups help the young to become independent in their
(a) Thought (b) Decision
(c) Both (a) and (b) (d) Family

656. There are following elements in the concept of transfer of learning.
(a) This is not always but may become a binding on other knowledge
(b) The use of knowledge already gained is "disuse" in new circumstances
(c) The knowledge in one subject is helpful in other subjects
(d) All of the above

657. The physiological theory of motivation has been advanced by
(a) Young (b) Murray
(c) Morgan (d) Hilgard

658. Which of the following facilitates learning according to Thorndike?
(a) Law of contiguity
(b) Transfer of training
(c) Mental set of the learner
(d) All of the above.

659. Gregariousness is related to
(a) inherited traits.
(b) biological factors.
(c) social conditioning.
(d) None of these.

660. "Theory of equal element" of Thorndike is based on following theory of learning.
(a) Changeable (b) Reinforcement
(c) Transfer (d) Fixation

661. In Hull's theory, for learning to occur, the S-R connection must be associated with the
(a) diminution of the need
(b) cognitive field of the learner
(c) Both (a) and (b)
(d) None of the above

662. Negative transfer of learning occurs when in other circumstances
(a) Obstructive (b) Destroyer
(c) Reinforcement (d) Helpful

663. Social motives are called
(a) Essential (b) Primary
(c) Secondary (d) None of these

664. If a high caste teacher adopts a discriminatory attitude towards a low caste students, his behaviour is
(a) against the national spirit, and need of the hour.
(b) correct according to his religion.
(c) not against the constitutional provisions.
(d) not against the code of teachers' professionalism of UNESCO.

665. Theory as an aspect of research does not
(a) describe the facts and relationships that exist.
(b) discard facts, specific and concrete observations.
(c) serve as a tool for providing a guiding frame-work for observation and discovery.
(d) serve as a goal providing explanation for specific phenomena with maximal probability and exactitude.

666. Hunger, thirst, sex are known as
(a) basic needs.
(b) psychological needs.
(c) secondary needs.
(d) None of these.

667. The following are the examples of "transfer of skill in learning".
(a) Skill of reading in writing
(b) Skill ofrunning in wrestling
(c) Skill of cycling in running scooter
(d) All of the above

668. Deductively reasoning out the consequences of the suggested solutions, is an aspect of thinking involved in the
(a) older methods of acquiring knowledge.
(b) psychological methods of acquiring knowledge.
(c) personal experiences as a method of acquiring knowledge.
(d) scientific methods of acquiring knowledge.

669. The main types of transfer of learning are
(a) Negative transfer
(b) Simple transfer
(c) Positive transfer
(d) Both (a) and (c)

670. Motive to keep contact with others is called.
(a) self-assertiveness.
(b) dependency.
(c) gregariousness.
(d) mastery.

671. Reinforcement in Skinner's theory is similar to drive reduction in
(a) Guthrie's theory (b) Lewin's theory
(c) Hull's theory (d) None of these

672. Self-actualization theory of motivation is
(a) Physiological (b) Psychological
(c) Hierarchical (d) Psychoanalytic

673. Zero transfer of learning will be when one talent of subject cannot be in other type of skill in this way.
(a) Neither unilateral nor bilateral
(b) Neither positive nor negative
(c) Neither vertical nor horizontal
(d) All of the above

674. Which of the following theories is most quantitatively measurable?
(a) Hull's (b) Pavlov's
(c) Skinner's (d) None of the above

675. Horizontal transfer of learning occurs when the acquired knowledge of one subject of a class is helpful in
(a) other subject of lower class.
(b) other subject of next class.
(c) other subject of same class.
(d) None of the above.

676 Curiosity is a ______ drive.
(a) social (b) personal
(c) psychological (d) organic

677. In drive reduction theory, the effective stimulus in leaning is the trace. It is formed
(a) by the bond of S-R
(b) in the nervous system
(c) in the brain
(d) None of the above

678. What should be done for constructing and standardizing a psychological test?

(a) It should be considered a research of value because the test so developed can be used later by others.
(b) It should be considered a valuable piece of research because a lot of labour and energy have gone into it.
(c) It should not be considered a research because it does not test any hypothesis.
(d) It should not be considered a research because it is a small-scale activity.

679. The motivational theory of emotion was developed by
(a) Garde (b) Atkinson
(c) Leeper (d) Hull

680. Bilateral transfer of learning occurs when the ability to do a work with one organ is ability to work with other organ
(a) is opponent (b) is helpful
(c) is obstructive (d) All of the above

681. While the religious attitude is emotional the philosophical attitude is
(a) Detached (b) Full of wonder
(c) Doubtful (d) All of the above

682. In drive reduction theory, habit formation is a function of
(a) reaction potential
(b) stimulus potential
(c) stimulus generalization
(d) All of the above

683. Example of bilateral transfer of learning is
(a) to focus the camera with one eye and both eyes are helpful to it.
(b) to focus the camera with one eye and the second eye is helpful to it.
(c) Both (a) and (b).
(d) None of the above.

684. The lie detector was devised by
(a) Detecty (b) Lyer
(c) Leonarde Killer (d) None of these

685. Hull may be considered superior to other S-R Theorists in the sense that he was able to measure
(a) reinforcement potential
(b) latency of response
(c) Both (a) and (b)
(d) None of the above

686. The kind of conflict in which both hopes and fears are associated with the same action is
(a) approach-avoidance conflict.
(b) approach-approach conflict.
(c) double approach-avoidance conflict.
(d) avoidance-avoidance conflict.

687. The role of teacher in transfer of learning is effected due to
(a) correlation of subjects.
(b) use of teaching aids.
(c) utility of previous knowledge.
(d) Both (a) and (c).

688. Which of the following statements is not correct?
(a) Drug addiction, drinking, and crimes are very common and are strong pollutants of social environment.
(b) Once a person gets addicted to the use of drugs and narcotics, he becomes useless for any type of work, cannot earn, but requires regular supply of drug to live.
(c) The problem of drug addiction can be best tackled only with the combined and determined efforts of the government, society and the educational institutions.
(d) None of the above is wrong.

689. For teacher transfer of learning, the child should develop the following powers instead of materialistic things.
(a) Skill
(b) Understanding
(c) Application of knowledge
(d) All of the above

690. If children are exposed to frequent rejection, punishment, teasing and oversolicitude by parents, usually it leads to
(a) suicide.
(b) inferiority feelings.
(c) brain disorders.
(d) mental retardation.

691. If you are irritated and show rashness because of the inadequate behaviour shown by others what do you think about your own behaviour?
(a) Your behaviour is also the sign of maladjustment and so try to control yourself when you are maltreated.
(b) Your behaviour is not good because elders have the right to behave with you in this way.
(c) It is justified because behaviours are echo like.
(d) None of the above.

692. In children, the frustration motive is primarily caused by
(a) encouragements.
(b) sibling rivalry.
(c) environmental obstacles.
(d) parental sanctions.

693. Teacher should stress this for the transfer of learning of acquired knowledge.
(a) To remember
(b) Utility of life
(c) Use in examination
(d) None of the above

694. Membership in a gang is often a cause of the members having poor attitude towards
(a) Culture (b) Religion
(c) Education (d) None of the above

695. If a student is constantly rubbing his eyes and is inattentive during blackboard work he is having
(a) adjustment problem
(b) visual problem
(c) hearing problem
(d) All of the above

696. For transfer of learning, teacher should clarify the teaching aims because aim develops the following in students.
(a) Change in behaviour
(b) Gaining of knowledge
(c) Success in examination
(d) All of the above

697. Temper tantrums occur among children due to
(a) inherited emotional instability.
(b) poor imagination.
(c) low intelligence.
(d) over protection.

698. Which of the following points differentiates Skinner from other S-R theorists?
(a) His schedule of reinforcement
(b) His way of shaping behaviour
(c) His operant conditioning (type R learning)
(d) All of the above.

699. The emotions of the child during the infancy are
(a) untrained.
(b) egoistic.
(c) mainly egoistic and untrained.
(d) mainly altruistic but of short duration.

700. Exceptional children are those, for which the following education method is done inspire of general class.
(a) Special
(b) Separate
(c) Both (a) and (b)
(d) None of the above

701. Skinner's theory is more objective in nature than the others because
(a) reinforcement is followed by responses.
(b) operant behaviour is external.

(c) reflexes never have zero strength.
(d) All of the above.

702. The class of exceptional children is
(a) Delinquent
(b) Gifted
(c) Mentally retarded slow learner
(d) All of the above

703. The term problem children is generally used to describe children who
(a) are specifically backward in one subject.
(b) have a low general intelligence.
(c) are maladjusted.
(d) have a physical defect.

704. Aversive stimuli in operant conditioning means
(a) individual will not do a particular act because of the disapproval from others.
(b) individual will not do a particular act because of fear of such stimuli.
(c) Both (a) and (b).
(d) None of the above.

705. A child has first experience of inter-group opposition from
(a) Cultural group (b) Social group
(c) Play group (d) Family group

706. The view that "Emotionality is by and large inherited" is
(a) Unrealistic (b) Realistic
(c) Acceptable (d) Not acceptable

707. The following child come under the category of exceptional child in view of physique.
(a) Mentally retarded (b) Delinquent
(c) Gifted (d) Physical

708. While the aim of religion is realisation of God, the aim of philosophy is
(a) Criticism
(b) Search for truth
(c) Reflection
(d) All of the above

709. "Gifted child is the best from normal child in physique, social adjustment, quality of personality, achievement in school, sports, information and variety of interests." This definition of gifted child is given by
(a) Terman and Oden
(b) Tyler
(c) Kirk
(d) Witty

710. Which is not true about the development of behaviour?
(a) It proceeds in a cephalo-caudal and proximo-distal direction
(b) It varies from child to child and the sequence is not uniform
(c) It is a gradual and a continuous process
(d) It proceeds from generalized mass activity to specific responses

711. In Skinner's theory, reinforcement is given to the learner when
(a) his response is 100% correct.
(b) his response is not correct.
(c) his response is closer to the correct behaviour.
(d) his response is regular and continuous.

712. Which of the following is most acceptable generalization about early and special training?
(a) It leads to an improvement in performance in certain cases
(b) It may actually be of great benefit
(c) It tends to be uneconomical and wasteful
(d) All of these are possible

713. The identification of gifted child is by following speciality.

(a) Power to obtain knowledge easily in large quantity
(b) Good health in his class
(c) Excellency in reading, language, maths, reasoning, etc.
(d) All of the above

714. Which of the following statements regarding S-R theories is not correct?
(a) Behaviour is overt and can be objectively measured.
(b) Learning proceeds from simple to complex.
(c) Things are perceived in the context of figure ground, i.e. in relation to other things.
(d) Man behaves like a machine.

715. Play group is heterosexual at the age of
(a) 7-8 years (b) 8-9 years
(c) 9-10 years (d) 10-12 years

716. Gifted children can be helped in giving education by following methods.
(a) Enriched curriculum
(b) Acceleration or quickly promoting in next class
(c) Both (a) and (b)
(d) None of the above

717. The term "developmental task" was popularized by
(a) Carmichael (b) E.G. Hurlock
(c) Havighurst (d) A. Gesell

718. A couple of research studies shows that the cinema encourages
(a) Anti-social conduct
(b) Educational values
(c) Positive education
(d) Social conduct

719. Which of the following statements regarding field theories are correct?
(a) Interaction between organism and the environment is essential for learning.
(b) Learning is not additive.
(c) Molar approach of behaviour is followed here.
(d) All of the above.

720. A highly creative man must be of high level of intelligence. This is claimed by
(a) Russian Psychologists
(b) Indian Psychologists
(c) British Psychologists
(d) American Psychologists

721. For helping gifted children an option of acceleration means
(a) permission to quality syllabus in less period than decided.
(b) admission in school in less age.
(c) to promote in next class twice or more in one year.
(d) All of the above.

722. Operant conditioning is different from respondent conditioning in which of the following points?
(a) A chain of responses is needed for shaping the behaviour (learning).
(b) In operant conditioning reinforcement is given after the response is made.
(c) In operant conditioning, behaviour is controlled by central nervous system.
(d) All of the above.

723. Gifted children can be given following help.
(a) Individualized teaching
(b) Education in special class or school
(c) Effective guidance
(d) All of the above

724. Adult creativity can be successfully measured by
(a) Anastasi Test (b) R.T.
(c) T.T.C.T. (d) Guilford's Test

725. Thorndike and Skinner do not differ at all in
(a) law of readiness
(b) law of contiguity

(c) the law of effect
(d) All of the above

726. Ruralization always
(a) stops creativity.
(b) cultivates creativity.
(c) fosters creativity.
(d) inhibits creativity.

727. There are following elements equivalent with concept of mentally retarded or slow learner children.
(a) Lack of self-confidence
(b) Slow speed of learning
(c) Physically handicapped
(d) Both (a) and (b)

728. A1 theory helps the researcher in
(a) determining how to make or record observations.
(b) identifying the facts needed to be considered in the context of the research problem.
(c) understanding the research procedure.
(d) understanding the technical terms used in research.

729. While the method of religion is emotional the method of philosophy is
(a) Reflective (b) Rational
(c) Logical (d) All of the above

730. The level of mentally retarded child on the basis of I.Q. is
(a) Morons—50 to 75
(b) Idiots—0 to 25
(c) Inbicile—25 to 50
(d) All of the above

731. Creativity increases with
(a) Practice (b) Experience
(c) Age (d) Education

732. What we have called behaviour is the activity of the individual organism in relation to
(a) Environment (b) Family
(c) Society (d) Nation

733. Creativity among poor children is always
(a) Cultivated (b) Unaffected
(c) Improved (d) Dead

734. One of the following is the I.Q. of dull normal child.
(a) 50 to 75 (b) 25 to 50
(c) 75 to 90 (d) All of the above

735. According to Gestalt psychologists, behaviour cannot be quantified because
(a) it is governed by the configuration produced in the mind.
(b) it is rarely overt.
(c) it is always changeable.
(d) All of the above.

736. Identification of mentally retarded children can be on following symptoms.
(a) Decrement of mental powers
(b) Physically handicapped
(c) Unhealthy
(d) All of the above

737. Items for identifying creative individuals is a scale which measures
(a) Creativity (b) Personality
(c) Interest (d) Intelligence

738. Law of pragnanz is the other name of the law of
(a) contiguity (b) continuity
(c) closure (d) None of the above

739. How does the law of similarity work according to field theorists?
(a) Similar objects or experiences are easily learnt.
(b) Similar ideas and experiences get associated to form a whole.
(c) Both (a) and (b).
(d) None of the above.

740. Relation of philosophy and religion can be said to be
(a) Complimentary
(b) Contradictory
(c) Both (a) and (b)
(d) Neither (a) nor (b)

741. Which of the following most influences the classroom behaviour of the child?
(a) The social groups in the class
(b) The monitor of the class
(c) The teacher
(d) The peers

742. The methods of identification or diagnosis of mentally retarded children is
(a) standardized diagnostic tests.
(b) achievement tests.
(c) Both (a) and (b).
(d) None of the above.

743. Which of the following does not belong to the group of the other three?
(a) Curricular validity
(b) Construct validity
(c) Logical validity
(d) Sampling validity.

744. We make use of general psychology in the several departments of life under
(a) abnormal psychology
(b) religional psychology
(c) applied psychology
(d) None of the above

745. By medical check up the identification of following special children can be
(a) Deliquent
(b) Gifted
(c) Mentally retarded
(d) All of the above

746. The view that "Learning, instead of being reinforced, should be self-rewarding" was expressed by
(a) Pavlov (b) Thorndike
(c) Skinner (d) Bruner

747. Learning by insight looks similar to some extent to which of the following theories?
(a) R type of learning
(b) Trial and error theory
(c) Need reduction theory
(d) None of the above.

748. Emotional reactions of an infant are determined by
(a) what frustrates him in his environment.
(b) the kind of self-concept he has.
(c) the treatment given to him by the parents.
(d) what he imitates from the people in his environment.

749. The following method should be used for the education of mentally retarded children.
(a) Special classes
(b) Special schools
(c) Enriched curriculum
(d) Both (a) and (b)

750. The other name of conditioned reflexes is
(a) physiological reflexes
(b) psychic reflexes
(c) motor reflexes
(d) None of the above

751. It is said that there are individual differences among students in a class. This fact is
(a) a suggestion for teachers to be careful in teaching.
(b) supported by lazy teachers to find execuses for their weaknesses.
(c) purely a historical evidence that is outdated today.
(d) a great hindrance to teachers in teaching.

752. "Personality is a total quality of a person". This definition of personality is given by
(a) Warran (b) Boring
(c) Valentine (d) Woodworth

753. Kobler wanted to prove that learning is
(a) a situation in which animals are superior to men.
(b) an autonomous random activity.
(c) the perception of different parts of the situation.
(d) the perception of the whole situation.

754. Which problems are included in the scope of Educational Research?
(a) Philosophical (b) Sociological
(c) Educational (d) Psychological

755. "The process by which practitioners attempt to study their problems scientifically in order to guide, correct and evaluate their decision and action is what a number of people have called Action Research". Who has given this definition?
(a) Sara Blackwell
(b) Stephen M. Corey
(c) McThrete
(d) John W. Best

756. Which of the following is not the part of the definition of the developmental task?
(a) Its failure leads to unhappiness and disapproval by the society
(b) It is something which is to be essentially achieved
(c) It is learning of a given task which arises at or about a certain period in the life of the individual
(d) Its successful achievement leads to success with later tasks

757. "To be affected by many factors" and "adjustment by environment"—these two qualities are of following.
(a) Learning
(b) Motivation
(c) Growth and development
(d) Personality

758. Zero transfer of training helps the teacher in the class when
(a) he teaches mathematics.
(b) he does not want one learning to be inhibited by other learning.
(c) he has to teach a lot in the class.
(d) None of the above.

759. According to Fried, the basic instigation of human-behaviour is
(a) Frustration
(b) Conflict
(c) Libido
(d) None of the above

760. "Achieving new and more mature relations with age-mates of both sexes" is the developmental task belonging to the period of
(a) Adolescence (b) Early childhood
(c) Adulthood (d) Late childhood

761. Theory of generalization is similar to the theory of
(a) Identical elements
(b) Transposition
(c) Both (a) and (b)
(d) None of the above

762. If rules of multiplication helps in learning correlation or regression, it is an example of
(a) negative transfer
(b) vertical transfer
(c) horizontal transfer
(d) sequential transfer

763. Which of the following ways does not help in securing pupil's emotional maturity?
(a) Providing the pupil with constructive outlets through which to channel emotional tension
(b) Providing the child with security
(c) Providing proper education of the emotions
(d) Training the pupil to repress emotions

764. The trait theory for personality was founded by
(a) Woodworth (b) Allport
(c) Fried (d) Jung

765. A stress situation may be dealt with by a defense mechanism which must be
(a) conscious
(b) unconscious

(c) unconscious but may be brought by constant fear or anxiety
(d) None of the above

766. Educational Psychology is regarded as a branch of
(a) Comparative psychology
(b) Applied psychology
(c) General psychology
(d) Both (a) and (c)

767. Allport has divided the traits of human personality into following series.
(a) Secondary traits (b) Central traits
(c) Cardinal traits (d) All of the above

768. Which is not correct about social develop ment of the child?
(a) It is child's attempt on not going against anything that prevails in the society
(b) It is individualization meaning, thereby, child's attempt to retain some of his individuality
(c) It is continuous process by means of which the child achieves social adequacy
(d) It is an attempt by society on having the child internalize certain of its regulations, values and mores

769. A projective test or technique is a method of collecting data about an individual's personality which
(a) uses direct observations of individuals behaviour.
(b) uses a short structured interview schedule.
(c) uses on-the-spot participant observations for measuring an individual's personality qualities.
(d) uses unstructured stimulus situations such as ink/blot, photographs, etc., to elicit individual's reactions.

770. What is absurd about the misbehaving child?
(a) He is one who is trying to satisfy some of his needs but is not going about it in the right way
(b) He is a born trouble-maker trying to be wicked
(c) He is one who is maladjusted in some way
(d) He is one who has not, yet, found socially acceptable solutions to some of his major problems

771. R.B. Cattell is supporter of which theory for development of personality.
(a) Type (b) Learning
(c) Psychoanalytic (d) Trait

772. Who is the chief contributor of the theory of transposition?
(a) Kohler
(b) Thorndike
(c) Max Wertheimer
(d) None of the above

773. Which of the following philosophies believe in the theory of identical element?
(a) Pragmatism (b) Idealism
(c) Existentialism (d) None of these

774. According to psychoanalytic theory personality is collaboration of
(a) Super-ego (b) Id
(c) Ego (d) All of the above

775. Social maturity does not mean
(a) attaining relative freedom from domination by the parents and the peers.
(b) to be well-accepted in the group.
(c) assuming responsibility for himself and his actions together with responsibility for others.
(d) participating effectively in social relations.

776. Analysis of research problem does not include
(a) proposing various explanations (hypotheses).

(b) idcntifying a problem.
(c) selecting and accumulating fact that might be related to the problem.
(d) None of the above.

777. Which is not included in the special provisions for dealing with the gifted children?
(a) Ability grouping
(b) Acceleration
(c) Adaptation or enrichment
(d) Schemes of special scholarships and awards

778. Allport has considered the following quality of the difference in intensity and quantity of traits.
(a) Uniformity (b) Uniqueness
(c) Static (d) Wholeness

779. A process by which conflicts between the demands of the individual and demand of the environment is normalized is called
(a) Social therapy (b) Adjustment
(c) Maladjustment (d) None of these

780. Studies of growth and development is
(a) Genetic psychology
(b) Animal psychology
(c) General psychology
(d) Physiological psychology

781. By Factorial analysis Cattell has decided the function of these factors in the development of traits of a person.
(a) Learning
(b) Heredity
(c) Both (a) and (b)
(d) None of the above

782. For dealing with the gifted child which is the most realistic and practicable approach
(a) segregation
(b) enrichment alone
(c) a combination of all these
(d) acceleration alone

783. Attempt to apply the knowledge to the field of education is
(a) Educational psychology
(b) Emotional psychology
(c) Comparative psychology
(d) None of the above

784. The physiological processes accompanying behaviour either as a cause or as an effect is
(a) Physiological psychology
(b) Genetic psychology
(c) Comparative psychology
(d) None of the above

785. Which is a more adequate definition of the exceptional child?
(a) He is one who deviates from the normal child in mental, physical and social characteristics to such an extent that he requires a modification of school practices
(b) He is socially much different from others
(c) He is emotionally undeveloped
(d) He is intellectually very superior

786. In the defined series of traits by Cattell the following are
(a) Source (b) Common
(c) Unique (d) All of these

787. Which of the following attitudes is required to remove the situation of maladjustment?
(a) The individual should alter the environment itself.
(b) The individual should adopt some mental mechanism to escape the situation.
(c) The individual should modify his own demand.
(d) All of the above.

788. The measurement of personality means which one of the following is in it by how much quantity.

(a) Quality (b) Trait
(c) Type (d) All of the above

789. A gifted child is never defined as one
(a) whose ability is within the range of the upper two per cent to three per cent of the population.
(b) whose IQ is 140 or above.
(c) who is extremely different from others of his age.
(d) whose performance is consistently remarkable in music, art, social leadership, and other forms of expression.

790. Which of the following is an important symptom of mental ill health?
(a) The person demands more from others than he pays to them.
(b) He considers himself a perfect person.
(c) He is irritated at petty situations.
(d) All of the above.

791. Which of the following is not a symptom of maladjusted children?
(a) Hyperactivity
(b) Sexual crimes
(c) Extreme timidity
(d) Aggression and bullying

792. Which of the following does not explain the true nature of adjustment?
(a) Adjustment is an individual's behaviour pattern directed towards tension-reduction
(b) Adjustment is the process by means of which, the individual attempts to maintain a level of physiological and psychological equilibrium
(c) Adjustment is an attempt on the part of the individual to maintain harmonious relationship between himself and the environment
(d) Only in death does the individual cease to adjust

793. Allport has also considered the following qualities of personality.
(a) Learning (b) Intelligence
(c) Socialization (d) Both (b) and (c)

794. If a student uses his knowledge obtained in class VIIth in understanding the subject matter of class Xth, it is an example of
(a) Sequential transfer
(b) Horizontal transfer
(c) Vertical transfer
(d) None of the above

795. The following are the main experiments in the measurement of personality by projective methods.
(a) CAT
(b) Rovschach or inkblot
(c) TAT
(d) All of the above

796. The view that "adjustment differs from maladjustment in degree rather than in kind" is psychologically
(a) correct sometimes.
(b) incorrect in certain situation.
(c) correct.
(d) incorrect.

797. Education means
(a) Change (b) Development
(c) Growth (d) All of the above

798. Education should teach us the right use of
(a) Fatigue (b) Self-expression
(c) Leisure (d) None of these

799. Which may not be a symptom of maladjustment?
(a) Selfishness
(b) Nail biting
(c) Excessive reading for vicarious excitement
(d) Daydreaming

800. "Play and Drama method" is which type of personality test?

(a) Projective (b) Objective
(c) Non-projective (d) None of these

801. Who said, "Educational research is that activity which is directed towards the development of science of behaviour in educational situation"?
(a) John W. Best (b) F.L. Whitney
(c) W.M. Traverse (d) W.S. Monroe

802. Movement of limbs and acts of hearing, seeing and smelling are
(a) skeleton movements
(b) biological functions
(c) behaviour
(d) All of the above

803. The following is main in the subjective methods of personality measurement.
(a) Interview (b) Autobiography
(c) Questionaire (d) All of these

804. Inadequate behaviour pattern of the individual by means of which he attempts to adjust or satisfy his needs is known as
(a) maladjustment.
(b) withdrawal mechanism.
(c) defence mechanism.
(d) adjustment mechanism.

805. Which of the following is not the social cause of maladjustment?
(a) Faulty social environment of the school
(b) Communal tension
(c) Injustice prevailing in the society
(d) Disability.

806. The habit of smoking in students cannot be the result of
(a) Inoculation
(b) Peer pressure
(c) Modelling
(d) Cigarete advertising

807. The objective methods of measuring personality are
(a) Sociogram (b) Observation
(c) Rating scale (d) All of these

808. A science which deals with the process of attaining mental health and preventing mental illness is called
(a) Mental hygiene
(b) Social medicine
(c) Adjustment psychology
(d) None of the above

809. Which are the psycho-analytical methods of personality measurement?
(a) Dream analysis
(b) Free association
(c) Both (a) and (b)
(d) None of the above

810. Socially undesirable behaviours are learned as a result of environment influences but not through
(a) latent learning.
(b) operant conditioning.
(c) observational.
(d) classical conditioning.

811. *A Mind That Found Itself* was written by Clifford Beers in
(a) 1917 (b) 1915
(c) 1908 (d) 1903

812. Who has defined the purpose of Educational Research in these words, "Educational research aims to make contribution towards the solutions of problems in the field of education by the use of the scientific and philosophical method, the method of critical reflective thinking."?
(a) W.S. Monroe (b) W.M. Traverse
(c) F.L. Whitney (d) John W. Best

813. Developing new behaviour and increasing the probability of a response by introducing reward or punishment is known as

(a) desensitization.
(b) classical conditioning.
(c) operant conditioning.
(d) shaping of behaviour.

814. In five points of rating scale of personality measurement if always honesty or truth is in first series then in its series 2, 4 and 5 respectively will be
(a) fifth series-never truthful.
(b) second series-almost truthful.
(c) fourth series-too less truthful.
(d) All of the above.

815. Which of the following sampling methods yields more efficient results when the population is heterogeneous?
(a) Cluster sampling
(b) Random sampling
(c) Purposive sampling
(d) Stratified sampling

816. Sociogram is on the basis of mutual relation of measurement group of the following of a person.
(a) Types (b) Traits
(c) Social qualities (d) All of the above

817. According to Freud, children pass through all the following psychosexual stages of development except
(a) Phallic (b) Autoerotic
(c) Genital (d) Oral

818. The purpose of mental hygiene is
(a) to help the individual to adjust in the environment.
(b) to enable the individual to use his potentialities effectively to achieve to the maximum.
(c) to make the individual healthy and happy.
(d) All of the above.

819. Lack of confidence and emotional security is caused by
(a) Rejection (b) Ill treatment
(c) Over affection (d) Under affection

820. Performance test method of personality measurement is used for which purpose.
(a) For establishing marrital relation
(b) For selection of special work
(c) For selection of special position
(d) None of the above

821. Which of the following is an important source of frustration for an adolescent?
(a) Regular failure in the competitive test
(b) Delay in sexual gratification
(c) Smoking prohibition
(d) All of the above.

822. The founder of ink blot test for personality measurement was
(a) Rourschach
(b) Moreno
(c) Murray and Morgan
(d) Bel lack

823. The children's nature is
(a) Imaginative (b) Distructive
(c) Imitative (d) Constructive

824. A student dreaming that he is pushing his way through a thick forest, pursued by wild animals can be most suitably analysed as
(a) a symbolic expression of his fear and anxiety about failing in an examination and being expelled from school.
(b) a symbolic expression of his fear towards his teachers.
(c) a symbolic expression of his fear and hatred towards his friends.
(d) a symbolic expression of his fear towards parents.

825. Who among the following is well-known personality theorist?
(a) Galton (b) G.Q. Allport
(c) Spearman (d) Freud

826. In Rourschach personality test on how many cards the shapes are of different colours?
(a) –3 (b) –5
(c) –2 (d) –10

827. A very important field that deals with the application of psychology in the solution of educational problems is
(a) Abnormal psychology
(b) Comparative psychology
(c) Physiological psychology
(d) Applied psychology

828. The following quality of a person can be known by Rourschach personality test.
(a) Obsession (b) Intelligence
(c) Socialization (d) All of these

829. Who developed Individual psychology?
(a) G.W. Allport (b) Alfred Adler
(c) Freud (d) Spearman

830. In which of the following situations conflict is created?
(a) When individual comes across two equally painful or enjoying situations simultaneously.
(b) When individual has two equally attractive options (goals) to follow.
(c) When individual wants to achieve two conflicting objectives at a time.
(d) All of the above.

831. Maladjusted children are mostly found in
(a) poor or joint families
(b) broken or unitary families
(c) Both (a) and (b)
(d) None of the above

832. Who said that two major components of "person's" psychology were the twin notions of basic anxiety and basic hostility?
(a) Freud (b) Adler
(c) G.W. Allport (d) Kareb Harney

833. In Rourschach personality test, the explanation of answers of a person is on basis of which principles?
(a) Assessed quality
(b) Time and response
(c) Ink blots
(d) Both (a) and (b)

834. By personality, which of the following is understood?
(a) Behaviour of the individuals
(b) Inner characteristics of the individuals
(c) Interaction between behaviour and situation
(d) The outer appearance of the individuals.

835. In Rourschach personality test this is required between examiner and subjective.
(a) Friendship (b) Respect
(c) Rapport (d) Confidence

836. Who put forward self-theory?
(a) Spearmanc (b) Freud
(c) G. Allport (d) Rogers

837. Motives are
(a) socially observed
(b) observed directly
(c) inferred from genes
(d) inferences from behaviour

838. Which of the following mechanism is used by a child in the school to escape punishment?
(a) Sublimation
(b) Denial of the fact
(c) Rationalization
(d) All of the above

839. R.B. Cattell made a personality test known as
(a) W.A.T. (b) CAVD
(c) T.A.T. (d) 16PF.

840. In TAT, out of 30 cards how many cards are used for both man women?

(a) 5 (b) 10
(c) 15 (d) 20

841. Which of the following is an important cause of mental ill health (maladjustment) of the teacher in the school?
(a) Hostile attitude of students
(b) Prejudices against him
(c) Poor service conditions
(d) All of the above.

842. The founder of TAT personality test was
(a) Morgan and Moreno
(b) Moreno and Murray
(c) Rourschach and Moreno
(d) Murray and Morgan

843. Who proposed transmutation of genetic material theory?
(a) Mendel (b) Lamark
(c) Darwin (d) Galton

844. Psychology seeks to study all
(a) National problems
(b) Social activities
(c) Human activities
(d) Human problems

845. Which technique is used by TAT?
(a) Analytical (b) Projective
(c) Inventory (d) Interviewing

846. In TAT, what is said to make on the basis of pictures?
(a) Picture story (b) Chapter
(c) Picture (d) Sentence

847. Ethics is a normative science of
(a) Thought (b) Satisfaction
(c) Action (d) Behaviour

848. What impels a person or animal to action?
(a) Motive (b) Drive
(c) Need (d) Goal

849. The founder of CAT was
(a) Morgan (b) Rouschach
(c) Murray (d) Bellack

850. Who used ink-block test first?
(a) Medongall (b) Freud
(c) Galton (d) Rorschach

851. Ectomorphic people according to Sheldon are
(a) Artistic (b) Self-controlled
(c) Introverted (d) All of the above

852. Spranger classified people on the basis of
(a) their interest in different fields
(b) their physique
(c) their psychology
(d) None of the above

853. Who designed the TAT?
(a) G.W. Airport (b) Mendel
(c) Murry (d) Karl Jung

854. The full name of CAT personality test is
(a) Children's Appreciative Test
(b) Children's Apperception Test
(c) Children's Attitude Test
(d) All of the above

855. Extroverts are
(a) tension free
(b) social and friendly
(c) Both (a) and (b)
(d) None of the above

856. Psychology deals with human
(a) Thoughts (b) Behaviour
(c) Feelings (d) All of the above

857. The full name of TAT personality test is
(a) Thematic Apperception Test
(b) Teaching Attitude Test
(c) Trial Attention Test
(d) None of the above

858. The most important scale for measurement of psychological traits is
(a) C.P. Scale (b) TAT
(c) CAVD (d) WAIS

859. Certainly introspection cannot be used in the behaviour of

(a) Insane persons (b) Old people
(c) Both (a) and (b) (d) Children

860. If fixation of libido takes place in the third stage of development, according to Freud, the person will be
(a) Dealing people high handedly
(b) Extreme lover of beauty
(c) Both (a) and (b)
(d) None of the above

861. The term personality has been derived from a
(a) Greek word (b) English word
(c) German word (d) Latin word

862. The method of CAT personality test is like the following test.
(a) Play and Drama Test
(b) Sentence Completion test
(c) TAT
(d) All of the above

863. Which of the following is not the property of traits?
(a) Traits are higher order habits
(b) Traits are directly observable
(c) Traits are quantifiable
(d) Traits change with time.

864. Who has defined Educational Research in these words, "The systematic and scholarly application of the scientific method interpreted in its broader sense, to the solution of educational problems; conversely, any systematic study designed to promote the development of education as science can be considered educational research"?
(a) Francis G. Cornell
(b) George J. Mouly
(c) W.S. Monroe
(d) John W. Best

865. By TAT personality test the knowledge of following is obtained, is not according to the quantity of
(a) Interests (b) Traits
(c) Aptitudes (d) Qualities

866. Both types and traits theories of personality focus on people's characteristics which are
(a) Motivational (b) Personal
(c) Attitudinal (d) Emotional

867. Which is a projective test?
(a) Allport-Vernon-Lindzey Study of Values
(b) Edwards Personal Preference Schedule (EPPS)
(c) Minnesota Multiphasic Personality Inventory (MMPI)
(d) Rorschach Test.

868. "Personality is the dynamic organization within the individual of those psychophysical systems that determine his unique adjustments to his environment". Who said this?
(a) G. Allport (b) Michael
(c) Medougall (d) Walter

869. The founder of the method of personality test by sentence of story completion was
(a) Tentlor (b) Ebinghaus
(c) Pine (d) All of these

870. The trait theories are not free from shortcomings as they are
(a) not quantified with zero reference point.
(b) subject to subjective interpretation.
(c) not universal.
(d) All of the above.

871. A question, a frown or a sneer from a friend is
(a) Action (b) Response
(c) Stimulus (d) Reaction

872. The founder of the method of personality test by "Play and Drama"
(a) Margan (b) Murray
(c) Bellack (d) Moreno

873. Who constructed the personality structure: Id, Ego, and Supergo?
(a) Freud (b) Krebs
(c) Eysenck (d) Crystal

874. The second cranial nerve is called the
(a) Abducens (b) Optic nerve
(c) Trigeminal nerve (d) Olfactory nerve

875. A hypothesis in educational research need not be
(a) logically consistent and pertinent to the question under consideration.
(b) compatible with well-attested theories and models.
(c) capable of establishing generalizations that can be applied in many areas of education or other fields.
(d) Both (a) and (b).

876. The sexual energy underlying Id, Ego and Superego urges is called
(a) Hunger (b) Thrust
(c) Drive (d) Libido

877. Moreno used the method of personality-test by "Play and Drama" for the elimination of
(a) dumb-deaf.
(b) for mentally retarded.
(c) depression due to mental illness.
(d) handicapped.

878. Individual psychology of personality was given by
(a) Jung (b) Eysenck
(c) Adler (d) None of the above

879. According to Erikson the process of personality development is completed in
(a) stage 6 (b) stage 7
(c) stage 8 (d) stage 10

880. In the non-projective methods of personality measurement subjective can hide the fact, hence they are
(a) Impracticable (b) Invalid
(c) Inveliable (d) All of the above

881. According to Freud, the Id operates according to what French called the
(a) Psychoanalytical principle
(b) Methodological principle
(c) Pleasure principle
(d) Sexual stimulated principle

882. Placing blame for difficulties upon others or attributing one's own unethical discussion to others, is
(a) Rationalization (b) Projection
(c) Identification (d) Repression

883. Psychology is a positive science because it is concerned with
(a) how we ought to behave
(b) how we actually do
(c) facts as they are
(d) All of the above

884. Most cases of impotence or frigidity are due to
(a) physical factors.
(b) sexual apathy.
(c) psychological factors.
(d) social factors.

885. In the projective methods of personality measurement a person has capability to read absent mind, hence the examiner need this.
(a) Training (b) Faith
(c) Study (d) Knowledge

886. Theory developed in reaction to phenomenological theories of personality is
(a) Cognitive theory
(b) Behaviour theory
(c) Both (a) and (b)
(d) None of the above

887. Walter's theory of personality emphasizes
(a) rewarded models to be immitated.
(b) good models to be imitated.
(c) Both (a) and (b).
(d) None of the above.

888. "In mental health science to discover for laws of mental health and to protect mental health is very much necessary". This statement is given by
(a) Drever
(b) Skinner
(c) Crow and Crow
(d) None of the above

889. The determinants of personality are
(a) Biological (b) Social
(c) Cultural (d) All of these

890. All that we do is to describe human activity as it is observed in different stages, aspects or phases without any regard to its moral worth. Science which follows this method of study are called
(a) Positive science (b) Psychology
(c) Negative science (d) Neutral science

891. As a vehicle of transmitting social norms and culture language is one of the many determinants of ______ personality.
(a) natural (b) genetic
(c) social (d) biological

892. To keep balance in life what a person has to do with his environment?
(a) Protection (b) Adjustment
(c) Equality (d) All of the above

893. Which of the following methods of study is an appreciative approach in which we try to judge behaviour in the light of some standard of worth or value and science?
(a) Psychology
(b) Formative science
(c) Social science
(d) Normative science

894. By what name zoologist call "adjustment"?
(a) Adoption (b) Organization
(c) Balance (d) Both (a) and (c)

895. Which famous psychologist believed in the collective unconscious?
(a) Alter (b) Adler
(c) Freud (d) Jung

896. Which type of behaviour of the model is imitated in social learning theory of personality?
(a) Touching behaviour which is applauded by the people
(b) Novel and unique behaviour
(c) Aggressive behaviour
(d) All of the above.

897. 'Erogenous zones' were referred as the parts of the body by
(a) Wundt (b) Pavlov
(c) Freud (d) Skinner

898. "Adjustment is a continuous process in life by it a person develops lot of moderation behaviour so as to establish a relation between him and environment." This definition of adjustment was given by
(a) Boring (b) Kulhan
(c) Langfield (d) Gates

899. The purpose of personality testing is
(a) to classify people into different groups.
(b) to apply behaviour/psycho therapy.
(c) to know the causes of maladjustment.
(d) All of the above.

900. In evaluating the significance of the research problem, an important social considerations is
(a) possibility of obtaining reliable and valid data by the researchers.
(b) the genuine interest of the researcher in the problem.
(c) necessary skills, abilities and background of knowledge of the researcher.
(d) practical value of the findings to educationists, parents and social workers, etc.

901. The following elements are in the concept of adjustment.
   (a) This exist according to necessity in environment
   (b) This is a continuous process
   (c) This is done for balancing purpose
   (d) All of the above

902. Freeman divided the personality inventory into
   (a) Six parts (b) Seven parts
   (c) Two parts (d) Five parts

903. In deductive method, teaching is done from
   (a) macro to micro level.
   (b) easy to difficult level.
   (c) general to specific level.
   (d) specific to general level.

904. "Specific" trait inventory' was made by
   (a) Rogers (b) Freeman
   (c) Tolman (d) Spearman

905. Adjustment reduces tension in the below mentioned situations
   (a) Opposition (b) Bluntness
   (c) Turmoil (d) All of the above

906. Play group of teenagers becomes more
   (a) Unorganized (b) Selective
   (c) Diselective (d) Can't say

907. Questions in the schedule are
   (a) few in number.
   (b) read by the respondent.
   (c) asked by the investigator in a face to face situation.
   (d) None of the above.

908. Two main steps of the process of adjustment are
   (a) Implementation of problem-solving.
   (b) Identification of tension state.
   (c) Both (a) and (b).
   (d) Remain away from problem solving.

909. Who was the first psychologist to make the personality inventory?
   (a) Frankman (b) Tolman
   (c) F. Galton (d) Freeman

910. Which of the following things should be done in order to make a good questionnaire?
   (a) Private questions should be asked only indirectly.
   (b) Number of questions should not be very large.
   (c) Language of questions should be clear and simple.
   (d) All of the above.

911. Minnesota Multiphasic personality inventory was developed for
   (a) Female (b) Male
   (c) Neither (d) Both (a) and (b)

912. As an adjustment which two methods are used by a person to reduce or eliminate tension?
   (a) To protection: rid of
   (b) To get away from problem
   (c) Visible method
   (d) All of the above

913. Questionnaire for collecting data is mailed when
   (a) a large number of respondents are to be covered.
   (b) it is not easy to approach the respondents personally.
   (c) respondent is an educated and responsible citizen.
   (d) All of the above.

914. In the visible methods of adjustment what is the meaning of 'changing path' is for success?
   (a) To adopt other path
   (b) To follow the instruction of others
   (c) To remain determined
   (d) To become disappointed

915. Study of family relations is the object of
(a) 16PF (b) GPL
(c) MPS (d) MMPI

916. The level of motivation is
(a) high when the task is of routine nature.
(b) high when the task is difficult.
(c) low when the task is interesting.
(d) low when the task is difficult.

917. Play groups of teenagers become
(a) Fully organized
(b) Partially organized
(c) Unorganized
(d) None of the above

918. The personality inventory to measure mental disorder was developed by
(a) Galton (b) Mowrer
(c) Terman (d) Sipply

919. The following are the main defence mechanism for adjustment.
(a) Day-dreaming (b) Withdrawal
(c) Regression (d) All of the above

920. If a child is appreciated by the mother only when he/she continuously sits and does his/her home work for two hours otherwise not, it is called
(a) fixed interval schedule of reinforcement.
(b) variable interval schedule of reinforcement.
(c) variable ratio schedule of reinforcement.
(d) fixed ratio schedule of reinforcement.

921. The meanings of adopting defence mechanism for rationalization of adjustment are
(a) to justify your attempt to success.
(b) to justify requirement of once's needs.
(c) search out reason for once's failure.
(d) None of the above.

922. Security Insecurity Inventory was developed
(a) Moslow (b) Hebb
(c) Galton (d) Freeman

923. Open end questionnaire is not preferred to fixed response questionnaire because
(a) respondents may ignore them.
(b) they cannot be statistically treated.
(c) subjectivity of interpretation may distort the result.
(d) All of the above.

924. What is the Test re-test reliability of Security Insecurity Inventory?
(a) .87 (b) .84
(c) .81 (d) .86

925. For adjustment, repression of defend mechanism means
(a) to regret over satisfied desires.
(b) to get rid of unsatisfied desires.
(c) to hide unsatisfied desires.
(d) to show unsatisfied desires.

926. Which of the following inventories is not used in schools?
(a) Social inventories
(b) Adjustment inventories
(c) Pathological trait inventories
(d) All of the above.

927. Woodworth's personal data sheet was developed in
(a) 1911 (b) 1914
(c) 1916 (d) 1918

928. What is the meaning of withdrawal of defend mechanism in repression?
(a) To become sad on unfulfilled desires
(b) Disappointment on unfulfilled desires
(c) Not to face the unsatisfied desires
(d) All of the above

929. MCI has
(a) 15 items (b) 355 items
(c) 25 items (d) 150 items

930. Sex drive can be classified as a
(a) Biological motive
(b) Sociological motive
(c) Security motive
(d) Psychological motive

931. Third ventricle is found in
(a) Brain of rabbit
(b) Heart of insect
(c) Heart of rabbit
(d) Brain of earthworm

932. 16PF study is the part of
(a) related personality test.
(b) personality inventory.
(c) behavioural technique.
(d) projective technique.

933. What is important regarding adjustment with respect to identification of defence mechanism?
(a) Try to forget the tension
(b) To satisfy even by unfulfilled desires
(c) Identification with tension problem
(d) Identification of a grand person to get rid of tension

934. Minnesota Counseling Inventory was developed by
(a) Bell
(b) Minnesota
(c) Berlie and Layton
(d) None of the above

935. For adjustment of day-dreaming, the meaning of defence mechanism is
(a) to get rid of the desire in disappointment.
(b) satisfaction of unfulfilled desires in imaginary world.
(c) to forgot pains of failure in dream.
(d) All of the above.

936. Uni-dimensional theory is a part of
(a) personality inventory.
(b) behavioural technique.
(c) projective technique.
(d) None of these.

937. Personality inventories are criticized on which of the following grounds?
(a) They have very poor diagnostic value.
(b) Their validity coefficient is very low.
(c) The individual may understand a question wrongly.
(d) All of the above.

938. To transform gang into worth-while youth organization, it can be given
(a) Adventure (b) Challenges
(c) Opportunity (d) All of the above

939. The term multi-dimensional is related to
(a) TAT technique.
(b) personality inventory.
(c) word association technique.
(d) behavioural technique.

940. How a person try to remove the tension developed due to adjustment by the projection defence mechanism
(a) To impose out fault on others
(b) To hide our fault in the fault of society
(c) To highlight one's faults
(d) Fault of other being the cause of tension

941. The first group of intelligence test was the
(a) Army Alpha Test
(b) Thematic Appreciation Test
(c) Army General Classification Test
(d) Stanford-Binet Test

942. Many students who form gang live in
(a) Posh colonies (b) Towns
(c) Slum areas (d) Any where

943. "For development of educational guided person the help rendered is consciously done effort". This definition is given by
(a) Bever (b) Jones
(c) Carter V. Good (d) Rutt Strang

944. Interview technique is the most important part of
(a) behavioural technique.
(b) questionnaire technique.
(c) projective technique.
(d) selection technique.

945. If a person is both hungry and sleepy at the same time then arises
(a) avoidance-avoidance conflict
(b) approach-avoidance conflict
(c) approach-approach conflict
(d) None of these conflicts

946. 'Case history' method is a part of
(a) diagnostic technique.
(b) gamma-technique.
(c) behavioural technique.
(d) study technique.

947. The need of vocational guidance is as per the following.
(a) Variety of profession opportunity
(b) Selection of right profession
(c) Educational weakness
(d) Both (a) and (b)

948. Interview is
(a) a psychological process
(b) an educational process
(c) a social process
(d) None of the above

949. The aim of personal guidance is
(a) to testify and rectify the personal problems of a person.
(b) to testify and rectify the professional ability of a person.
(c) to increase the capability of personal adjustment.
(d) Both (a) and (c).

950. How many objects are there in "Minnesota personality scale"?
(a) Five objects (b) Three objects
(c) Seven objects (d) None of these

951. The purpose of an interview may be
(a) to treat a psychological disease.
(b) to gather some facts.
(c) to assess and study the personality.
(d) All of the above.

952. Attempting to prove that one's behaviour is "rational" and justiciable and thus worthy of self and social approval is
(a) Rationalization (b) Sublimation
(c) Indentification (d) Projection

953. A profile stability score can be found by correlating the individual's odd and even scores in
(a) 16 variables (b) 10 variables
(c) 13 variables (d) 15 variables

954. What should be the role of sex-education in schools?
(a) Family planning (b) Sex-education
(c) Sex-hygiene (d) All of the above

955. Thinking analogously about hypotheses, a researcher should
(a) have no bets, but dice only.
(b) first bet and then roll the dice.
(c) change his bet after the data are in.
(d) first roll the dice and then bet.

956. Sex education is needed because in it absence students become
(a) suffer from sex diseases.
(b) they become notorious.
(c) they make other students notorious.
(d) All of the above.

957. Who said "A neurotic individual is one who deviates in his behaviour from the norms accepted by his culture because of anxiety and who feels lonely and inferior because of this deviation"?
(a) Hull (b) Brown
(c) Freeman (d) Coleman

958. A person can abase interview as a tool if
(a) he is unable to pool information into an integrated whole.

(b) he is obsessed by his own philosophy of life.
(c) he cannot mould and redirect questions.
(d) All of the above.

959. Interview is preferred to personality inventories because
(a) it can cover maximum aspects of personality.
(b) it involves greater flexibility between the two parties.
(c) Both (a) and (b).
(d) None of the above.

960. Spranger's typology is based on man's
(a) Body temperature
(b) Organs
(c) Behaviour
(d) Interests

961. The aim of sex-education in schools should be
(a) to save the students from sex diseases.
(b) impart education of social values to students.
(c) to impart fair sex education to students.
(d) Both (a) and (b).

962. The pin-prick is the
(a) Activity (b) Stimulus
(c) Response (d) Emotion

963. One aim of sex-education at secondary and higher secondary level is
(a) to know the importance of family planning.
(b) to impart appropriate knowledge of sex after marriage.
(c) to get sex-education from nature and other human beings.
(d) All of the above.

964. WAT was devised by
(a) Jung (b) Hull
(c) Freud (d) Adler

965. A harmonious and all-round growth and development of human powers or faculties, mental and physical comes through
(a) Physical health (b) Education
(c) Mental health (d) Society

966. The nature of personality can be defined as
(a) Motivational
(b) Attitudinal
(c) Psycho-physical
(d) Emotional

967. Which type of sex-education teacher should give to students in school?
(a) Expert in sex acts
(b) Respectable among students
(c) Efficient and good character
(d) Both (b) and (c)

968. Graphic rating scale is preferred to point scale because
(a) it can be plotted on a graph.
(b) it fills the gap between two scale points.
(c) Both (a) and (b).
(d) None of the above.

969. Q-sorting technique was developed by William Stephenson in
(a) 1974 (b) 1960
(c) 1858 (d) 1953

970. The average weight of mind at the time of birth of a child is
(a) 1400 gram (b) 450 gram
(c) 350 gram (d) 300 gram

971. Interview is the original method of
(a) personality make up.
(b) selection.
(c) attitude assessment.
(d) personality assessment.

972. The process in which, and by which the knowledge, character and behaviour of the young are shaped and moulded is known as

(a) Psychology (b) Education
(c) Exercise (d) All of the above

973. Which of the following is not a projective technique?
(a) Sentence-Completion Test
(b) Rorschach
(c) Maudsley Personality Inventory (MPI)
(d) T.A.T.

974. The term "Mental Hygiene" has been given to us by
(a) William James (b) James D. Page
(c) C.W. Bears (d) C.L. Pierce

975. In development cycle of child, the age of speedy development is
(a) 14 to 18 years (b) 10 to 12 years
(c) 2 to 4 years (d) 0 to 2 years

976. The teenage groups exist
(a) outside the society
(b) independently
(c) with play groups
(d) only in schools

977. The person unaware of his own hostile impulses but sees them in others is using the defence mechanism of
(a) reaction formation
(b) displacement
(c) insulation
(d) projection

978. "At the time of birth a child is neither social nor anti-social element but this state does not remain for much time". This statement is of
(a) Rousseau (b) Adler
(c) Crow and Crow (d) Hobbles

979. The word "Adjustment" is biological in origin. It actually means
(a) Life (b) Adaptation
(c) Survival (d) None of these

980. The performance of a person in a job is measured by
(a) Behaviourally Anchored Rating scale
(b) Group performance test
(c) Both (a) and (b)
(d) None of the above

981. The most fundamental characteristic of good adjustment's
(a) a sound and wholesome system of motives and goals.
(b) a high degree of acceptance of one's environment.
(c) keen insight.
(d) a sincere interest in people.

982. This is not a sign of adolescence.
(a) Interest in playing
(b) Group formation
(c) The thought of friendship
(d) Social consciousness

983. Error of 'Halo Effect' is caused when
(a) rater rates the person in the middle.
(b) rater is lenient in his rating.
(c) rater is influenced by one single favourable or unfavourable trait.
(d) None of the above.

984. The logical error in rating scale was first pointed out in
(a) 1911 (b) 1914
(c) 1924 (d) 1931

985. "Emotion is the provoked state of a person". This thought is of
(a) Jung (b) Allport
(c) Woodworth (d) Adler

986. The distinction between normality and abnormality is
(a) one of both kind and degree.
(b) essentially one of degree.
(c) just terminology.
(d) one of kind.

987. Which of the following is not measured by the TAT?

(a) Personality adjustment
(b) Personality needs
(c) Reasoning ability
(d) Emotions

988. A well-adjusted person should not have
(a) happiness at work.
(b) good health.
(c) emotional centre.
(d) unrealistic thinking.

989. The main reason of complex gland is
(a) subdued emotions.
(b) absence of feelings in a person.
(c) no real unification of emotions.
(d) None of the above.

990. Psychology is a systematic inquiry into man's relation with his
(a) Family (b) Environment
(c) Friends (d) All of the above

991. In order to improve the validity of rating scale which of the following methods should be adopted?
(a) Response options and different scales should be well defined.
(b) Rating should be done by independent raters.
(c) Traits to be measured should be defined in behavioural terms.
(d) All of the above.

992. First of all study of individual difference of heredity was done by
(a) Jung (b) Woodworth
(c) Crow and Crow (d) Galton

993. Wherever there is a barrier, there is
(a) Conflict (b) Mental illness
(c) Frustration (d) None of these

994. In socio-metric method, the super star is one who
(a) is chosen in multiple pairs.
(b) is chosen by maximum number of persons.
(c) Both (a) and (b).
(d) None of the above.

995. A conflict means or implies
(a) insecurity in feeling.
(b) incomparability in motives and for goals.
(c) incompetence.
(d) disorganisation of behaviour.

996. "All factors come in individual difference which can be measured". This recognitions is of below noted educationist.
(a) Milton (b) Murray
(c) Garton (d) Skinner

997. Projective technique is used for measuring
(a) Individual's need for self-actualization
(b) Individual's inventoried interests
(c) Individual's value-system
(d) Individual's dominant feelings, emotions, conflicts, needs which are, generally, repressed by the individual and are stored up in the unconscious mind

998. Situational test for assessing personality is used in
(a) military services for selecting officers.
(b) police department for identifying criminals.
(c) Both (a) and (b).
(d) None of the above.

999. Personality has been derived from the word
(a) Person (b) Personnel
(c) Personal (d) Persona

1000. Which of the following attempts to study not only growth and development of individual minds and behaviour but also of individual activities, habits and abilities?
(a) Comparative psychology
(b) General physiology

(c) Genetic psychology
(d) Physiological psychology.

1001. The classification of non-tangible, social and tangible intelligence was done by
(a) Smith (b) Good
(c) Garette (d) Thorndike

1002. With any conflict, the concept of is attached
(a) Need (b) Valency
(c) Force (d) All of these

1003. Operant conditioning is associated with
(a) Bleuler (b) Thorndike
(c) Hull (d) Skinner

1004. Which of the following is the most difficult and challenging step of project method for testing personality?
(a) Preparation of the test
(b) Scoring of the test
(c) Administration of the test
(d) Interpretation of the test

1005. In how many categories Best (1978) has classified projective techniques?
(a) Two (b) Three
(c) Four (d) Six

1006. Increasing feelings of worth by identifying self with person or institutions of illustrious standing, is
(a) Rationalization (b) Indentification
(c) Projection (d) Sublimation

1007. The most difficult type of conflict to solve is
(a) avoidance-avoidance
(b) approach-avoidance
(c) approach-approach
(d) None of these

1008. "One element theory" of intelligence was done in 1910 by
(a) Bine, Stern and Thurman
(b) Stern, Bine and Garette
(c) Bine
(d) Bine and Thurman

1009. The influence which the environment exercises on the organism and reuses it to activity is called the
(a) Response (b) Stimulus
(c) Both (a) and (b) (d) Emotion

1010. Positive science is known as
(a) Civics (b) Psychology
(c) Natural science (d) Sociology

1011. In how many stages the administration process of inkblot test gets completed?
(a) Three (b) Five
(c) Six (d) Seven

1012. "Multi-element theory" of intelligence was done in 1905 by
(a) Thuston (b) Turman
(c) Bine (d) Thorndike

1013. In order to adjust, we take help of mental or defence mechanisms. These are
(a) socially disapproved
(b) socially tolerated
(c) socially approved
(d) None of these

1014. In Rorschach test, vague responses of the examinee are clarified in
(a) testing of limit stage
(b) inquiry stage
(c) preparation stage
(d) None of the above

1015. When response is based on uncommon area of the blot, it is denoted by
(a) DW (b) DdW
(c) S (d) Dd

1016. Physics deals with
(a) Moment (b) Material
(c) Matter (d) Energy

1017. Compensation and rationalization are examples of

(a) defence mechanisms.
(b) non-adjustive emotions.
(c) distortion of reality.
(d) None of these.

1018. The founder of "group element theory" of intelligence was
(a) Bine (b) Watson
(c) Thomson (d) Thurston

1019. A science deals with a group of related
(a) Facts (b) Principles
(c) Both (a) and (b) (d) Composition

1020. Natural objects or things in inkblot tests are scored as
(a) No (b) N
(c) Na (d) Lm

1021. If number of D responses in an inkblot test is few, it indicates
(a) cheerfulness of the examinee.
(b) love for beauty of the examinee.
(c) stress and anxiety of the examinee.
(d) None of the above.

1022. The founder of sample theory related to intelligence was
(a) Turman (b) Bine
(c) Thomson (d) Thuston

1023. Boasting is a form of
(a) Compensation (b) Rationalisation
(c) Aggression (d) Substitution

1024. Third ventricle of brain is also known as
(a) Diacoel (b) Metacol
(c) Paracoel (d) Rhinocoel

1025. It is interested in the universal characteristics of behaviour and seeks not only to describe them but also to relate and explain them by reference to some general law. This is the scope of what may be called
(a) Experimental psychology
(b) Neurology
(c) General psychology
(d) Introspectim

1026. The eighth cranial nerve supplies structures in the
(a) Eye (b) Tongue
(c) Ear (d) Nose

1027. Rationalisation is of
(a) Three kinds (b) Four kinds
(c) Two kinds (d) None of these

1028. Who from the following made the first intelligence test in 1879?
(a) Thomson (b) Bine
(c) Galton (d) Budent

1029. Projective techniques are very poor measure of personality testing because
(a) their accuracy depends on the success of its inquiry stage.
(b) they are highly subjective.
(c) Both (a) and (b).
(d) None of the above.

1030. The success of TAT lies in the
(a) conclusion drawing power of the examiner.
(b) expression power of the examinee.
(c) Both (a) and (b).
(d) None of the above.

1031. The personality of the individual in TAT is reflected by
(a) the environment in which hero lives.
(b) the personality of the hero.
(c) Both (a) and (b).
(d) None of the above.

1032. Study of the behaviour of animals is
(a) Animal psychology
(b) Physiological psychology
(c) Genetic psychology
(d) None of the above

1033. Group intelligence test in 1917-18 in America, was started by

(a) Thurston (b) Turman
(c) John Dewey (d) Thomson

1034. "Grapes are sour" and "illness is a sign of greatness" are examples of
(a) Fantasy behaviour
(b) Compensation
(c) Rationalization
(d) Projection

1035. White matter is composed of bundles of
(a) non-myelinated nerve fibres
(b) nerve cells with blood vessels
(c) ependymal cells
(d) myelinated nerve fibres

1036. Word Association test for assessing personality was first used by Jung in
(a) 1898 (b) 1910
(c) 1912 (d) 1922

1037. Underlying assumption of figure drawing test is that
(a) the examinee expresses his feelings through these figures.
(b) the examinee projects himself and his surroundings in these figures.
(c) Both (a) and (b).
(d) None of the above.

1038. Somanbulism is a sign of
(a) Bedwetting (b) Narcolepsy
(c) Hysteria (d) Withdrawal

1039. The founder of active production theory of intelligence was
(a) Glasier (b) Thomson
(c) Guilford (d) Thurston

1040. A moralist, who believes in duty for the sake of duty
(a) will be considered as a successful teacher from a pragmatist's point of view.
(b) will be given preference in a pragmatist school as compared to an idealistic school.
(c) could be considered as an ideal teacher because he depends on the maxim of rewards and punishments.
(d) will find no place in a pragmatist school because a pragmatist regards discipline as an external force.

1041. The foundation of an individual's later development rests entirely on the outcome of his earlier stages and is the result of his
(a) Social life (b) Family life
(c) Cultural life (d) All of the above

1042. The calculation of IQ for idiot is
(a) 0 to 25 (b) 70 to 80
(c) 50 to 70 (d) 25 to 50

1043. Psychology's major contribution in education lie in
(a) identifying potentially successful educational procedures.
(b) providing a scientific foundation for the art of teaching.
(c) comparing the relative effectiveness of various teaching procedures.
(d) defining the goals on which the teacher should strive.

1044. Self report inventories are called
(a) Attitude scale
(b) Check list
(c) Both (a) and (b)
(d) None of the above

1045. Which of the following theories considers personality as the product of environmental factors?
(a) Learning Theories
(b) Trait theories
(c) Both (a) and (b)
(d) None of the above

1046. In India Equality of Educational opportunity is
(a) Reality (b) Illusionary
(c) Only in name (d) None of these

1047. Education psychology is oriented towards
(a) the formulation of hypothesis and theories relative to educations practice.
(b) the development on the part of the child of realistic goals and effective plans for their attainment.
(c) the study of the peculiarities of individual children.
(d) the application of the principles and techniques of psychology to the solution of the problems of the class room.

1048. First of all intelligence test was started in India in the year
(a) 1912 (b) 1922
(c) 1931 (d) 1950

1049. Education cannot be classified within the group of religious studies because
(a) religion speaks of traditions of the past which cannot cater to the requirements of education for culture today.
(b) there is scope for religious ideals in the modern education.
(c) the bases of religion are faith and belief which are by themselves inadequate for the development of education.
(d) religious studies cannot develop the personality of students in the present day.

1050. First quantitative study of human abilities was Galton's report prepared in
(a) 1869 (b) 1888
(c) 1904 (d) 1909

1051. First systematic intelligence test was prepared by Alfred Binet in
(a) 1901 (b) 1904
(c) 1905 (d) 1908

1052. The founder of "active conditioning theory" was
(a) Rousseau (b) Therston
(c) Werthemer (d) B.F. Skinner

1053. The primary aim of educational psychology is
(a) to provide a theoretical framework for educational research.
(b) to provide the academic background essential for effective teaching.
(c) to contribute to an understanding of sound educational practices.
(d) to provide the teacher with a greater appreciation of his role in the education of the child.

1054. The famous standard revision of Binet's scale of intelligence was first undertaken by
(a) Cyril Burt
(b) B.F. Skinner
(c) Levis Terman
(d) Edward Thorndike

1055. The distinction between moral and ethical instruction could be made as follows:
(a) Morals are long standing but ethics are slow in change.
(b) The morals emphasize knowledge and ethics stress performance.
(c) Ethics stress knowledge and morals emphasize performance.
(d) Ethics are fast changing but morals are slow in change.

1056. According to Renzuli, a gifted child is one
(a) who is committed to task and highly motivated.
(b) who is definitely creative.
(c) who possesses above average ability in almost every field.
(d) All of the above.

1057. According to psychology, all education is

(a) Functional (b) Self-education
(c) Deliberate (d) Purposive

1058. The IQ of a backward student is less than
(a) 40 (b) 50
(c) 85 (d) 90

1059. Gifted and talented children must be identified as early as possible because
(a) they are likely to create problems for others, if they are not given work according to their ability.
(b) ordinary level of curriculum will not suit these children.
(c) if their potentials are not developed by proper guidance of the teacher, it is a loss of the society.
(d) All of the above.

1060. After sometime the child develops 'the ego' which represents
(a) Rationality (b) Reality
(c) Reasoning (d) All of the above

1061. After taking over from other people—parents and teachers—certain socially accepted solutions of problems, a child develops the
(a) Super Ego (b) Id
(c) Ego (d) None of these

1062. The founder of mental health science was
(a) John Watson (b) Morgan
(c) W. John (d) W. Bier

1063. The best definition of educational psychology is a study of teaching and learning" has been given by
(a) James Ross
(b) W. Kolesnik
(c) N.L. Munn
(d) Charles E. Skinner

1064. Achievement test can be a good indicator of intellectual power if
(a) a student shows good performance consistently on different achievement tests.
(b) it is conducted immediately after the teaching is over.
(c) Both (a) and (b).
(d) None of the above.

1065. Which of the following skills does not require high intellectual ability?
(a) Teaching skills
(b) Technical skills
(c) Management skills
(d) Mechanical skills

1066. The third aim of education reflects the importance of
(a) Socialization
(b) Social aim in education
(c) Individual aim
(d) Both (a) and (b)

1067. Who said this, "The boundaries of Educational Psychology are unlimited and chan ging"?
(a) Gates (b) Hurlock
(c) William James (d) None of these

1068. "Learning is knowledge of habbits and adoption of attitudes." This opinion is of
(a) Jung (b) Gates
(c) Crow and Crow (d) Watson

1069. Education makes a person
(a) Socially acceptable
(b) Personally well adjusted
(c) Technically efficient
(d) All of the above

1070. Cognitive abilities related to giftedness are all except
(a) high retention power.
(b) high comprehensive and analytical abilities.
(c) high level of verbal intelligence.
(d) None of the above.

1071. A superior child is advanced to a normal child by at least
(a) 1½ years (b) 2½ years
(c) 3½ years (d) 4½ years

1072. "Readiness is like half victory over the war of learning". This saying is of
(a) Shelter (b) Mursel
(c) Bhatia (d) Turman

1073. The major contribution educational psychology might be expected to make towards modern education lies in area of
(a) a re-evaluation of the principles of progressivism.
(b) a clarification of the goals of modern education.
(c) a refinement of the research techniques through which educational problems might be solved.
(d) a reconsideration of educational experiences from the standpoint of their contribution to pupil growth.

1074. Erikson ties physical growth more closely to certain
(a) Cultural events
(b) Physiological events
(c) Psychological events
(d) Social events

1075. The personality of an individual is a
(a) concept developed by psychologists.
(b) psychological term for his character.
(c) dynamic and a continuous process.
(d) fixed state of one's behaviour.

1076. A gifted child is
(a) more frequently chosen by his age mates and peers.
(b) realistic in his approach.
(c) highly interested in solving social problems.
(d) All of the above.

1077. Educational psychology is branch of psychology. Psychology is a science. Who is the father of experimental psychology?
(a) Wundt (b) Tolman
(c) Boring (d) Hull

1078. "School is the best workplace of transfer of education". This saying is of
(a) Garret (b) Sorenson
(c) Crow and Crow (d) Bhatia

1079. Which of the following enrichment programmes is suitable for gifted children in the school?
(a) Map work during studies
(b) Mathematics or Science Olympiad
(c) Challenging home assignments
(d) All of the above.

1080. Who says that the individual's 'Id' is socialized in the framework of the family and in the wider social setting?
(a) Linton (b) E.H. Erikson
(c) Freud's theory (d) Moore

1081. The basic concept of personality is
(a) Id (b) Super Ego
(c) Ego (d) All of the above

1082. "Motivation is the process of starting a work, continuing it and making it permanent". This statement is of
(a) Crow and Crow (b) Garret
(c) James (d) Good

1083. Where was first experimental psychology laboratory set up?
(a) Frankfurt (b) Leipzig
(c) Berlin (d) Boston

1084. Which of the following does not come under the category of acceleration for gifted children?
(a) Extra laboratory work
(b) Skipping of classes
(c) Organizing summer camps
(d) Early admission.

1085. Under achievers are those who
(a) score low on intelligence tests.
(b) achieve low in the class consistently despite their superior intelligence.
(c) are unable to correspond their achievement to the level of their innate abilities.
(d) Both (b) and (c).

1086. Between the 'Id' and arbitrary society, represented in part by the
(a) demands of the outside world
(b) super ego
(c) Both (a) and (b)
(d) None of the above

1087. Which method has made educational psychology a science?
(a) Experimental method
(b) Observation method
(c) Clinical method
(d) Survey method

1088. The types of motivation as directed by Maslow are
(a) by birth or earned.
(b) punishment or reward.
(c) biological and non-biological.
(d) natural or artificial.

1089. Which of the following conditions must be satisfied in order to designate a person mentally retarded?
(a) Very poor adaptive ability
(b) Dependability on others
(c) Sub-normal intellectual functioning
(d) All of the above.

1090. The best measure of identifying mildly mentally retarded is
(a) administration of adjustment test.
(b) administration of standardized intelligence test.
(c) administration of behaviour test.
(d) a combination of all.

1091. Our behaviour is determined by such motives as
(a) Thirst (b) Hunger
(c) Sleep (d) All

1092. "Human health science is related to human welfare. This saying is of
(a) Crow and Crow (b) C. Borse
(c) Skinner (d) Good

1093. The oldest method in psychology is
(a) Observation (b) Clinical method
(c) Introspection (d) Case study

1094. Watson and Skinner are
(a) Physiological psychologists
(b) Behavioural psychologists
(c) Physical scientists
(d) None of the above

1095. Physical trauma during pregnancy may cause
(a) Deafness
(b) Mental retardation
(c) Blindness
(d) All of the above

1096. All of the following may cause mental retardation except
(a) action of toxic agent
(b) radio-activity
(c) blood incompatibility
(d) None of the above

1097. Introspection as a method stands rejected by
(a) Psychoanalysts
(b) Gesralt
(c) Functional school
(d) Behaviourists

1098. "Those parents who love their children give protection to them, are helpful to their mental health". This recognition is of
(a) Turman
(b) Wudnt

(c) Kuppu Swami
(d) None of the above

1099. Which of the following is an important postnatal cause of mental retardation?
(a) Severe malnutrition
(b) Brain injury
(c) Infection
(d) All of the above

1100. Who studied the way in which the child learns about the world and the people in it?
(a) Erikson (b) Skinner
(c) Watson (d) Piaget

1101. The intertwined psychological and biological aspects of growth and development occur in a social and cultural setting that finally makes
(a) the adult (b) the baby
(c) the old (d) None of these

1102. The following is not the element of memory.
(a) Recalling (b) Learning
(c) Assumption (d) All of the above

1103. Name the method which deals with only one person at a time and promotes his adjustment.
(a) Experimental method
(b) Case study
(c) Questionnaire
(d) Clinical method

1104. Dullers do not differ from normal children in
(a) level of social expectancy
(b) physical characteristics
(c) Both (a) and (b)
(d) None of the above

1105. Which of the following things is not required for educating mildly mentally retarded children?
(a) Modification in the curriculum
(b) Regular counseling
(c) Regular evaluation
(d) Remedial teaching

1106. Teaching of which of the following skills is not suitable to borderline cases?
(a) Repairing of electric or electronic equipments
(b) Activity based skills
(c) Electric fitting
(d) Oratory skills.

1107. Educational psychology is concerned with
(a) the learning process.
(b) the learning situation.
(c) the learner.
(d) All of these.

1108. "Intelligence is ability of thoughts about non-tangible things". This definition is of
(a) Turman
(b) Thorndike
(c) Berwinghan
(d) None of the above

1109. According to psychoanalytical thinkers the process of socialisation is closely identified with
(a) Id development
(b) Super ego development
(c) Ego development
(d) None of the above

1110. It is much better if discipline comes from the
(a) control of teacher
(b) control within the student
(c) control of society
(d) All of the above

1111. IQ of morons is in the range of
(a) 30-50 (b) 50-75
(c) 60-80 (d) 60-90

1112. According to Allport, personality is
(a) correlation with environment.
(b) union of mind and body.
(c) union.
(d) None of the above.

1113. Some authors classify methods of educational psychology as
(a) proximal method.
(b) distal method.
(c) (a) and (b) are true.
(d) Neither (a) nor (b) are true.

1114. Morons are slow in
(a) taking initiative
(b) physical growth
(c) thinking and planning
(d) All of the above

1115. Unsatisfactory relation of a mentally retarded child with the environment is technically called
(a) Pseudo-dullness
(b) Autism
(c) Maladjustment
(d) None of the above

1116. Everyone of us has to learn
(a) Age roles (b) Sex roles
(c) Job roles (d) All of the above

1117. The content of educational psychology includes
(a) wide ranging items concerning human motivation and learning.
(b) special items concerning processes of education in particular.
(c) special items concerning teaching and learning.
(d) None of these.

1118. Jung has classified the personality in this book.
(a) *Type of Man*
(b) *Psychological*
(c) *Behaviourism*
(d) None of the above

1119. Who saw 'Child growth as proceeding through an organized sequence of stages divided roughly by age'?
(a) Erikson (b) Skinner
(c) Watson (d) Piaget

1120. Each child has to pass through a series of developmental crisis' according to
(a) Erikson (b) Skinner
(c) Watson (d) Piaget

1121. All of the following are characteristics of morons except:
(a) They are educable upto normal level but at a slower rate.
(b) They have stronger sex drives than the normals.
(c) They are restricted to unskilled or semi-skilled occupations.
(d) They are likely to be delinquent more easily.

1122. Questionaire is the other name of
(a) project method.
(b) mixed questionaire method.
(c) projectile method.
(d) paper-pencil method.

1123. Which of the following is not a function of educational psychology?
(a) To define the goals for which education is to strive
(b) To promote a greater understanding of the learning process
(c) To promote a greater understanding of the learner
(d) To discover techniques by means of which educational goals can be attained effectively

1124. Which of the following modifications in the curriculum is needed for morons?
(a) Emphasis on social training
(b) Activity based curriculum
(c) Skill dominated curriculum
(d) All of the above.

1125. Which of the following things cannot be taught to Imbeciles?
(a) Unskilled job to be performed under supervision
(b) Writing skills
(c) Social skills
(d) Self-help skills.

1126. Human behaviour is determined by
(a) Society
(b) Sociogenic factors
(c) Biogenic factors
(d) Both (a) and (b)

1127. Which of the following is primary concern to educational psychologist?
(a) The development of professional insights into the principles underlying the teaching art
(b) The discovery of teaching procedures of maximum effectiveness
(c) The formulation of hypothesis
(d) The discovery of practical solutions to educational problems

1128. The propounder of "ink-blot test" Harman Rouseau was inhabitant of
(a) Switzerland (b) America
(c) Russia (d) England

1129. The Id is
(a) Primitive reasonable man
(b) Developed reasonable man
(c) Developed unreasonable man
(d) Primitive unreasonable man

1130. The psychological aspects of the classroom are best managed by
(a) the students themselves
(b) the class teacher
(c) the principal
(d) the subject teacher

1131. Creative products or ideas are
(a) Flexible to be remanipulated
(b) Novel and unique (previously unknown)
(c) Constructive or destructive
(d) All of the above

1132. Hindrance in once path of "will or necessity" creates
(a) Conflict (b) Tension
(c) Frustration (d) All of the above

1133. Educational psychology should provide prospective teachers with
(a) research procedures by means of which to evaluate correct teaching procedures.
(b) insight into the various aspects of modern education.
(c) validate procedures to use in their teachings.
(d) principles, insights and attitudes as points of departure for effective teaching.

1134. Originality in creativity refers to
(a) Cleverness
(b) Uncommonness
(c) Remoteness
(d) All of the above

1135. A person cannot be a creative one unless
(a) the product produced by him is a useful one.
(b) he is clever enough to think divergently deviated from the normal track.
(c) Both (a) and (b).
(d) None of the above.

1136. Character could be distinguished from personality in which of the following sense?
(a) Character is a patent objective of education for the society whereas personality is popular among education.
(b) Personality deals with over all disposition of a person which is inborn whereas character is cultivated.

(c) Personality includes physical and social aspects whereas character stresses on the intellectual and spiritual aspects.
(d) All of the above.

1137. The primary task of the teacher is
(a) to promote habits of conformity to adults demands and expectations.
(b) to teach the prescribed curriculum.
(c) to provide diagnostic and remedial aid wherever indicated.
(d) to stimulate and guide student learning.

1138. "The word Genius is used one percent of children who are super most intelligent". This statement is of
(a) Crow and Crow
(b) Skinner and Hariman
(c) Turman and Odem
(d) None of the above

1139. The gestalt psychologists brought out clearly the importance of
(a) the functional factors in perception.
(b) the functional factors in cognitive operations.
(c) the interactive factors in cognition.
(d) the structural factors in perception.

1140. In which of the following cases divergent thinking is required?
(a) Attempting a multiple choice item
(b) Writing an essay
(c) Doing a research activity
(d) Both (a) and (c).

1141. Remote Association Test (RAT) of creativity was developed by
(a) Spearman
(b) Sarnoff Mednick
(c) Fisher
(d) Hans Eysenck

1142. The general meaning of "mental weakness" is
(a) less than average mental ability.
(b) average mental ability.
(c) more than average mental ability.
(d) None of the above.

1143. Which of the following teacher traits and procedures is most often given by children as the reasons for not liking the teacher?
(a) Unfairness and favouritism
(b) Irritable and bad temperament
(c) Unreasonable demands on the children
(d) Ignorance of the subject matter

1144. Which of the following tests is similar to Guilford's test of cognitive abilities?
(a) Hidden shapes test
(b) Word association test
(c) Things test
(d) None of the above.

1145. Which of the following statements would be true about the attitudes of a person?
(a) They could be measured on the basis of the aptitude tests developed by psychologists.
(b) They are not biogenic, although they are based on biogenic motives.
(c) They are not measurable because they are so subjective.
(d) They are biogenic and receive further strength and support from the social environment.

1146. In an experiment there are variables. Variable is
(a) Dependent (b) Organismic
(c) Independent (d) All of these

1147. Minimum and maximum age of child-crime in India is
(a) 6 to 14 years respectively
(b) 7 to 16 years respectively
(c) 7 to 18 years respectively
(d) 8 to 17 years respectively

1148. In Hidden shapes test of creativity, which of the following things is used?
(a) Things (b) Pictures
(c) Words (d) None of these

1149. A creative child in the class cannot be satisfied unless
(a) he is allowed to ask questions in his own way.
(b) he is given freedom to manipulate ideas or things.
(c) Both (a) and (b).
(d) None of the above.

1150. A creative child is one who
(a) is all the time restless to do something uncommon and unique.
(b) is ideationally productive and unconventional.
(c) does not stick to social and religious norms in a hard manner.
(d) All of the above.

1151. The following is compared with unconscious mind.
(a) Heredity (b) Iceberg
(c) Heaven (d) Soul

1152. The first step in conducting an experiment is
(a) to formulate a hypothesis.
(b) to interpret data.
(c) to collect data.
(d) to setup a laboratory.

1153. Psychologists are in favour of including contents of therapeutic value in the reading material to be recommended for school children. This objective could be achieved by
(a) dealing with doubts and problems of students which cannot be asked in the classroom directly.
(b) explaining to students the problem being faced by schools in their administration.
(c) including lesson on treatment of physical ailments.
(d) simplifying the language of the books to enable students to understand what they read clearly.

1154. For the development of creative potential of a child, the teacher should
(a) give them chance of problem solving.
(b) allow him to be critical to ideas and people.
(c) Both (a) and (b).
(d) None of the above.

1155. The first book of psychology was written by
(a) Plato (b) Clark Hull
(c) William James (d) Kohler

1156. "Life description method" was first tested by
(a) Tideman
(b) T.P. Nunn
(c) Woodrow Wilson
(d) Davis

1157. Creativity is positively correlated to
(a) social and aesthetic values
(b) school achievement
(c) intelligence
(d) All of the above

1158. Which of the following statements about creativity is not correct?
(a) He can anticipate the problem which can emerge in future.
(b) He may be problematic in the class.
(c) A creative child is conformist.
(d) He does not accept religious values very much.

1159. Which of the following meanings of psychology would be correct today as per the views of experts?
(a) It is a science of consciousness.
(b) It is a science of the mind.
(c) It is a science of the soul.
(d) It is a science of behaviour.

1160. The relation of self-attachment is with following.
(a) Psychological analysis method
(b) Association method
(c) Dream analysis method
(d) All of the above

1161. The first book on Psychology titled *Principal Psychology* was published in
(a) 1890 (b) 1905
(c) 1895 (d) 1879

1162. New ideas (Eureka) suddenly comes in the minds of the creative children in the stage of
(a) Illumination (b) Incubation
(c) Preparation (d) Revision

1163. The technique to foster creativity in children is
(a) problem solving
(b) brain storming
(c) Both (a) and (b)
(d) None of the above

1164. Which of the following conclusions should be correct in your opinion? An individual's best opportunity for self-fulfilment lay
(a) in a state which takes complete responsibilities for individuals.
(b) in a social rather than in a narrowly individualistic context.
(c) in an individualistic rather than a wide social context.
(d) in the individual's struggle against the environmental forces.

1165. An emotionally person is one who
(a) has lack of patience.
(b) has proper emotion at proper time and expresses it in proper quantity in a proper way.
(c) does not express his emotions.
(d) is boastful.

1166. "Personality development is sum of inherited habits". This statement is of
(a) Martin Prince (b) Vallentine
(c) Munn (d) Boring

1167. A teacher can foster creativity in children by
(a) giving them opportunity to express.
(b) developing confidence in them.
(c) Both (a) and (b).
(d) None of the above.

1168. Which is the most difficult step in creativity testing?
(a) Construction of the test
(b) Administration of the test
(c) Scoring of the test
(d) None of the above.

1169. Founder of TAT was
(a) Balleck
(b) Harman Rousseau
(c) Shalden
(d) Moore and Morgan

1170. Which of the following is the most important factor underlying the success of beginning teacher?
(a) His verbal facility and organizational ability
(b) His personality and ability to relate to the class
(c) His scholarship and intellectual ability
(d) His attitudes and outlook on life

1171. The concept of motivation helps us to
(a) take special precautions to avoid safeguarding self interests.
(b) adopt measures to assess the achievements of individual.
(c) explain the behaviour of man or animals than can be observed.
(d) frame rules and regulations to control an educational situation.

1172. Motivation theories can be divided into the push and pull theories according to some experts. The pupil's theories deal with

(a) knowledge of the problems imposed by population growth.
(b) education for family planning.
(c) sex education from a scientific point of view.
(d) the characteristics of different population groups.

1173. Learning disabled children are
(a) low in intelligence
(b) slow in activity
(c) deficient is using potentials
(d) None of the above

1174. The greatest single cause of failure in beginning teachers lies in the area of
(a) subject matter background.
(b) general culture.
(c) inter-personal relations.
(d) general scholarship.

1175. The IQ co-relation between intelligence of child and creativity is
(a) 50 (b) 120
(c) 180 (d) 80

1176. Learning disability is related to
(a) poor ability of expression.
(b) poor ability of mathematical operation.
(c) low listening and comprehension power.
(d) All of the above.

1177. Learning disabled children perform very poorly in
(a) technical areas
(b) academic areas
(c) Both (a) and (b)
(d) None of the above

1178. Absolutism in philosophy can be interpreted as
(a) the possibility of gaining insight into perfect knowledge through spirituality.
(b) absolute contraction of each philosopher that his view alone is perfectly right.
(c) an approach to educational philosophy on the basis of empirical truths alone.
(d) belief in the existence of an absolute entity.

1179. The types of creativity according to external needs of creator are following.
(a) Inventor (b) Engineer
(c) Sculpturist (d) Both (a) and (b)

1180. Which of the following is most likely to be characterized the in-effective teacher?
(a) Emphasis upon pupil discussion in the clarification of group goals
(b) Emphasis upon standards
(c) Refusal to help children until they have helped themselves
(d) Emphasis upon the control of the immediate situation

1181. Problem of learning disability is more complex than that of other disabilities because
(a) it is associated to behaviour problems.
(b) its causes cannot be easily ascertained by applying usual tests.
(c) Both (a) and (b).
(d) None of the above.

1182. Educationally, learning disabled look similar to
(a) backward children
(b) dullers
(c) Both (a) and (b)
(d) None of the above

1183. In which of the following physical characteristics learning disabled children differ from the normal ones?
(a) Poor coordination of motor abilities
(b) Height, weight and health

(c) They are all the time clumsy and awkward
(d) All of the above.

1184. The teacher's major contribution towards the maximum self-realization of the child is best effected through
(a) strict control of classroom activities.
(b) sensitivity pupil needs, goals and purposes.
(c) strict reinforcement of academic standards.
(d) constant fulfilment of the child's needs.

1185. "The meaning of creativity is production of complete new thing or partially new thing". This definition was given by
(a) Rouch
(b) Guilford
(c) Sten
(d) Stenager and Karoskey

1186. The adjustment mechanisms in Psychology are so called because
(a) they are flexible and could be easily adjusted to any situation irrespective of persons involved.
(b) they create favourable conditions for adjusting an individual to a new situation.
(c) they suggest methods of locating the situations to which a person could be easily adjusted.
(d) they protect a person's self esteem against frustration and anxiety by suggesting alternative methods.

1187. Which of the following methods is most suitable for learning disabled children?
(a) Brain storming
(b) Behaviour guidance method
(c) Remedial teaching
(d) None of the above.

1188. Graham had told the following stages in the process of creativity
(a) Illumination (b) Preparation
(c) Inoculation (d) All of the above

1189. The field of education is permeated by conflicts and misconceptions largely because
(a) there are no best teaching methods and procedures.
(b) education has first to be practical and only secondarily to be scientific.
(c) the problems encountered in teaching call for subjectivity of interpretation.
(d) the problem encountered in teaching are not amenable to rigorous scientific investigation.

1190. In order to improve work habits of learning disabled what should be done?
(a) Close monitoring of the behaviour is needed
(b) Cues and prompt should be given
(c) Unattending behaviour should be penalized
(d) All of the above.

1191. The term 'Functional Literacy' regarding the education of adult means that
(a) the literacy provides him access to written communication without much difficulty.
(b) the literacy of the adult should enable him for thoughtful reading in his social and professional life.
(c) the adults should be able to function as members of the adult franchise scheme.
(d) None of the above.

1192. Those who are normal in intelligence but slow in academic achievement due to psycho-social reasons are called
(a) gifted under achievers
(b) backward children

(c) Both (a) and (b)
(d) None of the above

1193. Which method of research contributes most to the advancement of educational psychology as a science?
(a) Historical method
(b) Survey method
(c) Clinical method
(d) Experimental method

1194. Guilford had clarified the following abilities for creative thinking.
(a) Insculptured
(b) Basic
(c) Both (a) and (b)
(d) None of the above

1195. Consistent low achievement leads to low intelligence because
(a) learning develops thinking and reasoning power.
(b) 50% intellectual ability is expressed in verbal form.
(c) Both (a) and (b).
(d) None of the above.

1196. Which of the following situations may lead to educational backwardness?
(a) Motor disability
(b) Long diseases and health problems
(c) Sensory impairment
(d) All of the above.

1197. Educational Equality is a
(a) customary right only
(b) directive principle only
(c) fundamental right
(d) legal right only

1198. The quality of a creative child is
(a) High IQ (b) More eager
(c) More daring (d) All of these

1199. The basic characteristic of the experimental method in education is
(a) its complete analysis.
(b) the applicability of its outcome to relatively unlimited population.
(c) its centre of relevant extraneous factors.
(d) its isolation from the influence of one after the other factors inherent in total situation.

1200. Emotional disturbances may lead to educational backwardness because
(a) emotions will develop intellectual power, i.e. emotional intelligence.
(b) proper emotional development is necessary for social interactions.
(c) Both (a) and (b).
(d) None of the above.

1201. Which of the following factors will not lead to educational backwardness?
(a) Poor educational environment of the school.
(b) Occupation of the family.
(c) Poor emotional climate of the family.
(d) Poor socio economic status of the family.

1202. Which of the following is an important cause of educational backwardness at primary level of education in India?
(a) Lack of accountability
(b) Attitude of the masses towards education
(c) Poor school organisation
(d) All of the above.

1203. Experimental method has many designs such as
(a) Control group (b) Rotation group
(c) Single group (d) All of these

1204. For developing creativity the teacher should do the following.
(a) Children should be taught according to syllabus

(b) Child should be given enough independence
(c) Maintain strict discipline
(d) All of the above

1205. The writings which show that "the psycho analytical point of view can be used in a productive way" are related to
(a) Linton (b) Freud's theory
(c) E.H. Erikson (d) Spencer

1206. Primary education helps in
(a) course understanding
(b) democratisation of child
(c) socialisation of child
(d) All of the above

1207. Which of the following measures should be adopted by the teacher to check educational backwardness?
(a) Adjustment and behaviour training
(b) Continuous evaluation and regular feedback
(c) Remedial teaching
(d) All of the above.

1208. "Due to behaviour there is change in behavioural learning". This definition was given by
(a) Crow and Crow (b) Skinner
(c) Gattes (d) Guilford

1209. The basic foundations of physical, mental and personality development are laid in the period of
(a) Infancy (b) Childhood
(c) Adulthood (d) Adolescence

1210. Teaching by small steps and frequent short assignment techniques are useful for
(a) educationally backward children
(b) children of all types of disabilities
(c) learning disabled
(d) slow learners

1211. Special schools are required for backward children when
(a) the size of population of backward children in the society is very large as is the case of Gujarat where the achievement of students in mathematics is always seen very low.
(b) backwardness is due to any serious physical handicap.
(c) Both (a) and (b).
(d) None of the above.

1212. We usually avoid remembering some thing that is associated with fear or unpleasantness. In traditional language this avoidance is termed as
(a) Retrieving (b) Forgetting
(c) Suppressing (d) Repressing

1213. The span of years during which boys and girls move from childhood to adulthood—mentally, emotionally, socially and physically is called
(a) Adolescence (b) Adult years
(c) Infancy (d) Late Childhood

1214. The speciality of learning is
(a) it continues after life.
(b) it is motiveful.
(c) this is a change in behaviour.
(d) All of the above.

1215. Directive therapy was developed by
(a) Skinner
(b) Carl Roger
(c) Ellis
(d) None of the above

1216. Directive technique of counseling puts emphasis on
(a) applying direct remedial measures.
(b) developing counseling on the basis of learning theories.
(c) knowing the causes of the problem first.
(d) None of the above.

1217. Counseling based on learning theories and principles is known as

(a) Behaviour therapy
(b) Play therapy
(c) Eclectic therapy
(d) Shock therapy

1218. The following activity is effective to remove fatigue during learning
(a) to exercise.
(b) to give nourishing diet.
(c) Both (a) and (b).
(d) None of the above.

1219. Which is 'Why' age?
(a) Puberty
(b) Late adolescence
(c) Early childhood
(d) Late childhood

1220. Jung used the term "Collective Unconscious" to indicate
(a) the effects of all the unconscious urges which made a person's behaviour problematic.
(b) the unconscious tendencies inherited by an individual from primordial racial tendencies.
(c) all the factors that together constitute to strengthen an individual's unconscious.
(d) the unconscious potential of a group or mob.

1221. The term behaviour therapy was coined by Arnold Lazarus in
(a) 1932 (b) 1958
(c) 1976 (d) 1994

1222. According to Watson and Rayner learnt fear can be removed by which of the following techniques?
(a) Reconditioning through feeding the child in the presence of the feared objects
(b) Experimental extinction
(c) Constructive activities around the feared objects
(d) All of the above.

1223. Later childhood is also known as
(a) gang age.
(b) age of curiosity.
(c) spontaneous age.
(d) age of mental development.

1224. Sex education is necessary for children as due to lack of its knowledge the following bad habits develop in them.
(a) Social degradation
(b) Reproductive organs related diseases
(c) Anti-social sex feeling
(d) All of the above

1225. Bringing desirable changes in the behaviour of the client by reinforcing the behaviour close to the point of correction successively is called
(a) Extinction (b) Fading
(c) Generalization (d) Shaping

1226. A child in a school is called a problem child when
(a) he is very resourceful in suggesting good problems for the class to workout.
(b) he is able to solve the problems of other children.
(c) he suggests useful approaches to teachers when they are explaining any problem.
(d) he behaves such that it becomes a problem for the teacher to understand him.

1227. Which of the following is the best method of treating neurotic patient?
(a) Electric shock method
(b) Gradual desensitization
(c) Play method
(d) Eclectic method.

1228. Due to lack of sex-education and by bad company of children this unsocial habbit develops.
(a) Hand practice (b) Prostitution
(c) Homo-sexuality (d) All of these

1229. Can we predict development?
(a) Yes
(b) No
(c) Don't know
(d) None of the above

1230. The method used to release the blocked emotions and pent up motives is
(a) Socio drama
(b) Desensitization
(c) Psycho drama
(d) None of the above

1231. Which of the following terms is close to guidance?
(a) Group counseling
(b) Psychotherapy
(c) Professional advice
(d) All of the above.

1232. In teaching any class or subject, student's needs and interests also have to be borne in mind. Which of the following dimensions cover this aspect?
(a) The methodological dimension
(b) The psychological dimension
(c) The evaluation dimension
(d) The philosophical dimension.

1233. The real carriers of heredity are
(a) the nucleus of the cell.
(b) the chromosomes.
(c) the 'X' and 'Y' chromosomes.
(d) the genes.

1234. In the development of a child at which stage appropiate sex-education is necessary?
(a) Adolesence (b) Adulthood
(c) Infanthood (d) Childhood

1235. Which of the following statements about counseling is not correct?
(a) Counseling is a continuous process
(b) Counseling helps the pupil to solve his problem himself
(c) Every child needs counseling
(d) Same counseling procedure is needed for all the pupils.

1236. Which among the following tools of collecting psychological information about the pupil is the most objective?
(a) Interview
(b) Standardized tests
(c) Projective devices
(d) Rating scale.

1237. Who among the following is the contributor of rational approach of counseling?
(a) Ellis (b) Williamson
(c) Thorne (d) All of the above

1238. Actual age of a child is 12 years and he solves questions like a child of 15 years, then his mental age will be 15 years, then his Intelligence Quotient (IQ) will be
(a) (Mental age 12/Chronological age 15) × 100 = 80
(b) (Mental age 15/Chronological age 12) × 100 = 125
(c) Both (a) and (b)
(d) None of the above

1239. Human development is determined
(a) by a complex of inherited and environmental force.
(b) almost solely by the genetic make up of the individual.
(c) the factors vary from individual to individual.
(d) turning by individual resources over which the individual has no control.

1240. There is always confusion between personality and character. The so-called destination between them is that
(a) character speaks of moral behaviour while personality stands for the psychological aspect of behaviour.

(b) personality is external and character is internal as behaviour.
(c) personality is the moral aspect of behaviour and character is the psychological aspect of behaviour.
(d) personality depends more on the environment while character depends on heredity.

1241. In Williamson's directive technique of counseling, which of the following is the third step?
(a) Diagnosis (b) Counseling
(c) Synthesis (d) None of these

1242. Which of the following alternatives describes infant behaviour?
(a) Innate
(b) Specialized
(c) Differentiated
(d) Undifferentiated or generalised

1243. IQ of backward children according to Dr. Kamath is
(a) 50-59.5 (b) 69-69.5
(c) 80-99.5 (d) 130-139.5

1244. Learning theory approach of counseling is based on the assumption that
(a) behaviour changes with age.
(b) behaviour is acquired and hence can be modified.
(c) behaviour is genetic.
(d) None of the above.

1245. In behaviour therapy
(a) undesirable behaviour is desensitised.
(b) present behaviour is modified.
(c) the desired behaviour is conditioned.
(d) All of the above.

1246. Psychologists speak of 'Social heredity' of an individual while discussing the topic of heredity. It means
(a) the background and origin of the society from which the individual comes.
(b) influences that have shaped the individual social surroundings.
(c) the natural surroundings and climate conditions of the society in which a child is reared.
(d) the customs, habits and environmental effects of the hope and society from which the individual comes.

1247. Speciality of intelligence test of individual is
(a) effective from environment.
(b) vocational direction on basis of test.
(c) less chances of betraying.
(d) Both (b) and (c).

1248. Changes in behaviour remit from
(a) maturation alone.
(b) learning and maturation, both in important amounts.
(c) maturation primarily.
(d) learning alone.

1249. Psychoanalytic approach of counseling was first introduced by
(a) Jung (b) Freud
(c) Adler (d) None of these

1250. According to psychoanalysis theory of personality neurotic disorders are caused by
(a) Inactivity of libido
(b) Role of unconscious mind
(c) Repression of desires
(d) All of the above

1251. If a child fails again and again in a class, which of the following services will be most suitable to him?
(a) Information services
(b) Testing services
(c) Follow up services
(d) Orientation services.

1252. Which of the following aspects of individuals development is most clearly defined by heredity?

(a) The limits (b) The rate
(c) The direction (d) The level

1253. The drawback of group intelligence test is
(a) general intelligence measurement is not possible.
(b) being written are not effective on uneducated persons.
(c) Both (a) and (b).
(d) None of the above.

1254. According to Montessori
(a) teachers should interfere in the pupil's behaviours with keen interest.
(b) equipment of schools is more important than teachers.
(c) knowledge of experimental psychology is essential for teachers.
(d) knowledge of psychology will be a luxury for teachers.

1255. Behaviourism in psychology is the outcome of which of the following schools of thought, prevalent in education?
(a) Aristotelianism
(b) Structuralism
(c) Associationism
(d) Mechanical Naturalism

1256. A high school student is much more influenced by his
(a) Classmates (b) Society
(c) Reference group (d) Peer group

1257. Subsidiary law of learning is
(a) law of effect.
(b) law of multiple response.
(c) law of practice.
(d) None of the above.

1258. Which of the following is not characteristic of maturation?
(a) Increasing specificity of behaviour
(b) Uniformity in rate
(c) Directional tendencies
(d) Uniformity of sequence

1259. Peer-oriented is well developed in
(a) Boys (b) Adults
(c) Children (d) Girls

1260. Every teacher should know that shortage of vitamin 'A' in the children's food leads to
(a) night blindness
(b) loss of bodily weight
(c) loss of appetite
(d) None of the above

1261. While delivering lecture if there is some disturbance in the class, then a teacher should
(a) punish those causing disturbance.
(b) not bother of what is happening in the class.
(c) keep quite for a while and then go on.
(d) All of the above.

1262. In which of the following areas are sex differences around age 11 greatest?
(a) Personality development
(b) Height and weight
(c) Fine muscular co-ordination
(d) Physical strength

1263. "Difference as member of a group in mental, physical characteristics of average group is called individual difference". This definition is given by
(a) Terman (b) Tyler
(c) James Draver (d) Skinner

1264. The characteristics of a class may develop around
(a) Family (b) Occupation
(c) Wealth (d) All of the above

1265. For writing on the Black Board, which of the following methods would be correct for a teacher?

(a) Putting a question to students and then writing the answer as stated by them.
(b) Writing fast and as clearly as possible.
(c) Turning towards the Black Board and teaching along with writing at the same time.
(d) Writing the matter first and then asking students to read it.

1266. The reason of individual differences is
(a) Personality (b) Heredity
(c) Poverty (d) All of the above

1267. The concept of readiness of the learner is one of the fundamental importance to the teacher's of
(a) any new activity.
(b) children with academic difficulties.
(c) K.G. Class primarily.
(d) grade I.

1268. Experimental studies have shown that highly creative children in schools become behaviour problems. The reason is that
(a) such students feel proud of themselves.
(b) schools fail to give them challenging tasks.
(c) teachers become their favourites.
(d) schools give them higher regard.

1269. All of the following are the characteristic features of an effective teacher except
(a) emphasis upon the quick control of the problematic situation.
(b) emphasizing group discussion for the purpose of clarifying the objectives.
(c) emphasis upon standard.
(d) None of the above.

1270. The trait called negativism develops among young children due to
(a) indifference of adults
(b) neglect of peer groups
(c) extreme considerations from parents
(d) frustration by adult interference

1271. An emotion is best defined as
(a) an excited state arising in response to a stimuli for which the individual has no adequate ready-made reactions.
(b) individual's response to situation.
(c) the display of excessive behaviour as a result of intense stimuli.
(d) a reaction to emotional stimuli.

1272. This is the type of test projectile methods of personality.
(a) Knowledge test
(b) Questionnaire
(c) Individual history
(d) Interview

1273. Sensory involvement in visual approach is/are
(a) Auditory
(b) Visual
(c) Motor and tactile
(d) All of the above

1274. A new comer teacher who is maltreated in his class will deal with the students by
(a) changing his class after consultation with the principal.
(b) applying punitive measures.
(c) improving his qualities and expressing it before them in a good way.
(d) giving them a threat of expulsion.

1275. Which of the following interpretations would be correct about diagnostic tests in education?
(a) They help in eliminating selection of undeserving pupils.
(b) They guide teacher in selecting relevant test material.
(c) They reveal students' errors for corrective instruction.
(d) They are meant for locating lapses in the teaching process.

1276. The following are the main in the inventories made for personality valuation.
(a) Woodworth's Personality Data Sheet
(b) Bell's Adjustment Inventory
(c) Bernreuter's Personality Inventory
(d) All of the above

1277. Emotional experiences are
(a) Subjective (b) Impersonal
(c) Objective (d) Not Known

1278. When a student asks a question to which the teacher has no direct correct answer, he should
(a) ask the student to find out the answer himself from books in the library.
(b) tell the student not to ask such irrelevant questions.
(c) give some vague answer and satisfy the student.
(d) tell the student that he would give the correct answer later.

1279. Classroom discipline can be maintained effectively by
(a) putting on fancy clothes in the classroom.
(b) knowing the cause of indiscipline and handling it with stern hand.
(c) providing a programme which is according to the need and interest of the pupils.
(d) None of the above.

1280. Emotions rise abruptly but die
(a) Quickly (b) Never
(c) Slowly (d) Suddenly

1281. "Our personality is that which we have started, which we have enjoyed is only group of reactions". This definition is given by
(a) J.F. Dashial (b) Woodworth
(c) J.B. Watson (d) G.W. Allport

1282. If a student is mischievous and disturbing in the class with words and actions which of the following methods would be correct in your opinion to deal with him?
(a) Call him to your room and make him to understand his problems.
(b) Insult him in the class by pointing out his mistakes.
(c) Punish him by expelling him from the class to teach a lesson to others.
(d) Shout at him and warn him to correct himself.

1283. The educational philosopher must have knowledge of psychology because
(a) psychological principles arise out of philosophical maxims.
(b) psychology acquaints the philosopher with the world of reality in his theorizing.
(c) the question of 'why' and 'what' in philosophy is purely psychological at the root.
(d) psychology is after all a branch of philosophy.

1284. These elements are due to personality difiference.
(a) School
(b) Health
(c) Biological related
(d) Environment related

1285. Which is the master emotion?
(a) Fear (b) Anger
(c) Worry (d) Happiness

1286. A back bencher is unable to watch the black board clearly. As a result he stands, sees and sits repeatedly. What inference will you draw regarding the case?
(a) The blackboard is under-shining effect of light.
(b) The child is of short height as compared to his class mates.

(c) The child has defective vision.
(d) Both (a) and (c).

1287. In teaching the teacher will develop
(a) Constructive thinking
(b) Problem solving ability
(c) Both (a) and (b)
(d) All of the above

1288. If a child is afraid of school, he becomes
(a) Regular (b) Truant
(c) Punctual (d) Obedient

1289. One who divided personality into introvert and extrovert was
(a) Sprezer (b) Guilford
(c) Krashmer (d) Jung

1290. If students do not understand what is taught in the class, the teacher should.
(a) teach the lesson again giving more examples.
(b) check up the previous knowledge of the students in the topic.
(c) repeat the lesson once again.
(d) proceed to the next lesson so that syllabus could be covered.

1291. In the conditioning approach to learning
(a) the unnatural stimulus follows the natural stimulus.
(b) the natural stimulus follows the unnatural stimulus.
(c) the subject should be in readiness to receive the unnatural stimulus.
(d) response to natural stimulus is required to be reinforced.

1292. In the personality test of Rousseau how many cards are there of other colours besides black, brown and red?
(a) 2 (b) 5
(c) 10 (d) 3

1293. Which is the age in which a child laughs less and smiles more i.e. he has learnt to control his emotions?
(a) Later Childhood
(b) Babyhood
(c) Adolescence
(d) Early Childhood

1294. Boys in high school generally tend to get free from the influence of their
(a) Peer group (b) Society
(c) Family (d) None of these

1295. Peer groups develop certain status symbols which
(a) remain fixed
(b) change from time to time
(c) are flexible to a certain limit
(d) can't say

1296. Which of the following was a basis for rationalism?
(a) The development of knowledge from mathematical reasoning.
(b) The use of self-evident truths as first principles.
(c) Both (a) and (b).
(d) None of the above.

1297. Moods are formed during
(a) Adulthood (b) Infancy
(c) Childhood (d) Adolescence

1298. By looking unclear pictures on cards in TAT of personality the examinee has to make
(a) Booklet (b) Play
(c) Story (d) All of the above

1299. If students do not understand what is taught in the classroom, the teacher should
(a) feel pity for the students.
(b) feel terribly bored.
(c) feel that he is wasting time.
(d) try to explain it in a different way.

1300. The outstanding functional psychologist in Education during the first quarter of the present century was

(a) Alexander Bain
(b) William James
(c) Edward Thorndike
(d) Frederick Terman

1301. The best way to deal with a wrong answer given by a student is
(a) to ask another student to give the correct answer.
(b) to ignore the wrong answer and pass on to the next question.
(c) to scold him for not having learnt the lesson.
(d) to explain why the answer is wrong.

1302. The maker of instruments of play method of personality test was
(a) Morgan
(b) Rousseau
(c) Margret Lovanfeld
(d) Moure

1303. The period of heightened emotionality, elation and depression, formulation of moods and sentiments is known as
(a) Early childhood (b) Adolescence
(c) Old age (d) Babyhood

1304. In the final analysis, teaching must be thought of mainly as a process of
(a) directing the activities of the pupils.
(b) hearing the recitation of pupils.
(c) asking questions and evaluating the learning.
(d) All of the above.

1305. Which of the following statements regarding motivation is correct?
(a) Curiosity and level of aspiration are the motivating factors according to Berlyne.
(b) Inborn, unlearned tendencies, called instincts are the motivating forces according to James Burt.
(c) Freewill, intellect and reason are the motivating factors according to Plato.
(d) All of the above.

1306. The educational philosopher must have knowledge of psychology because
(a) the question of 'why' and 'what' in philosophy is purely psychological at the root.
(b) psychology is after all a branch of philosophy.
(c) psychology acquaints the philosopher with the world of reality in his theorizing.
(d) psychological principles arise out of philosophical maxims.

1307. The overprotected child will tend to display
(a) Immaturity (b) Aggressiveness
(c) Negativisim (d) Defensiveness

1308. The source of associated words in "Word Association Test" of personality test is
(a) Adolesence (b) Childhood
(c) Adult (d) Both (a) and (b)

1309. "The students describe an experiment demonstrated by the teacher in the classroom". This statement is an example of student's behaviour pertaining to the objective of
(a) Application (b) Knowledge
(c) Analysis (d) Understanding

1310. Which of the following statement is correct?
(a) Education is the influence of the environment on the individual with a view to producing a permanent change in his habits of behaviour, of thought and of attitude.
(b) In the modern complex society the basic problems concerns with the pollution of environment for which our society of today has shown lot of involvement.
(c) In educational process, we find there are good number of problems connected with the environment—

rather every type of environment—social, physical, natural and political.
(d) All are correct.

1311. Vablens Theory of change is related to
(a) Economic goal
(b) Human goal
(c) Both (a) and (b)
(d) None of the above

1312. "Ecstasy and Origin Theory" proposed by Thorndike is also known by
(a) Theory of effect
(b) Theory of readiness
(c) Stimulus response theory
(d) All of the above

1313. A teacher confronted with frequent emotional outbursts on the part of pupil should
(a) allow them to release tensions in this way.
(b) let them express this outside the class.
(c) consider the suitability of demands made upon them.
(d) None of these.

1314. 'Cultural Lag' is the term used by Ogburn to describe how
(a) one phase of culture may change more rapidly than another phase.
(b) morals change over a period of time.
(c) culture changes.
(d) None of the above.

1315. Which of the following concepts would correctly represent the objectives of the term 'Environmental Education'?
(a) Familiarizing children with the objectives and condition of their environment.
(b) Teaching children to develop capacities to modify their environment.
(c) Developing an attitude of patriotism and love towards leaders.
(d) Adopting education to suit children's environment.

1316. Skinner's Theory of Learning is centered around the principle of
(a) Reinforcement (b) Operationism
(c) Conditioning (d) Association

1317. "Emotions are the backbone of all development". Do you agree!?
(a) No (b) Yes
(c) Can't say (d) Not sure

1318. In the secondary law of learning by Thorndike—"Law of Multiple response"—stress is given on
(a) learn by changing association.
(b) learn by ecstasy and origin theory.
(c) learn by intimacy.
(d) None of the above.

1319. In order to understand students and their behaviour, one must know about and understand their
(a) Playing groups
(b) Social status
(c) Reference groups
(d) None of the above

1320. The ideal personality should be
(a) emotionally stable
(b) socially acceptable
(c) Both (a) and (b)
(d) None of the above

1321. Animals including insects transmit meaning through behaviour or sounds, much of this is by
(a) Error
(b) Trial
(c) Both (a) and (b)
(d) None of the above

1322. Other name of learning theory of oparant conditioning is
(a) operant conditioning.
(b) instrumental conditioning.
(c) operant conditioning.
(d) All of the above.

1323. Modern media is
(a) Digital (b) Electronic
(c) Print (d) Celluloid

1324. The preventive theory of punishment aims at
(a) controlling wrong doers through the cooperation of parents and social members.
(b) preventing the occurrence of situations which induce wrong behaviour and call for remedial measures.
(c) advising children about the preventive measures to be adopted by the school, in advance.
(d) preventing children from doing wrong through careful supervision.

1325. Reinforcement in learning is by following ways.
(a) Negative reinforcement
(b) Positive reinforcement
(c) Interdict reinforcement
(d) Both (a) and (b)

1326. Education is the .... controlled process
(a) psychologically (b) consciously
(c) unconsciously (d) uncontrolled

1327. A classroom could be called a collective behaviour group as long as
(a) the members want to establish their status as individuals.
(b) there is a common feeling with a task to face.
(c) there is a hierarchic organisations in the class.
(d) the group is sufficiently a large one.

1328. The psychoanalysts believe that in a majority of cases, people get blindness or paralysis because
(a) they are the hereditary weaknesses with a biological basis.
(b) these defects take root in childhood experience only.
(c) they are the outcome of wish fulfilment and motivated acts.
(d) such defects exist in all individuals in an unconscious state.

1329. "Motivation are those physical and psychological conditions which get originated by drive and end by adjustment." This definition was given by
(a) Thomson (b) Woodworth
(c) Rofer (d) Mc Dougal

1330. The learning process which is much more effective is
(a) Religional-directed
(b) Socially-directed
(c) Inner-directed
(d) Externally-directed

1331. What will you do as a teacher if the students do not attend your class?
(a) Blame the students for their absence
(b) Keep quiet considering the present attitude of students as the change of the culture
(c) Know the reasons and try to remove them
(d) Think of using some interesting methods of teaching.

1332. Pollution of air, land and water have resulted all over the planet due to
(a) Standardized goods
(b) Scientific technology
(c) Industrialisation
(d) All of the above

1333. "Original instincts are the motive powers of the thoughts and working of a person". This view is of
(a) Mc Dougal (b) Barnard
(c) Guilford (d) Johnson

1334. If a student becomes unconscious in the class what will you do first?
(a) Make arrangement to send him to his home.
(b) Telephone student's parents and wait for them.
(c) Rush to the principal's office and canvass for help impatiently.
(d) Give first aid to him and try to contact any nearby doctor.

1335. The major responsibility of a school is to
(a) make the child able to get job.
(b) harmonize the needs of the child and demands of the society for the benefit of both.
(c) prepare the school programme according to the need of the child.
(d) All of the above.

1336. The term 'Behaviour' includes
(a) external stimulation as an objective condition.
(b) external stimulus and response only.
(c) both external and internal stimulation.
(d) internal stimulation as the main cause.

1337. The theory of motivation is
(a) will power theory.
(b) stimulus response theory.
(c) original habbit theory.
(d) All of the above.

1338. While dealing with juvenile delinquents a teacher should
(a) complain to the principal against them.
(b) always punish them.
(c) talk with them frankly and guide and channelize their potentialities in constructive ways.
(d) None of the above.

1339. Change is necessary to eliminate unsatisfactory conditions and situations which are produced by the conflict between ends that are beneficial or which tend to exploit. The idea was given by
(a) Max Weber
(b) Auguste Comte
(c) Veblen's theory
(d) None of the above

1340. An effective teacher will ensure
(a) competition among students
(b) laissez faire role
(c) competition or co-operation as the situation demands
(d) co-operation among his students

1341. "Motive is that condition of a person which clarifies definite behaviour for completion of definite aim". This definition was given by
(a) C.L. Hull
(b) Cart Lawil
(c) Maslow
(d) Woodworth

1342. Observable behaviours which a teacher can use in the class to bring home to the pupil an idea or point is technically called
(a) demonstration abilities
(b) communication facilities
(c) teaching skills
(d) None of the above

1343. According to the modern view, the supervision programme in schools should
(a) be concerned with only the administrative aspect of school functions.
(b) aim at development of leadership qualities among teachers.
(c) be closely associated with the programmes of curriculum development.
(d) not mingle with the curriculum development work.

1344. Which of the following could be regarded as a principle of good discipline in educational institutions?
(a) Developing rules and policies in consultation with the students.
(b) Laying clearcut rules and principles for acts of indiscipline.
(c) Planning rules by teachers in co-operation with heads.
(d) Formulating rules and regulations in the beginning of the year.

1345. If remarks are passed by students on you, as a teacher, you will
(a) punish them
(b) be impartial at the time of evaluation
(c) expel them from the college
(d) take revenge while evaluating internal test copies

1346. If you come across to teach a blind student along with the normal students what type of behaviour you are expected to exhibit?
(a) Arrange the seat in the front row and try to keep your teaching pace according to him without making the other students suffer.
(b) Don't give any extra attention because majority of students may suffer.
(c) Take care of him with sympathy.
(d) None of the above.

1347. You have to give assignments to your students as a part of teaching. The precaution to be observed would be, to
(a) suggest that students might seek anybody's help in completing the work.
(b) give sufficient work so that students are fully engaged at home.
(c) give students the required clues and guidance in the class for completion of the work.
(d) select the assignment from a portion to be taught the next day.

1348. In the classification of motives by Maslow the following acquired class is in general social motives.
(a) Life goal (b) Interest
(c) Aspiration level (d) All of the above

1349. The subject matter of the school curriculum must be functional in relation to adult living and be adopted to the level of development of the
(a) Human beings
(b) Community
(c) Child
(d) None of the above

1350. Classroom discipline can be maintained effectively by
(a) providing a programme which is according to the need and interest of the pupils.
(b) by putting on fancy clothes in the classroom.
(c) knowing the cause of indiscipline and handling it with stern hand.
(d) None of the above.

1351. The functions of a teacher is in the order of
(a) checking homework, guiding him and assigning further task.
(b) guiding the child, helping him towards progress and evaluation.
(c) assigning further talk, evaluation and checking homework.
(d) None of the above.

1352. The most appropriate meaning of learning is
(a) acquisition of skills
(b) inculcation of knowledge
(c) modification of behaviour
(d) personal adjustment

1353. The following are important inborn motives of motivations
(a) Love (b) Hunger
(c) Sex (d) All of the above

1354. Dewey liked best the following definition of education?
(a) Acquisition of knowledge
(b) Recapitulation
(c) Reconstruction of experience
(d) Education as a product.

1355. Older children and youth live in the dual world of their
(a) Peers (b) Society
(c) Adults (d) Both (a) and (c)

1356. Environmental education should be
(a) optional
(b) compulsory at only postgraduate level
(c) compulsory at all levels of education
(d) no need of this education

1357. Adjunct programming is the method which
(a) combines programmed instruction with the understanding of textbooks.
(b) combines programmed instruction with classroom teachers.
(c) is follow up of programmed instruction.
(d) is a substitute for the project approach of teaching.

1358. Two systems exerting opposite influence on the same organ/organs are—
(a) Endocrine and digestive system
(b) Endocrine and nervous system
(c) Muscular and nervous system
(d) None of the above

1359. The knowledge of education psychology is necessary for a teacher
(a) for self-knowing of teacher.
(b) to learn the new techniques of valuation.
(c) for attaining knowledge of new educational techniques.
(d) for solving problems verbally.

1360. Connection between brain and spinal cord of frog is severed. The leg of such an animal is pricked with a sharp needle. The animal will
(a) move only the unpricked leg.
(b) move the pricked leg.
(c) not show any reaction.
(d) not move the legs.

1361. We usually avoid remembering some thing that is associated with fear or unpleasantness. In traditional language such avoidance is termed as
(a) Repression (b) Retrieval future
(c) Forgetting (d) Suppressing

1362. If some of your pupils misbehave with you in the college campus you must
(a) report to the principal.
(b) mobilize other teachers against these guys.
(c) report to their parents.
(d) improve their behaviour by your own character and scholarship.

1363. Psychologists speak of a plateau in learning process. This is
(a) an indication of fatigue and boredom to give a gap in our trails for learning.
(b) the final stage of learning, indicating that further attempts will lead to frustration.
(c) a stage when the learner is consolidating his previous learning and preparing for further learning.
(d) a stage at which an individual faces some difficulty in progressing further.

1364. Pseudo-maturity in life is the state of following.
(a) Young (b) Childhood
(c) Infanthood (d) Adolescence

1365. The Gestalt psychologists brought out clearly the importance of
(a) the functional factors in perception.
(b) the interactive factors of cognition.

(c) the functional factors in cognitive operations.
(d) the structural factors in perception.

1366. As chairman of a selection board, while selecting a teacher you should be
(a) fair and impartial.
(b) encouraging to those appearing for interview.
(c) able to judge the personality of candidates.
(d) All of the above.

1367. The problem of the single teacher schools
(a) need to be opposed as a social evil.
(b) should be solved by ending them.
(c) exists in our country only.
(d) should be mended but not ended.

1368. The teacher is concerned more about the educational process than with the formulation of its
(a) Goals
(b) Purposes
(c) Both (a) and (b)
(d) None of the above

1369. In the final analysis, teaching must be thought of mainly as a process of
(a) hearing the recitation of pupils.
(b) asking questions and evaluating the learning.
(c) directing the activities of the pupils.
(d) All of the above.

1370. Teachers primary responsibility lies in
(a) keeping students records.
(b) implementing policies.
(c) planning educational experiences.
(d) All of the above.

1371. The nerves carrying impulses to CNS are known as
(a) Motor (b) Mixed
(c) Afferent (d) Efferent

1372. IV, V and X cranial nerves are
(a) Olfactory, Optic and Oculamotor.
(b) Abducens, Facial and Hypoglossal.
(c) Oculamotor, Abducens and Hypoglossal.
(d) Trochlear, Trigeminal and Vagus.

1373. You are teaching a subject or a topic to your students. At the end of a unit you test their achievement. Which of the following would be called the dependent variable?
(a) The response of your students
(b) The background of your students
(c) The test that you prepared
(d) The subject that you teach.

1374. If majority of students in your class are weak you should
(a) keep your teaching slow along with some extra guidance to bright pupils.
(b) keep your speed of teaching fast so that students comprehension level may increase.
(c) not care about the intelligent students.
(d) keep your teaching slow.

1375. Which of the following skills has the largest share in communication time in schools/colleges?
(a) Writing (b) Reading
(c) Listening (d) Speaking

1376. In the process of personality difference there are following characteristics
(a) Diversity
(b) Equality
(c) Both (a) and (b)
(d) None of the above

1377. People of all age levels form
(a) Peer group (b) Team
(c) Society (d) Reference group

1378. Which of the following statements would be true in your opinion about creative teachers?

(a) They command good respect from colleagues, etc.
(b) They create problems for the school administrators.
(c) They are very friendly and predictable among their colleagues.
(d) There is a connection between their subject knowledge and creativity.

1379. A teacher who is not able to draw the attention of his students should
(a) resign from the post.
(b) evaluate his teaching method and improve it.
(c) start dictating.
(d) find fault in his pupils.

1380. If a teacher is not able to answer the question of a pupil he should
(a) rebuke the pupil.
(b) say that he will answer after consultation.
(c) feel shy of his ignorance.
(d) say that the question is wrong.

1381. The largest cranial nerve is
(a) Facial (b) Trigeminal
(c) Optic (d) Vagus

1382. Second cranial nerve supplies
(a) Ciliary muscles
(b) Retina and lens
(c) Retina and iris
(d) None of the above

1383. All of the following are the limitations of televised instruction except
(a) experts consume much time in planning and preparation of the programme.
(b) it does not permit the exchange of ideas between the teacher and taught.
(c) it moves at a fixed speed and thus cannot take the individual differences of students into account.
(d) it does not properly help the students in making the materials clearly understood.

1384. Which one is a simple reflex?
(a) Watering of mouth at the sight of delicious food
(b) Climbing stairs in the dark
(c) Tying laces while talking to and looking at another person
(d) Closing of eyes if an object suddenly approaches them.

1385. Which one does not involve brain?
(a) Voluntary action
(b) Cerebral reflex
(c) Spinal reflex
(d) Cranial reflex.

1386. Which of the following teachers will you like most?
(a) A teacher who often amuses his students
(b) A loving teacher
(c) A disciplined teacher
(d) A teacher of highly idealist philosophy.

1387. Which is the more desirable outcome of teaching in higher education?
(a) Increase in the level of independent thinking of students
(b) Increase in students achievement
(c) Higher percentage of result
(d) Increase in the number of students who opt for the subject.

1388. Heredity in personality theory provides the following thing.
(a) Present (b) Cultural
(c) Psychological (d) All of the above

1389. A college teacher will really help the students when she
(a) encourages students to ask questions.
(b) dictates notes in the class.
(c) is objective in her evaluation.
(d) covers the syllabus completely in the class.

1390. I.Q. is the ratio of mental age to
(a) chronological age divided by 100.
(b) chronological age only.
(c) chronological age multiplied by 100.
(d) chronological age multiplied by ten.

1391. It is recommended that the house system would be better for arranging sports and games in school. These houses are formed better if
(a) care is taken to see that the number of students is kept equal in all houses.
(b) different groups are formed in schools according to ages.
(c) different games are specified for different games and sports.
(d) students from all classes are represented in each house as a group.

1392 The concept of academic freedom for teachers, should be taken to mean that
(a) all the relative scholars alone should have freedom to teach truths.
(b) freedom should be given only at higher levels of academic learning.
(c) freedom should be given only to teachers and not to learners.
(d) teachers are completely free to teach whatever they feel as true.

1393. Better classroom management means
(a) getting the attention and cooperation of all the students before starting the class/task.
(b) punctuality of the teachers in coming in the class and finishing the course in time.
(c) performing group work and better interaction among pupils.
(d) All of the above.

1394. One function of parasympathetic nervous system is
(a) acceleration of heart beat.
(b) constriction of pupil.
(c) contraction of hair muscles.
(d) stimulation of sweat glands.

1395. Sympathetic nervous system is also called
(a) Mesenteric
(b) Visceral
(c) Carniosacral
(d) Thoracico lumbar

1396. We often hear about tripartite agreements being finalised in the field of industry. A similar agreement in education should mean agreement between
(a) government, management and parents.
(b) students, teachers and heads of school.
(c) society, schools and students.
(d) local authorities, government and schools.

1397. The culture epoch theory of organisation of the curriculum in the 19th Century suggests that
(a) human beings develop through education in the order in which human culture developed in nature.
(b) there should be greater concentration in education for the cultural development in our epoch.
(c) the curriculum should be framed in accordance with the development of human culture, epoch wise.
(d) culture of a nation from different epochs should find representation in the school curriculum.

1398. Guilford use the following assumption to explain the concept of intelligence.
(a) Product (b) Operation
(c) Content (d) All of the above

1399. Which of the following would you consider as a valid weakness of the experimental methods in education?
(a) They claim too much of authenticity for their approach.

(b) They lack the required competence and sophistication.
(c) They do not provide insight into the total behaviour of subjects.
(d) The experimenters usually lack insight into their problems.

1400. One of the important characteristic of successful school administration is
(a) rigidity for right principles.
(b) the rational soundness.
(c) non-concern with the political philosophy.
(d) None of the above.

1401. The term 'Curriculum' should really mean
(a) all the experiences provided by a school in the classroom teaching learning situations.
(b) subjects as a whole that are prescribed for examination purpose.
(c) the academic subjects taught in the school.
(d) all the experiences which pupils received in a school in and outside the classes.

1402. The intelligence of an individual can be rightly defined as
(a) a natural gift which is inherent in a person.
(b) a quality of his learned behaviour.
(c) a constant and unmodifiable quality of behaviour.
(d) a potentially fixed quality of the genes.

1403. If students are not able to follow, you should
(a) illustrate with examples.
(b) make the matter easy.
(c) give them hints.
(d) All of the above.

1404. Learning is the modification of the organism in response to other
(a) Group (b) Religion
(c) Society (d) Organism

1405. To make one's teaching more effective one should depend most on his
(a) Knowledge (b) Teaching aids
(c) Management (d) Feedback

1406. If some students fail in the examination it is the fault of
(a) text books
(b) the principal
(c) the teacher
(d) pupils themselves

1407. An effective teaching means all of the following except
(a) puting emphasis more on teaching than on class control.
(b) teaching with enthusiasm.
(c) finding fault in students.
(d) making the subject matter understood rather than completing the course.

1408. A serious minded teacher as a rule
(a) takes all precautions so that students never commit mistakes.
(b) never allow any mistakes on the part of his students.
(c) should mildly punish students who commit mistakes.
(d) allow the mistakes to be committed and then explain how to minimize those mistakes.

1409. Which of the following do you consider as cause for a teacher's maladjustment to the profession?
(a) Too much of leisure and wishful thinking.
(b) Not enough work to keep him engaged.
(c) Poor relationship with colleagues and administration.
(d) Limitations in his qualifications.

1410. An effective teacher is expected to
 (a) make students feel that education is their need.
 (b) reduce the anxiety level of students to moderate level.
 (c) encourage the students to make initiative.
 (d) All of the above.

1411. The person responsible for administration in a school is
 (a) Director of Education
 (b) Education officer
 (c) Principal
 (d) None of the above

1412. It is found in many experiments that the discussion method of teaching is more effective that the lecture method. This is the effect of
 (a) Socialisation
 (b) Group dynamics
 (c) Impressionism
 (d) Teacher's dynamism

1413. The number of pairs of cranial nerves in mammals that are purely sensory is
 (a) One (b) Two
 (c) Three (d) Five

1414. Which of the following approaches could be considered as progressive in the construction of curriculum?
 (a) Selecting the contents of the curriculum from the disciplinary and cultural values point of view.
 (b) Creating provision for promoting children to exert their potentialities for learning.
 (c) Providing knowledge from the past culture and achievements of the nation for inheritance.
 (d) Arranging the subject matter required for compulsory acquisition by students in the interests of the society.

1415. Acetylcholinesterase is connected with
 (a) digestion of polypeptides
 (b) synthesis of protein
 (c) digestion of protein
 (d) conduction of nerve impulse

1416. When you start teaching a new topic to a class, the foremost precaution to be observed would be to
 (a) prepare the teaching matter as thoroughly as possible.
 (b) see that students do not raise questions in the course of your teaching.
 (c) create the feeling among students that the new topic has logical relation with what they knew before.
 (d) see that you make a good first impression upon the class.

1417. Which of the following provides more freedom to the learner to interact?
 (a) Viewing Countrywide Classroom Programme on TV
 (b) Use of film projector
 (c) Lecture by Experts
 (d) Small group discussion.

1418. Teachers primary responsibility lies in
 (a) implementing policies
 (b) planning educational experiences
 (c) keeping students records
 (d) All of the above

1419. Which of the following teachers will you like most?
 (a) One who uses charts and maps.
 (b) One who uses film projector along-with the proper use of the board.
 (c) One who uses motion picture as a last resort.
 (d) One who uses board occasionally.

1420. Before starting instruction a teacher should

(a) know the existing knowledge of his students and their background knowledge.
(b) be competent enough to arouse the curiosity of his pupils.
(c) be aware of the environmental variables acting on the mind of the pupils.
(d) All of the above.

1421. The branch of psychology with which sociology has got maximum linkage is
(a) Social Psychology
(b) Child Psychology
(c) Industrial Psychology
(d) General Psychology

1422. If a teacher has to establish credibility in evaluating answer scripts he/she must be
(a) prompt (b) lenient
(c) strict (d) objective

1423. If back-benchers are always talking in the classroom a teacher should
(a) ask them to sit on the front benches.
(b) punish them.
(c) let them do what they are doing.
(d) None of the above.

1424. A student is able to learn playing of harmonium more easily than typewriting. Playing of harmonium is a case of
(a) conditioned reflex
(b) long term homeostasis
(c) residual learning
(d) short term homeostasis

1425. The curriculum suggested by Froebel for the kindergartens
(a) has no provision for languages.
(b) has no place for religious instruction.
(c) includes religion and religious instruction.
(d) None of the above.

1426. Closed circuit television is useful
(a) only for poor students of the class.
(b) for large group communication.
(c) only for a restricted audience residing at a particular place.
(d) None of the above.

1427. The American Council on Education's Design for General Education
(a) involved a careful analysis of the behaviour of different age groups in society.
(b) made a sharp distinction between general education and liberal education.
(c) identified 10 objectives of general education, each with its specific end products.
(d) rejected the empirical method of determining educational goals.

1428. Examination or evaluation of an educational process should have direct reference to
(a) the administrative competencies of an institution.
(b) the experiences of the personnel in charge of the process.
(c) the aims and objectives governing the process.
(d) the programmes adopted in the process.

1429. Televised educational programme is useful because
(a) it affords the opportunity for large audience in the same auditorium or in different locations to view it clearly.
(b) it can magnify the microscopic forms of life and can be presented on TV.
(c) it can present the natural phenomenon of the world in natural form.
(d) All of the above.

1430. Any effective communication system employs a feedback system in order to

(a) understand more about the content.
(b) make the necessary modifications in the process.
(c) find faults with the receiver (the student).
(d) find faults with the sender (the teacher).

1431. Education will no longer depend entirely on obtaining knowledge through the
(a) Digital mode
(b) Printed page
(c) Visual approach
(d) None of the above

1432. Visualization in the instructional process cannot increase
(a) stress and boredom
(b) retention and adaptation
(c) curiosity and concentration
(d) interest and motivation

1433. If a teacher comes across ideas difficult for others to understand, he should
(a) explain it to others only at a cost, be it money or favour.
(b) be happy and look forward to explain it to others.
(c) rather not explain it to a person who obviously does not wish to spend much time on it.
(d) keep this understanding to himself which would ensure him a special status.

1434. Which of the following groups of students can be most benefited through computer-based education programme?
(a) Small group of low IQ
(b) Heterogeneous groups in IQ
(c) Large group of moderate intelligence
(d) All of the above.

1435. Teaching on TV is superior to classroom instruction because
(a) teaching materials can be filmed for reuse.
(b) experts for teaching a difficult topic can be arranged and others can be benefited from them.
(c) very large classes are made possible and thus it is economically advantageous.
(d) All of the above.

1436. Eye muscles are innervated by
(a) oculomotor, facial and vagus
(b) oculomotor, trochlear and abducens
(c) oculomotor, abducens and vagus
(d) oculomotor, abducens and facial

1437. A teacher
(a) should have command over his subject.
(b) should have command over his language.
(c) should introduce the lesson before he starts teaching.
(d) All of the above.

1438. It is said that there are individual differences among students in a class. This fact is
(a) a suggestion for teachers to be careful in teaching.
(b) supported by lazy teachers to find excuses for their weaknesses.
(c) purely a historical evidence that is outdated today.
(d) great hindrance to teachers in teaching.

1439. I will appreciate the teacher who
(a) is friendly with the students.
(b) has strict control over his students.
(c) knows the problems of students and helps them.
(d) has charming personality.

1440. When a student commits a mistake in his presentation in the classroom the teacher

(a) should explain the mistake to the student after the class.
(b) should ask the students to find out and correct the mistake.
(c) should be silent.
(d) should immediately correct it.

1441. The projective techniques in education and psychology are intended to
(a) simplify the vocational and educational guidance.
(b) facilitate adoption of project methods.
(c) identify the unconscious tendencies of individuals.
(d) promote techniques of projecting individuals.

1442. Teacher's professionalism means
(a) a teacher must have completed professional teachers' training course before his appointment.
(b) a teacher has to teach to receive salary.
(c) the extent to which a teacher subscribes to a professional code.
(d) All of the above.

1443. Foramen of Monro is an aperture between
(a) Diacoel and metacoel
(b) Rhinocoel and diacoel
(c) Third and fourth ventricles
(d) Lateral and third ventricles

1444. The psychologist who was the forerunner of the Gestalt School of Psychology in Education, was
(a) James Watson (b) Wilhelm Wundt
(c) William James (d) Max Wertheime

1445. The trial and error method of learning is an offshoot of
(a) Conditioning (b) Purposivism
(c) Connectionism (d) Behaviourism

1446. Guidance services are recommended to be introduced in schools. This means that
(a) students should be given groper guidance in completing their assignments.
(b) students should be guided as to what courses or vocations would be suited to them.
(c) students must be guided for preparation for examinations through unit and term tests.
(d) teachers should guide the parents about the method to look after their children.

1447. Overhead projector is superior to short circuit TV in a classroom teaching because
(a) it is easy to use.
(b) it is cheap and self devised.
(c) information presented through it is easily retained.
(d) pictures in it may be shown in a desired sequence and with a minimum of lost motion (material).

1448. Which is the least important in teaching?
(a) Lecturing in impressive ways
(b) Punishing the students
(c) Drawing sketches and diagrams on the black-board if needed
(d) Maintaining discipline in the class.

1449. When a student is making noise in the classroom, the teacher should
(a) ignore the student.
(b) send the student outside the classroom.
(c) talk to the student privately after the class and should find out the reasons for his making noise.
(d) criticize the student.

1450. An area where the teacher-made tests cannot be pertinent is
(a) Intelligence (b) Attitudes
(c) Interests (d) Personality

1451. Thermoregulatory centre in the brain of homeothermic animals and man is found in
(a) Hypothalamus (b) Diencephalon
(c) Skin (d) Pituitary gland

1452. In order to be successful, a teacher should
(a) provide subject knowledge to students.
(b) help students in achieving their goals.
(c) prepare the students to score high marks in administrative activities.
(d) concentrate on syllabus completion.

1453. Faculty psychology was most widely accepted
(a) during the renaissance period but given up in the past renaissance period.
(b) during the post renaissance period.
(c) during the renaissance period.
(d) both during the renaissance period and the post renaissance period.

1454. All of the following statements regarding a teacher are correct except that s/he
(a) teaches what the students do not know.
(b) the leader of the class.
(c) changes his attitudes and behaviour according to the need of the society.
(d) a friend, guide and philosopher.

1455. A good teacher should have
(a) Conceptual clarity
(b) Interpersonal skills
(c) Communication skills
(d) All of the above

1456. Olfactory lobes of a rabbit are
(a) Fused and solid
(b) Free and hollow
(c) Free and solid
(d) Fused and hollow

1457. The auditory portion of the inner ear is
(a) Vestibule (b) Auditory nerve
(c) Cochlea (d) Ear ossicles

1458. On the first day of your teaching a class, the students remain quiet, which of the following would be your correct inference?
(a) They are wondering at your experiences in the subject.
(b) They are watching and studying your weak and strong qualities carefully.
(c) They are all well disciplined and obedient students.
(d) They are satisfied and impressed by your personality.

1459. Which is most desirable?
(a) The teacher should not allow students to make noise in the class.
(b) The teacher should explain as simply as possible difficult aspects of the subject matter.
(c) The teacher should make good use of the black-board.
(d) The teacher should speak clearly and loudly.

1460. Which of the following concepts is related to treating children as plants and the teacher as the gardener?
(a) Abhudaya Pathasalas
(b) Kindergartens
(c) Nursery Schools
(d) Bal Bhavans

1461. Suppose you are an ambitious teacher. You have high ideals for classroom teaching but your hard labour goes in vain. The reason underlying this problem may be
(a) your teaching level is above the ability level of students.
(b) individual differences among students make your efforts futile.

(c) Both (a) and (b).
(d) None of the above.

1462. One can be a good teacher, if he
(a) has good expression.
(b) has genuine interest in teaching.
(c) knows his subject.
(d) knows how to control students.

1463. Part of mammalian brain controlling muscular co-ordination is
(a) Cerebellum
(b) Medulla oblongata
(c) Corpus callosum
(d) Cerebrum

1464. There are recommendations for including a subject called 'Safety education' in schools of today, it means
(a) health education for safeguarding the health of students.
(b) instruction and practice in the road sense to escape from accidents.
(c) corrective education to protect the mental health of children.
(d) All of the above.

1465. If cerebral hemisphere of a man is removed he would
(a) Behave normally
(b) Die after some time
(c) Die immediately
(d) Stop eating

1466. Which of the following cranial nerves is mixed
(a) Olfactory (b) Trochlear
(c) Optic (d) Vagus

1467. To make teachers accountable, they should be given
(a) training in teaching and examining.
(b) transfer to places where they want to serve.
(c) freedom in the selection of content and methods of teaching.
(d) opportunities for professional growth.

1468. Hearing is controlled by
(a) Temporal lobes
(b) Frontal lobes
(c) Parietal lobes
(d) Occipital lobes

1469. All the functions of educational measurements are concerned, directly or indirectly with
(a) improvement of administration.
(b) facilitation of learning.
(c) selection of teachers.
(d) avoidance of conflicts.

1470. The Montessori schools insist on
(a) well equipped school buildings.
(b) the principle of natural, self-directed process.
(c) creativeness, the main objective of education.
(d) complete discipline and supervision.

1471. According to Alder, the primary cause for stresses and strains in an individual is
(a) the desire for knowledge of the self.
(b) the feeling of inferiority.
(c) the curiosity to know the mind of others.
(d) the desire for gratification of the sex impulse.

1472. Historically speaking, Thorndike's theory of learning was translated into classroom method following:
(a) John Locke's approach to children's state of mind.
(b) The scientific principles recommended by Rousseau.
(c) Herbartian steps with only slight modifications.
(d) None of the above.

1473. The horizontal enrichment programme of instruction means
(a) enrichment to be given in relating the topic with other related topics.

(b) enlisting the co-operation of all talented students to study together with a competitive spirit.
(c) grouping children of similar abilities for teaching advanced knowledge.
(d) selecting topics of equal difficulty level and presenting them together.

1474. Appetite and satiety centres of brain are present in
(a) Cerebellum
(b) Hypothalamus
(c) Medulla oblongata
(d) Cerebral hemisphere

1475. When you put a question in the class to check the knowledge of students, the best method would be
(a) to point to intelligent students first and then put the question.
(b) to put more than one question at a time to stimulate students.
(c) to pose the question to the whole class and then select somebody to answer.
(d) to frame the question as lengthy as you can.

1476. The theory of learning associated with connectionism was propounded by
(a) Pavlov (b) Skinner
(c) Socrates (d) Thorndike

1477. Evaluation in education insists on
(a) conducting periodical tests to detect students' weaknesses.
(b) examining students objectively for selection purpose.
(c) making tests more reliable and valid.
(d) clear cut behavioural objectives of teaching.

1478. A mixed cranial nerve is
(a) Auditory (b) Oculomotor
(c) Abducens (d) Facial

1479. Effective teaching means
(a) love, co-operation, sympathy, affection and encouragement given to students.
(b) corporal punishment given to students at the time of moral offences.
(c) individualized instruction and open classroom discussion.
(d) Both (a) and (c).

1480. School children are often victims of infection caused by
(a) carelessness of teachers in providing activities.
(b) mal-nutrition caused by undigested food particles.
(c) lack of proper exercise and drill.
(d) invasion of the body by the plant and animal organisms.

1481. Students should prefer those teachers who
(a) are themselves disciplined.
(b) can clear their difficulties regarding subject-matter.
(c) dictate notes in the class.
(d) give important questions before examination.

1482. Students learn more from a teacher who is
(a) affectionate
(b) hard working
(c) able to communicate his ideas precisely and clearly
(d) gentle

1483. The most important skill of teaching is
(a) covering the course prescribed in the subject.
(b) making students understand what the teacher says.
(c) taking classes regularly.
(d) keeping students relaxed while teaching.

1484. Parkinson's disearse is a degenerative disorder of the

(a) central nervous system
(b) circulatory system
(c) digestive system
(d) respiratory system

1485. If a girl student requests you to collect her posts at your address what would you like to do in this case?
(a) You will permit the girl to collect the posts at your address because as a teacher you should do it.
(b) You will never give her your own address suspecting a foul game.
(c) You will permit her because you have some attachment with her.
(d) You would not give permission as it is against your own principles.

1486. Which of the following definitions would be correct for the term "programmed instruction"?
(a) It is a planned sequence of arranging the material to be learned form simple to complex for self study.
(b) It is a schedule of instructions coupled with extra-curricular programmes in the school.
(c) It is an instructional procedure as per time table and monthly progress programme of the school.
(d) It is a project approach based on a programme of visits and observational studies by students.

1487. If students do not understand what is taught in the class, the teacher should
(a) check up the previous knowledge of the students in the topic.
(b) repeat the lesson once again.
(c) teach the lesson again giving more examples.
(d) proceed to the next lesson so that syllabus could be covered.

1488. Learning according to Watson's behaviourism is
(a) learning by selection of successful variants.
(b) learning by trial and error only.
(c) common among human beings only.
(d) based on the interpretation of the law of effects.

1489. Programmed learning involves
(a) well planned lesson material used for continuing education.
(b) a graded series of audio-tapes.
(c) collection of slides and film strips on the lesson.
(d) an ordered sequence of stimulus items.

1490. A child may have hearing impairment if
(a) he generally says, "Please repeat" to the teacher.
(b) he comes nearer to the speaker during conversion.
(c) he speaks loudly unusually.
(d) All of the above.

1491. Which of the following is an example of a software material?
(a) Nursery Rhymes set to music recorded on tapes
(b) Over head projector
(c) Teaching machine
(d) Computer.

1492. Which device do you use to project an opaque object?
(a) Film strip projector
(b) Magic lantern
(c) Epidiascope
(d) Slide projector

1493. An important principle of the play-way technique in education is that
(a) authoritarianism is a must for speedy learning and adaptation.
(b) children should learn on their own responsibility.

(c) opportunities for self-expression should be selective under guidance and supervision.
(d) learning should take place under disciplined conditions.

1494. Which of the following describes Micro-teaching?
(a) Explaining the lesson in minute detail
(b) Breaking up the subject matter into small divisions
(c) Teaching the basics of a selected unit
(d) Scaling-down teaching situation.

1495. When a student asks a question to which the teacher has no direct correct answer, he should
(a) give some vague answer and satisfy the student.
(b) tell the student that he would give the correct answer later.
(c) ask the student to find out the answer himself from books in the library.
(d) tell the student not to ask such irrelevant questions.

1496. Speaking about the problem method of teaching, Dewey asserts that
(a) problem should arise from some school subjects rather than from the child's behaviour.
(b) problem should start from some life experience rather than from school subject.
(c) teachers should first recognise a problem to pass it on to students.
(d) the problem should be for students and not for teachers.

1497. The trial and error method of learning according to Thorndike could be classified as the
(a) principle of Associative learning.
(b) principle of partial activity.
(c) principle of multiple response.
(d) law of exercise.

1498. The term 'Evaluation' and 'Assessment' could be discriminated as follows:
(a) Assessment is an attempt to measure the pupil as whole whereas evaluation is concerned with his achievement.
(b) Assessment is limited to achievement whereas evaluation is qualitative in character.
(c) Evaluation is concerned with the effective aspects of achievement whereas assessment judges the cognitive aspects.
(d) Evaluation involves the measurement as well as diagnosis of students' achievements, whereas assessment is concerned with only scholastic achievements.

1499. If a student is constantly rubbing his eyes and is inattentive during blackboard work he is having
(a) visual problem
(b) adjustment problem
(c) hearing problem
(d) All of the above

1500. Play therapy is adopted in the study of children in order to
(a) make education more activity centred.
(b) make the educational process joyful.
(c) highlight the importance of play activities in education.
(d) understand the inner motives and complexes of children.

1501. The most important challenge before a teacher is
(a) to prepare question paper.
(b) to maintain discipline in the classroom.
(c) to make teaching-learning process enjoyable.
(d) to make students do their home work.

1502. Suppose you want to teach your students to develop factual knowledge of a subject.

Which of the following methods would be suitable in your opinion?
(a) The lecture method
(b) The heuristic method
(c) The source method
(d) The demonstration method.

1503. Teaching in higher education implies
(a) helping students to prepare for and pass the examination.
(b) asking questions in the class and conducting examinations.
(c) helping students how to learn.
(d) presenting the information given in the text book.

1504. Effective teaching, by and large is a function of
(a) teacher's making students learn and understand.
(b) teacher's honesty.
(c) teacher's liking for the job of teaching.
(d) teacher's scholarship.

1505. To say that the adolescents are rebellious in nature, will be regarded by experts as
(a) an effect of the environment.
(b) a misconception.
(c) a necessary behaviour at that stage.
(d) an objective description of facts.

1506. The development of feelings of appreciation and interests come under the category of
(a) affective aspects of development.
(b) cognitive development of personality.
(c) psycho-motor development of emotions.
(d) None of the above.

1507. The state of the psyche designated as super ego by the psychoanalysts, is found
(a) among human beings alone.
(b) among men practising yogic exercises.
(c) in men and animals as well.
(d) in all mammals.

1508. Afferent nerve fibers carry impulses from
(a) CNS to muscles
(b) Effector organs to CNS
(c) CNS to receptors
(d) Receptors to CNS

1509. Nerve transmission is
(a) Biological process
(b) Physical process
(c) Mechanical process
(d) Chemical process

1510. If a curriculum maker follows the subjective theory of values in education, he will
(a) care more for the content aspects than for the methodological.
(b) not insist on the inclusiveness of any subject in the curriculum if pupils or parents are not interested in it.
(c) disregard the interests of children for the inclusive of any subject in the curriculum.
(d) implement the study of a subject for its inherent values to fulfill the needs of a student.

1511. Twelve pairs of ribs and twelve pairs of cranial nerves are found in
(a) Snake (b) Man
(c) Fish (d) Frog

1512. It is recommended by educationists that there should be a dynamic approach to teaching. It means that
(a) the students should be required to learn through activities.
(b) the courses of teaching should not remain static, but dynamic.
(c) teachers should be energetic and dynamic.
(d) teaching should be forceful and effective.

1513. Classroom discipline can be maintained effectively by

(a) providing a programme which is according to the need and interest of the pupils.
(b) by putting on fancy clothes in the classroom.
(c) knowing the cause of indiscipline and handling it with stem hand.
(d) None of the above.

1514. Which cranial nerve is motor in function
(a) Spinal accessory (b) Vagus
(c) Facial (d) Trigeminal

1515. According to Watson, the Behaviourist, sensations and feelings are
(a) elements on which his system actually developed.
(b) elements of conscious experience.
(c) not the elements of conscious experience.
(d) None of the above.

1516. Each learning experience aims at the total growth. This is possible because the learning teaching situations focus on
(a) Common problems
(b) Personal problems
(c) Social problems
(d) All of the above

1517. Which nerve depresses heart beat
(a) Spinal accessory
(b) Glossopharyngeal
(c) Vagus
(d) Trigeminal

1518. In the final analysis, teaching must be thought of mainly as a process of
(a) hearing the recitation of pupils.
(b) asking questions and evaluating the learning.
(c) directing the activities of the pupils.
(d) All of the above.

1519. At the time of impulse transmission, the potential on the inner side of nerve changes
(a) – + and – (b) – + and +
(b) + – and – (d) + – and +

1520. The most appropriate meaning of learning is
(a) acquisition of skills.
(b) inculcation of knowledge.
(c) personal adjustment.
(d) modification of behaviour.

1521. An injury in accident has disturbed regulation of body temperature, water balance and hunger in a person. The part of brain affected is
(a) Corpora quadrigemina
(b) Cerebellum
(c) Hypothalamus
(d) Medulla oblongata

1522. Which of the following teacher's qualities contributes most to good classroom discipline?
(a) Effective teaching
(b) Good behaviour and pleasant manners
(c) Simple way of living
(d) Charming personality.

1523. John Dewey's experimental school was called
(a) the community school
(b) the progressive school
(c) the free school
(d) the activity school

1524. The Core Curricula in education means
(a) knowledge as well as skills for further education and life.
(b) science and Mathematics, integrated.
(c) public examination subjects for certification.
(d) language subjects and skills.

1525. An autonomic nervous system has
(a) Brain and spinal chord
(b) Paired chain ganglia

(c) Cerebral hemisphere
(d) Sense organs

1526. The potential difference across the membrane of nerve fibre when it does not show any physiological activities is called resting potential. It is about
(a) +60 mv (b) –80 mv
(c) –60 mv (d) +90 mv

1527. Which of the following is a "whole-hearted purposeful activity proceeding in a social environment"?
(a) Project method
(b) Dalton plan
(c) Heuristic method
(d) Problem method.

1528. The most important teaching aid for a teacher is
(a) Black-board
(b) Maps and Charts
(c) Colour pictures
(d) Graphs and tables

1529. "Micro teaching", one of the recent trends in education, insists on
(a) finding out the subtle doubts in the minds of students.
(b) teaching students by dividing them into smaller groups.
(c) mastering of various skills of teaching with special attention.
(d) teaching of minutest points of a subject.

1530. Which is incorrect
(a) Na^+ helps in conduction of nerve impulses.
(b) Na^+ helps in retention of water in the body.
(c) Na^+ transports substances across membranes.
(d) Na^+ takes part in thermoregulation.

1531. Audio-visual aids are more effective because
(a) verbalism is not adequate usually.
(b) students are more attracted by TV and cinema.
(c) they provide a change.
(d) they make the learning experience more concrete, more realistic and more dynamic.

1532. The term 'Maturation' is specifically used for
(a) quantitative change in the organism not induced by learning.
(b) quantitative change in the organism induced by learning.
(c) qualitative change in the organism not induced by learning.
(d) physiological development induced by learning and situation.

1533. In a nerve if sodium pump is blocked, which of the following is most likely to happen?
(a) Na^+ and K^+ will increase outside the cell.
(b) Na^+ outside the nerve will increase.
(c) K^+ inside the nerve will increase.
(d) Na^+ inside the nerve will increase.

1534. Who of the following teachers is most desirable?
(a) One who is a moralist and preaches morals to students all the time.
(b) One who comes to the class on time, but does not mind students coming late in the class.
(c) One who just knows enough of his subject but motivates his students a lot to learn.
(d) One who comes to teach regularly, but does not care to know what the students are learning.

1535. Dalton Plan is associated with
(a) John Dewey
(b) Helen Parkhurst

(c) E.L. Thorndike
(d) John Dalton

1536. An axon has four terminals ends connected with dendrites of four different neurons. Its nerve impulse will
(a) pass on to one neuron only.
(b) travel in all the four neurons with equal strength.
(c) not travel because the movement of impulse is from dendrites to axon.
(d) become weak due to distribution in to four.

1537. Which of the following is the most indirect experience?
(a) Dramatised experience
(b) Visual symbols
(c) Verbal symbols
(d) Contrived experience.

1538. Good teaching is a function of
(a) high level scholarship of the teachers.
(b) sincerity and devotion to the profession of teaching.
(c) principal's powerful leadership in the college.
(d) high academic qualifications of the teachers.

1539. The site from which the nerve impulses for hearing originates in mammals is
(a) Cochlea (b) Vestibule
(c) Auditory nerve (d) Ear ossicles

1540. Who has the least chance of becoming an effective teacher?
(a) One who is a strict disciplinarian
(b) One who knows his subject well
(c) One who teaches moral values
(d) One who has no interest in teaching.

1541. Synaptic fatigue is due to
(a) repeated release of acetylcholine.
(b) exhaustion of acetylcholinesterase.
(c) repeated release of adrenaline.
(d) exhaustion of neurotransmitters.

1542. Organ of Corti sends information to brain through cranial nerve
(a) VII (b) V
(c) VIII (d) VI

1543. Third cranial nerve is
(a) Abducens (b) Oculomotor
(c) Olfactory (d) Optic

1544. In rabbit/mammal, the cranial nerve associated with the sense of body balance is
(a) VI (b) VII
(c) VIII (d) IX

1545. By origin brain is
(a) Endodermal (b) Peridermal
(c) Mesodermal (d) Ectodermal

1546. Which of the following cranial nerves helps regulate heart beat?
(a) VIII (b) VII
(c) IX (d) X

1547. Outermost covering of brain is
(a) Pia mater
(b) Dura mater
(c) Choroid mater
(d) Arachnoid mater

1548. The branched tree-like structure present in the cerebellum is
(a) Areola (b) Arbor vitae
(c) Arboreal (d) Archenteron

1549. Autonomic nervous system regulates all except
(a) Blood circulation
(b) Excretion
(c) Learning and memory
(d) Respiration

1550. A nerve has K^+ concentration
(a) more on the inside
(b) more on the outside
(c) less on the outside
(d) None of the above

1551. The chemical causing the transmission of the nerve impulse across synapse/and plate is
(a) Cholinesterase (b) Adrenaline
(c) Acetylcholine (d) Choline

1552. Vagus nerve is
(a) Sympathetic nerve
(b) Parasympathetic
(c) V-cranial nerve
(d) X-cranial nerve

1553. III, V and XII cranial nerves are
(a) trigeminal, vagus and glossopharyngeal.
(b) pathetic, trigeminal and gloss pharyngeal.
(c) olfactory, spinal accessory and vagus.
(d) oculomotor, trigeminal and hypoglossal.

1554. Which part of human brain is highly developed as compared to others?
(a) Cerebellum
(b) Cerebrum
(c) Medulla Oblengata
(d) Optic lobes

1555. An example of autonomic nervous system is
(a) Knee jerk response
(b) Peristalsis of intestine
(c) Pupillary reflex
(d) Swallowing food

1556. On stimulation, sympathetic nervous system
(a) increases tear secretion
(b) decreases saliva secretion
(c) increases sweat secretion
(d) All of the above

1557. Diencephalon does not control
(a) Heart beat (b) Love
(c) Anger (d) Heat

1558. Trigeminal nerve arises from
(a) medulla and divides into ophthalmic, maxillary and mandibular.
(b) medulla and divides into palatine, chorda tympany and hyomandibular.
(c) cerebellum and divides into ophthalmic, maxillary and mandibular.
(d) cerebellum and divides into palatine, chorda timpani and hyomandibular.

1559. Heuristic method is a method according to which
(a) the learner discovers things for himself.
(b) learning occurs without a teacher.
(c) learning occurs by doing.
(d) the learner follows the analytic method.

1560. The reflex arc is formed by
(a) Muscles - Receptor - Brain
(b) Muscles - Spinal cord - Receptor
(c) Receptor - Spinal cord - Muscles
(d) Brain - Spinal cord - Muscles

1561. Which is absent in mammalian brain?
(a) Dura mater
(b) Subdural space
(c) Subarachnoid space
(d) None of the above.

1562. Trochlear nerve supplies
(a) interior oblique eye muscle
(b) nasal epithelium
(c) superior oblique eye muscles
(d) superior rectus eye muscles

1563. On stimulation the inside of a nerve becomes
(a) filled with acetylcholine
(b) + vely charged
(c) – vely charged
(d) depolarised

1564. Number of spinal nerves in man is
(a) 12 pairs (b) 31 pairs
(c) 32 pairs (d) 33 pairs

1565. In the teaching of any subject, a unit means

(a) a topic which may require several lessons to be completed.
(b) the post of a presentation requiring demonstration.
(c) the portion covered by the teacher in the class period.
(d) a part of lesson plan such as introduction of assignment.

1566. Teaching method called the Dalton Plan is mentioned in Pedagogical literature as a successful experiment. It was concerned with
(a) an open school system, allowing students to learn for themselves from surrounding situations and people, through their own initiative.
(b) a play way techniques for development of physical and artistic skills, through manipulation.
(c) education through co-curricular and extra curricular activities within the school boundaries with indirect supervision and observation by teachers.
(d) abolition of the classroom teaching and encouraging children to learn according to their own speed in fulfilling the given assignments.

1567. It is said that teachers should adopt methods so that their pupils do not feel that teachers are always necessary for learning. Which of the following devices would substitute the teachers?
(a) The experimental method
(b) The seminar method
(c) The programmed learning method
(d) The discussion method.

1568. Which of the following is most important for a teacher?
(a) Classroom discipline
(b) Subject he is teaching
(c) Time available for teaching
(d) Students of the class.

1569. What I like about teaching is that it is the
(a) most lucrative job because of the scope for private tuition.
(b) most challenging job.
(c) resort of even the least competent persons.
(d) most peaceful job.

1570. The main pillar on which the edifice of psychoanalysis rests is the
(a) ego ideal principle
(b) super ego principle
(c) theory of repression
(d) theory of suggestion

1571. It terms of Spearman's two factor theory while comparing a mathematician with a musician we can say that
(a) the mathematician requires more of 'S' factor whereas the musician requires more of 'G' factor.
(b) the musician has more of 'G' factor as compared to the mathematician.
(c) the mathematician has more 'G' factor and musician has more of the 'S' factor.
(d) both of them require equal amount of 'G' and 'S' factors.

1572. A computer cannot be used
(a) as a systematic programmed learning technique.
(b) for reading and writing.
(c) as a machine for evaluating students progress.
(d) for demonstration.

1573. The heuristic method of teaching any subject insists on
(a) quantification of problems and planning for their solutions.
(b) the survey of a situation for arriving at conclusion.

(c) verification of facts through exploration and analysis.
(d) self-experimentation for observation and discovery.

1574. A teacher should
(a) teach well and think that his job is over.
(b) help the students to get good marks.
(c) maintain distance from his students.
(d) do whatever is needed to promote the welfare of his students.

1575. Listening is badly affected by
(a) a sizable hearing loss—physiological problem.
(b) high speed of speaking.
(c) message overload—excess of listened material.
(d) All of the above.

Question Nos. 1576 to 1578 are of Multi-statement type. Choose the correct code as given.

1576. Below are given some essentials of teaching competencies
1. Assisting in the conduct of co-curricular activities
2. Motivating students for learning
3. Improving classroom management
4. Knowing subject matter thoroughly
5. Taking interest in college administration

Which of these combinations is most appropriate for classroom teaching?

Codes:
(a) 1, 2, 3, 4 (b) 1, 2, 3, 5
(c) 1, 3, 4, 5 (d) 2, 3, 4, 5

1577. When there is a heterogeneous group of students consisting of slow learners and bright students it is better for the teacher to
1. keep the teaching level high so that slow learners will eventually catch up
2. keep the teaching level low so that every one understands
3. keep the teaching level moderate so that it is not too boring for the bright students
4. arrange remedial teaching for the slow learners

Codes:
(a) 1 only (b) 1 and 4
(c) 2 and 4 (d) 3 and 4

1578. Following are the experimental learning activities adopted by a teacher. Arrange them in cyclic order:
1. Accommodation 2. Converging
3. Assimilation 4. Diverging

Codes:
(a) 4, 3, 2, 1 (b) 3, 1, 2, 4
(c) 1, 2, 3, 4 (d) 2, 3, 4, 1

Question Nos. 1579-80 are Matching type. Choose correct code as given.

1579. **List I**
A. Classical conditioning
B. Drive reduction
C. Sign gestalt
D. Learning by insight

List II
1. Kohler 2. Hull
3. Pavlov 4. Tolman

Codes:	A	B	C	D
(a)	4	3	2	1
(b)	2	1	3	4
(c)	1	2	3	4
(d)	3	2	4	1

1580. **List I (Traits)**
A. Product of neuropsychic system
B. Structure of personality
C. Unconscious mind
D. Determine the type of personality

List II (Psychologists)
1. Sigmund Freud
2. Raymond Cattell

3. Hans Eysenck
4. Gordan Allport

Codes:	**A**	**B**	**C**	**D**
(a)	4	3	2	1
(b)	1	2	3	4
(c)	4	2	3	1
(d)	4	2	1	3

The following question consists of two statements, one labelled as 'Assertion (A)' and the other as 'Reason (R)'. You have to examine these two statements carefully and decide if the Assertion A and the Reason R are individually true and if so, whether the Reason is a correct explanation of the Assertion. Select your answer to these items using the codes given below:

(a) if both A and R are true and R is the correct explanation of A
(b) if both A and R are true but R is not the correct explanation of A
(c) if A is true but R is false
(d) if A is false but R is true

1581. **Assertion (A):** There is a powerful stabilizing factor to control and coordinate growth.

Reason (R): If it is not so body weight will not coordinate to body size.

ANSWERS

1. (a)	2. (d)	3. (b)	4. (c)	5. (d)	6. (b)
7. (c)	8. (d)	9. (c)	10. (d)	11. (b)	12. (d)
13. (c)	14. (a)	15. (a)	16. (d)	17. (b)	18. (b)
19. (a)	20. (c)	21. (d)	22. (a)	23. (c)	24. (b)
25. (d)	26. (b)	27. (b)	28. (c)	29. (b)	30. (d)
31. (c)	32. (c)	33. (d)	34. (b)	35. (a)	36. (a)
37. (c)	38. (a)	39. (d)	40. (c)	41. (d)	42. (a)
43. (d)	44. (b)	45. (b)	46. (a)	47. (d)	48. (a)
49. (d)	50. (d)	51. (a)	52. (b)	53. (b)	54. (d)
55. (d)	56. (d)	57. (c)	58. (d)	59. (a)	60. (d)
61. (d)	62. (a)	63. (c)	64. (c)	65. (b)	66. (d)
67. (c)	68. (d)	69. (a)	70. (b)	71. (d)	72. (c)
73. (b)	74. (c)	75. (d)	76. (b)	77. (c)	78. (b)
79. (a)	80. (a)	81. (a)	82. (c)	83. (d)	84. (b)
85. (b)	86. (a)	87. (d)	88. (d)	89. (c)	90. (d)
91. (b)	92. (c)	93. (c)	94. (b)	95. (b)	96. (d)
97. (d)	98. (c)	99. (b)	100. (b)	101. (a)	102. (b)
103. (a)	104. (b)	105. (c)	106. (c)	107. (a)	108. (a)
109. (a)	110. (b)	111. (d)	112. (c)	113. (c)	114. (d)

115. (d)	116. (a)	117. (d)	118. (b)	119. (a)	120. (d)
121. (d)	122. (b)	123. (c)	124. (b)	125. (c)	126. (d)
127. (c)	128. (a)	129. (c)	130. (d)	131. (b)	132. (a)
133. (d)	134. (b)	135. (b)	136. (c)	137. (a)	138. (a)
139. (d)	140. (d)	141. (d)	142. (d)	143. (d)	144. (d)
145. (d)	146. (c)	147. (c)	148. (b)	149. (a)	150. (d)
151. (a)	152. (d)	153. (a)	154. (c)	155. (a)	156. (a)
157. (a)	158. (a)	159. (d)	160. (b)	161. (d)	162. (a)
163. (c)	164. (a)	165. (a)	166. (d)	167. (b)	168. (d)
169. (c)	170. (a)	171. (c)	172. (b)	173. (d)	174. (d)
175. (a)	176. (b)	177. (b)	178. (a)	179. (a)	180. (b)
181. (c)	182. (c)	183. (d)	184. (b)	185. (d)	186. (b)
187. (d)	188. (c)	189. (a)	190. (b)	191. (d)	192. (d)
193. (d)	194. (a)	195. (d)	196. (d)	197. (d)	198. (c)
199. (b)	200. (d)	201. (d)	202. (c)	203. (b)	204. (a)
205. (c)	206. (c)	207. (d)	208. (c)	209. (a)	210. (d)
211. (d)	212. (d)	213. (b)	214. (b)	215. (d)	216. (c)
217. (c)	218. (d)	219. (d)	220. (c)	221. (b)	222. (b)
223. (a)	224. (d)	225. (d)	226. (d)	227. (c)	228. (c)
229. (b)	230. (a)	231. (d)	232. (d)	233. (a)	234. (a)
235. (a)	236. (c)	237. (a)	238. (d)	239. (c)	240. (c)
241. (a)	242. (c)	243. (d)	244. (d)	245. (d)	246. (c)
247. (b)	248. (c)	249. (b)	250. (b)	251. (a)	252. (d)
253. (d)	254. (d)	255. (c)	256. (a)	257. (c)	258. (b)
259. (a)	260. (d)	261. (c)	262. (d)	263. (d)	264. (d)
265. (d)	266. (c)	267. (a)	268. (c)	269. (c)	270. (c)
271. (d)	272. (a)	273. (d)	274. (d)	275. (c)	276. (d)
277. (d)	278. (c)	279. (b)	280. (a)	281. (d)	282. (a)
283. (b)	284. (d)	285. (c)	286. (a)	287. (b)	288. (c)
289. (a)	290. (d)	291. (d)	292. (a)	293. (c)	294. (d)
295. (d)	296. (b)	297. (d)	298. (b)	299. (c)	300. (c)
301. (b)	302. (b)	303. (b)	304. (d)	305. (c)	306. (b)
307. (c)	308. (d)	309. (c)	310. (c)	311. (b)	312. (d)
313. (d)	314. (d)	315. (a)	316. (c)	317. (c)	318. (a)

319. (a)	320. (a)	321. (a)	322. (d)	323. (c)	324. (d)
325. (c)	326. (c)	327. (b)	328. (c)	329. (d)	330. (d)
331. (a)	332. (a)	333. (b)	334. (b)	335. (d)	336. (d)
337. (a)	338. (d)	339. (c)	340. (d)	341. (d)	342. (a)
343. (d)	344. (c)	345. (a)	346. (c)	347. (d)	348. (b)
349. (a)	350. (d)	351. (a)	352. (d)	353. (d)	354. (c)
355. (d)	356. (d)	357. (d)	358. (d)	359. (a)	360. (a)
361. (b)	362. (c)	363. (a)	364. (d)	365. (d)	366. (a)
367. (b)	368. (d)	369. (b)	370. (b)	371. (b)	372. (d)
373. (a)	374. (a)	375. (a)	376. (c)	377. (d)	378. (c)
379. (d)	380. (d)	381. (d)	382. (d)	383. (b)	384. (c)
385. (d)	386. (a)	387. (b)	388. (d)	389. (b)	390. (d)
391. (c)	392. (a)	393. (c)	394. (c)	395. (a)	396. (a)
397. (d)	398. (b)	399. (d)	400. (a)	401. (b)	402. (a)
403. (a)	404. (b)	405. (d)	406. (a)	407. (d)	408. (c)
409. (a)	410. (d)	411. (c)	412. (d)	413. (d)	414. (b)
415. (a)	416. (b)	417. (a)	418. (d)	419. (b)	420. (d)
421. (c)	422. (c)	423. (b)	424. (d)	425. (a)	426. (c)
427. (b)	428. (c)	429. (d)	430. (d)	431. (b)	432. (a)
433. (a)	434. (b)	435. (d)	436. (a)	437. (d)	438. (c)
439. (c)	440. (d)	441. (b)	442. (d)	443. (b)	444. (b)
445. (a)	446. (d)	447. (d)	448. (c)	449. (d)	450. (d)
451. (d)	452. (c)	453. (a)	454. (c)	455. (a)	456. (d)
457. (d)	458. (c)	459. (a)	460. (b)	461. (d)	462. (c)
463. (d)	464. (d)	465. (d)	466. (b)	467. (c)	468. (a)
469. (b)	470. (a)	471. (c)	472. (c)	473. (b)	474. (d)
475. (a)	476. (d)	477. (d)	478. (d)	479. (b)	480. (d)
481. (b)	482. (b)	483. (c)	484. (d)	485. (d)	486. (b)
487. (c)	488. (c)	489. (d)	490. (b)	491. (c)	492. (b)
493. (c)	494. (a)	495. (b)	496. (b)	497. (c)	498. (d)
499. (c)	500. (c)	501. (c)	502. (c)	503. (b)	504. (c)
505. (a)	506. (b)	507. (d)	508. (c)	509. (d)	510. (b)
511. (c)	512. (c)	513. (c)	514. (a)	515. (d)	516. (b)
517. (d)	518. (c)	519. (c)	520. (a)	521. (a)	522. (c)

523. (d)	524. (c)	525. (d)	526. (c)	527. (c)	528. (d)
529. (d)	530. (a)	531. (d)	532. (d)	533. (c)	534. (c)
535. (b)	536. (c)	537. (a)	538. (d)	539. (c)	540. (d)
541. (c)	542. (d)	543. (c)	544. (d)	545. (d)	546. (c)
547. (d)	548. (d)	549. (c)	550. (b)	551. (c)	552. (c)
553. (c)	554. (c)	555. (d)	556. (d)	557. (d)	558. (a)
559. (b)	560. (a)	561. (a)	562. (c)	563. (d)	564. (c)
565. (d)	566. (d)	567. (d)	568. (d)	569. (d)	570. (b)
571. (b)	572. (b)	573. (b)	574. (c)	575. (b)	576. (d)
577. (c)	578. (b)	579. (c)	580. (a)	581. (a)	582. (b)
583. (d)	584. (c)	585. (c)	586. (c)	587. (c)	588. (d)
589. (d)	590. (a)	591. (d)	592. (a)	593. (b)	594. (c)
595. (a)	596. (c)	597. (d)	598. (d)	599. (c)	600. (c)
601. (a)	602. (b)	603. (c)	604. (d)	605. (b)	606. (c)
607. (d)	608. (b)	609. (b)	610. (b)	611. (b)	612. (c)
613. (a)	614. (c)	615. (a)	616. (b)	617. (c)	618. (c)
619. (d)	620. (b)	621. (b)	622. (c)	623. (c)	624. (b)
625. (a)	626. (b)	627. (c)	628. (c)	629. (b)	630. (d)
631. (a)	632. (b)	633. (c)	634. (c)	635. (d)	636. (c)
637. (a)	638. (b)	639. (d)	640. (d)	641. (b)	642. (d)
643. (a)	644. (a)	645. (c)	646. (c)	647. (c)	648. (d)
649. (c)	650. (a)	651. (d)	652. (c)	653. (d)	654. (b)
655. (c)	656. (d)	657. (c)	658. (d)	659. (c)	660. (c)
661. (a)	662. (a)	663. (c)	664. (a)	665. (a)	666. (a)
667. (c)	668. (d)	669. (d)	670. (c)	671. (c)	672. (c)
673. (b)	674. (a)	675. (c)	676. (c)	677. (b)	678. (a)
679. (c)	680. (b)	681. (d)	682. (b)	683. (b)	684. (c)
685. (b)	686. (a)	687. (d)	688. (d)	689. (d)	690. (b)
691. (a)	692. (c)	693. (b)	694. (c)	695. (b)	696. (a)
697. (a)	698. (d)	699. (c)	700. (c)	701. (b)	702. (d)
703. (c)	704. (b)	705. (c)	706. (c)	707. (d)	708. (d)
709. (a)	710. (b)	711. (c)	712. (d)	713. (d)	714. (c)
715. (a)	716. (c)	717. (c)	718. (a)	719. (d)	720. (c)
721. (d)	722. (d)	723. (d)	724. (c)	725. (c)	726. (c)

727. (d)	728. (a)	729. (d)	730. (d)	731. (b)	732. (a)
733. (a)	734. (c)	735. (a)	736. (d)	737. (a)	738. (c)
739. (b)	740. (a)	741. (d)	742. (c)	743. (d)	744. (c)
745. (c)	746. (d)	747. (b)	748. (d)	749. (d)	750. (b)
751. (a)	752. (d)	753. (d)	754. (a)	755. (b)	756. (b)
757. (d)	758. (b)	759. (c)	760. (a)	761. (a)	762. (b)
763. (d)	764. (b)	765. (a)	766. (d)	767. (d)	768. (a)
769. (d)	770. (b)	771. (d)	772. (c)	773. (a)	774. (d)
775. (b)	776. (b)	777. (d)	778. (b)	779. (b)	780. (a)
781. (c)	782. (c)	783. (a)	784. (a)	785. (a)	786. (d)
787. (d)	788. (a)	789. (c)	790. (d)	791. (b)	792. (d)
793. (d)	794. (c)	795. (d)	796. (c)	797. (d)	798. (c)
799. (a)	800. (a)	801. (c)	802. (c)	803. (d)	804. (d)
805. (d)	806. (a)	807. (d)	808. (a)	809. (c)	810. (a)
811. (c)	812. (c)	813. (c)	814. (d)	815. (a)	816. (c)
817. (b)	818. (d)	819. (a)	820. (b)	821. (d)	822. (a)
823. (d)	824. (a)	825. (b)	826. (a)	827. (d)	828. (d)
829. (b)	830. (d)	831. (b)	832. (d)	833. (d)	834. (d)
835. (c)	836. (d)	837. (d)	838. (d)	839. (d)	840. (b)
841. (d)	842. (d)	843. (b)	844. (c)	845. (b)	846. (a)
847. (d)	848. (b)	849. (d)	850. (d)	851. (d)	852. (a)
853. (c)	854. (b)	855. (c)	856. (d)	857. (a)	858. (b)
859. (c)	860. (b)	861. (d)	862. (c)	863. (b)	864. (b)
865. (b)	866. (b)	867. (d)	868. (a)	869. (d)	870. (d)
871. (c)	872. (d)	873. (a)	874. (b)	875. (c)	876. (d)
877. (c)	878. (c)	879. (c)	880. (c)	881. (c)	882. (b)
883. (d)	884. (c)	885. (a)	886. (a)	887. (c)	888. (a)
889. (d)	890. (b)	891. (d)	892. (b)	893. (d)	894. (a)
895. (d)	896. (d)	897. (c)	898. (d)	899. (d)	900. (d)
901. (d)	902. (a)	903. (c)	904. (b)	905. (d)	906. (b)
907. (c)	908. (c)	909. (c)	910. (d)	911. (d)	912. (d)
913. (d)	914. (a)	915. (d)	916. (b)	917. (a)	918. (d)
919. (d)	920. (a)	921. (c)	922. (a)	923. (d)	924. (d)
925. (c)	926. (c)	927. (d)	928. (a)	929. (b)	930. (a)

931. (a)	932. (d)	933. (d)	934. (c)	935. (b)	936. (a)
937. (d)	938. (d)	939. (a)	940. (a)	941. (a)	942. (c)
943. (a)	944. (a)	945. (c)	946. (c)	947. (d)	948. (c)
949. (d)	950. (a)	951. (d)	952. (a)	953. (d)	954. (c)
955. (b)	956. (d)	957. (b)	958. (d)	959. (c)	960. (d)
961. (d)	962. (b)	963. (a)	964. (a)	965. (b)	966. (c)
967. (d)	968. (b)	969. (d)	970. (c)	971. (d)	972. (b)
973. (c)	974. (c)	975. (d)	976. (b)	977. (b)	978. (c)
979. (b)	980. (c)	981. (a)	982. (a)	983. (c)	984. (d)
985. (c)	986. (b)	987. (c)	988. (d)	989. (c)	990. (d)
991. (d)	992. (d)	993. (c)	994. (b)	995. (b)	996. (d)
997. (d)	998. (c)	999. (d)	1000. (c)	1001. (c)	1002. (b)
1003. (d)	1004. (b)	1005. (c)	1006. (b)	1007. (b)	1008. (a)
1009. (b)	1010. (b)	1011. (a)	1012. (d)	1013. (a)	1014. (b)
1015. (d)	1016. (d)	1017. (a)	1018. (d)	1019. (c)	1020. (c)
1021. (c)	1022. (c)	1023. (a)	1024. (a)	1025. (c)	1026. (c)
1027. (c)	1028. (d)	1029. (c)	1030. (b)	1031 (b)	1032. (a,
1033. (b)	1034. (c)	1035. (d)	1036. (b)	1037. (b)	1038. (c)
1039. (c)	1040. (d)	1041. (d)	1042. (a)	1043. (c)	1044. (a)
1045. (c)	1046. (a)	1047. (d)	1048. (d)	1049. (d)	1050. (a)
1051. (c)	1052. (d)	1053. (c)	1054. (c)	1055. (c)	1056. (d)
1057. (b)	1058. (a)	1059. (d)	1060. (d)	1061. (a)	1062. (d)
1063. (d)	1064. (c)	1065. (b)	1066. (d)	1067. (a)	1068. (d)
1069. (d)	1070. (d)	1071. (b)	1072. (d)	1073. (c)	1074. (c)
1075. (c)	1076. (d)	1077. (a)	1078. (b)	1079. (d)	1080. (b)
1081. (d)	1082. (b)	1083. (b)	1084. (a)	1085. (d)	1086. (c)
1087. (a)	1088. (c)	1089. (d)	1090. (d)	1091. (d)	1092. (a)
1093. (c)	1094. (b)	1095. (d)	1096. (d)	1097. (d)	1098. (d)
1099. (d)	1100. (d)	1101. (a)	1102. (a)	1103. (d)	1104. (c)
1105. (a)	1106. (d)	1107. (d)	1108. (d)	1109. (b)	1110. (b)
1111. (b)	1112. (c)	1113. (c)	1114. (d)	1115. (b)	1116. (d)
1117. (a)	1118. (a)	1119. (d)	1120. (a)	1121. (a)	1122. (d)
1123. (a)	1124. (d)	1125. (b)	1126. (d)	1127. (b)	1128. (b)
1129. (d)	1130. (b)	1131. (d)	1132. (d)	1133. (b)	1134. (d)

1135. (b)	1136. (b)	1137. (d)	1138. (b)	1139. (d)	1140. (d)
1141. (b)	1142. (a)	1143. (b)	1144. (c)	1145. (b)	1146. (d)
1147. (b)	1148. (b)	1149. (c)	1150. (d)	1151. (a)	1152. (a)
1153. (a)	1154. (c)	1155. (c)	1156. (d)	1157. (d)	1158. (c)
1159. (d)	1160. (d)	1161. (c)	1162. (a)	1163. (c)	1164. (b)
1165. (b)	1166. (c)	1167. (c)	1168. (c)	1169. (d)	1170. (b)
1171. (c)	1172. (c)	1173. (d)	1174. (c)	1175. (c)	1176. (d)
1177. (b)	1178. (d)	1179. (d)	1180. (d)	1181. (b)	1182. (a)
1183. (b)	1184. (b)	1185. (d)	1186. (a)	1187. (b)	1188. (d)
1189. (d)	1190. (d)	1191. (b)	1192. (b)	1193. (d)	1194. (c)
1195. (c)	1196. (d)	1197. (c)	1198. (d)	1199. (b)	1200. (c)
1201. (b)	1202. (d)	1203. (d)	1204. (b)	1205. (c)	1206. (d)
1207. (d)	1208. (d)	1209. (b)	1210. (b)	1211. (c)	1212. (c)
1213. (a)	1214. (d)	1215. (d)	1216. (c)	1217. (a)	1218. (c)
1219. (c)	1220. (a)	1221. (b)	1222. (c)	1223. (a)	1224. (d)
1225. (a)	1226. (c)	1227. (b)	1228. (d)	1229. (a)	1230. (c)
1231. (d)	1232. (b)	1233. (d)	1234. (a)	1235 (c)	1236. (b)
1237. (d)	1238. (b)	1239. (a)	1240. (d)	1241. (a)	1242. (d)
1243. (c)	1244. (b)	1245. (d)	1246. (d)	1247. (d)	1248. (b)
1249. (b)	1250. (c)	1251. (b)	1252. (a)	1253. (b)	1254. (c)
1255. (d)	1256. (d)	1257. (b)	1258. (a)	1259. (a)	1260. (a)
1261. (c)	1262. (c)	1263. (c)	1264. (d)	1265. (a)	1266. (b)
1267. (a)	1268. (b)	1269. (a)	1270. (b)	1271. (a)	1272. (a)
1273. (d)	1274. (c)	1275. (c)	1276. (d)	1277. (a)	1278. (d)
1279. (c)	1280. (c)	1281. (c)	1282. (a)	1283. (a)	1284. (c)
1285. (a)	1286. (d)	1287. (c)	1288. (b)	1289. (d)	1290. (a)
1291. (a)	1292. (d)	1293. (a)	1294. (c)	1295. (b)	1296. (c)
1297. (d)	1298. (c)	1299. (d)	1300. (c)	1301. (d)	1302. (c)
1303. (b)	1304. (a)	1305. (d)	1306. (d)	1307. (b)	1308. (d)
1309. (d)	1310. (d)	1311. (c)	1312. (c)	1313. (c)	1314. (a)
1315. (a)	1316. (b)	1317. (b)	1318. (b)	1319. (c)	1320. (c)
1321. (c)	1322. (d)	1323. (a)	1324. (b)	1325. (d)	1326. (b)
1327. (b)	1328. (c)	1329. (c)	1330. (c)	1331. (c)	1332. (d)
1333. (a)	1334. (d)	1335. (b)	1336. (c)	1337. (d)	1338. (c)

1339. (c)	1340. (c)	1341. (d)	1342. (c)	1343. (c)	1344. (a)
1345. (b)	1346. (a)	1347. (c)	1348. (d)	1349. (c)	1350. (a)
1351. (b)	1352. (c)	1353. (d)	1354. (c)	1355. (d)	1356. (c)
1357. (a)	1358. (b)	1359. (a)	1360. (c)	1361. (d)	1362. (d)
1363. (c)	1364. (d)	1365. (d)	1366. (d)	1367. (d)	1368. (c)
1369. (c)	1370. (c)	1371. (b)	1372. (d)	1373. (a)	1374. (a)
1375. (c)	1376. (c)	1377. (a)	1378. (b)	1379. (b)	1380. (b)
1381. (a)	1382. (b)	1383. (d)	1384. (c)	1385. (d)	1386. (b)
1387. (a)	1388. (a)	1389. (c)	1390. (d)	1391. (d)	1392. (a)
1393. (d)	1394. (a)	1395. (d)	1396. (b)	1397. (c)	1398. (d)
1399. (c)	1400. (a)	1401. (d)	1402. (b)	1403. (a)	1404. (d)
1405. (d)	1406. (d)	1407. (c)	1408. (a)	1409. (c)	1410. (d)
1411. (c)	1412. (b)	1413. (c)	1414. (c)	1415. (c)	1416. (c)
1417. (d)	1418. (b)	1419. (b)	1420. (d)	1421. (a)	1422. (d)
1423. (a)	1424. (c)	1425. (c)	1426. (c)	1427. (c)	1428. (c)
1429. (d)	1430. (b)	1431. (b)	1432. (a)	1433. (b)	1434. (d)
1435. (d)	1436. (b)	1437. (d)	1438. (a)	1439. (c)	1440. (b)
1441. (c)	1442. (c)	1443. (d)	1444. (d)	1445. (c)	1446. (b)
1447. (d)	1448. (b)	1449. (c)	1450. (a)	1451. (a)	1452. (b)
1453. (d)	1454. (a)	1455. (d)	1456. (c)	1457. (c)	1458. (b)
1459. (b)	1460. (b)	1461. (c)	1462. (b)	1463. (a)	1464. (b)
1465. (c)	1466. (d)	1467. (c)	1468. (a)	1469. (b)	1470. (b)
1471. (b)	1472. (c)	1473. (a)	1474. (a)	1475. (c)	1476. (d)
1477. (d)	1478. (a)	1479. (d)	1480. (d)	1481. (b)	1482. (b)
1483. (b)	1484. (a)	1485. (d)	1486. (a)	1487. (c)	1488. (a)
1489. (d)	1490. (d)	1491. (a)	1492. (c)	1493. (b)	1494. (d)
1495. (b)	1496. (b)	1497. (c)	1498. (d)	1499. (a)	1500. (d)
1501. (c)	1502. (a)	1503. (c)	1504. (c)	1505. (b)	1506. (a)
1507. (a)	1508. (b)	1509. (b)	1510. (d)	1511. (b)	1512. (a)
1513. (a)	1514. (a)	1515. (c)	1516. (d)	1517. (a)	1518. (c)
1519. (d)	1520. (d)	1521. (d)	1522. (a)	1523. (d)	1524. (c)
1525. (d)	1526. (c)	1527. (a)	1528. (a)	1529. (c)	1530. (d)
1531. (d)	1532. (c)	1533. (d)	1534. (c)	1535. (b)	1536. (a)
1537. (c)	1538. (b)	1539. (a)	1540. (d)	1541. (d)	1542. (c)

1543. (b)	1544. (c)	1545. (a)	1546. (d)	1547. (b)	1548. (b)
1549. (c)	1550. (c)	1551. (c)	1552. (d)	1553. (d)	1554. (b)
1555. (d)	1556. (c)	1557. (b)	1558. (a)	1559. (a)	1560. (c)
1561. (b)	1562. (c)	1563. (a)	1564. (b)	1565. (c)	1566. (a)
1567. (c)	1568. (d)	1569. (b)	1570. (c)	1571. (d)	1572. (d)
1573. (d)	1574. (d)	1575. (d)	1576. (a)	1577. (d)	1578. (a)
1579. (d)	1580. (d)	1581. (b)			

4

Methodology of Educational Research

1. When the 'Population' is hetrogeneous, what should be the proper method of 'Sampling'?
   (a) Purposive Sampling
   (b) Stratified Sampling
   (c) Cluster Sampling
   (d) Random Sampling
2. What does randomization ensure in experimental research?
   (a) Uniformity and similarity of the groups
   (b) Uniformity of the groups
   (c) Uniformity, similarity and equalization of the groups
   (d) Similarity of the groups
3. No research is possible without
   (a) formulating a hypothesis.
   (b) applying scientific method.
   (c) using statistical techniques.
   (d) All of the above.
4. What should be the Independent Variable in a study of comparing the traits of creativity of the students taught with the "Attribute Listing" Method and "Brain Storming Method"?
   (a) One of both
   (b) Method of Facilitating Creativity
   (c) Attribute Listing Method
   (d) Brain Storming Method
5. Power of the test of significance means probability of what?
   (a) Incorrect acceptance of the null hypothesis
   (b) Correct acceptance of the null hypothesis
   (c) Incorrect rejection of the null hypothesis
   (d) Correct rejection of the null hypothesis
6. The value which cannot be determined graphically is
   (a) Frequency table
   (b) Median
   (c) Mean
   (d) None of the above
7. What does F-ratio mean?
   (a) A ratio between mean SS_T and mean SS_A
   (b) A ratio between mean SS_T and mean SS_w
   (c) A ratio which is always more than 1.0
   (d) A ratio between mean SS_A and mean SS_W
8. What will help the analysis of data concerning a corporation study of the Adjustment Achievement Mean of the students of Government Higher Secondary School and a Public School?
   (a) Analysis of Variance
   (b) T-test
   (c) Man Whiteruy V-Test
   (d) Co-variant Analysis

9. The most frequent item of the series around which other items are densely populated is known as
   (a) Harmonic mean
   (b) Geometric mean
   (c) Mode
   (d) Arithmetic mean
10. What affects the laboratory experiment?
   (a) Intrinsic Validity
   (b) Cross Validity
   (c) Internal Validity
   (d) External Validity
11. In which situation x^2 (Cbi square) test can be used?
   (a) df is greater than I, but more than 20 per cent of frequencies are smaller than S
   (b) k = 2, but some expected frequencies are less than S
   (c) Any expected frequency is smaller than I
   (d) None of the above is found to be a fact
12. The square of standard deviation is called
   (a) Co-efficient
   (b) Mean
   (c) Variance
   (d) None of the above
13. What is wrong about non-parametric tests or significance?
   (a) They make no assumption about the parameters
   (b) They do make certain assumptions, but these are fewer and less stringent
   (c) They are distribution-free techniques of analysis
   (d) They assume that groups should be homogeneous
14. What results in programmed learning?
   (a) Fundamental Research
   (b) Applied Research
   (c) Action-Research
   (d) Experimental Research
15. After passing your B.Ed. examination, you go back to the same school where you were working before. Which of the following changes should your students notice in your teaching?
   (a) There is a feeling of superiority in your movement and treatment of students.
   (b) They find you better respected among your colleagues.
   (c) They find your giving more opportunities to them to learn themselves.
   (d) You appear more stylish and better behaved than before.
16. A senior school student who is not well-adjusted with his family, is given a Word-Association Test, what will be his response to the word "Breakfast"?
   (a) Bad (b) Good
   (c) Late (d) Hunger
17. In evaluating the significance of the research problem, an important social consideration is
   (a) necessary skills, abilities and background of knowledge of the researcher.
   (b) possibility of obtaining reliable and valid data by the researchers.
   (c) the genuine interest of the researcher in the problem.
   (d) practical value of the findings to educationists, parents and social workers, etc.
18. Research is an honest, exhaustive and intelligent searching for facts and their meanings or implications with reference to a given problem. Who said this?
   (a) M. Fair Child (b) J.W. West
   (c) W.S. Monroe (d) P.M. Cook

19. A hypothesis in educational research need not be
    (a) logically consistent and pertinent to the question under consideration.
    (b) capable of establishing generalizations that can be applied in many areas of education or other fields.
    (c) a compatible with well-attested theories and models.
    (d) None of these.
20. What does the Relevance level of 5% indicate about the decision taken?
    (a) 5% will be correct
    (b) 5% of the time correct
    (c) 5% will be wrong
    (d) 95% will be wrong
21. Given the series below:

X	18	19	20	21	22	23	24	25
F	5	6	7	8	9	8	9	5

The mode is
    (a) 23 (b) 21
    (c) 20 (d) 22
22. The principles discuss
    (a) cause-effect relationship between variables which universally applicable.
    (b) empirically evident abstracted facts.
    (c) those which are universally adopted.
    (d) generalization based on the results of research.
23. Thinking analogously about hypothesis, a researcher should
    (a) first roll the dice and then bet.
    (b) change his bet after the data are in.
    (c) have no bets, but dice only.
    (d) first bet and then roll the dice.
24. The sum of the derivations of the items from Mean is always
    (a) Two (b) Six
    (c) One (d) Zero
25. If the population on which a study is based is such that all its units can be reached, it is termed as
    (a) homogeneous population.
    (b) target population.
    (c) heterogeneous population.
    (d) accessible population.
26. If a researcher wants to find out the relationship between sex and colour-blindness, what correlation will be most suitable?
    (a) Phi-Coefficient
    (b) Tetrachoric Coefficient
    (c) Bi-Serial Correlation
    (d) Point Bi-Serial Correlation
27. The average marks secured by 30 students are 60. If two more students join the class, the average comes down to 56.25. The total marks secured by these students were
    (a) 60 (b) Zero
    (c) 20 (d) 40
28. The "Null Hypothesis" is
    (a) formulated in all experimental studies.
    (b) tested in statistical form.
    (c) stated in negative form.
    (d) formulated in all types of research.
29. Sampling frame means
    (a) preparing a complete list of the units of a finite population for drawing a sample.
    (b) identification of target and accessible population.
    (c) fixing the sample size and drawing a sample.
    (d) defining sample unit and selecting units.
30. Problem of a research can be identified and selected by
    (a) studying fundamental researches.
    (b) surveying the literature.

(c) coming across a real problem in the field.
(d) All of the above.

31. Action research is ordinarily concerned with problems
(a) have long-range implications.
(b) are of immediate concern and call for immediate solutions.
(c) constituting universal truths.
(d) of general nature.

32. What should be the objective of Psychological Test?
(a) Construct Validity
(b) Concurrent Validity
(c) Content Validity
(d) Product Validity

33. Educational organisation is different from educational administration because
(a) administration is concerned with arrangements of things etc., while organisation deals with the management aspects.
(b) organization is concerned with arrangements of equipment etc., whereas administration has to manage which things to be organised.
(c) administration is concerned with persons whereas organisation is concerned with equipments.
(d) educational organisation is political whereas educational administration is a political.

34. To find correlation between two bi-category variables, the proper statistics is
(a) Tetrachoric Correlation
(b) Chi Square
(c) Biserial Correlation
(d) Phi Coefficient

35. What is the aim of educational research?
(a) Identifying the aims of education
(b) Identifying major problems that need to be solved
(c) Identifying the values that need to be inculcated in the pupils
(d) Searching for the new facts and principles underlying the process of education

36. If r is 0.5, $\Sigma xy = 120$, σ of $y = 8$ and $\Sigma x^2 = 90$, the value of n will be
(a) 10 (b) 12
(c) 15 (d) 20

37. Why is research in education important for teachers?
(a) It enables them to make best possible judgments about what should be taught and how
(b) It makes them better teachers
(c) It makes them wiser
(d) It adds to their academic qualifications

38. The "Null Hypothesis" is that which
(a) is tested by statistics.
(b) is always in the negative form.
(c) is without Type-1 error.
(d) is tested by two-tailed test.

39. The sum of the deviations of individual observation is zero from
(a) Median (b) Geometric mean
(c) Arithmetic mean (d) Mode

40. "Non-Parametric" tests are useful for
(a) Description and assumption
(b) Prediction
(c) Description
(d) Assumption

41. What does view of related research and literature not do?
(a) Make the researcher competent and perfect in doing research
(b) Provide the researcher with sufficient useful knowledge
(c) Make the researcher aware of the pitfalls that plagued his predecessors
(d) Help the researcher in identifying needed problems of research

42. Which of the following could be classified under the software of educational technology
(a) R.T.V. Telecast
(b) Radio Broadcasts
(c) Programmed instructional material
(d) Tape recorders

43. Who said that "the problem is a proposed question for solution"?
(a) J.C. Almak
(b) John C. Torensand
(c) John W. Best
(d) Fred N. Kurlinger

44. What type of test is association?
(a) Vocabulary (b) Projective
(c) Creativity (d) Memory

45. A research is
(a) a solution to the problem, local or universal.
(b) a goal directed activity.
(c) an effort to formulate new laws and principles or their applications.
(d) All of the above.

46. "Semantic Differendal' is a
(a) Achievement Test
(b) Group Difference Test
(c) Intelligence Test
(d) Attitude Test

47. What type of study means comparison of likeness and differences among phenomena to find out factors which seem to accompany or contribute to the occurrence of certain events?
(a) A causal comparative study
(b) A correlational study
(c) An ex post-facto study
(d) An experimental study

48. Skewness is present if
(a) quartile is equidistant from median.
(b) quartile is not equidistant from median.
(c) median is equal to 3rd quartile.
(d) None of the above.

49. Which of the following is not a correct statement?
(a) A test can be reliable without being valid
(b) A test can be valid without being reliable
(c) A test can be reliable and valid both
(d) A test cannot be valid without being reliable

50. "Quota Sampling" is like
(a) Double Sampling
(b) Cluster Sampling
(c) Stratified Sampling
(d) Systematic Random Sampling

51. The Law of Probability is applied in
(a) Geometry
(b) Random sampling
(c) Non-random sampling
(d) None of the above

52. Sufficiency of sample is determined by
(a) Validity level for decision-making
(b) Degree of Freedom
(c) Size of Population
(d) Availability of resources

53. Which of the following is undesirable in a questionnaire?
(a) Avoiding ambiguity in questions
(b) Asking for unnecessary information that lengthens the questionnaire
(c) Avoiding questions which the subjects will not answer or will not answer truthfully
(d) Simplest possible wording and suitable vocabulary

54. If from all the items in a distribution, a value X is subtracted, the arithmetic mean of the new series will be
(a) $\bar{X} + \frac{X}{N}$ (b) $\bar{X} + \frac{N}{X}$
(c) $\bar{X} - X$ (d) $\bar{X} \cdot X$

55. Which of the following is desirable in a questionnaire?
   (a) Two ideas in one question
   (b) Emotionally toned questions
   (c) Questions which will elicit valid and reliable answers
   (d) Too broad questions

56. What hypothesis is tested by one-tail test?
   (a) At higher secondary level, the girls are more achievement-oriented than the boys
   (b) There is difference between the exam-anxiety in the boys and girls
   (c) There is difference between the achievements of boys and girls in science subject
   (d) There is difference between achievements of the boys in Maths and Science subjects

57. When a pure research is applied to new situation after careful inquiry it is called
   (a) action research
   (b) applied research
   (c) Both (a) and (b)
   (d) None of the above

58. One-way Anova compared the achievements of four groups of 20 students in each group. Here in the group the degree of independent will be
   (a) 3 (b) 4
   (c) 76 (d) 79

59. What does the face validity of a questionnaire not involve?
   (a) Seeing that there is an adequate coverate of the overall topic
   (b) Relating each question to the topic under investigation
   (c) Seeing that questions are clear and unambiguous
   (d) Checking the responses which the questionnaire elicits against an external criterion

60. Mode is
   (a) most frequent value.
   (b) least frequent value.
   (c) middle most value.
   (d) majority out of total frequency.

61. Projective technique is used for measuring
   (a) individual's inventoried interests.
   (b) individual's need for self-actualization.
   (c) individual's value-system.
   (d) individual's dominant feelings, emotions, conflicts, needs which are, generally, repressed by the individual and are stored up in the unconscious mind.

62. The result of Applied Research is
   (a) Problem-solving (b) New policies
   (c) Discovery (d) Invention

63. If all the items in a distribution are multiplied by a value X, the arithmetic mean of the next series will be
   (a) $\bar{X} + \frac{X}{N}$ (b) $\bar{X} - X$
   (c) $\bar{X} \cdot X$ (d) $\bar{X} + \frac{N}{X}$

64. The coefficient of correlation between two variables is 0.5, it means
   (a) 25% variance in one variable may be explained by the variance in the other.
   (b) both variables have equal 50% variance.
   (c) 50% relationship between the variables.
   (d) 50% variance one variable may be explained by the variance in the other.

65. Which of the following is not a projective technique?
   (a) T.A.T.
   (b) Rorschach
   (c) Maudsley Personality Inventory (MPI)
   (d) Sentence-Completion Test

66. The mean of 9 items is 16. One more value is added, the mean is now 17. The value of the 10th item is
(a) 26 (b) 25
(c) 24 (d) 21

67. Which of the following is not measured by the T.A.T. test?
(a) Personality adjustment
(b) Reasoning ability
(c) Personality needs
(d) Emotions

68. The half reliability of a test is 0.6, if it is further used then the value of test-reliability will be
(a) 0.3 (b) 0.9
(c) 0.75 (d) 1.2

69. An extreme item or a lowest item will always have a bearing upon
(a) Mode (b) Mean
(c) Median (d) None of these

70. The personality-study or the case-study is like
(a) Development Study
(b) Casual Comparative study
(c) Survey-Study
(d) Study of Inter-personal relationship

71. Which is a projective test?
(a) Allport Vemon-Lindzey Study of Values
(b) Edwards Personal Preference Schedule (EPPS)
(c) Minnesotta Multiphasic Personality Inventory (MMPI)
(d) Rorschach Test

72. Which of the following situations will motivate a researcher to conduct a fresh study?
(a) When some doubt is there in the mind of the researcher regarding a particular practice.
(b) When pace of social change is much faster than the pace of education causing adjustment problems.
(c) When he finds a gap in two researches conducted in the field.
(d) All of the above.

73. What is the meaning of Data?
(a) Truths
(b) Facts
(c) Marks obtained
(d) Observation

74. Descriptive research does not include
(a) Development Study
(b) Ex-Post Fact Study
(c) Survey Study
(d) Inter-personal Study

75. The arithmetic mean of the direct 100 natural numbers is
(a) 25.7 (b) 50.5
(c) 55.2 (d) 60.1

76. The following is not correct about Field Studies.
(a) It researches behaviour
(b) It regularises definite variables
(c) It is Ex-post Facto Study
(d) It is a study of situations related to real life

77. What are the types of data according to nature?
(a) Quantitative (b) Qualitative
(c) Both (a) and (b) (d) None of these.

78. The term wastage is used to denote that
(a) a lot of amount meant for school education is wasted by authorities.
(b) children have to waste a lot on materials other than prescribed books for study.
(c) most rural parents think it a waste of time for their children to attend schools.

(d) children leave schools before they complete the prescribed age or class in education.

79. What are the kinds of variables?
(a) Discrete (b) Continuous
(c) Both (a) and (b) (d) None of these

80 "Action-research" is related to this problem.
(a) Immeate problem and its immediate solution
(b) Problem having implications for the long time
(c) Problem of general nature
(d) Problem related to all persons

81. Studying the social status of a population a researcher concluded that Mr. X is socially backward. His conclusion is
(a) Inaccurate (b) Wrong
(c) Right (d) Biased

82. The scientific method used in educational research is
(a) Deductive reasoning
(b) Inductive reasoning
(c) Any one or both (a) and (b)
(d) None of the above

83. On what basis data are classified?
(a) Stability (b) Flexibility
(c) Clarity (d) All of these

84. All of the following are characteristics of a research problem except
(a) problem will satisfy the mind of the researcher.
(b) problem is socially significant.
(c) problem is new.
(d) problem is feasible for the researcher.

85. What is the meaning of population in Educational Research?
(a) Observation of all the units
(b) Elites
(c) Male, Female, Children
(d) All of these

86. The Randomization of a sample in experimental research determines
(a) uniformity and equality of the group.
(b) uniformity and equality and equal ratio.
(c) uniformity of the group.
(d) equality of the group.

87. The population census will have the primary data from
(a) Gram panchayats
(b) Municipalities
(c) Registrar General and Census Commissioner
(d) None of the above

88. F-Ratio means
(a) ratio which is between Mean SSt and Mean SSo.
(b) ratio which is between Mean SSt and Mean SSw.
(c) ratio between Mean SS and Mean SSw.
(d) ratio which is always more than 1.0.

89. Who has called sample an element of facts?
(a) John W. Best
(b) W.G. Kokaran
(c) W.S. Travers
(d) George J. Mouley

90. In a moderately skewed distribution
(a) $\bar{X} = M = 2Z$ (b) $M = 2\bar{X} - Z$
(c) $Z = 3M - 2\bar{X}$ (d) $Z = \bar{X} = M$

91. High intelligence combined with high motivation raises the levels of academic achievement and high intelligence combined with low motivation lowers academic achievement, this indicates that
(a) intelligence interacts with motivation.
(b) intelligence and motivation are equally important as factors of achievement.

(c) intelligence is more important a factor of achievement.
(d) motivation is more important a factor of achievement.

92. The main aim of educational research is
(a) to identify the objectives of education.
(b) to discover the facts and principles related to the field of educational process.
(c) to identify the problem which need to be solved.
(d) to identify the values to be developed in the siudents.

93. Data collected from published books are called
(a) Primary data
(b) Secondary data
(c) Tertiary data
(d) None of the above

94. The teachers research-work in the field of education is useful because
(a) it makes the teachers the better teachers.
(b) it enables the teachers to make good professional decisions.
(c) it raises the teaching-standard of the teachers.
(d) it makes the teachers intelligent.

95. Which of the following does not determine the size of an adequate sample?
(a) The degree of precision desired
(b) The nature of the population
(c) Researcher's insight into sampling
(d) The type of sampling design

96. The sum of the squared deviations of the items from Arithmetic mean is always
(a) One (b) Five
(c) Minimum (d) Zero

97. Which of the following does not belong to the group of the other three?
(a) Sampling validity
(b) Curricular validity
(c) Logical validity
(d) Construct validity

98. The study of related literature does not provide the researcher
(a) knowledge about the researches previously done.
(b) efficiency in research work.
(c) help in identifying the problem.
(d) enough useful knowledge.

99. Which of the following is the best method of defining a problem?
(a) Logical definition
(b) Idealistic definition
(c) Conceptual definition
(d) Operational definition.

100. The IV survey of Educational Research includes the research-works done up to the year
(a) 1998 (b) 1991
(c) 1988 (d) 1983

101. Which of the following is not correct about inventories?
(a) They list items relating to the factor being appraised and request subjects to indicate preferences or check items that describe their typical behaviour.
(b) The responses obtained on the inventories are evaluated to obtain descriptions of certain fundamental predic-positions of the subjects
(c) They are instruments that attempt to "take stock" of one or more aspects of an individual's behaviour rather than to measure in the usual sense
(d) They require subjects to perform at their maximum level

102. A teacher encounters various problems during his professional experiences. He should

(a) take the help of head of the institution.
(b) avoid the problematic situations.
(c) do research on that problem and find a solution.
(d) resign from his post in such situations.

103. With whom is the sociometric technique closely identified?
(a) Henry A. Murray
(b) P.V. Young
(c) Helen Jennings
(d) J.F. Moreno

104. The first Ph.D. degree in India was awarded in the year
(a) 1945 (b) 1943
(c) 1940 (d) 1951

105. A research problem is feasible only when
(a) it has utility and relevance.
(b) it is new and adds something to knowledge.
(c) it is researchable.
(d) All of the above.

106. The Ph.D. degree in Education for the first time in India was awarded by
(a) Madras University
(b) Punjab University
(c) Calcutte University
(d) Bombay University

107. In which study sociometric methods cannot be used with advantage?
(a) Group structure
(b) Social adjustments
(c) Personality
(d) Leadership

108. Which of the following is a positional average?
(a) Harmonic mean
(b) Arithmetic mean
(c) Geometric mean
(d) Median

109. Which of the following is not employed in sociometric studies?
(a) Interviews (b) Observations
(c) Rating scales (d) Questionnaires

110. India from 1941 to 1983 how many Ph.D. degree in Education were awarded by the university?
(a) 2407 (b) 1507
(c) 1423 (d) 1017

111. Which of the following variables is manipulated by the researcher?
(a) Discrete variables
(b) Independent variable
(c) Dependent variable
(d) Continuous variables

112. What does the better "Re" in the word "Research" indicate?
(a) Only depth
(b) Reputation
(c) Frequency
(d) Frequency and depth

113. What is "MAXMINCON"?
(a) A method of statistical analysis
(b) A combination of three key words each pointing out to a separate principle of designing experimental research
(c) A design of experimental research
(d) None of these

114. A researcher wants to study the future of the Congress Party in India. For the study which tool is most appropriate for him?
(a) Schedule (b) Rating scale
(c) Questionnaire (d) Interview

115. What are the characteristics of a good measuring technique?
(a) Reliability (b) Usability
(c) Objectivity (d) All of these

116. What does the word "Search" mean in the word "Research"?

(a) Discovery (b) Investigation
(c) Enquiry (d) Both (b) or (c)

117. Seeing a very big rally it was reported that a party will win the election. The conclusion was based on
(a) purposive sampling
(b) systematic sampling
(c) cluster sampling
(d) random sampling

118. In "Research" only that man can be regarded as successfully who has
(a) explained new relationship based on data collected.
(b) discovered new facts.
(c) presented old facts in a new way.
(d) All of the above.

119. "In general words questionnaire refers to a device for securing answers to questions by using a form which the respondent fills in himself". Who has defined questionnaire in these words?
(a) Goode and Scates
(b) John W Best
(c) Goode and Hatt
(d) Barr, Davis and Johnson

120. If to all the items in a distribution, a value X is added, the arithmetic mean of the new series will be
(a) $\bar{X} + X . N$ (b) $\bar{X} + \Sigma X . N$
(c) $\bar{X} + X$ (d) $\bar{X} + \frac{N}{X}$

121. Which is the technique of investigation involving face-to-face conversation?
(a) Sociometry (b) Observation
(c) Questionnaire (d) Interview

122. "The aim of research is to understand the state of the past and present events." Who has made this statement?
(a) Turney and Roch
(b) Crow and Crow
(c) Turney
(d) Roch

123. In a normal distribution, the distance of one standard deviation above and below the Mean shows the limits of middle
(a) 64.26% of the distribution.
(b) 66.26% of the distribution.
(c) 68.26% of the distribution.
(d) 86.20% of the distribution.

124. The "Intellectual Research" is related to
(a) man's intellectual ability.
(b) man's desire.
(c) man's curiosity.
(d) None of the above.

125. Which techniques are most used in Educational Research?
(a) Observation (b) Sociometry
(c) Questionnaire (d) Interview

126. Why is definition of the research problem necessary?
(a) It limits the study to a particular boundary.
(b) It determines the direction of research.
(c) Both (a) and (b).
(d) None of the above.

127. Which is the best technique of measuring the internal feelings of a student?
(a) Projective technique
(b) Sociometry
(c) Interview
(d) Questionnaire

128. "Practical Research" is related to
(a) man's curiosity.
(b) man's skill.
(c) man's desire.
(d) None of the above.

129. "Statistics is the science of Estimates and Probabilities", is said by
(a) Secrist (b) Croxton
(c) Bowley (d) Boddington

130. The main aim of "Fundamental Research" is to
(a) simplify the facts.
(b) telate natural events to the results of the research.
(c) Both (a) and (b).
(d) None of these.

131. Which is the best measurement of social status?
(a) Interview (b) Sociometry
(c) Questionnaire (d) Observation

132. While writing research report a researcher
(a) must compare his results with those of the other studies.
(b) must arrange it in logical, topical and chronological order.
(c) must not use the numerical figures in numbers in the beginning of sentences.
(d) All of the above.

133. Which is not described by Kerlinger as a method of controlling extraneous variables?
(a) Randomization
(b) Purposive sampling
(c) Matching
(d) Selection

134. The nature of research does not contain the following.
(a) It is based on inter-disciplinary method
(b) It is not based on personal belief or loyalty
(c) It is based on philosophy
(d) It is based on information and assumption

135. The sum of deviations of the items from Median, ignoring the signs is
(a) Zero (b) Maximum
(c) Least (d) None of these

136. The following is not the method of getting knowledge.
(a) Indicative-Deductive method
(b) Discovery method
(c) Authority
(d) Personal Experiences

137. What determines whether a researcher should use .05 or .01 level of significance for testing the hypothesis?
(a) How much risk is involved in incorrect finding
(b) How much precision is required
(c) How important are the findings
(d) All of these

138. Which of the following things is first done before the selection of a problem?
(a) Discussion with experts
(b) Selection of area of study
(c) Both (a) and (b)
(d) None of the above.

139. What determines the choice of statistical test to be used in the analysis of the data of the quantitative research?
(a) Kind of sampling used
(b) Nature of population
(c) The power of test
(d) All of these

140. The following is not the characteristic of a scientific Method.
(a) Sentimental assumption
(b) Systematic thinking
(c) Objectivity
(d) Not to use Hypothesis

141. The difference between the frequency polygon and the histogram is that
(a) the histogram represents cumulative frequencies of measures whereas the frequency polygon represents the percentile ranks of measures.
(b) in a histogram the measures interval are represented by a rectangle whereas in a frequency polygon all the measures are represented by the mid-point of the interval.

(c) the frequency polygon represents the percentile ranks while the histogram represents the measures in an interval in the form of rectangles.
(d) the frequency polygon represents all the measures of an interval while the histogram shows the curve joining all midpoint of an interval.

142. Out of the following facts which of them is not a characteristics of research?
(a) It is Empirical
(b) It is knowledge-oriented
(c) It is systematic
(d) It is controlled

143. What is a research describing developmental changes in personality characteristics by studying the same group at different age levels?
(a) Longitudinal growth study
(b) Developmental study
(c) Cross-sectional growth study
(d) Trend study

144. If the two Regression lines are 3x + 2y – 26 = 0 and 6x + y – 31 = 0; the values of $\bar{x}, \bar{y}$ =
(a) 11, 13 (b) 9, 11
(c) 5, 8 (d) 4, 7

145. What is studying different groups of children of different ages simultaneously and describing their developmental characteristics?
(a) Trend study
(b) Longitudinal growth study
(c) Cross-sectional growth study
(d) Time series study

146. Which of the following characteristics is the main characteristics of an "Experimental Research"?
(a) Generalization
(b) Manipulation of the variables
(c) Randomization
(d) None of the above

147. Statistics does not deal with
(a) Groups (b) Mass data
(c) Aggregates (d) Individuals

148. Which of the following research-type is widely used in laboratory?
(a) Historical Research
(b) Descriptive Research
(c) Fundamental Research
(d) Applied Research

149. What do correctional studies reveal?
(a) How much relationship is there and of what kind between the variables
(b) Which variable is the cause and which is the effect
(c) Whether there is relationship between the variables or not
(d) None of these

150. Educationists attach great importance to 'experience' in education. What would be the correct interpretation of this suggestion?
(a) Appointing experienced teachers
(b) Teaching through activities and experimental methods in the school
(c) Teaching the experiences of great teachers in education
(d) Providing actual life experience in schools as suited to outside life.

151. The case study is the study of a
(a) single individual.
(b) single group.
(c) single unit done intensively to bring out the processes and dynamics underlying its problems and functioning.
(d) single community or family.

152. What is "Action Research"?
(a) Research which is conducted to find immediate solution to a problem in the local setting

(b) Research to find relationship between variables
(c) Research in controlled situation of the laboratory
(d) Research whose aim is to develop a principle

153. Multistage sampling is recommended in large scale surveys because
(a) it may help overcome the problem of non-response.
(b) it is convenient.
(c) it is less time consuming.
(d) All of the above.

154. "Psychological Research" begins with
(a) search for variables.
(b) search for related literature.
(c) any problem.
(d) any hypothesis.

155. What does Descriptive Research include according to Van Dalen?
(a) Inter-relationship studies
(b) Developmental studies
(c) Survey studies
(d) All of these

156. Total error in a research is equal to
(a) $\sqrt{[(\text{sampling error}) + (\text{non-sampling error})]^2}$
(b) sampling error × 100
(c) only sampling error
(d) sampling error + non-sampling error

157. What is the aim of Survey Research?
(a) Comparing the current status of these with some available standards and making suggestions for improving the status
(b) Studying a small sample and drawing inferences about the larger population
(c) Describing the current status of a phenomenon, a group or an institution
(d) All of these

158. If in the psychological research the related literature is not reviewed then what would happen?
(a) It will finish its utility
(b) It will lower its validity
(c) The generalization of its results will be defective
(d) It will lower the reliability of the study

159. The coefficient of variation is always
(a) Average
(b) Ratio
(c) A percentage
(d) None of the above

160. "The learning process accelerates by award". This statement comes in the following category.
(a) Research Results
(b) Research Problem
(c) Research Hypothesis
(d) None of the above

161. Which of the following is not correct about ex-post facto research?
(a) It is possible to exercise much rigorous control in this and obtain highly valid results
(b) It is not possible in this research to assign the subjects to the treatment groups randomly
(c) It provides support for any number of different and sometimes contradictory hypothesis
(d) The dependent variable is measured first, and after that the independent variable or variables are studied

162. By breaking the scale on X or Y axis in a graphical representation we will be creating
(a) Bar diagram (b) Line graph
(c) False base line (d) None of these

163. Which of the following statements is most correct about the difference between Applied and Action Research?
(a) While applied research and action research both are undertaken to solve immediate practical problems, in action research the researcher is the same person as the practitioner who will use the findings of the research
(b) While applied research adds to an organized body of scientific knowledge, action research does not do that
(c) The difference between them is that of nomenclature only; otherwise they are the same
(d) While the findings of applied research have practical implications for educational practices, action research is not concerned with that

164. Suppose a researcher has prepared two groups of 10 years and 20 years old persons to see the effect of an independent variable on dependent variable. In this example what is the category of age?
(a) Dependent Variable
(b) Independent Variable
(c) Type-E in Independent Variable
(d) Type-S in Independent Variable

165. If the data is plotted on a graph and a bell shape is obtained it is an indication of
(a) No skewness (b) No correlation
(c) Skewness (d) None of these

166. What is that variable in a psychological experiment about which prediction is made?
(a) Extraneous Variable
(b) Independent Variable
(c) Dependent Variable
(d) None of these

167. What is the importance of the correlation coefficient?
(a) The fact that it is one of the most valid measures of education
(b) The fact that it is a non-parametric method of statistical analysis
(c) The fact that there is linear relationship between the correlated variables
(d) The fact that it allows one to determine the degree or strength of the association between two variables

168. Cluster method is employed when
(a) lists of all units of populations is not available.
(b) it is easier to form groups of individuals.
(c) Both (a) and (b).
(d) None of the above.

169. Which will be the most appropriate method of statistical analysis if a researcher wants to know how much contribution a JRF test makes to the over-all success of the candidates?
(a) t-test
(b) Product-movement correlation
(c) F-test
(d) Linear regression method

170. The group which contains independent variable is called
(a) Observed Group
(b) Main Group
(c) Control Group
(d) Experimental Group

171. When two or more variables are studied, it is called
(a) Partial correlation
(b) Positive correlation
(c) Linear correlation
(d) None of the above

172. The other name of controlled variable is
(a) Irrelevant Variable
(b) Quantitative Variable

(c) Manipulated Variable
(d) Extraneous Variable

173. What does the validity of psychological test mean?
(a) The test measures what it purports to measure
(b) The test measures certain predetermined values
(c) The test yields scores that are stable
(d) The test measures something consisting

174. In the matter of curriculum teachers should
(a) be quite active participants in its development.
(b) be mainly concerned with the tasks of its implementation.
(c) understand the main objectives of every subject.
(d) understand its historical development to be able to teach.

175. Which is the most objective psychological tool?
(a) Interviews
(b) Thematic Apperception Test
(c) Intelligence Test
(d) Rorschach Test

176. What category would you give to the age of an individual?
(a) Sequence Relevant Variable
(b) Subject Relevant Variable
(c) Situational Relevant Variable
(d) None of these

177. Stagnation in education means that
(a) children do not progress from class year by year.
(b) methods followed for teaching have lost attraction for children.
(c) the curriculum studies have become old and outmoded.
(d) teachers have got no inclination to refresh their knowledge.

178. The number of the members of a family is an example of
(a) Non-Continuous variable
(b) Qualitative Variable
(c) Sequence Continuous Variable
(d) None of these

179. A set of questions asked and filled in by the interviewer in a face-to-face situation with another person is called
(a) a questionnaire.
(b) a schedule.
(c) an opinionnaire.
(d) a checklist.

180. For doing external criticism (for establishing the authenticity of data) a researcher must verify
(a) style of prose writing of that period.
(b) the paper and ink used in that period which is under study.
(c) the signature and handwriting of the author.
(d) All of the above.

181. When is type-I error increased?
(a) When the sample size increases
(b) When alpha-level decreases
(c) When the sample size decreases
(d) When alpha-level increases

182. Quota Sample is a sort of
(a) Mixer of Probability and Non-Probability Sample
(b) Snowball Sample
(c) Random Sample
(d) Non-Probability Sample

183. Sampling is preferred to studying the entire population because
(a) it is possible to control a sample as compared to the entire population.
(b) sample may have the same characteristics as of the population.
(c) Both (a) and (b).
(d) None of the above.

184. When an experimenter rejects a correct Null Hypothesis then it is called
(a) Type-Two Error
(b) Rosanthal Effect
(c) Experimenter's bias
(d) Type-One Error

185. Sampling results into
(a) high precision
(b) greater accuracy
(c) reduced cost, and item
(d) control of extraneous variables

186. Where informants are literate and are spread over a vast area, the most suitable method of collecting data is
(a) interview by investigator.
(b) direct personal interview.
(c) mailed questionnaire method.
(d) All of the above.

187. Which is the most important characteristics of the survey method of research?
(a) It studies characteristics of a group instead of an individual
(b) It relies on a small sample
(c) It focuses on studying the cause effect relationship between variables
(d) It aims at developing some theory or the scientific laws

188. In Uniform Internal Method, the scale value of each unit is the following of the distribution.
(a) Mode
(b) Standard Deviation
(c) Mean
(d) Median

189. If two or more characters are shown in a table it is called
(a) Complex table (b) Variable table
(c) Simple table (d) None of these

190. In the Uniform Interval Method, the prepared scale contains the following numbers.
(a) 50 to 52 (b) 40 to 42
(c) 30 to 32 (d) 20 to 22

191. What consideration a rating procedure involves?
(a) The continuum on which rating is to be done
(b) The persons who will do rating
(c) The trait to be rated
(d) All of the these

192. It is said that in the course of a child's education his feeling and emotions also must be looked after. This aspect of education can be termed as
(a) Affective Education
(b) Congnitive Education
(c) Psychological Education
(d) Value Orientation

193. To which are the concepts of internal external criticisms associated?
(a) Historical research
(b) Literary research
(c) Descriptive research
(d) Validity of experimental designs of research

194. The main defect of Uniform Internal Method is that this method
(a) cannot be used when the number of statements is more.
(b) requires more energy and time in preparing attitude.
(c) has no scientific basis of selecting the statements.
(d) has the subjectivity of the evaluaters.

195. Population differs from sample in which of the following respects?
(a) Sample can never be hypothetical.
(b) Sample is always finite.

(c) Both (a) and (b).
(d) None of the above.

196. Who was the enunciater of "Method of Successive Interval"?
(a) Edwards (b) Likert
(c) Thurstone (d) Guilford

197. It is undesirable on the part of the researcher
(a) getting the full meaning out of the author's ideas and paraphrasing them in his own language.
(b) to present a research report based on investigator's own ideas and written in his own words.
(c) concentrating on written material, eliminating unessential details.
(d) stringing lots of quotations together.

198. The process of grouping of related facts into classes is called
(a) Pie diagram (b) Tabulation
(c) Classification (d) None of the above

199. Which is the purpose of theory building?
(a) Fundamental research
(b) Applied research
(c) Survey research
(d) Action research

200. When the cumulative proportion is 50 then its Normal Deviation will always be
(a) –1 (b) +2
(c) Zero (d) +1

201. A set of vertical bars whose areas are proportional to the frequencies represented is called
(a) Histogram
(b) Pie chart
(c) Frequency polygon
(d) None of the above

202. When the cumulative proportion is more than 0.50 then its Normal Deviation will always be
(a) Zero (b) Perfect
(c) Positive (d) Negative

203. If the findings of a research have practical implications for improving educational patterns, it is called
(a) applied research.
(b) experimental research.
(c) pure research.
(d) descriptive research.

204. The term 'Supervised study' in schools means that
(a) it is curricular subject of study like the social studies.
(b) teachers are required to supervise slow students study after school.
(c) it is a term used by inspectors to supervise low teachers study for their daily work.
(d) students effort in learning is encouraged by teachers with their guidance.

205. On the spot research aimed at the solution of an immediate problem is called
(a) fundamental research.
(b) survey research.
(c) pure research.
(d) action research.

206. For measuring 'Attitude Scale' Likert had enunciated a specific method which is called
(a) Method of Summated Ratings
(b) Scalogram Analysis Method
(c) Uniform Internal Method
(d) Scale Discrimination Technique

207. Sampling technique is based on
(a) Deductive method
(b) Analysis method
(c) Inductive method
(d) None of the about

208. As a social scientist what method would you regard as important for the collection of valid data?

(a) Only Schedule
(b) Only Questionnaire
(c) Both Questionnaire and schedule
(d) None of these

209. Research concerned with the derivation of generalizations of broad applicability and only secondarily with any practical value is called
(a) fundamental research.
(b) applied research.
(c) practical research.
(d) action research.

210. The objective behind population education in schools is to
(a) explain how educational facilities should be improved for our country's population.
(b) make students understand the dangers of the growing of population in our country.
(c) teach about the nature and magnitude of the population of different countries.
(d) give an idea of the size of population of different states in our country.

211. Which of the following is not relevant to analysis of the research problem?
(a) Attending seminars on research methodology
(b) Isolating the variables that are involved in the problem and clarifying their relationships
(c) Proposing various relevant explanations (hypothesis) for the cause of the difficulty
(d) Accumulating the facts that might be related to the problem

212. Who tried to measure attitude on the basis of Social Distance?
(a) Gattman (b) Likert
(c) Thurstone (d) Bogardus

213. Which of the following is an example of negative correlation?
(a) Corruption in India is increasing.
(b) Poor working condition retards output.
(c) An increase in population will lead to a shortage of foodgrains.
(d) Poor intelligence means poor achievement in school.

214. Likert's Attitude scale the number of units is about
(a) 10 to 45 (b) 40 to 45
(c) 20 to 25 (d) 30 to 35

215. To which aspect are related questioning assumptions underlying the problem?
(a) Defining the problem
(b) Identifying the problem
(c) Stating the problem
(d) Analysing the problem

216. Some researches have revealed that the headmasters of schools really do not like the parents to come to school and talk to them. What would be your assumption about this attitude?
(a) They fear that parents come always with complaints against the schools, etc.
(b) They feel it is a waste of time to talk to parents.
(c) They feel inferior to parents and want to avoid them.
(d) They feel it as a disturbance in their work.

217. What does description of the research problem not include?
(a) Theories on which it is based
(b) Assumptions underlying it
(c) Review of research done
(d) Background of the study

218. Usually the form of Individual Test is
(a) Performance
(b) Performance and Oral

(c) Verbal
(d) Non-Verbal

219. An example of scientific knowledge is
(a) laboratory and field experiments.
(b) religious scriptures.
(c) social traditions and customs.
(d) authority of the Prophet or great men.

220. The Arithmetic Test prepared for class III will prove to be this for class X students.
(a) Speed Test (b) Objective Test
(c) Power Test (d) None of these

221. Which of the following is the least helpful to locating and analyzing problems?
(a) Examining everyday experiences
(b) Critical analysis of the existing theories and practices
(c) Discussing with the research guide
(d) Exploring the literature in an area of interest

222. Non-probability sample is used when
(a) researcher wants to get some idea about the population in a very short period of time.
(b) researcher wants to collect information only from informed people.
(c) Both (a) and (b).
(d) None of the above.

223. To find out the relationship between intelligence and achievement after eliminating the effect of motivation, an investigatorshould use
(a) $r_{12.3}$ (b) r_{bis}
(c) $R_{1.23}$ (d) r_{xy}

224. "Raven Progressive Matrices" in this type of test
(a) Non-Lingual (b) Performance
(c) Non-Verbal (d) Verbal

225. The Co-efficient of concurrent deviations from the following data: No. of pairs of observation = 96, No. of pairs of concurrent deviations = 36, will be
(a) 0.577 (b) –0.577
(c) –0.482 (d) 0.482

226. Which of the following objectives items contains the minimum objectivity.
(a) Completion Item
(b) Matching Item
(c) Two alternative Item
(d) Muti alternative Item

227. The correlation between two variables in which the effect of some other variable or variables on their relationship is controlled is called
(a) partial correlation.
(b) contingency coefficient of correlation.
(c) product-moment correlation.
(d) multiple correlation.

228. Direct personal interviews constitute
(a) Primary data
(b) Secondary data
(c) Tertiary data
(d) None of the above

229. What is the nature of the statement that experimental genealizations are statistical inferences; they can only attain a degee of probability somewhere along a continuum between truth and falsity ?
(a) Wholly true
(b) Incorrect entirely
(c) Not wholly true
(d) None of these

230. "The best test has many qualities." Which of the following cannot be its quality?
(a) Validity (b) Self-Correlation
(c) Subjectivity (d) Norms

231. Indirect oral interviews are called
(a) Mock tests (b) Viva Voice
(c) Primary data (d) Secondary data

232. What is the "Lowest Common Denominator" of a psychological test?
(a) Norm (b) Item
(c) Reliability (d) Validity

233. Which of the following is not an advantage of non-parametric statistical tests?
(a) They can be used in situations where parametric tests are applicable
(b) They can be used when data are in the forms of ranks or categories
(c) They are less powerful than the parametric tests
(d) They yield statements of exact probabilities irrespective of the shape of the population distribution

234. In a moderately skewed distribution
(a) $M = 3Z + 2\bar{X}$ (b) $2M = Z + 2\bar{X}$
(c) $3M = Z + 2\bar{X}$ (d) $2M = 2Z + \bar{X}$

235. ANOVA does not assume that
(a) the treatment groups are homogeneous.
(b) the treatment groups are selected at random from the same population.
(c) the treatment groups are drawn from a larger population.
(d) the adjusted scores within groups have normal distibution.

236. If the difficulty level of any item is 90% it means that it is
(a) of medium difficulty.
(b) very easy.
(c) very difficult.
(d) None of these.

237. Which of the following does not belong to the category of non-probability sample?
(a) Purposive sample
(b) Quota sample
(c) Incidental sample
(d) Multi-stage sample.

238. Discriminatory Indicator can be best known by the following method.
(a) A NOVA
(b) Coefficient of concordance
(c) Item sum Correlation
(d) J. Proportion

239. Some activities described as 'research' like some M.Ed., and Ph.D. dissertations should not be so designated because
(a) they just compile information which is already available and hence, do not add to existing knowledge.
(b) the infonnation they collect is of no value.
(c) the research they conduct cannot be classified into any standard type of research.
(d) they just describe something and do not explain anything.

240. A moving average is calculated by using
(a) Median (b) Mode
(c) Mean (d) None of these

241. What is not correct about research?
(a) Research may involve venturing into areas of thought about which little is known
(b) Research is begun because someone has asked a question and it has to answer it
(c) Research is needed if the aim is to increase the extent of knowledge or to make it more complex
(d) Research has to be planned and conducted because it is a scientific way of gathering information

242. Reliability is the quality of
(a) Test-examiner (b) Test
(c) Test-scores (d) None of these

243. Middle quartile is known as
(a) Mode (b) Median
(c) Geometric mean (d) Harmonic mean

244. When two variables have much relationship their correlation coefficient is
(a) Around .20 and –.20
(b) Around –1.00
(c) Around +1.00
(d) Around +1.00 and –1.00

245. What should be done for constructing and standardizing a psychological test?
(a) Should not be considered a research because it does not test any hypothesis
(b) Should not be considered a research because it is a small-scale activity
(c) Should be considered a valuable piece of research because a lot of labour and energy have gone into it
(d) Should be considered a research of value because the test so developed can be used later by others

246. Given the following distribution

X	F
0-10	4
10-20	6
20-30	5
30-40	10
40-50	20
50-60	22
60-70	24
70-80	6
80-90	2
90-100	1

The model class in the distribution is
(a) 40-50 (b) 50-60
(c) 50-60 and 60-70 (d) 60-70

247. What is the modern method of acquiring knowledge?
(a) Personal experience
(b) Authority
(c) Expert opinion
(d) Scientific method

248. Predictive Validity is a sort of
(a) Construct Validity
(b) Content Validity
(c) Criteria Validity
(d) None of these

249. Froebel, the well-known child educationist was a
(a) psychologist of the progressive education movement.
(b) realist from the United Kingdom.
(c) german educationist with poor education.
(d) french psychologist.

250. What does 2-score indicate?
(a) Distance in Quarterlie unit
(b) Distance of score from the Median
(c) Distance of score from the Median in the unit of standard deviation
(d) None of these

251. Deductively reasoning out the consequences of the suggested solutions is an aspect of thinking involved in the
(a) personal experience as a method acquiring knowledge.
(b) scientific method of acquiring knowledge.
(c) older methods of acquiring knowledge.
(d) psychological methods of acquiring knowledge.

252. Which of the following methods of study will need a very small sample?
(a) Field Experiment (b) Surveys
(c) Clinical studies (d) All of the above

253. What is not the goal of scientific method of acquiring knowledge?
(a) Fact-finding (b) Prediction
(c) Explanation (d) Control

254. Standard score's median is always
(a) +1 (b) –1
(c) +2.58 (d) Zero

255. The following cannot be located with the help of an ogive
(a) Decile (b) Median
(c) Mode (d) Quartile

256. According to Speraman and Brown, which of the following equations is correct?
(a) Whole test reliability = 2 + 1 – Reliability ofhalf test /2x Reliabilities of half test
(b) Whole test reliability = 1 + 2x Reliability ofhalf test /2x Reliabilities of half test
(c) Whole test reliability = 1 + Reliability of half test /2x Reliabilities of half test
(d) Whole test reliability= 1 – Reliability of half test/2x Reliabilities of half test

257. Theory, as an aspect of research, does not
(a) serve as a goal providing explanation for specific phenomena with maximal probability and exactitude.
(b) discard facts, specific and concrete observations.
(c) serve as a tool for providing a guiding framework for observation and discovery.
(d) describe the facts and relationships that exist.

258. Find the odd one out:
(a) Decile (b) Deviation
(c) Percentile (d) Quartile

259. "Theory" helps the researcher in
(a) understanding the technical terms used in research.
(b) determining how to make or record observations.
(c) understanding the research procedure.
(d) identifying the facts needed to be considered in the context of the research problem.

260. Which of the following statements is false?
(a) The applied research for human welfare is more useful than the pure research
(b) Cause-effect relationship is always verified in scientific research
(c) More efforts are made in the development of principles in psychology because they do not properly interpret the events
(d) Scientific research is regarded more as a method of problem-solving and less in the form of knowledge

261. Introspection is a method of educational psychology which helps us to collect data about the
(a) structural aspects of a subject.
(b) conscious experiences of a subject.
(c) unstructural aspects of a subject.
(d) unconscious experiences of a subject.

262. The scientific method has some qualities. Which of the following is regarded as its quality?
(a) This method involves replication
(b) This method has a controlled situation
(c) This method has involved generalization of its results
(d) All of these

263. What type of statistical data are used in educational research?
(a) Inferential statistical analysis
(b) Descriptive statistical analysis
(c) Both of them
(d) None of these

264. The observational method in all social situations
(a) requires experimental facilities to observe large groups at a time.
(b) involves considerable training in the method of observation.
(c) can be adopted in the case of adult 'literate persons only'.
(d) is the easiest to be adopted by teachers who observe children every time.

265. What are the functions of statistical analysis?
   (a) Presentation of data
   (b) Explanation of results
   (c) Both of them
   (d) None of these

266. "Replication" is needed in psychological researches for
   (a) increasing the external validity of the present research.
   (b) increasing the validity and reliability of the previous researches.
   (c) verifying the results of previous researches or raising some questions about them.
   (d) increasing the internal validity of the present research.

267. Which of the following methods of writing hypothesis is correct?
   (a) They are formulated before defining the problem.
   (b) They are always written in directional form.
   (c) They are formulated before the collection of data.
   (d) None of the above.

268. Descriptive research has many characteristics which of the following is not its characteristic?
   (a) Finding the correlation between variables
   (b) Manipulating the variables to their effect
   (c) Analysis and description of present events
   (d) Shows the contradiction in the comparison of the relations of variables

269. Which tests are used in explanation of results?
   (a) Non-parametric tests
   (b) Parametric tests
   (c) Both of them
   (d) None of these

270. Nine years old children are taller than 7 years old ones. It is an example of
   (a) cross-sectional studies
   (b) vertical studies
   (c) case studies
   (d) experimental studies

271. Which types of correlation are used in educational research?
   (a) Partial correlation
   (b) Multiple cumulative correlation
   (c) Co-efficient correlation
   (d) All of these

272. Which of the following is not the limitation of laboratory experimental research?
   (a) It cannot study all types of variables
   (b) Some situations can not be created in this research
   (c) Its situations is artificial
   (d) It lacks internal validity

273. The measure which divides a distribution in ten equal parts is known as
   (a) Decile (b) Quartile
   (c) Deviation (d) Percentile

274. Which of the following is not in the category of non-experimental research?
   (a) Case Study
   (b) Survey Research
   (c) Field Study
   (d) Field Experiment

275. What is the meaning of Null Hypothesis?
   (a) The difference is due to error in sampling
   (b) Difference between two parametric mean is zero
   (c) Both of them
   (d) None of these

276. If both the variables are varying in the same direction it is called
(a) Negative correlation
(b) Positive correlation
(c) Multiple correlation
(d) None of the above

277. In t-test when separate samples are selected in two groups in one population or in two populations, the test used is
(a) one-tailed test.
(b) analysis of variance.
(c) two-tailed test.
(d) All of these.

278. Which of the following is not in the category of the experimental research?
(a) Field Study
(b) Laboratory Experiment Research
(c) Field Experiment Research
(d) All of these

279. In a research, conclusions are drawn
(a) after verifying the results
(b) after testing the hypothesis
(c) before testing the hypothesis
(d) None of the above

280. If a psychologist in the classroom uses some specific principles to find a solution to a student's psychological problem then his research will be called as
(a) Applied Research
(b) Action Research
(c) Educational Research
(d) Fundamental Research

281. When the achievement and degeneration of one group is to be tested in t-test, the test used is
(a) one-tailed test.
(b) analysis of Variance.
(c) two-tailed test.
(d) All of these.

282. $\bar{X} = X(3M - Z)$, Then X is
(a) 2 (b) 1
(c) 3 (d) 1/2

283. In case of ANOVA what is the variance caused by treatment?
(a) SS_A (b) SS_w
(c) SS_{AXB} (d) SS_T

284. In psychological researches, the research design has certain definite objective. Which of the following is regarded as the most unsuitable objective?
(a) The design provides best opportunity for proper statistical analysis
(b) The design increases the experimental variance and decreases error variances
(c) It possibly answers in a specific way the problems of the research
(d) Design works as a control mechanism

285. Epistemology is a field which is concerned with
(a) the social aspects of knowledge to be imparted in schools.
(b) goals of knowledge to be achieved through mental processes.
(c) the practical considerations as aims of education.
(d) the real nature of knowledge and its achievement.

286. A pigion was trained to pick at a point where the green light was on and not to pick when the red was on. After it gave a right response it was given food. Out of the following which one is dependent variable?
(a) Intensity of the light
(b) Reward (food)
(c) Colour of the light (red or green)
(d) Number of picks

287. In case of ANOVA, what is SS_W?
(a) The variance caused by the difference within the subjects
(b) Total variance between the groups

(c) The variance caused by the treatments
(d) The variance caused by the extraneous factors

288. Logic of induction is very close to the logic of
(a) the controlled variable
(b) observation
(c) sampling
(d) None of the above

289. Which is not correct about non-parametric test of significance?
(a) They make strong assumptions of homogeneity of variance qf the groups to be compared
(b) They compare population distributions rather than the parameters
(c) They are small-sample tests
(d) They are distribution free tests

290. Suppose a social psychologist conduct an experiment to observe the feeling of discomfort in men and women when six persons collect in a telephone booth.

Which of the following is an independent variable in this experiment?
(a) Basis of telephone-booth
(b) Number of persons in the booth
(c) Sex of the persons
(d) Experience of discomfort

291. Hypothesis cannot be stated in
(a) general terms
(b) directional terms
(c) null and question form terms
(d) declarative terms

292. In any experiment the main reason of 'Null Result' is
(a) lack of enough control on extraneous variables.
(b) unreliability of dependent variable.
(c) unreliability of the independent variable.
(d) any deficit in the controlled variable.

293. When the questions are presented to the respondents in a face-to-face situation, and the interviewer rather than the subjects, fills out the query, it is called
(a) a schedule.
(b) an inventory.
(c) a test.
(d) a questionnaire.

294. All are example of qualitative variables except
(a) interest of the subject
(b) sex
(c) religion and castes
(d) observation

295. An unguided interview of psycho-analytical nature permitting the subject to talk freely with a view to obtain insight into hidden motives is called
(a) a directive interview.
(b) a focussed interview.
(c) a structured interview.
(d) a non-directive depth interview.

296. Which of the following differences is most appropriate in null hypothesis and null results?
(a) Null hypothesis shows zero difference while null result is zero-result event
(b) Null hypothesis is an assumption while null result is an observation
(c) Null hypothesis indicates the independent variable will affect the dependent variable while null result indicates that dependent variable is unaffected by the independent variable
(d) Null hypothesis is an assumed condition while null result is the condition obtained

297. All of the following purposes are served by hypothesis except they
(a) help to relate theory to observation and vice versa.

(b) help to determine the sample.
(c) determine the direction of research.
(d) None of the above.

298. What is not the reason underlying the importance of research in education?
(a) It is a potent means of creating new knowledge
(b) It is a tool for verifying, testing and validating knowledge
(c) It provides answers to many problems faced by educators
(d) It has moved to the centre of the bahavioural sciences

299. Independent variable is divided into different categories according to the forms of variables. Which of the following is not such a category?
(a) Environment Variable
(b) Quantitative Variable
(c) Task Variable
(d) Subject Variable

300. To study the distribution of wealth and income
(a) Lorenz curve is used
(b) Only capitalistic theory is used
(c) Standard deviation is used
(d) Only Marxian theory is used

301. A variable which is determined by counting the value is called
(a) Continuous Variable
(b) Discrete Variable
(c) Qualitative Variable
(d) Qualitative Variable

302. What is not essential about a research problem?
(a) It should lead to new knowledge
(b) It should be amenable to research
(c) It should lead to theory building
(d) It should be significant

303. In a symmetrical distribution the interval between mean & median and the mean & mode is equal to
(a) 1/2 (b) 3/4
(c) 1/3 (d) 2/3

304. The age of an individual is an example of
(a) Discrete Variable
(b) Continuous Variable
(c) Qualitative Variable
(d) None of these

305. If $\beta_2 > 3$ the curve is called
(a) platykurtic
(b) mesokurtic
(c) positively skewed
(d) teptokurtic

306. Which of the following is a primary source of data?
(a) Personal records, letters, diaries, autobiographies, wills, etc.
(b) Oral testimony of traditions and customs.
(c) Official records—governments documents, information preserved by social and religious organizations, etc.
(d) All of the above.

307. In a given distribution $\bar{X} = 20$, ♦ = 16, the coefficient of variation is
(a) 80% (b) 4%
(c) 320% (d) 36%

308. Any psychological problem can be regarded as solvable when
(a) its formal test is possible.
(b) it possesses the quality of systematization.
(c) its empirical test is possible.
(d) its objective observation is possible.

309. Which of the following is an important characteristics of hypothesis?
(a) They should be limited in scope
(b) They should be testable
(c) They should express relationship between variables
(d) All of the above.

310. The main difference between research problem and research hypothesis is

(a) research problem is not testable in itself while research hypothesis is a testable statement.
(b) research problem is a beginning point of research while research hypothesis is a middle point of research.
(c) research problem indicates the problem while research hypothesis shows how the problem can be solved.
(d) research problem is an introgative statement while research hypothesis is a declarative statement.

311. Q.D. equals
(a) 1s (b) Zero
(c) 1/3s (d) 2/3s

312. Some thinkers rightly feel that under the guise of the feeling of nationalism there is the fear of
(a) hiding our prides and weaknesses and giving too much importance to a few virtues.
(b) self praise and feelings of indifference, increasing among people.
(c) developing over-confidence in our work and neglecting the progress process of improvement.
(d) developing feeling of pride and selfishness among people.

313. Mean deviation equals
(a) 4/5s (b) 1/3s
(c) 5/6Q.D. (d) 1/5Q.D.

314. The hypothesis which psychologist wants to test are called
(a) Research Hypothesis
(b) Statistical Hypothesis
(c) Universal Hypothesis
(d) Eistential Hypothesis

315. Educational technology is a process that is concerned with
(a) equipping the technical institutions for better methods of instructions.
(b) improving the schools through implementation of science and technological subjects.
(c) explaining the progress of technology through education.
(d) using the modern methods of technologies in teaching and learning in schools.

316. Which of Lite following is not the characteristics of a good research hypothesis?
(a) It should be have consensus with other hypothesis of related field
(b) It should be based on relation of variable
(c) It should be economic
(d) It should be testable

317. In a normal distribution, 100 per cent of observations are covered by the following
(a) 3s (b) s
(c) 3.09s (d) 2s

318. In a positive skewed distribution
(a) $Z > M > \bar{X}$ (b) $M > Z > \bar{X}$
(c) $Z = M = \bar{X}$ (d) $Z < M < \bar{X}$

319. In a moderately skewed distribution = 100, V = 35 and j (coefficient of skewness) = 0.2, the value of mode is
(a) 93 (b) 103
(c) 35 (d) 67

320. In psychological researches, there are many functions of the hypothesis. Which of the following is not such a function?
(a) To describe an event
(b) To verify the facts previously obtained
(c) To test the principles
(d) To enunciate new principles

321. Hypothesis is related to all of the following except
(a) Research objectives
(b) Sample

(c) Research tools
(d) None of the above

322. In psychological experiments, there are many methods of controlling extraneous variables. Which of the following is not an adequate method?
(a) Randomization (b) Constantly
(c) Elimination (d) Balancing

323. Karl Pearson's coefficient of skewness of a distribution is 0.4. Its mean is 30. The value of mediun will be
(a) 34.15 (b) 25.63
(c) 28.93 (d) 31.25

324. The number of times a value is repeated is called
(a) Sample
(b) Class interval
(c) Frequency
(d) None of the above

325. What can Statistics do?
(a) Disprove anything
(b) Neither prove nor disprove anything is just a tool
(c) Prove anything
(d) None of these

326. Which of the following cannot be regarded as pre-experimental design?
(a) Static group comparison design
(b) Counter balancing design
(c) One shot case-study design
(d) One group protest-postest design

327. Which of the following is the most unstable average?
(a) Geometric mean (b) Mode
(c) Arithmetic mean (d) Median

328. The sample which is easily available for an experiment is called as
(a) Incidental Sample
(b) Quota Sample
(c) Random Sample
(d) Stratified Sample

329. Who said, Statistics has been defined as "The Science of Counting"?
(a) R.A. Fisher (b) Stephen King
(c) Galton (d) Bowley

330. The lowest and the highest values that can be included in a class are called
(a) Class limit
(b) Frequency table
(c) Class interval
(d) None of the above

331. On what is placed reliance in most investigations?
(a) Primary data
(b) Secondary data
(c) Both primary and secondary data
(d) None of these

332. Research design has some criteria on the basis of which it is tested. Which of the following is not a best criteria?
(a) Generalization
(b) Potentiality of increasing the reliability
(c) Potentiality of the solution of research problem
(d) Control of extraneous variable

333. Review of the related literature helps the researcher to
(a) determine the limits of his field of research.
(b) avoid duplication.
(c) find the gap between different facts.
(d) All of the above.

334. What design is regarded best for use in singh subject research?
(a) Multiple treatment design
(b) Factorial design
(c) A-B-A design or reveral design
(d) Multiple baseline design

335. What should be the number of questions in a questionnaire?
(a) As small as possible keeping in view the purpose of the survey

(b) 20
(c) 15
(d) 5

336. The ends of a class interval are called
(a) Frequency distribution
(b) Class limits
(c) Class marks
(d) None of the above

337. What is the reliability of primary data?
(a) Depends on the care with which data have been collected
(b) Always more reliable compared to secondary data
(c) Depends on the agency collecting the data
(d) Less reliable compared to secondary data

338. When the objective of an experiment is not only to study the effect of independent variable on dependent variable but also on the dependent variable, then for this condition the best suited research design is the following.
(a) Factorial Design
(b) Posttest only/Equivalent groups Design
(c) Counter Balance Design
(d) Equivalent time Design

339. "Statistics may be called the science of counting", is said by
(a) Bowley (b) Karl Marx
(c) Cowden (d) Pearson

340. What is Hawthrone effect?
(a) It is an effect in which the subject do not know for which experiment they are being used
(b) It is an effect in which the experimentator unconsciously affects the results of the experiment
(c) It is an effect which facilitates control over extraneous variable
(d) It is a situations in which the subjects are affected with the feelings of their being interesting

341. The only thing to be seen before using secondary data is that they are
(a) adequate for the purpose in hand.
(b) representative.
(c) reliable.
(d) All of these.

342. Given the following series, the value of mode is

5, 6, 3, 2, 8, 4, 7, 9, 1, 10, 11, 12, 13
(a) 12 (b) 13
(c) 9 (d) not defined

343. Which average is affected most by extreme observations?
(a) Arithmetic mean
(b) Median
(c) Geometric mean
(d) Mode

344. A statement which indicates that the stated relationship between the variables will be correct in all places and every time is called as
(a) Existential Hypothesis
(b) Statistical Hypothesis
(c) Universal Hypothesis
(d) None of these

345. While taking deviations the signs are ignored in
(a) Mean deviation
(b) Quartile deviation
(c) Range
(d) All of the above

346. When a statement indicates that there is no difference in the mean scores of one pair of participating groups on dependent variable then this statement will be called as
(a) Research Hypothesis
(b) Existential Hypothesis

(c) Null Hypothesis
(d) Partial Null Hypothesis

347. Mode is
(a) most frequent value.
(b) represents majority out of total frequency.
(c) middle most value.
(d) least frequent value.

348. Which of the following is an elaborated form of the title?
(a) Hypothesis
(b) Objectives
(c) Statement of problem
(d) None of the above

349. Which of the following are positional averages?
(a) Geometric mean
(b) Harmonic mean
(c) Median
(d) Arithmetic mean

350. The experiment whose aim is to identify the difficulties of the main experiment, is called as
(a) Confirmatory Experiment
(b) Pilot Experiment
(c) Crucial Experiment
(d) Exploratory Experiment

351. If the variables are varying in the opposite directions, it is called
(a) Linear correlation
(b) Positive correlation
(c) Negative correlation
(d) None of the above

352. What is External Validity?
(a) The method of control of extraneous variables
(b) The internal control technique of the experiment
(c) The adequacy of the design of the experiment
(d) That extent to which the results of the experiment related to behaviour in natural environment are adequate

353. An average should be used to typify
(a) a distribution showing a clear, single concentration of observations.
(b) V-shaped distribution.
(c) multimodel distribution.
(d) a biodal distribution.

354. The first step for making a statistical investigation is
(a) Collection of data
(b) Samples
(c) Organisation
(d) None of the above

355. The sum of absolute deviations of items is minimum from
(a) geometric mean.
(b) median.
(c) harmonic mean.
(d) mode.

356. When the null hypothesis is continuous but the experimentator fails to reject it then it is called as
(a) One Tailed Test
(b) Two Tailed Test
(c) Type One Error
(d) Type Two Error

357. An average should be used to typify
(a) a distribution showing a clear, single concentration of observations.
(b) U-shaped distribution.
(c) multimodal distribution.
(d) a biodal distribution.

358. What does confounding in psychological researches mean?
(a) A situation in which the effect of all 4-5 on DV is indrect
(b) A situation in which the effect of c.ily extraneous variables on DV is observed

(c) Situation in which the experimentator fails to remove 4 or DV and the difference of effects on other similar variables
(d) A situation in which 4 and DV interact with each other

359. Which of the following statement is correct?
(a) A.m. > G.m. > H.m.
(b) A.m. < G.m. < H.m.
(c) G.m. > A.m. < H.m.
(d) A.m. > G.m. < H.m.

360. Evaluation of the research proposal is necessary because it
(a) can determine the competence of the researcher.
(b) can determine the method and procedure of research.
(c) determines the significance of the study.
(d) All of the above.

361. The value of mean, mediun and mode coincide in case of
(a) negatively skewed distribution.
(b) symmetrical distribution.
(c) positively skewed distribution.
(d) All of these.

362. What is cross over interaction?
(a) When the effects of one 4 and the other 4 on dependent variable are opposite eachf other
(b) When 4 and extraneous variable together affect the dependent variable
(c) Joint effect of two 4s
(d) When the dependent variable's effectt contradictory

363. Herbert Spencer favoured Pestalozzi's learning theory as a process of
(a) Internal self-instruction
(b) Programmed instructional material
(c) Serving the cause of nation
(d) Self-activity

364. That variable which is measured and recorded by the experimentator is
(a) Extraneous Variable
(b) Dependent Variable
(c) Independent Variable
(d) None of these

365. Which of the following is the most unstable average?
(a) Mode
(b) Geometric mean
(c) Median
(d) Arithmetic mean

366. Which average is affected most by extreme observations?
(a) Arithmetic mean (b) Mode
(c) Geometric mean (d) Median

367. Step deviation method to estimate arithmetic mean can be applied only when
(a) it is a discrete series.
(b) it is an individual series we are examining.
(c) deviations are divisible by a common factor.
(d) it is continuous series.

368. When the independent variable uniformly affects all the levels of the other variable then it is called as
(a) Hawthorne Effect
(b) Rosenthal Effect
(c) Main Effect
(d) Interaction Effect

369. Graphically, mode can be estimated from
(a) Histogram (b) Historigram
(c) Ogive (d) Bar diagram

370. An experimental result obtained when on DV the effect of level of an independent variable is different from that of the other independent variable then it is called
(a) Interaction Effect
(b) Main Effect

(c) Hawthorn Effect
(d) Recency Effect

371. The average age of 10 students in a class is 17 years. If one of them who is 26 years old leaves the school, the average age will be
(a) 16 years (b) 15 years
(c) 18 years (d) 17 years

372. Given below is the Charlier's check of accuracy of computation of arithmetic mean *f*(dx + 1) = S*f*dx + x
(a) S*f*dx (b) *f*(Sdx)
(c) S*f* (d) S*f*dx

373. The research proposals sent to research institutes for financial assistance must have
(a) definite objectives of research.
(b) the whole plan and procedure.
(c) budget requirements and time schedule.
(d) None of the above.

374. In the series given below

Marks	No. of students
More than	50
10	46
20	40
30	26
40	10
50	3

The number of students securing upto 40 marks is
(a) 30 (b) 46
(c) 20 (d) 40

375. The scaling method which indicates the relation between psychological feelings and physical stimuli is called
(a) Direct Scaling
(b) Psychological Scaling
(c) Multidimensional Scaling
(d) Psychological Scaling

376. The mean age of 40 students is 16 years and the mean age of another group of 60 students is 20 years. The mean age of all the 100 students is
(a) 18.4 years (b) 18.8 years
(c) 18 years (d) 16.8 years

377. In a Psychological Scale
(a) physical and psychological both qualities are measured.
(b) the relationships between psychological and physical qualities are analyses.
(c) psychological qualities are measured.
(d) physical qualities are measured.

378. If from all the items in a distribution, a value X is subtracted, the arithmetic mean of the new series will be
(a) $\bar{X} + \frac{N}{X}$ (b) $\bar{X} - X.N$
(c) $\bar{X} + \bar{X} + \frac{X}{N}$ (d) $\bar{X}.X$

379. Graph of frequency distribution is called
(a) Histogram
(b) Frequency polygon
(c) Curve
(d) None of the above

380. The average weight of a group of 25 boys was calculated to be 78.4 lbs. It was later discovered that the weight of one boy was misread as 69 lbs instead of 96 lb. The correct average is
(a) 79.48 (b) 79.84
(c) 79.00 (d) 78.48

381. Who enunciated the "Law of Comparative Judgement"?
(a) Edwards (b) Bogardes
(c) Thurstone (d) Likert

382. Given below is the Charlie's check of accuracy of computation of arithmetic mean. $\Sigma f(dx + 1) = \Sigma fdx + X$
The letter x stands for

(a) $\Sigma f(dx)$ (b) Σfdx
(c) Σf (d) $f(\Sigma dx)$

383. In the Thurstone's terminology an individual's reaction to a stimulus is called
(a) Discriminal Dispersion
(b) Discriminal Process
(c) Model Discriminal Process
(d) None of these

384. In the formula given below

$$X \frac{\bar{X}_1 N_1 X N_2 \ \ldots \bar{X}_N N_N}{N_1 \ \ N_2 \ \ldots \ N_N}$$

X stands for
(a) X_2 (b) X_2
(c) r (d) s

385. Selection of research tool depends on the nature of
(a) sample selected
(b) hypothesis
(c) Both (a) and (b)
(d) None of the above

386. The mean age of 40 students is 16 years and the mean age of another group of 60 students is 20 years. The mean age of all the 100 students is
(a) 18.4 years (b) 18.8 years
(c) 18 years (d) 16.8 years

387. For preparing an "Attitude Scale" Likert constructed a specific scale which is called
(a) Method of Stimulated Ratings
(b) Scalegram Analysis
(c) Equal Appearing Interval
(d) Method of Successive Interval

388. An auto-ride costs Rs. 5 for the first 1.6 km and Re. 0.50 per each additional 100 metres. The cost for each distance unit is incurred at the beginning of the unit, so that the rider pays for the whole unit. The average cost for a 8 km ride is
(a) Rs. 4.54 (b) Rs. 4.75
(c) Rs. 5.25 (d) Rs. 4.62

389. In Thurstone's Method of equal appearing interval" the evaluators have to select each unit in
(a) any one category out of 7-point categories.
(b) any one category out of 5-point categories.
(c) any one category out of 11-point categories.
(d) any one category out of 9-point categories.

390. An auto-ride costs ₹ 5 for the first 1.6 km and ₹ 0.50 per additional 100-metres. The cost for each distance unit is incurred at the beginning of the unit, so that the rider pays for the whole unit. The average cost for a 8 km ride is
(a) ₹ 4.62 (b) ₹ 4.54
(c) ₹ 5.25 (d) ₹ 4.75

391. With which of the following propositions about research you do not agree?
(a) Research contributes to social progress of the country.
(b) Research improves the quality of teaching.
(c) Research is a joy in itself.
(d) Research leads to finding solution to many problems of the society.

392. The arithmetic mean of the direct 100 natural, numbers is
(a) 50.5 (b) 60.1
(c) 25.7 (d) 55.2

393. In Thurstone's method some assumptions are made which is the main hypothesis out of the following.
(a) The evaluator's own attitude does not affect the selection of the statements in different categories
(b) The evaluator's own attitude affects the selection or sorting work very much

(c) The evaluator's own attitude generally affects the selection of the statements in different categories
(d) The psychological distance of different intervals is equal

394. Median is
(a) middle most value
(b) least frequent value
(c) most frequent value
(d) centre of gravity

395. In the "Equal appearing interval", it indicates the disagreement of the evaluators about each unit.
(a) Average Deviation
(b) Variance
(c) Quartile
(d) Standard Deviation

396. The sum of deviations taken from actual arithmetic mean is
(a) Positive (b) Infinite
(c) Zero (d) Negative

397. Classification of quantitative data into categories is not needed when
(a) experimental studies are conducted.
(b) the group is highly homogenous.
(c) tool is faulty and defective.
(d) None of the above.

398. In the given series 71, 72, 64, 68, 70, 76, 73, 75, the median is
(a) 72 (b) 72.5
(c) 71 (d) 71.5

399. When the evaluators do not agree with one another about the scaling value of any statement then in this situation the deviation's.
(a) Median is greater
(b) Quartile is greater
(c) Standard Deviation is greater
(d) Both quartile and S.D. are greater

400. The experimental study is based on the law of
(a) occupation
(b) interest of the subject
(c) single variable
(d) replication

401. Which is mdoern method of research?
(a) Authority
(b) Case Study
(c) Discussion
(d) Scientific Method

402. Thurstone in his "Equal appearing interval" method for 130 statements used a definite number of evaluators which became a standard. Although later on some psychologists used the evaluators in less or more number than Thurstone.
(a) 250 (b) 300
(c) 450 (d) 350

403. Given the following distribution

X	F
0-20	0
20-40	5
40-60	22
60-80	25
80-100	16

The value of median is
(a) 65.0 (b) 66.6
(c) 60.5 (d) 65.6

404. In the given series
71, 72, 64, 68, 70, 76, 73, 75
The median is
(a) 71 (b) 72
(c) 71.5 (d) 72.5

405. The difference between a personality inventory and an intelligence test is
(a) of style.
(b) of foreign make.

(c) of length.
(d) of right and wrong answers.

406. What is the "Criteria of Relevance"?
(a) In it the subjects have to express their agreement or disagreement with the statements of definite scaling value
(b) A criteria determined by the judges on which the validity of the statements is tested
(c) It is a criteria which tests favourableness and unfavourableness of the evaluator towards each statement
(d) The constructor of a scale prepares an objective criteria which tests the reliability of each individual

407. In a positively skewed distribution the value of mode is
(a) Same (b) Zero
(c) Maximum (d) Minimum

408. In the "Equal appearing Interval Method" if a subject expresses his agreement with certain statement and also with the similar statement but having different scaling value then such statement is
(a) Reliable and valid
(b) Meaningless
(c) Proper and relevant statement
(d) Improper and Irrelevant statement

409. Which of the following is not related to increasing the sensivity of the t-test?
(a) Increasing the reliability of measures
(b) Reducing the level of noise
(c) Increasing the sample size
(d) All of these

410. Which of the following is not an approach of analysis of qualitative data?
(a) Inductive analysis
(b) Logical analysis
(c) Criterion analysis
(d) Content analysis

411. When a researcher conducts an experiment he or she wants to be sure that any differences between the conrol and experiment groups are due to
(a) differences among the subjects.
(b) the operational definition.
(c) the hypothesis.
(d) the experimental manipulation.

412. "Equal appearing method" has this special advantage over "Method of poired comparison".
(a) It has more objectivity
(b) Its scale has more reliability and validity
(c) Its use is efficient inspite of large number of units
(d) Its use takes less time

413. If $\overline{x} = 18$, $\overline{y} = 100$, $\sigma x = 14$, $\sigma y = 20$, $r = 0.8$. Regression line of y on x =
(a) Y = 1.134x + 72.92
(b) Y = 1.341x + 74.29
(c) Y = 1.341x + 72.49
(d) Y = 1.143x + 79.42

414. What defect of "Equal appearing interval Method" was removed by "Method of successive Interval"?
(a) Low validity
(b) The effect of Evaluator's personal attitudes
(c) Less scienticity of different intervals
(d) None of them

415. In an experiment, the dependent variable
(a) is the aspect of the expriment that is controlled and manipulated by the expreimenter.
(b) represents the effect and is measured by the experimenter.
(c) is an extraneous variable.
(d) provides a standard on which group differences can be measured.

416. The one method which satisfies the factor reversal test under the price index method is
   (a) Fisher's Ideal Method
   (b) Paasche's Method
   (c) Laspeyres Method
   (d) None of the above

417. By substracting the lowest score from the highest score, researchers are able to deter mine the
   (a) mode.
   (b) range of scores.
   (c) standard deviations.
   (d) median score.

418. How is "Cumulative Proportion" is found by the method of "Successive Intervals"?
   (a) By multiplying cumulative frequency by N
   (b) By dividing cumulative frequency by N
   (c) By dividing cumulative frequency by reciprocal of N
   (d) By multiplying cumulative frequency by reciprocal of N

419. Positional Average is called
   (a) Chart table (b) Mean
   (c) Median (d) Mode

420. How many categories are there of Attitude Statements in the "Simmulated Rating Method"?
   (a) –7 (b) –11
   (c) –5 (d) –9

421. Stephen M. Corey is associated with
   (a) pure research.
   (b) action research.
   (c) scientific research.
   (d) applied research.

422. Which of the following will provide qualitative data?
   (a) Non-structured interview
   (b) Observation
   (c) Open end questionnaire
   (d) All of the above

423. The scope of educational research is very vast. The problems included are
   (a) Educational (b) Sociological
   (c) Philosophical (d) All of these

424. Which of the following is given the highest positive weight in Likert's Method?
   (a) Strongly disagree (b) Disagree
   (c) Strongly agree (d) Agree

425. The average weight of a group of 25 boys was calculated to be 78.4 lbs. It was later discovered that the weight of one boy was misread as 69 lbs. instead of 96 lbs. The correct average is
   (a) 79.48 (b) 79.00
   (c) 78.48 (d) 79.84

426. In the Likert's Method the scoring sequence for totally disagree, disagree indefinite, agree and totally agree response categories for suitable units will be as follows:
   (a) 1, 2, 3, 4 and 5 (b) 2, 3, 4, 1 and 5
   (c) 5, 4, 3, 2 and 1 (d) 5, 1, 4, 3 and 2

427. Most of the beginners in research suffer from
   (a) too many problems.
   (b) lack of training to tend a problem.
   (c) problem blindness.
   (d) None of these.

428. The process not needed in experimental researches is
   (a) reference collection
   (b) controlling
   (c) observation
   (d) manipulation and replication

429. How many sources of educational research have been identified by or admitted by Good, Barr and Scates?
   (a) Five (b) Seven
   (c) Three (d) Four

430. In the Likert's method "High Scale" indicates an individual's
(a) Neutral Attitude
(b) Favorable Attitude
(c) Unfavorable Attitude
(d) None of these

431. The average age of 10 students in a class is 17 years. If one of them who is 26 years old leaves the school, the average age will be
(a) 15 years (b) 16 years
(c) 17 years (d) 18 years

432. If a psychologist wants to know the ideas of respondents in less time then he will prefer the following method.
(a) Case-Study (b) Projective Test
(c) Schedule (d) Questionaire

433. Delimitation of a problem means
(a) why of research.
(b) drawing a boundary round it.
(c) what of research.
(d) how many of research.

434. Qualitative data are preferred when
(a) a researcher wants to study the attitudes and values of the population.
(b) it is not possible to collect quantitative data.
(c) a researcher wants to study a problem more comprehensively.
(d) All of the above.

435. "Hypothesis, is a tentative information or provisional guess which seems and explains the situation under observation. Who defined hypothesis as this?
(a) Lokesh Kaul
(b) John W. Best
(c) K.S. Sidhu.
(d) James E. Greetan

436. What task needs our most attention while preparing an interview-schedule?
(a) Pre-testing of questions
(b) Specifying the procedure relating to the use of a questionaire
(c) Construction of questions
(d) Re-examination and revision of questions

437. The value of mean, median and mode coincide in case of
(a) positively skewed distribution.
(b) symmetrical distribution.
(c) negatively skewed distribution.
(d) All of the above.

438. Which of the following defects is the main defect of a interview-schedule?
(a) The presence of the interviewer embarrasses the interviewer in answering the questions
(b) It takes much time to administer it
(c) Its administration needs a trained and experienced interviewer
(d) Its administration needs more expenses

439. Null, Prediction, Declaration, Question are
(a) types of hypothesis.
(b) variations.
(c) forms of hypothesis.
(d) None of these.

440. In the series given below

Marks	No. of students
more than 0	50
10	46
20	40
30	26
40	10
50	3

The number of students securing upto 40 marks is
(a) 40 (b) 26
(c) 46 (d) 20

441. A research hypothesis is generally converted into null hypothesis.

(a) It is a general statement
(b) It is safer
(c) It is a vague statement
(d) It cannot be tested statistically

442. Which of the following facts is not the quality of a schedule?
(a) It requires "face to face" situation for its use
(b) It includes questions of different forms-fixed closed items and open ended items
(c) It is a list of questions
(d) The respondent reads each question and answers it

443. Step deviation method to estimate arithmetic mean can be applied only when
(a) it is an individual series we are examining.
(b) deviations are divisible by a common factor.
(c) it is a discrete series.
(d) it is continuous series.

444. The interview in which an interviewer asks the respondent some standardized questions in a definite sequence is called as
(a) Focussed Interview
(b) Selection Interview
(c) Structured Interview
(d) Unstructured Interview

445. Explain F Ratio.
(a) A ratio between mean SS_T and mean SS_A.
(b) A ratio between mean SS_A and mean SS_W.
(c) A ratio between mean SS_T and mean SS_W.
(d) A ratio which is always more than 1.0.

446. Index of topics and sub topics is prepared in which of the following stages?
(a) Interpretation stage
(b) Data organizing stage
(c) Conclusion stage
(d) Data analysis stage.

447. In the list of shortcoming of Educational Research in India presented in the 4th survey, which of the following was not included?
(a) Inadequate understanding of research process
(b) Absence of clear educational perspective
(c) Absence of reliability and validity of research
(d) Absence of conceptual framework

448. The questionnaire used in "Structure Interview" is called as
(a) Observation Schedule
(b) Interview Schedule
(c) Interview Questionnaire
(d) None of these

449. The mean monthly salary paid to all employees of a company is Rs. 5000. The mean monthly salary paid to male and female employees is Rs. 5,250 and Rs. 4,000 respectively. The percentage of females in total employees is
(a) 20 per cent (b) 40 per cent
(c) 60 per cent (d) 10 per cent

450. The interview schedule has many characteristics which of the following is not a characteristic of interview schedule?
(a) It contains only the standardized questions
(b) It contains only fixed or closed questions
(c) Its questions are in a definite sequence
(d) It is conducted only in the presence of the interviewer

451. What is the main purpose of survey of related studies?
   (a) To know methods of attack
   (b) To avoid duplication
   (c) Insight into methods
   (d) To know what is already known

452. The sum of deviations taken from actual arithmetic mean is
   (a) Infinite (b) Negative
   (c) Zero (d) Positive

453. Which is the don't in survey of related literature?
   (a) In taking notes, be as brief as possible
   (b) Turn the summary of the journal or the article
   (c) Be accurate
   (d) Do not hurry

454. Which of the following scaling techniques is modeled on undiversanality?
   (a) Guttman Scale (b) Bogards Scale
   (c) Likert Scale (d) Thurstone Scale

455. The formula for the calculation of the Mode is
   (a) Mode = 4 Mdn. – 3 Mean
   (b) Mode = 3 Mean – 2 Median
   (c) Mode = 2 Mdn. – 2 Mean
   (d) Mode = 3 Mdn. – 2 Mean

456. Which of the following "Reproducibility Coefficients" according to Guttman cannot be included in the category of "Reproducible Scale"?
   (a) 98 (b) 88
   (c) 95 (d) 93

457. The method of research may be selected on the basis of
   (a) type of control.
   (b) source of data.
   (c) purpose of research.
   (d) All of these.

458. The purpose of content analysis is to
   (a) give a systematic description of data.
   (b) express data quantitatively.
   (c) express data objectively.
   (d) All of the above.

459. Data means
   (a) Observationss (b) Marks obtained
   (c) Facts (d) Truths

460. Who tried to measure attitude on the basis of "Social Distance"?
   (a) Guttman (b) Likert
   (c) Thurstone (d) Bogardus

461. In the formula given below

$$\bar{X} = \frac{\bar{X}_1 N_1 + \bar{X}_2 N_2 + ... + \bar{X}_N N_N}{N_1 + N_2 + ... + N_N}$$

X stands for
   (a) $\bar{X}_2$ (b) σ
   (c) r (d) X_2

462. The highest category of the "Attitude Scale" developed by Bogardus indicates
   (a) very much favorable effect.
   (b) very much unfavorable effect.
   (c) very much social closeness.
   (d) less social closeness.

463. What is the basis of collection of data?
   (a) Flexibility (b) Clarity
   (c) Stability (d) All of these

464. Which one is not a primary data?
   (a) Material from Govt. Records
   (b) Direct personal interview
   (c) Mailed questionnaire
   (d) None of the above.

465. Level of significance means
   (a) probability of accepting null hypothesis.
   (b) probability of accepting the research hypothesis.
   (c) probability of rejecting research hypothesis.
   (d) probability of rejecting small hypothesis.

466. What is the 5th category on Bogardus Scale?
(a) To give employment in my occupation
(b) To citizenship in my country
(c) To my street as neighbour
(d) To visitors in my country

467. The entrance tests for admission to educational institutes is intended to
(a) find out whether the candidates remember what they have learnt in their first degree.
(b) test the scholastic abilities of the candidates.
(c) know whether they can quickly guide and decide about their desire to work as teachers.
(d) boost minority representation.

468. If you are asked to measure attitude towards a Paskistan individual what scale would you like to work with?
(a) Bogardus Scale (b) Thurstone Scale
(c) Likert Scale (d) Guttman Scale

469. What is population?
(a) Males and Females
(b) Only the choosen ones
(c) Totality of objects or individuals
(d) All of these

470. The Root-Mean square deviation is also called
(a) Quartile deviation
(b) Mean deviation
(c) Standard deviation
(d) None of the above

471. A sample represents
(a) Crowd (b) Population
(c) Audience (d) None of these

472. If there is an unfavorable item in the Likert's method and its reaction is written as totally disagree neutral agree and totally agree then its respective scores will be
(a) 3, 2, 4, 5 and 1 (b) 1, 5, 4, 3 and 2
(c) 5, 4, 3, 2 and 1 (d) 1, 2, 3, 4 and 5

473. Variables and categories are specified in
(a) the third stage of content analysis.
(b) the first stage of content analysis.
(c) the second stage of content analysis.
(d) None of the above.

474. In Likert Method, a specific process is adopted for final selection of the units which is called as
(a) Cluster Analysis
(b) Content Anafysis
(c) Item Analysis
(d) Scalogram Analysis

475. Why should we select a sample?
(a) Economy of time
(b) Not possible to study total population
(c) Economy of money
(d) All of these

476. In a positively skewed distribution the value of mean is
(a) Minimum (b) –1
(c) Maximum (d) Zero

477. What is the disadvantage of sampling?
(a) Suitable in limited resources
(b) Better scrutiny of data
(c) Greater speed
(d) Chances of bias

478. The main difference in Likert Method and Thurstone Method is
(a) in Thurstone Method, the units or items are tested by the "Criteria of Irrelevance", but no such criteria exists.
(b) Thurstone Method is more complex while Likert Method is much simple.
(c) In Likert Method, the number of reactions is 5 while in Thurstone method this number is 11.

(d) Likert Method the selection of units is based on a scientific method of unit-analysis while in Thurstone Method no such scientific criteria exists for selection of units.

479. The per capita income of India increased four times from 1950 to 2000. This study is
   (a) Longitudinal (b) Social
   (c) Factorial (d) Horizontal

480. What is main defect of Likert Method?
   (a) It has less validity
   (b) It has also less reliability
   (c) The meaning of scores of 'Neutrality' in Likert method are not clear
   (d) "Item Analysis" in Likert Method is complex process

481. What is the advantage of random sample?
   (a) It is free from bias and prejudice
   (b) It is free of errors in classification
   (c) If the units are widely dispersed, the selection of sample becomes impossible
   (d) It is simple to use

482. Picking up small variable units and making a general prediction upon their study is called
   (a) Census (b) Sample
   (c) Secondary data (d) Primary data

483. Reliability in a test refers to
   (a) consistency in results.
   (b) objectivity in administering and scoring.
   (c) adequacy of standardization.
   (d) None of the above.

484. The psychologists have prepared a scale for measuring attitude which is the mixture of the method of thurstone Likert and Gutthman. The name of this scale is
   (a) Scale discrimination technique
   (b) Cumulative scaling
   (c) Method of absolute scaling
   (d) Quasi scales

485. Data analysis is guided by
   (a) the number of categories into which data has been classified.
   (b) statistical technique available.
   (c) hypothesis formulated.
   (d) All of the above.

486. Thurstone has inundated both the methods equal appearing interval and successive interval. Both these methods have similarities besides dissimilarities. What is the main similarity which is scientific?
   (a) Both methods divide the statements in known intervals
   (b) Both methods have more numbers of statements
   (c) Both methods are enunciated by the same person
   (d) Both methods have its mid to point Neutrality

487. What is an ideal sample in term of numbers?
   (a) 4,000 (b) million
   (c) 10 (d) 1,000

488. Which of the following statement is correct?
   (a) G.m. > A.m. < H.m.
   (b) A.m. > G.m. < H.m.
   (c) A.m. < G.m. < H.m.
   (d) A.m. > G.m. > H.m.

489. Which of the following does not determine the size of a sample?
   (a) Type of sampling design
   (b) Nature of population
   (c) Knowledge of sampling
   (d) The degree of precision

490. In the Likert method whether the items are favourable or unfavorable a definite score is meant for the neutral point and this score is

(a) 2 (b) 3
(c) 4 (d) 5

491. Which of the following is the weighted Aggregative Index (indices)?
(a) Laspeyres Index (b) Fisher's Index
(c) Paasche's Index (d) All of the above

492. The objective of "critarion of irrelevance" in thurstone's scale is
(a) to find out undimensionality of statements.
(b) to find out reproducibility of statements.
(c) to find out internal consistency of statements.
(d) item analysis of statements.

493. Who said that "the problem is a proposed question for solution"?
(a) J.C. Almak
(b) John C. Torensand
(c) John W. Best
(d) Fred N. Kurlinger

494. A symmetrical distribution is one where
(a) Mean = Mode
(b) Mean = Median
(c) Median = Mode
(d) Mean = Median = Mode

495. Who said that the problem is an interrogative sentence or description in which correlation is found out between two or more variables?
(a) George J. Mouley
(b) J.C. Almak
(c) John C. Torensand
(d) Fred N. Kurlinger

496. The psychologists test means
(a) a test which tests a person's intelligence.
(b) a test which tests a person psychologically.
(c) a standard technique which measures the sample's behavioural in an objective and standardized way.
(d) a standard technique which tests a person's intelligence and his personality.

497. The study of history is useful to us in which of the following ways?
(a) To predict future on the basis of the trends available.
(b) To avoide the mistakes of our forefathers.
(c) To take the benefit of past experiences.
(d) All of the above.

498. The psychologists test in which the specialists agree with the scores of its units is called as
(a) Subjectivity Test
(b) Power Test
(c) Objective Test
(d) Standardized Test

499. Who said that there are four criteria sources for identifying the problem of educational research?
(a) George J. Mouley
(b) J.C. Almak
(c) Fred N. Kurlinger
(d) John C. Torensand

500. Cumulative frequency curve is known as
(a) Histogram
(b) Frequency polygon
(c) Historigram
(d) Ogive

501. How many sources of Educational Research have been admitted by Goode, Barr and Scates?
(a) Six (b) Seven
(c) Four (d) Five

502. The test in which the time limit is related for the units to answer so that most of the

examinees may answers correctly is called as

(a) Essay Test (b) Objective Test
(c) Power test (d) Speed Test

503. Combination of Laspeyres and Paasche's Method is
(a) Aggregate Method
(b) Simple average of price relatives method
(c) Fishers Ideal Index
(d) None of the above

504. What is the adequate difference between non-verbal intelligence test and performance intelligence test?
(a) In non-verbal test instruction is given by proto-mine while in performance test instruction is given orally
(b) In non-verbal test figures are used in the units while concrete objects are used in performance test
(c) Less use of written words and sentences in non-verbal test while no such use in the performance test
(d) Actual manipulation in the units is not possible in non-verbal test while it is possible in performance test

505. The meaning of defining a problem is that it should be widely and properly determined. Who said this?
(a) George J. Mouley
(b) J.C. Almak
(c) W.S. Monroe
(d) F.L. Whitney

506. In the following data:

X	10	11	12	13	14	15	16
F	2	7	11	15	10	4	1

arithmetic mean is
(a) 12 (b) 13.2
(c) 12.8 (d) 13.0

507. What are the types of Educational Research Problems?
(a) Historical (b) Theoretical
(c) Applied (d) All of these

508. There is difference between teacher-made test and standardized test. Which of the following facts is not regarded as a difference?
(a) The former has definite norms while in the latter no definite norm is there
(b) In the former teachers conduct the test and write their scores while in the latter test publishers determine the rules for scoring
(c) The former has specific objectives while the latter has general objectives
(d) The evaluation in the former is done by teacher while in the latter this is done by evaluation-experts

509. System analysis in curriculum development applies
(a) Survey researches
(b) Historical researches
(c) Both (a) and (b)
(d) None of the above

510. In the multiple choice items one option is correct answer and the other options are partially correct which is called as
(a) Inappropriate Answer
(b) Distractor
(c) Wrong Option
(d) None of these

511. Which of the following cannot be considered a quality of good hypothesis?
(a) Plausibility (b) Verifiability
(c) Clarity (d) Modifiability

512. In a positively skewed distribution the value of
(a) mode is maximum
(b) mean and mode are same
(c) mean is maximum
(d) None of the above

513. What is the name of an unknown variable that correlates with the independent variable and explains the outcome of the experiment in the same way as the specified independent variable does?
(a) An extraneous variable
(b) A controlled variable
(c) An implicit variable
(d) A confounded variable

514. Which of the following statements is false?
(a) In essay-test, the thinking and writing are important while in objective test reading and thinking is important
(b) In essay-test, the quality of items depends on the skill of scoring while in objective test the quality of items depends on the skill of test constructor
(c) In essay-test, the examinee writes his answer in his own words while in objective test the examinee selects the correct option
(d) In essay-test, the experts agree to a great extent while in objective test they agree to a less extent

515. Individual Extreme values cannot influence
(a) Average (b) Mean
(c) Median (d) None of these

516. Which of the following suggestions would you prefer for writing a good test-item?
(a) The item writer should be conversant with technical aspects of item-writing
(b) The item writer should have knowledge of subject matter
(c) The item writer should keep in his mind the ability of the examinee
(d) All of these

517. Why is it essential to convert the research hypothesis into null hypothesis?
(a) It is a very general statement and does not indicate the specified direction of research
(b) Because it does not express the relationship existing between the dependent and the independent variable
(c) It is not a scientific statement
(d) It cannot be tested statistically

518. The average weekly wage of a group of 50 workers was Rs. 400. It was later discovered that two entries were misread as Rs. 230 and Rs. 140 instead of Rs. 320 and Rs. 410. The correct average is
(a) Rs. 395.6 (b) Rs. 409.7
(c) Rs. 409.3 (d) Rs. 407.2

519. The first Ph.D. in education in India was awarded by
(a) Bombay University
(b) Madras University
(c) Punjab University
(d) Calcutta University

520. The main objective of item-analysis is
(a) to make the language of the item more effective.
(b) to make the language items easy.
(c) to give informaticn about the difficulty-level of items and discrimination index.
(d) to make the items more meaningful.

521. Findings of historical researches can be criticized on which of the following grounds?
(a) The investigator cannot manipulate the source of information.
(b) The investigator's dependence on secondary sources of data.
(c) The investigator does not have control over treatment of data.
(d) All of the above.

522. The test-development has some systematic steps. Identify the correct sequence which construct an item
(a) Planning, preliminary administration, item validity reliability and constructing of norm-mannual

(b) Planning, item-writing, preliminary administration, reliability and construction of norm-mannual
(c) Planning, item writing, reliability, validity, preliminary administration and preparation of norm-manual
(d) Planning, item-writing, preliminary administration, relability, validity and norm-manual

523. Who has called sample an element of facts?
(a) John W. Best
(b) W.G. Kokaran
(c) W.S. Travers
(d) George J. Mouley

524. In any research one should
(a) not try out anything blindly but wait until a sudden flash appears in his mind.
(b) know everything in the area without bothering to learn the details if any.
(c) know more and more about less and less in certain specific sub areas.
(d) None of the above.

525. What is the advantage of selecting sample?
(a) Economy of money
(b) Knowledge of more truth
(c) Economy of time
(d) All of these

526. What is an identification item?
(a) That item whose correct answers are evaluated subjectively
(b) That item whose correct answer is to given in a fixed time
(c) It is an item whose correct answer is to be selected by the examinee
(d) That item whose correct answer is given by the examinee himself

527. Attributes of objects, events or things which can be measured are called
(a) Qualitative measure
(b) Variables
(c) Data
(d) None of the above

528. What is the meaning of "Difficulty level of Item"?
(a) Percentage of that number which is obtained by subtracting number of failures from the number or successful examinees
(b) The number of examinees who could not answer the item
(c) Percentage of successful examinees for the item
(d) Percentage of failing examiners for the item

529. What are the characteristics of good sample?
(a) Flexibility (b) Clarity
(c) Stability (d) All of these

530. Which of the following is used to study the public opinion?
(a) Direct interviews
(b) Judgement sampling
(c) Quota sampling
(d) Random sampling

531. What are the main methods of selecting samples?
(a) Stratified sample
(b) Multiple sample
(c) Systematic sample
(d) All of these

532. What should be the difficulty level of a good item?
(a) 20 (b) 70
(c) 50 (d) 80

533. Which of the following is the best approach of writing historical findings?
(a) Expository
(b) Descriptive
(c) Narrative
(d) A combination of all

534. A test containing items of difficulty level 4 to 6 is called as
(a) Dichotomous Test
(b) Power Test
(c) Peaked Test
(d) None of these

535. Which of the following is not true about hypothesis?
(a) They provide direction to research and prevent review of irrelevant literature and collection of useless data
(b) They prejudice the researcher in favour of certain results
(c) They act as a framework for stating the conclusions
(d) They enable the researcher to clarify the procedure and methods to be used in the research

536. The mean of 5 observations is 4.4 and the variance is 8.24. If the first three observations are 1, 2, 6, the last two observations will be
(a) 8, 7 (b) 3, 5
(c) 9, 4 (d) 4, 2

537. The view that a hypothesis is never proved; but merely sustained or rejected only tentatively, is
(a) a wrong assumption about hypothesis.
(b) a misconception.
(c) a correct and valid statement.
(d) a fact not accepted by all.

538. What is discriminating index?
(a) Characteristics of an item which check the guess work of the examinees
(b) The potentiality of an item to identify those examinees who could not answer it because they did not know its correct answer
(c) The potentiality of the item which can discriminate between the best and the low achiever examinees
(d) The potentiality of the item to show how much percentage of examinees agreed with that item

539. All causes non sampling errors except
(a) defect in data collection
(b) non response
(c) inadequate sample
(d) faulty tools of measurement

540. There are many methods of finding out 'Discrimination Index'. In one method the discrimination index is determined by selecting 27% examinees from above the score of the examinees and 27% from below this score. This method was enunciated by
(a) Lord (b) Hales
(c) Guilford (d) Kelly

541. Which of the following is not true about hypothesis?
(a) They are statements consisting of elements expressed in an orderly system relationships
(b) They are known facts discovered by the researcher from the forest of knowledge
(c) They are the eyes of the researcher through which he looks into the disorder that is a problem and sees the possibilities of order
(d) They are intelligent guesses that offer possible solutions to problems

542. If the Regression Equation of y on x is: $y = 1.143x + 79.42$, and if the values of x is given at 70. The value of y will be
(a) 159.43 (b) 160.43
(c) 160 (d) 149.63

543. Which of the following statement is wrong about the data of the Descriptive Research?
(a) It may be qualitative, in verbal symbols
(b) It is only qualitative, never quantitative

(c) It may be qualitative and quantitative both
(d) It may be quantitative, in mathematical symbols

544. When on any item more upper group examinees are successful and less examinees from the lowest group are successful then it is called
(a) Zero discrimination
(b) No discrimination
(c) Positive discrimination
(d) Negative discrimination

545. Restricting the study to a particular age or region is called
(a) analysing the problem
(b) delimiting the problem
(c) defining the problem
(d) None of the above

546. Sometimes the successful candidates on an item from the lower is more than that of upper group then the discrimination in the item is
(a) Zero
(b) No discrimination
(c) Positive
(d) Negative

547. Which of the following methods should be used for establishing reliability of the questionnaire?
(a) Split-half method
(b) Rational equivalent method
(c) Test-retest method
(d) Parallel form method

548. The co-efficient value is always a
(a) Average
(b) Ratio
(c) Percentage
(d) None of the above

549. Which of the following statements is applicable to the unstructured interview?
(a) It is most appropriate for getting insight into a particular situation in the early stages of investigation
(b) It is less flexible than the structured interview
(c) It is one that operates on the basis of an interview schedule
(d) It is not suited to getting varied responses

550. Which of the following information is not detained by the item's difficulty level and discrimination index?
(a) Whether the item distractors are working properly or not
(b) Whether any item is working properly or not
(c) The item is difficult or easy
(d) Whether the item is discriminating between good and bad students or not

551. Boarding schools are considered to be better than the day schools because they
(a) save the trouble for children to walk to school from homes.
(b) help children in their social development.
(c) are meant for homeless and parentless children.
(d) are helpful in freeing parents from their responsibilities.

552. If any item is administered on 200 students out of which 50 students answered correctly or 150 students gave wrong answer. In such situation the difficulty level of that item is
(a) .25 (b) .30
(c) .45 (d) .50

553. Which of the following is not the strength of the unstructured interview?
(a) Its usefulness in probing into attitudes and motives of which even the respondent may not be aware

(b) Its flexibility
(c) Its simplicity
(d) Its getting below the level of cliche's in the instance

554. Field study is related to
(a) Laboratory situations
(b) Experimental situations
(c) Real life situations
(d) None of the above

555. Observing the behaviours, customs and ways of living of the group by way of becoming a regular member of the group, is known as
(a) participant observation.
(b) direct observation.
(c) natural observation.
(d) non-participant observation.

556. If the optimal level of discriminatory index of an item is +1 which is obtained when the difficulty level of the item is
(a) 1.0 (b) .50
(c) .30 (d) .85

557. Which of the following is secondary source of data?
(a) Will and deeds
(b) Relics
(c) Novels written in the past
(d) None of the above

558. Generally, the high discrimination index of a test indicates its good quality but it is regarded as adequate only when it is
(a) 2.0 (b) .80
(c) .30 (d) .60

559. Identifying a factor to be measured by placing units or categories on a scale to differentiate varying degrees of that factor and describing these units in some manner is known as
(a) a test. (b) a rating scale.
(c) a checklist. (d) a schedule.

560. Independent variables are not manipulated in
(a) Normative researches
(b) Ex-post facto researches
(c) Both (a) and (b)
(d) None of the above

561. If a researcher conducts a research on finding out which administrative style contributes more to institutional effectiveness, it is an example of
(a) applied research.
(b) fundamental research.
(c) action research.
(d) basic research.

562. If there are such items in a test which measure different abilities then their discrimination index is a bit distorted and becomes low. The solution to this problem is
(a) some items be added in the items of the test and their D.I. be found out.
(b) such items be removed from the test.
(c) the item of a test be devided into no generous unit and its discrimination index be found out.
(d) the discrimination index of such items be found out separately.

563. If $\bar{x}$ = 36, $\bar{y}$ = 85, σx = 11, σy = 8, r = 0.66. The Regression line of x upon y will be
(a) X = 0.2709y – 41.13
(b) X = 0.9075y – 41.13
(c) X = 0.9072y – 43.11
(d) X = 0.7590y – 41.31

564. The good distractors in the multiple choice items is that which
(a) is selected as correct answer by more students of the higher group than those of the lower group.
(b) is selected by the equal number of students from each group.

(c) resembles the correct answer but they are not as such.
(d) is selected as correct answer by more students of lower group than those of the higher group.

565. What is the variance calculated by averaging the squared deviations of the group from the grand mean and dividing it by the degrees of freedom?
(a) SS_A (b) SS_T
(c) SS_w (d) None of these

566. Internal criticism is done to verify the
(a) authenticity of the source.
(b) accuracy of the source.
(c) Both (a) and (b).
(d) None of the above.

567. Who developed method of equal appearing intervals forming the basis of constructing attitude scales?
(a) Bogardus
(b) Likert
(c) Guttman
(d) Thurstone and Chave

568. The coefficient obtained by test-retest method is called
(a) Contengency coefficient
(b) Internal consistency coefficient
(c) Temporal stability coefficient
(d) None of these

569. The progressive education movement that started in the beginning of this country, emphasizes the
(a) individualistic approach to education.
(b) socialistic approach to education.
(c) moralistic attitude of behaviour.
(d) problem solving attitude of mind.

570. Which of the following facts is not required for finding reliability by test-retest method?
(a) The interval between two administrations of a test should be of at least 14 days
(b) Possibility of finding correlation between two distributions
(c) Minimum two groups of students
(d) Administration of one test on a group two times

571. What is an attitude scale with five points on it varying from strongly approved to strongly disapproved?
(a) Guttman type
(b) Bogardus type
(c) Thurstone type
(d) Likert type

572. If $\Sigma xy = 025$, $\Sigma x^2 = 100$, $\Sigma y^2 = 25$; then $r =$
(a) 0.4 (b) 0.25
(c) 0.5 (d) 0.24

573. What is an attitude scale in which each item's value is calculated by finding out the mean or median of the ratings of a large number of judges on an eleven-point rating scale?
(a) Bogardus type
(b) Likert type
(c) Guttman type
(d) Thurstone type

574. Which of the following facts is not required for finding out reliability by internal consistency method?
(a) Possibility of dividing the units of a test into two equal parts
(b) When the reliability of the test is to be obtained in the last time
(c) Administration of test on the group atleast two times
(d) Homogenity characteristics in the item of a test

575. Women employees reported a mean weight of 148 pounds. Men employees reported a mean weight of 162 pounds. The mean weight of both groups together is 155 pounds. The proportion of women employees in the total is

(a) 40 per cent (b) 70 per cent
(c) 60 per cent (d) 50 per cent

576. Which of the following methods is the most popular method of finding reliability?
(a) Flanagan Formula
(b) Kuder-Richadrson Formula
(c) Split Half Reliability Method
(d) Rulon Formula

577. Which of the following situations calls for the use of a ratio-scale?
(a) He wishes to state that the attitude of one person 'X' is more favourable than that of 'Y'
(b) He wants to show that 'X' is twice as much in favour of nationalization as 'Y'
(c) A researcher waits to assert that the two persons X and V differ in their attitudes towards nationalization of education
(d) He wishes to make a statement that as compared to Y, 'X' is much more in favour of nationalization than he is, as compared to 'Z'

578. An important criterion to judge the success of a lesson by a teacher in the class would be, to see whether the
(a) teacher encourages questions and answers in the class.
(b) lesson is completed in time.
(c) students listen to the teacher clearly.
(d) teacher maintains discipline in the class.

579. What is the scale on which the distance between scale positions are equal?
(a) Interval scale (b) Ratio scale
(c) Ordinal scale (d) Nominal scale

580. The formula used in "Split half formula method" of finding Reliability is
(a) Spearman-Brown Properly Formula
(b) Flangan Formula
(c) Kudar Richardson Formula
(d) Rulon Formula

581. If a researcher notices a gap in his historical studies, he should
(a) give all possible explanations of the gap.
(b) point out the gap.
(c) Both (a) and (b).
(d) None of the above.

582. "The Reliability of Test-scores" means
(a) internal consistency with the test.
(b) self-correlation of test.
(c) correlation of test with external criterion.
(d) None of these.

583. Which of the following is an example of the criterion-reference test?
(a) The test is such as the score on it reveals how much an individual has acquired in some specific area of learning as judged against some external criterion
(b) The test is such as the score on it reveals what the position of an individuals is in the group on which it has been standardized
(c) The test is such as its reliabilities and validities have been established extensively
(d) The test is such as its norms have been prepared on a sufficiently large sample

584. If the ratio of change between two variables is same then it is called
(a) Linear correlation
(b) Non-linear correlation
(c) Both (a) and (b)
(d) None of the above

585. Which is the characteristic of a norm-reference test?
(a) It has items which cluster around a few well-specified objectives

(b) It is objective-referenced or domain referenced
(c) It reveals where a particular individual stands in the group in regatd to the trait being measured by the test
(d) It tells to what extent instructional objectives have been achieved

586. Which of the following is the logical or technical meaning of reliability?
(a) The ratio of true variance in the obtained variance
(b) The ratio of error-variance in the obtained variance
(c) Consistency of scores
(d) Self-correlation of scores

587. Researches have revealed the following distinction between the average and the talented students the
(a) average students work with a genuine zeal even when there is no modernisation.
(b) average students are less boring than the talented students.
(c) talented students work with a zeal if they are given motivation.
(d) talented students are more grade conscious.

588. Which of the following is not the characteristic of random error?
(a) Random error in also called error of measurement
(b) A definite part of each score is a random error
(c) Random error pulls the score in one direction
(d) Random error pulls the score in both positive and negative sides

589. Qualitative analysis is not, at all, used in
(a) ethnographical research.
(b) descriptive research.
(c) historical research.
(d) experimental research.

590. If Median = 4400, M.D. = 571.4, Coefficient of Mean Deviation is
(a) 0.027 (b) 0.045
(c) 0.054 (d) 0.123

591. Which of the following indicates that it is a parameter, not a statistics?
(a) n (b) s
(c) X (d) S

592. Which of the following facts cannot be included in the method of finding reliability?
(a) Fuder Rechardson Formula
(b) Item-total Correlation Method
(c) Test-Retest Method
(d) Split-half Method

593. Which of the following studies is used for prediction?
(a) Trend analysis
(b) Correlation studies
(c) Both (a) and (b)
(d) None of the above

594. What is discriminant validity?
(a) When the test is not correlated with expected referents
(b) When the items of the test have much differences
(c) When the test is correlated with expected refrents
(d) When the test can discriminate between the expected criteria

595. Which of the following statements is correct?
(a) (mew) is used for the mean of the total population
(b) N is used for the number of cases or subjects in the sample
(c) S is used for the standard deviation of the population
(d) s is used for standard deviation of a sample

596. If $Q_3 = 40$, $Q_1 = 20$, Co-efficient of QD will be
(a) 0.222 (b) 0.44
(c) 0.111 (d) 0.333

597. What should we do, if we want to reduce both the type-I and type II errors?
(a) Increase the size of the sample
(b) Increase the level of significance
(c) Reduce the size of the sample
(d) Decrease the level of significance

598. What is sampling validity?
(a) The extent to which the test indicates that the items represents the intended content area
(b) The extent to which the test indicates that the items do not represent the intended content area
(c) It is the extent to which the test finds it represents the content area
(d) The extent to which the test can discriminate between the good sample and inferior sample

599. The most important area of schools supervision should be
(a) Instructional work
(b) School environment
(c) Pupil growth
(d) Developmental aspects

600. If the two forms of a test are administered at different times then the coefficient obtained is called as
(a) Equivalence Coefficient
(b) Stability Coefficient
(c) Internal Test Coefficient
(d) Stability and Equivalence Coefficient

601. The level of significance (alpha) gives the probability of
(a) correctly rejecting H_0.
(b) mistakenly or falsely accepting H_0.
(c) correctly accepting H_0.
(d) mistakenly or falsely rejecting H_0.

602. A good hypothesis should be
(a) precise, specific and consistent with most known facts.
(b) of limited scope and should not have global significance.
(c) formulated in such a way that it can be tested by the data.
(d) All of the above.

603. $(r-1) \times (k-1)$ gives the degrees of freedom of
(a) Chi-square value in case of chi-square test.
(b) SS_T incase of ANOVA.
(c) t-value in case of uncorrelated samples test.
(d) SS_{AXB} in case of factorial design of experiment.

604. One of the assumptions of Classical Test Theory is that an individual's test-scores are made up two factors. These two factors are
(a) Error Score and Standard Score
(b) True Score and T Score
(c) True Score and Error Score
(d) True Score and Means Score

605. Which of the following researches provides information about status quo of a phenomenon?
(a) Case studies
(b) Survey studies
(c) Follow up studies
(d) All of the above

606. The two forms of a test are regarded equivalent only when
(a) the inter-item correlation of both the forms is equal.
(b) the means of both the forms are equal.
(c) the variance of both the forms are equal.
(d) All of these.

607. Given the scores of 50 students on a test of intelligence and only the information who of them gets which category, i.e. I, II, III divisions and fall in the annual examination, which method of statistical analysis may reveal whether intelligence is related to achievement or not?
(a) Chi-square
(b) t-test
(c) Rho (r), i.e. Ran Order Correlation
(d) Median test

608. Where 'X' stands for raw scores and 'F' for frequency, formula for calculating the Arithmetic Mean for scores in a frequency institution would be
(a) FX^2-1/N (b) FX/N
(c) x^2/N (d) FX^2/N

609. What method should be used if a researcher wants to know how different levels of an independent variable affect the dependent variable at different levels of another independent variables?
(a) Multiple correlation method
(b) Factorial analysis of variance method
(c) Two-way analysis of variance
(d) Analysis of covariance method

610. The equivalent form reliability measures the following of the test-scores
(a) Temporal Consistency
(b) Interval Consistency
(c) Both (a) and (b)
(d) None of them

611. The amount of change in one variable does not bear a constant ratio to the amount of change in other variable. It is called
(a) Partial correlation
(b) Linear correlation
(c) Non-linear correlation
(d) None of the above

612. If the length of a test is increased by increasing the number of equivalent items then its
(a) true variance is increased.
(b) error variance is increased.
(c) reliability is increased.
(d) validity is increased.

613. Various factors operating and interacting simultaneously at the same time affect human behaviour. This can be studied more appropriately through the
(a) non-parametric tests of analysis.
(b) t-test.
(c) two-way analysis of variance.
(d) factorial designs of statistical analysis.

614. There was movement called negative education recommended by a well known naturalist called Rousseau. What do you think would be the correct interpretation?
(a) The world is a mixture of right and wrong qualities so education should negate the wrong and teach what is right.
(b) The purpose of education is to prevent children from doing wrong things, so check them from the beginning.
(c) Human beings are born with wrong tendencies to commit sins from the Biblical point of view. So education must adopt a negative approach to check.
(d) Nature is good while the society is full of vices. So keep the child away from the society and take him to nature.

615. A major limitation of the projective tests is that they
(a) are very costly.
(b) are individual tests.
(c) are not reliable and valid.
(d) require a highly specialized training in the administration, scoring and interpretation of these tests.

616. If a test is administered on such a group which has much group-variability then test-score's
(a) error variance is diminished.
(b) reliability is increased.
(c) validity is increased.
(d) All of these.

617. School surveys are conducted
(a) to compare the performance of the school with that of other schools.
(b) to give recommendations for improvement.
(c) to know the real position of the school at present.
(d) All of the above.

618. Which of the following suggestions would you regard as more important for increasing the reliability coefficient?
(a) The discrimination-index of test-items should be high and the difficulty-level should be of medium size
(b) The test should be administered on hetrogeneous group as far as possible
(c) The length of the test be increased
(d) The scoring of the test-items should be objective

619. Which is the technique used for measuring interpersonal relationships within a group?
(a) Sociogram (b) Psychogram
(c) Scalogram (d) Psychodynamics

620. The square of standard deviation is called
(a) Co-efficient (b) Percentage
(c) Variance (d) None of these

621. Which is the device for a graphic and straightforward portrayal of the total configuration of relations among the members of a group at some given point in time?
(a) Group dynamics
(b) Psychodynamics
(c) Sociometry
(d) Psychometry

622. When a test correctly measures the trait or characteristics for which it was meant then it is called its
(a) Test-Norm (b) Test-Validity
(c) Test-Reliability (d) None of these

623. Survey study does not aim at
(a) knowing facts about the existing situation.
(b) comparing the present status with the standard norms.
(c) criticising the existing situation.
(d) identifying the means of improving the existing situation.

624. There are many characteristics of Test-scores. Which of the following is not such characteristic?
(a) Validity is expressed in degree
(b) Validity means the reproductibility of the test-scores
(c) Validity is a relative term
(d) Validity is not a definite characteristic of validity

625. A research hypothesis cannot take the following form
(a) Problem form
(b) Declarative form
(c) Null form
(d) Question form

626. We learn from newspapers and reports that the national average of the literacy rate in our country is about
(a) 40 per cent (b) 45 per cent
(c) 39 per cent (d) 36 per cent

627. What is most correct about the necessary conditions that are conducive to the formulation of hypothesis?
(a) Researcher's creative imagination
(b) Analogy and consultations with experts and the guide

(c) Richness of researcher's background knowledge
(d) All of these

628. According to "Standards for educational and psychological tests and manuals" validity is of many types. Which of the following is not a type of validity?
(a) Constructs Validity
(b) Face Validity
(c) Content Validity
(d) Criteria-related Validity

629. Consultant surveys are conducted to
(a) give recommendations for solution of the problem.
(b) give expert opinion on the problem.
(c) Both (a) and (b).
(d) None of the above.

630. What type of validity is most needed in an achievement test?
(a) Predictive Validity
(b) Construct Validity
(c) Content Validity
(d) Concurrent Validity

631. What is irrelevant in the context of the criteria of acceptable hypothesis?
(a) A hypothesis should state the expected relationship between the variables
(b) A hypothesis should be such that it can be proved
(c) A hypothesis should be testable
(d) A hypothesis should be clearly and precisely stated

632. If $\bar{x}$ = 100, C.V. is 4 and skewness is 0.15, the value of mode is
(a) 80.40 (b) 89.40
(c) 90.40 (d) 99.40

633. A good or adequate hypothesis should
(a) not be a bunch of relationships.
(b) be consistent with known theories and facts.
(c) be limited in scope.
(d) have all these characteristics.

634. Which of the following things is most needed besides other things for the content Validity in a test?
(a) Sampling Validity
(b) Item Validity
(c) Only Homogenieity of items
(d) Both (a) and (b)

635. If median is 28.9 and mean is 30, the value of mode will be
(a) 19.2 (b) 25.2
(c) 26.8 (d) 24.8

636. When for finding the validity of a test another similar test is selected as an independent criteria then this type of validity is called
(a) Predictive Validity
(b) Circular Validity
(c) Content Validity
(d) Concurrent Validity

637. What is irrelevant in the context of the fcasibiliy consideration of research problem?
(a) Supervisor's willingness, if he is required to guide the research work
(b) Researcher's competencies
(c) Researcher's financial, time and energy resources
(d) Researcher's interest and enthusiasm

638. Given $\bar{x}$ = 120, variance of wages for employee is 9; then C.V. is equivalent to
(a) 4 (b) 3.5
(c) 2.5 (d) 3

639. While defining the research problem, the researcher is not required to state
(a) the questions to be answered so as to make the problem clearer and more understandable.
(b) the scope of the problem.

(c) personal and special interests the researcher has in the problem.
(d) the special terms used in the title mean.

640. What is the meaning of "Face Validity"?
(a) It is that characteristic of a test which shows it measuring
(b) It is that characteristic of a test which as to what it predicts for an individual score
(c) It is that characteristic of a test which shows what a test is measuring
(d) It is that characteristic of a test that it is going to measure

641. The positive welfare state must
(a) see that people obtain freedom from restraints of regulations and planning.
(b) be natural regarding the clashing interests of its citizens.
(c) take only positive but not negative action to maintain social welfare.
(d) take both positive and negative actions to balance the welfare of its citizens.

642. It is evident from the studies of psychometric experts that if a test's concurrent validity and predictive validity both are obtained then
(a) predictive validity will always be lower than concurrent validity.
(b) concurrent validity will always be lower than predictive validity.
(c) both types of validity will not be different in a direction.
(d) both types of validity will be equal.

643. To define a problem does not mean
(a) to put a fence around it.
(b) to give its standard meaning and definition as understood universally.
(c) to specify and state questions and subordinate questions to be answered.
(d) to specify it in detail and with precision.

644. Which of the following statistical techniques is used in opinion surveys for analysis of data?
(a) R Test (b) T Test
(c) X^2 Test (d) None of the above

645. If data collection stands for 1, formulation of hypothesis for 2, selection of the problem for 3, methodology for 4, analysis and interpretation of data for 5 and reporting the results for 6, which is the correct sequence of the steps in educational research in code numbers?
(a) 3, 2, 5, 1, 6, 4 (b) 3, 2, 4, 1, 5, 6
(c) 1, 3, 2, 5, 6, 4 (d) 3, 2, 4, 1, 6, 5

646. Which of the following types of validity is the most difficult to be calculated?
(a) Predictive Validity
(b) Construct Validity
(c) Content Validity
(d) Concurrent Validity

647. The term social facilitisation is meant to indicate
(a) the facilities offered by the society for the performance of a task by an individual.
(b) the influence of the presence of others on a person's performance.
(c) the facilities available in a society for the successful performance of an individual.
(d) the need for creating facilities for members of the society in their attempts for an achievement.

648. Which of the following types of validity is the most easy to be calculated?
(a) Face Validity
(b) Predictive Validity
(c) Content Validity
(d) Concurrent Validity

649. For what is the Thematic Appreciation Test (TAT) most useful?

(a) Assessment of intellectual level
(b) Differential diagnosis
(c) Assessment of motivational variables
(d) Predicting suitability for psychotherapy

650. If median is 12, and D = 36, N = 48, the mean deviation is
(a) 0.48 (b) 0.52
(c) 0.75 (d) 0.45

651. Which of the following is not an example of projective tests?
(a) Draw-man Test (b) MMPI
(c) TAT (d) Rorschach Test

652. If there is low correlation between a test and its criteria then it would always mean that
(a) validity of test is enough.
(b) validity of test may be high or low.
(c) validity and reliability both are enough.
(d) validity of test is low.

653. Which of the following is the most essential characteristic of a research worker?
(a) Open mindedness
(b) Emotional control
(c) Patience
(d) Sympathy

654. Causal comparative studies are similar to
(a) Correlation studies
(b) Social surveys
(c) Both (a) and (b)
(d) None of the above

655. When a test is correlation with its referents then it is called
(a) Intrinsic Validity
(b) Concurrent Validity
(c) Convergent Validity
(d) Discriminant Validity

656. In the assessment of personality, the normative and objective method refers to
(a) prediction of behaviour on the basis of intensive interviewing.
(b) prediction of behaviour on the basis of data from personality tests.
(c) the use of projective techniques.
(d) the use of sophisticated techniques for measuring the accuracy of a person's perception of reality.

657. Validity of a research can be improved by
(a) eliminating extraneous factors.
(b) taking the true representative sample of the population.
(c) Both of the above measures.
(d) None of the above.

658. Which is the best format to use if content and material gathered for certain number of students by different interviews have to be compared in a piece of research?
(a) Structured (b) Projective
(c) Analytical (d) Unstructured

659. The fundamental difference between Rulon Formula and Flangan formula is
(a) in Rulon formula, reliability is calculated from the variance of the whole test while in Flangan formula the test is divided into two parts and their variance is used.
(b) in Rulon formula, the reliability has a technical meaning while in Flangan formula it has simple meaning.
(c) in Rulon formula, reliability is calculated based on the scores-variable on two equal parts of test while in Flangan formula reliability of test depends on the variance of the whole test.
(d) the calculation of reliability by Rulon formula takes less time but by Flangan formula it takes much time.

660. Which of the following is a non-probability sample?

(a) Simple random sample
(b) Quota sample
(c) Purposive sample
(d) Both (a) and (c)

661. Kendar and Richandson had constructed many formula for finding reliability coefficient. Which of the following formula has become most popular?
(a) K-R 10411 (b) K-R 25428
(c) K-R 30431 (d) K-R 20421

662. What best describes the Likert technique of attitude measurement?
(a) Subjects indicate on five point scales the extent of their agreement with a set of attitude statements
(b) Subjects judge a particular concept on a series of bipolar semantic scale
(c) Subjects response to an open-ended interview are coded by content analyst
(d) Subjects indicate whether they agree with each of a series of attitude statements which are equally spaced along an attitude continuum

663. A researcher divides his population into certain groups and fixes the size of the sample from each group. It is called
(a) Stratified sample
(b) Quota sample
(c) Cluster sample
(d) All of the above

664. What can increase the power of a statistical test?
(a) Designing for small error effects
(b) Avoiding random sampling
(c) Decreasing the size of the sample
(d) Avoiding the use of the null hypothesis

665. Which of the following assumptions is not needed in the use of Keeder and Rechardson formula?
(a) Instead of being a power test it should be a speed test
(b) The difficulty level of the items of a test should not differ much
(c) All the items of the test should be homogeneous
(d) The items of the test should be written in the form of +1 and 0

666. A researcher selects only 10 members as a sample from the total population of 5000 and considers it good because
(a) the population was homogeneous.
(b) he was guided by his supervisor.
(c) he was a good researcher.
(d) All of the above.

667. K-R 20 and K-R 21 mainly differ in this respect.
(a) K-R 20 takes less time than L-R 21 for finding reliability
(b) For the use of K-R 20 the difficult levels of items may be different but for the use of K-R 21 this level should be uniform
(c) The items should be written in form +1 and 0 in K-R 20 but it is not necessary in K-R 21
(d) The validity of K-R 20 is more than K-R 21

668. Which is not the effective way of controlling a nuisance variable in an experimental design?
(a) Exercising statistical control
(b) Random assignment of subjects
(c) Holding the nuisance variable constant for all subjects
(d) Excluding the variable as one of the factors in the experiment

669. Formulation of hypothesis is not necessary in
(a) Growth studies
(b) Survey studies
(c) Both (a) and (b)
(d) None of the above

670. Who has defined Ex-Post Facto Research by saying that it is a systematic scientific exploration in which the scientist (researcher) does not have direct control on the independent variable?
(a) George J. Mouly
(b) Fred Karlinger
(c) W.S. Monroe
(d) John W. Best

671. In which situation the validity of test depends directly on the reliability?
(a) In Hetrogeneous Test
(b) In Homogeneous Test
(c) Both (a) and (b)
(d) None of these

672. The research antagonistic to ex-post facto research is
(a) normative researches
(b) experimental studies
(c) library researches
(d) All of the above

673. Which of the following situations is necessary for high reliability?
(a) Diversity of the groups
(b) Small test
(c) Items of same difficulty-level
(d) Inter correlation between the items

674. What are the types of variables?
(a) Controlled variables
(b) Independent variables
(c) Both of them
(d) None of these

675. The final result of a study will be more accurate if the sample drawn is
(a) representative to the population
(b) taken randomly
(c) purposive
(d) fixed by quota

676. What is the difference between Laboratory Experiement and Field Experiment?
(a) Difference of samples
(b) Difference of variables
(c) Difference of place
(d) All of these

677. Which of the following situations is necessary for high validity?
(a) Enough length of the test
(b) Limited capacity of the sample
(c) Items of different difficulty level
(d) Low inter-correlation between the items

678. In order to ensure moral freedom in the younger generation the social culture must
(a) ensure that children avoid abuse of authority and stick to it.
(b) be binding on students so that they should be within its limits.
(c) not be a binding chart, but a ladder on which they may climb.
(d) not allow deviations from the legitimate restrictions of the authority.

679. The standard fact about the standard score is
(a) it has a definite Mode.
(b) it has a definite Median and Standard Deviation.
(c) it has a definite Median.
(d) it has a definite Quartile.

680. Which experiments are more popular in Educational Psychology?
(a) Field Studies
(b) Historical Researches
(c) Laboratory Experiments
(d) Field Experiments

681. In the conditioning approach to learning
(a) the unnatural stimulus follows the natural stimulus.
(b) the subject should be in readiness to receive the unnatural stimulus.

(c) the natural stimulus follows the unnatural stimulus.
(d) response to natural stimulus is required to be reinforced.

682. Which technique of research is applied in Educational Sociology?
(a) Historical Researches
(b) Field Studies
(c) Laboratory Experiments
(d) Field Experiments

683. If the half test reliability of test-scores is 70, then the reliability of the whole test would be according to Spearman-Brown formula as
(a) .283 (b) .382
(c) .826 (d) .882

684. Which of the following is similar to case studies?
(a) Social surveys
(b) Follow up studies
(c) Longitudinal studies
(d) None of the above

685. For some special reasons Guillford and Fructer has called split-half-reliability as
(a) Internal Consistency Reliability
(b) On the Spot Reliability
(c) Delayed Reliability
(d) None of these

686. What is Survey Method?
(a) Field Studies
(b) Historical Researches
(c) Field Experiments
(d) Laboratory Experiments

687. Frequency is not taken into consideration in
(a) continuous series
(b) individual observation
(c) discreet series
(d) None of the above

688. What is not correct about hypothesis?
(a) Even in case of status-studies, the investigator is likely to need some tentative hypothesis to guide him
(b) Its absence, essentially, means no research or poor research
(c) It is essential in studies where cause effect relationships are to be discovered
(d) It is less crucial in studies in which the task is one of determining the status of a given phenomenon

689. The main defect of discriminatory method is that
(a) it gives reliability coefficient which is lower than the real value.
(b) it gives reliability coefficient which is affected more by the individual's maturity level.
(c) it cannot find speed-test reliability.
(d) it takes more time in finding reliability.

690. Which of the following approaches could be considered as progressive in the construction of curriculum?
(a) Arranging the subject matter required for compulsory acquisition by students in the interests of the society.
(b) Creating provision for promoting children to exert their potentialities for learning.
(c) Providing knowledge from the past culture and achievements of the nation for inheritance.
(d) Selecting the contents of the curriculum from the disciplinary and cultural values point of view.

691. The basis of finding reliability by Rulon formula is
(a) the relevance of test-scores with the test-reliability.
(b) the division of all test-items into two parts.

(c) the technical meaning of test-reliability.
(d) None of these.

692. What does representative sample mean?
(a) A sample which is smaller in size than the population
(b) A miniature or replica of the population at least with respect to the characteristic under investigation, if not in all respects
(c) A sample whose mean is estimated to be within sampling errors of the population mean
(d) A sample similar to the population in all respects

693. If co-efficient of skewness is 0.64; $\bar{x}$ = 82, and σ is 50, the value of mode is
(a) 40 (b) 70
(c) 60 (d) 50

694. If an examiner, inadvertently, allows three minutes extra time to some subjects in the group on a test of intelligence used in a research, this will introduce in the experiment
(a) measurement error of random nature.
(b) measurement error of constant nature.
(c) sampling error of constant nature.
(d) sampling error of random nature.

695. The norm on a test is the following of the score of representative sample.
(a) Mode
(b) Median
(c) Standard Deviation
(d) None of these

696. The press reports collected by correspondents can be classified as
(a) Secondary data
(b) Tertiary data
(c) Primary data
(d) None of the above

697. Which of the following norms is mostly used in the psychological tests as a measure?
(a) Percentile Norms
(b) Standard Score Norms
(c) Age Norms
(d) Grade Norms

698. Level of significance means the probability of
(a) accepting the research hypothesis.
(b) rejecting the null hypothesis.
(c) rejecting the research hypothesis.
(d) accepting the null hypothesis.

699. Field experiment differs from field studies in which of the following respects?
(a) Formulation of hypothesis is a must in field experiment but it is not always needed in later case.
(b) Former is a controlled study and later is a status quo study.
(c) Both (a) and (b).
(d) None of the above.

700. Historical research has nothing to do with
(a) formulating hypothesis to explain events and conditions.
(b) collecting source material.
(c) testing hypothesis statistically to draw inferences.
(d) internal and external criticism of source material.

701. Which of the following is required to get the correct meaning of the score of a test?
(a) High Validity
(b) High Item Validity
(c) Norm
(d) High Reliability

702. Which of the following areas of co-operation should be regarded as more basic in your opinion?

(a) Parents and teachers
(b) School and community
(c) Teachers and supervisors
(d) Students and community.

703. If your are preparing a norm for the height of 16 years old girls of Bihar, then out of the following norms which are would you like to find?
(a) Standard Score Norm
(b) Grade Norm
(c) Age Norm
(d) Percentile Norm

704. The best measuring tool for research is
(a) highly valid.
(b) well-standardized.
(c) highly reliable.
(d) both sufficiently reliable and sufficiently valid.

705. The formula for calculating the product moment co-efficient of correlation with x and y deviations will be
(a) $r = xy/x^2\ xy^2$
(b) $r = zxy - 2/xy$
(c) $xy/x^2\ xy^2$
(d) $xr = xy - 1$

706. In true experimental research, the investigator is always required to make a compromise between
(a) "internal validity" and "external validity".
(b) control of extraneous variables and building the correlated variable into design.
(c) "randomization" and "manipulation" which of the above four is not correct.
(d) "contrived setting" and natural "setting".

707. For which one of the following the construction of Age-Norm is suitable?
(a) Such traits whose development-rate is equal to other traits
(b) Such traits which show a graded change in the individual as the age advances
(c) Such traits which are stable in spite of the advancing age
(d) None of these

708. The sum of absolute deviations of items is minimum from
(a) Geometric mean (b) Median
(c) Harmonic mean (d) Mode

709. If any individual's extraversion is PR 70 based on the test-score it means
(a) there is 30% persons score below this individual.
(b) all person's score is 70% equal to this individual.
(c) there is 70% persons score above this individual.
(d) there is 70% persons score below this individual.

710. What is not possible to achieve in case of the field experiment?
(a) Control of extraneous variables
(b) Randomization and control of extraneous variables both
(c) Randomization
(d) Manipulation

711. Which of the following statements about experimental research is not correct?
(a) Controlling of extraneous factors is a must here.
(b) Only single variable can be manipulated by using factorial design.
(c) More than one variables can be manipulated by using factorial design.
(d) All of the above.

712. Causal-comparative studies are classified under
(a) descriptive research.
(b) experimental research.

(c) developmental research.
(d) historical research.

713. What is coefficient Alpha?
(a) A method of finding inter-analysis
(b) A norm which is used only in achievement test
(c) A method of finding reliability of a test
(d) A method of finding validity of a test

714. If σ is – 22.5, mean is 45, median is 48, the coefficient of skewness will be
(a) –0.4 (b) –0.3
(c) –0.2 (d) –0.5

715. If in a test the items scores are not written in the form of 0 and 1 and other method is used then the best method of finding the test reliability will be
(a) Coefficient Alpha
(b) Coefficient Beta
(c) Kuder-Richardson
(d) Internal Consistency Method

716. Which is the most correct among the following statement?
(a) Parametric tests are less powerful when the assumptions underlying them are not satisfied
(b) Non-parametric tests are most powerful when the assumptions underlying them are fully satisfied
(c) Non-parametric tests are always preferable to parametric tests because they are simple, easy and require a small sample
(d) Parametric tests are always preferable to non-parametric tests as they are most powerful

717. If Q_3 = 37.5, Q_1 = 30.6, QD
(a) 3.45 (b) 2.48
(c) 2.47 (d) 3.46

718. Which of the following is not effective in reducing the error in experimental research?
(a) Random selection and random assignment of subjects to groups
(b) Increasing the sample size
(c) Matching the subjects in the group
(d) Building the variable in the experiment itself

719. If for finding the validity of a test a sample is selected which had not been previously used but it selected from the same population from which the previous sample had been selected this process is called
(a) Cross Reliability
(b) Cross Validation
(c) Cross Test-score
(d) None of these

720. In order to augment the accuracy of the study a researcher should
(a) increase the size of the sample.
(b) keep the variance high.
(c) be honest and unbiased.
(d) All of the above.

721. What is scorer reliability?
(a) Prejudices of the persons writing the scores
(b) Relevance between the persons writing the scores
(c) Irrelevance between the persons writing the scores
(d) None of these

722. Why is the hypothesis not acceptable that "The number of tables and chairs in the school influences positively the academic achievement of its students"?
(a) It is not testable
(b) It is not precisely stated
(d) It is not based on any rational relationship between dependent and independent variables
(d) It is not scientifically developed

723. Which of the following statistical techniques is not used in controlling extraneous factors?

(a) ANOVA
(b) T Test
(c) Multiple Regression analysis
(d) Correlation coefficient.

724. What is not related to increasing sensitivity of the test?
(a) Increasing sample size
(b) Reducing the level of noise
(c) Using computer for making calculations
(d) Increasing reliability of measures

725. What is Deviation Intelligence Quotient?
(a) A sort of standardized score norm
(b) A sort of I.Q. which is the basis of measuring others I.Q.
(c) I.Q. of the mentally gifted persons
(d) I.Q. of the mentally weak persons

726. The validity and reliability of a research will be at stake when the
(a) author who is the source of information is biased, incompetent or dishonest.
(b) researcher himself is not competent enough to draw logical conclusions.
(c) incident was reported after a long period of time from that of its occurrence.
(d) All of the above.

727. What is the main object of Percentile Norm?
(a) The computation of percentile norm is difficult
(b) It is a subjective norm
(c) This norm creates confusion at the time of percentage
(d) The scale based on this norm is not uniform

728. What helps most in identification of the research problem?
(a) Researcher's own experience
(b) Discussion with the supervisor
(c) Review of related literature
(d) All of these

729. If $\bar{x} = 65$, $\bar{y} = 67$, $r = 0.8$, $\sigma x = 2.5$, $\sigma y = 3.5$, the Regression Equation of y upon x will be
(a) $Y = 1.21x - 5.8$
(b) $Y = 1.12x - 5.8$
(c) $Y = 0.21x - 8.5$
(d) $Y = 1.21x - 8.5$

730. Random sampling does not
(a) reduce error and increase precision of the experiment.
(b) make the sample representative of the population.
(c) maximize experimental variance.
(d) ensure generalization of results.

731. What is Percentile Band?
(a) It is such an expansion of percentile category out of which it lies
(b) It is such an expansion of percentile category in which it lies
(c) It is percentile category which estimates the achievements level of examinee
(d) It is such an expansion of percentile category which gives correct meaning to the scores

732. Who is regarded as the father of scientific social surveys?
(a) Darwin (b) Best
(c) Booth (d) None of the above

733. The psychologists use three criteria to evaluate the appropriateness of any norm these are three R's as follows.
(a) Realism, Reasonableness, Rationalization
(b) Realism, Reasonableness, Reliance
(c) Representativeness, Relevance, Recency
(d) Representativeness, Rational, Realism

734. Which of the following does not clarify the nature of the problems?

(a) Underlying assumptions
(b) Precise and exact statement
(c) Definition of technical terms used in the statement of the problem
(d) Its theoretical background

735. Which of the following is an easiest method of matching the two groups of subjects?
(a) Matching by means and SD of scores
(b) Matching by ranking
(c) Subject to subject matching
(d) None of the above.

736. From what do problems for research emerge?
(a) Review of research already done
(b) Discussion of theories and principles
(c) Puzzling experiences
(d) Extensive reading

737. The main difference between norm and standard is
(a) norm indicates about the present of the examinee while standard indicates about his future.
(b) the norm show how an examinee should be while standard shows how his performance is.
(c) norm predicts about the future of examinees while the standard about the present only.
(d) norm indicates how the examinee has performed while the standard shows performance's quality.

738. In a school the administrator of the curriculum is the
(a) Class teacher (b) Sports teacher
(c) Principal (d) All of the above

739. The difference between reliability and validity is that
(a) reliability is test's self-relationship while validity is correlated with some outside criteria.
(b) reliability is quality of test-scores while validity is quality of the test.
(c) reliability is correlation of test with outside criteria while validity is self-related.
(d) reliability is a desired quality of the best while validity is undesirable quality of the test.

740. What is not correct about non-parametric tests of statistical analysis?
(a) They are wasteful of data
(b) They are less economical
(c) They require much larger a sample to obtain the power efficiency which is yielded by a parametric test with a particular size
(d) Their power efficiency is always low

741. Where X means original scores, N means the number of persons in the group and M means the actual means of the scores, the formula for the calculation of the standard deviation would be

(a) $\sqrt{\frac{\Sigma X^2}{N} + M^2}$ (b) $\sqrt{\frac{\Sigma X^2 - M^2}{N}}$

(c) $\sqrt{\frac{\Sigma M^2}{N} - X^2}$ (d) $\sqrt{\frac{\Sigma X^2}{N} - M^2}$

742. Chi-square test can be appropriately used as
(a) df greater than 1, but 22 per cent of the expected frequencies are either 2 or 3 or 4.
(b) K = 2, df = 1, one expected frequency = 3.
(c) df = 6, but one expected frequency is 7.
(d) df = 6, no expected frequency is smaller than 9.

743. If you have to measure the organizational capacity of examinees then which one of

the following types of the items of test would you like to select?

(a) Test's of objective items
(b) Test's of essay-items
(c) Both (a) and (b)
(d) Only an oral examination

744. In a normal distribution, 100 per cent of observations are covered by

(a) $\bar{X} + 2\sigma$ (b) $\bar{X} + 3\sigma$
(c) $\bar{X} + 309\sigma$ (d) $\bar{X} + \sigma$

745. Which of the following validities cannot be regarded criteria related validity?

(a) Predictive Validity
(b) Construct Validity
(c) Concurrent Validity
(d) All of these

746. In which Non-Parametric Test, following formula is used?

$$\text{Rho } \tilde{n} = 1 = \frac{6\Sigma D}{N(N-1)}$$

(a) Sign Test
(b) Chi-square Test
(c) Median Test
(d) Rho correlation

747. Criterion for formulating a hypothesis is that

(a) they should specify the dependent and independent variables.
(b) they should be closer to the known facts.
(c) they should be verifiable after experiment.
(d) All of the above.

748. If the purpose of research is to discover the relative incidence, distribution and inter-relationship of sociological and psychological variables it is called

(a) ex-post facto research.
(b) field experiment.
(c) survey research.
(d) experimental research.

749. When a researcher accepts the effect of one variable on the other variable because these two variables often appear together then it is called

(a) Cause-effect Relationship
(b) Empirical Research
(c) Ex-post Facto Research
(d) Post-Hock Fallacy

750. A negative coefficient of skewness implies that

(a) mean is greater than mode.
(b) mean is less than mode.
(c) mean is equal to mode.
(d) mean is equal to median.

751. Which of the following methods is best suited to control the extraneous variables?

(a) Randomization
(b) Counter Balancing
(c) Constancy
(d) Elimination

752. What is the essential difference between the laboratory experiment and the field study experiment?

(a) Testing of hypothesis
(b) Randomization
(c) The logic and purpose of the research
(d) Manipulation of independent variable

753. Among the following the least observations are covered by

(a) $\bar{X} + \sigma$ (b) $\bar{X} + 3\sigma$
(c) $\bar{X} + 309\sigma$ (d) $\bar{X} + 2\sigma$

754. What is internal validity of experimental research?

(a) The extent to which control of extraneous variables is made rigorous
(b) The extent to which the results can be generalized to other populations

(c) The extent of which manipulation of independent variable is ensured
(d) The extent to which the results obtained are due to differences in the treatments

755. Which of the following sampling methods has sample which does not represent the population best?
(a) Sample Random Sampling
(b) Stratified Random Sampling
(c) Quota Sampling
(d) Area or cluster Sampling

756. In a given distribution, x = 20, a = 16. The coefficient of variation is
(a) 320% (b) 4%
(c) 36% (d) 80%

757. The fundamental necessity for determining a research problem is
(a) Only need (b) Resources
(c) Only problem (d) None of these

758. What are the main functions of analysis of data?
(a) Testing null hypothesis
(b) Acquiring meaningful results
(c) Making the data meaningful
(d) All of these

759. In a series the range AM + 3σ and AM – 3σ will cover
(a) 50 per cent of the values
(b) some values
(c) most of the values
(d) None of the above

760. "A research-problem is an interrogative sentence which finds mutual relationship of two dynamic terms." Whose statement is it?
(a) Crow and Crow
(b) Fred Er Kilanger
(c) Jone C. Townsed
(d) None of these

761. Given the following distribution

X	F
0-20	0
20-40	5
40-60	22
60-80	25
80-100	16

The value of median is
(a) 65.0 (b) 60.5
(c) 66.6 (d) 65.6

762. In single group experimentation which of the following is not needed?
(a) Observation
(b) Matching of subjects
(c) Keeping all variables constant except the experimental one
(d) Calculation of D.

763. According to J.W. Best, it is not among the sources of the research problem.
(a) Technological change and 'Social development'
(b) Class and School
(c) Society and Curriculum
(d) All of these

764. Cumulative frequency curve is known as
(a) Hysterogram
(b) Ogive
(c) Frequency polygon
(d) Histogram

765. In a given distribution $\bar{X}$ = 800, σ = 120. The coefficient of variation is
(a) 15% (b) 920%
(c) Zero (d) 680%

766. Middle quartile is known as
(a) Geometric mean
(b) Median
(c) Harmonic mean
(d) Mode

767. "In respect of achievement boys are better than the girls." This hypothesis is
(a) Two tailed (b) Directed
(c) Zero (d) Undirected

768. Mean deviation equals
(a) 1/3 σ (b) 5/6 Q.D.
(c) 1/5 Q.D. (d) 4/5 σ

769. The correct formula to find out term C for ANOVA is
(a) $(\Sigma X)^2/N$ (b) $(\Sigma X^2)/N$
(c) $\Sigma X2/N$ (d) $\Sigma X^2/N$

770. The measure which divides a distribution in ten equal parts is known as
(a) Percentile (b) Quartile
(c) Deviation (d) Decile

771. Q.D. equals
(a) 1/3 σ (b) 0 σ
(c) 2/3 σ (d) 1 σ

772. The following cannot be located with the help of an ogive
(a) Quartile (b) Decile
(c) Median (d) Mode

773. Find the chi-square value from the following options

	A	B	C	D
0	3	4	1	8
E	2	1	5	8

(a) 2.0 (b) 12.7
(c) 2.5 (d) 2.25

774. Experimental researches are superior to other studies because
(a) subjectivity does not have any role to play here.
(b) they can be replicated to verify the result.
(c) they will always give correct result.
(d) All of the above.

775. In the context of measurement by research tool the following is relevant.
(a) Only high valid
(b) Only good standardized
(c) Only high reliable
(d) Both enough reliability and validity

776. The most frequent item of the series around which other items are densely populated is known as?
(a) Harmonic mean
(b) Arithmetic mean
(c) Mode
(d) Geometric mean

777. If $\beta_2 > 3$ the curve is called
(a) Platykurtic
(b) Mesokurtic
(c) Leptokurtic
(d) Positively skewed

778. Given the following series, the value of mode is

5, 6, 3, 2, 8, 4, 7, 9, 1, 10, 11, 12, 13

(a) 12 (b) 9
(c) 13 (d) Not defined

779. Where was the VI All India Training College Union conference held in 1961?
(a) Baroda (b) Ahmedabad
(c) Delhi (d) Banglore

780. Bowley's coefficient of skewness is ... Karl Pearson's coefficient of skewness
(a) not related to (b) less than
(c) equal to (d) greater than

781. In 1969 under the auspices of U.G.C. a seminar was hold at this place to determine areas of Educational research.
(a) Banglore (b) Poona
(c) Mumbai (d) Delhi

782. Graphically, mode can be estimated from
(a) Histogram (b) Bar diagram
(c) Historigram (d) Ogive

783. For a symmetrical distribution the coefficient of skewness is

(a) +1 (b) zero
(c) +3 (d) –1

784. In a positive skewed distribution
(a) 2 < M > (b) $M > Z >$
(c) $Z = M = \bar{X}$ (d) $Z < 3M >$

785. How many areas of educational research have been mentioned in Dr. Buch's book *Survey of Educational Research* published in 1974?
(a) 14 (b) 18
(c) 26 (d) 16

786. Bowley's coefficient of skewness is given by

(a) $\dfrac{Q_3 - Q_1 + 2\text{ Med}}{Q_3 + Q_1}$

(b) $\dfrac{Q_3 + Q_1 - 2\text{ Med}}{Q_3 - Q_1}$

(c) $\dfrac{Q_3 + Q_1 + 2\text{ Mode}}{Q_3 - Q_1}$

(d) $\dfrac{Q_3 + Q_1 + 2\text{ Mode}}{Q_3 + Q_1}$

787. That statistical value is known by the people by the name of "Average Value" is
(a) Median (b) Mode
(c) Central Tendency (d) Mean

788. In a moderately skewed distribution
(a) M = 2 – Z (b) $M = 2Z$
(c) $Z = 3M - 2$ (d) $Z = M$

789. Who gave the idea of Factorial design?
(a) R.A. Fisher
(b) C.S. Peiree
(c) Campbell and Stanley
(d) None of the above

790. Which of the following measures of central tendency cannot be represented graphically?
(a) Quartile (b) Median
(c) Arithmetic mean (d) Mode

791. "National Science Foundation" has classified research into the following types.
(a) Survey Technique and Fundamental Research
(b) Fundamental Applied and Experimental Research
(c) Action Fundamental and Intellectual Research
(d) None of these

792. Karl Pearson's coefficient of skewness
(a) can be both positive and negative.
(b) is always negative.
(c) is always positive.
(d) cannot be zero.

793. According to Edward and Crombek, the proper classification of research is as follows.
(a) Only Survey and Technique Research
(b) Only Critical and Survey Research
(c) Survey Technique Applied Critical Research
(d) Critical Action Fundamental Experimental Research

794. Given the N values in a series, the geometric mean is
(a) the third root of the product of N values.
(b) the square root of the product of N.
(c) the Nth root of the product of N values.
(d) the fourth root of the product of N values.

795. When coefficient of skewness is positive the distribution is said to be
(a) Positively skewed
(b) Platykurtic
(c) Leptokurtic
(d) Symmetrical

796. Harmonic mean of a series of data is
(a) the reciprocal of the arithmetic average of the values of various items.
(b) always ill-defined.
(c) the reciprocal of the arithmetic average of the reciprocals of the values of its various items.

797. "The main aim of fundamental research is to construct new principles about the concept of fundamental research". This is the statement of
(a) M.P. Cook (b) J.W. Best
(c) Davors (d) Andriaska

798. In a moderately skewed distribution $\bar{X}$ = 100, V = 35 and *j* (coefficient of skewness) = 0.2. The value of mode is
(a) 93 (b) 67
(c) 35 (d) 103

799. The proper research-method to solve the problems related to class education and school organization in the field of education is
(a) Historical Research
(b) Applied Research
(c) Survey Research
(d) None of these

800. Which of the measures given here are based on every item of the series?
(a) Quartile deviation
(b) Range
(c) Standard deviation
(d) All of these

801. Variation of sample mean from the population mean is due to
(a) biased attitude of the researcher.
(b) sampling error.
(c) wrong method of data collection.
(d) All of the above.

802. Which of the measures of dispersion is more useful in case of open-end distributions?
(a) Quartile deviation
(b) Standard deviation
(c) Average deviation
(d) Range

803. Action is regarded the alternative of research in
(a) 1926 (b) 1936
(c) 1906 (d) 1916

804. According to Piaget, the stage of concrete operations in children's development occurs between the ages of
(a) 2 to 5 years (b) 5 to 7 years
(c) 7 to 11 years (d) 11 to 16 years

805. The first step of research is
(a) to select the problem.
(b) to prepare the outline of research.
(c) to collect data.
(d) to formula hypothesis.

806. Standard deviation is always computed from
(a) Median (b) GM
(c) Mean (d) Mode

807. Validity of a test means
(a) consistency of results
(b) discriminating ability
(c) predictive quality
(d) level of difficulty

808. Under a normal curve X σ covers
(a) 95.85 per cent
(b) 95.54 per cent of the area
(c) 95.45 per cent
(d) 94.55 per cent

809. The main difference of selecting the sample in action research and fundamental research is
(a) the knowledge of the techniques of selecting sample in fundamental research.
(b) in action research there is no problem of selection of sample while in

Fundamental research pure sample is selected from the population.

(c) in action research sample is a difficult task while in Fundamental research it is easy task.

(d) None of these.

810. Karl Pearson's coefficient of skewness of a distribution is 0.4. Its mean is 30. The value of median will be

(a) 25.63 (b) 31.25
(c) 34.15 (d) 28.93

811. V.V. Kanath in his article has mentioned the main areas of research for this country.

(a) Germany (b) Sri Lanka
(c) India (d) America

812. Which of the following measures is least affected by extreme items?

(a) Standard deviation
(b) Quartile deviation
(c) Mean deviation
(d) Range

813. According to central limit theorem, if large sample is selected randomly from an infinite population then the

(a) average value of the sample means will be same as that of the population mean.
(b) standard deviation of the sample mean will be the standard error of means (SEn).
(c) distribution of sample mean is normal.
(d) All of the above.

814. Variance is given by

(a) s^2 (b) $\frac{s}{N}$
(c) $\frac{\sigma}{\overline{X}}$ (d) $\frac{\overline{X}}{6}$

815. There no practical recognition of the research problem of the following.

(a) Possibility of data
(b) Expenditure
(c) Time
(d) All of the above

816. The examination oriented system of education in India emphasizes extra homework and leaves little time for

(a) Social service activities
(b) Clubs
(c) Games
(d) All of the above

817. 'It is necessary to reform the researcher's interest personal ambition and educational situations in selecting research problem." You regard this statement as

(a) Not Clear
(b) Beyond the aims of Research
(c) Meaningless
(d) Relevant and Meaningful

818. Which of the following is a computed measure of absolute variation?

(a) Standard deviation
(b) Quartile deviation
(c) Range
(d) All of these

819. Mean deviation equals

(a) 1/3 σ (b) 6/5 Q.D.
(c) 5/6 Q.D. (d) 1/5 Q.D.

820. Coefficient of variation is given by

(a) $\frac{\sigma}{\overline{X}}$ (b) $\frac{A-Z}{\sigma}$
(c) $\frac{Q_3-Q_1}{Q_3-Q_1}$ (d) None of these

821. "Hypothesis describes what we want to observe it looks forward to the future. This is a logical sentence and its validity can be tested. It can prove to be correct or incorrect." This is the statement of

(a) Good and Scates (b) Barr and Scates
(c) Good and Hatt (d) Lundburg

822. If N = 100, P 85 shall lie in
(a) 80th item (b) 90th item
(c) 70th item (d) 85th item

823. "Educational achievements will increase if all the children get awards." This hypothesis has more predictively value it comes under the category of following type
(a) Existential Hypothesis
(b) Zero Hypothesis
(c) Universal Hypothesis
(d) None of these

824. When coefficient of skewness is positive, the distribution is said to be
(a) Platykutic.
(b) Symmetrical.
(c) Leptokutic.
(d) Positively skewed.

825. When the given data is divided into two equal parts to calculate the time series it is called
(a) Moving average method
(b) Sampling method
(c) Semi average method
(d) None of the above

826. A negative coefficient of skewness implies that
(a) mean is less than mode.
(b) mean is equal to median.
(c) mean is greater than mode.
(d) mean is equal to mode.

827. "In the research statistical terms the statistical relations are regulated." The type of this hypothesis is
(a) Precise Hypothesis
(b) Existential Hypothesis
(c) Universal Hypothesis
(d) Statistical Hypothesis

828. 1.96 level of significance for a large sample means
(a) 5% chance is there that the result obtained will not match the population mean.
(b) 2.5% on each side of the normal curve out of range of the investigation.
(c) Both (a) and (b).
(d) None of the above.

829. The following method is used to test the meaningfulness of hypothesis.
(a) Only Z-test
(b) Only T-test
(c) Only Parametric Test
(d) All of these

830. Where informants are literate and are spread over a vast area, the most suitable method of collecting data is
(a) direct personal interview.
(b) interview by investigator.
(c) mailed questionnaire method.
(d) None of these.

831. If 4 or 6 or 8 years moving average is secured to draw a trend line it is called
(a) Sampling method
(b) Even period of moving averages
(c) Semi average method
(d) None of the above

832. Who have made the greatest contribution in the development of statistical methods?
(a) Businessmen
(b) Mathematicians
(c) Scienstists
(d) Economists

833. To measure the quantity of variable, the smallest factors are called
(a) Scale (b) Unit
(c) Measure (d) None of these

834. The long term movements when studied in statistics are called
(a) Data collection
(b) Secular trend

(c) Range trends
(d) None of the above

835. The sample is required for
(a) more knowledge of truth.
(b) economy of money.
(c) administrative convenience.
(d) All of these.

836. Who is the real giant in the development of the theory of statistics?
(a) R.A. Fisher (b) Galton
(c) Gauss (d) Bowley

837. The word 'Education' as derived from its root terms means to
(a) develop the environment
(b) train in literacy
(c) develop children
(d) give instruction

838. Statistics can be best considered
(a) as a science.
(b) as an art.
(c) Both art and science.
(d) Neither art nor science.

839. In the research problem, there is possibility of representation of population this sample is of this type.
(a) Non-Probability
(b) Probability Sample Sample
(c) Both (a) and (b)
(d) None of these

840. Link relative method is used to study
(a) Cyclical variations
(b) Seasonal variations
(c) Both (a) and (b)
(d) None of the above

841. What is that type of research-sample in which there is possibility of inclusion of each gloup of the population in it?
(a) Improbable Sample
(b) Probable Sample
(c) Both (a) and (b)
(d) None of these

842. Which is not a correct statement?
(a) A test can be both valid and reliable
(b) A test can be reliable without being valid
(c) A test can be valid without being reliable
(d) A test cannot be valid without being reliable

843. 't' formula has been given by
(a) B.F. Skimmer (b) Karl Pearson
(c) Fisher (d) None of the above

844. 'Structured' and 'Unstructured' are two types of
(a) Introspection (b) Interview
(c) Observation (d) None of these

845. Which of the following types of research is appropriate for solving the local problem?
(a) Action Research
(b) Applied Research
(c) Survey Research
(d) Fundamental Research

846. The mathematical method of measuring trend value is called
(a) Semi averages method
(b) Moving averages method
(c) Least squares method
(d) None of the above

847. What is that type of research with which Stepphen M. Corey was associated?
(a) Survey Research
(b) Fundamental Research
(c) Action Research
(d) Applied Research

848. Closed form of questionnaire means
(a) checking an item out of given responses.
(b) yes or no response.

(c) restricts the choice of response for the respondent.
(d) a short response.

849. Which technique is generally followed when the population is finite?
(a) Area sampling technique
(b) Systematic sampling technique
(c) Purposive sampling technique
(d) None of the above.

850. A good questionnaire is
(a) as short as possible.
(b) significant, novice, clear topic.
(c) easy to tabulate, summarize and interpret.
(d) psychological and biologically arranged.

851. Who has written the book *Research for Teachers* about the action research?
(a) Kurt Lewin
(b) Bankingham
(c) Mc Grethare
(d) Stephen M. Corery

852. A researcher divides his population into certain groups and fixes the size of the sample from each group. It is called
(a) Cluster sample
(b) Stratified sample
(c) Quota sample
(d) All of the above

853. What type of research is "Paolov's Conditioned Response Principle" associated with?
(a) Survey Research
(b) Applied Research
(c) Fundamental Research
(d) Action Research

854. Condition for preparing a questionnaire is
(a) to explore hypothesis, to cover the whole topic, approval of authorities, related to some known educationists.
(b) problem selected from one and a halftimes more items than needed.
(c) to present a preliminary card asking whether the subject is willing to participate and two copies of questionnaire.
(d) take help from other studies, related literature and experts of related field.

855. In the formula of 't' = $\frac{M_D}{SE_{MD}}$, SE_{MD} is
(a) standard error of mean deviation.
(b) standard error of mean of difference.
(c) standard error of mode deviation.
(d) None of the above.

856. Advantage of questionnaire is
(a) confidential, less strain, focussing all the significant ideas.
(b) economical, nationwide or International coverage.
(c) esay to plan, construct and administer.
(d) All of these.

857. What type of research is the beginning of "Basic Education in India" associated with?
(a) Fundamental Research
(b) Survey Research
(c) Applied Research
(d) Action Research

858 If you are doing experiment on a large group of sample which method of controlling will you adopt?
(a) Elimination
(b) Matching
(c) Elimination and matching both
(d) Randomization

859. "Most of the problems related to teaching-behaving process are behavioural. Their analysis and generalization is called 'Applied'." Who has given this statement?
(a) Hotten and Hunt
(b) John W. Best

(c) Hotten
(d) Hunt

860. The mass of data collected needs to be systematized and organised through
(a) Classifying (b) Tabulating
(c) Editing (d) All of these

861. Some of the sources of secondary data are
(a) confidential records of the Government.
(b) internal records of a firm's sales, production, etc.
(c) reports and publications of Central and State Governments.
(d) the data obtained by a firm in a survey conducted by it.

862. Good Barr and Scates suggest helpful mode to start with the analysis of data
(a) to examine carefully the statement of the problem, earlier analysis and to study original record of the data.
(b) to think in terms of significant tables that the data permit.
(c) to make simple statistical calculations from the data.
(d) to discuss the problems with others.

863. Action research is the contribution of democratic age. Its concept originated from psychology. Who is that psychologist who suggested action research?
(a) Thormdike (b) Skinner
(c) Kurt Lewin (d) Hull

864. If the marks obtained by 5 students are 40, 60, 70, 80, 90 the modal marks are
(a) 40 (b) 80
(c) 60 (d) 90

865. What type of research are Thorndike's principle of learning and Kohler's Gestalt principles associated with?
(a) Survey Research
(b) Applied Research
(c) Fundamental Research
(d) Action Research

866. Statistical method of analysis
(a) correlation, co-efficient of reliability and validity
(b) ranks and percential ranks, measures of central tendency.
(c) error and probable error—difference or significant difference.
(d) measures of variability—range, quartile deviation, average deviation and standard deviation.

867. If we have five random samples and we want to determine whether there are significant differences among their means, we would have to use
(a) $5\frac{(5-1)}{2} = 10$ t tests
(b) $\frac{5 \times 5 \times 4}{2} = 50$ t tests
(c) $5\frac{(5-3)}{2} = 5$ t tests
(d) None of the above

868. Common error of interpretation
(a) failure to recognise limitations in the research evidence misinterpretation due to unstudied factors.
(b) ignoring selective factors, difficulties and interpretative evaluation.
(c) failure to see the problem in proper perspective, to appreciate the relevance of various elements.
(d) All of these.

869. Which of the following facts is not included in the description of research-problem?
(a) Study of related literature
(b) Defining the problem
(c) Historical background of study
(d) Basic principle

870. The historical research is different from experimental research in the process of
(a) the hypothesis testing
(b) the formulation of the hypothesis
(c) replication
(d) All of the above

871. Which of the following facts is not included in the statement of the research-problem?
(a) Defining the Terms
(b) Objectives of Research
(c) Review of Research
(d) Area of Research

872. Common fallacy of reasoning leading to erroneous generalization
(a) errors incidental to classification, nomenclature and terminology.
(b) errors commonly arising out of the use of the inductive methods, false analogy including argument from final cause.
(c) fallacy of non-observation and mal-observation.
(d) All of these.

873. Statistical observations arranged in chronological order is called
(a) Progression
(b) Regression
(c) Time services
(d) None of the above

874. Hint is a formulating generalization
(a) that conclusions should be based on the evidence of sound adequate data, must answer the questions asked in the problem.
(b) must prove or disprove hypothesis, recognize the limitations of the study, accompanied by suggestions for application and implementation and suggestion of problems for further investigation.
(c) to summarise the findings and compare them with the hypothesis.
(d) All of these.

875. How many parts have the source of research-data is divided?
(a) Four (b) One
(c) Two (d) None of these

876. Which of the following is not the characteristic of a researcher?
(a) He is a specialist rather than a generalist.
(b) He is not versatile in his interest and even in his native abilities.
(c) He is industrious and persistent on the trial of discovery.
(d) He is not inspirational to his chosen field but accepts the reality.

877. The example of primary data is
(a) the material obtained by the research work of others.
(b) the material obtained by researcher's research-work.
(c) reliability of data.
(d) All of these.

878. Main body of the research report includes
(a) assumptions and delimitations and assumptions underlying the hypothesis.
(b) definition of important terms, statement of hypothesis.
(c) introduction—statement, significance and purposes.
(d) All of these.

879. Bibliography given in a research report
(a) shows the vast knowledge of the researcher.
(b) makes the report authentic.
(c) helps those interested in further research and studying the probiem from another angle.
(d) None of the above.

880. Reference section of a research report includes
(a) Appendix (b) Index if any
(c) Bibliography (d) All of these

881. What is a Sample?
(a) To give justice by research
(b) To find the value of variable some of its units are selected
(c) Group of persons
(d) All of these

882. Formula for standard error of Z (σ_Z) is
(a) $\frac{1}{\sqrt{N-3}}$ (b) $\frac{1}{\sqrt{N-2}}$
(c) $\frac{1}{N-3}$ (d) None of these

883. The quality or characteristic of condition which is the objective of research-study is called
(a) Population (b) Sample
(c) Variable (d) Tool

884. Projective technique is used for measuring
(a) individual's dominant feelings, emotions conflicts, needs repressed and stored up in the unconscious mind.
(b) individual's need for self-actualization.
(c) individual's value-system.
(d) individual's inventoried interests.

885. The quartile deviation in a frequency distribution is
(a) the distance between the 75th and 25th percentiles.
(b) the distance between the 70th and the 30th percentiles.
(c) half of the distance between the 75th and 25th percentiles.
(d) half of the distance between the 70th and 30th percentiles.

886. Where does importance of projective tests lie?
(a) Reliability and validity
(b) They reveal deeper layers of personality, i.e. emotions, conflicts, feelings, etc.
(c) Non-verbal and can be used even in case of illiterates and children
(d) Indirect methods of knowing and the potentials of a person

887. When the value of the characteristic selected for study is the same in all the units, then it is called
(a) Heterogeneous Population
(b) Homogeneous Population
(c) Both (a) and (b)
(d) None of these

888. If $\Sigma fx = 2461$, $N = 60$, $\overline{x} =$
(a) 40 (b) 43
(c) 42 (d) 41

889. When the value of variables in unit-2 changes then it is called
(a) Heterogeneous Population
(b) Homogenous Population
(c) Variable Population
(d) All of these

890. Not measured by TAT test is
(a) reasoning ability.
(b) personality needs.
(c) emotions.
(d) personality adjustment.

891. Index number is always a
(a) Absolute number
(b) Primary number
(c) Relative number
(d) None of the above

892. A projective technique uses
(a) unstructured stimulus situations such as ink-blots, photographs, etc.
(b) direct observations of a persons behaviour.
(c) a short structured interview schedule.
(d) on the spot participants observations for measuring an individual's qualities.

893. The population of 10 students of class XII for Intelligence Test will be
(a) Heterogeneous (b) Homogeneous
(c) Both (a) and (b) (d) None of these

894. The other name of non-parametric tests is
(a) X test
(b) distribution free test
(c) X^2 test
(d) None of the above

895. Usually what form of the sample is used for study in the fields of psychology and education?
(a) Homogeneous Population
(b) Heterogeneous Population
(c) Any form
(d) All of these

896. Opinionnaire is defined as a special form of inquiry to collect
(a) to quantify, analyse and interpret the collected data.
(b) the opinion of a sample of population on certain facts.
(c) Both (a) and (b).
(d) Neither (a) nor (b).

897. The Regression lies of x upon y is expressed as
(a) $X_c = ay + b$ (b) $Y_c = b + ay$
(c) $Y_c = ab + y$ (d) $X_c = a + by$

898. In case of true experiemntal research the investigator is always required to make a compromise between which of the following four is not correct?
(a) Randomization and manipulation
(b) Control of extraneous variables and building the correlated variable into design
(c) Internal validity and external validity
(d) Contrived setting and natural setting

899. When the counting and numbering of the units of the defined population is possible, then it is called
(a) Unlimited Population
(b) Limited Population
(c) Both (a) and (b)
(d) None of these

900. Calculus was developed by
(a) Descartes (b) Francis Bacon
(c) Spinoza (d) Leibniz

901. When the counting and numbering of the units of population is impossible, then it is called
(a) Unlimited Population
(b) Limited Population
(c) Both (a) and (b)
(d) None of these

902. While writing a research report investigators mostly arrange items in bibliography in
(a) in a single alphabetized list.
(b) heading like—books, perdiocals, newspaper reports, public documetns and miscellaneous.
(c) Both (a) and (b).
(d) Neither (a) nor (b).

903. Free hand method is used in
(a) Histogram
(b) Pie diagram
(c) Time services
(d) None of the above

904. When researchers refer to a significant difference, they mean that the
(a) results of a study occurred by chance.
(b) scores of two groups shows great variability.
(c) results of a study can be replicated by another similar study.
(d) experiental results have social importance.

905. The example of unlimited population in research is
(a) teachers of primary schools.
(b) number of planets in the sky.

(c) students of secondary level.
(d) None of these.

906. Non-parametric tests are used when
(a) variables are expressed in ordinal form.
(b) population from which sample is drawn is not normal.
(c) variables are expressed in nominal form, i.e. represented by frequency counts.
(d) All of the above.

907. When there is not a physical basis of population units then population is determined on assumptions, it will be called
(a) Assumed Population
(b) Real Population
(c) Limited Population
(d) Unlimited Population

908. Free Association in psycho-analysis means
(a) focussed interview.
(b) a structured interview.
(c) allowing a subject to talk freely.
(d) None of the above.

909. A test of "Shiftability of Base" is called
(a) Circular test
(b) Factor reversal test
(c) Time reversal test
(d) None of the above

910. There is only person who has defined Educational Research. He is
(a) W.M. Travers
(b) George Mouly
(c) John W. Best
(d) None of these

911. When all the units of population are real then it is called
(a) Mixed Population
(b) Real Population
(c) Assumed Population
(d) All of these

912. The Regression line of y upon x is expressed as
(a) $Y_c = a + bx$ (b) $X_c = b + ax$
(c) $X_c = a + bx$ (d) $Y_c = ax + b$

913. In the use of sample in research the following is not the advantage
(a) Repetition in research
(b) Accuracy of result
(c) Economy in expenditure
(d) Increase in the skill of the researcher

914. The device to measure the differences in the magnitude of a group of related variable is called
(a) Corelation
(b) Regression
(c) Index number
(d) None of the above

915. In the research work, the size of sample determines
(a) inclusion of total population
(b) representation of sample
(c) non-representation of sample
(d) All of these

916. The test used with discrete data in the form of frequencies is
(a) 't' test (b) ANOVA
(c) X^2 test (d) Z test

917. Statistically how much number of population can be the minimum large sample?
(a) Sample of less then 30
(b) Sample of more then 100
(c) Sample of more then 30
(d) Sample of more then 50

918. If N = 80, D_2 shall lie in
(a) 15th item (b) 14th item
(c) 18th item (d) 16th item

919. In research studies, the size of sample depends on
(a) tools of research.
(b) population of the research.

(c) nature of research.
(d) topic of research.

920. The problem solving method in the teaching of any subject is best adopted when the
   (a) students can solve the problem by their previous knowledge.
   (b) problem is presented in the form of an assignment by the teacher.
   (c) students previous knowledge is insufficient and the solution is possible only after acquiring new knowledge.
   (d) problem is selected out of the initiative of the teachers.

921. For a research study formulation of hypothesis norm is
   (a) it is not compulsory to formulate hypothesis to solve all problems.
   (b) in the statement of problem only one hypothesis is formulated for its solution.
   (c) in the statement of problem hypothesis having more than one solution is formulated.
   (d) Both (a) and (c)

922. Attributes of objects, events or things which can be measured are called
   (a) Qualitative measure
   (b) Variables
   (c) Data
   (d) None of the above

923. "Prizes increases the achievements in study". What type or category is for this statement of hypothesis?
   (a) Baseless Hypothesis
   (b) Hypothesis with direction
   (c) Hypothesis without direction
   (d) All of these

924. In plotting a frequency polygon, it is important to see that
   (a) mid point of all class intervals are joined together.
   (b) the mid point of an interval is always taken to represent the entire interval.
   (c) each class interval is represented by a separate rectangle.
   (d) None of the above.

925. "Prizes do not affect study-achievement". What is the category of this hypothesis?
   (a) Baseless
   (b) Zero or Null
   (c) With direction
   (d) Without direction

926. In a 2 × 2 table comprised of four cells with (2–1) (2–1) = 1 formula used for calculating X^2 is
   (a) $X^2 = \frac{(AD-BC)^2}{(A+B)(C+D)(A+C)(B+D)}$
   (b) $X^2 = \frac{N(AD-BC)}{(A+B)(C+D)(A+C)(B+D)}$
   (c) $X^2 = \frac{N(AD-BC)^2}{(A+B)(C+D)(A+C)(B+D)}$
   (d) None of the above

927. One of the characteristics which does not relate to good hypothesis is
   (a) to obtain results proper statistical techniques are used for analysis.
   (b) hypothesis is basis of verifying research work.
   (c) enough data may be collected patiently.
   (d) its results can be generalized.

928. If A = 35, $\Sigma fd = -200$, N = 100x =
   (a) 33 (b) 30
   (c) 32 (d) 40

929. What type of sample in research work first the size of the sample and population in determined?
   (a) Random Sample
   (b) Double Sample

(c) Organised Sample
(d) Proportionate Sample

930. The review of the related study is important while undertaking a research because
(a) it helps the researcher not to draw illogical conclusions.
(b) it helps in understanding the gaps.
(c) it avoids repetition or duplication.
(d) All of the above.

931. In research-work whatever units are conveniently available in the population are studied. This type of sample is called
(a) Objective-oriented
(b) Organised Sample
(c) Random Sample
(d) Incidental or Casual Sample

932. A researcher divides the populations into PG, graduates and 10 + 2 students and using the random digit table he selects some of them from each. This is technically called
(a) representative sampling
(b) stratified sampling
(c) stratified random sampling
(d) None of the above

933. The research-tools classification depends on
(a) sociology psychology basis and interview.
(b) enquiry size and observation.
(c) interview enquiry and size.
(d) All of these.

934. To measure the changed purchasing power of currency, the index number that is used is called
(a) Cost of living index
(b) Quantity index
(c) Both (a) and (b)
(d) None of the above

935. The enquiry form of research-tools include
(a) Intelligence Test
(b) Schedule Test
(c) Questionnaire
(d) Achievement Test

936. Median test is used for testing whether
(a) two independent samples differ in central tendencies.
(b) two samples differ from the population mean.
(c) two independent samples differ in SD.
(d) None of the above.

937. In research the question—what how and why—about the problem under study are related to
(a) Research Summary
(b) Research Report
(c) Research outline or proposal
(d) Research Process

938. A researcher selects a probability sample of 100 out of the total population. It is
(a) a systematic sample
(b) a random sample
(c) a cluster sample
(d) a stratified sample

939. It is not a necessary elements of Research-outline.
(a) Unscientific draft
(b) Writing sentences in present and future tense
(c) Its language should be simple
(d) Sentences be written in the third person

940. The process not needed in experimental researches is
(a) observation
(b) reference collection
(c) controlling
(d) manipulation and replication

941. For grouped sample, it is not correct.
(a) The results obtained are accurate and true
(b) It requires a lot of time and money
(c) It represents the population properly
(d) This method is objective

942. The experimental study is based on the law of
(a) interest of the subject
(b) occupation
(c) single variable
(d) replication

943. It is not correct about grouped sample.
(a) It is very useful and practical method
(b) It involves errors
(c) It is an easy method
(d) It saves time and money

944. Significance of contingency coefficient is calculated by the formula
(a) $C = \frac{X^2}{N + X}$ (b) $C = \frac{\sqrt{X^2}}{N + X^2}$
(c) $C = \sqrt{\frac{X^2}{N + X^2}}$ (d) None of the above

945. It is irrelevant about the stratified sample.
(a) It is a an objective sample
(b) It is a comprehensive technique for research
(c) It is a complex and different method
(d) It is a good sample

946. The period against which comparisons are made in Index number is called
(a) Coming year (b) Current year
(c) Base year (d) None of the above

947. For graded sample, it is an irrelevant aspect.
(a) This method saves money
(b) Its results can be generalized
(c) This method is free of error
(d) This method is easy

948. A statistical measure based upon the entire population is called parameter while measure based upon a sample is known as
(a) statistics
(b) sample parameter
(c) inference
(d) None of the above

949. The irrelevant aspects about undetermined sample is
(a) correctness about estimate depends on size of sample.
(b) an easy method.
(c) free from personal prejudice.
(d) represented the population.

950. Field study is related to
(a) laboratory situations
(b) experimental situations
(c) real life situations
(d) None of the above

951. The fact that is not correct about incidental sample is
(a) totally free from errors.
(b) not need a plan to select it.
(c) an easy method.
(d) useful for practical science.

952. The degree of relationship between a bivariate data is called
(a) correlation (b) data analysis
(c) regression (d) None of the above

953. It is not relevant about objective oriented sample.
(a) The units are properly controlled
(b) It can compare the groups properly
(c) Its technical method is not defective
(d) It can study its groups properly

954. The other name of independent variable for an experimental research is/are
(a) manipulated variable
(b) experimental variable

(c) treatment variable
(d) All of the above

955. This statement is not relevant about a complete sample.
(a) It is an easy method
(b) It is widely used in social surveys
(c) It is a form of grouped sample
(d) It is completely free from error

956. The approach to the concept of learning was different for Dewey and White Head in the following sense:
(a) Dewey thought learning as an end in itself whereas White Head thought about it as a means.
(b) Dewey thought of learning in pragmatic terms whereas White Head thought in terms of cultural aspects.
(c) Dewey thought of learning in experimental terms whereas White Head thought of it in more aesthetic terms.
(d) Dewey's approach was logical whereas White Head's approach was philosophical.

957. This is not relevant to say about determined sample.
(a) The research himself selects the definite units for his own purpose
(b) It can properly be used in research process
(c) It is an objective method
(d) None of these

958. If the sample drawn does not specify any condition about the parameter of the population, it is called
(a) census
(b) selected statistics
(c) distribution free statistics
(d) None of the above

959. If a group of students having low intelligence has low level of achievement, it is an example of
(a) positive high degree correlation
(b) zero correlation
(c) negative correlation
(d) negative high degree correlation

960. It is not the basis of stratification in the random stratified sampling.
(a) If the population is divided into coordinated sub-groups then the stratification is meaningless
(b) More possibility of the representativeness of the sample
(c) The knowledge about the units of different levels of population is needed
(d) Stratification is also done for administration convnience

961. If N = 100, D_4 shall lie in
(a) 90th item (b) 10th item
(c) 40th item (d) 50th item

962. Which of the following types is not stratified random sampling?
(a) Cluster Stratified
(b) G.C.M. Division
(c) Proportionate
(d) Non-Proportionate

963. Which of the following will be acceptable for establishing a fact?
(a) Reference in the ancient literature
(b) Traditionally in practice over a long period of time
(c) Opinion of a large number of people
(d) Availability of observable evidence.

964. When sometimes the units of sample are not natural units but are natural group or cluster then the sample is called
(a) Stratified Sample
(b) Graded Sample
(c) Cluster Sample
(d) Double Sample

965. Which of the following is a non-probability sample?

(a) Simple random sample
(b) Quota sample
(c) Purposive sample
(d) Both (a) and (c).

966. Questionnaire is a written form of interview technique this statement is
(a) Confusing
(b) Correct
(c) Not according to the facts
(d) None of these

967. Which of the following type of desks would you prefer as being convenient for students to write?
(a) The plus desk (b) The zero desk
(c) The minus desk (d) The flat desk

968. "Questionnaire is a technique of measurement used for getting responses written by the members of the sample". This definition is given by
(a) Good and Davis
(b) Good and Barr
(c) Good and Hatt
(d) Good and Scates

969. Coefficient of correlation ranges from
(a) 0.7 to –0.7 (b) 1 to 2
(c) –1 to +1 (d) None of the above

970. The field of descriptive and survey research-works is so comprehensive that for the collection of its data the following tool is most appropriate
(a) Check-List (b) Rating Scale
(c) Interview (d) Questionnaire

971. The plus two stage in our education ladder, is intended to
(a) be devoted for purely diversified vocational courses.
(b) divert a part of students towards vocational courses.
(c) provide for education as a substitute for the earlier intermediate education.
(d) All of the above.

972. This area or field does not relate to interview tool.
(a) In the view of participants
(b) In the view of work
(c) In the view of depth of study
(d) All types of research-work

973. Generalised conclusion on the basis of a sample is technically known as
(a) data analysis and interpretation.
(b) statistical inference of external validity of the research.
(c) parameter inference.
(d) All of the above.

974. The first step in the sequence of steps for interview is
(a) specification of the objectives of interview.
(b) real interview.
(c) conclusion of interview.
(d) meeting with the interviewee.

975. Which of the following assumptions would be correct from a statistical point of view?
(a) Measures of physical and mental traits cannot be accepted to follow the normal probability curve.
(b) Errors of observation will have frequencies that cannot approximate the normal probability curve.
(c) Linear magnitudes have measured frequencies that are always skewed.
(d) Linear magnitudes have measured frequencies closely following the normal probability curve.

976. Attitude is always
(a) Negative
(b) Positive
(c) Both positive and negative
(d) None of these

977. Direction of relationship between two variables is expressed by

(a) percentage of the coefficient
(b) degree of the coefficient
(c) the sign of the coefficient
(d) None of the above

978. If an attitude scale contains 30 opinions then an individual's minimum and maximum score will be between
(a) 0 and 150 (b) 30 and 90
(c) 30 and 150 (d) All of these

979. The device through which the functional relationship is studied and forecasting is made is called
(a) Time series
(b) Corelation
(c) Regression
(d) None of the above

980. If the observation is done from such a place that the observed group or persons are not aware of it then such observation is
(a) Objective (b) Subjective
(c) Uncontrolled (d) Controlled

981. Variance is given by
(a) $\frac{\sigma^2}{N}$ (b) $\frac{\overline{x}}{\sigma}$
(c) $\frac{\sigma}{\overline{x}}$ (d) σ^2

982. Hall Jenings name is associated with this tool of research
(a) Check-list (b) Sociomtry
(c) Score-card (d) Rating scale

983. The quartile deviation includes the
(a) first 50 per cent of the items
(b) last 50 per cent
(c) central 50 per cent
(d) All of the above

984. Standard deviation is always computed from
(a) Mode (b) Median
(c) Mean (d) G.M.

985. The following type of research-method is not according to the classification of George J. Mulley
(a) Historical Research
(b) Experimental Research
(c) Survey
(d) Action Research

986. The other name of Pearson correlation coefficient is
(a) phi coefficient of correlation.
(b) rank difference correlation.
(c) product moment correlation.
(d) None of the above.

987. Descriptive research is a part of survey research in how many sub-categories has it been divided?
(a) Three (b) Four
(c) Two (d) None of these

988. Which of the following measures is least affected by extreme items?
(a) Quartile deviation
(b) Standard deviation
(c) Mean deviation
(d) Range

989. Coefficient of variation is given by
(a) $\frac{\sigma}{\overline{x}}$ (b) $\frac{Q_3 - Q_1}{Q_3 + Q_1}$
(c) $\frac{A - Z}{\sigma}$ (d) None of the above

990. The research method by which we understand the present in the light of the past remains and facts is
(a) Survey Method
(b) Constitutional Method
(c) Experimental Method
(d) Historical Method

991. Which of the following is a computed measure of absolute variation?
(a) Quartile deviation
(b) Range

(c) Standard deviation
(d) All of the above

992. A good researcher lays his hands on
(a) any area as long as manpower and fundings are available in plenty.
(b) several areas and tries to understand them at fundamental level.
(c) a specific area and tries to understand it in minute details.
(d) All of the above.

993. The research in which prediction is made on the basis of finding the fundamental relations of events and used in their control is
(a) Analytical Method
(b) Historical Method
(c) Experimental Method
(d) Interview Survey Method

994. Partial correlation is calculated when
(a) we want to know the partial relationship between two variables.
(b) we want to nullify the effect of third variable on other two variables.
(c) Both (a) and (b).
(d) None of the above.

995. It is not related to the informations obtained from survey method
(a) Controlled Projection
(b) How can we get them
(c) What do we want
(d) What is the present state

996. Harmonic mean of a series of data is
(a) the reciprocal of the arithmetic average of the values of various items.
(b) the reciprocal of the arithmetic average of the reciprocals of the values of its various items.
(c) Always ill-defined.
(d) None of the above.

997. The speed of Rajdhani Express, Tamil Nadu Express and Kerala Express are 250 km, 200 km and 175 km per hour respectively. A passenger travelled 4800 km by Rajdhani, 3000 by TN Express and 2500 km by Kerala Express. The coverage of distance per hour is
(a) 212.37 km (b) 207.60 km
(c) 200.17 km (d) 217.17 km

998. The research method which prepares the basis of determination and planning, is
(a) Experimental Study
(b) Records Study
(c) Descriptive Study
(d) Historical Study

999. If by obtaining two curves one for X variable and other for Y variable we see the both curves moving in the same direction, it indicates
(a) Negative corelation
(b) Partial corelation
(c) Positive corelation
(d) None of the above

1000. "Some behaviours are generally observable but the behaviour cannot be described in words like differences of husband and wife family feuds and delivery of women." This statement indicates this reality of the tool of observation.
(a) Criticism of Observation
(b) Limits of Observation
(c) Characteristics of Observation
(d) None of these

1001. The nature of relationship is studied through
(a) Progression
(b) Co-relation
(c) Regression
(d) None of the above

1002. The formula for the Mean in the ungrouped data is
(a) M = A.M./N (b) M = SX/N
(c) M = S/X/N (d) None of these

1003. Mean deviation is ... standard deviation
(a) not related to (b) more than
(c) less than (d) equal to

1004. In the word 'Research', the word 'Search' is synonym of
(a) Investigation (b) Frequency
(c) Both (a) and (b) (d) None of these

1005. Coefficient of correlation is used to
(a) analyse factors
(b) make predictions
(c) evaluate the degree of reliability and validity of tests
(d) All of the above

1006. Which of the following research types is related to the curiosity of man?
(a) Fundamental Research
(b) Action Research
(c) Practical Research
(d) Intellectual Research

1007. Which of the measures of dispersion is more useful in case of open-end distributions?
(a) Range
(b) Quartile deviation
(c) Average deviation
(d) Standard deviation

1008. "National Science Foundation" has not included this type of research in its classification.
(a) Action Research
(b) Experimental Research
(c) Applied Research
(d) Fundamental Research

1009. Under a normal curve X + 2s covers
(a) 95.85 per cent (b) 94.55 per cent
(c) 95.45 per cent (d) 95.54 per cent

1010. When the average value of a number of years is taken as a trend to plot a trend line it is called
(a) Semi Average Method
(b) Moving Average Method
(c) Both (a) and (b)
(d) None of the above

1011. Edward and Cronback has not included this type of research in their classification.
(a) Technical Research
(b) Critical Research
(c) Historical Research
(d) Survey Research

1012. The following measure of central tendency cannot be represented graphically
(a) Median (b) Quartile
(c) Arithmetic mean (d) Mode

1013. It is not characteristic of the nature of the 'Educational Research'.
(a) Educational research is accurate like scientific research
(b) Educational research is based on subjectivity
(c) It is based on education and philosophy
(d) It is based on information and assumption

1014. The co-efficient value of co-relation lies between
(a) –1 to 1 (b) 1 – 10
(c) 0 to 1 (d) 0 to –1

1015. The following method is not the accepted method of getting knowledge.
(a) Deduction Method
(b) Knowledge
(c) Authority
(d) Individual Experience

1016. On matters of academics (knowledge) a researcher should consider himself as
(a) a status quo maintainer.
(b) entirely dependent on the teacher.

(c) fairly knowledgeable.
(d) open minded and radical.

1017. "The proposed question is for the solution of the problem." This statement was given by the following scholar relating to the research problem.
(a) Buch
(b) Turno and Rob
(c) Kalinger
(d) John C. Townsend

1018. Given the N values in a series, the geometric mean is the
(a) Nth root of the product of N values.
(b) fourth root of the product of N values.
(c) square root of the product of N values.
(d) third root of the product of N values.

1019. "The problem is such a question which can be answered by the use of an individual's general abilities." This is the statement is this scholar.
(a) Good and Scates
(b) N. Kalinger
(c) Mc Goodgan
(d) John Best

1020. Which of the measures given here are based on every item of the series?
(a) Standard deviation
(b) Quartile deviation
(c) Range
(d) All of the above

1021. The following is not the source of research problem according to John W. Best.
(a) Curriculum (b) School
(c) Society (d) All of these

1022. In regression equation of Y on X, YC = a + bx the values of
(a) a, b are constant
(b) a, b are variable
(c) Both (a) and (b)
(d) None of the above

1023. A good teacher is one who
(a) cooperates well with the principal
(b) teaches well
(c) reads a lot
(d) publishes lot of research papers

1024. Which of the following causes is not the cause of selection of research problem?
(a) To reform the educational situations
(b) Not to make the research basis of large research
(c) Researchers interests
(d) Researchers personal ambition

1025. A researcher selects a probability sample of 100 out of the total population. It is
(a) a random sample
(b) a stratified sample
(c) a cluster sample
(d) a systematic sample

1026. It is not included in the practical assumptions of research-problem.
(a) Moral problem
(b) Non-availability of data
(c) Expenditure
(d) Time

1027. If x is 4 and the distribution is 2, 3, 4, 5, 6, the sum of squared deviations from the x will be
(a) 12 (b) 6
(c) 8 (d) 10

1028. If in any research-work in the relation of problem Hypothesis and solution any hypothesis does not find its solution then
(a) nothing can be said about it.
(b) hypothesis will not be tested.
(c) hypothesis will be accepted.
(d) hypothesis will be rejected.

1029. A statistical measure based upon the entire population is called parameter while measure based upon a sample is known as
(a) Inference
(b) Statistics
(c) Sample parameter
(d) None of the above

1030. Such assumed Hypothesis which expresses the relation of two factors is called
(a) Zero Hypothesis
(b) Existential Hypothesis
(c) Fundamental Hypothesis
(d) Statistical Hypothesis

1031. Who said that members of the same species are not alike?
(a) Herbert Spencer
(b) Charles Booth
(c) Francis Bacan
(d) Charles Darwin

1032. The exponent of Zero Hypothesis is
(a) Hatt
(b) Kalinger
(c) Sir Ronald Fisher
(d) Good

1033. In a scatter diagram if the points come to a straight line it is an indication of
(a) no correlation
(b) skewness
(c) perfect correlation
(d) None of the above

1034. Such hypothesis which regulates the statistical relationship of fundamental hypothesis and the items is
(a) Fundamental Hypothesis
(b) Zero Hypothesis
(c) Universal Hypothesis
(d) Statistical Hypothesis

1035. The x height of 25 male workers in a factory is 61 cms; and the x height of 35 female workers in the same factory is 58 cms. The x height of 60 workers in the factory will be
(a) 28 (b) 49.25
(c) 59.25 (d) 43

1036. The test of hypothesis which is not a standardized test is called
(a) Z-test (b) T-test
(c) F-test (d) All of these

1037. A contractor employs 20 male, 15 female and 5 children in his factory. Male wages are ₹ 10 per day, female ₹ 8 per day, and children ₹ 3 per day. The weighted x of wages paid per day will be
(a) 8.37 (b) 10.63
(c) 3.86 (d) 9.21

1038. The following is not included in the fundamental research/data material
(a) Questionaire and schedule
(b) Record
(c) Researcher's or individual's own experiments
(d) Representative survey

1039. If x is 48, Median is 47, Mode value will be
(a) 45 (b) 49
(c) 50 (d) 44

1040. Find the median of the following data: 160, 180, 200, 280, 300, 320, 400
(a) 300 (b) 280
(c) 140 (d) 180

1041. Under a normal curve X + 3s covers area of
(a) 99.23 per cent (b) 99.37 per cent
(c) 99.32 per cent (d) 99.73 per cent

1042. If N = 150, L_1 = 40, L_2 = 50, f_1 = 51, c = 56. Median shall be

(a) 44.36 (b) 46.34
(c) 44.63 (d) 42.36

1043. If $\angle$ = 44, D_1 = 15, D_2 = 29, i = 4, Z =
(a) 45.37 (b) 45.27
(c) 45.47 (d) 45.17

1044. In research, 'Population' means
(a) the population which sees researcher.
(b) group of units things or men.
(c) the present population.
(d) None of these.

1045. In a frequency distribution the last cumulative frequency is 300, Median shall lie in
(a) 130th item (b) 140th item
(c) 150th item (d) 160th item

1046. The 'Variable' in research means
(a) that characteristics or state which is the aim of research.
(b) steps of research.
(c) steps of research-problem.
(d) None of these.

1047. The average monthly production of a factory for the first 8 months is 2,500 units, the next 4 months 1,200 units, the average monthly production of the year will be
(a) 3012.11 units (b) 2066.55 units
(c) 5031.10 units (d) 4021.12 units

1048. In a distribution of 10, 20, 30, 40, 50, the x is 30, the sum of deviations from x will be
(a) 60 (b) 15
(c) 0 (d) 30

1049. If N = 120, Sf/x = 5.975, H.M.=
(a) 20.08 (b) 20.06
(c) 28.02 (d) 19.08

1050. The degree of variable that is measured in the smallest unit is called
(a) Variable (b) Test
(c) Unit (d) None of these

1051. In a frequency distribution the last cumulative frequency is 500. Q_3 must lie in
(a) 275th item (b) 175th item
(c) 475th item (d) 375th item

1052. In a week the prices of a bag of rice were 350, 280, 340, 290, 320, 310, 300. The range is
(a) 60 (b) 100
(c) 60 (d) 70

1053. If Sfx = 825, N = 30, $\overline{x}$ =
(a) 25.2 (b) 25.7
(c) 22 (d) 27.5

1054. Verbal guidance is least effective in teaching
(a) attitude
(b) skills
(c) concept and facts
(d) relationship

1055. When the value of the characteristic selected for the research study is the same in each unit, then is called
(a) Sample
(b) Homogeneous Population
(c) Heterogeneous Population
(d) All of these

1056. Maximum participation of students is possible in teaching through
(a) audio-visual aids
(b) lecture method
(c) textbook method
(d) discussion method

1057. When in a research-study the value of variable changes in the units, then it is called
(a) Saming
(b) Homogeneous Population
(c) Heterogeneous Population
(d) None of these

1058. The essential role of the teacher in a class room is to

(a) give information
(b) motivate the students to learn
(c) develop learning competencies
(d) Both (b) and (c)

1059. Quality of education in a school/college can be measured through
(a) students' achievement.
(b) availability of manpower, teachers and principal.
(c) infrastructural facilities available.
(d) All of the above.

1060. In a research when the counting and numbering of the units of population is not possible then it is called
(a) Unlimited Population
(b) Homogeneous Population
(c) Heterogeneous Population
(d) Limited Population

1061. If you are planning to write a book for school children which of the following should be your main consideration?
(a) It should logically cover the entire field of the subject.
(b) It should be of the question-answer type.
(c) It should be examination oriented.
(d) It should provide the latest material on the subject.

1062. What is that method of sampling in which each unit has the probability of being selected?
(a) Representative Sample
(b) Random Sampling
(c) Probability Sampling
(d) Non-Probability Sampling

1063. Research has shown that maladjustment among teachers is
(a) relatively non-existent.
(b) exceedingly widespread, especially among women teachers.
(c) of greater incidence than in comparable professional groups.
(d) relatively rare among 'Career' teachers.

1064. The essential elements of any good curriculum are
(a) plans and activities
(b) content and structure
(c) content and text books
(d) teachers and text books

1065. The curriculum prepares the child for living in a
(a) Global society
(b) Regional society
(c) Both (a) and (b)
(d) None of the above

1066. What is that type of sample when the sample's Standard Deviation is less than the other deviation?
(a) Simple Sample
(b) Representative Sample
(c) Random Sample
(d) None of these

1067. Educational technology is a process concerned with
(a) the modern methods of technologies in teaching and learning in schools.
(b) equipping the technical institutions for better methods of instructions.
(c) improving the schools through implementation of science and technological subjects.
(d) explaining the progress of technology through education.

1068. What is that method of sampling in which the size of the sample and population is determined?
(a) Random Sample
(b) Incidental Sample
(c) Organised Sample
(d) Representative Sample

1069. By the term 'independent variable' in conducting any educational research we mean the
   (a) factors that are beyond the reach of the experiments for conducting a research.
   (b) freedom and independence of the experiments in formulating a research approach.
   (c) conditions or situations which the experiments can manipulate or change.
   (d) conditions which the experiments cannot manipulate or change.

1070. The topic method in education should be interpreted as a
   (a) method suited better for arts subjects as compared to science subjects.
   (b) substitute for the project method of teaching.
   (c) method of development of the syllabus in a subject.
   (d) concentric approach of teaching in the classroom.

1071. What is that method of sampling in which any unit is conveniently obtained for study?
   (a) Random Sample
   (b) Incidental Sample
   (c) Representative Sample
   (d) Organised Sample

1072. If I do not get a satisfactory explanation to certain occurrences
   (a) I would not be at rest until I get an appropriate explanation.
   (b) I would wait until I come across a right person who may explain it to me.
   (c) I give a damn to it, perhaps it is not worth knowing.
   (d) I would visit a nearby research institute to find out whether an answer could be obtained.

1073. The following is not the characteristic of research-tools.
   (a) Discrimination
   (b) Its reliability and validity
   (c) To fulfil the objective by the tool
   (d) Incomprehensiveness of the tool

1074. Educational Administration
   (a) is concerned with the what of education.
   (b) tells about the 'Ro' of educational objectives.
   (c) sets the goals for education.
   (d) explains the methods of schools and class control.

1075. "Questionnaire is a tool of getting responses and its form is such that the respondent answers himself." This is the statement of the following.
   (a) Good and Hatt (b) Good
   (c) Stern (d) Hatt

1076. Which is the most important characteristic of the survey method of research?
   (a) It aims at developing some theory or the scientific laws.
   (b) It relies on a small sample.
   (c) It focuses on studying the cause-effect relationship between variables.
   (d) It studies characteristics of a group instead of an individual.

1077. What is that type of questionnaire which requires definite reponse?
   (a) Open Questionnaire
   (b) Restricted Questionnaire
   (c) Mixed Questionnaire
   (d) Closed Questionnaire

1078. The aptitude of a person for taking teaching profession could be tested on the basis of
   (a) his attitude towards persons whom he has to teach.

(b) his enthusiasm to display his knowledge.
(c) his achievement standards in his courses of study.
(d) his imposing personality for controlling classes.

1079. "The rating scale presents a qualitative description of limited aspects of any person quality or thing." This is the statement of
(a) Good (b) Hatt
(c) John W. Best (d) Campher

1080. The main difference between an administrator and a researcher is in fact that the
(a) former is more interested in social outcomes while the latter in finding out as to why things happen as they do.
(b) former approaches problems in a practical manner while the latter is purely theoretical.
(c) former is more concerned only with the what of things while the researcher is interested both in the why and what of things.
(d) former takes a global view of things while the latter penetrates deep into specific issues.

1081. What will be the Chi-square value in the following

L	O	E
Low	4	5
Average	9	10
High	7	5

(a) 6.0 (b) 1.4
(c) 1.2 (d) 1.1

1082. It is not the type of rating scale.
(a) Statistical scale
(b) Social Distance scale
(c) Graph scale
(d) Standard scale

1083. The word 'statistics' has been derived from the ... word 'status'
(a) Russian (b) Latin
(c) Roman (d) Greek

1084. In the development of statistical methods, the greatest contribution is that of
(a) Economists (b) Businessmen
(c) Mathematicians (d) Scientists

1085. An absolute is defined as that which
(a) is said to be universally valid.
(b) requires proof of its validity.
(c) has been found to be true.
(d) everyone believes is true.

1086. The Rank difference coefficient of correlation is
(a) more reliable than the product movement when the number of cases is larger.
(b) almost the same as the product movement *r*, because the difference is so small.
(c) less reliable than the product movement *rx*.
(d) more reliable than the product movement *r*.

1087. "Observation in the controlled conditions can be conducted by the experementator and the results can be generalized." It is this type of observation.
(a) Participatory observation
(b) Laboratory observation
(c) Area observation
(d) None of these

1088. When an investigator uses two or more variables in combination to predict a single variable, he has to use
(a) product moment correlation, r
(b) partial correlation $r_{12.3}$
(c) rank order correlation
(d) multiple correlation, $R_{1.23}$

1089. Before using secondary data the only thing to be seen is that they are
(a) representative
(b) adequate for the purpose in hand
(c) reliable
(d) All of the above

1090. What is that type of observation which is only are inspection done in social conditions?
(a) Area observation
(b) Participatory observation
(c) Laboratory observation
(d) Non-participatory observation

1091. As a plural noun, statistics refers to
(a) interpretation of numerical data.
(b) statistical methods.
(c) compilation of numerical data.
(d) numerical statements of facts.

1092. The concepts of internal and external criticisms are associated with
(a) Literary research
(b) Descriptive research
(c) Experimental research
(d) Historical research

1093. What is that observation method in which the observer adjusts himself with the variables being observed and behaves like those variables?
(a) Laboratory observation
(b) Non-Participatory observation
(c) Area observation
(d) Participatory observation

1094. In any discipline, theories and their related experimental results
(a) should compensate each other.
(b) should complement each other.
(c) need not have anything to do with each other.
(d) more often than not should contradict each other.

1095. The inventor of sociometric technique was
(a) John Best (b) John Dewey
(c) Kilpatrick (d) Kegards

1096. Whom do you consider as the real giant in the development of the theory of statistics
(a) R.A. Fisher (b) Galton
(c) Bowley (d) Gauss

1097. Statistics has been defined as "The Science of Counting" by
(a) Karl Pearson (b) Bowley
(c) Galton (d) R.A. Fisher

1098. Most investigations rely on
(a) primary data
(b) secondary data
(c) both primary and secondary data
(d) None of the above

1099. In a test administrated to 50 boys and 50 girls, the means were 34.5 and 34.6 respectively. In the case of boys, the scores ranged from 15 to 49 and in the case of girls the range of scores was 20 to 40. We may, therefore conclude that
(a) the boys were less heterogenous than girls.
(b) the girls were more homogeneous than boys.
(c) there was greater uniformity among boys than girls.
(d) the girls were less heterogenous than boys.

1100. The research approach adopted by the persons for a study related to agriculture economy and product marketing is
(a) Complete Survey
(b) Sample Survey
(c) Survey Research
(d) Historical Survey

1101. In its present usage the word statistics is

(a) 10 centuries old
(b) 3 centuries old
(c) a century old
(d) a decade old

1102. Statistics can
(a) prove anything
(b) disprove anything
(c) neither prove nor disprove anything is just a tool
(d) None of the above

1103. If a test measures successfully what it attempts to measure, it is termed as
(a) Diagnostic (b) Reliable
(c) Valid (d) Objective

1104. What is that survey approach which conducts a comprehensive statistical study of the whole population?
(a) Complete sample system
(b) Area use system
(c) States or census system
(d) Sample survey system

1105. The first question that a researcher interested in the application of statistical techniques to his problem has to ask is
(a) whether worthwhile inferences could be drawn.
(b) whether the data could be quantified.
(c) whether analysis of data would be possible.
(d) whether appropriate statistical techniques are available.

1106. The synonym of "Zero Hypothesis" is
(a) Un-Directed Hypothesis
(b) Statistical Negative Hypothesis
(c) Directed Hypothesis
(d) None of these

1107. Statistical methods
(a) have to be used with caution
(b) are foolproof
(c) can be used by anyone
(d) are always definite and certain

1108. Statistics implies
(a) only data
(b) only statistical methods
(c) both data and statistical methods
(d) None of the above

1109. Chi-square was first used in 400 A.D. by
(a) Kil Patrick (b) Campher
(c) Karl Pearson (d) John Best

1110. The number of questions in a questionnaire should be
(a) a minimum of five.
(b) as small as possible keeping in view the purpose of the survey.
(c) limited to a maximum of twenty.
(d) around fifteen.

1111. A set of questions asked and filled in by the interviewer in a face-to-face situation with another person is called
(a) a schedule (b) a questionnaire
(c) an opinionnaire (d) a check list

1112. The information about behaviours and mental activities collected by the methods of observation experiment interview and questionnaire are in this form.
(a) Numerical form
(b) Quantitative form
(c) Both (a) and (b)
(d) None of these

1113. Type I error is also known as
(a) error of the first kind
(b) alpha error
(c) false positive
(d) All of the above

1114. To study the relationship of family size to income, a researcher classifies his population into different income slabs and then takes a random sample from each slab. Which technique of sampling does he adopt?
(a) Systematic sampling
(b) Random sampling

(c) Stratified random sampling
(d) Cluster sampling

1115. Which of the following statistics aim at describing correctly the quantitative or numerical data obtained from large units?
(a) Correlated Statistics
(b) Descriptive Statistics
(c) Assumed Statistics
(d) All of these

1116. The most important question for a researcher interested to use statistical technique in his problem to see
(a) whether analysis of data would be possible.
(b) whether appropriate statistical techniques are available.
(c) whether worthwhile inferences could be drawn.
(d) whether the data could be quantified.

1117. A good piece of research is the product of
(a) collective scholarship.
(b) a penetrating and analytical mind.
(c) a touch of genius.
(d) a good research library.

1118. Research is
(a) data gathering, processing and analysis.
(b) data gathering only.
(c) moving from a broad area to a narrow and focussed area.
(d) a systematic process of finding the truth.

1119. Which of the following statistics aim at measuring the mutual relation of two or more measures or variables?
(a) Correlated Statistics
(b) General Statistics
(c) Assumed Statistics
(d) Descriptive Statistics

1120. Which of the following skills/qualities is most important for a researcher?
(a) Ability to gather data
(b) Ability to work hard
(c) Communication skills
(d) Desire to discover the truth.

1121. The case study method is adopted to find out the
(a) family history of a person.
(b) cases of a child's maladjustment.
(c) effects of heredity on education of a child.
(d) personality development of an individual.

1122. The first question that a researcher interested in the application for statistical techniques to his problem has to ask is
(a) whether worthwhile inferences could be drawn.
(b) whether the data could be quantified.
(c) whether appropriate statistical techniques are available.
(d) whether analysis of data would be possible.

1123. What is that statistics in which on the basis of obtained data the two process of predicting about the population are—Hypothesis testing and computation?
(a) Descriptive Statistics
(b) General Statistics
(c) Correlated Statistics
(d) Assumed Statistics

1124. Which statement is not correct?
(a) All researches contribute to the existing knowledge.
(b) One research gives birth to another research.
(c) A good researcher is expected to be a knowledgeable person.
(d) None of the above.

1125. The quality of research is judged by the
(a) depth of the research
(b) experience of the researcher
(c) relevance of research
(d) methodology followed in conducting the research

1126. What is the simplest method of measuring things or events for classifying them into different types on the basis of some specific characteristic?
(a) Interval Scale
(b) Proportional Scale
(c) Nominal Scale
(d) Categoric Scale

1127. The objectives of a research can be written
(a) only in question form
(b) only in statement form
(c) both in question and statement form
(d) in hypothetical form

1128. Quality of research depends on
(a) dedication on the part of researchers
(b) available facilities
(c) use of high technology
(d) training in research methodology

1129. What is that scale which can measure the distance or difference of distance between the characteristics of two things?
(a) Interval Scale
(b) Categorical Scale
(c) Proportional Scale
(d) None of these

1130. Which of the following is a measure of variability?
(a) Standard deviation
(b) Mean
(c) Median
(d) Correlation coefficient

1131. My reaction to the statement: "A good teacher is essentially a good researcher" is that this is
(a) only a hypothesis
(b) only an opinion
(c) difficult to agree
(d) my firm belief

1132. Which of the following measuring scales organises in a sequence the things, events, characteristics and reactions on the basis of their some quality?
(a) Categorical Scale
(b) Proportional Scale
(c) Interval Scale
(d) Nominal Scale

1133. One undertakes research
(a) to describe and explain a new phenomenon.
(b) to refute what has already been accepted as a fact.
(c) to verify what has already been established.
(d) All of the above.

1134. What is that scale of physical or mental measurement which provides in it Zero point?
(a) Proportional Scale
(b) Interval Scale
(c) Nominal Scale
(d) Categorical Scale

1135. Which of the following will be acceptable for establishing a fact?
(a) Availability of observable evidence
(b) Traditionally in practice over a long period of time
(c) Reference in the ancient literature
(d) Opinion of a large number of people.

1136. When the scores are written in a column in ascending or descending order and the frequency of getting a score is noted against each score, then it is called
(a) Histogram
(b) Line Graph
(c) Frequency Distribution
(d) Pi Chart

1137. Comparison, contrasts and associations lead to

(a) Generalisation (b) Motivation
(c) Recapitulation (d) Application

1138. Sometimes the questions are classified into different groups on the basis of Nominal Scàle. What figure or chart is used to show these scores?

(a) Line graph
(b) Cumulative frequency curve
(c) Pi chart
(d) Column figures

1139. In a frequency distribution of scores of 'N' measures if 'X' stands for deviations in the units of class intervals and 'C' stands for correlation in the class intervals from the assumed means, the standard deviation should be calculated by the formula

(a) $fx^2 - C^2/N-2$ xi (interval)
(b) $fx - C^2/N-1$ xi (interval)
(c) $fN^2 - C^2/2$ xi (interval)
(d) $fx^2 - C^2/N$ xi (interval)

1140. When the cumulative frequencies are changes into percentages then the curve built by percentile frequencies is called

(a) Percentile cumulative curve
(b) Cumulative frequency curve
(c) Score-frequency
(d) Histogram

1141. Several surveys conducted by medical councils and school health committees have revealed that the biggest deficiency percentages among school children are due to

(a) postural disorders
(b) nutritional disorders
(c) lack of parental attention
(d) lack of recreational facilities

1142. If mode is 52, mean is 48, median value will be

(a) 49.3 (b) 51
(c) 49 (d) 48

1143. What is the method of computing Median besides the Algebric formula?

(a) Median from graph
(b) Score cumulative method
(c) Median from grouped data
(d) None of these

1144. The mean weight is 160 lbs, standard deviation 7 lbs, coefficient of variation will be

(a) 0.01 (b) 0.02
(c) 0.03 (d) 0.044

1145. The population of a state was 300 million in 1991, it became 640 million in 2001. The percentage compound rate of growth per annum will be

(a) 5% (b) 4%
(c) 3% (d) 3.9%

1146. What is that measure of central tendency which is used in large size of data and it has a score occuring with highest frequency?

(a) Mode (b) Median
(c) Mean (d) None of these

1147. If the industrial production in the country increased by 5% in the first year, 6% in the second year, and 7% in the third year, the average increase for three years will be

(a) 5% (b) 7%
(c) 6% (d) None of these

1148. Which of the following forms is the basis of the similarity or closeness of Mean, Median and Mode?

(a) Median
(b) Frequency Distribution
(c) Scores
(d) None of these

1149. The measure called the 'Mean Deviation' is used when

(a) we want to compute coefficients of correlation between two set of scores.
(b) we want to know the total spread of scores in a distribution.
(c) it is desired to weight all deviations according to size.
(d) we want a quick measure of variability in a distribution of scores.

1150. While preparing frequencies distribution the highest and the lowest limits of the scores are determined. What measure shows the interval between the highest and lowest scores?
(a) Quality of Variance
(b) Standard Deviation
(c) Frequency Distribution
(d) Complete Variance

1151. The $\overline{x}$ is 80, s is 25, the coefficient of variance shall be
(a) 31.10 (b) 30.96
(c) 32.10 (d) 31.25

1152. The most significant measure based on deviation of the variance is
(a) Variance (b) Mean
(c) Data Collection (d) Mode

1153. The mean height of a group of children is 70 cm and standard deviation 1.3 cm. The coefficient of variation will be
(a) 0.017 (b) 0.018
(c) 0.019 (d) 0.006

1154. If mean is 40, median is 42, the value of absolute skewness is
(a) 6 (b) 5
(c) –5 (d) –6

1155. If mode is 27, s is 6, and Coefficient of skewness is 0.33 the value of x will be
(a) 28.98 (b) 28.21
(c) 27.82 (d) 30

1156. What is the mean of ignored values with position and negative signs of the deviation of scores of a data-collection from the mean?
(a) Mean Deviation
(b) Variance Measure
(c) Mean
(d) Standard Deviation

1157. Which of the following cannot be a good way of communication in promoting literacy among villagers?
(a) Providing material on TV and film projector
(b) Demonstration
(c) Reading and Writing
(d) Large group discussion.

1158. If $Q_3 - Q_1$ is 40, median is 32, and SKb is 0.5, find out the value of Q_1 and Q_3
(a) 12, 52 (b) 22, 62
(c) 20, 60 (d) 22, 42

1159. What is that statistic which describes the quantitative relation of the determined quality and the variance of the values of two variables?
(a) Variance and Standard Deviation
(b) Complete Variance
(c) Correlation Statistics
(d) Standardized Score

1160. Kurtosis of a frequency distribution means that the
(a) frequency distribution is peaked or flat as compared to normal distribution.
(b) measures are grouped more towards the left end.
(c) frequency distribution is flatted than the distribution in the frequency polygon.
(d) measures are grouped more towards the right end.

1161. What is closely related to correlation?
(a) Complete Statement
(b) Complete Variance

(c) Standardized Score
(d) All of these

1162. You want to find out the reading interests of children and for this purpose you select representative sample of children of different ages in your area. This survey would be called
(a) Cross-sectional case study approach
(b) Development case study approach
(c) Genetic case study approach
(d) Longitudinal case study approach

1163. The correlation coefficient can be compluted directly from the raw scores without finding the deviation. This computation method is known as
(a) Ungrouped Computation Method
(b) Standard Score Method
(c) Correlation Difference Method
(d) Raw Score Method

1164. If SKp is 0.52, mean is 80, mode is 60, the value of s will be
(a) 35.22 (b) 37
(c) 38.46 (d) 28.52

1165. What is the mean of the sample?
(a) Confidence Level
(b) Large Sample
(c) Point Computation
(d) Confidence Interval

1166. T-distribution was originated in the year
(a) 409 (b) 410
(c) 1808 (d) 408

1167. In a research when it is formulated or assumed that a mean is not equal to other mean or there is real difference between their values, then this hypothesis is called
(a) Directed Hypothesis
(b) Null Hypothesis
(c) Non-directed Hypothesis
(d) All of these

1168. The statistical process used in testing the significance of the difference of independent mean the same process is used in testing the significance of the difference of the following.
(a) Standard error of the difference of dependent means
(b) The significance of the difference of correlated means
(c) Significance test
(d) None of these

1169. Which of the following tests is used when both the means are based on large samples?
(a) ANOVA Test (b) T-test
(c) Critical Ratio (d) F-test

1170. What type of the measure of the degree of difference of probable frequencies is chi-square?
(a) Qualitative Measure
(b) Numerical Measure
(c) Descriptive Measure
(d) Quantitative Measure

1171. Like T-Ratio frequency chi-square is also a statistics of this type.
(a) Probability (b) Sample
(c) Sample selection (d) None of these

1172. Which of the following tests is used when the number of samples in a research is less?
(a) Sign-test (b) T-test
(c) F-test (d) None of these

1173. When the behaviour or trait of an individual is measured more than one after different intervals and the measurement remains the same, then this test is regarded as
(a) Standard Test (b) Valid Test
(c) Reliable Test (d) None of these

1174. The most widely used test of reliability is

(a) General relevance method
(b) Retest method
(c) Internal relevance method
(d) None of these

1175. What method is used to know the reliability of test in which the test is divided into equal parts and the correlation between the scores obtained from these tests is computed?
(a) Internal Relevance Method
(b) Retest Method
(c) Alternate Method
(d) Half Split Method

1176. The following is not the necessity of educational research.
(a) Productivity of education
(b) Multifaced view of education
(c) Revolution and extension in education
(d) Technical traditionalism

1177. The number of areas of educational research as shown by Dr. Buch in his edited book *Survey of Research in Education* in 1974, is
(a) Twenty-six (26) (b) Sixteen (16)
(c) Ten (10) (d) Six (6)

1178. What method is used when all the items of a test are homogeneous?
(a) Alternate Method
(b) Internal Relevance Method
(c) Half split Method
(d) None of these

1179. Observe the following statements of Bogrades which according to him is fixed?
(1) To close kinship by marriage
(2) To give employment in my occupation
(3) To visitors in my country
(4) To citizenship in my country
The right sequence of these statements according to Bogradus is
(a) 1, 2, 3, 4 (b) 1, 2, 4, 3
(c) 3, 2, 1, 4 (d) 4, 3, 2, 1

1180. Who have given the following suggestions about the analysis of data?
(i) Thinking over data through Meaning Table
(ii) Carefully examining the problem statements
(iii) Thinking over the problem like an ordinary person
(iv) Using various ordinary statistical analysis
(a) George J. Mouly
(b) John W. Best
(c) Goode, Barr and Scates
(d) W.S. Munroe

ANSWERS

1. (b)	2. (c)	3. (b)	4. (a)	5. (d)	6. (b)
7. (d)	8. (b)	9. (c)	10. (a)	11. (d)	12. (c)
13. (d)	14. (b)	15. (c)	16. (a)	17. (d)	18. (d)
19. (b)	20. (c)	21. (d)	22. (a)	23. (d)	24. (d)
25. (d)	26. (c)	27. (b)	28. (b)	29. (a)	30. (a)
31. (b)	32. (a)	33. (b)	34. (c)	35. (d)	36. (a)
37. (a)	38. (a)	39. (d)	40. (d)	41. (c)	42. (d)
43. (b)	44. (b)	45. (d)	46. (b)	47. (a)	48. (b)

49. (d)	50. (d)	51. (b)	52. (c)	53. (b)	54. (c)
55. (c)	56. (a)	57. (b)	58. (a)	59. (c)	60. (a)
61. (d)	62. (a)	63. (c)	64. (b)	65. (c)	66. (a)
67. (b)	68. (c)	69. (b)	70. (d)	71. (c)	72. (d)
73. (d)	74. (b)	75. (d)	76. (c)	77. (c)	78. (b)
79. (a)	80. (a)	81. (a)	82. (c)	83. (d)	84. (a)
85. (a)	86. (b)	87. (c)	88. (d)	89. (b)	90. (c)
91. (a)	92. (b)	93. (b)	94. (b)	95. (c)	96. (a)
97. (a)	98. (b)	99. (d)	100. (c)	101. (d)	102. (c)
103. (d)	104. (b)	105. (d)	106. (d)	107. (c)	108. (d)
109. (b)	110. (c)	111. (b)	112. (d)	113. (b)	114. (c)
115. (b)	116. (a)	117. (c)	118. (d)	119. (d)	120. (c)
121. (d)	122. (a)	123. (c)	124. (c)	125. (a)	126. (c)
127. (c)	128. (c)	129. (d)	130. (c)	131. (b)	132. (d)
133. (b)	134. (b)	135. (c)	136. (b)	137. (d)	138. (b)
139. (d)	140. (d)	141. (b)	142. (b)	143. (a)	144. (d)
145. (c)	146. (b)	147. (d)	148. (c)	149. (a)	150. (d)
151. (c)	152. (a)	153. (d)	154. (c)	155. (d)	156. (a)
157. (d)	158. (a)	159. (c)	160. (c)	161. (a)	162. (c)
163. (a)	164. (d)	165. (a)	166. (c)	167. (d)	168. (c)
169. (d)	170. (d)	171. (a)	172. (d)	173. (a)	174. (a)
175. (c)	176. (b)	177. (a)	178. (a)	179. (d)	180. (d)
181. (b)	182. (d)	183. (c)	184. (d)	185. (c)	186. (a)
187. (a)	188. (d)	189. (a)	190. (d)	191. (d)	192. (a)
193. (a)	194. (c)	195. (d)	196. (c)	197. (d)	198. (c)
199. (a)	200. (c)	201. (a)	202. (c)	203. (a)	204. (d)
205. (d)	206. (a)	207. (c)	208. (c)	209. (a)	210. (b)
211. (a)	212. (d)	213. (c)	214. (c)	215. (d)	216. (a)
217. (c)	218. (b)	219. (a)	220. (a)	221. (a)	222. (c)
223. (a)	224. (c)	225. (b)	226. (a)	227. (d)	228. (a)
229. (a)	230. (c)	231. (c)	232. (b)	233. (d)	234. (c)
235. (c)	236. (b)	237. (d)	238. (b)	239. (b)	240. (c)
241. (d)	242. (c)	243. (b)	244. (d)	245. (d)	246. (c)
247. (d)	248. (c)	249. (c)	250. (c)	251. (b)	252. (c)

253. (d)	254. (d)	255. (c)	256. (d)	257. (d)	258. (b)
259. (b)	260. (b)	261. (b)	262. (d)	263. (c)	264. (b)
265. (c)	266. (c)	267. (c)	268. (b)	269. (c)	270. (a)
271. (d)	272. (d)	273. (a)	274. (a)	275. (d)	276. (b)
277. (c)	278. (a)	279. (b)	280. (a)	281. (a)	282. (d)
283. (a)	284. (a)	285. (d)	286. (d)	287. (a)	288. (c)
289. (a)	290. (d)	291. (a)	292. (a)	293. (a)	294. (a)
295. (d)	296. (a)	297. (d)	298. (d)	299. (b)	300. (a)
301. (a)	302. (c)	303. (c)	304. (b)	305. (d)	306. (d)
307. (a)	308. (c)	309. (d)	310. (a)	311. (d)	312. (a)
313. (a)	314. (a)	315. (d)	316. (c)	317. (c)	318. (d)
319. (b)	320. (b)	321. (d)	322. (c)	323. (d)	324. (c)
325. (b)	326. (b)	327. (b)	328. (a)	329. (d)	330. (a)
331. (b)	332. (b)	333. (d)	334. (b)	335. (a)	336. (b)
337. (a)	338. (a)	339. (a)	340. (d)	341. (d)	342. (d)
343. (a)	344. (c)	345. (a)	346. (d)	347. (a)	348. (c)
349. (c)	350. (b)	351. (c)	352. (d)	353. (a)	354. (a)
355. (b)	356. (d)	357. (a)	358. (c)	359. (a)	360. (d)
361. (b)	362. (a)	363. (d)	364. (d)	365. (a)	366. (a)
367. (c)	368. (c)	369. (a)	370. (a)	371. (a)	372. (c)
373. (c)	374. (d)	375. (d)	376. (a)	377. (c)	378. (b)
379. (b)	380. (d)	381. (c)	382. (b)	383. (b)	384. (a)
385. (c)	386. (b)	387. (c)	388. (d)	389. (c)	390. (a)
391. (c)	392. (a)	393. (d)	394. (a)	395. (c)	396. (c)
397. (b)	398. (d)	399. (b)	400. (c)	401. (d)	402. (b)
403. (d)	404. (c)	405. (d)	406. (a)	407. (d)	408. (d)
409. (a)	410. (c)	411. (d)	412. (c)	413. (d)	414. (c)
415. (b)	416. (a)	417. (b)	418. (d)	419. (c)	420. (c)
421. (b)	422. (d)	423. (d)	424. (c)	425. (c)	426. (d)
427. (c)	428. (a)	429. (b)	430. (b)	431. (b)	432. (d)
433. (b)	434. (d)	435. (d)	436. (d)	437. (b)	438. (a)
439. (c)	440. (a)	441. (d)	442. (d)	443. (b)	444. (c)
445. (b)	446. (b)	447. (c)	448. (b)	449. (a)	450. (b)
451. (b)	452. (c)	453. (d)	454. (a)	455. (d)	456. (b)

457. (d)	458. (d)	459. (a)	460. (d)	461. (a)	462. (c)
463. (d)	464. (a)	465. (a)	466. (b)	467. (a)	468. (a)
469. (c)	470. (c)	471. (b)	472. (c)	473. (c)	474. (c)
475. (b)	476. (c)	477. (d)	478. (d)	479. (a)	480. (c)
481. (c)	482. (b)	483. (a)	484. (a)	485. (d)	486. (d)
487. (a)	488. (d)	489. (c)	490. (b)	491. (d)	492. (c)
493. (b)	494. (d)	495. (d)	496. (c)	497. (d)	498. (c)
499. (b)	500. (d)	501. (b)	502. (c)	503. (c)	504. (d)
505. (c)	506. (c)	507. (d)	508. (a)	509. (c)	510. (b)
511. (d)	512. (c)	513. (d)	514. (d)	515. (c)	516. (d)
517. (d)	518. (d)	519. (a)	520. (c)	521. (d)	522. (d)
523. (b)	524. (c)	525. (d)	526. (c)	527. (b)	528. (c)
529. (d)	530. (c)	531. (d)	532. (c)	533. (d)	534. (c)
535. (b)	536. (c)	537. (c)	538. (c)	539. (c)	540. (d)
541. (b)	542. (a)	543. (b)	544. (c)	545. (b)	546. (d)
547. (c)	548. (b)	549. (a)	550. (b)	551. (b)	552. (a)
553. (c)	554. (c)	555. (a)	556. (b)	557. (c)	558. (c)
559. (b)	560. (c)	561. (a)	562. (c)	563. (b)	564. (c)
565. (a)	566. (b)	567. (d)	568. (c)	569. (d)	570. (d)
571. (d)	572. (c)	573. (d)	574. (c)	575. (d)	576. (c)
577. (b)	578. (d)	579. (a)	580. (a)	581. (c)	582. (b)
583. (a)	584. (a)	585. (c)	586. (a)	587. (c)	588. (c)
589. (d)	590. (c)	591. (b)	592. (b)	593. (c)	594. (a)
595. (c)	596. (d)	597. (a)	598. (c)	599. (a)	600. (d)
601. (a)	602. (d)	603. (a)	604. (c)	605. (d)	606. (d)
607. (d)	608. (d)	609. (b)	610. (c)	611. (c)	612. (c)
613. (d)	614. (d)	615. (a)	616. (b)	617. (d)	618. (a)
619. (a)	620. (c)	621. (c)	622. (b)	623. (d)	624. (b)
625. (a)	626. (d)	627. (a)	628. (b)	629. (c)	630. (c)
631. (b)	632. (d)	633. (d)	634. (d)	635. (c)	636. (d)
637. (a)	638. (d)	639. (c)	640. (a)	641. (d)	642. (a)
643. (b)	644. (c)	645. (b)	646. (b)	647. (b)	648. (a)
649. (c)	650. (c)	651. (b)	652. (b)	653. (a)	654. (a)
655. (c)	656. (b)	657. (c)	658. (a)	659. (a)	660. (d)

661. (d)	662. (a)	663. (a)	664. (a)	665. (a)	666. (a)
667. (b)	668. (d)	669. (c)	670. (b)	671. (b)	672. (b)
673. (b)	674. (c)	675. (a)	676. (d)	677. (b)	678. (c)
679. (b)	680. (c)	681. (a)	682. (b)	683. (c)	684. (c)
685. (b)	686. (a)	687. (b)	688. (b)	689. (c)	690. (c)
691. (c)	692. (a)	693. (d)	694. (b)	695. (b)	696. (c)
697. (a)	698. (b)	699. (c)	700. (c)	701. (c)	702. (b)
703. (c)	704. (d)	705. (a)	706. (a)	707. (b)	708. (b)
709. (d)	710. (d)	711. (b)	712. (a)	713. (c)	714. (a)
715. (a)	716. (a)	717. (a)	718. (d)	719. (b)	720. (d)
721. (b)	722. (d)	723. (b)	724. (c)	725. (a)	726. (d)
727. (d)	728. (d)	729. (b)	730. (c)	731. (b)	732. (c)
733. (c)	734. (b)	735. (a)	736. (a)	737. (d)	738. (c)
739. (a)	740. (d)	741. (d)	742. (d)	743. (b)	744. (a)
745. (b)	746. (d)	747. (d)	748. (c)	749. (d)	750. (b)
751. (a)	752. (d)	753. (b)	754. (d)	755. (c)	756. (d)
757. (d)	758. (d)	759. (c)	760. (b)	761. (d)	762. (b)
763. (d)	764. (b)	765. (a)	766. (b)	767. (b)	768. (d)
769. (a)	770. (d)	771. (c)	772. (d)	773. (b)	774. (b)
775. (d)	776. (c)	777. (c)	778. (d)	779. (d)	780. (a)
781. (d)	782. (a)	783. (b)	784. (d)	785. (d)	786. (b)
787. (d)	788. (c)	789. (a)	790. (c)	791. (b)	792. (a)
793. (c)	794. (c)	795. (a)	796. (c)	797. (d)	798. (a)
799. (b)	800. (c)	801. (b)	802. (a)	803. (a)	804. (c)
805. (a)	806. (c)	807. (c)	808. (c)	809. (b)	810. (d)
811. (a)	812. (d)	813. (d)	814. (a)	815. (d)	816. (d)
817. (d)	818. (a)	819. (b)	820. (a)	821. (c)	822. (d)
823. (c)	824. (d)	825. (c)	826. (a)	827. (d)	828. (c)
829. (d)	830. (b)	831. (b)	832. (b)	833. (b)	834. (b)
835. (d)	836. (a)	837. (c)	838. (c)	839. (b)	840. (b)
841. (a)	842. (d)	843. (c)	844. (b)	845. (a)	846. (c)
847. (c)	848. (a)	849. (b)	850. (d)	851. (b)	852. (b)
853. (c)	854. (a)	855. (b)	856. (d)	857. (a)	858. (d)
859. (b)	860. (d)	861. (c)	862. (d)	863. (c)	864. (d)

865. (c)	866. (a)	867. (a)	868. (d)	869. (a)	870. (d)
871. (c)	872. (d)	873. (c)	874. (d)	875. (c)	876. (b)
877. (b)	878. (d)	879. (c)	880. (d)	881. (b)	882. (a)
883. (c)	884. (a)	885. (c)	886. (b)	887. (b)	888. (d)
889. (a)	890. (a)	891. (c)	892. (a)	893. (a)	894. (b)
895. (b)	896. (c)	897. (d)	898. (c)	899. (b)	900. (d)
901. (a)	902. (a)	903. (c)	904. (c)	905. (b)	906. (d)
907. (a)	908. (c)	909. (a)	910. (a)	911. (b)	912. (d)
913. (a)	914. (c)	915. (b)	916. (c)	917. (c)	918. (d)
919. (c)	920. (c)	921. (d)	922. (b)	923. (b)	924. (a)
925. (d)	926. (c)	927. (b)	928. (a)	929. (c)	930. (d)
931. (d)	932. (c)	933. (d)	934. (a)	935. (c)	936. (a)
937. (c)	938. (a)	939. (a)	940. (b)	941. (b)	942. (d)
943. (b)	944. (c)	945. (c)	946. (c)	947. (c)	948. (a)
949. (a)	950. (c)	951. (a)	952. (a)	953. (c)	954. (d)
955. (d)	956. (c)	957. (c)	958. (c)	959. (a)	960. (a)
961. (c)	962. (a)	963. (d)	964. (b)	965. (d)	966. (b)
967. (c)	968. (d)	969. (c)	970. (d)	971. (b)	972. (d)
973. (b)	974. (d)	975. (d)	976. (c)	977. (c)	978. (c)
979. (c)	980. (a)	981. (d)	982. (b)	983. (c)	984. (c)
985. (d)	986. (b)	987. (a)	988. (b)	989. (a)	990. (d)
991. (c)	992. (c)	993. (c)	994. (b)	995. (a)	996. (b)
997. (a)	998. (c)	999. (c)	1000. (b)	1001. (c)	1002. (b)
1003. (c)	1004. (a)	1005. (d)	1006. (d)	1007. (b)	1008. (a)
1009. (c)	1010. (b)	1011. (c)	1012. (c)	1013. (a)	1014. (c)
1015. (b)	1016. (d)	1017. (d)	1018. (a)	1019. (c)	1020. (b)
1021. (d)	1022. (a)	1023. (b)	1024. (b)	1025. (a)	1026. (b)
1027. (d)	1028. (d)	1029. (b)	1030. (c)	1031. (d)	1032. (c)
1033. (c)	1034. (d)	1035. (c)	1036. (d)	1037. (b)	1038. (b)
1039. (a)	1040. (b)	1041. (d)	1042. (c)	1043. (a)	1044. (c)
1045. (c)	1046. (a)	1047. (b)	1048. (c)	1049. (a)	1050. (c)
1051. (d)	1052. (d)	1053. (d)	1054. (b)	1055. (b)	1056. (d)
1057. (c)	1058. (d)	1059. (c)	1060. (a)	1061. (a)	1062. (b)
1063. (c)	1064. (a)	1065. (a)	1066. (b)	1067. (a)	1068. (c)

1069. (c)	1070. (b)	1071. (b)	1072. (a)	1073. (d)	1074. (d)
1075. (a)	1076. (d)	1077. (b)	1078. (a)	1079. (c)	1080. (a)
1081. (d)	1082. (b)	1083. (b)	1084. (c)	1085. (a)	1086. (b)
1087. (b)	1088. (d)	1089. (d)	1090. (a)	1091. (d)	1092. (d)
1093. (d)	1094. (b)	1095. (d)	1096. (a)	1097. (b)	1098. (b)
1099. (b)	1100. (b)	1101. (d)	1102. (c)	1103. (c)	1104. (c)
1105. (b)	1106. (c)	1107. (a)	1108. (c)	1109. (c)	1110. (b)
1111. (d)	1112. (c)	1113. (d)	1114. (c)	1115. (b)	1116. (d)
1117. (b)	1118. (a)	1119. (a)	1120. (b)	1121. (b)	1122. (b)
1123. (d)	1124. (a)	1125. (c)	1126. (c)	1127. (c)	1128. (a)
1129. (c)	1130. (a)	1131. (d)	1132. (a)	1133. (c)	1134. (a)
1135. (a)	1136. (c)	1137. (a)	1138. (d)	1139. (d)	1140. (a)
1141. (a)	1142. (a)	1143. (a)	1144. (d)	1145. (d)	1146. (a)
1147. (c)	1148. (b)	1149. (b)	1150. (d)	1151. (d)	1152. (b)
1153. (c)	1154. (d)	1155. (a)	1156. (a)	1157. (c)	1158. (c)
1159. (c)	1160. (a)	1161. (a)	1162. (a)	1163. (d)	1164. (c)
1165. (c)	1166. (c)	1167. (c)	1168. (b)	1169. (c)	1170. (c)
1171. (c)	1172. (a)	1173. (c)	1174. (b)	1175. (d)	1176. (d)
1177. (b)	1178. (b)	1179. (b)	1180. (c)		

Model Test Papers

PAPER-II
SET-1

1. Match the following—

   List I (Characteristic)

   A. Learning by doing
   B. Education through environment
   C. Realization of truth, beauty and goodness
   D. "World as it is here and now"

   List II (Philosophy)

   1. Naturalism
   2. Idealism
   3. Pragmatism
   4. Realism
   5. Existentialism

Codes:	A	B	C	D
(a)	1	3	2	4
(b)	3	2	4	5
(c)	3	1	2	4
(d)	1	4	2	3

2. "No disinterested pursuit of knowledge and no intellectual education for its own sake" was the slogan of the
   (a) Pragmatists (b) Naturalists
   (c) Realists (d) Idealists

3. **Assertion (A):** Marx advocated the creation of a classless society.

   Reason (R): There are too many classes which are struggling with each other.

   Codes:
   (a) Both (A) and (R) are false
   (b) Both (A) and (R) are true
   (c) Only (A) is true
   (d) Only (R) is true

4. The process of attaining one's existence as per existentialism is
   (a) lonliness, pain and pleasure, struggle, essence.
   (b) essence, struggle, pain and pleasure, lonliness.
   (c) essence, pain and pleasure, struggle, lonliness.
   (d) lonliness, struggle, pain and pleasure, essence.

5. Which philosophy says "Do not care to know various theories about God and Soul; do good and be good; that will take you to whatever truth there is"?
   (a) Jainism (b) Vedanta
   (c) Sankhya (d) Buddism

6. The originaltor of coefficient of correlation to know the degree of liner correlation between two variables was
   (a) Kil Patric (b) Bloom
   (c) John Best (d) Pearson

7. Which statement/s is/are true as per Buddhist philosophy?
   1. Maya is root cause of all troubles
   2. Sorrow is the root cause of all troubles

3. Birth and death are causes of troubles
4. Getting involved in worldly pursuits is the cause of all troubles

(a) 2, 3 and 4 are true
(b) 2 and 3 are true
(c) 1 and 2 are true
(d) 1, 2, 3 and 4 are true

8. Which philosophy developed the monitorial system in classrooms?

(a) Buddhism (b) Islam
(c) Vedant (d) Vedic

9. **List I (Thinker)**

A. Gandhi
B. Tagore
C. Aurobindo
D. Vivekananda

List II (Type of Education)

1. Shantiniketan
2. Integral Yoga
3. Gurukul
4. Man-making education
5. Wardha Scheme

Codes:	**A**	**B**	**C**	**D**
(a)	3	4	2	5
(b)	5	1	2	4
(c)	4	2	3	5
(d)	5	1	4	2

10. The aim of basic education, as per the dream of Gandhiji is to

1. create a classless society.
2. create a Sarvodaya Society.
3. create a society respecting all religions.
4. create a society where a rich and poor can live together.

(a) 2, 3 and 4 are correct
(b) 1, 2 and 4 are correct
(c) 1, 2, 3 and 4 are correct
(d) 1, 2 and 3 are correct

11. Which part of Indian Constitution allows every citizen to impart education as per ones own religion?

(a) Democratic Rights
(b) Fundamental Rights
(c) Directive Principles
(d) Concurrent List of Centre and the States

12. Who is not in favour of logical analysis?

(a) Ludwig Wittgenstein
(b) G.E. Moore
(c) Kant
(d) Bertrand Russel

13. The great sociologist who held the view that "education doesn't bring about social change; rather the social change results into an educational change" was

(a) Durkheim (b) Dewey
(c) McDougal (d) Aristotle

14. Why is school considered a miniature society?

(a) Like a chicken develops into an adult, school children develop into adult, society members.
(b) Though small in number, school inmates come from society only.
(c) The number of school inmates is less than the number of society members.
(d) School children are of lower age group than society members.

15. Why is mother regarded as the first teacher of a child?

1. The basic learning of the child occurs in the company of mother only.
2. Informal learning of the child with the mother is more effective than the formal learning in later years of life.
3. The child lives in the womb of the mother for nine months.
4. The mother tries to impart her bets to the child.

(a) 2 and 4 are correct
(b) 1 and 2 are correct
(c) 2 and 3 are correct
(d) All of the above four statements are correct

16. By community, we mean a group of people with
    (a) similar aim and at least one factor as common among caste, class, religion, profession or belief.
    (b) same caste, class, religion or profession.
    (c) people with similar aim.
    (d) None of the above
17. Teaching Political Science to learners helps in
    1. developing leadership skills in them.
    2. developing political consciousness among them.
    3. inculcating democratic values in them.
    4. developing awareness about social issues in them.
    (a) 1, 2 and 3 are correct
    (b) 2, 3 and 4 are correct
    (c) 1, 2 and 4 are correct
    (d) All of the above statements are correct
18. Religion is an institution because
    (a) it imparts moral and spiritual education to people.
    (b) it gives respect to the individual in society.
    (c) it teaches religion to people.
    (d) it discharges an important social function.
19. Which of the following mobility is not related to modernization?
    (a) Physical mobility
    (b) Social mobility
    (c) Psychic mobilty
    (d) Scientific mobility
20. Teaching how to respect elders and talk to them is an example of
    (a) Socialization
    (b) Social adjustment
    (c) Social cohesion
    (d) Social change
21. Which of the following is not a factor for social change in India?
    (a) Regionalism (b) Census
    (c) Caste (d) Language
22. Religion acts as a great barrier in social change because
    (a) it expects participation of all age groups.
    (b) it preached values.
    (c) it is based on faith.
    (d) it depends on social gathering.
23. Equality of educational opportunities is possible by
    (a) privatizing the education system in the country.
    (b) public funding of education.
    (c) extending portals of educational institutions to all without any discrimination.
    (d) opening more educational institutions.
24. Children of some minority communities are unable to fully participate in Indian educational institutions because
    (a) minority communities lack faith in Indian education system.
    (b) Indian educational institutions do not have required infrastructure.
    (c) there is exclusion process in educational institutions.
    (d) minority communities have not been spending on education of their children.
25. "Give me a dozen of healthy children I can make them Doctor, Judge, Beggar and even a Thief"—comment made by
    (a) Hull (b) Guthrie
    (c) J.B. Watson (d) Jung
26. Which doesn't belong to the group of the other three?

(a) Guthrie's Theory of Learning
(b) Operant Conditioning Theory of Learning
(c) Classical Conditioning Theory of Pavlov
(d) Learning Theory of Watson

27. The view that "Anything can be taught at any stage of development" was expressed by
(a) Bruner (b) Gagne
(c) Piaget (d) Asubel

28. The IQ of a 25 years old boy, whose mental age 16 will be
(a) 80 (b) 100
(c) 64 (d) 75

29. Which of the following is an incorrect pair?
(a) Field Theory of Learning — Lewing
(b) Sign Theory of Learning — Tolman
(c) Trial and Error Theory of Learning — Thorndike
(d) Social Learning Theory — Bruner

30. **Assertion (A):** Pleasure or displeasure resulting from a learning experience decides the degree of its effectiveness.

Reason (R): All pleasant experiences have a lasting influence and are remembered for a long-time while the unpleasant ones are soon forgetten.

Codes:
(a) Both (A) and (R) are correct and (R) is the correct explanation for (A)
(b) Only (R) is correct
(c) Both (A) and (R) are incorrect
(d) Both (A) and (R) are correct and (R) is not the correct explanation for (A)

31. The Rorschach-Inkblot Test consists of
(a) five black and white and five multicoloured cards.
(b) ten multicoloured cards.
(c) five black and five coloured cards.
(d) ten black and ten white cards.

32. If Ram is taller than Mohan and Mohan is taller than Sohan, Ram is the tallest. This statement comes under which type of reasoning?
(a) Conditioned Reasoning
(b) Linear Reasoning
(c) Inductive Reasoning
(d) Deductive Reasoning

33. **List I**
A. Theory of Instinct
B. Drive Reduction Theory
C. Social Urges Theory
D. Self-actualization Theory

List II
1. McDougal 2. Hall
3. Adler 4. Maslow
5. Freud

Codes:	**A**	**B**	**C**	**D**
(a)	5	4	1	2
(b)	1	2	3	4
(c)	1	3	4	2
(d)	1	5	2	4

34. Which one of the statements is incorrect in the context of determinants of attention?
(a) It is always better to introduce novelty to secure attention.
(b) Moving stimulus catches our attention quickly.
(c) Too much repetition of a stimulus captures our attention.
(d) All types of stimuli are not able to bring forth the same degree of attention.

35. In the conditioning approach to learning,
   (a) the natural stimulus follows the unnatural stimulus.
   (b) response to natural stimulus required to be reinforced.
   (c) the subject should be in readiness to receive the unnatural stimulus.
   (d) the unnatural stimulus follows the natural stimulus.

36. If a group of children learns a lot of arithmetic skills by way of completing a project on 'Celebration of Deepawali festival'. This will be known as a kind of
   (a) Informal learning
   (b) Incidental learning
   (c) Non-formal learning
   (d) Formal learning

37. Which of the following is a method of qualitative research?
   (a) Ethernomethodology
   (b) Experimental Research
   (c) Ex-post factor Research
   (d) Normative Survey

38. Which of the following is not common to experimental and ex-post facto designs of research?
   (a) Controlling extraneous variables
   (b) Observation of dependent variable
   (c) Cause and effect relationship.
   (d) Manipulation of independent variable

39. An operational definition of a construct is the one which defines it in terms of
   (a) other equivalent words in the dictionary.
   (b) other constructs.
   (c) implied behaviour pattern.
   (d) activities necessary to measure it.

40. Which of the following is not a characteristic feature of research process?
   (a) Systematic endeavour
   (b) Critical analysis
   (c) Empirical approach
   (d) Uncontrolled conditions

41. The method of measuring many characteristics of the reactions occuring by only one stimulus is
   (a) Standardized Deviation
   (b) Mean
   (c) Correlation
   (d) None of these

42. The synonym of "Probability" is
   (a) Natural (b) Possibility
   (c) Natural priority (d) Sample

43. Which of the following is not correctly matched?
   (a) KR-20 : Stability
   (b) Parallel Form : Equivalence
   (c) Test-Retest : Stability
   (d) Split-Half : Internal Consistency

44. **List I**
   A. Intelligence
   B. Attitude
   C. Projective Techniques
   D. Semantic Differential

   List II
   1. Alfred Binet
   2. LL Thurstore
   3. Rorschach
   4. Osgood
   5. Guilford

Codes:	**A**	**B**	**C**	**D**
(a)	5	2	1	4
(b)	1	2	3	4
(c)	2	4	3	1
(d)	4	3	2	5

45. Which of the following is not a measure of dispersion?
   (a) Standard Deviation
   (b) Mean Deviation
   (c) Range
   (d) Mode

46. The variance reflecting a systematic difference between groups of measures is termed as
   (a) Withing Groups Variance
   (b) Experimental Variance
   (c) Total Variance
   (d) Error Variance
47. The difference between a statistical average based on the entire population and the one based on a sample is known as
   (a) Sampling Error
   (b) Mean Deviation
   (c) Standard Error
   (d) Mean Difference
48. The Standard Deviation of Sampling Distribution of a Statistic is known as
   (a) Sampling Error
   (b) Standard Variance
   (c) Sampling Variance
   (d) Standard Error
49. In the process of statistical inference, the Type II Error is committed when we
   (a) accept a false null hypothesis.
   (b) reject a false null hypothesis.
   (c) accept a true null hypothesis.
   (d) reject a true null hypothesis.
50. If a researcher conducts a research on finding out which administrative style contributes more to institutional effectiveness. This will be an example of
   (a) Fundamental Research
   (b) Applied Research
   (c) Basic Research
   (d) Action Research

ANSWERS

1. (c)	2. (c)	3. (a)	4. (a)
5. (a)	6. (d)	7. (d)	8. (b)
9. (d)	10. (c)	11. (b)	12. (a)
13. (a)	14. (a)	15. (d)	16. (b)
17. (d)	18. (a)	19. (c)	20. (c)
21. (d)	22. (a)	23. (c)	24. (c)
25. (c)	26. (c)	27. (c)	28. (c)
29. (d)	30. (d)	31. (d)	32. (a)
33. (a)	34. (c)	35. (c)	36. (c)
37. (b)	38. (c)	39. (c)	40. (d)
41. (c)	42. (b)	43. (a)	44. (b)
45. (d)	46. (d)	47. (c)	48. (d)
49. (b)	50. (a)		

PAPER-II
SET-2

1. Which of the following is not a task of Philosophy?
   (a) Prescription
   (b) Observation
   (c) Speculation
   (d) Description and Analysis
2. Which of the following is not a unique feature of education envisaged by Swami Vivekananda?
   (a) Residential programme of education
   (b) Importance to concentrations
   (c) Cultivation of heart and physical strength
   (d) Intelligent productive manual labour
3. 'Intuitive Knowledge' is attained through
   (a) External experiences
   (b) Internal experiences
   (c) Both internal and external experiences
   (d) Neither internal nor external experiences
4. "The child is an integral part of the ultimate universe" is the viewpoint of
   (a) Existentialism (b) Idealism
   (c) Realism (d) Pragmatism
5. Which of the following is not a suited connotation for 'Equality of educational opportunity'?

(a) Equitable rationing and distribution of available resources to all.
(b) Investing more funds on education.
(c) A policy of open access to education to all.
(d) Equalisation of educational attainment by providing resources in favour of less able and less motivated group.

6. 'Learning in communion with nature' was propagated by
(a) Sri Aurobindo
(b) Mahatma Gandhi
(c) Swami Vivekananda
(d) Rabindranath Tagore

7. The founder of Pragmatism was
(a) Kilpatrick
(b) Charles Sanders Peirce
(c) John Dewey
(d) William James

8. Rousseau's conception of 'freedom' was not accepted by
(a) John Dewey (b) Paulo Freire
(c) Pestalozzi (d) Jean Paul Sartre

9. "Discipline through direct consequence" was propagated by
(a) Naturalist (b) Realist
(c) Existentialist (d) Pragmatist

10. The School of Philosophy which upholds the primacy of 'mind' over 'matter' is
(a) Pragmatism (b) Idealism
(c) Realism (c) Existentialism

11. The teacher is very much concerned with epistemology because his aim is to promote
(a) Knowledge (b) Skills
(c) Values (d) Truth

12. Which School of Philosophy maintains that the "universe is an expression of intelligence and will"?
(a) Pragmatism (b) Idealism
(c) Existentialism (d) Realism

13. "Education according to interest rather than the caste, creed, race or religion" was propagated by
(a) Jainistic Education
(b) Buddhistic Education
(c) Vedantic Education
(d) Islamic Education

14. The major constraint of social change is
(a) Religion (b) Poverty
(c) Education (d) Caste

15. Modernisation of 'educational programmes' has posed many issues in the society. Which one of the following is not applicable?
(a) Increasing number of suicides in students
(b) Reduced status of teachers
(c) Increasing numbers of crimes in teenagers
(d) Misuse of media by youngsters

16. Analysis of the sociological processes involved in the educational institutions could be known as
(a) Sociology of Education
(b) Educational Sociology
(c) Social Science of Education
(d) Social foundations of Education

17. According to Talcott Parson, social change deals with
(a) Cultural revolution
(b) Functional needs of the society
(c) Spiritual upliftment
(d) Economic upliftment

18. Caste system can create a
(a) Changing society
(b) Open society
(c) Closed society
(d) Dead society

19. It is often complained that there is a 'brain drain' in our country. The implication is that

(a) education today is creating strain to the brains of students.
(b) the brains of educated persons are being washed in unnecessary pursuits.
(c) educated and capable people are seeking jobs in other countries for better opportunities and economic benefits.
(d) students' brains are burdened with education unnecessarily.

20. Some sociologists have given importance to the functioning factors of social interaction. These factors are concerned with
(a) the purpose and common facts of societies.
(b) the needs and past experiences of the societies.
(c) goodness, common cause and economy of the societies.
(d) the proximity and similarity of the societies.

21. National reconstruction in any country should be based on
(a) weeding out the unsocial and unscientific practices at the top level.
(b) developing ambitious outlooks among administrator.
(c) familiarising the children with the nation's culture and philosophy.
(d) improvement of adjustability and adaptability of people.

22. Which of the following is not an attribute of culture?
(a) Innate (b) Learnt
(c) Transmittable (d) Shared

23. The Kothari Commission's report was entitled as
(a) Diversification of Education
(b) Education and Social Change in Democracy
(c) Education and National Development
(d) Learning to Be

24. Acculturation is the process of
(a) following the latest trends of a culture as opposed to the past traditions.
(b) developing qualities affecting the culture of a nation.
(c) accepting the innovations required for the development of nation's culture.
(d) being influenced by the cultural imperatives of a nation.

25. The SUPW has been introduced in the school curriculum due to the recommendation of
(a) The Ishverbhai Patel Educational Review Committee
(b) The University Education's Committee Report
(c) The Kothari Education Commission's Report
(d) The Secondary Education Commission's Report

26. For harmonious development of the personality of the child, parents should
(a) provide conducive environment at home.
(b) engage qualified teachers for the child.
(c) regularly compare the child with other children.
(d) over-protect the child.

27. During early phases of development, educational psychology has drawn its content from the researches in
(a) Medical Sciences
(b) Natural Sciences
(c) Physical Sciences
(d) Social Sciences

28. Who among the following described the intellectual development as age-related development?
(a) Jean Piaget
(b) Hilda Taba

(c) Jerome S. Bruner
(d) David Ausubel

29. Most important factors in the development of child are
(a) educational and social status of parents.
(b) socio-economic and intellectual environment of the child.
(c) physical and moral environment of the child.
(d) social and economic status of the family.

30. Differences in 'Learning Styles' among learners may be attributed to
(a) economic conditions of the family.
(b) parenting of the child.
(c) socialisation process of learner.
(d) thinking strategies adopted by learner.

31. Two-factor theory of intelligence is given by
(a) L.M. Terman
(b) J.P. Guilford
(c) Alfred Binnet and L. Simon
(d) C.E. Spearman

32. Children whose mental age is lower than chronological age are called
(a) Normal children
(b) Retarded children
(c) Gifted children
(d) Learning disabled

33. Concepts are important vehicles in
(a) motivating the learner.
(b) learning communication.
(c) achievement of learner.
(d) thinking processes.

34. The meaningful reception learning was explained by
(a) David Ausubel
(b) Jerom S Bruner
(c) Robert Gagne
(d) Jean Piaget

35. The type of learning explained by Albert Bandura is also known as
(a) Sign learning
(b) Insight learning
(c) Verbal learning
(d) Observational learning

36. A child is working very hard for her examination. Her behaviour is an indicator of her
(a) very busy schedule.
(b) desire to impress her parents.
(c) high achievement motivation.
(d) sharp cognitive abilities.

37. The purpose of instructional theory is
(a) Evaluative (b) Prescriptive
(c) Descriptive (d) Instructive

38. The quality of questions in a test is assessed by using the method of
(a) Content Analysis
(b) Trend Analysis
(c) Item Analysis
(d) Task Analysis

39. The size of a population is 100 and every 5th person is selected to form a sample. This technique of sampling is known as
(a) Systematic (b) Cluster
(c) Random (d) Stratified

40. The operational definition of a variable indicates as to how that variable may be
(a) Measured (b) Observed
(c) Explain (d) Described

41. If a test measures mastery level achievement in a subject, it is known as
(a) Norm-referenced test
(b) Criterion-referenced test
(c) Prognostic test
(d) Diagnostic test

42. In an ethnographical study which of the following techniques is most appropriate?
(a) Observation
(b) Sociometry

(c) Psychological testing
(d) Questionnaire

43. The correlation between X and Y is significant. It means that
(a) Y causes variation in X.
(b) X and Y vary independently.
(c) X causes variation in Y.
(d) X and Y vary together.

44. If Q_1, Q_2 and Q_3 represent 1st, 2nd and 3rd quartiles respectively and Q semi-intrinsic quartile, then Q may be written as—
(a) $\frac{Q_3 + Q_1}{2}$ (b) $Q_2 - Q_1$
(c) $Q_1 - Q_3$ (d) $\frac{Q_3 - Q_1}{2}$

45. If K is added to every score of a distribution with mean 'M' and standard deviation 's' the new standard deviation will be
(a) Ks (b) K
(c) s (d) s + K

46. If each z-score of a distribution of scores is multiplied by 10 and the result increased by 50, the standard deviation of the resulting numbers would be
(a) 40 (b) 5
(c) 50 (d) 10

47. Which of the following types of test-items make a 'supply type' test?
(a) Completion (b) Classification
(c) Multiple choice (d) Matching

48. Which of the following purposes demands Action Research?
(a) Solving a classroom problem
(b) Testing a theory
(c) Developing a theory
(d) Writing a thesis

49. What type of the measure of the degree of difference of probable frequencies is chi-square?
(a) Qualitative Measure
(b) Numerical Measure
(c) Descriptive Measure
(d) Quantitative Measure

50. **List I (Type of Correlation)**
A. Biserial correlation
B. Pie coefficient
C. Point-biserial correlation
D. Tetrachoric correlation

List II (Nature of Variables)
1. Continuous *vs* Continuous
2. Continuous *vs* Dichotomous
3. Dichotomous *vs* Dichotomous
4. Dichotomized *vs* Dichotomized
5. Continuous *vs* Dichotomized

Codes:	A	B	C	D
(a)	3	2	5	2
(b)	5	4	2	1
(c)	4	1	5	2
(d)	5	3	2	4

ANSWERS

1. (a)	2. (a)	3. (c)	4. (b)
5. (b)	6. (d)	7. (b)	8. (c)
9. (b)	10. (c)	11. (a)	12. (b)
13. (c)	14. (d)	15. (d)	16. (b)
17. (b)	18. (c)	19. (c)	20. (c)
21. (a)	22. (d)	23. (c)	24. (c)
25. (d)	26. (a)	27. (d)	28. (a)
29. (b)	30. (d)	31. (d)	32. (b)
33. (d)	34. (d)	35. (d)	36. (c)
37. (a)	38. (a)	39. (a)	40. (b)
41. (a)	42. (b)	43. (d)	44. (d)
45. (c)	46. (d)	47. (a)	48. (a)
49. (c)	50. (c)		

PAPER-II
SET-3

1. Who has said this—"Education is the manifestation of divine perfection already existing in Man"?
   (a) Tagore
   (b) Sri Aurobindo
   (c) Mahatma Gandhi
   (d) Swami Vivekananda
2. Which philosophy believes in the five principles of conduct—Truth, Non-stealing, Non-violence, No sex life, Non-attachment?
   (a) Vedic (b) Islamic
   (c) Buddhism (d) Jainism
3. Which one of the following is the main source of educational progress?
   (a) Educational History
   (b) Educational Philosophy
   (c) Educational Theory
   (d) Educational Practice
4. Functions of Educational Philosophy is
   (a) Critical (b) Speculative
   (c) Normative (d) All the above
5. Weakest point of idealistic education is ________.
   (a) methods of teaching
   (b) discipline
   (c) aims
   (d) curriculum
6. The moral values of life are associated with which problem of philosophy?
   (a) Axiology (b) Cosmology
   (c) Metaphysics (d) Epistemology
7. Which one of the following is not a form of Naturalism?
   (a) Mechanical Naturalism
   (b) Biological Naturalism
   (c) Physical Naturalism
   (d) Psychological Naturalism
8. The main aim of idealistic education is ________.
   (a) creation of intuition
   (b) to be practical
   (c) self-realization
   (d) physical development
9. "Integration of the learning process" is the key note of the philosophy of the school
   (a) Pragmatism (b) Idealism
   (c) Realism (d) Existentialism
10. Which school of philosophy describes philosophy as an activity having no content?
   (a) Sankhya Darshan
   (b) Marxism
   (c) Logical Positivism
   (d) Naturalism
11. Education should be vocational in character is advocated by
   (a) Pragmatism (b) Idealism
   (c) Naturalism (d) Realism
12. **List I** **List-II**
   A. Sankhya 1. Swami Mahavira
   B. Vedanta 2. Gautam Buddha
   C. Buddhism 3. Kapil
   D. Jainism 4. Shankaracharya
   5. Kanad

Codes:	A	B	C	D
(a)	4	1	2	5
(b)	1	5	3	2
(c)	5	2	1	3
(d)	3	4	2	1

13. **List I**
   A. Navodaya Vidyalaya
   B. Home
   C. Changing way of life
   D. Social stratification

   List II
   1. Culturally Decided
   2. Socialisation

3. Equality of educational opportunities
4. Modernisation

Codes:	A	B	C	D
(a)	3	4	2	1
(b)	1	3	4	2
(c)	1	2	3	4
(d)	3	2	4	1

14. **Assertion (A):** Girls from poor families usually drop out of the school.

    Reason (R): Girls look after their younger brothers and sisters at home.
    (a) (A) and (R) both are correct
    (b) (A) and (R) both are wrong
    (c) Only (A) is correct
    (d) Only (R) is correct

15. The skills and knowledge acquired in the classroom are actually utilised by the individual in his/her adjustment to
    (a) Social Culture
    (b) Social Behaviour
    (c) Social Science
    (d) Social Situation

16. Which of the following is informal agency of education?
    (a) Classroom (b) Seminar
    (c) Library (d) Playground

17. Which one of the following is not an agency of socialisation?
    (a) Printed material
    (b) Kin group
    (c) Neighbourhood
    (d) Playmates

18. Which of the following is a barrier to social changed?
    (a) Pragmatic (b) Poverty
    (c) Aristocracy (d) Thinking

19. The concept of 'Continuous learning' is the outcome of
    (a) need to apprise oneself with latest knowledge.
    (b) dynamics of expansion of knowledge.
    (c) need to educate large number of illiterates.
    (d) people's desire to learn more.

20. Sociology of education includes
    (a) society and its relationship with the individual.
    (b) communication of individual with society.
    (c) social relations by which an individual gains experiences.
    (d) social development in the country.

21. Which of the following is included in the implied concept of school as a social agency?
    (a) Curriculum should be organized in terms of local needs
    (b) Curriculum should be organized as per needs of the individual child
    (c) Curriculum should be organized in terms of development of knowledge
    (d) Curriculum should be organized in terms of social values

22. Which of the following is not one of the pillars of education?
    (a) Learning to work
    (b) Learning to know
    (c) Learning to be
    (d) Learning to live peacefully with others

23. "Educational change and social change are independent, but which is the cause and which is the effect cannot be determined" are the views of
    (a) Ottoway (b) Auguste Comte
    (c) Dewey (d) Gandhiji

24. Stratification in society is based on
    (a) motivation, mobility and material possession.
    (b) education, earning and empowerment.
    (c) power, property and prestige.
    (d) culture, caste and class.

25. Educational psychology is not
   (a) a normative science
   (b) a social science
   (c) a behavioural science
   (d) an applied science

26. Identify the true statement from the following.
   (a) A person with low intelligence can be creative.
   (b) Intelligence and creativity are not related to each other.
   (c) A highly intelligent person is highly creative.
   (d) A certain level of intelligence is essential for being creative.

27. "Negative reinforcement" means
   (a) punishment.
   (b) terminating an unpleasant stimulus.
   (c) not presenting any stimulus.
   (d) presenting an unpleasant stimulus.

28. 'Programmed learning' is based on
   (a) Operant conditioning
   (b) Classical conditioning
   (c) Field theory
   (d) Gestalt learning theory

29. Enquiry learning is conducive for develop ment of
   (a) Cognitive skills (b) Creativity
   (c) Memory (d) Imagination

30. **List I**
   A. Schedules of Reinforcement
   B. Equilibration
   C. Student centred learning
   D. Self actualisation

   List II
   1. Maslow
   2. Carl Rogers
   3. Piaget
   4. Skinner
   5. Bandura

Codes:	**A**	**B**	**C**	**D**
(a)	4	1	5	3
(b)	5	2	1	4
(c)	4	3	2	1
(d)	3	2	1	4

31. Experimental learning is advocated by
   (a) Gestaltians
   (b) Cognitive psychologists
   (c) Humanists
   (d) Behaviourists

32. Which of the following is not a defence mechanism?
   (a) Association (b) Compensation
   (c) Regression (d) Sublimation

33. It is a self-reporting technique of assessing personality
   (a) Questionnaire
   (b) Observation
   (c) Draw-a-man test
   (d) Rorschach inkblot test

34. 'Learning disabled' children are mostly
   (a) Underachieves (b) Consistent
   (c) Aggressive (d) Organised

35. A child's attitude 'I don't care' is a type of behaviour which can be called
   (a) Defence (b) Retrogression
   (c) Aggression (d) Denial

36. Which of the following statements is not correct about guidance?
   (a) Group guidance is a co-operative venture
   (b) Minimum guidance programme depends only on budget available in the school
   (c) Guidance worker maintains confidentiality of information
   (d) Guidance workers does not need any special training

37. A researcher wants to test the hypothesis that "there is no significant difference

between means of control and experimental groups". At the time of analysing the data, he noticed that there is a constant error in the score where real score is higher than the observed. What should he do?

(a) Rescore the data
(b) Add error in each score
(c) Ignore the mistake
(d) Any of the above

38. Which one of the following statements is not true?
(a) Randomization procedures in experimental designs provide sufficient experiment control.
(b) Findings of an experimental study can be reverified.
(c) Historical research uses criticism of data.
(d) Correlational studies have low validity.

39. Which one of the following does not belong to the construct that other three belong to?
(a) *r* (b) χ^2
(c) *t*-test (d) F-test

40. A researcher has decided to test his one-tailed hypothesis at 01 level of significance. The critical value expected for rejection of Null Hypothesis would be a value equivalent to ________ level of significance for a two-tailed hypothesis.
(a) .005 (b) .01
(c) .02 (d) None of these

41. A researcher is developing items bank for an achievement test in subject A, where item can be either right or wrong. He has selected upper (top 27%) and lower (bottom 27%) of the group for item analysis. Which of the following would be the most appropriate method for determining directly validity of an item?
(a) Chi-square (b) Tetrachoric
(c) Phi-coefficient (d) Point Bi-serial

42. A researcher wants to study association between variable X and variable Y whereas there is a variable Z which influences both. If he wants to study the real value, he can do so by
(a) calculating multiple correlation.
(b) using χ^2.
(c) calculating partial correlation.
(d) calculating product-moment correlation.

43. If a researcher wants to study achievement in a school subject with respect to the intelligence then he has to take
(a) one variable in Interval scale and other in Ratio scale.
(b) one variable in Nominal scale and other in Interval scale.
(c) Both (a) and (c).
(d) None of these.

44. Purposeful sampling refers to
(a) the least desirable strategy of comprehensive sampling.
(b) strategies to find information-rich cases simultaneously.
(c) a type of probability sampling.
(d) sampling procedure designed before data collection.

45. **List I**
A. Tests theories and explains relations in behavioural sciences
B. Tests usefulness of scientific theories in a given field
C. Establishes an accepted body of research-based knowledge in a given field
D. Assesses the merit and worth of a particular practice at a given site

List II
1. Applied research
2. Basic research
3. Evaluation research

Codes:	A	B	C	D
(a)	3	1	2	2
(b)	3	1	2	3
(c)	2	1	3	2
(d)	1	2	2	3

46. Two characteristics of expost facto research are
    (a) non-manipulation and non-randomization.
    (b) randomization and comparison of groups.
    (c) non-manipulation and randomization.
    (d) non-randomization and manipulation of independent variable.
47. Which of the following circumstances necessitates the use of a quasi experimental design?
    (a) When more than one independent variable has to be introduced
    (b) Experimenter cannot assign subjects randomly
    (c) Experimenter has to collect data by himself
    (d) A pretest has to be administered
48. Preparation of a research proposal involves
    (a) using a unique format and style.
    (b) letting the typist decide the format and style.
    (c) carefully following the required format and style.
    (d) using the first person voice in writing.
49. List I
    A. Construct validity
    B. Content validity
    C. Concurrent validity

    List II
    1. Measure of fair representation
    2. Measure of theoretical processes
    3. Measure of product/performance
    4. Measure of agreement with known results

Codes:	A	B	C
(a)	2	3	4
(b)	3	4	1
(c)	2	1	4
(d)	1	2	3

50. For quantitative research, the external validity refers to
    (a) the characteristics of the subjects of the study.
    (b) the generalizability of the results of the study.
    (c) the use of research results in only the setting of that study.
    (d) how well the research was done.

ANSWERS

1. (d)	2. (d)	3. (d)	4. (d)
5. (c)	6. (a)	7. (d)	8. (c)
9. (a)	10. (d)	11. (d)	12. (d)
13. (d)	14. (c)	15. (b)	16. (d)
17. (a)	18. (c)	19. (b)	20. (b)
21. (c)	22. (d)	23. (a)	24. (d)
25. (d)	26. (d)	27. (b)	28. (a)
29. (a)	30. (a)	31. (c)	32. (a)
33. (a)	34. (a)	35. (d)	36. (d)
37. (a)	38. (d)	39. (b)	40. (b)
41. (c)	42. (c)	43. (b)	44. (b)
45. (d)	46. (d)	47. (a)	48. (c)
49. (a)	50. (b)		

PAPER-III
SET-1

1. It is recommended by educationists that there should be a dynamic approach to teaching. It means that
    (a) teachers should be energetic and dynamic
    (b) teaching should be forceful and effective

(c) the students should be required to learn through activities
(d) the courses of teaching should not remain static, but dynamic

2. Classroom discipline can be maintained effectively by
(a) knowing the cause of indiscipline and handling it with stem hand
(b) providing a programme which is according to the need and interest of the pupils
(c) by putting on fancy clothes in the classroom
(d) None of the above

3. Which cranial nerve is motor in function?
(a) Facial (b) Trigeminal
(c) Spinal accessory (d) Vagus

4. According to Watson, the Behaviourist, sensations and feelings are
(a) not the elements of conscious experience
(b) elements on which his system actually developed
(c) elements of conscious experience
(d) None of the above

5. Each learning experience aims at the total growth. This is possible because the learning teaching situations focus on
(a) Social problems
(b) Common problems
(c) Personal problems
(d) All of the above

6. The mathematical method of measuring trend value is called
(a) Least squares method
(b) Semi averages method
(c) Moving averages method
(d) None of the above

Direction: Read the passage carefully and answer the question no. 7-10.

The errors are termed as unbiased errors, if the estimated or approximated values are likely to err on either side, i.e., if the chances of making an over-estimate is almost same as the chance of making an under-estimate. Since, these errors move in both the directions, the errors in one direction are more or less neutralised by the errors in the opposite direction and consequently, the ultimate result is not much affected.

Thus, if the number of observations is quite large, these unbiased errors will not affect the final result. Since, the errors in one direction compensate for the errors in the other direction, unbiased errors are also termed as compensatory errors.

Thus, we observe that the unbiased errors do not grow with the increase in the number of observations but they have a tendency to get neutralised and are minimum in the ultimate analysis and the magnitude of the unbiased errors is inversely proportional to the number of items.

Measures of Statistical Errors (Absolute and Relative Errors): A measure of the statistical errors is provided by absolute and relative errors.

Absolute Error: An absolute error (A.E.) is the difference between the true value of any particular observed item or variable and its estimated or approximated value. Symbolically, we may write;

$$\text{A.E.} = |a - e|,$$

where, a is the actual value and e is the estimated value and $[a - e]$ represents the modulus value $(a - e)$ after ignoring the negative sign.

Relative Error (R.E.) is defined as the ratio of the absolute error to the actual value. Symbolically,

$$\frac{\text{A.E.}}{\text{Actual Value}} = \frac{a-e}{a}$$

7. Which technique is generally followed when the population is finite?

(a) Purposive sampling technique
(b) Area sampling technique
(c) Systematic sampling technique
(d) None of the above

8. A researcher divides his population into certain groups and fixes the size of the sample from each group. It is called
(a) Quota sample
(b) Cluster sample
(c) Stratified sample
(d) All of these

9. In the formula of 't' $= \frac{M_D}{SE_{MD}}$, SE_{MD} is
(a) standard error of mode deviation
(b) standard error of mean deviation
(c) standard error of mean of difference
(d) None of the above

10. If you are doing experiment on a large group of sample which method of controlling will you adopt?
(a) Matching
(b) Elimination
(c) Elimination and matching both
(d) Randomization

11. Some of the sources of secondary data are
(a) reports and publications of Central and State Governments.
(b) the data obtained by a firm in a survey conducted by it.
(c) confidential records of the Government.
(d) internal records of a firm's sales, production, etc.

12. If the marks obtained by 5 students are 40, 60, 70, 80, 90 the modal marks are
(a) 60 (b) 90
(c) 40 (d) 80

13. If we have five random samples and we want to determine whether there are significant differences among their means, we would have to use
(a) $5\frac{(5-3)}{2} = 5t$ tests
(b) $5\frac{(5-1)}{2} = 10t$ tests
(c) $\frac{5\times5\times4}{2} = 50t$ tests
(d) None of the above

14. The historical research is different from experimental research in the process of
(a) replication
(b) the hypothesis testing
(c) the formulation of the hypothesis
(d) All of the above

15. Statistical observations arranged in chronological order is called
(a) Time services
(b) Progression
(c) Regression
(d) None of the above

16. Which of the following is not the characteristic of a researcher?
(a) He is industrious and persistent on the trial of discovery.
(b) He is not inspirational to his chosen field but accepts the reality.
(c) He is a specialist rather than a generalist.
(d) He is not versatile in his interest and even in his native abilities.

17. Bibliography given in a research report
(a) helps those interested in further research and studying the problem from another angle.
(b) shows the vast knowledge of the researcher.
(c) makes the report authentic.
(d) None of the above.

18. Formula for standard error of Z (σ_7) is

(a) $\frac{1}{N-2}$ (b) $\frac{1}{\sqrt{N-3}}$

(c) $\frac{1}{\sqrt{N-2}}$ (d) None of these

19. The quartile deviation in a frequency distribution is
(a) half of the distance between the 75th and 25th percentiles.
(b) half of the distance between the 70th and 30th percentiles.
(c) the distance between the 75th and 25th percentiles.
(d) the distance between the 70th and the 30th percentiles.

20. If $\Sigma fx = 2461$, N = 60, x =
(a) 42 (b) 41
(c) 40 (d) 43

21. Index number is always a
(a) Relative number
(b) Absolute number
(c) Primary number
(d) None of the above

22. The other name of non-parametric tests is
(a) X^2 test
(b) X test
(c) distribution free test
(d) None of the above

23. The Regression lies of x upon y is expressed as
(a) $Y_c = ab + y$ (b) $X_c = a + by$
(c) $X_c = ay + b$ (d) $Y_c = b + ay$

24. Calculus was developed by
(a) Spinoza (b) Leibniz
(c) Descartes (d) Francis Bacon

25. Free hand method is used in
(a) Pie diagram (b) Time services
(c) Histogram (d) None of the above

26. Indian philosophers like Manu opined that philosophy leads to
(a) salvation
(b) a disciplined life
(c) practical perfection
(d) thinking in the abstract

27. Acts and movements for progress have been set afloat to achieve what we had hoped for after gaining independence. It is in the
(a) Five year plans
(b) Foreign Policy
(c) Creations of States
(d) Twenty year plans

28. Under the Satellite Instructional Television Experiment, the Govt. of India developed
(a) Student training material
(b) Teacher training material
(c) Data Bank
(d) Multi-media package

29. Educational Philosophers feel that the conflict between capitalism and communism
(a) gives a definite shape to common policies.
(b) creates gaps in many different stages of education.
(c) creates a healthy competitive spirit in education.
(d) leaves important educational issues without solving the conflict.

30. What is now-a-days termed as non-formal education, is really?
(a) not a substitute for formal education
(b) non-technical education
(c) a substitute for higher education
(d) a substitute for formal education

31. The main recommendation of the Sadler Commission appointed in 1917 was that

(a) the intermediate course was for the better students completing their matriculation and qualifying for higher education.
(b) the intermediate colleges should be attached to Universities.
(c) the intermediate colleges were dividing line between the University and the Secondary Education.
(d) None of the above.

32. The Industrial Revolution, whose effects shook the world took place in the
(a) 19th century (b) 20th century
(c) 17th century (d) 18th century

33. Which of the following statements would be correct in comparing the educational methods of Froebel and Montessori?
(a) Froebel favours development of imagination while Montessori provides no scope for this.
(b) Both favour classroom instructional approach.
(c) There is greater scope for social development in the Montessori method as compared to Froebel's method.
(d) There is scope for development of imagination in both methods.

34. The Renaissance in Europe which brought about tremendous social, cultural and intellectual changes was the result of many new and explosive
(a) Politics (b) Ideas
(c) Actions (d) Culture

35. The Secondary Education Commission, 1952-53, took the lead for introduction of technical education in the country, from
(a) the Abbot-Wood report of 1936-37.
(b) the Sargent report of 1944.
(c) the Hunter Commission report of 1882.
(d) the Hartog Committee report of 1929.

36. The subjects included in the late medieval studies of the West under quadrivium were
(a) Logic, Grammar, Music and Arithmetic
(b) Music, Arithmetic, Geometry and Astronomy
(c) Philosophy, Logic, Arithmetic and Grammar
(d) Logic, Astronomy, Arithmetic and Grammar

37. The main objective of education according to Acharya Vinoba Bhave is to
(a) train students in intellectual self-reliance and make them endependent thinkers.
(b) make a clear distinction between learning and doing.
(c) make a student self-dependent within the shortest possible time.
(d) None of the above.

38. The group of philosophers who call themselves as reconstructionlists
(a) think that the present is more important for reconstructing the society.
(b) object to progressive education as the only approach for the reconstruction of the society.
(c) object to Utopian view of the education and blindly support the status quo approach.
(d) recommend progressive education as the only approach for the reconstruction of the society.

39. Socrates was executed in Greece on the complain that
(a) he was encouraging the youth to revolt against the government of the day.
(b) he was teaching men to be skeptical without refining their convictions.

(c) he was conservative in the sense of the Athenian notions of knowledge.
(d) he was corrupting the youth by teaching them disrespect for gods.

40. The 1968 National Policy on Education stressed
(a) the importance of continuing educational programmes for the needy.
(b) the need for expansion of correspondence courses of education.
(c) the need of functional literacy at the elementary and secondary levels.
(d) the need for spread of literacy and Adult Education.

41. The facial expressions of students relate to which element of the communication process?
(a) Message (b) Sender
(c) Channel (d) Receiver

42. In the eyes of the educational sociologists, schools can best contrast prejudice by
(a) developing the intellect.
(b) asserting loyalty to the 'in-group' and hostility to others.
(c) developing and extending primary group values.
(d) imparting the knowledge.

43. The term 'sub-culture' is used to indicate
(a) the culture of the lower strata of the society.
(b) the culture of different groups of societies.
(c) the traditions and ideas of tribal groups of societies.
(d) the belief and customs of traditional social groups.

44. Which of the following is not a method or approach commonly used in intergroup education?
(a) Criticism of the customs of minorities
(b) Socio-drama and role-playing
(c) Emphasis placed upon the contributions or minorities
(d) None of the above

45. Naturalism in education means
(a) introduction of physical sciences in education.
(b) making discrimination between mind and consciousness.
(c) giving more importance to mind than to matter.
(d) supporting both mind and consciousness equally.

46. Any deterrents are negative in character
(a) when they are administered with a negative motive.
(b) when they prevent doing wrong but do not reform children.
(c) when they are administered owing to some misunderstanding.
(d) when they prevent children from doing wrong.

47. Industries near the towns cause
(a) Pollution
(b) Security concerns
(c) Happiness
(d) Employment problems

48. It is absurd to say that
(a) pollution occurs due to land noise.
(b) education causes pollution.
(c) transport vehicles cause pollution.
(d) All of the above.

49. Which of the following will not hamper effective communication in the class?
(a) A lengthy statement
(b) A precise statement
(c) A statement which allows the listener to draw his own conclusions
(d) An ambiguous statement

50. The most powerful barrier of communication in the classroom is

(a) more outside disturbance in the classroom.
(b) confusion on the part of the teacher.
(c) lack of teaching aids.
(d) noise in the classroom.

51. It is said that there is an urgent need of articulation among schools and colleges. This problem of articulation is concerned with
(a) better facilities for in-service training of teachers.
(b) appointment of talented teachers.
(c) communication and closer relationship among teachers.
(d) provision of better administrative facilities.

52. The idea that Basic Education is education through crafts is
(a) true to some extent only because the concept is deeper.
(b) the complete truth even for urban areas.
(c) true so far as the rural areas are concerned.
(d) Not true at all.

53. The term prejudice in a person is coloured by
(a) pre-judgement of a situation with a view to settle a conflict in haste.
(b) judgement and assessment of a situation without any favoritism.
(c) partial observation and acquaintance of a situation without any motives.
(d) a hasty judgement about a situation without due examination of facts.

54. Suppose you are teaching in a minority college where casteism and narrow mindedness victimize you, for better adjustment you should
(a) rebel against such attitudes as it is against the norms of the Indian society.
(b) be submissive and save your job at all costs.
(c) uplift the humanistic values beyond those narrow walls and develop scientific temper in your students.
(d) None of the above.

55. The sociologist feels that, if men expect to put an end to prejudice and race conflict, they will have to give major attention to
(a) remedying social abuses and reducing conflict.
(b) legislating human rights for minorities.
(c) putting into effect the 'melting pot theory.'
(d) re-establishing ethnocentrism.

56. Boarding schools are considered to be better than the day schools because
(a) they are meant for homeless and parent-less children.
(b) they save the trouble for children to walk to school from homes.
(c) they are helpful in freeing parents from their responsibilities.
(d) they help children in their social development.

57. Cultural pluralism is based on the concept that
(a) culture differs from individual to individual.
(b) culture vanishes due to intermingling of people.
(c) our culture is variegated and dynamic, with each group of immigrants contributing towards its enrichment.
(d) America is the 'Melting Pot' for various foreign stocks.

58. As an idealist, which of the following maxim would you think to correct the problem of discipline?

(a) The child should be subjected to fear and control to train him to desist from doing wrong.
(b) Discipline should be imposed from outsiders and teachers with full control.
(c) The child should be allowed full freedom without any restraint.
(d) The child should be trained to practice restraint with only limited freedom.

59. Which of the following statements is incorrect?
(a) 'Population Education' was first used in Sweden in 1935, the population education commission of the country to generate public awareness about the increase of the rate of growth.
(b) The purpose of population education is to develop awareness and understanding of the relations between population growth and national development both in short and long run and to develop an understanding of the consequences of individual decisions in the important area of reproductive behaviour.
(c) The term population education is applied either to increase or to decrease the rate of growth of population as per the need of situation of a nation of the world.
(d) None of the above.

60. A student centred plan is most favourable in the matter of
(a) Balance (b) Continuity
(c) Articulation (d) All of these

61. The trial and error method of learning according to Thorndike could be classified as the
(a) principle of multiple response
(b) law of exercise
(c) principle of Associative learning
(d) principle of partial activity

62. The term 'Evaluation' and 'Assessment' could be discriminated as follows:
(a) Evaluation is concerned with the effective aspects of achievement whereas assessment judges the cognitive aspects.
(b) Evaluation involves the measurement as well as diagnosis of students' achievements, whereas assessment is concerned with only scholastic achievements.
(c) Assessment is an attempt to measure the pupil as whole whereas evaluation is concerned with his achievement.
(d) Assessment is limited to achievement whereas evaluation is qualitative in character.

63. If a student is constantly rubbing his eyes and is inattentive during blackboard work he is having
(a) hearing problem
(b) visual problem
(c) adjustment problem
(d) All of the above

64. Play therapy is adopted in the study of children in order to
(a) highlight the importance of play activities in education.
(b) understand the inner motives and complexes of children.
(c) make education more activity centred.
(d) make the educational process joyful.

65. The most important challenge before a teacher is
(a) to make teaching-learning process enjoyable.
(b) to make students do their home work.
(c) to prepare question paper.
(d) to maintain discipline in the classroom.

66. Suppose you want to teach your students to develop factual knowledge of a subject. Which of the following methods would be suitable in your opinion?

(a) The source method
(b) The demonstration method
(c) The lecture method
(d) The heuristic method

67. Teaching in higher education implies
(a) helping students how to learn
(b) presenting the information given in the textbook
(c) helping students to prepare for and pass the examination
(d) asking questions in the class and conducting examinations

68. Effective teaching, by and large is a function of
(a) teacher's liking for the job of teaching
(b) teacher's scholarship
(c) teacher's making students learn and understand
(d) teacher's honesty

69. To say that the adolescents are rebellious in nature, will be regarded by experts as
(a) a necessary behaviour at that stage.
(b) an objective description of facts.
(c) an effect of the environment.
(d) a misconception.

70. The development of feelings of appreciation and interests come under the category of
(a) psycho-motor development of emotions.
(b) affective aspects of development.
(c) cognitive development of personality.
(d) None of the above.

71. The state of the psyche designated as super ego by the psychoanalysts, is found
(a) in men and animals as well.
(b) among human beings alone.
(c) among men practising yogic exercises.
(d) in all mammals.

72. Afferent nerve fibers carry impulses from—
(a) CNS to receptors
(b) Receptors to CNS
(c) CNS to muscles
(d) Effector organs to CNS

73. Nerve transmission is
(a) Mechanical process
(b) Chemical process
(c) Biological process
(d) Physical process

74. If a curriculum maker follows the subjective theory of values in education, he will
(a) disregard the interests of children for the inclusive of any subject in the curriculum.
(b) implement the study of a subject for its inherent values to fulfill the needs of a student.
(c) care more for the content aspects than for the methodological.
(d) not insist on the inclusiveness of any subject in the curriculum if pupils or parents are not interested in it.

75. Twelve pairs of ribs and twelve pairs of cranial nerves are found in
(a) Fish (b) Frog
(c) Snake (d) Man

ANSWERS

1. (c)	2. (c)	3. (b)	4. (b)
5. (a)	6. (a)	7. (c)	8. (c)
9. (c)	10. (d)	11. (a)	12. (b)
13. (b)	14. (d)	15. (a)	16. (d)
17. (a)	18. (b)	19. (a)	20. (b)
21. (a)	22. (c)	23. (b)	24. (b)
25. (b)	26. (a)	27. (a)	28. (d)
29. (d)	30. (a)	31. (a)	32. (d)
33. (a)	34. (b)	35. (a)	36. (b)
37. (a)	38. (a)	39. (c)	40. (d)
41. (a)	42. (c)	43. (b)	44. (a)

45. (a)	46. (b)	47. (a)	48. (b)
49. (b)	50. (b)	51. (c)	52. (a)
53. (d)	54. (c)	55. (b)	56. (d)
57. (c)	58. (d)	59. (d)	60. (c)
61. (c)	62. (d)	63. (d)	64. (d)
65. (a)	66. (a)	67. (d)	68. (d)
69. (c)	70. (a)	71. (a)	72. (b)
73. (a)	74. (a)	75. (a)	

PAPER-III
SET-2

1. If N = 80, D_2 shall lie in
   (a) 18th item (b) 16th item
   (c) 15th item (d) 14th item
2. The problem solving method in the teaching of any subject is best adopted when the
   (a) students previous knowledge is insufficient and the solution is possible only after acquiring new knowledge.
   (b) problem is selected out of the initiative of the teachers.
   (c) students can solve the problem by their previous knowledge.
   (d) problem is presented in the form of an assignment by the teacher.
3. Attributes of objects, events or things which can be measured are called
   (a) Variables
   (b) Data
   (c) Qualitative measure
   (d) None of the above
4. In plotting a frequency polygon, it is important to see that
   (a) the mid-point of an interval is always taken to represent the entire interval.
   (b) each class interval is represented by a separate rectangle.
   (c) mid-point of all class intervals are joined together.
   (d) None of the above.
5. In a 2 × 2 table comprised of four cells with (2 – 1) (2 – 1) = 1 formula used for calculating X^2 is
   (a) $X^2 = \frac{N(AD-BC)^2}{(A+B)(C+D)(A+C)(B+D)}$
   (b) $X^2 = \frac{N(AD-BC)}{(A+B)(C+D)(A+C)(B+D)}$
   (c) $X^2 = \frac{(AD-BC)^2}{(A+B)(C+D)(A+C)(B+D)}$
   (d) None of the above
6. If A = 35, $\Sigma fd = -200$, N = 100x =
   (a) 32 (b) 40
   (c) 33 (d) 30
7. The review of the related study is important while undertaking a research because
   (a) it avoids repetition or duplication.
   (b) it helps the researcher not to draw illogical conclusions.
   (c) it helps in understanding the gaps.
   (d) All of the above.
8. A researcher divides the populations into PG, graduates and 10 + 2 students and using the random digit table he selects some of them from each. This is technically called
   (a) stratified random sampling.
   (b) representative sampling.
   (c) stratified sampling.
   (d) None of the above.
9. To measure the changed purchasing power of currency, the index number that is used is called
   (a) Quantity index
   (b) Cost of living index
   (c) Both (a) and (b)
   (d) None of the above
10. Median test is used for testing whether

(a) two independent samples differ in SD.
(b) two independent samples differ in central tendencies.
(c) two samples differ from the population mean.
(d) None of the above.

11. A researcher selects a probability sample of 100 out of the total population. It is
(a) a cluster sample.
(b) a stratified sample.
(c) a systematic sample.
(d) a random sample.

12. The process not needed in experimental researches is
(a) controlling
(b) manipulation and replication
(c) observation
(d) reference collection

13. The experimental study is based on the law of
(a) Single variable
(b) Replication
(c) Interest of the subject
(d) Occupation

14. Significance of contingency coefficient is calculated by the formula

(a) $C = \frac{\sqrt{X^2}}{N+X}$ (b) $\frac{\sqrt{X^2}}{N+X^2}$

(c) $C = \frac{X^2}{N+X}$ (d) None of the above

15. The period against which comparisons are made in Index number is called
(a) Current year (b) Base year
(c) Coming year (d) None of the above

16. A statistical measure based upon the entire population is called parameter while measure based upon a sample is known as
(a) Sample parameter
(b) Inference
(c) Statistics
(d) None of the above

17. Field study is related to
(a) experimental situations.
(b) real life situations.
(c) laboratory situations.
(d) None of the above.

18. The degree of relationship between a bivariate data is called
(a) Regression
(b) Correlation
(c) Data analysis
(d) None of the above

19. The other name of independent variable for an experimental research is/are
(a) Treatment variable
(b) Manipulated variable
(c) Experimental variable
(d) All of the above

20. The approach to the concept of learning was different for Dewey and White Head in the following sense
(a) Dewey thought of learning in experimental terms whereas White Head thought of it in more aesthetic terms.
(b) Dewey's approach was logical whereas White Head's approach was philosophical.
(c) Dewey thought learning as an end in itself whereas White Head thought about it as a means.
(d) Dewey thought of learning in pragmatic terms whereas White Head thought in terms of cultural, aspects.

21. If the sample drawn does not specify any condition about the parameter of the population, it is called

(a) Selected statistics
(b) Distribution free statistics
(c) Census
(d) None of the above

22. If a group of students having low intelligence has low level of achievement, it is an example of
(a) negative correlation.
(b) negative high degree correlation.
(c) positive high degree correlation.
(d) zero correlation.

23. If N = 100, D_4 shall lie in
(a) 40th item (b) 50th item
(c) 90th item (d) 10th item

24. Which of the following will be acceptable for establishing a fact?
(a) Opinion of a large number of people
(b) Availability of observable evidence
(c) Reference in the ancient literature
(d) Traditionally in practice over a long period of time.

25. Which of the following is a non-probability sample?
(a) Purposive sample
(b) Simple random sample
(c) Both (a) and (b)
(d) Quota sample

26. The philosophy behind the progressive education movement could be designated as
(a) individualistic philosophy of education.
(b) personalistic philosophy of education.
(c) developmental philosophy of education.
(d) realistic philosophy of education.

27. The philosophy known as mechanical naturalism considers that
(a) the purpose of education is only to understand the nature of man and his activities.
(b) education is governed by the purpose of understanding nature and its mechanism.
(c) there is no purpose of aim of education except making education a mechanical process.
(d) it is much better than naturalism because its suggests a materialistic philosophy.

28. Arrange the Pestalozzi's stages of intellectual development given below in sequence—
1. Function of mind starts with impression.
2. Sense impression makes form and qualities of things clear.
3. Images of things are transformed into ideas.

Codes:
(a) 1, 2, 3 (b) 2, 1, 3
(c) 3, 1, 2 (d) 3, 2, 1

29. **List I** **List II**
A. Republic 1. Descartes
B. Emile 2. Rousseau
C. Modern theory 3. John Dewey of dualism
D. Experimentalism 4. Plato

Codes:	**A**	**B**	**C**	**D**
(a)	4	2	1	3
(b)	1	2	3	4
(c)	1	3	4	2
(d)	4	1	2	3

30. **List I (Role of the teacher)**
A. Guide and helper
B. Instructor
C. Autocrat
D. Disciplined

List II (Philosophy)
1. Marxism 2. Existentialism
3. Pragmatism 4. Idealism

Codes:	A	B	C	D
(a)	1	2	3	4
(b)	3	4	1	2
(c)	2	3	4	1
(d)	4	3	2	1

31. The term 'Co-curricular activities' is a popular one for all educational institutions. Which of the following would you regard as a co-curricular activity?
   (a) Football matches
   (b) Collection of funds for school building
   (c) Debating competitions
   (d) None of the above

32. The interaction between teachers and students or between buyers and sellers is classified by the sociologists as a social interaction of
   (a) The responsive type
   (b) The primary type
   (c) The secondary type
   (d) The multiple type

33. A sentiment could be correctly defined as
   (a) a weak point in individual's emotional life.
   (b) a link between the likes and dislikes of an individual.
   (c) a sum total of a person's feeling and emotions about some object.
   (d) a strong desire for an action with an inner motive.

34. Learning is a
   (a) Organic process
   (b) Dynamic process
   (c) Reflective process
   (d) Both (b) and (c)

35. The process of expansion of an individual's capacities qualitatively, should be termed as
   (a) Growth (b) Maturation
   (c) Development (d) Equilibration

36. The term 'curriculum' is used in education to indicate
   (a) the sum total of all experiences provided for students by an educational institution.
   (b) the field covered by a particular course of study.
   (c) the courses prescribed for an examination.
   (d) the contents of a broad subject selected for a particular class or grade.

37. Elements of the core concept is/are
   (a) co-operative pre-planning by teachers.
   (b) ideas to develop resource units.
   (c) teacher-pupil planning daily.
   (d) All of the above.

38. Who criticized the subject-centred traditional curriculum?
   (a) Sigmund Freud
   (b) Rabindranath Tagore
   (c) Alfred North Whitehead
   (d) John Dewey

39. Which of the following distinctions between instruction and education would meet your approval as a teacher?
   (a) Instruction requires a content matter whereas education requireds a methodical approach.
   (b) Education is for grown ups, but instruction is for younger ones.
   (c) Instruction is specific whereas education is comprehensive.
   (d) Education depends upon the students abilities while instruction requires teacher's abilities.

40. The emphasis in core concept is on total growth of the pupil
   (a) Socially (b) Physically
   (c) Intellectually (d) All of these

41. The approach of core pattern is
   (a) Objective centred
   (b) Problem centred

(c) Core centred
(d) All of these

42. Educational Administration is concerned with
(a) the 'how' of achieving educational objectives.
(b) the 'what' of educational programme.
(c) the goals of educational practices.
(d) the 'why' of educational processes.

43. A school complex means
(a) the superiority or inferiority complexes of schools.
(b) schools within easily accessible radius.
(c) a number of schools with in a single building.
(d) number of schools situated in any community area.

44. Which group of communication aspects does not distort the communication process in the class?
(a) Reversing – evaluating – focussing
(b) Evaluating – focussing – exaggerating
(c) Focussing – illustrating – exaggerating
(d) Evaluating – focussing – illustrating

45. The difference between moral and ethical education is that
(a) morals can prematurely hinder ethical development whereas ethics need support of religion.
(b) morals emphasize performance whereas ethics emphasize knowledge.
(c) morals emphasize knowledge while ethics emphasize performance.
(d) teaching ethics can hinder moral stagnation while teaching morals advances discrimination.

46. Social stratification and rigid class structures brought about the
(a) Caste system
(b) United system
(c) Cultural system
(d) National integration

47. Social changes may be speeded up by
(a) Economy (b) Education
(c) Industrialization (d) All of the above

48. Educational inspection is different from educational supervision ih the sense that
(a) inspection assumes correction whereas supervision assumes status quo.
(b) inspection is static whereas supervision is dynamic in approach.
(c) inspection is prutive whereas supervision is corrective.
(d) None of the above.

49. One is most likely to lead to the desired goal through
(a) Marriage (b) Election
(c) Education (d) Service

50. The most important factors in bringing about social change which may be found in inventions are
(a) Ideas (b) Acculturation
(c) Diffusion (d) None of the above

51. Which nerve depresses heart beat
(a) Vagus
(b) Trigeminal
(c) Spinal accessory
(d) Glossopharyngeal

52. In the final analysis, teaching must be thought of mainly as a process of
(a) directing the activities of the pupils.
(b) hearing the recitation of pupils.
(c) asking questions and evaluating the learning.
(d) All of the above.

53. At the time of impulse transmission, the potential on the inner side of nerve changes
(a) + – and – (b) + – and +
(c) – + and – (d) – + and +

54. The most appropriate meaning of learning is

(a) personal adjustment
(b) modification of behaviour
(c) acquisition of skills
(d) inculcation of knowledge

55. An injury in accident has disturbed regulation of body temperature, water balance and hunger in a person. The part of brain affected is
(a) Hypothalamus
(b) Medulla oblongata
(c) Corpora quadrigemina
(d) Cerebellum

56. Which of the following teacher's qualities contributes most to good classroom discipline?
(a) Simple way of living
(b) Charming personality
(c) Effective teaching
(d) Good behaviour and pleasant manners

57. John Dewey's experimental school was called
(a) the free school
(b) the activity school
(c) the community school
(d) the progressive school

58. The Core Curricula in education means
(a) public examination subjects for certification.
(b) language subjects and skills.
(c) knowledge as well as skills for further education and life.
(d) science and mathematics, integrated.

59. An autonomic nervous system has
(a) Cerebral hemisphere
(b) Sense organs
(c) Brain and spinal chord
(d) Paired chain ganglia

60. The potential difference across the membrane of nerve fibre when it does not show any physiological activities is called resting potential. It is about
(a) –60 mv (b) +90 mv
(c) +60 mv (d) –80 mv

61. Which of the following is a "whole-hearted purposeful activity proceeding in a social environment"?
(a) Heuristic method
(b) Problem method
(c) Project method
(d) Dalton plan

62. The most important teaching aid for a teacher is
(a) Colour pictures
(b) Graphs and tables
(c) Black-board
(d) Maps and Charts

63. 'Micro teaching', one of the recent trends in education, insists of
(a) mastering of various skills of teaching with special attention.
(b) teaching of minutest points of a subject.
(c) finding out the subtle doubts in the minds of students.
(d) teaching students by dividing them into smaller groups.

64. Which is incorrect?
(a) Na + transports substances across membranes
(b) Na + takes part in thermoregulation
(c) Na + helps in conduction of nerve impulses
(d) Na + helps in retention of water in the body

65. Audio-visual aids are more effective because
(a) they provide a change.
(b) they make the learning experience more concrete, more realistic and more dynamic.
(c) verbalism is not adequate usually.
(d) students are more attracted by TV and cinema.

66. The term 'Maturation' is specifically used for
(a) qualitative change in the organism not induced by learning.
(b) physiological development induced by learning and situation.
(c) quantitative change in the organism not induced by learning.
(d) quantitative change in the organism induced by learning.

67. In a nerve if sodium pump is blocked, which of the following is most likely to happen?
(a) K^+ inside the nerve will increase.
(b) Na^+ inside the nerve will increase.
(c) Na^+ and K^+ will increase outside the cell.
(d) Na^+ outside the nerve will increase.

68. Who of the following teachers is most desirable?
(a) One who just knows enough of his subject but motivates his students a lot to learn.
(b) One who comes to teach regularly, but does not care to know what the students are learning.
(c) One who is a moralist and preaches morals to students all the time.
(d) One who comes to the class on time, but does not mind students coming late in the class.

69. Dalton Plan is associated with
(a) E.L. Thorndike (b) John Dalton
(c) John Dewey (d) Helen Parkhurst

70. An axon has four terminals ends connected with dendrites of four different neurons. Its nerve impulse will
(a) not travel because the movement of impulse is from dendrites to axon.
(b) become weak due to distribution in to four.
(c) pass on to one neuron only.
(d) travel in all the four neurons with equal strength.

71. Non-parametric tests are used when
(a) variables are expressed in nominal form, i.e., represented by frequency counts.
(b) variables are expressed in ordinal form.
(c) population from which sample is drawn is not normal.
(d) All of the above.

72. A test of "Shiftability of Base" is called
(a) Time reversal test
(b) Circular test
(c) Factor reversal test
(d) None of the above

73. The Regression line of y upon x is expressed as
(a) $X_c = a + bx$ (b) $Y_c = ax + b$
(c) $Y_c = a + bx$ (d) $X_c = b + ax$

74. The device to measure the differences in the magnitude of a group of related variable is called
(a) Regression (b) Index number
(c) Corelation (d) None of these

75. The test used with discrete data in the form of frequencies is
(a) X^2 test (b) Z test
(c) 't' test (d) ANOVA

ANSWERS

1. (b)	2. (a)	3. (a)	4. (c)
5. (b)	6. (c)	7. (d)	8. (a)
9. (b)	10. (b)	11. (c)	12. (d)
13. (b)	14. (b)	15. (b)	16. (c)
17. (b)	18. (b)	19. (d)	20. (a)
21. (b)	22. (c)	23. (a)	24. (b)
25. (c)	26. (b)	27. (a)	28. (a)
29. (a)	30. (b)	31. (c)	32. (c)

33. (c)	34. (d)	35. (c)	36. (a)
37. (d)	38. (c)	39. (c)	40. (d)
41. (b)	42. (a)	43. (b)	44. (c)
45. (b)	46. (a)	47. (b)	48. (b)
49. (c)	50. (a)	51. (a)	52. (d)
53. (a)	54. (a)	55. (a)	56. (c)
57. (a)	58. (a)	59. (d)	60. (b)
61. (c)	62. (d)	63. (a)	64. (d)
65. (a)	66. (a)	67. (d)	68. (b)
69. (c)	70. (a)	71. (d)	72. (b)
73. (b)	74. (b)	75. (a)	

PAPER-III
SET-3

1. The age level at which the child cannot pass any of the items of particular subtest is called
   (a) Ceiling age (b) Mental age
   (c) Basal age (d) Specific age
2. Intelligence is the property of recombining our behaviour pattern so as to act better in a novel situation. This definition is given by
   (a) Hull (b) Binet
   (c) Wells (d) William Stern
3. As the infant grows his mental ability
   (a) Fluctuates (b) Stagnates
   (c) Decreases (d) Increases
4. The most widely used test for adults was developed by
   (a) Guilford (b) Wechsler
   (c) Stanford (d) Terman
5. Which group test was designed during World War I for persons who could not read or who did not speak English?
   (a) WAIS (b) Stanford-Binet
   (c) Army Alpha (d) Army Beta
6. Which group test was designed during World War I for persons who could read?
   (a) WAIS (b) Army Beta
   (c) Stanford-Binet (d) Army Alpha
7. "Intelligence is the ability to adjust oneself to a new situation." This definition was given by
   (a) Merrill (b) William Stern
   (c) Wells (d) Terman
8. The WAIS like the Stanford-Binet is a/an ______ test.
   (a) individual (b) social
   (c) school (d) general
9. The deviation IQ is a type of
   (a) Average score (b) Raw score
   (c) Standard score (d) Mean score
10. Wechsler set the mean of the scores equal to an IQ of
    (a) 100 (b) 120
    (c) 150 (d) 50
11. When is type-I error increased?
    (a) When the sample size increases
    (b) When the sample size decreases
    (c) When alpha-level decreases
    (d) When alpha-level increases.
12. Sampling results into
    (a) control of extraneous variables.
    (b) high precision.
    (c) greater accuracy.
    (d) reduced cost, and item.
13. Which is the most important characteristics of the survey method of research?
    (a) It aims at developing some theory or the scientific laws.
    (b) It focuses on studying the cause effect relationship between variables.
    (c) It relies on a small sample.
    (d) It studies characteristics of a group instead of an individual.
14. What consideration a rating procedure involves?

(a) The continuum on which rating is to be done
(b) The persons who will do rating
(c) The trait to be rated
(d) All of the these.

15. To which are the concepts of internal external criticisms associated?
(a) Historical research
(b) Literary research
(c) Validity of experimental designs of research
(d) Descriptive research.

16. It is undesirable on the part of the researcher
(a) getting the full meaning out of the author's ideas and paraphrasing them in his own language.
(b) concentrating on written material, eliminating unessential details.
(c) to present a research report based on investigator's own ideas and written in his own words.
(d) stringing lots of quotations together.

17. Which is the purpose of theory building?
(a) Fundamental research
(b) Survey research
(c) Applied research
(d) Action research

18. If the findings of a research have practical implications for improving educational patterns, it is called
(a) descriptive research
(b) experimental research
(c) pure research
(d) applied research

19. On the spot research aimed at the solution of an immediate problem is called
(a) action research
(b) pure research
(c) survey research
(d) fundamental research

20. Research concerned with the derivation of generalizations of broad applicability and only secondarily with any practical value is called
(a) action research
(b) practical research
(c) applied research
(d) fundamental research

21. Which of the following is not relevant to analysis of the research problem?
(a) Attending seminars on research methodology
(b) Proposing various relevant explanations (hypothesis) for the cause of the difficulty
(c) Isolating the variables that are involved in the problem and clarifying their relationships
(d) Accumulating the facts that might be related to the problem.

22. To which aspect are related questioning assumptions underlying the problem?
(a) Analysing the problem
(b) Stating the problem
(c) Identifying the problem
(d) Defining the problem

23. What does description of the research problem not include?
(a) Assumptions underlying it
(b) Review of research done
(c) Background of the study
(d) Theories on which it is based.

24. Which of the following is the least helpful to locating and analyzing problems?
(a) Examining every day experiences
(b) Critical analysis of the existing theories and practices
(c) Exploring the literature in an area of interest
(d) Discussing with the research guide.

25. To find out the relationship between intelligence and achievement after eliminating the effect of motivation, an investigator should use
    (a) r_{xy} (b) r_{bis}
    (c) $R_{1.23}$ (d) $r_{12.3}$
26. Who was the nineteenth century founder of Existentialism?
    (a) Rousseau
    (b) D.J. O'Connor
    (c) Hegel
    (d) Soren Kierkegaard
27. Who was twentieth century Existentialist?
    (a) D.J. O'Connor
    (b) Jean Paul Sartre
    (c) Soren Kierkegaard
    (d) None of the above.
28. Which of the following is more generally acceptable by modern educationists?
    (a) Contribution to the welfare of the society should be the only aim of education.
    (b) Education is bound to have several aims since its concerns are several such as the individual, the society, the family, the nation and so on.
    (c) There should be one single aim of education unchangeable over time and space.
    (d) There is one grand objective of education; and that is the development of the inner nature of the child.
29. What is development of human potentialities in education?
    (a) Individual as well as social aim
    (b) Specific aim
    (c) Individual aim
    (d) Social aim

Direction: Read the passage carefully and answer the question no. 30-35.

Education is a process of initiating the child into the ways of adult life. An educator not only holds certain beliefs and ideals of life, he also tries to convert his pupils to his own views and his own way of life. The influence of a person, holding a vital belief, brought to bear upon another person with the object of making him also to hold that belief, is *education*. Thus education means to lead out, through the modification of the native behaviour of the child. In the words of Redden, "Education is the deliberate and systematic influence, exerted by the mature person upon the immature, through instruction, discipline and systematic influence, exerted by the mature person upon the immature, through instruction, discipline, and harmonious development of physical, intellectual, aesthetic, social spiritual power of the human being. Mahatma Gandhi and education as "*an all-round drawing out of the best in child and man-body, mind and spirit*".

After discussing the meaning and concept of both education and philosophy, it is not very difficult to describe the relationship between the two. Apparently, there seems to be little connection between them. One is science while the other is an art. One is speculative while the other is practical. But philosophy determines the supreme aim of life and sets standards and values that should guide and direct man's educational efforts to achieve them. Thus philosophy is a major concern of education. There is, in fact, an intimate relationship between philosophy and education which may be described briefly as under.

We have already said, education means modification of the child's native behaviour. But the problem is in which direction modification should be carried out and what should be the standards and values, to strive for. This problem is solved by philosophy which points out the way to be followed by the educator in the modification of the child's behaviour. Philosophy, thus, deals with the ends and education is a laboratory' in which philosophic theories and speculations are tested and made concrete. Education may, therefore, be rightly called applied philosophy. Philosophy is wisdom, education transmits that wisdom from one generation to the other. Philosophy is in reality the theory of education. In other words, education is the dynamic side of philosophy, or application of the fundamental principles of philosophy. Philosophy formulates the method, education its process. Philosophy gives ideals, values an principles. Education works out those ideals, values and principles.

30. What is development of social sense and co-operation among the individuals through education?
    (a) National aim
    (b) Constitutional aim
    (c) Individual aim
    (d) Social aim
31. Which among the following is not an acceptable criticism of social aims of education?
    (a) They hinder the growth and development of art and literature
    (b) Man, in them, becomes only a means to an end
    (c) They are anti-individual
    (d) They are unpsychological as they do not take into account the capacities and interests of the individual.
32. Which among the following is not emphasized by the individual aims of education?
    (a) Development of inner potentialities
    (b) Development of values of tolerance and non-violence
    (c) Individual freedom
    (d) Self-expression.
33. Which of the following statements does not go in favour of the individual aims of education?
    (a) Every individual is unique; development of his potentialities is essential.
    (b) Society is supreme and all individuals are only parts of it.
    (c) The individual is an asset to the society; his development and growth are necessary.
    (d) The society is strong if the individual is strong.
34. Which among the following is the most correct view about social and individual aims of education?
    (a) Individual aims are implied in the social aims of education.
    (b) Individual and social aims are only two sides of the same coin.
    (c) Individual aims should be given preference to social aims.
    (d) Social aims should be preferred to individual aims.
35. Which statement is most acceptable to the academicians about "Bread and butter aim" of education?
    (a) It is only partly acceptable.
    (b) It is important for only a section of the society.
    (c) It is the most important aim and should be given top priority by educationists.
    (d) It is equally important alongwith other aims of education.
36. Which of the following does not pertain to intellectual development aim of education?
    (a) Development of cognitive powers
    (b) Training and "formation" of mind
    (c) Cultivation of intelligence
    (d) Spiritual development.
37. Preparing the child for future life as an aim of education is preparing child for

(a) facing all kinds of emergencies and situations of future life.
(b) a happy married life.
(c) some suitable vocation.
(d) some particular course of study.

38. The most effective method of character-formation is
(a) teaching by high character teachers.
(b) rewarding virtuous behaviours and presenting high character models in the schools.
(c) teaching virtues through religious books.
(d) organizing specialists lectures on importance of values in life.

39. Harmonious development of the child aim of education means
(a) development of physical, mental, moral and spiritual potentialities of the child in a balanced manner.
(b) development of the adjustment capacities of the child.
(c) development of all the qualities of the mind to the maximum possible extent.
(d) development of a sound mind in a sound body.

40. The social aims of education imply that
(a) the state is superior to the individual transcending all his desires and aspirations
(b) the state has to give not to take anything from the individual
(c) the state is ah idealized metaphysical entity
(d) the state is above the individual citizen

41. Rigid system of state-education is justified on the basis that the state
(a) has a right and a bounden duty to mould the citizen to a pattern which makes for its own preservation and enhancement.
(b) has better resources to manage education.
(c) is supreme to dictate what shall be taught and how shall be taught.
(d) has absolute control over the lives and destinies of its individual members.

42. Social aims of education imply the training of
(a) the individuals according to their capacities.
(b) the individuals according to the facilities.
(c) the individuals for the purpose of serving the needs of the society.
(d) individuals according to their needs.

43. What does the individual aim of education imply?
(a) It should have more and more institutions every year.
(b) It should be by and large the concern of the private sector.
(c) Education must secure for everyone the conditions under which the individuality is most completely developed.
(d) It must contribute to the peace and happiness of the whole society.

44. According to which philosophy of education, childhood is some thing desirable for its own sake and children should be children?
(a) Naturalism (b) Realism
(c) Idealism (d) Pragmatism

45. Who emphasized that education should be a social process?
(a) Dewey (b) Pestalozzi
(c) Vivekananda (d) Rousseau

46. A situation where a student is expected by his parents to study his lessons and is expected by his roommates to visit a movie-house illustrates

(a) role conflict
(b) culture conflict
(c) status conflict
(d) primary-secondary group conflict

47. Individual and society are considered as
(a) Complementary (b) Supplementary
(c) Interdependent (d) Contradictory

48. Human nature develops in man as a
(a) member of an organisation.
(b) member of a society.
(c) member of a religion.
(d) citizen of a state.

49. Man's behaviour in society is determined mainly by two forces, namely
(a) physical and social.
(b) psychological and philosophical.
(c) formal and informal.
(d) natural and unnatural.

50. Identify a quasi-group among the following
(a) Mob (b) Crowd
(c) Status groups (c) Trade union

51. An individual starts learning from
(a) Childhood (b) Adolescence
(c) Mother's womb (d) Adulthood

52. Suggestion is one of the basic principles of
(a) Class (b) Socialization
(c) Human behaviour (d) Caste

53. One of the basic principles of socialing individuals is
(a) Education (b) Imitation
(c) Religion (d) Caste

54. When the child is able to judge the response of a group as a whole, he is responding to a
(a) 'generalised other'
(b) 'significant other'
(c) 'particular other'
(d) 'insignificant other'

55. Internalization means that the individual
(a) has adopted the norms and values of the group and uses them.
(b) has standards to judge his own behaviour.
(c) conforms to group norms.
(d) has identity, social location, aspiration and values.

56. The concept of the looking-glass self may be summarised as follows:
(a) what ego thinks, alter thinks, ego is
(b) what ego thinks alter is
(c) what ego thinks ego is
(d) what alter thinks ego is

57. The process which aims to destroy the opponent is
(a) Competition
(b) Accommodation
(c) Co-operation
(d) Conflict

58. When a group of clans get merged together, then the resultant grouping is called
(a) Family (b) Gotra
(c) Lineage (d) Siblings

59. The preferences and aversions amongst the various members of a group is shown by
(a) social psychology
(b) interactional analysis
(c) sociogram
(d) sociological analysis

60. The technique of measurement of the patterns of social behaviour in a group is known as
(a) social distance scale
(b) sociometry
(c) sociogram
(d) interactional, analysis

61. "Birds of the same feather flock together" refers to the idea of a socialising process known as

(a) Identification (b) Sympathy
(c) Imitation (d) Suggestion

62. The price paid to the Muslim bride is called
(a) Mehar (b) Compensation
(c) Dowry (d) Bride price

63. In early Hindu society, widow remarriage was
(a) Promoted (b) Prohibited
(c) Permitted (d) Protected

64. The laws of Muslim marriage are based on
(a) Indian contract act
(b) Constitution of India
(c) Quran
(d) Muslim law

65. Mehar given by husband to the wife immediately after marriage is known as
(a) Muwajjal Mehar
(b) Dower after dissolution of marriage
(c) Settled Dower
(d) Meharul Misl

66. The first intelligence test was developed by
(a) David Wechsler
(b) Alfred Binet
(c) Lewis Terman
(d) Albert Sidney Beckham

67. Who invented the correlation coefficient and developed the ideas behind finger-printing and eugenics?
(a) Alfred Binet
(b) Wechsler
(c) Charles Darwin
(d) Sir Francis Galton

68. The Binet scale for Intelligence which was published in 1905 was revised in the years
(a) 1906 and again in 1910
(b) 1908 and again in 1911
(c) 1909 and again in 1912
(d) 1907 and again in 1913

69. A bright child's MA is above his CA; a dull child has a MA below his CA. This statement is
(a) Partly right (b) Can't be said
(c) True (d) False

70. The formula for calculating IQ is
(a) $\frac{CA}{MA} \div 100$ (b) $\frac{CA}{MA} \div 200$
(c) $\frac{MA}{CA} \times 100$ (d) $\frac{MA}{CA} \times 200$

71. According to the Guilford's (1967) model of Intelligence the number of identifiable abilities are
(a) 100 (b) 130
(c) 120 (d) 110

72. "Intelligence is the aggregate or global capacity of the individual to act purposefully, to think rationally, and to deal effectively with his environment." The above definition was given by
(a) Wechsler (b) Anastasi
(c) Ebbinghaus (d) Terman

73. Intelligence is the ability of
(a) adjusting in new situations.
(b) availing of past experiences.
(c) abstract thinking.
(d) All of these.

74. To understand the intelligence, scientific approaches started around
(a) hundred years back.
(b) recently.
(c) two hundred year back.
(d) quarter of a century back.

75. For testing purposes, the highest level at which all items of Binet's test are passed by a given child is that child's
(a) Ceiling age (b) Ground age
(c) Mental age (d) Basal age

ANSWERS

1. (a)	2. (c)	3. (d)	4. (b)	37. (a)	38. (b)	39. (a)	40. (b)
5. (d)	6. (d)	7. (b)	8. (a)	41. (a)	42. (c)	43. (c)	44. (a)
9. (c)	10. (a)	11. (c)	12. (d)	45. (a)	46. (a)	47. (c)	48. (b)
13. (d)	14. (d)	15. (a)	16. (d)	49. (c)	50. (a)	51. (c)	52. (b)
17. (a)	18. (d)	19. (a)	20. (d)	53. (b)	54. (a)	55. (b)	56. (a)
21. (a)	22. (a)	23. (b)	24. (a)	57. (d)	58. (c)	59. (b)	60. (b)
25. (d)	26. (d)	27. (b)	28. (b)	61. (a)	62. (a)	63. (c)	64. (c)
29. (c)	30. (d)	31. (c)	32. (b)	65. (a)	66. (b)	67. (d)	68. (b)
33. (b)	34. (b)	35. (a)	36. (d)	69. (c)	70. (c)	71. (c)	72. (a)
				73. (d)	74. (a)	75. (d)	

Previous Years Papers

PAPER-II
DECEMBER 2012

Note: This paper contains fifty (50) objective type questions, each question carrying two (2)

1. Epistemology is the branch of philosophy which deals with the theories of
   (a) Reality (b) Existence
   (c) Knowledge (d) Values
2. Given below are two statements, one labelled as Assertion (A) and the other labeled as Reason (R).
   Assertion (A): Philosophy helps in determining aims of education.
   Reason (R): Education depends mostly on Philosophy.
   In the context of the two statements, which one of the following is correct?
   Codes:
   (a) Both (A) and (R) are true.
   (b) Both (A) and (R) are false.
   (c) (A) is true, but (R) is false.
   (d) (A) is false, but (R) is true.
3. "Things as they are and as they are likely to be encountered in life rather than words" was the slogan of the
   (a) Pragmatists (b) Realists
   (c) Idealists (d) Existentialists
4. An existentialistic teacher should emphasize on
   I. Freedom
   II. Responsibility
   III. Subjective feelings
   IV. Cooperative living
   In the above which combination is correct?
   Codes:
   (a) I & II are correct.
   (b) I & III are correct.
   (c) I, II & III are correct.
   (d) II, III & IV are correct.
5. Who advocated the creation of a classless society?
   (a) Plato (b) Auguste Comte
   (c) M.K. Gandhi (d) Karl Marx
6. The Vedas teach us that
   (a) Creation is without beginning.
   (b) Creation is without an end.
   (c) Creation is without beginning and without an end.
   (d) Creation has a definite beginning and also an end.
7. According to Samkhya philosophy, the sequence of creation is as under:
   (a) Purusa, Prakrati, Ahankar, Mahat
   (b) Prakrati, Purusa, Ahankar, Mahat
   (c) Prakrati, Purusa, Mahat, Ahankar
   (d) Purusa, Prakrati, Mahat, Ahankar

8. Match the following:
List - I (Buddhist Concept)
a. Arya Satya
b. Dwadash Nidan
c. Ashtanga Marg
d. Nirvana
List - II (Meaning/Example)
1. Namrupa
2. Samadhi
3. Samyaka Vyayam
4. Controlling of breath
5. Sorrow in life

Codes:	**a**	**b**	**c**	**d**
(a)	2	4	1	3
(b)	5	1	3	2
(c)	5	1	4	2
(d)	1	5	4	3

9. Critically judge the following:
Assertion (A): All Muslim Women need to go to school.
Reason (R): Muslim Philosophy lays emphasis on the equality of all-men or women.
Codes:
(a) Both (A) and (R) are true.
(b) Both (A) and (R) are false.
(c) Statement (A) is true, but (R) is false.
(d) Statement (A) is false, but (R) is true.

10. In Tagorian Education System the child learns better by
I. Debates and Discussion
II. Reading, Writing and Speaking
III. Dance, Drama and Music
IV. Travelling and interacting with nature.
In the context of the above, which statements are true?
(a) All I, II, III and IV are true.
(b) Statements I, III and IV are
(c) Statements I, II and III are true.
(d) Statements II, III and IV are true.

11. The right to free and compulsory education for children between age group of 6 to 14 has been inserted in Indian Constitution as
(a) Article 46 (b) Article 16
(c) Article 45A (d) Article 21A

12. Who advocated the logical analysis of language for getting the true meaning?
(a) A.J. Ayer (b) Bertrand Russel
(c) Morris L. Biggie (d) G.E. Moore

13. Sociology of Education is
(a) A branch of Anthropology.
(b) A study of the Society.
(c) An analysis of Sociological processes involved in the institutions of Education.
(d) A science which studies primitive societies.

14. Schools are basically social institutions as
(a) They preserve and instil the values of our culture in future generations.
(b) They suggest ways and means for social progress.
(c) They suggest solutions to social problems.
(d) They are established by the society.

15. Which is not a criterion used consistently for placing people in a particular social class?
(a) Race (b) Religion
(c) Knowledge (d) Wealth

16. Beginning with family as the lowest unit which of the following constitutes correctly sequenced hierarchy of social group?
(a) Nation – Race – Class – Tribe – Family.
(b) Family – Class – Tribe – Race – Nation.
(c) Family – Tribe – Race – Class – Nation.
(d) Family – Race – Class – Tribe – Nation.

17. Use of Science and Technology in replacing existing social practices is termed as

(a) Socialization (b) Westernization
(c) Sanskritization (d) Modernization

18. The process of imbibing one's own culture in one's personality is termed as
(a) Enculturation (b) Acculturation
(c) Socialization (d) Sanskritization

19. Critically judge the following:
Assertion (A): My religion is the best religion.
Reason (R): The democratic philosophy allows me to think and live with freedom.
Codes:
(a) Both (A) and (R) are true and (R) is the correct explanation.
(b) Both (A) and (R) are false.
(c) Only (A) is true, but (R) is false.
(d) Only (R) is true.

20. Which of the following chains represents the change processes underlying educational system of Free India?
(a) Psychological change – Social change – Political change – Educational change.
(b) Political change – Social change – Psychological change – Educational change.
(c) Social change – Psychological change – Political change – Educational change.
(d) Educational change – Social change – Psychological change.

21. The son of a rickshaw puller struggles and becomes an engineer. This is an example of
(a) Social change
(b) Social stratification
(c) Social mobility
(d) Social cohesion

22. An example of Social Stratification is
I. People with different status living in an area.
II. A society divided into different social status.
III. A separate colony in which only class III government employees live.
IV. A society consisting of upper and lower castes.
(a) All the above statements are correct.
(b) Statements I, II and IV are correct.
(c) Statements I, II and III are correct.
(d) Statements II, III and IV are correct.

23. Equality of opportunities in education implies that each student
(a) passes examination with first division.
(b) gets equal number of books and stationery.
(c) gets facilities according to his abilities and interests.
(d) gets facilities according to his potential and level in the society.

24. Disadvantaged sections of society consist of
I. Scheduled Castes and Scheduled Tribes
II. Women
III. Physically handicapped
IV. Rural people
(a) All the above
(b) Only I, II and III
(c) Only II, III and IV
(d) Only I, II and IV

25. Introspection method lacks in
(a) Reliability (b) Validity
(c) Objectivity (d) All the above three

26. Which of the following is not a principle of development?
(a) Principle of continuity.
(b) Principle of individual difference.
(c) Principle of proceeding from specific to general response.
(d) Principle of integration.

27. Development of language in children, according to B.F. Skinner, is the result of
    (a) Training in grammar
    (b) Imitation and reinforcement
    (c) Innate abilities
    (d) Maturation
28. Behaviour pattern that increases in frequency when followed by a reward is known as
    (a) Shaping
    (b) Classical Conditioning
    (c) Generalization
    (d) Operant Conditioning
29. Find out the odd one:
    (a) Originality (b) Punctuality
    (c) Flexibility (d) Fluency
30. Who propounded Self Theory of Personality?
    (a) Kretschmer (b) Allport
    (c) Eysenck (d) Roger
31. Archimedes found the solution of his problem when he was in his bath tub. This will come under which step of process of creativity?
    (a) Preparation (b) Incubation
    (c) Illumination (d) Verification
32. **Assertion (A):** Motivation is important in the process of teaching and learning.

    Reason (R): Motivation is attraction towards a goal and clarifies it's meaning.

    Codes:
    (a) Only (A) is correct and (R) is incorrect.
    (b) Only (A) is correct.
    (c) Only (R) is correct.
    (d) Both (A) and (R) are correct.
33. The pioneer of functionalism is
    (a) Wilhelm Wundt
    (b) William James
    (c) J.B. Watson
    (d) Kurt Lewin
34. Names of different types of intelligence tests are given in List – I and examples of questions are given in List – II. Match the correct name of the test to questions.

    List – I
    a. Vocabulary test
    b. Memory test
    c. Information test
    d. Association test

    List – II
    1. In what ways animals and plants are a like?
    2. Where is Taj Mahal situated?
    3. What is the meaning of the word "Eventually"?
    4. What is the mobile number of your class teacher?
    5. Why are nights longer and days shorter in winter?

Codes:	**a**	**b**	**c**	**d**
(a)	3	5	4	1
(b)	3	1	5	2
(c)	1	4	2	5
(d)	3	4	2	1

35. Re-arrange the following steps of social learning theory as given by Bandura.
    a. Remembering the behaviour.
    b. Converting the memory into action.
    c. Reinforcement of the imitated behaviour.
    d. Attending to and perceiving the behaviour.

    (a) a, b, d, c (b) d, a, b, c
    (c) d, a, c, b (d) a, d, b, c
36. Nihar fails in the examination and attributes his failure to the framing of the faulty question paper. Which defence mechanism does he use?
    (a) Projection (b) Compensation
    (c) Identification (d) Rationalisation

37. Which of the following is not a characteristic of Naturalistic Inquiry?
   (a) Multiple Realities
   (b) Generalisation
   (c) Human Relations
   (d) Value Based Research

38. **Assertion (A):** Longer tests are more reliable than shorter ones.
   Reason (R): Each item adds to test reliability.
   Which of the following is correct?
   Codes:
   (a) Both (A) and (R) are correct.
   (b) Only (A) is correct.
   (c) Only (R) is correct.
   (d) None of the (A) and (R) is correct.

39. Which of the following variances is not controlled or manipulated in a research design?
   (a) Variance of independent variable.
   (b) Variance of dependent variable.
   (c) Variance of extraneous variables.
   (d) Error variance.

40. Which of the following is not a criterion for the statement of a good research problem?
   (a) Expression of relationship between/among variables.
   (b) Clarity and unambiguousness.
   (c) Possibility of empirical testing.
   (d) Possibility of use of statistical analysis.

41. Which of the following variables is continuous?
   (a) Attitude towards school
   (b) Family size in a locality
   (c) Marital status of College students
   (d) Religious affiliation of workers.

42. Read the following statements about a laboratory experiment.
   I. It has relatively complete control of extraneous variables.
   II. Its results are applicable to real life situations.
   Which of the following is correct?
   Codes:
   (a) Both I and II are correct.
   (b) I is incorrect, but II is correct.
   (c) Neither of I and II is correct.
   (d) I is correct, but II is incorrect.

43. Which of the following is not correctly matched?
   (a) Achievement Test – Content validity
   (b) Aptitude Test – Predictiv validity
   (c) Reasoning – Content Test validity
   (d) Personality – Concurre test validity

44. Read the following two lists of items:
   List – I
   a. Historical Research
   b. Action Research
   c. Survey Research
   d. Experimental Research
   List – II
   1. Current status
   2. Control of variables
   3. Natural setting
   4. Local problem
   5. Past oriented
   Which of the following matching is correct?

Codes:	**a**	**b**	**c**	**d**
(a)	3	4	1	2
(b)	5	4	1	2
(c)	4	3	2	5
(d)	1	2	3	4

45. In the context of a Survey Research, the following steps are taken in a certain order:
   1. Sampling
   2. Inference
   3. Data analysis
   4. Data collection

Which of the following is the right order of these steps?

(a) 2, 3, 1, 4 (b) 1, 4, 3, 2
(c) 3, 2, 4, 1 (d) 4, 1, 2, 3

46. Which of the following is a measure of location?

(a) Mode
(b) Mean
(c) Percentile
(d) Standard Deviation

47. An investigator wants to study the vocational aspirations of visually challenged children in a wide geographical area. He should select his sample by using

(a) Sample Random sampling
(b) Stratified sampling
(c) Purposive sampling
(d) Convenient sampling

48. The distribution of a large number of means based on samples of the sample size selected from the same population is known as

(a) normal distribution
(b) sampling distribution
(c) standard distribution
(d) rectangular distribution

49. Two variables X and Y are correlated. This means that the two variables

(a) cause variation in each other
(b) measure the same trait
(c) vary together
(d) vary independently

50. When the questions are presented to the respondents in a face-to-face situation and the interviewer fills out the query rather than the subjects it is known as

(a) An inventory (b) A questionnaire
(c) A schedule (d) A test

ANSWERS

1. (c)	2. (a)	3. (b)	4. (c)	5. (d)	6. (c)
7. (d)	8. (b)	9. (d)	10. (b)	11. (d)	12. (a)
13. (c)	14. (a)	15. (c)	16. (b)	17. (d)	18. (a)
19. (d)	20. (b)	21. (c)	22. (b)	23. (c)	24. (a)
25. (d)	26. (c)	27. (b)	28. (d)	29. (b)	30. (d)
31. (c)	32. (d)	33. (b)	34. (d)	35. (b)	36. (d)
37. (b)	38. (b)	39. (b)	40. (d)	41. (a)	42. (d)
43. (c)	44. (b)	45. (b)	46. (c)	47. (c)	48. (b)
49. (c)	50. (c)				

PAPER-III
DECEMBER 2012

Note: This paper contains seventy five (75) objective type questions of two (2) marks each. All questions are compulsory.

1. Who said this "Education is man-making. It is that by which character is formed, strength of mind is increased, intellect is expanded and by which man can stand on his own feet"?
   (a) Vivekananda
   (b) Tagore
   (c) Dayanand Saraswati
   (d) None of these

2. In List – I the name of the philosopher and philosophy is given and in List – II statements regarding the philosophy is given. Match the List – I with List – II in correct order:

   List – I
   a. Tagore b. Vivekananda
   c. Mahatma Gandhi d. Buddhism

   List – II
   i. Harmonious development of personality
   ii. The doctrine of karma
   iii. Child is more important than all kinds of books
   iv. Yoga as a method of education
   v. The doctrine of dharma

Codes:	a	b	c	d
(a)	v	i	ii	iv
(b)	iii	iv	i	ii
(c)	iii	iv	ii	v
(d)	iv	ii	i	iii

3. Purpose of creation of the universe and its relation to man and god is discussed in
   (a) Metaphysics (b) Ethics
   (c) Epistemology (d) None of these

4. Which of the following agency regulates education?
   (a) Church (b) State
   (c) School (d) Library

5. "The greatness of a nation is to be measured not by its material power and wealth but by the intercultural relationship of its people." Who said this?
   (a) Dr. Radhakrishnan
   (b) Tagore
   (c) Vivekananda
   (d) Gandhi

6. Which of the following does not specify Max Weber's concept of social stratification?
   (a) Educational Status
   (b) Income and Wealth
   (c) Political Power
   (d) Social Prestige

7. If rules of multiplication helps in learning correlation or regression, then it is an example of
   (a) Sequential transfer
   (b) Horizontal transfer
   (c) Negative transfer
   (d) Vertical transfer

8. According to Freud, Super Ego is properly developed during
   (a) latency period (b) anal period
   (c) phallic period (d) None of these

9. When response is based on uncommon area of the blot, it is denoted by
   (a) S (b) Dd
   (c) DW (d) DdW

10. Individual psychology of personality was given by
    (a) A. Adler (b) Jung
    (c) Eysenck (d) None of these

11. Which of the following theories is most quantitatively measurable?
    (a) Pavlov's (b) Skinner's
    (c) Hull's (d) None of these

12. Maladjusted children are mostly found in
    (a) Broken families or unitary families
    (b) Poor or joint families
    (c) Both of these
    (d) None of these
13. Theory of generalization is similar to the theory of
    (a) Transposition
    (b) Identical elements
    (c) Both of these
    (d) None of these
14. Which is the highest level of concept formation?
    (a) Formal level (b) Sensory level
    (c) Concrete level (d) None of these
15. Which of the following is the apex body in the area of Teacher Education in India?
    (a) UGC (b) MHRD
    (c) NCTE (d) NCERT
16. Who have signed MOU for accreditation of Teacher Education Institutions in India?
    (a) NAAC and UGC
    (b) NCTE and NAAC
    (c) UGC and NCTE
    (d) None of the above
17. As per NCTE norms, what should be the pattern of teaching staff for a unit of 100 students at B.Ed. level?
    (a) 1 + 7 (b) 1 + 9
    (c) 1 + 10 (d) 1 + 5
18. There are three phases of teaching given by P. Jackson, which of the following is incorrect one?
    (a) Pre-active phase
    (b) Underactive phase
    (c) Interactive phase
    (d) Post-active phase
19. Which of the following is the least important aspect of the teachers' role in the guidance of learning?
    (a) The development of insight into what constitutes an adequate performance.
    (b) The development of insight to overcome the pitfalls and obstacles.
    (c) The provision of encouragement and moral support.
    (d) The provision of continuous diagnostic and remedial help.
20. Which of the following qualities of a teacher will be liked most by you?
    (a) Idealistic philosophy
    (b) Compassion
    (c) Discipline
    (d) Entertaining
21. The most important challenge for a teacher is
    (a) to maintain discipline in the classroom.
    (b) to make students do their homework.
    (c) to prepare the question-bank.
    (d) to make teaching process enjoyable.
22. Techno-Pedagogic competency is
    (a) a science of using technology in teaching.
    (b) a technique of combining principles of technology and principles of teaching.
    (c) a set of skills of interweaving technology into teaching and learning both scientifically and aesthetically.
    (d) a competence to develop techno-pedagogic systems in education.
23. Which of the following skills are needed for present-day teacher to adjust properly with the classroom teaching?
    1. Knowledge of technology
    2. Use of technology in teaching learning
    3. Knowledge of student's needs
    4. Content mastery

    (a) 1 and 3 (b) 2 and 3
    (c) 2, 3 and 4 (d) 2 and 4

24. Psycho-analytic approach of counselling was first introduced by
    (a) Adler (b) Jung
    (c) Freud (d) None of these
25. Which of the following tools of collecting psychological information about pupils is the most objective?
    (a) Rating scale
    (b) Interview
    (c) Standardized tests
    (d) Projective devices
26. According to psycho-analysis theory of personality, neurotic disorders are caused by
    (a) Repression of desires
    (b) Inactivity of libido
    (c) Role of unconscious mind
    (d) All of these
27. Which of the following does not belong to the category of non-probability sample?
    (a) Quota sample
    (b) Multi-stage sample
    (c) Purposive sample
    (d) Incidental sample
28. The research proposals sent to research institutes for financial assistance must have
    (a) The whole plan and procedure
    (b) Budget requirements and time schedule
    (c) Definite objectives of research
    (d) None of the above
29. Which of the following is not an approach of analysis of qualitative data?
    (a) Logical Analysis
    (b) Criterion Analysis
    (c) Content Analysis
    (d) Inductive Analysis
30. Internal criticism is done
    (a) to verify the accuracy of the source.
    (b) to verify the authenticity of the source.
    (c) Both of these
    (d) None of these
31. Which of the following commissions suggested silent meditation as a part of moral values?
    (a) Secondary Education Commission
    (b) University Education Commission
    (c) National Education Commission
    (d) Indian Education Commission
32. Which of the following is described as Magna-Carta of Indian Education?
    (a) Sargent Commission
    (b) Wood's Despatch
    (c) Macaulay Minutes
    (d) Hunter Commission
33. "Rising knowledge to wisdom is real education" was said by
    (a) Rigveda
    (b) Chhandogya Upanishad
    (c) Samaveda
    (d) Bhagvadh Geeta
34. The Oriental School of Thought is related to
    (a) knowledge of science
    (b) classical literature
    (c) conservation of fashion
    (d) learning of natives
35. *Leviathan* was written by
    (a) Locke (b) Hobbes
    (c) Rousseau (d) Hegel
36. "Project is a whole-hearted purposeful activity proceeding on a social environment", it was defined by
    (a) John Dewey (b) Ballard
    (c) Kilpatrick (d) Adamson
37. Who said that the school be made as miniature society?

(a) Skinner (b) Thorndike
(c) Herbert (d) Dewey

38. 'Socialization' is a process by which the individual is adapted to his
(a) classroom environment
(b) social environment
(c) political environment
(d) cultural environment

39. The movement from one social class to another is known as
(a) social status (b) social control
(c) social change (d) social mobility

40. 'Cultural Lag' is the term used by
(a) Ogburn (b) Pyne
(c) Weber (d) Marx

41. District Primary Education Programme (DPEP) was started in
(a) 1990 (b) 1994
(c) 1998 (d) 1996

42. Supervision is a continuous activity whereas Inspection is a
(a) general activity in a common place
(b) special activity in a given moment
(c) complex activity in a situation
(d) specific activity in a specific time

43. Who propounded the 'self' theory of personality?
(a) Kretschmar (b) Allport
(c) Eysenck (d) Roger

44. Match the following List – I with List – II in correct order:

List – I
a. Classical conditioning
b. Drive reduction
c. Sign Gestalt learning
d. Learning by insight

List – II
i. Kohler ii. Hull
iii. Pavlov iv. Skinner
v. Tolman

Codes:	**a**	**b**	**c**	**d**
(a)	iv	ii	v	i
(b)	iii	ii	v	i
(c)	iv	ii	i	v
(d)	iii	ii	i	v

45. In the List – I name of the Psychologists are given and in List – II the theories developed by them. Match the List – I with List – II in correct order:

List – I	**List – II**
a. Freud	i. Two factor theory
b. Spearman	ii. Creativity
c. Rorschach	iii. Psycho-analysis
d. Torrance	iv. Projective technique
	v. Multifactor theory

Codes:	**a**	**b**	**c**	**d**
(a)	i	iii	ii	iv
(b)	ii	v	iii	iv
(c)	iv	iii	v	ii
(d)	iii	i	iv	ii

46. University Education Commission constituted in 1948 was appointed by
(a) Ministry of Human Resource Development
(b) Ministry of Education
(c) NCERT
(d) ICSSR

47. Rearrange the following steps of social learning theory as given by Bandura:
a. Remembering the behaviour.
b. Connecting the memory in action.
c. Reinforcement of the imitated behaviour.
d. Attending and perceiving the behaviour.
(a) b, a, d, c (b) d, a, b, c
(c) a, b, d, c (d) d, a, c, b

48. Education falls under the
(a) Concurrent List
(b) Fundamental Rights

(c) Constitution of India
(d) State List

49. Critically judge the following:
Assertion (A): Motivation is important in the process of teaching and learning.
Reason (R): Motivation is attraction towards a goal and clarifies its meaning.
(a) Both (A) and (R) are incorrect.
(b) Only (A) is correct.
(c) Only (R) is correct.
(d) Both (A) and (R) are correct.

50. Curriculum means
(a) all the experiences which students get in school.
(b) subject that are transferred by the faculty.
(c) syllabus prescribed for the course.
(d) class experiences, sports and games.

51. Programmed learning is based on the principles of
(a) Conditioned Learning Theory
(b) Cognitive Learning Theory
(c) Gestalt Learning Theory
(d) Operant-conditioning

52. According to Piaget, at what stage does abstract thinking begin to develop?
(a) Sensory motor
(b) Pre-operational
(c) Concrete operational
(d) Formal operational

53. Which of the following is the incorrect pair?
(a) Sign Theory of - Tolman Learning
(b) Field Theory of - Lewin Learning
(c) Social Learning - Bruner Theory
(d) Trial and error - Thorndike Theory

54. Match the following:

List – I
a. Sentence Completion Test
b. Multiple Choice
c. Match the following
d. Read the passage and answer the question

List – II
1. Association
2. Recognition
3. Comprehension
4. Recall

Codes:	a	b	c	d
(a)	4	2	1	3
(b)	4	3	2	1
(c)	4	2	3	1
(d)	3	2	1	4

55. Which is the most effective reinforcement schedule according to operant conditioning theory of learning for stable learning?
(a) Continuous reinforcement
(b) Fixed ratio reinforcement
(c) Variable ratio reinforcement
(d) Fixed interval reinforcement

56. Xerophthalmia is a result of insufficient amount of
(a) Vitamin C (b) Vitamin B
(c) Vitamin D (d) Vitamin A

57. A child who has unusual difficulty in oral instruction may have the following impairment
(a) Intellectual disability
(b) Cerebral Palsy
(c) Hearing impairment
(d) Visual impairment

58. The child who reads numbers wrongly has the following learning disability
(a) Dyscrasia (b) Dyslexia
(c) Dyspepsia (d) Dyscalculia

59. The child having the difficulty in picking up objects is suspected to have
(a) Lower level of intellectual function
(b) Sight impairment

(c) Speech impairment
(d) Locomotor impairment

60. Delinquency is committed by the children of the age group
(a) 8 – 18 years (b) 6 – 14 years
(c) 7 – 15 years (d) 9 – 19 years

61. Which of the following philosophies are most tilted to individualism?
(a) Jainism (b) Samkhya
(c) Buddhism (d) None of these

62. Research means
(a) Searching again and again
(b) Finding solution to any problem
(c) Scientific approach to new truth
(d) Conducting experiment

63. Which of the following is the first step in the research process?
(a) Searching sources of information.
(b) Survey of related literature.
(c) Identification of a broad area of research.
(d) Searching for solution to problem.

64. If a researcher conduct a research on finding out which administrative style contributes more to institutional effectiveness, this will be an example of
(a) Expost facto research
(b) Action research
(c) Applied research
(d) Fundamental research

65. A researcher is generally expected to
(a) study the existing literature in a field.
(b) generate new principles and theories.
(c) synthesize the ideas given by others.
(d) evaluate the findings of a study.

66. The process of educational research involves the following steps:
(1) Collection of data
(2) Statement of objectives
(3) Selecting the problem
(4) Method/Procedure
(5) Analysis and Interpretation of data
(6) Reporting the results
Which of the following sequence is correct?
(a) 3, 2, 4, 1, 5, 6 (b) 1, 3, 2, 5, 6, 4
(c) 3, 2, 4, 1, 6, 5 (d) 3, 2, 5, 1, 6, 4

67. The Government of India conducts Census after every 10 years. The method of research used in this process is
(a) Case Study (b) Developmental
(c) Survey (d) Experimental

68. Items of List – I and List – II given below have one-to-one relationship on some basis. Identify the inherent relationship and select the correct matching from the given options:

List – I	List – II
a. Experimental	1. Sampling
b. Historical	2. Meta-analysis
c. Philosophical	3. Internal criticism
d. Descriptive	4. Content analysis
	5. Internal validity

Codes:	a	b	c	d
(a)	3	5	2	3
(b)	1	4	2	5
(c)	3	4	2	1
(d)	5	3	4	1

69. Two variables X and Y are significantly correlated. This means that
(a) X causes variation in Y.
(b) Y causes variation in X.
(c) X and Y vary together.
(d) No such conclusion may be drawn.

70. Which of the following types of studies results in findings which could not be generalized to other situations?
(a) Descriptive
(b) Historical
(c) Experimental
(d) Causal Comparative

71. The Rosarch Inkblot test consists of
   (a) Five black and five coloured cards
   (b) Ten black and ten white cards
   (c) Five black and white & five multi-coloured cards
   (d) Ten multi-coloured cards
72. Which of the following terms is relevant to a qualitative study?
   (a) Comparison (b) Prediction
   (c) Correlation (d) Exploration
73. Which of the following is a characteristic feature only of experimental studies?
   (a) Control of extraneous variables.
   (b) Study of cause and effect relationship.
   (c) Observing variation in the dependent variable.
   (d) Manipulation of treatment variable.
74. When a researcher checks the genuineness and authenticity of the source material, it is known as
   (a) External validity
   (b) External criticism
   (c) Concurrent validity
   (d) Internal consistency
75. An investigator studied the census data for a given area and prepared a write-up based on them. Such a write-up is called
   (a) Research Paper
   (b) Article
   (c) Thesis
   (d) Research Report

ANSWERS

1. (a)	2. (b)	3. (a)	4. (b)	5. (a)	6. (a)
7. (d)	8. (a)	9. (b)	10. (a)	11. (c)	12. (a)
13. (b)	14. (a)	15. (c)	16. (b)	17. (a)	18. (b)
19. (b)	20. (b)	21. (d)	22. (c)	23. (c)	24. (c)
25. (c)	26. (a)	27. (b)	28. (b)	29. (b)	30. (a)
31. (b)	32. (b)	33. (b)	34. (b)	35. (b)	36. (c)
37. (d)	38. (b)	39. (d)	40. (a)	41. (b)	42. (d)
43. (d)	44. (b)	45. (d)	46. (b)	47. (b)	48. (a)
49. (d)	50. (a)	51. (d)	52. (d)	53. (c)	54. (a)
55. (c)	56. (d)	57. (c)	58. (b)	59. (d)	60. (c)
61. (a)	62. (c)	63. (c)	64. (c)	65. (b)	66. (a)
67. (c)	68. (d)	69. (c)	70. (b)	71. (c)	72. (d)
73. (d)	74. (b)	75. (b)